MEDIEVAL HERESY

TO MY WIFE

# MEDIEVAL HERESY

*Popular Movements from the Gregorian Reform to the Reformation*

THIRD EDITION

## MALCOLM LAMBERT

**Blackwell**
Publishing

Editorial Offices:
108 Cowley Road, Oxford OX4 1JF, UK
Tel: +44 (0)1865 791100
350 Main Street, Malden, MA 02148–5018, USA
Tel: +1 781 388 8250

First published 1977 by Edward Arnold as *Medieval Heresy: Popular Movements from Bogomil to Hus*
Second edition published 1992 by Blackwell Publishers Ltd 1992
Third edition published 2002 by Blackwell Publishers Ltd, a Blackwell Publishing company

*Library of Congress Cataloging-in-Publication Data*

Lambert, Malcolm (Malcolm D.)
    Medieval heresy : popular movements from the Gregorian reform to the Reformation / Malcolm Lambert – 3rd ed.
        p. cm.
    Includes bibliographical references and index
    ISBN 0–631–22275–8 (alk. paper) – ISBN 0–631–22276–6 (pb. : alk. paper)
        1. Heresies, Christian – History – Middle Ages, 600 – 1500. I. Title.

BT1319 .L35 2002
273'.6–dc21                                                                            2001043102

A catalogue record for this title is available from the British Library.

Typeset in 10 on 11.5 pt Baskerville
by Kolam Information Services Pvt. Ltd, Pondicherry, India
Printed in Great Britain by MPG Books Ltd, Bodmin, Cornwall
This book is printed on acid-free paper

For further information on
Blackwell Publishers, visit our website:
www.blackwellpublishers.co.uk

# Contents

# List of Maps

# List of Illustrations

# Acknowledgements

I owe the idea of writing on medieval heresy to Professor N. Cantor. The Alexander von Humboldt Stiftung, most generous of scholarship funds, gave me the opportunity to study at the Monumenta Germaniae Historica in Munich. I am indebted to Mitarbeiter and staff for many kindnesses both personal and scholarly, especially to Dr C. Lohmer for untiring pursuit of photocopies, and to Dr H. Schneider and Dr M. Polock; also to librarians Dr H. Lietzmann and Frau M. Becker and the late President, Professor H. Grundmann, for initial guidance. I remember here my father, who first interested me in historical research.

At the University of Bristol, I was indebted to the late Professor Douglas for encouragement and for a grant from the Colston Research Fund; to Professor D. Turner, head of the Department of Theology 1986–9, and his staff for the happiest years of my university career; to the library staff, especially Mr J. Edwards, for their help; and to Margaret Aherne, of Bristol, freelance editor.

I owe generous gifts of unpublished work to Professor M. Barber, Dr P. Biller, Dr J. Bird, Dr C. Dutton, Dr J. V. Fearns, Dr J. Fines, Dr M. Frassetto, Rev. Dr J. M. Henderson, Professor R. I. Moore, Dr M. Pegg, Dr A. Roach, Rev. Dr N. Tanner S. J., who demonstrate that the barbarisms of governments have not destroyed a long tradition of trust among academic researchers.

I am grateful for gifts of books from Dr A. Brenon, Dr G. Dickson, Professor W. Eberhard, Dr A. Fössel, M. M. Roquebert, Professor F. Seibt, Dr Y. Stoyanov, Professor B. Töpfer, the late Professor E. Werner and Sutton Publishing. May the many historians who have sent offprints and photocopies accept my gratitude collectively. I thank Dr J. Duvernoy, Professor R. I. Moore, Mr A. Murray, Professor J. B. Russell, Professor P. Segl and Rev. Dr S. Tugwell O. P. for answers to queries and Professor K. Walsh for bibliographical help.

To my wife I owe more than I can say. In a real sense she has been a co-author and I do not think I would have finished this book or its later editions without her.

M.D.L.
The Yews, Eastcombe, Stroud, GL6 7DN

# *Part I*

## The Beginnings

# 1

# The Problem of Heresy

Heresy, and the horror it inspires, intertwines with the history of the Church itself. Jesus warned his disciples against the false prophets who would take His name and the Epistle to Titus states that a heretic, after a first and second abomination, must be rejected. But Paul, writing to the Corinthians, said, 'Oportet esse haereses', as the Latin Vulgate translated his phrase – 'there must be heresies, that they which are proved may be manifest among you'[1] – and it was understood by medieval churchmen that they must expect to be afflicted by heresies.

Heresy was of great importance in the early centuries in forcing the Church progressively to define its doctrines and to anathematize deviant theological opinions. At times, in the great movements such as Arianism and Gnosticism, heresy seemed to overshadow the Church altogether. Knowledge of the individual heresies and of the definitions which condemned them became a part of the equipment of the learned Christian; the writings of the Fathers wrestled with these deviations, and lists of heresies and handbooks assimilated this experience of the early centuries and handed it on to the Middle Ages.

Events after Christianity became the official religion of the Empire also shaped the assumptions with which the Church of the Middle Ages met heresy. After Constantine's conversion, Christians in effect held the power of the State and, despite some hesitations, they used it to impose a uniformity of belief. Both in the eastern and in the western portions of the Empire it became the law that pertinacious heretics were subject to the punishments of exile, branding, confiscation of goods, or death. These regulations survived the fall of the Empire, and so did the assumption that it was the right of the Church to call on the State to put down heresy.

1  Titus 3: 10; 1 Cor. 11: 19. H. Grundmann, 'Oportet et haereses esse: Das Problem der Ketzerei im Spiegel der mittelalterlichen Bibelexegese', *AKG* xlv (1963), pp. 129–64. For the Greek term see L. Goppelt, *Apostolic and Post-Apostolic Times*, tr. R. A. Guelich (London, 1970), pp. 165–77. For heresy in the early Christian centuries, E. Peters, *Heresy and Authority in Medieval Europe* (1980) (*PHA*) (trans. extracts with intro.), pp. 1–3, 13–56.

Heresy was not thought to be the product of the individual speculative intelligence, or of devout men and women seeking a higher ethical life – still less of oppressed lower classes demanding better conditions and masking their economic objectives in the outwardly religious forms of their age. All these interpretations have been put forward by modern historians of medieval heresy, but they are quite alien to the assumptions of churchmen, whether of the Middle Ages or of the early centuries of the Church. They believed that heresy was the work of the devil. Descriptions of heretics were couched in sets of favourite adjectives and texts, passed on from author to author, and only too often imposed with scant discrimination on the heretics, their beliefs and practices.[2] Some were an inheritance passed on to the Middle Ages from the age of the Fathers; others were developed in the Middle Ages themselves. The descriptions served primarily to develop a set of conventional characteristics of the type-figure of the heretic: his pride, which must be a feature, for he has set himself up against the teaching of the Church; his superficial appearance of piety, which must be intended to deceive, and cannot be real, since he is in fact the enemy of the faith; and his secrecy, which is contrasted to the openness of Catholic preaching. He may well be described as unlettered (even if this is not entirely true), since *a priori* he lacks the equipment of the orthodox churchman; he may be accused of counterfeiting piety while actually indulging in libertinism – an accusation which strangely repeats those made by pagan writers against early Christians, and sometimes appears to feed on the same material. His beliefs may be crudely assimilated to the heresies of the patristic age, even when they are quite unrelated, though this tendency fades as more accurate knowledge of actual medieval heresy penetrates the conventions. The bulk of sources emanate from the repressing forces or the chroniclers on the Catholic side, and their descriptions are thus shaped by these conventions. Surviving work of the heretics, in which we can see for ourselves the nature of their teaching, is very much less, either because the heresy was conveyed more often by word of mouth than by writing, or because repression has destroyed documents.

The historian thus faces acute problems of evidence when he wishes to study the behaviour, motives and beliefs of the medieval heretic. He is dealing much of the time with underground movements existing behind a barrier of secrecy – and because Church and State are most often combined against them, they are willy nilly secret opposition movements hostile to authority. As a modern historian, he must elucidate motives from sources which are very rarely concerned with them, and scrape off layers of convention and prejudice from his originals in order to reach a true delineament of the heretics.

2   H. Grundmann, 'Der Typus des Ketzers in mittelalterlichen Anschauung', *Kultur- und Universalgeschichte. Festschrift für Walter Goetz* (1927), pp. 91–107 (fundamental for approach to sources); for coll. articles, of fundamental importance, see *Ausgewählte Aufsätze* I: *Religiöse Bewegungen* (1976), II: *Joachim von Fiore* (1977), III: *Bildung und Sprache* (1978); obituary assessment: A. Borst in I, pp. 1–25, bibliography: H. Lietzmann, I, pp. 26–37. A Patschovsky, 'Der Ketzer als Teufelsdiener', *Papsttum, Kirche und Recht im Mittelalter*, ed. H. Mordek (1991), pp. 317–34. P. Biller, 'The *Topos* and reality of the heretic as *illiteratus*', Id., *Waldenses* (below p. 158, n. 1 ), pp. 169–90. Id., 'Through a glass darkly: seeing medieval heresy', *The Medieval World*, ed. P. Linehan, J. Nelson.

The subject is also two-sided. It takes two to create a heresy: the heretic, with his dissident beliefs and practices; and the Church, to condemn his views and to define what is orthodox doctrine. It was in the persistent resistance to the teaching of the Church that heresy consisted: error became heresy when, shown his deviation, the obstinate refused to obey and retract. In the thirteenth century Robert Grosseteste's definition stated that 'a heresy is an opinion chosen by human perception contrary to holy Scripture, publicly avowed and obstinately defended'. The Church, confronted from the twelfth century onwards with a challenge from hostile sects, was forced, step by step, to recognize how these sects differed from those of late antiquity, and to take new measures to deal with them. A machinery was created both for defining doctrine and for uncovering and putting down those who refused to accept the decisions of authority. It came to be accepted that Christianity was a system of beliefs 'that were self-evidently true, so that rejection of any of them implied ignorance or malice'.[3] Not all of these developments have been fully studied by medievalists, for, although we have known much since Lea of the origins and workings of one of the instruments of repression, the inquisition, much more needs to be known about the doctrinal decision-making of ecclesiastical authority and the way in which the medieval concept of heresy was built up. Moreover, the search for understanding of the motives of the heretic will take the historian into the study of medieval societies and economic changes and into the issues of the morale of the faithful, the conditions in regional Churches and the effect of abuse in stimulating heresies. All are subjects open to investigation, where often enough no final word, even within the limitations of our sources, has yet been said.

Not only the existence of the assumption that State and Church have a duty to persecute, and the emergence of a machinery to detect and examine religious dissidents, shaped the conditions of existence of the medieval heretic. He was also subject to one basic principle of medieval Christianity generally: that the heretic who wilfully persisted in his error was condemned to the pains of Hell for eternity. The persistent dissident was thus not only defying a visible authority – and, as we shall see, that authority was not always very clearly in evidence, or actively pursuing heretics; he was also challenging the fear of damnation, and backing his own judgement or that of his group against a spiritual authority with the power to decide his eternal future. That groups of men and women in medieval society were prepared to make this defiance is one of the striking facts to record, and one major theme of this book will be the examination, where possible, of the motives which led them to do it. Second only in interest to this question is that of the failure of all medieval heretical movements that made this defiance to survive in the long term. Why, we may ask, having once challenged authority, were these heretics severally unable to maintain the independence of their beliefs?

---

3  N. Tanner's comment, 'Penances', *LG*, p. 236 (see below, p. 266, n. 1). On the medieval notion of heresy, see *MBPH*, pp. 1–7 and *The Concept of Heresy in the Middle Ages (11th–13th C.)*, ed. W. Lourdaux, D. Verhelst (1976). See also prologue to G. Leff, *Heresy in the Later Middle Ages* (1967), 2 vols (survey stressing intellectual factors). A. S. McGrade, 'The medieval idea of heresy: what are we to make of it?' *SCH* Subsidia xi, pp. 111–39 (see esp. for varied views in Augustine).

The search for salvation, coupled with the conviction that the Church no longer channelled the means of salvation or had distorted the teaching of Christ or was temporarily in the hands of evil men, was the most important single factor impelling the leaders of heretical movements to challenge ecclesiastical authority. Conviction that their reading or hearing of Scripture or an inner illumination or the instruction of a holy man and the conferring of a valid sacrament where the Church's sacraments had become valueless, overrode the decisions of priests, bishops or popes.

The search for salvation moved the rank and file of such movements as well as the leaders: we have a vivid demonstration of this in the battle for souls at the deathbed between the Cathar *consolamentum* and the Catholic last rites, and the wavering of the sick and their relatives between rival claims.

Eloquence could change lives – briefly or permanently. If the preacher could fuse through his exhortation social and economic grievance and a religious exaltation, extraordinary events became possible. For a moment at Le Mans in 1116, Henry the Monk, blending Lenten revivalism with anticlerical emotions, broke down social barriers, brought prostitutes to repentance and induced young men to marry them; on a far wider scale in Bohemia three centuries later, radical Hussite preachers led peasant families to go *en masse* on pilgrimage to the hills, joining large-scale preachings and celebrations of communion in both kinds, breaching the normal barriers of society and creating the manpower for the most effective of Hussite armies.

The appeal of the great heresies, Cathar, Waldensian, Lollard, was perennial, supra-regional and transcended the personalities of their leaders. Given that this was so, it is necessary to look at local and regional conditions in order to understand why a heretical movement survived or even prospered in one area rather than another; to explain this, the political, social or economic circumstances of a region will be decisive.[4] Northern Italy was the land of heresy *par excellence* because of its social pressures and its intellectual vitality, and above all because its cities prized their independence so highly that they preferred to tolerate heretics rather than surrender to the demands of their bishops or of popes. Parts of Languedoc were a seed-ground for Catharism because of its chronic political anarchy, which deterred secular authority from repression of religious dissidence, and because of a certain casual, meridional tradition of tolerance, which gave time for its missionaries to gain recruits and build up their Churches. The city of Rome's material grievances gave Arnold of Brescia a political and religious platform for his teaching on poverty and the disendowment of the Church. It was no accident that Milan was at one and the same time a fast-growing industrial centre and the cradle of proliferating heretical groups. The

4 Anthropology shows itself fruitful; for general comments, see J. L. Nelson, 'Society, theodicy and the origins of heresy: towards a reassessment of the medieval evidence', *SCH* ix, pp. 65–77; another view: T. Asad, 'Medieval heresy: an anthropological view', *Social History* xi (1986), pp. 354–62; survey of hypotheses: J. B. Russell, 'Interpretations of the origins of medieval heresy', *MS* xxv (1963), pp. 26–53.

clash of Czech and German speakers in Prague and the social tensions of the New Town account for much in the history of Hussitism.

And yet, however much the fate of the movements with mass support rested on these varying terrestrial circumstances, the actions of the dedicated heretic were dictated far more by conscience and his conviction that he was doing the will of God as he braved persecution. Some historians have been inclined to see in the chroniclers' accounts of heretics accepting their fate with equanimity, even with joy, literary *topoi* with an insecure basis in fact. Not so: better-recorded narratives of the bearing of dedicated men and women before the fire, and some modern medical information, make these stories wholly credible. The stake was the last and fiercest test; the courage of the heretical missionaries and the strongest of their supporters developed over the years made them ready, when all opportunities of escape failed, to face a cruel death. Their religious convictions account for the longevity of the movements for which they sacrificed their days.

Defiance none the less ended either in destruction or at least in the cowing and marginalizing of these movements. Repression makes martyrs, but, efficiently conducted, it is also largely successful. In a sufficient number of cases, orthodoxy commanded the services of the secular arm, the emperors, kings and aristocrats with military and economic power. Studies devoted to the analysis of medieval heresies may often unwittingly conceal this point, because they are concerned with the exceptions, the occasions when repression was ineffective or not even attempted. At most times and in most places orthodoxy had support, and not only the support of the leadership in society, but of rank and file too. In the Albigensian Crusade, for example, volunteers repeatedly came to serve in the south of France in order to repress heresy, and although some came in the expectation of winning land, others came out of religious conviction and served the time needful to gain the crusading indulgence, then went home. In the long history of Lollardy, the bulk of the English populace remained indifferent to the heresy. Some were positively hostile, as is demonstrated by the grim evidence of the will of a London goldsmith, bequeathing money to buy faggots for the burning of heretics. That hostility lasted in some quarters into the Reformation epoch. In Exeter sticks and gorse were thrown on to the burning fire of a heretic in 1533.[5]

More than that of any other scholar, the work of Herbert Grundmann has shaped the approach of this book. His insistence that, in order to understand the rise and influence of heresies, the historian must look at the history of orthodoxy, his determination to avoid the constricting influence of denominationalism and denominational history and to look beyond the well-recorded story of Catholic religious orders to the lesser, often short-lived medieval experiments in religious life so revealing of general trends in Church and society and, finally, his understanding that heresy is born primarily of religious conviction, are keynotes in my exposition. An initiative of R. E. Lerner has brought Grundmann's classic work,

5   M. E. Aston, *Faith and Fire* (1993) (coll. articles), p. xiv.

the *Religiöse Bewegungen im Mittelalter* of 1935,[6] coupled with a historiographical essay, to English readers, who can now judge for themselves why the book has been so durable a guide to its subject.

My first edition provided a working synthesis of the state of research on popular heretical movements from the eighth to the fifteenth centuries, designed both for the undergraduate reader who needed a one-volume introduction and as a handbook for the scholar working in one portion of this vast field, for quick reference on the subject as a whole. 'Popular' was taken to mean movements with a substantial following among laymen: individual heretical episodes involving small numbers were only included in so far as they revealed a stage in the growth of a movement on a larger scale. Intellectual heresy would have made another book: it was not analysed except in those cases where it gave a direct impetus to a popular heresy. So Abelard, despite the general interest aroused, was excluded while Wyclif, because of his effect on the Lollards, was given a chapter, and space was devoted to learned disputes about Wyclif and his teaching in the University of Prague as essential to the understanding of the popular movement of the Hussite revolt.

Heresy was taken to mean whatever the papacy explicitly or implicitly condemned during the period.[7] The growth of heresies and the failure of local authorities to deal effectively with them was one factor in the extension of papal power in the Church and it was some time before a clear legal concept of heresy emerged from the uncertainties of the eleventh and twelfth centuries: nevertheless, this definition served as a convenient working tool. It may incidentally lead to criticism in relation to the Hussites: some historians, not without reason, regard the moderate wing of the Hussites as reformers rather than heretics and note that the condemnation of Hus was the work of a Council that itself had unorthodox views on the papacy. Yet Hus denied the medieval doctrine of the papacy and even the moderate Utraquists received papal condemnation. I, therefore, with consistency, treated the Hussite movement as heretical. Where Byzantine heresy was concerned, I followed the decisions of the patriarch of Constantinople; for early heresy the decisions of the undivided Church.

When dealing with certain Western heresies, I felt justified in making a distinction between 'real' heresies that involved a major distortion of orthodox belief or practice and 'artificial' heresies, which as an ensemble in a living context did not exist, as in the case of the Free Spirit. The heresy of the *fraticelli* and the

6   1st edn, Berlin, 1935; 2nd, Darmstadt, 1961, trans. S. Rowan as *Religious Movements in the Middle Ages* (1995), intro. R. E. Lerner, pp. ix–xxv (on Marxism, pp. xvii–xviii, xxiii–xxv); reflections, J. L. Nelson, 'Religion in "histoire totale": some recent work on medieval heresy and popular religion', *Religion* x (1980), pp. 60–84.

7   H. Kaminsky, 'The problematics of later-medieval heresy', *Husitství–Reformane–Renasence*, ed. J. Pánek *et al.* (1994) (essays for F. Šmahel), pp. 132–54, criticizes historians defining the term 'heresies' 'as whatever the papacy condemned' on the grounds that they 'will see them under the same aspect in which they appeared to the medieval inquisitor' (p. 137). The inference is incorrect. A condemnation is merely a starting-point for investigation, seeking to establish the factors behind the condemnation, what the heretics believed, who they were and why they so acted.

case of the poverty of Christ occupy a curious position. The distortions of the ideal of poverty threatened to overturn the balance of Christian ethics; yet the actual decisions whereby the pope of the time condemned them and tried to uproot their basis in the Franciscan order were in fact based on technical issues and may fairly be called 'artificial'. The concept of 'artificial' heresy also enabled me to give attention to the cases in which unpopular groups or individuals were smeared with slanderous charges by authority at various levels or by local opinion and to allude, but no more, to the closely allied subject of witchcraft.

The second edition maintained the assumptions of the first but extended the scope in time, carrying the story of the Hussites from 1436 to the Reformation and extending the slim epilogue of the first edition to a full chapter on the sixteenth century. New scholarship also induced me to alter my view on the importance of Bogomil infiltration from Byzantium as a factor in the rise of heresy in the eleventh century, to give place instead to indigenous Western factors and to rewrite much of the Lollard chapter to incorporate the fruits of manuscript research by Anne Hudson and others.

The third edition keeps the shape and the time-scale of the second but remodels parts of the chapters on the Cathars, the Waldensians after 1218 and the Lollards, and makes significant additions on the eleventh-century emergence of heresy.

Eleventh-century origins continue to intrigue historians. About a half dozen episodes give material for analysis; one writer has argued that the sources are too few and too frail to justify the volume of research which has descended on them since Grundmann published seven pages on the subject in an appendix to *Religiöse Bewegungen*. That view is misguided. One needs only to glance at the expositions of two distinguished historians in the 1940s and 1950s which set controversy alight, A. Dondaine and R. Morghen, now outpaced by exploration of the social context and deeper analysis, to see that this most opaque of subjects has advanced. Chronicles and trial reports are now viewed with more sceptical and perceptive eyes; the major movements of secular history, expounded by Duby and Barthél-emy, have been brought into play to explain or, better, deconstruct heresy reports; the Peace of God movements and the strange thought-world of Adémar of Chabannes have been recreated; finally, a number of historians have lately turned back to the thesis of Bogomil infiltration as partial explanation of these early outbreaks and made cogent points in its favour. Reading the latest work, I feel like Mr Toad being talked to by Badger in the smoking room – entirely convinced when inside, but somehow not so certain after a lapse of time. I continue to believe that events and emotions in the West provide the major explana-tions, but have modified my analysis to give scope to fresh theories of Eastern missionizing.

Deconstruction has been a growing theme of heresy research, not only in analysis of the eleventh century. *Inventer l'Hérésie?*, a collection of articles edited by Professor Monique Zerner in 1997, repeatedly asks the question: when is heresy really heresy? Guy Lobrichon, who has successfully redated the letter of Heribert de Périgord from the twelfth to the eleventh century, queries the trial report of the bishop of Cambrai/Arras as true evidence of heresy in 1025 in a more thorough-going fashion than anyone else; Zerner herself demonstrates that Manselli muddled the sources for Henry the Monk, casts doubt on the exact nature of his relationship to Peter of Bruis and makes it likely that Henry was a fiery Donatist preacher of repentance and never at any stage as profound a heretic as Peter; Dr. Iogna-Prat convincingly notes how the MS tradition of transmission of the text of the Arras trial fits into a Cistercian tradition of seeking to master heresy by persuasion; M. Rubellin attempts to put Valdes himself into a new relation to the work and ideals of an orthodox, reforming archbishop.

However far deconstruction may go in the future – and M. G. Pegg's *The Corruption of Angels* is an intriguing example[8] – the fact remains that the faint springs in heretical episodes of the eleventh and early twelfth centuries have turned into great torrents by the early thirteenth century. While some heresy in the twelfth and thirteenth centuries may yet be deconstructed, other research has begun to give a little more body to Catharism in Northern Europe, long a mysterious subject, as P. Biller looks again at Cathars in England and at the evidence for a once fertile Catharism in Northern France, and B. Delmaire draws out the implications of sermons denouncing 'Bougres' in Arras and at La Charité sur Loire. G. Rottenwöhrer's fourth volume crowns his encyclopaedic analysis of Cathar sources and doctrines, drawing together the threads of his earlier investi-gations and demonstrating beyond doubt that the fissiparous nature of Cathar faith and its internal dissensions were realities and not figments of the imagin-ation of inquisitors and hostile polemicists.

English readers are now well served, with accounts of the Albigensian Crusade and Catharism in Languedoc by M. Costen and M. Barber, and an overall survey of my own, designed to supplement and bring up to date A. Borst's *Die Katharer*, still a major source of references and now translated into French. Janet Shirley has translated *The Song of the Cathar Wars* and the Siblys, Pierre des Vaux de Cernay's chronicle, with extensive notes. M. Roquebert's five-volume narrative history of the crusade, its aftermath and the end of Catharism in Languedoc concludes with a moving exposition of the last century of their existence, 1244–1329. In her *Les Femmes Cathares*, Anne Brenon recreates from a pro-Cathar standpoint the day-to-day life of Cathar women, especially towards the end, again in Languedoc. Some novel points may be expected from P. Jiménez-Sanchez's thesis, lately defended, on the development of Cathar doctrine in the University of Toulouse-Mirail.

Italy has been less well served, but now, in addition to synthesizing the valuable but fragmentary work of Italian scholars, Carol Lansing has produced a close investigation of Orvieto. Short articles can be illuminating: B. Hamilton explains convincingly the extraordinary resolution of so many of the Cathar perfect, rank and file as well as leaders, who died bravely. 'They came', he says, 'to fear life more than death.'[9] Similarly, L. Paolini, in his article on Italian Catharism and

---

8    Below, p. 147; also p. 36, n. 79.
9    B. Hamilton, 'The Cathars and Christian perfection', *SCH* Subsidia XI, pp. 5–23.

written culture, throws a new, clear light on the major Cathar texts discovered by Dondaine.

My Waldensian chapter has undergone more changes than any other. The English reader is again well served. The broad reflections of G. Audisio on Waldensianism, based on his masterly researches into the Waldensian underground, have been translated; Euan Cameron has given an account with full emphasis on the varying doctrines and geographical settings of Waldensian groups from Valdes into the Reformation epoch. Peter Biller's articles, long valued by professionals, are gathered into one volume and completed by his unpublished work on the *Liber Electorum*, a key text for understanding fourteenth-century Waldensianism and its time of troubles.

Pierrette Paravy's two volumes on Catholicism, witchcraft and heresy in Dauphiné, a definitive, Gallic research project covering a multitude of themes within the dioceses of Embrun and Grenoble in the late Middle Ages, has brought the Waldensians of Dauphiné into the light in a work which ranks beside Audisio's *Luberon*. In a series of articles and an edition of sources, Katrin Utz Tremp has clarified the Waldensianism of Fribourg. My earlier version did scant justice to the Waldensianism of the towns and, together with Biller's articles, Utz Tremp's work has enabled me to fill the gap.

I open the revised chapter 8 with Bishop Fournier's interrogation of the Waldensian deacon Raymond de Sainte Foy, because his answers reveal the nub of the Waldensian challenge to the Church. Fournier perceived that in many things the deacon accepted Catholic belief, but all attempts to convert him broke down on his rejection of purgatory – because he could not accept that it had any base in Scripture. Authority in the last resort was Scripture, not the Church; on that the bishop burnt him. Modern researchers rightly stress the degree to which Waldensians were still anchored in medieval Catholicism. They insisted on access to Scripture, in its bare text, but made relatively few challenging inferences from it, in striking contrast to sixteenth-century Protestants; yet Scripture remained the authority.

The study of Wyclif and Lollardy continues apace and is a tribute to the one book that K. B. McFarlane, a master of later medieval English political history, published in his lifetime, a slim but pungent life of Wyclif and his followers – a curious choice for a political historian who was professedly no theologian. He reacted against hagiographic work of the Methodist H. B. Workman, who carefully investigated Wyclif's writings but lacked historical experience: he is belaboured anonymously in the body of the book. McFarlane's work acted like a stone flung into a quiet pool and stimulated waves of research by himself, his pupils and others, the 1990s carrying common judgement on Wyclif, his motivation and the movement he founded farther away from the McFarlane biography.

The nuanced account of Wyclif and Wycliffism in J. Catto's contribution to the history of the University of Oxford, while never explicitly rejecting McFarlane (the evidence is seldom decisive), has quite a different tone. Anne Hudson, her colleagues and pupils have by their editing and analysis of the massive corpus of vernacular Lollard texts revealed the earnest, scholarly tone of so much of their missionizing, and forced a revision on the potential threat posed by Lollardy. A major work of transcription of Lollard vernacular sermons by Anne Hudson and Pamela Gradon was concluded with the issue of volumes 4 and 5 in 1996. There are now two volumes of perceptive articles by Margaret Aston in print, and N. Tanner, who has put all scholars in his debt by his edition of the Norwich and Kent heresy trials, is, with Shannon McSheffrey, preparing a text with analysis of the Coventry trials. Pertinaciously analyzing Lollard meetings and cells in the light of sociology in her *Gender and Heresy*, McSheffrey concludes that, by and large, women had no more significant role in Lollardy than in ordinary society, a view which can be compared to existing analyses of women in Catharism and Waldensianism.[10] A conference on *Lollardy and the Gentry* grappled with politics, Lollardy and class adherence, and carried work on the Lollard knights a stage further. R. Lutton introduces us to the inner world of the Lollard-influenced Wealden village of Tenterden and the particular character of wills in Lollard-inclined families. D. Plumb's researches have spanned the Reformation age and given an intriguing glimpse of an apparent continuity in one region between Lollardy and seventeenth-century early Protestantism. Lollardy merged into the new Protestantism, but the exact nature of its contribution and the degree to which it influenced opinion remains uncertain.

No one who writes on heresy can leave the inquisition out of account. Bayreuth University has established itself as a centre for the study of heresy, inquisition and witchcraft under the leadership of P. Segl. Papers at a conference published in 1993 wrestled with the problem of the beginnings of inquisitorial proceedings, taking as the criterion that, to be a true inquisitor, the churchman must combine the duties of investigating and judging in one office.[11] Herein, of course, lay both the source of a new efficiency and the open road to arbitrary injustice. The conference also gave publicity to W. Trusen's pioneer work exposing the quirks whereby Innocent's passion for disciplining the higher clergy and speeding investigation and judgement by proceeding *per inquisitionem* led, in other hands, to the development of inquisition against heresy. J. B. Given has used the rich Languedoc material against a background of sociology to establish in detail the reasons for inquisitors' successes. In a too-little known Denis Bethell Memorial Lecture, A. Murray points out how, by the end of the thirteenth century, some friars seconded to inquisitorial duties acted as a force on their own, no longer punishing heresy but procuring gain, abetted by Italian municipalities. The history of the inquisition and heresy diverges.

In a collection entitled *Religious Enthusiasm in the Medieval West* and an article on revivalism as a medieval religious genre, G. Dickson, with good ground, establishes a new subject, drawing sustenance from a close scrutiny of chronicles and the study of modern revivalism and such concepts as the 'burnt-over district'. Revivalism straddled the worlds of heresy and orthodoxy and Dickson's work has been decisive for my expositions on the Amalriciani and Flagellants.

10   Below, p. 292; cf. Cathars, pp. 124–6, Waldensians, 162, 178, 181.
11   Segl, *Die Anfänge der Inquisition*, below, pp. 106–7, 109.

The story of Hussitism has been altered less than any other part of the book. Writing from a pro-Taborite view, T. A. Fudge makes Taboritism more understandable and adds a contribution on Hussite propaganda and a full bibliography. Especially in his comments on Bohemian climate and temperature on the occasions of the alleged Adamite orgies, A. Patschovsky convinces me that these stories are nothing other than slander. The conference proceedings, *Jan Hus. Zwischen Zeiten, Völkern, Konfessionen*, edited by F. Seibt in 1997, contains a wealth of articles, not least the editor's own reflections, fruit of decades of his own work and reading. In his European articles and the conference he led in Munich, F. Šmahel remains a leading figure in modern Hussite studies in Prague; the German translation of his *Hussite Revolution* is anticipated at the end of 2001.[12]

The end of Marxist governments has liberated scholars from the rigidities of party dogma, and from the thunder of quotations from Marx, Engels and others previously necessary for publication. E. Werner devoted his last book on Jan Hus to a subject from his native Czechoslovakia. M. Erbstösser will be found in the Waldensian chapter elucidating the leading class of laymen in Germany who were intermediaries between masters and their congregations; B. Töpfer has published a definitive work on propertylessness and the concept of the state of innocence. 'Deconstruction' has, in a manner of speaking, taken over from orthodox Marxism: both approaches argue that heretical movements have as their driving force other factors, political or economic, rather than religious.

Experienced historians inevitably come to resemble undertakers: they deal only too often in loss and tragedy and must develop resistance to emotions which would prevent them carrying out their duties. Nowhere is this more true than in the study of heresy. Pleasure at the continual volume of valuable investigation in this field should never cause us to lose sight of the human disasters which lie behind the research. The pioneer of the study of medieval heresy in modern times for the English reader was H. C. Lea, the historian of the inquisition; seriously outdated in many aspects, his three volumes remain the most comprehensive treatment of the subject and may still be used with profit. He wrote with a powerful indignation. He hated the Middle Ages and its Church and he lacked any sympathetic understanding of the persecuting churchmen and their ideals. Yet the reader who, while admiring Lea's detailed scholarship, disagrees with him and his lack of perspective, must still be reminded that the history of medieval heresy is a terrible story – one of persecution of men and women for their religious opinions.[13]

---

12  *Husitská revoluce*, 2nd edn, I–IV (Prague, 1996); review, F. Seibt, *Bohemia* XL (1999), pp. 529–34.
13  H. C. Lea, *A History of the Inquisition of the Middle Ages* (1888); review, J. Dahlberg-Acton, *EHR* III (1888), pp. 773–88; E. Peters, 'Henry Charles Lea 1825–1909', *Medieval Scholarship* I, ed. H. Damico, J. B. Zařadil (1995), pp. 89–99.

# The Revival of Heresy in the West: The Eleventh Century

## Heresy and Politics at Orléans

Sometime after a fire in the year 1078 Paul, a monk of the community of St Père de Chartres, celebrating the memory of Aréfast, a Norman aristocrat, benefactor and former member of the community, inserted in the cartulary which he was compiling a vivid account of the startling events in which his hero had been involved some sixty years previously. His narrative has circumstantial details which suggest the evidence of an eye-witness, conceivably Aréfast himself; or Paul may have had a *libellus* in front of him, written by an Aréfast supporter much closer to the events to edify and to praise his achievement.[1] We shall never know exactly from where Paul got his information; what we have from the *excursus* in his cartulary is a moral tale, the spiritual odyssey of a layman, who set out on a chivalrous quest[2] on behalf of the Church, survived the trials and dangers of a heretical circle and played a major part, when the efforts of the natural authorities, king and bishops, were in danger of foundering, in unmasking an evil sect.

These events have been freshly analysed by R. H. Bautier in a publication of 1975.[3] In the narrative which follows, Paul's exposition has been put side by side with the facts about the political and ecclesiastical allegiances of the protagonists, as Bautier has elucidated them.

---

1    *Gesta Synodi Aurelianensis* in Bouquet, x, pp. 536–9; tr. *WEH* (largest collection of translated texts, with historical sketch, pp. 1–55), pp. 76–81, also *MBPH*, pp. 10–15 (working selection of translated texts up to triumph of Catharism; introduction to medieval attitudes, pp. 1–7); *libellus* hypothesis in B. Stock, *The Implications of Literacy* (1983) (illuminating analysis of chroniclers' thought); Paul of St Père prime source; orgy story excised as legendary digression; other sources in my 1st edn (1977), pp. 343–7, abandoning hypothesis of Bogomil infiltration; essential revision in R. H. Bautier, 'L'hérésie d'Orléans et le mouvement intellectuelle au début du xɪe siècle', *Actes du 95e Congrès National des Sociétés Savantes* (1970): *Section philologique et historique* (1975) ɪ, pp. 63–88; *libellus* and analysis of Paul, pp. 67–9, 76–7; H. Fichtenau, *Ketzer und Professoren* (1992) (*FK*) (parallel discussion of pop. heresy and academic development), pp. 33–43; tr. D. A. Kaiser as *Heretics and Scholars* (1998).
2    Stock, *Literacy*, p. 109.
3    Bautier, *Actes du 95e Congrès*.

Orléans was a centre of education, and of critical importance in a long-running battle for power between Robert the Pious, king of France, and his rival, Eudes II, Count of Blois, who needed the city to establish links between his holdings in the Sancerrois and his counties of Blois, Chartres and Tours. He who controlled the bishopric was a fair way towards controlling the city and its surrounding territory. Robert imposed on the chapter his candidate, Thierry, a protegé of his queen, Constance. The disappointed rival, Odalric, was a nephew of the bishop of Beauvais and, probably, of Eudes II: in any case, he was Eudes' man. Robert's intervention was controversial, but he got his way. Some of the chapter appealed for assistance to the honoured figure of Fulbert, bishop of Chartres, who condemned Robert's intervention and declined to take part in the consecration of Thierry. Some years passed. Suddenly, most likely late in 1022, Thierry was displaced. Odalric reigned in his place and Thierry took flight, first to his former monastery, St Pierre-le-Vif at Sens, and then to Rome. He died on the way.

Thierry's departure was a major defeat for Robert the Pious's party. At Christmas 1022 Robert journeyed with Queen Constance to Orléans to preside over a synod of bishops. A scandal had been uncovered in Orléans and the backlash from it had led to a shift of power. The bishops proceeded to interrogate a distinguished group of clergy, its core lying in the canons of the Church of Holy Cross. The total may have been as many as twenty, including, as well as the canons, nuns and other women, clergy, members of the nobility and Stephen, one-time confessor to Queen Constance. Aréfast, who was of the lineage of the dukes of Normandy and vassal to Duke Richard II, a member of the alliance of Eudes II of Blois, had got wind of heresy through his chaplain, Heribert, who had studied in Orléans and had learnt heresy in the house of Stephen, the queen's confessor, and Lisois, a canon of Holy Cross. Aréfast took action. When Heribert tried to ensnare him, he contacted his duke, who alerted King Robert. A trap was set. Posing as a potential convert, Aréfast set out for Orléans, turning in by the way to consult Fulbert, bishop of Chartres, the opponent of Thierry and a natural supporter of Eudes II. In Fulbert's absence, he took advice from Evrard, sacristan of Chartres, who recommended him to dissimulate, to listen and in due course to expose, while all the time availing himself of the protection afforded by Christ and the Church, praying, making the sign of the cross and doing what would have been unusual in a layman of the time, receiving holy communion every day.

It turned out to be a thoroughgoing heresy, traces of which in Orléans apparently went back to about 1015. The core of the heretics' beliefs lay in a *gnosis*, entry to which was conferred by a ceremony of laying-on of hands. Initiates, relieved of the stain of all sin, were filled by the gift of the Holy Spirit, which gave them full understanding of Scripture. Orthodox doctrines connected with Christ's possession of a human body were denied in the group: 'Christ was not born of the Virgin Mary. He did not suffer for men. He was not really buried in the sepulchre and was not raised from the dead.'[4] There was wholesale denial of the validity of the sacraments of the Church. 'In baptism there was no washing

4   These and subsequent quotations are from *MBPH*; another tr.: *WEH*, pp. 76–81.

away of sins.' Ordination was rejected, as was the mass. 'There is no sacrament', it was reported to be their belief, 'in the consecration by a priest of the body and blood of Christ.' Penance was also rejected. The initiate who had gained inner illumination was superior to these things, having entered on another level of being where he fed on heavenly food and saw angelic visions. Priesthood and Church were thus demoted by the experience of illumination. The 'heavenly food' Paul interpreted as meaning a devilish viaticum made of the ashes of a murdered baby, the child of the group's secret and nocturnal orgies, in which each of the men 'grabbed whatever woman came to hand'.

King, queen and bishops assembled. The heretics were captured, then interrogated in the Church of Holy Cross. Aréfast, in chains with the rest, revealed himself. It was essential in such cases to have a confession, and Aréfast's inner knowledge finally secured that. As the heretics attempted to hide their true beliefs behind cloudy phrases, he challenged them to reveal the nature of the teaching they had given him. Then, when Bishop Guarin of Beauvais questioned Stephen and Lisois, they turned on him, admitting Aréfast's accusations and explaining their denial of orthodoxy in terms of a blend of scepticism and an other-worldly rejection of earthly things. To the bishop's exposition of the reality of Christ's suffering and resurrection, they replied, 'We were not there, and we cannot believe that to be true', and to his question on the Virgin Birth, 'What nature denies is always out of harmony with the Creator'. When he asked them whether they believed in the doctrine of creation by the Father through the Son, they defied him, contrasting their knowledge of the Law written on the heart by the Holy Spirit and derived directly from the Creator with the bishop's teaching, fit to be related to 'those who have earthly wisdom and believe the fictions of carnal men, scribbled on animal skins'. 'Do with us what you will', they concluded. 'Now we see our king reigning in heaven, He will raise us to His right hand in triumph.' The assembly argued with them, trying to persuade them to recant; they resisted 'with the obstinacy of iron'. The clergy were then vested, solemnly stripped of their vestments by the bishops, and condemned. The queen, at the king's command, stood before the door of the Church 'to prevent the common people from killing them inside the church', and as Stephen, her former confessor, passed, struck out his eye with a staff. One clerk and a nun recanted; the rest were burnt in a cottage outside the walls of Orléans.

With the living, Paul tells us, were burned the 'evil ashes', the diabolical viaticum that issued from the nocturnal orgies. Punishment extended to the dead; after the executions, Odalric the bishop exhumed the body of the dead cantor, Theodatus, who had once been a member of the heretical circle, and threw it on waste ground.[5] Every trace of heresy was to be destroyed or removed, lest it imperil souls and damage the kingdom.

5   Adémar of Chabannes, *Chronique* III. lix, ed. J. Chavanon (Paris, 1897), pp. 184–5; *WEH*, p. 75. On Adémar as source, see Stock, *Literacy*, pp. 97, 115–17 and see below n. 36. New edns by J. France, N. Bulst and P. Reynolds (1989), G. Cavallo and G. Orlandi (1989).

No-one can say exactly what was in the mind of the king when he condemned the heretics to burn, for he had no near precedent for execution of any kind.[6] No Capetian king of France had ever burned heretics, and there had been no capital punishment for heresy in the West for centuries, since the execution of Priscillian of Avila in 383. Priscillian was suspect of the dualist heresy of Manichaeism, which excited fear and anger among both Christians and pagans; but in fact the official reason for burning him was witchcraft.

Had Robert been influenced by the popular custom of burning for sorcery? Or did the memory linger on among his councillors of the punishment of burning in Roman law for certain kinds of heretics? To the Romans, sorcery and religious deviation alike were political offences: both damaged the order and welfare of the State. The offence of heresy came to be assimilated to that of *lèse-majesté*, and punishment reached beyond the grave: hence, perhaps, at Orléans the exhumation of the dead cantor. Or was the dominant influence the notion that fire purged, and would most completely rid his kingdom of the taint of the heretical? Robert, an insecure ruler, could not afford to tolerate a heresy whose adherents openly defied orthodoxy: he was taking up the traditional Carolingian role of corrector and protector of the Church, destroying its enemies. A proper order was to be restored in society by the utter destruction of the heresy – even though that proceeding would bring damage to the king's immediate political interests.

And so it did. Thierry had had to go. A blow had been struck at the king and at the queen, whose marriage originally had been to the detriment of the Blois interest.[7] The heresy had come dangerously close to the court circle, since Lisois had been on close terms with the king, who was said to have admired his sanctity, and Stephen, revealed as a master in the heresy, had been the queen's confessor. The queen, a resourceful virago, distanced herself from the danger when she assaulted Stephen, repudiating his beliefs and no doubt giving vent to her own anger at the damage done by his folly. The king by his sentence could not have repudiated the heresy more emphatically. Burning vividly displayed him in the role of a Catholic ruler putting down heresy with resolution.[8]

Aréfast, when he reported his suspicions to Duke Richard, was putting a powerful weapon into the hands of the duke and the party of Eudes II of Blois, and by his dangerous role as spy ensured that it was effectively used. None the less, Aréfast's weapon would not have worked had not a genuine horror of heresy been present among clergy and people. Heresy in this episode stirred the common man: the crowd wanted to lynch the guilty, moved no doubt by their drastic denials of orthodoxy and by the conviction that they were (as the chroniclers said) servants of Satan, who should be eliminated from the earth.

---

6   R. Gorre, *Die ersten Ketzer im 11. Jahrhundert* (1985 edn) (analysis, with fine bibliography, of cases of Leutard, Orléans, Arras, Monteforte), pp. 102–16; burning: p. 274, n. 133.
7   R. I. Moore, *The Origins of European Dissent* (1977; 1985; references are all to 1985 edn) (forceful, well-written analysis from *c.* 1000 to early Cathars, with use of anthropology, sociology; classic introduction); summary on Bautier, Stock and Orléans: pp. 285–9, this reference: p. 287.
8   For some of the reactions which followed, see Bautier, *Actes du 95ᵉ Congrès*, p. 79; *FK*, p. 35.

Was a real heresy at work in Orléans, or had heresy accusations been artificially confected in the interests of a conspiracy? Bautier's analysis of the power-struggle over the bishopric which accompanied the scandal of heresy might suggest the latter:[9] the discrediting and condemnation of clergy close to the king and queen was convenient and excitable accusations had been made before. No-one would now accept that there was any genuine basis, for example, for accusations of heresy against Gerbert of Aurillac, the pioneer scholar, yet they were made. On this interpretation, Odalric, when he exhumed the body of the dead cantor and threw it on to waste ground, was exercising revenge on the plea of heresy on a former chapter member who had worked against his candidature.

Paul, or his source, was unaware of any conspiracy. He does not name the bishops who were present, or allude to the crisis over the episcopal election: his focus is solely on the battle between Aréfast, advised by Evrard the sacristan (a possible author for a *libellus* on the episode), and the heretics.[10] The assumption of Paul, which runs through his narrative, is that heresy must be of diabolical inspiration, and his *excursus* displays much of the prejudice and typecasting of heretics which bedevils most eleventh-century sources. Heresy, for Paul, is 'depravity', 'poison', 'the path of error', 'depths of wickedness', 'madness and devilish error'. The heretics are 'enemies of all truth', 'doomed and wretched'. Heribert is 'intoxicated with a deadly draught of evil'. There is an analogy with sickness: the heresy is described as 'the disease that was lurking in his [i.e. Robert's] kingdom'. These are heavily emotive, dehumanizing terms: R. I. Moore has shown us the effect which terms relating to medical disorders are liable to have.[11] They arouse fear, demand urgent remedies, conjure up frightening images and distract the observer from reporting or explaining.

When Paul reaches the climax of his story and the bishop of Beauvais at last, given the lead by Aréfast, elucidates the real views of the heretics, he shows himself quite uninterested in explaining how the heretical ideas had reached the guilty men, precisely the questions which intrigue the modern historian. There is an inner logic about this. If heresy is the work of the devil, it does not matter greatly what instruments he chances to use.

For Paul, the magical ash made from the dead baby had a well-nigh irresistible force: 'whoever', he says, 'had partaken of no matter how small a portion . . . was scarcely ever afterward able to direct his mind away from heresy'. A logical confutation – which was attempted in vain by the bishops – was no answer. What was effective was the superior power of Christ in the Host, protecting Aréfast.

9   R. I. Moore, 'The birth of popular heresy: a millennial phenomenon', *JRH* xxiv (2000), pp. 8–25 (see esp. for sweep of historiography), speaks of 'trumped-up heresy charges against political opponents': see also Id., *The Formation of a Persecuting Society* (1987) (wide-ranging hypotheses on origins of persecution of heretics, Jews, homosexuals, lepers), p. 16.
10   For illuminating analysis, see Stock, *Literacy*, pp. 108–15 (focusing on chronicler); assessment, R. I. Moore, 'New sects and secret meetings', *SCH* xxiii, pp. 47–68 at pp. 52, 59.
11   R. I. Moore, 'Heresy as disease', *Concept*, ed. Lourdaux and Verhelst, pp. 1–11.

This ash was so dangerous, it had to be destroyed along with the recalcitrant in the cottage outside the walls.[12]

The heretical group, in Paul's account, behaved exactly as heretics in the medieval stereotype were expected to behave, deceiving their judges about their beliefs, concealing them 'behind a shield of words'. Paul compares the respondents evading questions to a serpent 'which the more easily eludes the grasp the more tightly it is held in the hands'.[13] Only Aréfast's painstakingly acquired inner knowledge forced the guilty into confession. The trial did not, apparently, elucidate the secret libertinism of the adepts of the sect: Paul throws this in by way of explanation and admonition 'so that Christians should beware'. The link with the diabolical is explicit: only with the descent of a demon 'in the guise of some wild beast' are the lights extinguished and the orgy begun, the effects of which lead first to a birth and then to 'the test of the flames after the manner of the ancient pagans' of the baby, and the confecting of the diabolical ash-viaticum, the counterpart of the orthodox last rite.

Gnostics of the early centuries sometimes were libertines. Epiphanius's shame-faced yet circumstantial account of a sect he knew in the fourth century, man and woman copulating, then taking the man's sperm in their hands and looking up to heaven, has a ring of truth,[14] which Paul's account does not. At this point in his narrative, his concern with the diabolical has entirely detached him from the realities of the eleventh century – an impression reinforced by the discovery of a close and incongruous correspondence between Paul's orgy narrative and the work of the Christian apologist Justin Martyr, describing slanderous accusations by pagans against early Christian communities.[15]

For a modern observer, the combination of Paul's account of the secret orgy with his prejudices, and implicit evidence for conspiracy springing from the electoral conflict, might well lead to the conclusion that his testimony (albeit sincere) is fatally biased, and that a true group heresy at Orléans never existed.

The issue is complicated by the existence of five other chronicles of varying dates, which describe the doctrines of the Orléans group, sometimes in terms corresponding to those of Paul, sometimes not – and one of these, the letter by Jean de Fleury, was written only months after the synod.[16]

And yet, for all Paul's emotive terminology, his description of the manner in which the leaders of the Orléans circle carried Aréfast step by step towards their inner secrets corresponds so well to the technique of a Gnostic, illuminist sect, in which the core of doctrine is only revealed to a select few, taken on 'from the

---

12  On ashes, Gorre, *Ketzer*, pp. 64–7; on burning generally, *FK*, p. 35.
13  I here follow *WEH*, p. 80.
14  G. Filoramo, *A History of Gnosticism* (Oxford, 1990).
15  R. L. Poole, *Illustrations of the History of Medieval Thought and Learning* (repr. New York, 1960), p. 85; N. Cohn, *Europe's Inner Demons* (1975). Did the heretics' views on marriage provide a starting-point for the orgy story? (Duby's hypothesis.) Andreas of Fleury (see his *Vie de Gauzlin, Abbé de Fleury*, ed. R. H. Bautier and G. Labory (1969) attributed to them the view that 'marriages do not need blessing; let every man take any woman he likes, whoever she is'.
16  See appendix to Lambert, *Medieval Heresy* (*LMH*), 1st edn, pp. 343–8.

Charybdis of false belief' until illumination is attained and the neophyte has begun 'to open his eyes to the light of the true faith'.[17] The approach is well known, both from the history of the Gnostic sects of the early centuries and that of the Cathar movement in the twelfth and thirteenth centuries in the West. No other source has the telling details of Aréfast's search, his consultation with Evrard, the challenge to his erstwhile colleagues or the assault by the queen on her confessor. The physical details have an authenticity: should we dismiss, by contrast, *all* the exposition of doctrine contained in the same source? Paul, or his source, casts the narrative of the synod in the form of a dialogue between interrogators and heretics, in which the latter are finally pushed into revealing their beliefs; at the end of his drama we have the sentence of defiance to the bishop: 'You may spin stories in that way to those who have earthly wisdom and believe the fictions of carnal men, scribbled on animal skins.' It has all the idiosyncratic character of *ipsissima verba*. The trial ended in recalcitrance: the little group, with a leadership of trained minds, refused to recant and make an orthodox profession of faith, as they could have done. Death followed. There is no suggestion in the sources of torture or private mental pressure to elicit designed responses, as in later heresy trials in the Middle Ages.[18] The accused in the end were defiant; according to one source they 'laughed as they were bound to the pyre':[19] probably the effect of a strange state of exaltation which, as modern medical investigations suggest, confers immunity to pain and fear.

Few heresy accusations were ever launched out of pure concern for purity of doctrine; in this case the occasion for the unmasking of the heretics was political – but the heresy itself was real. It had spread from clergy to laity and embraced, as well as the intellectual core, members of the nobility. Heribert's attempt on Aréfast shows that they were ready to missionize. The fire extinguished them and there is no record of any subsequent tradition in Orléans. Authority had cut them off.

The heresy was *sui generis*, probably an amalgam of neoplatonic speculation and of inferences made from the search, familiar to biblical scholars of the time, for an inner meaning beneath the literal surface of the text of Scripture 'written on animal skins'.[20] Extreme though the views of the Orléans elite turned out to be, with their Docetism, their belief that the body of Christ was an illusion and their rejection of a bodily resurrection – doctrines which, together with Gnostic-type emphasis on mysteries known only to initiates, curiously resembled the tenets of the heretical movement of the Bogomils,[21] then spreading from its

---

17  Key passages: *MBPH*, pp. 11–12.
18  See e.g. the case of the Templars, below, pp. 198–9.
19  Adémar: *WEH*, p. 76.
20  B. Smalley, reviewing Moore, *Origins*, *EHR* xciii (1978), pp. 853–6 at p. 855; books gave confirmation of pre-existing beliefs, in Fichtenau's view (*FK*, p. 34).
21  See below, p. 63; Moore, *Origins*, pp. 26–8 (on Orléans, 25–39, 40–4, 285–9) rejects Bogomil influence; he convinced me, *LMH* 2nd edn, pp. 9–32 in contradistinction to 1st edn, pp. 7–23. For debate between Bogomil and Western interpns. see *RB*, pp. 476–83; Ilarino da Milano, 'Le Eresie popolari del secolo xi nell' Europa occidentale', *Studi Gregoriani*, ed. G. B. Borino, ii (1947), pp. 43–89; most exclusively Western interpn., R. Morghen, *Medioevo Cristiano* (1953) from *ADRSP* lxvii (1944), pp. 97–151, arousing controversy in Dondaine, 'L'Origine de l'hérésie médiévale', *RSCI* vi (1952),

cradle-land in Bulgaria into other parts of the Byzantine Empire[22] – the heresy is most likely to have evolved spontaneously, an aspect of the reawakening of learning in the West in the late tenth and early eleventh centuries. Gerbert of Aurillac, dogged by accusations of heresy and necromancy, had felt himself compelled to issue a declaration of orthodoxy derived from the fifth-century *Statuta Ecclesiae antiqua*, a declaration aimed, among other items, at dualist heresy on the legitimacy of marriage and the eating of meat.[23] Liery, archbishop of Sens who took part in the synod at Orléans, had been involved earlier in the century in eucharistic controversy and, when he changed the words of consecration in the mass, had received a letter from Robert the Pious threatening him with deposition. Odorannus, a protégé of Thierry at St Pierre-le-Vif, was persecuted on grounds of heresy in the aftermath of the Orléans affair.

Fears of heresy were aroused by the work of scholars and their discussions; accusations circulated, could be, and were, used in politico-ecclesiastical battles. The suspects of Orléans, however, in the hot-house atmosphere of their little circle had incubated a heresy of their own and through Heribert had begun to missionize. Challenged, they were defiant. The first burning in the West was a burning of true heretics.

## Heresy at Monteforte

So was the second, at Milan about 1028. Archbishop Aribert of Milan, accompanied by some of his clergy and *capitanei*,[24] the leading class of Milan and its *contado*, had embarked on a pastoral tour of his suffragan dioceses, designed to knit them more closely to the see of St Ambrose, when in the diocese of Turin he

pp. 43–78; further work by Morghen, *HS*, bibliography and pp. 121–38 (see esp. Delaruelle's quotation, p. 137); facts, C. Thouzellier, 'Tradition et résurgence dans l'hérésie médiévale', *HS*, pp. 105–20; J. B. Russell, *Dissent and Reform in the Early Middle Ages* (1965) (central theme of Western generation but with added dimension of pre-1000 heresy); accepting partial Bogomilism, A. Borst, *Die Katharer* (1953) (*BK*) (succinct, classic account, emphasis on doctrine), pp. 71–80; criticism of Bogomil interpn., H. C. Puech, 'Catharisme médiévale et Bogomilisme', *Oriente ed Occidente nel Medio Evo* (1957), pp. 84–104; E. Werner, 'Häresie und Gesellschaft im 11. Jahrhundert', *SSAWL Philologischhistorische Klasse* CXVII, V (1975), pp. 5–83; for Bogomil influence based on subtle dogmatic analysis, J. V. Fearns, 'Peter von Bruis und die religiöse Bewegung des 12. Jahrhunderts', *AKG* XLVII (1966), pp. 311–35. Helpful surveys, C. N. L. Brooke, 'Heresy and religious sentiment 1000–1250', *BIHR* XLI (1968), pp. 115–31, repr. Id., *Medieval Church and Society* (1971), pp. 139–61; G. Cracco, 'Riforma ed Eresia in momenti della cultura Europa tra X e XI secolo', *RSLR* VII (1971), pp. 411–77. Recent work by Moore, below p. 25, n. 36; for partial revival of Bogomil hypothesis, below, pp. 36–7; B. Töpfer, reviewing Fichtenau in *Mediaevistik* VIII (1995), pp. 366–88 believes Bogomil influence understated (see also *Jahrbuch für Geschichte des Feudalismus* XII (1988), p. 381); M. Barber, *The Cathars* (2000) (*BC*), pp. 21–30 suggests revision; B. Hamilton, 'Wisdom from the East', *BHL* (ref. below, p. 62, n. 38), pp. 38–60, argues for possible influence via Orthodox monks visiting Western shrines.

22 D. Obolensky, *The Bogomils* (Cambridge, 1948); for a subtle account of doctrines in analysis of Cosmas the Priest, see H. C. Puech and A. Vaillant, *Le Traité contre les Bogomils de Cosmas le Prêtre* (1945); survey: M. Loos, *Dualist Heresy in the Middle Ages* (1974); summary: *LMH*, 1st edn, pp. 12–23; below, p. 63, n. 41 Hamilton notes that Bogomilism was evolving in Byzantium in the eleventh century and not 'fully-fledged' either there or in the West, where he believes it had begun to make itself felt.

23 For argument and examples, see Bautier, *Actes du 95e Congrès*, pp. 82–6.

24 *Capitanei* rather than 'a troop of brave knights' (*WEH*, p. 86): Gorre, *Ketzer*, p. 184 and p. 312, n. 5.

received news of a suspected heresy at the castle of Monteforte, in the diocese of Asti, three days' journey from the city.[25] Their leader, Gerard, was brought to Turin to be interrogated. It is not clear whether he was a layman or a cleric. He had certainly undergone some intellectual training and, unlike the Orléans leadership, did not wish to conceal his views from authority. Indeed, in the account given by Landulf Senior, a reputable Milanese historian, writing some seventy-five years after the event, but apparently with some record of Aribert's investigation in front of him, Gerard responded to the archbishop with all the bright confidence of an adept. 'To God Omnipotent...', Landulf reports him as saying, 'I give boundless thanks that you take the pains to examine me so carefully. And may He who knew you from the beginning in the loins of Adam grant that you live unto Him and die unto Him and be glorified.'[26]

He then proceeded to expound the group's belief and inner discipline. It was austere indeed. Sexual intercourse was prohibited as wrong in itself. Virgins were expected to preserve virginity, married men to treat their wives as though they were their mothers or sisters. The group never ate meat, allowed no private property, and fasted. Gerard mentioned elders ('majores') who took turns in praying, night and day, 'that no hour may pass without prayer', and a single leader ('major noster') who gave 'permission' for those who had lost their virginity to observe perpetual chastity. In a mysterious phrase he said: 'None of us ends his life without torments, that we may thus avoid eternal torments.' His conclusion sounded conventional. 'We believe in and confess', he said, 'the Father, Son and Holy Spirit. We believe truly that we are bound and loosed by those who have the power of binding and loosing. We hold to both the Old and New Testament and to the holy canons, and we read them daily.' Apart from the oddity of the 'torments', Gerard's group sounded like an ascetic monastic community, based on an individualistic reading of Scripture, exactly of the kind then spreading in Italy, albeit with the important qualification that Gerard and his group's teaching made the celibate, monastic way of life compulsory for all.

Aribert scented heresy: 'recognizing his astuteness and evil genius from certain phrases', he pressed Gerard on the Trinity. Gerard's replies, which to a modern historian suggest neoplatonism from Eriguena or Augustine,[27] almost certainly appeared to Aribert and his companions to be heretical definitions of the Persons of the Trinity. 'The Father', he said, 'is the eternal God, who created everything in the beginning and in whom all things exist. The Son is the spirit of man ['animus hominis'], beloved by God. The Holy Spirit is the understanding of

---

25    *Landulphi senioris Mediolanensis historiae*..., ed. A. Cutolo, Muratori IV, 2, pp. 67–9, tr. *WEH*, pp. 86–9; *MBPH* (using *MGH* edn), pp. 19–21; C. Violante, *La Società Milanese nell'eta precommunale* (Bari, 1953), pp. 176–86, Stock, *Literacy*, pp. 174–215, esp. pp. 188–9 on portrait of Aribert; H. E. J. Cowdrey, 'Archbishop Aribert', *History* LI (1967), pp. 1–15; dating of episode from R. Glaber, from his allusion to crowning of Conrad II. Glaber, Burgundian Cluniac, unreliable on doctrines, provides factual material. Stock, *Literacy*, p. 139, rejects attempts to reconcile Glaber and Landulf. On Glaber and class of heretics ('miles'), see Gorre, *Ketzer*, p. 218; geographical setting: pp. 212–13.

26    *WEH*, p. 87, for this and the following four quotations.

27    Gorre, *Ketzer*, pp. 185–204; *FK*, p. 46, doubts a diffusion of Eriguena, preferring neoplatonism via Augustine.

divine matters ['intellectus divinarum scientiarum'] by which individual things are governed.'[28] Aribert probed further: 'What do you say of Christ, the Word of God, born of a virgin?' Had Gerard clung to the kind of accepted ecclesiastical formulae which underlay Aribert's questioning, he might yet have saved himself, but he chose not to. He replied, 'The Jesus of whom you speak is the spirit, born sensibly ['sensualiter'] from the Virgin, that is the understanding of sacred Scripture.' The phrases are reminiscent of Eriguena's commentary on St John's Gospel, where he uses a mode of discussion of the doctrine of the Trinity based on analogies rather than definitions, and there are echoes in Gerard's replies of Eriguena's double similitudes.[29] But Aribert is likely to have seen nothing other than a denial of the existence of Christ as a historical person, and a voiding of orthodox doctrine.

A question followed about the implications of Gerard's views on marriage for procreation and the future of humanity. Gerard answered that if the human race agreed 'not to experience corruption' (i.e. engage in sexual intercourse) it would then be begotten 'without coition, like bees'. This was another intellectual reminiscence, for Ambrose, Isidore of Seville and Alcuin had all used the bees as an image of purity.[30] 'In whom', Aribert went on, 'is absolution of our sins – in the Pope, in a bishop or in any priest?' Gerard in reply dismissed all the hierarchy in favour of the direct experience of the Spirit. 'We do not have that Roman pontiff, but another who daily visits our brothers, scattered throughout the world, and when he brings God to us, pardon is granted.' Aribert asked how life ended 'in torments'. The answer implied murder. 'If we expire through torments inflicted upon us by the wicked, we rejoice, but if nature at any time brings us near death, the one nearest us kills us in some way ['quoquo modo'] before we yield up our soul.' A last question in Landulf's account was a catch-all, covering the faith of the Roman Church, the nature of Christ, 'truly the Son of God, who was born of the Virgin Mary according to the flesh', and the validity of the sacrament of the body and blood of Christ, as administered by a Catholic priest 'though a sinner'. The reference to the priesthood only elicited a repetition of Gerard's denial of papal authority. 'There is no other pontiff beside our Pontiff, though he is without tonsure of the head or any sacred mystery.'

Heresy was manifest. Aribert sent a strong force to arrest the heretics of the castle and bring them to Milan. Landulf describes them as 'milites', rough men, castellans, often engaged in local war. The haul included both men and women, among whom was a countess. The attempt was made to convert them to orthodoxy, but without success; on the contrary, Landulf says, 'those most wicked persons, who had come into Italy from some unknown part of the world' missionized among curious peasants who had come into the city from the countryside.

---

28   Tr. in Stock, *Literacy*, p. 142, preferred to *WEH*; my capitals.
29   Gorre, *Ketzer*, as above; see esp. pp. 198–9; H. Taviani, 'Naissance d'une hérésie en Italie du nord au xie siècle', *Annales* xxix (1974), pp. 124–52; criticism: Gorre, *Ketzer*, p. 318, n. 54.
30   Moore, *Origins*, p. 14; pungent account of Monteforte: pp. 31–5.

The *capitanei* acted, in Landulf's interpretation against the wishes of Aribert,[31] and forced the heretics to choose between a pyre and a cross. Some chose the cross and recanted; 'many, covering their faces with their hands, leaped into the flames'. Landulf, like Paul of St Père for the Orléans affair, described a duel between good and evil, in which heresy is disclosed and punished; his hero is an archbishop, not a devout layman, penetrating the true nature of the heresy where his companions could not. It forms part of Landulf's depiction of a faithful spiritual leader, the repression of a heresy being one of the multifarious duties of his position, successfully carried out. For the chronicler heresy is wickedness, but Landulf's account lacks the demonological overtones of Paul.

The heresies were in each case illuminist: the experience of the group or the leader overrode the teaching of the Church. At Orléans, at first reluctantly, and then openly in the final exchanges with the bishop of Beauvais, and at Monteforte without shame from the outset, a spokesman for the accused rejected the Church. Gerard expounded his Trinitarian views wholly in personal terms. A threefold 'dixi' in Landulf's narrative, 'What I called the Father', 'What I called the Son', 'What I called the Holy Spirit', makes plain where Gerard's authority lay – in his own inner understanding. In both cases the spur to heresy seems to have been intellectual, in a neoplatonist tradition; but how and where Gerard acquired his knowledge or evolved his views remains unknown. Perhaps even the 'torments' of the group, which Landulf and Aribert found so strange, owe their origins to a strained understanding of Eriguena's exposition of Paul's saying in Galatians about being crucified with Christ.[32]

Puzzles remain. The 'torments' set up echoes in the mind of the much later practice of *endura* in Catharism.[33] Did dualist, as well as neoplatonic, influences play on Gerard's group? At the core of the inner discipline lay an exasperated asceticism, perhaps derived from Western monastic tradition, or perhaps from the Messalian heresy, a feature of Byzantine monasticism.[34] A Byzantine colony still existed in the south of Italy, a possible source of contacts.

What clearly differentiates the Monteforte group from the circle uncovered at Orléans is the degree of lay participation. The heretics at Orléans were churchmen, with a certain overspill into the lay world at a high level; it is a membership wholly compatible with an intellectual heresy, developed secretly among scholars in a closed study circle. At Monteforte there is no certain clerical membership at all, and the core of the incipient movement lay in the *milites* and their dependants.[35] The heresy reached as high as a countess, and could also touch peasants (taking Landulf's *rustici* in its most literal sense) from the *contado* of Milan. Landulf, who appreciated diligence, recorded an unceasing activity on the part of the heretics, 'who behaved as though they were good priests, and daily spread false

---

31  Gorre, *Ketzer*, p. 226, is sceptical about this; Moore, *Origins*, p. 35, is not.
32  Gorre, *Ketzer*, p. 201.
33  Below, p. 152.
34  Moore, *Origins*, pp. 31–4.
35  Gorre argues that poverty and isolation predisposed to a life of renunciation, *Ketzer*, p. 225; I am not convinced.

teachings wrenched from the scriptures'. It was a threat to souls and to stability of authority in the *contado*; on that the *capitanei* acted.

## Heresy and the Peace of God in Aquitaine

In Aquitaine in the same epoch the chronicler Adémar of Chabannes recorded a heretical movement on a scale dwarfing the episodes at Orléans and Monteforte. He gave his movement a label, recalling one of the most infamous names in the constellation of ideas of medieval churchmen, that of the third-century heretical preacher, Mani. 'Shortly thereafter', he wrote, 'Manichees arose throughout Aquitaine seducing the promiscuous populace, negating holy baptism and the power of the cross, the Church and the Redeemer of the World, marriage and the eating of meat – whatever was sound doctrine. Abstaining from food, they seemed like monks and faked chastity. But in fact among themselves they practised every depravity and were the messengers of the Antichrist; and they turned many simple people from the faith.'[36] In the earliest extant manuscript Adémar's account of the rise of the Manichees follows on the heels of a tragedy at the shrine of St Martial in the basilica at Limoges, in which fifty-two men and women were accidentally trampled to death in a panic before dawn in mid-Lent 1028. In that manuscript he wrote at the beginning of his Manichee sentences 'e vestigio' (translated above as 'shortly thereafter'), a phrase which elsewhere in his chronicle carries an element of causality. He changed his mind about linking the basilica tragedy to the Manichees and in two subsequent versions replaced 'e vestigio' by 'paulo post', which has no hint of causality, and introduced material after the account of the trampling, separating it from the story of the Manichees, and so concealing any connection.[37] Why did he come to do this?

One hypothesis is that he came to see the episode as discreditable to the shrine of St Martial and its reputation on which he had spent so much effort. A very late tradition had it that Abbot Geoffrey II attempted to molest a woman in the basilica, and that the scandal turned to panic amongst a great crowd.[38] The tragedy, at a critical point in the febrile history of religious revival in Aquitaine, caused a breakdown in confidence between excited masses and the monastic and ecclesiastical establishment. The rise, perhaps, better, the popularizing of a 'Manichee' movement outside the Church, was the result.

36   Edn of Adémar, as above, n. 5; R. Landes, 'The dynamics of heresy and reform in Limoges: a study of popular participation in the "Peace of God" (994–1033)', *Essays on the Peace of God: The Church and the People in Eleventh Century France*, ed. T. Head, R. Landes, *Historical Reflections / Réflexions Historiques* XIV (3) (1987), pp. 467–511 at p. 499, translates a conflated version of three texts of the chronicle. See also p. 502, n. 118. Landes, *Relics, Apocalypse and the Deceits of History* (1995) (fine-drawn analysis of Adémar's thought-world, with recreation of conditions in Aquitaine), pp. 24–49, 67–8; R. I. Moore, 'Heresy, repression and social change in the age of the Gregorian reform', *Christendom and Its Discontents*, ed. S. J. Waugh, P. Diehl (1996), pp. 19–46.
37   Landes, *Relics*, pp. 175–7.
38   Landes in *Essays*, ed. Head, Landes, p. 502, n. 120; development of a 'Christian community', Id., *Relics*, p. 128.

'They seemed like monks', Adémar wrote of the heretics. Disillusioned with official monasticism, they turned to a fiercely ascetic monasticism of their own outside the Church. Popular enthusiasm, in sum, outran the leadership of churchmen. This was the more significant as news began to travel further and faster. What Landes calls a 'culturally charged Christian community' was emerging.

That deep passions were aroused by St Martial emerges from Adémar's description, for the panic took place at nocturnal vigils, that is before dawn, and the numbers at this early hour must have been great to issue in so many deaths. Hagiographers, Adémar prominent among them, had so developed the cult of Martial that he came for a time to be accepted in Aquitaine as an apostle, one who held the towel for Jesus at the Last Supper. The bubble burst in 1029, on the very day on which the saint's remains were to be translated and an apostolic liturgy sung in his honour. Adémar, challenged by a speaker, the Lombard Benedict of Chiusa, on the accuracy of Martial's claim to apostolic status in the presence of listening crowds, could not make a convincing defence. Support for Martial's apostolicity vanished. It was a sign that the adherence of the masses could not be taken for granted – they could listen to arguments, exercise choice and accept or reject religious leadership.[39]

So in the Peace movement as a whole. Born, probably, at the Council of Le Puy under Bishop Guy in 975 with oath-taking from the assembled laity to preserve peace, protect Church property and the poor, the Peace of God had some of its most effective life in Aquitaine under the patronage of William v, duke 990–1031, who with the bishops and the magnates commanded a remarkable response from the mass of the laity.[40] Adémar described the scene at the Council of Limoges under the duke in 994 in the presence of the relics of the saints, with solemn oath-taking to keep the peace and the threat of excommunication and interdict to enforce compliance, and 'a huge crowd of people filling all the places to twelve miles around the city, rejoicing under open, brilliant skies'.[41] Eschatological expectations heightened enthusiasm at the millennium of Christ's birth in the year 1000 and again at the millennium of the crucifixion in 1033.[42] The sacral power of the saints was used to enforce peace and break the habit of brigandage and private war on the part of *milites* profiting by the weakness of

---

39   Landes, *Relics*, pp. 228–50; see also on Adémar, D. F. Callahan, 'Ademar of Chabannes, millennial fears and the development of Western anti-Judaism', *JEH* XLVI (1995), pp. 19–35 at 27–9; Id., 'The Manichaeans and the Antichrist in the Writings of Ademar of Chabannes: the Terrors of the Year 1000', *Studies in Medieval and Renaissance History* XV (1995), pp. 163–223.
40   F. S. Paxton, 'The Peace of God in modern historiography: perspectives and trends', *Essays*, ed. Head, Landes, pp. 385–404; B. Töpfer, *Volk und Kirche zur Zeit der beginnenden Gottesfriedensbewegung in Frankreich* (Berlin, 1957); H. E. J. Cowdrey, *The Peace and the Truce of God in the eleventh century*, *PP* XLVI (1970), pp. 42–67; outline: J.-P. Poly and E. Bournazel, *La Mutation Féodale X–XIIe Siècles* (Paris, 1980), pp. 234–50, maps: pp. 241, 243; heresy: p. 390. *The Feudal Mutation 900–1200*, trans. C. Higgitt (1991).
41   Landes, in *Essays*, ed. Head, Landes, p. 467.
42   For Glaber as chronicler and the millennium, see Stock, *Literacy*, pp. 466–72; G. Duby, *L'An mil* (Paris, 1967). See *The Peace of God*, ed. T. Head, R. Landes (1992); postscript by R. I. Moore, pp. 308–26.

royal power and the breakdown of Carolingian structures of authority in the south of France. Councils roused fervour, in which for a time duke, magnates and the 'pauperes', those without a share in power,[43] were united in common endeavour. To an unusual degree a wide social alliance, which included the common people, was forged by religious zeal. Unarmed crowds played a significant part. Miracle stories at the time of the councils emerged from among the common people.[44]

But inner tensions whittled away this unity, and brittle enthusiasm turned among some to dissent and heresy. When Abbot Geoffrey's death occurred, the bishop, who was his nephew, declined to consecrate his successor as abbot and kept the abbot's revenues for himself for two years and, although public opinion compelled the bishop to take action and consecrate, it was the kind of episode which weakened the alliance between churchmen and the masses. Adémar's challenger, who worsted him in public debate about St Martial, claimed openly that the monks pursued the cult of the saint out of pride, arrogance and the desire for money. In the 1020s the effectiveness of excommunication and interdict, which rested on public opinion, showed signs of breaking down. If some did turn against their ecclesiastical leaders, the very meetings of enthusiastic crowds in the open air which accompanied the Peace could point the way to a heresy, of the type of the alleged Manichees, which dispensed with hierarchy, buildings and religious apparatus.[45]

Temporal factors also mattered. The Peace of God offered a vision of unity, peace and order from which all would benefit. In practice the rewards were not available for those without power. Lords, churches, monasteries, not the small men gained from the upheavals then taking place in the south, whether connected or not with the Peace.[46] The fall of the Peace movement and the rise of the seigneurie were connected. There was disillusionment. Towards the end of his life Duke William seems to have accepted that the Peace was no longer a mass-movement – or perhaps he no longer wished that it should be so in his Duchy. Its law-enforcing function continued, with the pact and the oaths; but directed by the magnates. St Martial was still honoured. Great crowds were present at the consecration of a new basilica in his honour, and the duke came to venerate his relics in 1028. But the intimate link between the Peace and widespread religious enthusiasm had frayed. At about the same time as the translation of St Martial and the consecrating of the basilica the duke determined on action against the 'Manichees' and summoned a council of bishops and abbots at Charroux 'to wipe out the heresies which the Manichees had been spreading among the people'.[47]

---

43   For this interpretation of 'pauperes', see R. I. Moore, 'Family, community and cult on the eve of the Gregorian Reform', *TRHS*, 5th ser. xxx (1980), pp. 49–69.

44   Landes, in *Essays*, ed. Head, Landes, p. 488.

45   Ibid., pp. 505 (bishop and revenues), 495 (monks' motives), 506 (open-air meetings).

46   G. Duby, *The Three Orders: Feudal Society Imagined* (London, 1980), pp. 147–66.

47   *MBPH*, p. 10; Landes, in *Essays*, ed. Head, Landes, pp. 507–8. Id., *Relics*, pp. 198–9.

## The Trial at Arras

In 1025 a group of heretics was seized at Arras; Bishop Gerard of the diocese of Cambrai and Arras, most probably on a pastoral visitation, got wind of their presence and had them imprisoned. He wrote to his fellow bishop Roger I of Châlons, upbraiding him for being deceived by them and failing to act effectively when warned of the presence of 'wicked men, bewitched by the spirit of error', whose missionaries, he claimed, came to spread their errors in Arras.[48] Report said they came from Italy and they acknowledged a master, Gundolfo, who was not captured. Gerard kept them in prison for three days, where they may have been tortured, and ordered a day's fast by the monks and clergy of his diocese in hopes that the heretics might be restored to orthodoxy. On the third day, a Sunday in January, the bishop, in the majesty of his office, processed with his archdeacons carrying crosses and copies of the gospels and 'a great throng of all the clergy and people' to a formal hearing in church.

It must have lasted at least a day. As the report of the synod describes it, the heretics were interrogated by the bishop, revealed their beliefs and their dependence on Gundolfo, 'by whom they had been instructed in the precepts of the Gospels and of the apostles', and, with the assembled clergy and people, the archdeacons, abbots and monks seated in order of rank, were treated to a long exposition of orthodoxy by the bishop.

The report was written up, no doubt by order of Gerard, some time after the event; the bishop's sermon, almost 20,000 words in length,[49] cannot all have been delivered as it stands: it was enlarged, probably greatly enlarged, and then published. The reproachful letter to Roger of Châlons promised him a *libellus* on the heresy, and this was very likely it. To one modern historian, the bishop's statement reads like a summary from some handbook for the education of priests, deploying, though not acknowledging, for example, the Carolingian theologians Radbert and Hrabanus Maurus, to refute at length the heretics' views on baptism.[50]

A veteran imperialist bishop with traditionalist views, the enemy of the Peace of God movement, which he regarded as subverting the order of society, he seized the

---

48 *Acta Synodi Atrebatensis*, orig. ed. Luc d'Achery, *Spicilegium* (Paris, 1677), pp. 1–63; see Migne, *PL* CXLII; for the following quotations, see *MBPH*, pp. 15–19; tr. extracts synodal proceedings: *WEH*, pp. 82–5; E. van Mingroot, 'Acta Synodi Atrebatensis (1025): problèmes de critique de provenance', *Studia Gratiana* XX (1976), pp. 202–30, for dating, and identification of Gerard's addressee as Roger I of Châlons, eliminating doubts of J. B. Russell, 'A propos de synode d'Arras en 1025', *RHE* LVII (1962), pp. 66–87; Gorre, *Ketzer*, p. 276, n. 2, p. 310, n. 164 (diocesan history); analysis of sources: J. B. Russell, *Dissent*, pp. 21–7, Stock, *Literacy*, pp. 120–39, Moore, *Origins*, pp. 9–18, Gorre, *Ketzer*, pp. 132–62 (dissects influences on bishop's speech); *LMH*, 1st edn, p. 27, n. 16, is superseded. Evidence for the torture of the suspects lies in the term 'supplicia' used by the bishop in his letter to Roger I.
49 Moore's estimate: *MBPH*, p. 15.
50 Gorre, *Ketzer*, pp. 133, 163; I have not accepted Gorre's view, p. 169, that the Arras group were not heretics. G. Lobrichon, 'Arras, 1025, ou le vrai procès d'une fausse accusation', *Inventer l'Hérésie?*, ed. M. Zerner (1998), pp. 67–85, describing Gerard's sermon as 'the manifesto of a great servant of the Empire' (p. 85), reduces the 'heretics' to almost nothing; I cannot agree.

opportunity to launch a defence of the sacramental system of the Church, aimed as much at the instruction of the assembled orthodox audience, and especially the monks and clergy, as at the heretics themselves. A phrase in the synod's report which may well go back to the sermon actually preached, gives a clue to the bishop's intentions. 'The day was now wearing to a close and the lord bishop said . . . "There are other things, brothers, which I ought to say to strengthen you in your faith, but in case I oppress you with a great burden of words let that suffice." '[51] The brothers ('fratres') can only be the monks and clerks in the bishop's audience.

Gerard believed that the accused heretics rejected the legitimacy of marriage. They may, in fact, not have done so, but the bishop put forward a defence of matrimony in which he is breaking a lance in a long controversy over the status of marriage, which troubled the eleventh-century Church. On the one hand, ecclesiastical authority wished to enforce celibacy on the clergy – and this was widely resisted. On the other, authority wished to eliminate concubinage amongst the laity and enforce monogamy. That, too, was widely resisted, partly on the ground that sexual union was not the business of the Church. Gerard was as grudging as contemporary churchmen generally were on marriage. 'God is not pleased', he wrote, 'by marriages that incite men to sensuality and pleasure as if they were beasts.' But, none the less he was quite clear that a total rejection of marriage, a dualist, Manichaean view, was to be avoided: 'anyone who uses marriage so that, in the fear of God, its intent is the love of children rather than the satisfaction of the flesh, cannot, merely for the fault ['culpa'] of marriage, be excluded from the community of the faithful'.[52]

What the accused at Arras seem to have inculcated was, simply, the restraint of the flesh 'from carnal longings', not necessarily the same thing as a rejection of marriage *per se*, though that inference cannot be excluded. Accusations of dualism and the total rejection of the legitimacy of matrimony, however, were in the air, and Bishop Gerard is not likely to have been careful to pinpoint exactly what the heretics before him believed.

The safest entry-point to their teachings lies early on in the report of the synod, where the bishop interrogated them. Their answers to his queries put Scripture first – in the interpretation by Gundolfo of 'the precepts of the Gospels and of the apostles'. 'They accepted no other Scripture than this', says the report. The bishop had heard that they rejected the sacraments, baptism, the mass, confession and penance and 'legitimate matrimony'. He cited Christ's words to Nicodemus about being born again of water and the Spirit, as a proof text out of Scripture that they so valued, for the necessity of baptism, and they replied summarizing their way of life, which they insisted to be in accord with Scripture. Their 'law and doctrine' was 'to abandon the world, to restrain our flesh from carnal longings, to earn our bread by the labour of our hands, to wish harm to

51  *MBPH*, p. 17.
52  G. Duby, *The Knight, the Lady and the Priest* (London, 1984); see esp. pp. 114, 116. Controversy over the Church's role in marriage may lie behind statements attributed to the Orléans heretics by certain chroniclers. Andreas of Fleury's witness is the key point (p. 111); see also above, p. 19 and n. 15.

none, to show loving-kindness to all who are gripped by zeal for our way of life'.[53] The practice of this moral life, which they described as *justitia*, the way of righteousness, did away with any necessity for baptism. If *justitia* was observed, they argued, baptism was superfluous; if not, it could not save. Anticlerical feeling and insistence on individual responsibility influenced them against baptism in a way that was to become familiar in the twelfth century in the West. It was invalid because of the evil life of its ministrants, the certainty that sins renounced in it would be repeated in later life and the impossibility of an adult making renunciations on behalf of a child.

Gerard brought the power of his office to bear – although, interestingly enough, he was prepared to argue texts with them, and that at length. He made plain in the body of his sermon that the right interpretation lay with the priest and not the layman, and expounded what *justitia* consisted in. At the end, the synod report described the heretics as 'stupefied'. They were illiterate. Their master Gundolfo was not with them. They submitted. Bishop and clergy made a declaration of orthodoxy in Latin, including the sentence 'The Lord and his disciples and the apostle of the gentiles gave licence for marriage and ordained it to be observed by those to whom it is permitted'. The heretics asked for translation into the vernacular, then put their cross against an attestation of faith and were allowed to go home unpunished, for they had submitted. This was significant. The only extant text of these proceedings is in a late twelfth-century compilation, conceivably of Cistercian origin, together with treatises directed against Catharism. Arguably the compiler drew into his *vade mecum* against heretics an account of a much older heresy, firstly to demonstrate its ubiquity and secondly to show a case where the heresy was dealt with victoriously by persuasion and not by force.[54] 'Polemic can win' is his message. Arras was, in this, unusual.

### Early Western Heresy

Heresy had reappeared in the West after a long gap. The effects of the barbarian invasions in Western Europe had provided a kind of *tabula rasa* for orthodoxy. Catholicism under the pope at Rome came to win almost total victory in the territories under his jurisdiction.[55] Arianism, the fourth-century heresy which

53  I have preferred *WEH*, p. 84, at this point to *MBPH*, p. 17. Did the Arras group reject marriage, either for themselves or for all believers on the lines of Monteforte group? Their will to restraint from 'carnal longings' runs side by side with the will to abandon the world: it is therefore likely that they were a quasi-monastic group, as Monteforte was. There is no evidence that they, as opposed to Bishop Gerard, had any concern with the debate about the sacralization of marriage. The bishop assumed that they did condemn matrimony *per se* (perhaps in his view, as part of the wholesale rejection of sacraments, their characteristic feature): I agree with Moore, Stock and Gorre in thinking his speech is not evidence either way. On the bishop's motives, see Moore, *Origins*, p. 15.

54  *MBPH*, p. 18. On submission of the Arras group, R. I. Moore, 'Literacy and the making of heresy, c.1000–c.1150', *Heresy and Literacy 1000–1530*, ed. P. Biller, A. Hudson (1994) (*BHL*), pp. 19–37 at p. 32; MS history, Lobrichon, 'Arras', pp. 70–2.

55  H. I. Marrou, 'L'héritage de la Chrétienté', *HS*, pp. 51–4, at p. 53 (see *HS* for wide-ranging articles on heresies and society); on historiographical sequel to *HS*, A. Vauchez, 'L'Historiographie des hérésies médiévales', *L'Ogre historien. Autour de Jacques Le Goff*, ed. J. Revel, J.-C. Schmitt (1998), pp. 243–58.

denied the true divinity of Christ, brought to central German tribes by the preaching of Wulfilas, had for a time hindered the achievement of uniformity but was finally overcome. Events had altered the environment in which the heresies of the early centuries had once spread. Churchmen were occupied with the needs of defence and the spread of the gospel among the heathen barbarians. There was no longer a cultivated laity. The centuries following the fall of Rome were filled with warfare. Heresy of the old pattern virtually ceased to exist, its place being taken by the resistance to Christianity of paganism and superstition.[56]

Such outbreaks of doctrinal dissidence that did occur were treated mildly by the authorities, presumably because they presented no significant challenge to the Church:[57] they tend either to be the work of individual theologians who develop a real heresy but gather no movement, or that of rustic preachers who hold crowds in their hands but are themselves hardly more than isolated rebels and eccentrics. Four such episodes, dating from the eighth and early ninth centuries, a time of greater order and tranquillity, may be taken to illustrate the point.

One is the case of the ascetics whom Boniface met in Germany, some being abstainers from foods 'ordained by God for our use', others men who lived on milk and honey, perhaps recalling God's promises for the land of Canaan or adapting John the Baptist's diet of locusts and wild honey.[58] Two others are rural preachers. Aldebert, from Boniface's time, who first emerged in the region of Soissons, declared himself a saint, distributed his hair clippings and nail parings to followers, and, claiming to lead the apostolic life, travelled round preaching to large crowds. Theuda in the ninth century followed a similar career in the villages round Mainz, claiming a special revelation and a knowledge of the date of the imminent end of the world.[59] A fourth and very different case is that of Claudius, bishop of Turin, one-time master of a school in Aquitaine, who was appointed to his see by the favour of Louis the Pious between 814 and 820.[60] He denounced the use of images in Christian worship, and ordered them to be removed from his diocese. The cult of the cross excited his disapproval: in a *reductio ad absurdum* he asked why, if the cross was venerated, all virgin girls should not on similar grounds be paid reverence, since Christ was nine months in the womb of a virgin and only six hours on the cross. He rejected the cult of the saints, and questioned the value of pilgrimages. The pope's authority was put in doubt on the grounds that Peter's primacy was personal to him and ceased at his death; apostolic authority rested on good life rather than any institutional position. Thus uncannily a ninth-century theologian anticipated a part of the English Lollard heresy of the fifteenth century.[61]

56  A. Giesztor, 'Mouvements para-hérétiques en Europe centrale et orientale du 9e au 11e siècle: apostasies', *HS*, pp. 159–67.
57  For early Western heresy, see Russell, *Dissent*, esp. pp. 251–2.
58  The latter is Russell's suggestion (ibid., p. 11); for the episode see ibid., pp. 10–11, and further his 'St Boniface and the Eccentrics', *CH* xxxiii (1964), pp. 3–15.
59  Russell, *Dissent*, pp. 102–8.
60  Ibid., pp. 13–17.
61  See below, ch. 14.

Of the four, Theuda was an eccentric prophetess of a kind recurrent at all periods of the Church's history. Aldebert had a little more positive doctrinal content in his preaching – a rejection of wealth seems implicit in his simple costume and his claim to the apostolic life. The German ascetics are hard to place. It is natural to assume a scriptural basis for their behaviour but, unless they were arguing that their diet was necessary for all Christians, they were not strictly heretics. All differ from Claudius, who was giving vent to a dogmatic heresy, if not a very profound one; he, however, left no following and no tradition.

At this stage popular impulses to dissidence are not combining with doctrinal heresy to form movements against the Church. The Adoptionism taught by Felix of Urgel in the eighth century in his diocese of Toledo, though it reached the people, hardly qualifies as an exception. There, as elsewhere in this period, we do not meet the dedicated sectary with doctrinal apparatus and organization, of the kind that existed in the early centuries and was still to be found in Byzantium. Heresy in the West at this time remains rare, sporadic and formless.

In the renewed period of disorder which followed the death of Louis the Pious and the breakdown of the Carolingian Empire, we meet no recorded cases of heresy at all in the West for a period of one hundred years.[62] Western churchmen used the traditional texts of the Fathers and the councils of the early centuries in which heresy is denounced and categorized, and continued to believe that it was a deadly sin and a principal weapon of the devil against the Church; but by the late tenth century there was no-one among them with any personal experience of a living heresy.

### Challenge and Response

Then in the eleventh century dogmatic heresy with both lay and clerical support, missionizing, with some spectacular deviations from orthodoxy, reappeared in sporadic outbreaks. There was a violent and hostile response. Recalcitrant heretics from Orléans and Monteforte were burnt to death. The group at Arras escaped because they made a full submission. At Goslar in 1051 the Emperor Henry III hanged heretics who had been brought to the imperial court for judgement by Godfrey II, duke of Upper Lorraine. The accused, required to kill a chicken, had refused; apparently their refusal led to conviction and execution, presumably on the ground that their attitude implied a dualist-type belief in the transmigration of souls through the animal kingdom.[63] Both Adémar of Chabannes and Raoul Glaber, a Cluniac chronicler who also had a passionate interest in the Peace of God movement, allude to acts of violence against heretics elsewhere, sometimes by official tribunals, sometimes by popular

---

62   Russell, *Dissent*, pp. 17–18.
63   Ibid., p. 42; *BK*, p. 79, dating: n. 23; for Goslar, *MBPH*, p. 21; for tr. of Anselm of Liège, with Bishop Wazo's reflections on this episode, see *MBPH*, pp. 21–4; form of test derived from Augustine (*FK*, p. 103); Godfrey was exiled from Upper Lorraine; heretics, probably from elsewhere, were brought to him because of his linguistic skill for interrogation (*op. cit.*, p. 31); correction on Goslar, *FK*, p. 31.

action.[64] Anselm of Liège reported that among the French pallor had come to be seen as a sign of heresy (presumably because pallor would be produced by the extravagant fastings of the 'Manichees') and that because of this innocent Catholics had been put to death.[65] There was a flurry of fear and repression.

Leading laity were as active as the clergy in imposing violent punishment. At Orléans the king gave the order, the queen struck out her confessor's eye, the mob wanted to lynch the convicted; at Milan the *capitanei* took the heretics from Monteforte to the pyre to choose their fate; at Goslar the emperor hanged heretics probably after interrogation by Godfrey of Upper Lorraine.

The clergy assented to capital sentences, although Aribert at Milan was apparently reluctant. Where a properly constituted tribunal was at work, they must have been the authorities to make the decision as to whether heresy was present. It was the bishop's right and duty to recognize heresy, confute it and put it down. The tribunal of bishops exercised that right at Orléans, as did Archbishop Aribert of Milan and Gerard, bishop of Arras. One voice was raised against violence: that of Wazo, bishop of Liège. Let the wheat grow with the tares till the time of harvest, he said.[66] It was advice which went unheeded in the Middle Ages.

Fear was part of the impulse to violence. Authority assumed that heresy and rebellion went together. There was a fear of the laity *en masse*, the *rustici* of the chroniclers, and what they might do under a leadership hostile to churchmen. At Milan the impact of dedicated preachers on the common people coming in from the countryside was the decisive event, leading the *capitanei* to destroy the group from Monteforte with the threat and the reality of death. The monks of St Martial, a central point in the initially orthodox movement of enthusiasm for the Peace of God, wished for a wide participation of the laity in the prayers of the Church. Gerard of Arras would have no truck with this approach. His *libellus* made plain what he thought: that the peasant should work and the priest and monk should pray. The growth of lay literacy and a widening society gave new opportunities to the inquiring layman. Not all would be content with the passive role indicated for them by Gerard.

Beside fear there was care for souls in a hierarchical and paternalist Church. Scabby sheep could not be left to infect the flock. The group detected at Arras, when they put their cross to an affirmation of faith, were being given both a protection and a warning. 'Each of them made a certain mark in the form of a cross . . . so that if they held to this faith this sign might be presented for them at the Last Judgement for their salvation, but if they should violate it, it would bring about their confusion.'[67] At Orléans, in Milan for the Monteforte group and at Arras authority wrestled with the accused in order to secure submission to orthodoxy and save them from the power of Satan.

---

64   Landes, in *Essays*, ed. Head, Landes, p. 500, n. 112. Id., *Relics*, p. 39, n. 91.
65   *MBPH*, p. 24. Anselm of Liège, reporting Wazo's attempt to stop violence against heresy, recalled St Martin of Tours, opposing Priscillian's execution, and the use of pallor (allegedly produced by abstinence from meat) as a sign of heresy.
66   Ibid., p. 23.
67   Ibid., p. 19.

Behind the heresies lay a challenge to the Church. The clergy at Orléans and the leader of the Monteforte group preferred their own inner understanding to the decisions of bishops or the formal declarations of faith inherited from the past. At Arras the accused based themselves on Gundolfo and his interpretation of Scripture: the text as he expounded it to them, together with their group experience of the way of righteousness seemed to them to be sufficient without the intervention of the priesthood as ministers of the sacraments. They seemed surprised when this was challenged. 'Anyone who chooses to examine carefully our law and doctrine', they are reported as saying, 'which we have learned from our master, sees it to be contrary neither to evangelical principles nor to apostolic sanctions.'[68] Adémar of Chabannes's Manichees rejected the externals of contemporary religion, the cross, baptism, the Church itself, to follow their own way. Apostolicity was sought, not in monasteries, shrines or churches, but in the shared experience of their own communities outside the Church.

The eleventh century in the West was the age of the formation of communities *par excellence* – ascetic groupings in abundance leading to the formation of new orders, often with a stress on the eremitical aspect of monasticism; guilds in towns; communes; new villages, the product of the drive to colonize the waste lands. Heretical communities run parallel to this widespread process and are another facet of a fast-changing society. A new ability to read and understand texts; the emergence of charismatic interpreters, a Gundolfo at Arras, a Gerard at Monteforte; the fall-out from the brittle enthusiasm of the Peace of God movement in Aquitaine; the incubation of a heresy in the secret circle of illuminist clergy at Orléans; all played a part in the emergence of these new and alarming communities.

Social and economic changes also had a role: developing economic life created routes for trade which aided the diffusion of heretical ideas. Texts, preached from, repeated, studied in small groups, brought into being what Brian Stock has called 'textual communities',[69] within which the allegiance to the group or the leader came to transcend every other kind of allegiance. A nexus of thought and action was created, revolving round a number of sentiments or quotations, written or unwritten, with a transforming power, leading an association's members into resistance to authority, even willing death. Sporadic doubts about aspects of the Church's teaching or the conduct of its priests which touched individuals in earlier epochs could be taken up and incorporated in the teaching of a group, which thus gave them durability. Burchard of Worms in his canon law collection at the beginning of the eleventh century had felt it needful to include a penance for those who held the Donatist view that sacraments administered by unworthy priests were not valid.[70] It must have been widespread enough to have justified a set penance in Burchard, but without the teaching and companionship of a heretical group to sustain such beliefs they remain transient and individual, without major effects on Church life.

---

68　*WEH*, p. 84; see also *MBPH*, p. 17.
69　Stock, *Literacy*, p. 90.
70　On the absence of specific rulings on heresy, see Moore, *Origins*, p. 252.

Other heresies were reported. Raoul Glaber wrote of the grammarian Vilgard of Ravenna who 'began to preach many things contrary to the faith', notably that 'the words of the poets [i.e. classical authors] ought to be believed in all cases';[71] Glaber said that he gained supporters in Sardinia, Italy and Spain and violence was used to suppress them. This seems improbable.

He also described the career of the peasant Leutard from the village of Vertus in the diocese of Châlons-sur-Marne who, after being tormented in a dream by bees who entered his body through his private parts, stinging him as they made their way out through his mouth with a loud noise, then 'bidding him to do things impossible to men', went home from the fields.[72] He dismissed his wife 'as though he affected the separation by command of the gospel' ('quasi ex precepto evangelico'), went to the village church and broke the crucifix and thereafter gathered a hearing for his views among the peasants – aided no doubt by his welcome belief that it was not necessary to pay tithes. Part of his appeal was based on Scripture, used selectively: he is said to have taught 'that the prophets had set forth some useful things, and some not to be believed'. The bishop exposed the weaknesses of this rustic agitator who committed suicide by throwing himself into a well; his following lingered on for years after his death. Historians have suggested at various times that he was an isolated rural fanatic,[73] that he had been affected by fragments of Bogomil belief,[74] or was a victim of ergotism, the symptoms of which may include the sensation of burning in the genitals.[75] It has been wisely noted that the diocese of Châlons-sur-Marne was struck three times by heresy, once in the case of Leutard, once more c.1025, when Bishop Roger I failed to deal satisfactorily with heretics who sent their emissaries on to Arras, and for a third time when a successor of Roger wrote to Wazo of Liège in the 1040s asking for advice about peasants who 'followed the perverse teaching of the Manichees'. In each instance, whatever the exact nature and motivation of the heresy, it was marked by a rigorous concern for personal purity.[76]

But the stories of Leutard and Vilgard lie buried beneath the assumptions of the chronicler. Glaber wrote at a distance from the episodes he describes, and he is unlikely to have had anything other than oral report to guide him. He placed the Vilgard affair c.970 and Leutard c.1000: the episodes formed a pair of heresies lying at the extremes, one a learned, the other a peasant heresy, twin menaces to the Church in the millennial epoch.[77] Glaber's symbolism enfolds the Leutard story. The bees, often seen as symbols of purity, or treated by Bede as symbols of the Fathers themselves, interpreters of Scripture who make the honey of the spiritual understanding of the Word of God, in the growth of heresy have their

71  *WEH*, p. 73; Moore, *Origins*, p. 24; pungent comment, Russell, *Dissent*, p. 111.

72  *Rodulfus Glaber Opera* (1989) ed. J. France *et al.*, pp. 88–91; trans. from earlier edn, *WEH*, pp. 72–3; comment on Leutard, Landes, *Relics*, p. 308.

73  P. Alphandéry, 'De quelques faits de prophétisme dans les sectes latines anterieures au Joachimisme', *RHR* LII (1905), pp. 177–218, esp. p. 185.

74  *BK*, p. 73.

75  Moore, *Origins*, p. 36.

76  Ibid., pp. 36–8.

77  Landes, in *Essays*, ed. Head, Landes, p. 500, n. 110.

good functions reversed.[78] They become messengers of evil and they enter the body of Leutard through a shameful gate, just as a party of demons, who had left Orléans after the trial, attempted in a vision of a monk to enter the monastery of Fleury via the latrines, till they were stopped by the relic of the staff of St Benedict from coming up into the cloisters.[79] Once inside Leutard, the bees drive him to a false understanding of Scripture, dividing the message of the Prophets where orthodoxy would see all their teaching as a unity.

A collection made by the monks of St Germain d'Auxerre in the eleventh century, including St Augustine's classic work on heresies and a ninth-century treatise on the legitimacy of receiving tithes and offerings – an all-purpose compilation designed to defend monks against all their enemies – includes a denunciation of heresy. It takes the form of a letter by a monk, Heribert, addressed to all Christians at the four points of the compass, warning them of a heresy in Périgord whose adepts claimed to follow the apostolic life, eating no meat, drinking no wine beyond a measure every third day, refusing to handle money and making a hundred genuflections daily. They rejected the veneration of the cross and denounced liturgical chants as a vain invention. Some of these pseudo-apostles might chant the mass as a means of deception, throwing down the Host beside the altar or thrusting it into a missal. They possessed a remarkable capacity for educating those who joined them. The most 'rustic' among them would become so wise in eight days as to be impregnable in argument. The devil gave them supernatural powers. Heribert was witness to strange feats in which the adepts, bound with shackles and put overnight in an inverted wine tun, escaped, Houdini-like, by morning. There was no trace of them then until they disclosed themselves once more. A vase containing a little wine was found full next day.

The miracles have apocalyptic overtones: inspired by the devil, they are symptomatic of the intensification of evils preceding the End. The letter is a warning. What intercession to the saints can do, the devil can do for his servants. These faintly ludicrous episodes, Claire Taylor has lately argued, have parallels in contemporary orthodox miracles, especially miracles of liberation, in the lives of the Aquitainian saints, the child St Faith of Conques and St Léonard of Noblat. They reinforce the magical, other-worldly flavour of the whole letter, directed not to the bishop or a secular authority, but to all the faithful. It is imprecise on the heretics, embracing men of property who abandon their goods, priests, monks, nuns and the 'rustici'; the defiant reappearance of the prisoners is not explained, nor the function of the wine barrel.[80]

---

78   Gorre, *Ketzer*, p. 23.
79   T. Head, 'Andrew of Fleury and the Peace League of Bourges', in *Essays*, ed. Head, Landes, p. 522. For demons and excrement, see E. Le Roy Ladurie, *Montaillou*, tr. B. Bray (1978), p. 472, n. 1.
80   G. Lobrichon, 'Le clair-obscur de l'hérésie au début du xie siècle en Aquitaine: une lettre d'Auxerre', *Essays*, ed. Head, Landes, pp. 422–44; texts, 441–4; tr. *WEH*, pp. 138–9; *LMH*, 1st edn should be corrected; C. Taylor, 'The letter of Heribert of Périgord as a source for dualist heresy in the society of early eleventh century Aquitaine', *JMH* xxvi (2001), pp. 313–49; discussion, rejecting Bogomil influence and attacking any widespread attribution of dualism to heresies normally labelled Cathar, M. Pegg, 'On Cathars, Albigenses, and Good Men of Languedoc', *JMH* (2001) (witty account

Guy Lobrichon, whose MS discovery redated the original text from the twelfth to the eleventh century, argued that it had a strongly literary flavour, was not to be taken as a report of a real heresy but was an encoded attack on the enemies of the Cluniac reform. Claire Taylor rejects this and believes it to be a true report of a heresy in Périgord, influenced, at least in part, by a Bogomil mission, which worked with some success in an area and at a time disturbed by political and social problems. The aim of Bogomilism was not simply drastic reform but a total subversion of the Church. The subverting of the mass, the extreme asceticism, the rejection of the veneration of the cross (a rare feature in Western heresy), the genuflections (reminiscent of the Bogomils' bobbing up and down in worship reported by Euthymius of Peribleptos in the eleventh century), and, above all, the use of an Eastern doxology seem to her to be better explained by a Bogomil influence working on a disaffected population than by anything else.[81]

Her view is reinforced by Michael Frassetto's analysis of Adémar's unpublished sermons, giving greater depth to his well-known denunciation of Manichaean heretics in the *Historia*. These sermons, written at the end of his life after he had been worsted by Benedict of Chiusa but before he set off to Jerusalem in 1032, show him taking seriously the doctrinal errors of these heretics on the mass, baptism and the cross, working at refutations and exposition of orthodoxy. Adémar's assumptions that the heretics blasphemed the cross, believed its veneration was idolatry and that celebration of such suffering and death was contrary to the Divine will, seem to Frassetto to echo beliefs of the Bulgarian Bogomils attacked in the classic treatise of Cosmas the Priest. Moreover, he does not believe that Adémar's knowledge of dualism was derived solely from Augustine: there is by implication an element of direct observation. The missionaries postulated by both authors, he argues, 'helped focus the opposition to the established Church', which sprang from the breakdown of the Peace movement and the rise of the seigneurie.[82] As a factor in Western heresy, the Bogomils have thus again put their heads above the parapet.

---

of Conybeare and historiography; doubts authenticity of Council of S. Félix de Caraman; fails to weigh sufficiently ritual as well as doctrinal likenesses between Bogomilism and Catharism, and procedural approach of inquisitors of 1245–6, preferring place/date facts of heretical contacts to doctrinal interrogation; amusing aperçus, useful corrections, but I am not convinced of central thesis).
81  For Euthymius, J. and B. Hamilton, *Christian Dualist Heresies* (1998), pp. 142–64 at 14; doxology, *LMH*, 1st edn, p. 63. I mentioned this as clue to Bogomil influence when I believed his letter twelfth-century and omitted it when I accepted it as eleventh in my 2nd edn (p. 30). I accept Claire Taylor's reproach on this point. See also M. Frassetto, 'The sermons of Ademar of Chabannes and the letter of Heribert. New sources concerning the origins of medieval heresy', *Revue Bénédictine* CIX (1999), pp. 324–40, who prefers my arguments for Bogomilism in my 1st edn. Doctrinal analysis of Heribert, *GRK* III, pp. 369–82.
82  Frassetto, art. cit., p. 339; Id., 'Reaction and reform: reception of heresy in Arras and Aquitaine in the early eleventh century', *CHR* LXXXIII (1997), pp. 386–400 (see esp. comment p. 400); Id., 'Heresy, celibacy and reform in the sermons of Ademar of Chabannes', *Medieval Purity and Piety*, ed. Frassetto (1998), pp. 131–48 (esp. p. 135, n. 28: though Adémar was ready to forge material on St Martial, he is not likely to have been inaccurate on the canons of the Councils of Bourges and Limoges. Clerical celibacy is their target: Gregorian reform is foreshadowed); Id., 'The Manichaeans in the writings of Ademar of Chabannes and the origins of medieval heresy', *Revue des Études Augustiniennes* (forthcoming) (Adémar not subservient to Augustine); Id., 'The writings of Ademar

Adémar used the term 'Manichaean' vigorously. He was not alone. Landulf applied it to the Monteforte sectaries, another chronicler to the accused from Upper Lorraine, and a bishop of Châlons-sur-Marne, in his letter to Wazo of Liège, damaged his account of heretics in his diocese by recording that they believed that Mani was the Holy Spirit.[83] It is not likely that they had ever heard of Mani; it is universally accepted that Manichaeism itself had died out in the West some five centuries earlier; authority knew of it through Augustine and generally assumed that the heretics in front of them were a recrudescence of the ancient heresy. What is common to the heresies which the chroniclers put down to Manichaeism is the stress on flight from the world, a will to purity, a positive repugnance for the material and for human flesh and its desires.

Stress on renunciation is plainly related to the existence of the monastic reform movement, which was at this time beginning to stir the laity. Starting with the foundations of Cluny and Gorze in the previous century, a revival of monasticism was purging moribund houses over Western Europe, and by a natural overspill affecting the lay world as well. Increasingly, the desire for reform made itself felt in the secular Church, with a call to greater purity and devotion among the clergy. Monks were often instigators of reform and their ideals most widely diffused, with a concomitant tendency to consider the world of little worth. A radical pessimism about the natural order is a strong feature of this reform.[84] So, too, is the contrast preached by reformers between the Church of the apostles as evidenced in Scripture, and the state of the contemporary priesthood and hierarchy.

These two features help to account for the reaction in these heresies against the material world, towards an ascetic withdrawal, and also for the appeal which they made, however confusedly, to Scripture as against the contemporary Church and its practices. In a sense, a segment of the lay world in the more advanced countries of the West was experiencing a conversion in the eleventh century. The fortress Christianity of the Dark Ages was giving way, in the more propitious social circumstances of the age, to a religion which could touch the intellect of the layman. There are signs of this in some of the outbreaks: it is especially marked at Arras, with the insistence on adult responsibility in the refusal of infant baptism.

Heresy did not last. Only in the diocese of Châlons-sur-Marne and Liège, as far as our records run, does it appear more than once in any given site. It seems to have been snuffed out by repression, extinguishing heretical circles once they are discovered, without leaving a remnant of proselytizers to revive their heresy when publicity was over. After the hanging of the accused from Upper Lorraine in 1051 silence descends.

---

of Chabannes, the Peace of 994 and the "Terrors of the year 1000" ', *JMH* (forthcoming) (sermons show force of his apocalyptic ideas on eve of millennium; ergotism and 994; excellent biblio.).

83   *MBPH*, p. 22.

84   Background in Moore, *Origins*, ch. 2; Russell (pers. comm.) reminds me of some hard sayings in the Fathers about sexual activity. R. Bultot, *La Doctrine du mépris du monde* (Louvain and Paris, 1963), is informative.

The heresies themselves are individual compositions – in a sense collectors' pieces – with features not repeated later. Reconstruction is made difficult by the brevity and prejudice of many of the reports, and by the capacity of some churchmen for outright slander. Some historians believe that the eleventh century in the West witnessed a re-emergence, not of heresy, but of heresy accusations – a very different matter.[85] There is plainly a rhetorical use of heresy labels. When Duke William v of Aquitaine in 1016 denounces canons of St Hilaire of Poitiers who sell the saint's property as guilty of the sin of Arius, he does not mean that some anti-Trinitarian heresy has established itself, only that it is wicked to disobey his reform, establishing celibacy and the common life, as wicked as Arius, who divided the Church; married canons selling off property are also dividing the Church.[86] Other imperfectly recorded episodes of heresy may also spring from such casual phraseology: we have no means of telling.

In the thirteenth century, an age of established heretical movements, close examination of evidence for Provence and the Rhône valley demonstrates that anticlerical movements concerned with tithes, property and episcopal powers wre stigmatized too readily as driven by heresy. They were not: there were few heretics and the drive for change came from political and economic factors.[87] The same may be true in the much less well recorded eleventh century: the 'Manichees' of the chroniclers may be, as often as not, the fruit of the populace turning against a Church establishment with its own seigneurie, which had not fulfilled the promise of the Peace of God movement in its early days, rather than a true doctrinal revolt, its motives not so much religious as predominantly economic.[88]

And yet the scattering of episodes of recorded heresy c. 1000–1051 includes cases analysed above, at Orléans, Arras and Monteforte, where a true, doctrinal heresy is described or implied in some detail. That the unmasking of the Orléans group, for example, was of utility to the opposition to Robert the Pious and his queen is not in question, but it does not follow that the charges launched against the accused were mere inventions; similarly at Arras, bishop Gerard's massive sermon, certainly not delivered in the form in which it reaches us, and so useful for the stating of his own conservative position in face of change and reform, need in no way imply that the authorities were not in reality faced with doctrinal dissidents.

The fact that our sources are written by clergy and include the strange personality of Adémar of Chabannes may indeed give a one-sided slant to our

85   R. I. Moore, 'Heresy and enthusiasm in "the millennial generation"', *Imagining the End: Millennial Faith from Ancient Middle East to Contemporary America*, ed. A. Amanat, M. Bernhardsson (I. P. Tauris, 2001) (gives sweep of historiography); Id., 'The birth of popular heresy: a millennial phenomenon?', pp. 8–25.
86   Comment of Moore, 'Religious enthusiasm', citing P. Bonnassie, R. Landes, 'Une nouvelle hérésie est née dans le monde', *Les sociétés méridionales autour de l'an mil*, ed. M. Zimmerman (1992), pp. 435–59; see Frassetto, 'The sermons', above, p. 37, n. 81.
87   J. Chiffoleau, 'Vie et mort de l'hérésie en Provence et dans la vallé du Rhône du début du XIIIe au début du xive s.', *CF* xx, pp. 73–99.
88   Moore, 'Heresy and enthusiasm' See R. I. Moore, *The First European Revolution, c.970–1215* (Oxford, New York, 2000).

material; they may well have exaggerated the role of eschatological expectations. And yet eleventh-century society is a febrile one. Jeffrey Russell's re-creation of the strange cult of the Ship of Fools – which owes nothing to clerical manipulation – should remind us how odd and excitable an illiterate peasant population, subject to the uncertainties and pressures of the time, could be.[89] Later on, the flagellants of 1260 were marching and beating themselves, as Gary Dickson has demonstrated, because a popularized reading of an Italian prophetic writer, Joachim of Fiore, made that date a crucial one: prophecy and eschatology were stimulant to a massive, supra-national penitential movement.[90] The popular crusade of Peter the Hermit at the end of the century showed the force of an idea, the vision of Jerusalem. In this context, expectations stimulated by the dates 1000 and 1033 do not seem impossible – even if we make some allowances for sources dominated by churchmen.

Western heresy (and heresy accusations) in the eleventh century have all the fascination of beginnings, but the frailty of the sources makes it hard for any one interpretation of origins to knock out its rivals.[91] Heresy in this century is likely to remain particularly obscure. Perhaps the reason lies not only in the inadequacy of the literary equipment of the age, or the inexperience of the interrogators; it may also lie in the lack of developed, logical understanding of their own beliefs by the heretics themselves, innocent, ill-equipped seekers after purity. Unable to explain themselves adequately, they leave a blurred imprint on the sources.

Heresy thus reappears in the West after a gap of a hundred years, creates alarm in the 1020s, fades, then disappears as mysteriously as it had come.

---

89   *Dissent*; see index, St Truiden.

90   G. Dickson, *Religious Enthusiasm in the Medieval West* (2000) (coll. articles with major implications, illustrating author's views of medieval revivalism), ch. 8.

91   Moore's expositions justly describe difference of emphasis between his hypotheses and those of Landes; Id., *The First European Revolution, c.970–1215* (Oxford, New York, 2000).

*Part II*

---

# The Twelfth Century

# 3

# Orthodox Reform and Heresy

## The Nature of Twelfth-Century Heresy

Early in the twelfth century half a century's silence in the history of Western heresy was broken. A new rhythm becomes apparent:[1] heretical episodes occur more frequently. Heresy changes character. The heretical groups of the eleventh century sought a flight from the world to practise their austerities. They were generally content with a personal abnegation and a set of idiosyncratic views to be discussed within the closed circle of the chosen. The new breed of heretics are aggressive reformers who insist on changes in the Church that will bring Catholicism into line with their own ideas. The eleventh-century groups spread their views quietly, through personal contacts; in the best-documented example, at Orléans, a heretical group among the clergy existed secretly, expanding through quiet missionizing for years before attracting notice from authority. Twelfth-century heretics have other assumptions. Heresy is spread more by open and aggressive preaching. Hearers are stimulated to positive action. It may be that crosses are torn down and burnt, that women give up their jewellery, or, as in the case of Henry the Monk at Le Mans, a whole town rebels against its overlord. Heresiarchs are not afraid to use physical force: Eon de l'Étoile mobilizes a peasant force to rob churches in Brittany; Arnold of Brescia allies himself with the forces of republicanism to hold Rome against the pope; Tanchelm of Antwerp, whether suspect reformer or heretic leader, uses a bodyguard of soldiers.

The heretics and their supporters demand that the Church as a whole shall hear them and stir itself to follow. There is a new concern for the social implications

---

1 *BK*, p. 83; H. Grundmann, *Ketzergeschichte des Mittelalters, Die Kirche in ihrer Geschichte: Ein Handbuch* ed. K. D. Schmidt, E. Wolf, II, G. pt I (Göttingen, 1963), pp. 15–20; his 'Neue Beiträge zur Geschichte der religiösen Bewegungen im Mittelalter', *AKG* xxxvii (1955), pp. 129–68 (research report) also in *Relazioni* iii, pp. 357–402, *RB*, pp. 487–524 (2nd edn only); Moore, *Origins*, esp. ch. 3; A. Vauchez, *Les Laïcs au moyen âge* (1987), ed. D. J. Bornstein, trans. M. J. Schneider, as *The Laity in the Middle Ages* (1993), illuminates the effects of Gregorian reform. See also A. Roach, *The Devil's World: Heresy and Society 1100–1320* (forthcoming, 2001).

of the gospel, or a desire for radical changes among the clergy and in the relations between the Church and society.

We will not have far to seek the reasons for this change. An orthodox reform movement, first issuing from monks and from inferior strata in the hierarchy, then taken up vigorously by the papacy, had begun to stir the consciences of the laity at large.[2] Pamphlet and preaching warfare between the imperial and papal parties had taken discussion of the rightful place of the Church in the world into circles hitherto unaffected by such matters. Under Gregory VII the papacy had been led by a dominating personality prepared to open issues of principle to general discussion and to offer support for enthusiasts in rebellion against a simoniacal clergy.

The case of the lay movement of the Pataria in Milan, whose origins pre-dated the investiture controversies, is especially illuminating for the forces stirred by the reform movement.[3] The preaching of the deacon Ariald unleashed a formidable rebellion against the power of a simoniacal and unchaste upper clergy. Social tensions played a part as humbler citizens[4] attacked the power of a feudal nobility allied with the cathedral clergy, who lived an unregenerate life hardly distinguishable from that of their fellow nobles. Other cross-currents were the patriotism of a city and archbishopric with a distinguished past, and the rival interests of pope and emperor. Held together by an oath like a communal movement, the Pataria continued their inflammatory agitation from 1057 to 1075, and carried their influence into the cities of Brescia, Piacenza and Cremona. From Florence and the reform movement of St John Gualbert they drew uncorrupt priests to serve their needs in Milan.[5]

Lay participation was considerable, though lower clergy as well came to support the agitation, and two laymen, the knight Erlembald and his brother Landulf, notary of the Milan church, were leaders. In the fiercest language unworthy clergy were attacked, their houses were plundered, and the sacraments which they administered were boycotted. Landulf was quoted as saying that the people should think of their masses as if they were dogs' dung, and their churches as if they were cattle sheds; layman as he was, he preached, it would seem,

---

2   G. Volpe, *Movimenti religiosi e sette ereticali nella società medievale Italiana* (1926) (a stimulating survey, still of use); *RB*, pp. 13–16.

3   C. Violante, *La Pataria milanese e la riforma ecclesiastica* I: *Le Premesse (1045–57)* (1955) (the standard work); H. E. J. Cowdrey, 'The papacy, the Patarenes and the Church of Milan', *TRHS*, 5th ser. XVIII (1968), pp. 25–48; G. Miccoli, 'Per la storia della pataria milanese', *BISIAM* LXX (1958), pp. 43–123; E. Werner, *Pauperes Christi* (Leipzig 1956), pp. 114–64 (Marxist survey with hypothesis of Bogomil influence); comment in E. Dupré-Theseider, *Introduzione alle eresie medievali* (1953), pp. 77–94; Stock, *Literacy*, pp. 151–240 (fresh analysis with comparison to heresies in early eleventh century); Moore, *Origins*, pp. 55–62, 266–8; note comment on sources: p. 77, references: p. 296, n. 13. C. Thouzellier, *Hérésie et hérétiques* (1969), pp. 204–21; definitive work, H. E. J. Cowdrey, *Pope Gregory VII* (Oxford, 1998). See also U.-R. Blumenthal, *Gregor VII* (Darmstadt, 2001).

4   It used to be thought that the names Pataria and Patarene were derived from the rag-market. G. Cracco, 'Pataria: *opus e nomen*', *RSCI* XXVIII (1974), pp. 357–87 at pp. 357–62, argues that this is not so.

5   C. Violante, 'Hérésies urbaines et hérésies rurales en Italie du 11e au 13e siècle', *HS*, pp. 171–98 (individual hypothesis on the social reasons for Italy's fertility in heresy) at p. 177.

without specific authorization, and was attacked by a chronicler for doing so. Accusations of heresy were flung about, the conservatives in Milan accusing the reformers of being heretics, while distinguished members of the reform party in Rome in the same period made free with the word 'heresy' as a term of abuse for moral faults in the clergy.[6] The reformers wrote as controversialists at a time when scant attention had been given to setting a strict and technical boundary between heresy and orthodoxy; nevertheless the use of the word was important. If simony in the clergy was to be equated with heresy, extreme action to bring it to an end might seem justified. At the end of his career Erlembald went close to usurping a clerical function for himself, when he made a decision about the administration of baptism. To avoid use of chrism consecrated by the unworthy, he had a chrism made and administered by a Patarene priest.

Strictly, no action of the Patarenes went beyond the lines authorized by orthodox reformers in the Easter synod at Rome in 1059, which forbade laymen to hear the masses of married priests. They were not heretics: they lacked the will to proceed against the sacramental and doctrinal system of the Catholic Church.[7] But the reservations which even that most radical reformer St Peter Damiani expressed about the actions of the Pataria had some justification, for their reforming zeal tended to shake all Church authority, and set forces in motion whose direction could not be foreseen. This did not check the support which Gregory VII gave to the movement before and during his pontificate: influenced by him, Alexander II had given a banner to Erlembald, making him a kind of *gonfalonier* of the Roman Church. When Erlembald was killed in street fighting in 1075, Gregory honoured him as a martyr. The same public justification for action against unreformed clergy and the boycott of their sacraments was explicit in Gregory's rehabilitation of Ramihrdus, a priest in Cambrai burnt as a heretic after refusing to receive the sacrament from the hands of unworthy clergy. Ramihrdus roused a movement in Cambrai and its region that had affinities with the Pataria, burnt by a bishop, supporter of Henry IV, making an example of a Gregorian.[8] Yet the line was perilously thin between the boycott of the masses of unreformed clergy and the heresy, to which we may refer for convenience as Donatist, that the masses of unworthy clergy were invalid, and in the atmosphere of reform, with preaching and pamphlets stressing the vices of the unreformed clergy, the step into that heresy was easy to take. By calling on him to take action against unworthy clergy, the Gregorian movement demanded from the layman a certain personal responsibility. This, a relatively new sentiment in the West, was to be fateful for the future development of heresy.

Church reform and heresy have important links. The revolutionary programme of the Gregorians set before the Church ideals which could never be wholly realized, and gave to some clergy and numbers of laymen a vision of

---

6  J. Leclercq, 'Simoniaca haeresis', in *Studi Gregoriani* I, pp. 523–30.
7  Dupré-Theseider, *Introduzione*, p. 77.
8  Russell, *Dissent*, pp. 43–4; *MBPH*, pp. 24–6; Moore, *Origins*, pp. 62–3, 260; *FK*, p. 51.

a free Church that, in the social and political circumstances of the time, could never be expected to be wholly realized. At first, the Gregorians, as in the Pataria and elsewhere, could work with popular lay movements: thus the zeal of the common man who had been awakened to reform in the more advanced centres of Western Europe found an orthodox channel. That fact will explain the relative absence of heresy in the half century that lay between the executions at Goslar and the reappearance of popular heresy.[9]

But in time the direction of papal reform tended to change, and its aims became more narrowly clerical and juridical. At worst, it might separate clergy from laity without necessarily raising the devotion and efficiency of the former. The momentous question of the freedom of the Church and the worthiness of candidates for bishoprics tended to contract into the lesser issue of the right to deliver to the bishop the symbols of his sacred office; and, as compromise was reached on this at the Concordat of Worms in 1122, it might well be felt that some of the early call to purification had failed in its effect, and that the orthodox reform movement was turning into disputes over minutiae. Before Worms, reform in its most immediate impact on the lay world was beginning to run into the sands, and as this happened the number of heretical episodes began to rise. A first cause for the recrudescence of heresy in the West lay in the expectations roused by Gregorian reform and its failure to fulfil them.

Where the papacy scored its most lasting popular success was in the crusades. Here Urban II and his successors aroused a genuine popular enthusiasm, the driving force which outlasted so many military and political failures, and found expression in such obviously spontaneous and unrehearsed movements as the crusade of Peter the Hermit, which preceded the first crusade proper, or the children's crusade of the thirteenth century. How deep into the popular consciousness the crusades had penetrated is apparent from the belief of the inhabitants of the primitive region of western France on the borders of Brittany, Anjou and Maine, that the hermits of the woods who emerged as wandering preachers in shaggy attire were Saracens who had arrived by a concealed tunnel from their own land to betray the West from within.[10]

Crusade preaching stirred millennial enthusiasms. The Holy Land was represented as being literally a land flowing with milk and honey; the success of the crusade would, it was believed, issue in the new kingdom at Jerusalem that would reconcile men's quarrels, and usher in the era of plenty that would precede the End. The crusades aroused a deep popular feeling for the sufferings of Christ at the crucifixion and a corresponding hatred for the Jews: pogroms accompanied the summons to the crusade in a number of towns, and aided the spread of a mood of eschatological enthusiasm, in which the slaughter of the enemies of Christ was expected to lead to the events preceding the end of the world. A mood

9    *RB*, p. 483; Brooke, 'Heresy and religious sentiment', p. 119.
10    Bernard of Tiron, *Vita* (*PL* CLXXII, col. 1409b); comment, G. Dickson, 'Medieval Christian crowds and the origins of crowd psychology', *RHE* CXV (2000), pp. 45–75 at 59–60.

of religious enthusiasm was created that could lead to the rise of extravagant leaders and might easily run into unorthodox channels.[11]

The machinery of the crusades and the setting up of crusaders' kingdoms in Palestine that was their most obvious result, led to a renewed contact with Eastern heresy. Direct contact of crusaders with heresy is hardly recorded. In only one instance do we have such information, and that was when they came across a *castrum* inhabited by heretics, most probably Paulicians. The crusaders' reaction was to destroy the place and its inhabitants.[12] Yet the crusades were an important link in the chain binding closer the peoples of western Europe to Byzantium and the Balkans,[13] and the increased commercial activity stimulated, in part, by the existence of the crusader States would no doubt have facilitated formal and informal contacts with underground Bogomil churches in Constantinople, Asia Minor and the Balkans.

Nevertheless, dualism would never have made its re-entry into the West had not the soil been well prepared for the reception of heresy. A reaction against orthodoxy, an undogmatic dissatisfaction with the Church, was the necessary first stage if dissentient circles were ever to be able to accept, *en masse* and for a long period of time, elements of drastically ascetic religion well on the margins of Catholicism. This dissatisfaction was the product of a reform that for some had gone sour, or the effects of a rigidity and conservatism in the Church that was unable to accept new interpretations of the Christian life.

Most of a century was required before ecclesiastical authority was able to adapt its outlook and establish a coherent policy; in the doubts and hesitations, in the reaction to crude and sweeping condemnations, themselves the products of the uncertainty of authority, heretical groups found occasion to cut themselves off from the Church. The long, simmering crisis found for the first time the outline of a solution in the hands of Innocent III in the early thirteenth century. Till then, the anxieties of churchmen about the spread of heresy were not unjustified, for the Church of the twelfth century as a whole did not understand the forces at work behind the popular heretical movements, and had no effective answer to them.

---

11    On aberrations linked to the crusades, see N. Cohn, *The Pursuit of the Millennium* (1957); summary of Cohn's theory and definition of terms in his 'Medieval millenarism: its bearing on the comparative study of millenarian movements', *Millennial Dreams in Action*, ed. S. L. Thrupp (1962), pp. 31–43. Cohn's second edition of *The Pursuit of the Millennium* (1970) offers a profound revision of his first, which occasions me to withdraw my first-edition criticism, pp. 47–8; he no longer adopts a stress so exclusively urban; revolutionary millenarianism, he says (p. 281), appealed most to peasants who were not 'firmly integrated in the life of village or manor' or to artisans who were not 'firmly integrated in their guilds'. It appealed to those on the margins, whether in town or country.

12    N. Garsoïan, *The Paulician Heresy* (1967), p. 15, n. 9; *LMH*, 1st edn, pp. 23, 34.

13    C. Thouzellier, 'Hérésie et croisade au XIIe siècle', *RHE* XLIX (1954), pp. 855–72 (hypothesis linking development of heretical doctrine to crusaders from second crusade; for its weakness, see A. Borst, *DA* XI (1954–5), pp. 617–18, R. Manselli, in *BISIAM* LXVII (1955), p. 221n., S. Runciman, in *JEH* XVIII (1967), pp. 89–90); see now revised version of Thouzellier's article in her *Hérésie et hérétiques*, pp. 17–37 (note diagram on p. 37).

## Orthodox Wandering Preachers

What made the heresy of the twelfth century insidious was its relatively unformed nature, its lack (at least until Catharism began to solidify towards the end of the century) of concise dogmatic positions, and its close relationship to the ideals and preoccupations of orthodox piety. Most popular heresies were initiated, before the rise of the printing press, by a period of spontaneous wandering preaching. Those of the twelfth century were no exception. But the preaching, which stirred the populace and unconsciously helped to make them ready for the reception of the principal 'evangelical' and dualistic heresies of the century, often had an orthodox origin. We have seen it in operation in the Milan Pataria. In France it was carried on by wandering hermits well known in Catholic history as the founders of religious congregations. It was not a work of planned missionizing by some organized sect. Its aim was the entirely orthodox one of the preaching of penance, the call of clergy and people to reform. Here we have a kind of spontaneous overspill of the fierce asceticism of the woods of western France, the work of reformers and monks who had not found full satisfaction in the normal outlets of cloister, canons or life among the secular clergy. Their work of preaching was not disapproved by the Church; some could show a papal permission for wandering preaching, analogous to the permission given to preach for the first and second crusades; but the preachers themselves were fiery and idiosyncratic and their preaching tours had consequences that were not always comfortable.

The earliest to be discussed by Johannes von Walter in his pioneer work on the wandering preachers of France was Robert of Arbrissel, and the case was typical for the reaction against the conventional ways of religion.[14] Robert was once in the household of the bishop of Rennes, and had been a participant in the Gregorian reform movement, but he threw up a conventional career in the Church for the life of a hermit in the great wood of Craon, where he attracted followers and set out on preaching tours. Another case of reaction against a customary pattern of religious life is that of his follower Bernard of Tiron, who had become a monk, then prior of St Savin-sur-Gartempe where he came into conflict over the simony issue with Abbot Gervasius, then again abbot of St Cyprian near Poitiers, where he clashed with his monks who did not want to accept reforms. After an unsuccessful dispute with Cluny, he was forced to leave. His solution was to turn his back on the unprofitable world of monastic communities and suits at Rome, and flee to the woods at Craon.

Another of the wandering preachers, Vitalis of Savigny, had been chaplain to Count Robert of Mortain and canon of the Church of St Ebrulf at Mortain; but a love of poverty drove him into the waste and made him a hermit at Dompierre, east of Mortain, for seventeen years. He was evidently a devastating preacher of

---

14  *Die ersten Wanderprediger Frankreichs* (1903–6), 2 vols. Full modern exposition by J. Becquet, 'L'érémitisme clérical et laie dans l'ouest de la France', in *L'Eremitismo nei secoli* XI *e* XII (1965), pp. 182–211; and his 'Érémitisme et hérésie au moyen âge', in *HS*, pp. 139–45; H. Leyser, *Hermits and the New Monasticism* (1984).

penance 'bringing terror with the rolling thunder of divine rebuke'.[15] The best known of von Walter's group was Norbert of Xanten, who had found the work of reform in circles of canons insufficient and took to the roads as a wandering preacher. As with the others, his zeal was not easy to incorporate into existing religious structures – an early attempt to make him leader of a group of Augustinian canons in Laon failed because of the canons' resistance to his reforms and he was led, in co-operation with the bishop of Laon, to found a new association which flowered into the Premonstratensians.

Though the backgrounds might differ, there are similarities within the group of wandering preachers which bear witness to some interesting new strands in popular piety. Their love of poverty is striking. Robert appeared on the preaching tours in rags almost to the point of indecency, with a beard and a grey cowl, going barefoot; Bernard of Tiron in shaggy attire, barefoot or riding on a donkey as a sign of humility. In the woods they lived on fruits and berries or on the product of rough manual labour, like turning, or the products of simple gardens, worked by themselves without any lay brothers or hired labour. There were eccentricities: Robert of Arbrissel had a special calling for the religious care of women, and was accused by an opponent of undue intimacies – which in fact reflected no more than a characteristic lack of discretion. Bernard wept continually in his reflections on the sufferings of Christ all through the mass, and went about with his shoulders perpetually damp from his tears.

The audiences that these idiosyncratic figures drew on their preaching tours are a tribute, not only to their preaching power, but also to a diffused reverence for extreme asceticism and poverty. Poverty and preaching were closely linked: the lack of a stipend and the complete dependence of the preacher on the spontaneous offerings of his hearers were a guarantee of the preacher's independence and sincerity. Followers were speedily attracted, partly in the normal fashion, as the hermit who flees to the woods is seldom long there without attracting some visitors who come to seek a holy man's blessing and advice,[16] partly as mixed bodies of men and women attached themselves to the preachers as they travelled round the countryside. The preachers sought peace, the reform of the Church and the end of simony, mingling denunciations of the evils of society with the preaching of penance to individuals. The denunciations of a married clergy and the general abuses of the pre-Gregorian world which were so much part of Robert's sermons probably drew to him the cast-off wives of reformed clergy, which a reformer might well describe as prostitutes.[17]

These mixed bodies created some not wholly unjustified alarm on the part of authority. There were questions about the permission to preach; Norbert, for example, was queried in 1119 about the legitimacy of his wandering tours. Hermits who preached would be aware of the sending of the Twelve and the

---

15  Leyser, *Hermits*, p. 76, quoting Ordericus Vitalis, *Historia Ecclesiastica*, ed. M. Chibnall (London, 1973), p. 332.
16  H. Grundmann, 'Zur Vita S. Gerlaci eremitae', *DA* xviii (1962), pp. 539–54; economic interpn. in Werner, *Pauperes Christi*, pp. 25–52.
17  Böhmer, in *TLZ* xxix (1904), pp. 330–4.

Seventy. Both Robert of Arbrissel and Norbert were conscious of the instructions to have neither scrip nor purse nor shoes. Influence was brought to bear on the preachers to cause their followers to settle down and choose a stable form of religious life in community. Thus, partly out of a normal zeal, partly at the instance of a reforming diocesan concerned for the spiritual benefit of his own locality – as in the case of Hermann of Laon,[18] and partly out of the pressure of anxious authorities, wandering preachers became founders of monasteries and orders.

The idiosyncracy prevailed, however, here: the foundations were not of a conventional kind. Some, like Robert, revived the long disused idea of the double monastery. All were distinguished by a special care for poverty and a rejection of certain kinds of property. The foundations contributed to the variety of religious life in the first half of the twelfth century. Prémontré developed on the Slav frontier a missionary aim. But this was the exception. Robert of Arbrissel's foundation at Fontevrault, beginning as a pioneering work, with an unusual care for the status of women, ended as a religious house for the daughters and widows of the French court and nobility. But clearly wandering preaching and poverty could not be realized within these monasteries. That life was replaced for the followers of the preachers by withdrawal from the world in a stable pattern of life under vows.

A new stress on poverty is a major feature, partly explained by the ascetic roots of these movements, with a strong semi-monastic tinge, partly by the post-Gregorian reaction against an over-endowed Church. That poverty had extraordinary popularity is apparent, for example, from the existence of an order like the Grandmontines, with its frail constitution and overwhelming emphasis on renunciation of wordly goods. A few entered to share the austerities; many more in the world remained outside to admire.

The poverty movements represented a reaction against the wealthy Church and a developing bourgeoisie in a time of rapid economic growth.[19] Wealth was notably concrete and visible, displayed in the finery of a merchant and his family. Behind the criticism of the Church as over-wealthy lay also an increasing popular rationalism, capable in a groping way of making comparisons with a new historical sense between the simple Church of the apostles and the elaborate hierarchical Church of the twelfth century. What a leader and prophet of the Church in St Bernard of Clairvaux might set down for the pope in the *De consideratione*, urging on him the example of the simplicity of the early Church, might also be understood in a cruder way at more popular levels, and, mis-

---

18   C. Dereine, 'Les origines de Prémontré', *RHE* xlii (1947), pp. 352–78; for the Seventy, Leyser, *Hermits*, pp. 73–4.
19   It has been held that in the twelfth century the instructions at the sending of the Seventy in Matthew 10 and Luke 9 formed the pattern of apostolic life based on poverty and preaching, displacing an older one based on the community of goods among the apostles at Jerusalem in Acts 4, seen as a model for monastic life. Rev. Dr S. Tugwell O. P. warns me that his researches on St Dominic lead him to doubt the existence of this *apostolica vita* of poverty and preaching as a driving force in the formation of Dominic's ideal; this doubt has in turn caused re-examination of Acts 4 as the model for monastic life. His references, he tells me, 'may make us wonder whether *vita apostolica* is as

handled, turn towards heresy. A historian describing an encounter he had with a heretic at Bonn in the first half of the century described his scorn for the members of the Church hierarchy who lived so wrongfully (*irrationabiliter*) – the word is illuminating for the forces which operated below the surface against a traditional, conservative-minded hierarchy.[20]

Against this diffused advance in understanding, the dissemination of a new logic at more popular levels, the Church had relatively slight defences. The great crowds which turned out for a popular preacher expressed the need for more coherent instruction, which the Church was in substance not meeting at the lower levels. As is well known, proposals to set up training centres for the clergy and to use cathedrals as foci for a popular theology broke down. Before the coming of the friars standards of training remained low. Systematic instruction of the laity was rare. Contemporary descriptions reveal sometimes in a flash the nature of the situation in the growing towns, against which reformers had to contend. A startling example is the new industrial town of Antwerp in the early twelfth century in the time of Tanchelm, where the only church for the entire town was allegedly served by a simoniac who lived in sin with his niece. Only relatively slowly did the Church begin to cope with the problems caused by the lack of a developed cure of souls within the towns.[21]

Here lay, in outline, the opportunities for the heretics – in the existence of much popular zeal, which reacted against a conservative Church still much in need of reform, a kind of primitive rationalism no longer satisfied with the fortress Church of the barbarian age, a new understanding of certain texts of Scripture, which had entered the popular consciousness[22] and could not be brought into accord with the ecclesiastical practices that the zealous few saw around them and, again among the few, a rejection of a still coarse and bloodstained age, with its crude materialism. Their yearning for a new way of apostolic life becomes explicable when set against this background. A preacher of skill, who came out of an ascetic background and denounced abuses, was sure of a hearing, and this remained true whether his views were essentially within the bounds of orthodox reform or not. These facts explain the success of the wandering preachers of France – but also the success of the heretical preachers nearly contemporary with them.

---

coherent or constant an inspiration as is often alleged . . . We may find that apostles or the "apostolic community" of the early church may be mentioned together with coenobites in all kinds of different ways, for all kinds of different purposes', and he proceeds to demonstrate this with reference to Pachomius, Augustine, Cassian, Bede and others. I am very grateful to him for use of his work and have modified my own text. Von Walter saw the understanding of apostolic life based on the sending of the Seventy as a force in his *Wanderprediger*; *RB*, pp. 15–27 follows him; see Leyser, *Hermits*, pp. 26–8 and her chapter on hermits and preaching, pp. 69–77. I have been unable to see P. Henriet, '*Verbum Dei Disseminando*: la parole des ermites prédicateurs d'après les sources hagiographiques (xie–xiie siècles)', *La Parole du prédicateur*, ed. R. M. Dessi, M. Lauwers (Nice, 1997), pp. 153–85.

20  Morghen, *Medioevo Cristiano*, p. 253; Ekbert of Schönau, *PL* cxcv, col. 88. *Ratio* can mean 'right'; Morghen argues for the meaning of illogicality implicit here as well as of moral fault.

21  Russell, *Dissent*, pp. 60, 283; C. N. L. Brooke, 'The Church in the towns, 1000–1250', in *SCH* vi, pp. 59–83, esp. p. 79; fuller discussion below, pp. 94–6.

22  Morghen, *Medioevo Cristiano*, pp. 204–81 *passim*.

# Heretical Preachers and the Rise of Catharism

## Henry the Monk and Peter of Bruis

Henry the Monk provides a good example of a development in one wandering preacher from the ideas of drastic reform, largely still on the lines of the Gregorians, to a theological heresy, in which, nevertheless, issues of practical conduct still held first place.[1] In this he was typical of the theologically unformed protest of the twelfth century, in contradistinction to the more developed ideas of the thirteenth.

His origins are unknown. His success as a preacher in French-speaking areas suggests strongly that he himself was born somewhere in France or in a French-speaking part of the Empire. Henry was an apostate monk, probably also a priest, who had taken to the roads as a preacher of penance. The first detailed account of his activities comes from Le Mans, where he entered the city in 1116 preceded by two disciples carrying a cross on an iron-tipped staff, bearded, barefoot, and with poor clothing. He was at first welcomed by the bishop, who unwisely left him in freedom there while he set off for Rome. On his return he found that the city had been turned upside down, the clergy denounced, boycotted by shop-keepers and stripped of all reverence among the people, who were brought to repentance by Henry's extraordinary eloquence.

Henry was at this stage a radical Gregorian reformer, full of scathing denunciation for the sins of the clergy. But he showed some particular social concern and in Le Mans he had an eminently suitable milieu, both for that and for clerical denunciation. It was a town which had failed in its attempt to set up a commune

---

1   R. Manselli, 'Il monaco Enrico e la sua eresia', *BISIAM* LXV (1953), pp. 1–63; Id., *Studi sulle eresie del secolo* XII (1953), pp. 45–67 (survey linking evangelical heresies of Henry, Peter of Bruis, Valdes; criticized by Ilarino da Milano, *RSCI* IX (1995), pp. 424–31), superseded by M. Zerner, 'Du "Contra Hereticum" aux "Contra Hereticos"', Id., *Inventer l'Hérésie?*, pp. 119–56. Zerner upends Manselli's interpn.: *Contra Hereticum* (Nice MS) is the early source attacking Henry's heresy, not a subsequent partial summary; Manselli misdates *Contra Hereticos*, not only aimed at Henry but a composite, and misreads 'Henrico' for 'heretico' (p. 125). Only the Nice MS and the Le Mans chronicle can now be used for Henry's beliefs.

in 1070 and it was dominated by the clergy. It lacked men of substance. The commerce or industry which might have enabled the citizens to wrest a degree of independence from bishop and clergy were wanting.

A long resentment accounts for the violent espousal of Henry's leadership and the ferocity to the clergy which accompanied it. Hildebert the bishop was a reforming Gregorian and, it is likely, imposed the orthodox reformers' novel rules on the prohibited degrees of marriage, insisted that marriage was a sacrament of the Church and required clerical control of it. Later Henry in controversy attacked that view and said that 'the consent of the persons alone makes a marriage'. The rules were onerous and Henry gained support by rejecting them. In a meeting he vividly set forth his programme for the reform of marriage procedures, linking his ideas on Christian marriage with the need to rescue the prostitutes of the city. 'He proclaimed the new dogma', the chronicler said, 'that women who had not lived chastely must, naked before everyone, burn their clothes and their hair. Nobody should accept any gold or silver or goods or wedding gifts with his wife, or receive any dowry with her: the naked should marry the naked, the sick marry the sick and the poor marry the poor, without bothering about whether they married chastely or incestuously.'[2] 'Incestuously' for the chronicler meant within the prohibited degrees. In the exhilaration of emotional revivalism the hair and clothes of the prostitutes, polluted by their calling, were burnt, a collection was taken up to buy new clothes, and young men came forward to marry them. The chronicler might grumble that the prostitutes went back to their old ways, but, for a moment, in the fire of Henry's eloquence and the city's repentance, old social barriers, the dowries and the novel Gregorian rules were swept away. Such a breaking of the social code was rare, but while it lasted it had great potency: three centuries later it occurred with such force on a wider scale as to mould Bohemian peasants into the victorious fighting forces of Hussitism.

Henry was an individualist: in appearance he resembled other preachers of repentance, but he was a marriage reformer rather than a preacher of celibacy. He rejected divorce. He stressed poverty and sponsored the burning of ornaments, but he did not give the same emphasis as other preachers did to asceticism, particularly in diet. As a preacher he had a long career, reappearing to move the populace against the clergy at various times in Lausanne, Poitiers and Bordeaux, as well as Le Mans, before moving into the lands of the count of Toulouse, where his traces are lost after 1145. An attempt was made to divert him from heresy at the Council of Pisa in 1135, where he promised to enter a monastery and give up wandering preaching, the council handling him relatively mildly and denouncing only three tenets.

This restrained treatment by the council, at a time when churchmen were not specially disposed to leniency towards heresy, may well be significant. Henry's ferocious attacks on the Le Mans clergy recorded by the chronicler, and his views

---

2 Tr. of original text, the *Actus pontificum Cennomannis*, *WEH*, pp. 108–14; *MBPH*, pp. 33–8 (this tr.). Social context finely recreated, R. I. Moore, 'New sects', pp. 54–7; *Origins*, pp. 82–101; reflections, E. Werner, M. Erbstösser, *Ketzer und Heilige* (1986), pp. 233–71.

as discussed in a treatise directed against him, the *Contra Hereticum*, by an otherwise unknown monk, William, sprang from anger at their way of life. He was a Donatist, who rejected the power of the clergy to 'bind and loose' because of their sins and insisted on the necessity of poverty among them: the preacher of repentance crossed the line to heresy out of indignation at relaxed clergy and their possessions. The appeal to Scripture appears to be behind his doubts about the role of the clergy in confession – the accusation was that he had said that it was not a precept of the Gospel to go to a priest for penance – and an emphasis on the individual's responsibility behind the beliefs attributed to him, rejecting prayers for the dead and affirming that salvation was available for infants who died unbaptized. The last tenet was the most idiosyncratic – and unusual – since he was said to have spoken about children of Jews and Saracens as well as Christians.[3]

Peter of Bruis's heresy was much more profound.[4] He began his career as a village priest in the mountains of the Embrun region. He was ejected from his cure: it was probably after this that he began a career as a heretical agitator, which lasted some twenty years from about 1119 to his death in approximately 1139–40. Towards the end of his life, he roved through the prosperous towns of south-western France addressing great gatherings. At the time his opponent, Peter the Venerable, abbot of Cluny, wrote his treatise *Contra Petrobrusianos*, the heresy had spread into the province of Narbonne, westwards to Toulouse and the surrounding plain and finally, by the time he had completed his prefatory letter, into Gascony and the diocese of Arles. At St Gilles, Peter ended his career with a violent death.

Henry, meanwhile, was taken by the archbishop of Arles to the Council of Pisa, and thus may be presumed to have been active as a preacher in his province. After his return from Pisa, he began a second career in Languedoc, reaching the end of his tours in Toulouse, where St Bernard, if we believe his panegyrist, robbed Henry of his hold on the populace.[5] But the damage had been done. It can hardly be accidental that the area of Peter and Henry's success in the third decade of the century bears some similarity to that infiltrated by Catharism in the latter half of the century, where the Church had to face its greatest crisis.[6]

The origins of Peter's heresy raise problems. Bruis was a small village in the canton of Rosans in the Hautes-Alpes; it was either Peter's birthplace or his parish. Peter's early years of preaching were spent in the mountainous regions of Embrun, Gap and Die. What surprises us is the geographical origins of this heresy: the Hautes-Alpes one would expect to be a backward area, a possible fount for heathen

---

3   Reconstr. from Zerner, 'Du "*Contra Hereticum*"', p. 125; *WEH*, pp. 116–17, 677 n. 10.

4   See Peter the Venerable's *Contra Petrobrusianos hereticos*, ed. J. Fearns (Turnhout, 1968); Fearns, 'Peter von Bruis und die religiöse Bewegung des 12. Jahrhunderts', *AKG* XLVIII (1966), pp. 311–35; Id., 'The *Contra Petrobrusianos* of Peter the Venerable' (PhD, Univ. Liverpool, 1963); J-P. Torrell, D. Bouthillier, *Pierre le Vénérable et sa vision du monde* (1986).

5   See texts tr. *WEH*, pp. 122–6; *MBPH*, pp. 39–46. The *Vita prima* (*PL* CLXXXV, col. 313) says Henry was captured and brought to the bishop in chains. This may have been in 1145; see *WEH*, p. 680.

6   E. Griffe, *Les Débuts de l'aventure cathare en Languedoc (1140–1190)* (1969) (strong feel for locality), pp. 21–48.

survivals, but not for a 'modern' heresy in the twelfth century. Of course, Peter could himself have incubated his own heresy. He is too shadowy a figure in our sources for us to be able to come to any useful conclusions on his personality and capacities. A clue, however, on a possible source is to be found in the geography of Bruis. It lies on one of the Alpine routes to Italy. Here would be a passage-way to the mountain villages for novel heretical ideas, disseminated by travellers to and from that part of western Europe that was most open to external influences.[7]

Only a part of Peter's teaching resembled the common ideas of earlier and contemporary twelfth-century sects. It was radical and violent. Views were conveyed by vigorous practical demonstration, and it was in the course of one of these, while inciting the people at St Gilles to make a bonfire of their crucifixes, that Peter met his end, being pushed in himself and burnt by his opponents. At other times he and his followers would drag monks from their monasteries and force them to marry or, in a ceremony which foreshadows some actions of the radical group of Lollards at Norwich in the fifteenth century, would eat meat on Good Friday.[8]

Beneath these tenets lay a belief in the Church as the spiritual unity of the congregation of the faithful.[9] The accretions of later ages are all stripped away to reveal the underlying true nature of the Church. The keynote was a rejection of all external forms. The negative tenets of the sect are the repudiation of the authority of the Old Testament, of the Fathers and all the traditions of the Church, the rejection of infant baptism, of the doctrine of the eucharist and the sacrifice of the mass and of prayers for the dead. The use of church buildings was condemned, as was the veneration of the cross and the practice of singing in church. But behind the denials lay some varied strands of thought, not all readily reconcilable with the common ferment of popular religious ideas of Peter's own time. The rejection of so many of the externals of worship springs from the desire for a de-materialization of worship. The formal objects of veneration – buildings, crosses, altars – are seen as positive incumbrances to true religion, and violently cast aside.

Behind the rejection of the eucharist, as celebrated in the contemporary Church, and the practice of infant baptism, lay the literal appeal to the gospels. The eucharistic denial did not spring from the usual rejection of the unworthiness of the ministers of the sacrament, but from an extremely literal reading of Scripture. As they understood the gospels, the transformation of the bread and wine into the Body and Blood took place once only at the Last Supper, and was a miracle never since performed by anyone else. Christ had no intention of instituting a rite to be repeated on the altars of the Church; not even a symbolic rendering of the act was open to consideration in their group. This is an exceptionally radical viewpoint, not easy to parallel: it will not fit a strictly dualist viewpoint, for the Petrobrusians were not denying that Christ did offer his body

---

7  Fearns, 'Peter von Bruis', p. 329, n. 92; on possible contact with Bogomil-infected regions, cf. p. 332 and n. 100.
8  Below, p. 293.
9  Fearns, '*Contra Petrobrusianos*', p. xlvii (congregation of faithful); lvii–lix (eucharist); for dynamism unleashed by town life, *FK*, p. 63.

and blood in the Upper Room. They were not forced by a rejection of matter to interpret Christ's actions on that occasion purely figuratively. The likelihood seems, as J. V. Fearns suggests, that on this issue Peter made a personal contribution to heresy.[10] He was not a dualist, but he did act as a kind of John the Baptist to the organized dualist churches of the second half of the century, preparing a way for them among the people. When he wrote his treatise, Peter the Venerable believed that Henry was a faithful member of Peter's sect: later, when he wrote his introductory letter, he gave Henry greater independence. Exactly what the relationship was is made harder to elucidate by recent important revisions of our sources for Henry's teaching. What is clear is that both Henry and Peter prepared the way for the more profound and long-lasting heresy of Catharism.

Peter the Venerable was also a pioneer, who ventured beyond the existing tradition of invective based on the Fathers, Gregorian polemics and classical rhetoric to write a treatise opening new techniques of exposition and persuasion. His work had little immediate effect: in the 1140s the trend was not towards persuasion but coercion.[11]

In one other outbreak, two peasants, Clement and Ebrard, from the village of Bucy-le-Long near Soissons in about 1114, preached a heresy which appeared to have dualist undertones.[12] Christ did not in reality take on flesh; the bread and wine were not really transformed into the Body and Blood; the mouth of the priest was the opening of hell. The chronicler was convinced they were Manichaeans, as described by Augustine, and went on to say. 'Though this heresy had its origin in former times among learned persons, its dregs sank down to the countryfolk, who, boasting that they held to the way of life of the apostles, choose to read only their Acts'. They lived in a rigid asceticism which the chronicler believed cloaked libertinism.[13] The mention of the way of life of the apostles and the denunciation of the unworthy priesthood place them in the Western stream of heresy; but the Docetism, if correctly reported, is not common in spontaneous Western heresy. Especially significant is the nature of their renunciations. They refused everything that had been procreated as a result of sexual intercourse. Clement was subjected to the ordeal and failed it; when he was thrown into the vat and 'floated like a stick' there was rejoicing, perhaps because of his link with a 'rapacious' count, John of Soissons.[14] The bishop did not carry out sentence on the basis of the verdict of the ordeal but went to seek advice. The crowd broke into the prison and burnt Clement and Ebrard.[15]

10   Fearns, '*Contra Petrobrusianos*', pp. lvii–lix.
11   D. Iogna-Prat, 'L'argumentation défensive de la polémique grégorienne au *Contra Petrobrusianos* de Pierre le Vénérable', *Inventer l'Hérésie?*, ed. Zerner, pp. 87–118, citing G. Cracco, 'Bernardo e i movimenti ereticali', *Bernardo Cisterciense*, ed. E. Menesto (1990), pp. 165–86.
12   *WEH*, pp. 102–4.
13   Ibid., p. 103.
14   Interesting alternative interpn., Russell, *Dissent*, pp. 78–81 (with comment on Bishop Joscelin's creed).
15   R. I. Moore, 'Popular violence and popular heresy in Western Europe *c.* 1000–1179', *SCH* xxi (1984), pp. 43–50 at p. 49. *BK*, p. 84; see R. I. Moore, 'Guibert de Nogent and his world', *Studies . . . to R. H. C. Davis*, ed. H. Mayr-Harting, R. I. Moore (1975), pp. 107–17.

In another rural setting at the village of Ivoy in the first quarter of the century, a group of heretics met secretly and taught their followers to reject the eucharist and the baptism of infants.[16] The case may be taken as typical of the episodes in which the sources are inadequate to reveal fully the nature of the heresy. We catch only a gleam of the popular concern for the individual's religious responsibility – the usual motive for the rejection of infant baptism.

## Tanchelm and Arnold of Brescia

Tanchelm of Antwerp and Arnold of Brescia show how the ferment of reform ideals in the post-Gregorian age could lead to heresy.[17] According to the traditional account, Tanchelm owed his rise to the glaring neglect of the Church authorities for the developing town of Antwerp.[18] Disgusted by the state of the Church, Tanchelm began his preaching, soon held a dominance over the religious life of the town and carried his preaching into Flanders, Zeeland and Brabant. His hearers came from the lower classes, but the success of his sermons in Zeeland must prove that they were far from exclusively drawn from townsmen, for this remained economically a relatively undeveloped land of fishermen and farmers. Tanchelm totally rejected the Church and its sacraments, and said that the Church had become a brothel. The best-known source, a letter of the cathedral chapter at Utrecht, describes some fantastic scenes as Tanchelm declared himself God, entered into a symbolic marriage with a statue of Mary, and, accompanied by a former priest and a smith, made his way through Antwerp dressed in golden robes and with an armed guard.[19] The common people revered him as God, and drank his bathwater. But the interlude of fantasy came to an end after only three years, in 1115, when he was struck down by a priest.

Tanchelm had a gift for self-projection.[20] The size of following which he drew to him ensured the continuation of his preaching tours for years unmolested: it would have been too dangerous to put him down by force.

The odd episode of the bathwater has been variously interpreted, as a sign of the overwhelming reverence of credulous followers or as a misunderstanding by the writer, who had not understood Tanchelm's distribution to his followers of a watered wine;[21] connoisseurs of the twilight of popular cults may recall in favour of the first hypothesis that Garibaldi's servant found a good sale, all unknown to his master, for his bathwater. But other features in the usual description are not quite convincing. Why, if Tanchelm's original platform was the wickedness of the orthodox Church and the immorality of its priesthood, was he a libertine, who used his sway over women to satisfy his sexual needs?[22] Libertinism is almost an

---

16  Russell, *Dissent*, pp. 54–6; source in *WEH*, pp. 105–7.
17  Discussion by Grundmann, in *HZ* cxcvi (1963), pp. 661–6.
18  For a hypothesis based on reaction to industrial conditions, see Cohn, *Millennium*, 1st edn, pp. 35–8.
19  Tr. in *WEH*, pp. 96–100; *MBPH*, pp. 28–31.
20  Moore, *Origins*, p. 64 ('talent for manipulation').
21  *BK*, p. 85, n. 13.
22  Ibid.; Russell, *Dissent*, p. 65 (the best account of sources and dating, pp. 265–9, 282–3).

automatic accusation for a popular heretic who influences his women hearers. The principal source emanates from the enemies of Tanchelm in the chapter of Utrecht who sought to denounce him in 1112 to Frederick, archbishop of Cologne, and might be expected to press any possible hostile rumour on Tanchelm into service. Not everything in the case meets the eye. Behind the accusations of heresy could well lie an episode in the Gregorian–anti-Gregorian contest, much as accusations of heresy without much cause had been bandied about in the affairs of the Pataria in Milan and Ramihrdus in Cambrai, and were again to be in the case of Lambert le Bègue in Liège.[23] Such an interpretation is made more plausible by the evidence of direct borrowing of detail in the letter from Utrecht from the sixth-century chronicler Gregory of Tours.[24]

Pirenne brought some light when he inferred that Tanchelm was an agent of Count Robert II of Flanders, a supporter of the Gregorians, who wanted to use his party support in order to gain for the Flemish bishopric of Tournai a part of the bishopric of Utrecht, then in the hands of the imperialist party.[25] Tanchelm, on this view, played the part of the demagogue, stirring the populace against a lax imperialist clergy, and making manifest the need for a Gregorian reform in this area, which in turn might facilitate the diocesan rearrangements which the count desired. Pirenne made the connection too close: he was mistaken in thinking that Tanchelm was a layman, and a one-time notary of the count.

It now appears that Tanchelm is to be numbered among the heretical leaders who sprang from the clergy. But was he already a Gregorian when he appealed to the count for aid? Much rests on timing.[26] The letter of Utrecht can be read not as a hostile and discrediting account of a popular preacher with Gnostic undertones, but as a collection of slanders which wilfully distort Tanchelm's reforming activities. The letter might enable us to conclude that Tanchelm was first active in Zeeland,[27] not in Antwerp, and that he was active there in the first instance because this was the area which it was intended should be taken from the bishopric of Utrecht. The letter says that Tanchelm rejected the Church; for that one might understand the local Church, tainted by immorality and its imperialist connections. The rejection of Transubstantiation one might read as a rejection of the ministrations of unworthy priests, and the alleged union with God supposed to give Tanchelm divine powers one might read as an orthodox exhortation to mystical union with Christ. The betrothal with Mary, using rings, might be a version of a campaign to persuade women to give up luxuries and bestow their rings on a statue of Mary. Difficulties remain, even if this revision is

23    Russell, *Dissent*, pp. 90–6; on Lambert, see *MBPH*, pp. 101–11; L. K. Little, *Religious Poverty and the Profit Economy in Medieval Europe* (1978), p. 129.
24    W. Mohr, 'Tanchelm von Antwerpen, eine nochmalige Überprüfung der Quellenlage', *Annales Universitatis Saraviensis* III (1954), pp. 234–47; rejected by Werner (*Pauperes Christi*, pp. 205–7); Moore, *Origins*, is inclined to accept an element of extravagance as part of Tanchelm's technique to attract followers.
25    H. Pirenne, 'Tanchelin et le project de démembrement du diocèse d'Utrecht vers 1100', *ARBB*, 5th ser. XIII (1927), pp. 112–19; see further, Russell, *Dissent*, pp. 265–9.
26    I follow Russell (*Dissent*, p. 282).
27    Not first aroused by clerical deficiency (as *BK*, p. 84); correction by Russell (p. 283).

accepted; there is still a hostile tradition, not necessarily dependent on the Utrecht letter, in other sources. The truth will never be quite clear, but we are on secure ground if we assume that there was much less heresy and excess than the sources suggest, and that we are probably right if we think of Tanchelm as a Gregorian who, especially at the end, slipped into Donatism.[28]

In the case of Arnold of Brescia the sources are not obscure, although they lack the confirmation of the direct words or writing of the heresiarch himself. Arnold first showed his hand when ruling a community of canons regular in his native city of Brescia, once influenced by the Pataria agitation, and in the 1130s the scene of a struggle for the bishopric between Villano and Manfred, supporters of the rival claims to the papal tiara of Anacletus II and Innocent II.[29] In the absence of Manfred, the successful candidate, from his city, Arnold allied himself with the supporters of a commune, and used the opportunity to set about a drastic reform of the clergy. Manfred incurred Arnold's hostility, not because he was some idle nobleman in episcopal orders, but simply because his moderate reforming plans, which had already come up against the hostility of the local clergy, did not go far enough. For Arnold the pattern of apostolic life was realized in the lives of strict canons regular, and the solution to the problems of wealthy, simoniacal and unchaste clergy was to impose on them *tout court* what was in effect the life of canons regular.

Arnold's movement, though it loosely resembled the Pataria and the agitation of Ramihrdus of Cambrai, went beyond their ideas in some respects. Nor did Innocent II give Arnold the support Gregory VII had once given to the Pataria. Condemned in 1139, Arnold was forced to leave Italy and make for Paris, where he had formerly studied under Peter Abelard. There his attacks on the clergy and, surprisingly, on St Bernard of Clairvaux earned him a condemnation at the Council of Sens in 1140, somewhat rhetorically associated as pupil with the ruin of his master Abelard. In flight, he was befriended by Guy, papal legate to Bohemia, who persuaded him to submit and accept penance. Misguidedly, Pope Eugenius III invited him to Rome to keep him under his eye, only to discover that the spectacle of abuses of the curia and the involvement of the papacy in temporal affairs caused a revival of his agitation in a fiercer form. 'The pope himself', he came to believe, 'was not what he professed to be – an apostolic man and shepherd of souls – but a man of blood who maintained his authority by fire and sword.'[30] The grievances of Rome's citizens offered him a better platform than the communal movement at Brescia, and with their aid he expelled the

---

28   Russell (p. 64) goes farther in attributing heresy than I, partly on the analogy of the eccentric backwoods prophet Aldebert in the eighth century. I am more impressed by the possibilities of slander, and think excess more likely in a man of Aldebert's than Tanchelm's background.

29   A. Frugoni, *Arnaldo da Brescia* (1954) (stresses influence of gospel on Arnold in Morghen tradition); comment: Dupré-Theseider, *Introduzione*, pp. 134–7; Violante, *HS*, p. 177, discusses relative absence of heresy in Italy before Arnold. G. G. Merlo, ' "Heresis Lumbardorum e filii Arnaldi": note su Arnaldismo e Arnaldisti', *Nuova Rivista Storica* LXXVIII (1994), pp. 87–102.

30   John of Salisbury, *Historia Pontificalis*, tr. M. Chibnall (London, 1956) (under 1149); and *WEH*, p. 148. See also texts tr., *MBPH*, pp. 66–71.

pope and declared the independence of the city, where he attempted to realize his idea of the poor clergy – preaching, administering the sacraments, wholly unencumbered by possessions or political power. For a time his views, especially his rejection of the Donation of Constantine and his belief that the emperor should receive his crown from the citizens of Rome rather than the pope, recommended him to the imperial party. The pope, though he returned with the aid of military force, was again expelled in 1150. But Arnold's reform plans of that year revealed what a radical he was, and he could only retain his place through a conspiracy of faithful followers of the inferior class and without further aid from the nobles. The logic of his own radical religious positions led him into an extreme democratic position in politics. It was as a revolutionary holding on to power with limited numerical support that he was finally hunted down under Pope Hadrian IV and executed in 1155.

His eloquence and appeal to the crowds assimilate him to the inspired wandering preachers of France, and he is fully in accord with the ideas of the time in his stress on the overwhelming value of poverty. But he differed from the wandering preachers in his readiness to use political force to gain his ends, and in the fact that he offered a programme, not merely for the salvation of the individual, but also for the Church at large – a programme he was prepared to enforce with the sword. Its fundamental tenet was that clergy and monks who had possessions could not be saved. There were other, sacramental errors in his beliefs, which linked with the central position on poverty. The sacraments were not denied in themselves, but there was a sweeping application of the common post-Gregorian position, that the sacraments had become invalid through the unworthiness of ministers. As one might expect from the pragmatic nature of Arnold, there was no deep dogmatic difference with orthodoxy, and in fact he was never formally arraigned for heresy.[31] The spiritual power of Rome was denied because of its involvement with the things of this world. Preaching was open to all, and depended, not on a particular training or authorization, but simply on the life of the preacher.

In practice nearly all shrank from the drastic renunciations which Arnold demanded of the hierarchy. He was too radical to be at ease with reformers within the Church. The sympathy of Guy, the cardinal legate in Bohemia, and his earlier readiness to repent showed that initially he was not far from the Church. But the emotional experience of contact with the darker side of Rome and his own temperament carried him beyond reconciliation.

The Arnoldists as an organized force never again played a significant part in Italy, for their power was broken by the events which followed the re-establishment of the commune in 1150. Arnold, however, was one of those dissident leaders whose power is derived, not from any great originality of thought, but from their ability to focus widespread discontents, and these long outlived his movement. The tenets of Arnoldists were thought worthy of refutation by Bonacursus of Milan in his polemical work, the *Manifestatio haeresis Catharorum*, written between

31   Grundmann, *Ketzergeschichte*, p. 20; see A. Frugoni, 'Filii Arnaldi', *BISIAM* LX (1958), 521–4.

1176 and 1190, which included a section attacking the belief that evangelical poverty was obligatory, that laymen who practised it had full rights of preaching, and that their sins incapacitated priests and hierarchy from administering the sacraments and holding the power of binding and loosing.[32] Though at that date Arnoldism may well have represented a current of thought rather than a sect, the name passed into the catalogue of heresies to be periodically denounced by popes, continuing to exist in bulls, though surely not in reality, down to 1511.[33]

## Eon (or Eudo) de l'Etoile

The case of Eon carries us back to the wild rural agitators, Aldebert, Theuda and Leutard.[34] Though lettered and probably a younger son of the Breton nobility, Eon's following consisted exclusively of credulous peasants. The sources say that he gathered his followers to pray in secluded places, that he was opposed to church buildings, and with his followers attacked them and stripped them of ornaments. He believed himself the Son of God, and persuaded his followers into believing that he was 'eum' of the Latin phrase probably known to him from the formula of an exorcism: Jesus Christ who would return in glory – 'per eum qui venturus est cum gloria judicare vivos et mortuos et seculum per ignem'.[35] His disciples he called by the names of angels, prophets and apostles. His staff was, as it were, a sceptre shaped in the form of a Y – as long as the Y pointed upwards, two-thirds of the world belonged to God the Father, one to Eon; if he inverted the fork, the position would be reversed. The Council of Rheims in 1148 heard these revelations with laughter, and banished Eon to prison, where he soon died.

Some commentators have, reasonably, thought that he was mad; others have noted apparently Gnostic elements.[36] Werner notes the deep superstitions of Brittany, which had established so strong a hold that in the seventeenth century part needed in effect to be freshly converted by the Jesuits.[37] Russell depicts him as sincere but deranged. Mad, or only 'mad north north west', with an eye to church plunder and escaping the death sentence at Rheims, one certain feature of the case is the pitiable condition of the followers of Eon. Their heresy was manifestly based on a profound ignorance.

---

32 Ilarino da Milano, 'La "Manifestatio heresis catarorum"', *Aevum* XII (1938), pp. 281–333 (see third section of treatise); Arnoldists discussed in his *L'Eresia di Ugo Speroni* (1945), pp. 444–52. Note warning by W. L. Wakefield, *WEH*, p. 146, that the links between Arnold and the Arnoldists are not wholly assured.

33 D. Kurze, 'Die festländischen Lollarden', *AKG* XLVII (1965), p. 68, n. 1 (article important for terminology and study of popular religion).

34 Russell, *Dissent*, pp. 118–24; note discussion of his name: pp. 120–1, 289.

35 *BK*, p. 87n. Or derivation from 'per eundem dominum nostrum Jesum Christum' (Russell, *Dissent*, p. 120). Sources tr. in *WEH*, pp. 141–6; *MBPH*, pp. 62–6. Did he take on a new name, like a novice entering monastic life (*FK*, p. 54)?

36 References in *WEH*, pp. 685–6; Russell, *Dissent*, p. 120 and n. I agree with Russell in thinking there is little in this.

37 *Pauperes Christi*, p. 180.

## The Early Cathars

Heresy in the first three decades of the century tended to depend heavily on the personality of one preacher; his influence removed, the following he collected falls back into obscurity, or disappears completely. In Eon's time (the 1140s), the first signs appear that this phase in the history of Western dissent is coming to an end as writers and chroniclers describe the stirrings of a fully international movement, named differently in different countries, but having distinctive elements of belief and organization in common.[38] These betray a connection with the Bogomils of Byzantium and the Balkans.

The anonymity of the new heresy alarmed some orthodox observers. St Bernard, on hearing of it, exclaimed at the contrast between it and the heresies of the early Church, named after their founders, Mani and the Manichees, Sabellius and the Sabellians, Arius and the Arians.[39] Events bore out his fears, as over the following two decades this Bogomil-influenced heresy spread widely in the West.

The first outbreak to be recorded took place in the Rhineland, where in 1143–4 the Premonstratensian provost Everwin of Steinfeld described to St Bernard of Clairvaux the traits of a heresy detected at Cologne which had its own bishop and organization.[40] There were three ranks of adherents – auditors, believers and elect, entry from the lowest category to that of believers, and from believers to elect, being gained by a ceremony of laying-on of hands and a process of testing. The baptism thus obtained through the laying-on of hands 'in fire and the Spirit' was contrasted with the baptism by water of John the Baptist. The group refused to drink milk or consume anything produced as a result of coition, and rejected marriage. At daily meals, Everwin reported, they 'consecrated' their food and drink with the *Pater Noster*. They claimed their belief went back to the time of the martyrs, and that they had fellow adherents in 'Greece' (i.e. Byzantium) and 'certain other lands'. The bishop, his assistant and some others stood their ground in debate, and when they refused to recant were burnt by the people.

The distinctions among adherents, the existence of a category of adepts, the elect, the double initiation ceremony with the laying-on of hands, like the *baptisma* and the *teleiosis* known in Byzantium as rituals of the Bogomils to the orthodox twelfth-century writer Euthymius Zigabenus, the contrast between this and the baptism in water of John, the rejection of milk, the products of coition and the repudiation of marriage, and finally the belief in the existence of co-religionists in

---

38   *BK*, pp. 89–96; perceptive comments in B. Hamilton, 'Wisdom from the East: the reception by the Cathars of eastern dualist texts', *BHL*, pp. 38–60.

39   *Sermo* 66, *PL* CLXXXIII, col. 1094; *RB*, p. 50n.; for discussion of long-term effect of orthodox realization of the appearance of a rival Church inside Christendom, see P. Biller, 'Words and the medieval notion of religion', *JEH* XXXVI (1985), pp. 351–69; note p. 363.

40   *PL* CLXXXII, cols 676–80; tr. in *WEH*, pp. 127–32; on this correspondence, Manselli, *Studi*, pp. 89–109; *MBPH*, pp. 74–8; comment on punishment by the people, in Moore, 'Popular violence', pp. 47, 48.

Byzantium – all are good evidence of an infiltration of the Balkan and Byzantine heresy of Bogomilism.[41] Bogomil himself was a tenth-century Bulgarian village priest (his name, 'worthy of the pity of God', was probably a pseudonym), who organized and gave new shape to dualist ideas floating in his backward country, newly and shakily converted from paganism. He gave a voice to a peasantry oppressed by its Byzantine conquerors, its alien Byzantine priesthood and the Bulgarian aristocracy. So far from being weeded out in Bulgaria, the heresy developed and spread into Byzantium proper and Constantinople, carried forward by the strong, superficial attractions of the dualist interpretation of the world with its initial simplicity and its apparent solutions to the problem of the presence of evil in a world created by a good God. At the centre of the Bogomils' experience was the conviction that what is seen is evil: flesh itself is the creation of a fallen angel, Satan, given over to evil. What is unseen is spiritual. Initiates, who might appear like the most ascetic of Byzantine monks, lived a life as far removed from the fleshly world as was conceivable, eschewing eggs, milk, cheese, meat, all the products of coition, remaining celibate and fasting ruthlessly. Supporters venerated the initiates, gave them the opportunity to continue their renunciations and listened to their preaching, but were under no obligation themselves to renounce the products of coition, marriage or parenthood. A high ideal existed for the few; the many had very limited commitments.

The Bogomil ascetic ideal appealed in the West in the age of St Bernard and the Cistercians, when asceticism was given so high a value. Everwin's description tells us why Bogomil enthusiasts gained converts – they followed the pattern of the poor, wandering preacher. The Cologne heretics claimed, he said, that 'theirs alone is the Church, inasmuch as only they follow in the footsteps of Christ. They continue to be the true imitators of the apostolic life, seeking not those things which are of the world, possessing no house, or lands, even as Christ had no property... "You, however," they say to us, "add house to house, field to field, and seek the things that are of this world. You do this to the point that they who are considered the most perfect among you, such as monks and canons regular, although owning nothing of their own and holding everything in common, nevertheless possess all these things." Of themselves they

---

41   H. C. Puech, A. Vaillant, *Le Traité contre les Bogomiles de Cosmas le Prêtre* (1945) (subtle analysis); Y. Stoyanov, *The Other God* (2000) (wide-ranging survey of dualist religions with rich bibliography, superseding his *The Hidden Tradition* (New Haven and London, 1994)), Bogomils, pp. 158–83; mythology, pp. 260–86; B. and J. Hamilton with Stoyanov, *Christian Dualist Heresies* (1998) (*CDH*) (originals translated; see esp. intro. and new text of Cosmas, pp. 114–34); Periblepton, pp. 142–64; Zigabenus, pp. 180–207; M. D. Lambert, *The Cathars* (1998) (comprehensive account; Bogomils and Cathar origins, pp. 23–32) (*MLC*); Hamilton, 'Wisdom', *BHL*, pp. 38–60; M. Angold, *Church and Society in Byzantium* (1995), pp. 468–501; J. V. A. Fine Jr, 'The Bulgarian Bogomil Movement', *EEQ* xi (1977), pp. 384–412 (pungent critique); I. Dujčev, 'I Bogomili nei paesi slavi e loro storia', *Medioevo Bizantino-Slavo* i (1965), pp. 251–82; H. I. Marrou, 'Un Ange déchu, un Ange pourtant', *Satan, EC* xxvii (1948), pp. 28–43; E. Turdeanu, 'Apocryphes bogomiles et pseudo-bogomiles', *RHR* cxxxviii (1950), pp. 22–52, 176–218; *Interrogatio Johannis*, see below, p. 117, n. 8; *GRK* iii (*Die Herkunft der Katharer*) elucidates relation to Cathars; Dr Lydia Denkova, Sofia, in a private letter, argues for Bogomil as 'friend of God', marking the priest's ascent to a higher perfection.

say, "We, the poor of Christ, who have no fixed abode and flee from city to city like sheep amidst wolves, are persecuted as were the apostles and the martyrs." [42]

The way of life was the turning-point.[43] Where authority claimed apostolicity for the Church because of the succession of its bishops from the apostles and the tradition of its doctrine from the early Church, the heretics bypassed that claim by their plea for realization of the apostolic life. It is conceived by the heretics, and plainly also by their hearers, as the wandering insecure life of the disciples, based on the poverty texts of Scripture and the pattern of the sending of the Seventy. Orthodox Gregorian preachers, of whom the hermits of western France are the best-known examples, helped to create a demand for this pattern of living. Through conservatism this demand was never met by orthodoxy in this period. The heretics were the beneficiaries.

Not all of the Cologne heretics accepted the Bogomil influence, however. Another group described by Everwin had beliefs of a 'Western' type, rigorist in morality, pleading for a simple spiritual Church free of the tainted Catholic clergy and putting weight on the response of the individual conscience. They denied the validity of Catholic masses, Everwin said, 'because no priests of the Church are validly ordained. For, they say, the apostolic office has been corrupted through involvement in secular business... he who sits in the chair of Peter has lost the power to ordain which was bestowed upon Peter. And because the apostolic see does not have this power, the archbishops and bishops, who lead worldly lives within the Church, cannot receive from that see the power to ordain anyone.' They accepted the baptism of adults, 'baptized by Christ, no matter who may actually administer the sacrament', but rejected infant baptism as not in accord with Scripture. Texts again buttressed their idiosyncratic doctrine that only marriage between virgins was lawful, and also their rejection of purgatory. Penance they found unnecessary, 'because, on whatever day the sinner shall have lamented his sins, all are forgiven'.[44] Only observances established by Christ or the apostles were acceptable.

Alike in their ethical concern and their attacks on the clergy, the groups thus diverged markedly in their more positive beliefs. Dissension between them led to their discovery.

In 1145 St Bernard of Clairvaux, engaged on his few days' preaching against the followers of Henry the Monk in Toulouse, may have brushed another heresy, described in an imprecise phrase apparently as that of 'weavers and Arians'.[45] At Liège a group was discovered with its own hierarchy and with a division among its adherents between initiates, called 'believers', and 'auditors', who were

---

42   WEH, p. 129.
43   RB, pp. 18–27.
44   WEH, pp. 130–1.
45   PL CLXXXV, col. 411; Manselli, 'Una designazione dell'eresia Catara "Arriana Haeresis"', BISLAM LXVIII (1956), pp. 233–46; Griffe, Débuts, pp. 33–7. R. I. Moore ('St Bernard's mission to the Languedoc in 1145', BIHR XLVII (1974), pp. 1–10) argues that Bernard did not meet the type of heresy of the first Cologne group there, as is sometimes alleged. Hamilton, 'Wisdom', p. 45 does not exclude this.

neophytes in the heresy. They rejected wholesale the sacraments, including marriage.[46]

A profession of faith and formula for abjuration amongst the manuscripts of the abbey of Moissac in the south of France dating from mid-century implies the existence of a heresy rejecting baptism, the eucharist, marriage and meat eating, which laid stress on the imposition of hands.[47]

In the Rhineland a trial at Cologne in 1163[48] showed that the burnings two decades earlier had been ineffective; a Western-type heresy still existed there, but it had, according to the description of the prime source, Ekbert, later Benedictine abbot of Schönau, blended with the Bogomil-influenced group.[49] Amongst their errors, some held the belief that only marriage between virgins was legitimate – a sign that the 'Western' heresy still had its influence. But dissension between the groups seemed to have disappeared, and the 'Westerners' now existed as an outer circle, taught dissenting evangelical beliefs, while an inner circle of adepts had a secret doctrine which included belief in a Docetic Christology, transmigration of souls, and the creation of the world by an evil god. Initiation to the circle of adepts was obtained in a secret ceremony by the laying-on of hands. Ekbert believed that the heresy had an international character. In Flanders, whence the heretics had come, he said, they were called 'Piphles', in France 'Texerant' because of their weaving, and in Germany 'the Cathars', a Greek term meaning the 'pure ones'. The latter has been taken most widely by modern writers as a term for the new heresy of the twelfth century, formed by the coalescence of Western evangelical heresy and Bogomil influences from the East. But Ekbert's learning deceived him. He harked back to Augustine for the term 'Cathar'; a more likely derivation is from 'cat' and the wholly slanderous belief that the heretics, worshipping Lucifer in the form of a cat, kissed its posterior.[50]

Ekbert's sermons in one way represented a step forward in the progress of the Church's polemic against heresy, for they attempted to expound in full the dogmatic basis on which the Cologne heresy rested. Yet, progressive as this attitude was by contrast with that of the mass of writers hitherto, content with fleeting and

---

46   *WEH*, pp. 139–41; *MBPH*, pp. 78–9. I have preferred H. Silvestre, in *RHE* LVIII (1963), pp. 979–80; P. Bonenfant, in *LMA* LXIX (1963), pp. 278–9, on dating to J. B. Russell ('Les Cathares de 1048–54 à Liège', *BSAHDL* XLII (1961), pp. 1–8) who places the source, a letter from the faithful of Liège to the pope 'L', in the pontificate of Leo IX (1048–54).

47   Manselli, *BISIAM* LXVII (1955), pp. 212–34, corrected by *JDR*, p. 166, n. 93; for a summary see Manselli, *L'Eresia del Male* (1963), pp. 165–8. I have not been able to see the 2nd edn of 1980; *MLC*, p. 241.

48   For discussion of this trial and others in the dioceses of Cologne, Trier, Liège, with analysis of major source, Ekbert, see Moore, *Origins*, pp. 175–82.

49   *Adversus Catharos*, *PL* CXCV, cols 11–102; extract tr. in *MBPH*, pp. 88–94; reconstruction of events in Russell, *Dissent*, pp. 220–4.

50   'Hos nostra Germania Catharos, Flandria Piphles, Gallia Texerant ab usu texendi appellat', *PL* CXCIII, col. 1993; terminology for heretics generally in *RB*, pp. 29–38. But I think Grundmann underestimates the significance of references here and elsewhere to weaving; see below, p. 123. The term 'Cathar' should strictly only be applied to the leading class in the heresy; I have used the term as a generic one for the sect because it is so well established. *FK*, pp. 95–6, discusses cellars; Patschovsky, 'Der Ketzer,' is convincing on derivation from cat.

superficial notices of denials of orthodoxy, Ekbert's work was largely vitiated by his fatal penchant for transferring bodily the doctrines of the Manichees of the fourth century, attacked by Augustine, to the account of the Cologne sectaries.[51] His description of the teachings of the adepts, with their thoroughgoing dualism, must be treated with scepticism: it is possible to infer merely that the first group at Cologne described in the 1140s by Everwin had survived, that it had dualist beliefs and, further, that rationalist propaganda was being used to attract follow-ers. Although the true basis for the rejection of the mass lay in their rejection of bread and wine as part of an evil creation, the heretics used a primitive logic. Christ's body, they said, must have been as big as a mountain to feed the faithful for so long.[52]

Two years after the Cologne outbreak, a conference held at Lombers, a castle near Albi, in the south of France, revealed the relative freedom of Cathar heretics on a favourable terrain.[53] Local heretical leaders, known as 'the good men', debated with their opponents before a distinguished gathering which included, as well as William, the diocesan, the archbishop of Narbonne, other bishops, the viscount of Béziers, in whose lands Lombers lay, and Constance, countess of Toulouse and sister of the king of France.

The representatives of orthodoxy had to restrict their exposition so as to cite proof-texts only from the New Testament, since the heretics did not recognize the Old. The 'good men' stressed the evils of the way of living of churchmen, and their own superiority in this sphere. 'They said also', the record of the assembly runs, 'that Paul stated in his Epistle what kind of bishops and priests were to be ordained in the churches, and that, if the men ordained were not such as Paul had specified, they were not bishops and priests, but ravening wolves, hypocrites and seducers, lovers of salutations in the market place . . . desirous of being called rabbis and masters contrary to the command of Christ, wearers of albs and gleaming raiment, displaying bejewelled gold rings on their fingers, which their Master Jesus did not command.'[54] The ecclesiastics tried to draw their opponents on to the fields of dogma, in order to expose their deviations from orthodoxy. But the heretics were not to be drawn. They are reported as saying that they did not want to be forced to reply about their faith. Eventually, as the bishops seemed to be getting the better of it, the 'good men' appealed to the people, and made a declaration which sounded quite Catholic. But they refused to swear to it since, following texts in James and the gospels, they held that all oaths were unlawful. In any case they had said enough to be convicted of heresy, though the bishops never penetrated to the core of their beliefs.

The debate, it is plausibly argued, was intended to be a kind of legal pleading in the presence of eminent laity, in which the fact that the 'good men' were preaching heresy should be made manifest, and the secular authority conse-

51   *BK*, pp. 6–7; Manselli, *Eresia*, pp. 163–4.
52   Noticed by Manselli, *Eresia*, p. 164; see *MLC*, pp. 161, 249.
53   Bouquet, xiv, pp. 431–4; tr. *WEH*, pp. 190–4; *MBPH*, pp. 94–8; the best analysis is by Griffe, *Débuts*, pp. 59–67.
54   *WEH*, p. 191.

quently moved to action.[55] At Cologne there had been formal trial, which led instantly to punishment; at Lombers adjudication against the beliefs of the 'good men' had no effect at all.

A similar demonstration of the strength and independence of Catharism in the Midi took place some two years after Lombers in the international council of dualists held at the village of Saint Félix in the Lauragais, at which the territory most affected by Catharism was divided up into bishoprics, delimited territorially on the Catholic pattern.[56] In Lombardy a Cathar mission established itself in the fifth, or early in the sixth, decade of the century. A narrative, probably based on oral tradition, recounted a century later by the inquisitor Anselm of Alessandria, described how a party of heretics from northern France, led by a notary, made their way into northern Italy, and converted a gravedigger called Mark from the Milan area who became the apostle of Cathar Italy, and with his friends John Judeus, a weaver, and Joseph, a smith, established a base for mission at Concorezzo near his birthplace.[57] Under Mark's leadership, the heresy spread in Lombardy and then into the March of Treviso and Tuscany.

The story about the mission from Northern France is one of a series of pieces of evidence suggesting that the strength and potential of the Cathars of Northern France in the twelfth century has been underestimated.[58] In his *Summa Aurea* of *c.*1220, William of Auxerre, on internal evidence, was arguing, not simply against dualists whose views were enshrined in the Fathers, but against contemporary or near-contemporary Cathars. The 'Manichee' propositions which he rejected appear again as statements made by Cathars in the late polemical work of the Dominican Moneta of Cremona. Other Northern writers, Alan of Lille and Everard of Béthune, show knowledge of Cathars and their beliefs, Everard betraying knowledge of living Cathar arguments and the manner in which their polemicists handled Scripture. He had been in contact with them near Peronne.

There is good evidence from Ivo of Narbonne, formerly of Bordeaux, who moved among Cathars in Lombardy *c.*1214–15, that the heretics then regularly sent students to study Arts and Theology in Paris; they were evidently free to enter the schools and to return safely. If they could do this, it is likely that the Northern French Cathar families could do the same.

The Northern French Church, moreover, threw up one of the rare cases of an indigenous ecclesiastic of rank openly going over to Catharism, when the nephew of Evrard of Châteauneuf, a knight burnt for heresy, abandoned his canonry at Nevers, fled to Languedoc, changed his name and participated on the Cathar side in debates with Catholics. Evrard himself was a distinguished catch for

---

55   Griffe, *Débuts*, pp. 60–1.
56   See below, pp. 137–42.
57   A. Dondaine, 'La hiérarchie cathare en Italie', *AFP* xix (1949), pp. 282–312; xx (1950), pp. 234–324 (MS discoveries with analysis, lists of heretical bishops, important for internal history of Italian Cathars). Discussion of Anselm in *AFP* xx (1950), pp. 259–62; this text is in *TDH*, pp. 308–9; tr. in *WEH*, pp. 168–70. See below, p. 138; A. Dondaine, *Les Hérésies et l'inquisition* (Aldershot, 1990) (coll. papers); on Anselm, contrast *MLC*, pp. 34–7 and *BC*, pp. 27–8.
58   P. Biller, 'Northern Cathars and higher learning', *SCH* Subsidia xi, pp. 25–53.

Catharism and, when arraigning him, authority put up a notable body of ecclesiastics in council at Paris to condemn him.

Northern French Catharism in general had some recruits of rank, which stiffens the evidence that it included trained minds. Moreover, this Church had missionary zeal – the French notary brought Catharism to Italy and it is quite possible that it was Northern French who brought Catharism to Languedoc and that it was to a French bishop that quarrelling Italians turned in the aftermath of the Council of St Félix to settle their differences.[59] Northern Catholicism persecuted more vigorously and consistently than did orthodox authority in many parts of Languedoc and Italy, finally snuffing out the Church. This early fall and the chance that it has left so light an imprint on our sources leaves it largely in the shadows. But it once mattered.

One other major service of the Northern French in the twelfth century may also have been the translation and adaptation from the Greek ritual of the Bogomils for the initiation of adepts. Modern analysis of the Cathar ritual of initiation, the *consolamentum*, contained in thirteenth-century MSS, strongly suggests that it stemmed from a twelfth-century Latin archetype; what could be more natural than its translation from the Greek in the context of an early French bishopric in Constantinople?[60] Anselm is explicit. Greeks returning to Constantinople from Bulgaria set up what they called a bishop of the Greeks; Frenchmen ('Francigeni') who arrived 'intending to conquer the land and discovered this sect' set up their own bishop, 'who is called the bishop of the Latins'. It is arguable that Catharism, the child of Bogomilism, was born in Constantinople under North French auspices and there equipped itself with one of its most notable and characteristic features, the ritual of the *consolamentum* in the solemn liturgical language of the West.

Anselm gives pride of place to the Northern French for the beginnings of the Cathar evangelization of the West. He continues, 'Later on, the French who had gone to Constantinople returned to their homeland and preached and, as their numbers grew, set up a bishop of France....'

In addition to these established cases, there are other outbreaks imperfectly recorded, such as that of the clerk Jonas in Cambrai[61] and one in Vézelay in 1167.[62] England, too, was touched by Catharism.[63] Thirty German-speaking strangers entered the country to evangelize under their leader Gerard. Authority was uncertain how to deal with them; the king called a Council at Oxford in 1166, bishops interrogated and the Council resolved that they should be scourged, branded and set adrift. They were refused food and died. Describing the episode,

---

59　Cathars are found inland in Languedoc rather than on the seaboard, suggesting evangelization overland from the north; see also distribution of bishoprics. Italians' consultation, below, p. 141 n. 98; *MLC*, p. 50.
60　Hamilton, 'Wisdom' (strong and attractive hypothesis).
61　Russell, *Dissent*, pp. 217–18.
62　H. Maisonneuve, *Etudes sur les origines de l'Inquisition* (1960).
63　P. Biller, 'William of Newburgh and the Cathar mission to England', *SCH* Subsidia xii, pp. 11–30; text tr. *WEH*, pp. 345–7. Biller supersedes all others.

William of Newburgh rejoiced that England had been kept from heresy. But it may not have been quite so impervious as is sometimes stated. Certainly the strangers made one woman convert, possibly consoled, who recanted. Moreover, William's language could imply that the heretics had been in England some time before their capture. At the end of the century Peter of Blois exhorted the archbishop of York to action over heresy in a letter suggesting its existence in his province, and two chroniclers' entries for 1210 and 1211 concern the burning of Albigensian heretics. There were heresy scares later in the thirteenth century, at York in 1236 and in the diocese of Salisbury some time between 1238 and 1244, when the bishop spoke of heresies 'spreading anew'. Insular authority kept infiltration at bay, but England was not a *tabula rasa* for heresy.

At Arras we have concrete evidence from a sermon preached *c.*1200 denouncing the heresy of the 'Bougres', a pejorative term for Cathars derived from 'Bulgar' and reflecting the common understanding that the heresy came from Bulgaria. In 1183–4 there was a substantial investigation, uncovering a community of heretics including nobles and clergy. The ordeal by water and hot iron was used to establish guilt. The preacher alluded to other heretics, also Bougres, of La Charité sur Loire, whose beliefs included a rejection of the Old Testament and the orthodox doctrine of creation, and who were headed by an elite class of the perfect who would not eat meat, eggs or cheese. This is unmistakable Catharism, backed by adherents of rank, resilient in avoiding suppression by the bishop of Auxerre; despite harassment, a community lived on well into the thirteenth century.[64]

We have inevitably, a fragmentary picture of the beginnings of Catharism. Crusading was but one of the links drawing the West to Byzantium. There may well have been other strands of dualist missionary activity of which we know nothing. But of the success of the new heresy there can be no doubt. In roughly two decades from the undoubted appearance of Bogomil influence at Cologne, it was disseminated from the Rhine to the Pyrenees and into the Italian peninsula.[65]

---

64    B. Delmaire, 'Un sermon arrageois inédit sur les "Bougres" du nord de la France', *Heresis* XVII (1991), pp. 1–15.
65    *BK*, p. 92.

# The Waldensians and the Deepening Crisis

In the last thirty years of the twelfth century Catharism was the heresy which preoccupied authority. It was not put down: in northern and central Italy and in Languedoc it actually succeeded in increasing its hold. At the same time, the other currents of heresy maintained themselves and, within the evangelical tradition, two new groups emerged: the Humiliati and the Waldensians, simple gospel-based movements whose members desired the right to exhort their fellow Christians. Both fell foul of authority on the issue of the right to preach; both, though at the outset apparently untainted by heresy, passed after their experience of rejection from disobedience into unorthodoxy. The papacy under Lucius III made a more strenuous and broader-based attempt to grapple with the problem of efficient repression of heresy, but could not find a solution;[1] at the end of the century there was more heresy than ever before. The zeal of the Humiliati and Waldensians had been lost to the Church, and in the two most dangerous regions in Italy and Languedoc heretical teachers were able to spread their ideas almost in freedom.

## The Waldensians and the Humiliati

The Waldensians, the last and the most tenacious of the twelfth-century wandering-preacher movements, are the classic example of the would-be reform movement drawn into heresy by the inadequacies of ecclesiastical authority. Valdes, the founder,[2] was a rich businessman of Lyons who was touched by a

1  See the discussion of *Ad abolendam* below, pp. 74–6. Survey on papal policy in B. Bolton, 'Tradition and temerity: papal attitudes to deviants, 1159–1216', in *SCH* IX, pp. 79–91; see *RB*, pp. 50–69.
2  E. Cameron, *The Waldenses* (2000), pp. 1–60 (critical account to 1565, maps, biblio.; comprehensive with sharp queries); G. Audisio, trans. C. Davison, *The Waldensian Dissent* (1999), pp. 6–25 (reflections by master-researcher on nature of Waldensianism; no footnotes; trans. 1989 original); K. V. Selge, *Die ersten Waldenser* I: *Untersuchung und Darstellung*; II: *Der Liber antiheresis des Durandus von Osca* (1967), see I, ch. 3 (edn of major Waldensian treatise with history and analysis); Id., 'Caractéristiques du premier mouvement vaudois et crises au cours de son expansion', *CF* II, pp. 110–42; G. Gonnet, 'La figure et l'oeuvre de Vaudès dans la tradition historique et selon les dernières recherches', *CF* II, pp.

jongleur's version of the life of St Alexius, the penitent son of a rich man who rejected a bride and went away to live in poverty, returning after many years to die unrecognized, destitute in his father's house. The sequel was that Valdes, after consulting a master of theology, decided to give up his wealth and the world. There was a Franciscan touch in his religious passion, throwing money on the street, rejecting the usurious business methods that had brought him wealth, insisting on receiving his food from others and having to be forced by the archbishop to eat with his wife. He made provision for his wife, endowed his daughters so that they might enter Fontevrault, but did not himself enter a monastery. He insisted on staying a layman. From the outset Valdes showed an individualist, pragmatic streak. For more than two months in a famine, probably in 1176, he operated a soup-kitchen. His aim was the apostolic life of poverty and preaching on the lines of the gospel texts.[3] What distinguishes him from earlier wandering preachers, however, is his concern as a layman for self-instruction through vernacular translations of Scripture and the Fathers. Etienne de Bourbon, who supplements the edifying account of his conversion in the anonymous chronicle of Laon, tells us that he 'was not well-educated, but on hearing the gospels was anxious to learn more precisely what was in them', 'not only for many Books of the Bible but also for many passages from the Fathers',[4] set about commissioning translations, then drew followers. He desired to preach, and he and his followers set about doing so.

Soon he came into conflict with authority. The traditional interpretation of orders in the Church gave the right of preaching and of the cure of souls to the pope and the bishops, as successors of Peter and the Twelve, and to the priests, as successors of the Seventy.[5] Canon law restricted preaching to the clergy, and

---

87–109; G. Gonnet, A. Molnár, *Les Vaudois au Moyen Age* (1974) (older standard work, partly reassembling articles); sources, *EFV* (standard collection), see also A. Patschovsky, K. V. Selge, *Quellen zur Geschichte der Waldenser* (1973); H. Böhmer, 'Die Waldenser', *RPTK* xx, cols 799–840 (still of value though partly outdated by MS discoveries); *Les Vaudois des origines à leur fin (xiie–xvie siècles)*, ed. G. Audisio (1990) (surveys by researchers; see G. G. Merlo on early years, pp. 15–35); *Les Vaudois, RHR* ccxvii fasc. 1 Jan.– March 2000 (1998 colloquy); M. Rubellin, 'Au temps où Valdès n'était pas hérétique: hypothèses sur le rôle de Valdès à Lyon', *Inventer L'Hérésie?*, ed. M. Zerner (1998), pp. 193–217 (argues for working alliance between Valdes and Guichard, reforming Archbishop of Lyons. Intriguing, but only a hypothesis. Reform of urban clergy and sympathy for lay preaching do not necessarily coincide); Prescot Stephens, *The Waldensian Story* (1998) (popular, clear-headed account from Valdes to the present).
3   *Chronicon universale anonymi Laudunensis*, ed. G. Waitz, in *MGH Scriptores* xxvi, p. 447; *WEH*, pp. 200–2; *MBPH*, pp. 111–13; conversion 1173 (Laon), 1176 (Böhmer, in *RPTK* xx, col. 806); 1176 preferred; on soup-kitchen, see P. Biller, in *SCH* xix, pp. 55–77 at p. 58; *re topoi* in Anonymous of Laon, Biller (in *Les Vaudois*, ed. Audisio, pp. 39–40) notes *topoi* do not necessarily mean falsification – see bibliography, Ibid., p. 67.
4   A. Lecoy de la Marche, *Anecdotes historiques*, SHF Publications clxxxv (Paris, 1887), p. 291; *WEH*, p. 209; M. Carrières, 'Sur la langue de la Bible de Valdo', *BSSV* lxxxv (1946), pp. 28–34; A. Patschovsky, 'The literacy of Waldensianism from Valdes to c.1400', *BHL*, pp. 112–36 (subtle analysis). The 'passages from the Fathers' would form a *Florilegium*, grouped under topics; the 'books' and reference to the gospels imply translations of books of the Bible and gospels as a whole, not mere extracts. See p. 115 for record of Valdes's bakehouse in the will of one of his translators.
5   *RB*, p. 63; A. Dondaine, 'Aux origines de Valdéisme: une profession de foi de Valdès', *AFP* xvi (1946), pp. 191–235 (document and survey of background); see below, pp. 72–3.

there were few exceptions.[6] Valdes's movement was a popular success, likely to arouse both the fears and the jealousies of the local clergy. From a controversial local situation the group appealed to the pope,[7] and sent representatives to the third Lateran Council in 1179 at Rome, showing their translations, and asking for his authorization of preaching. The response, according to Walter Map, the chronicler and servant of Henry II, was a theological examination designed to show their fitness to preach, in which that worldly cleric exposed their weaknesses by asking them in turn whether they believed in God the Father, the Son, the Holy Spirit, and then the mother of Christ. To each question they replied, 'We do', only to be laughed at when they gave the same response to the question about Mary, whether through their naïvety in seeming to put Mary on equality with the Trinity, or because of Nestorian implications in their answer. They withdrew, Map said, in confusion.

Map need not be taken seriously. He intended to make fun of the Waldensians, just as he deliberately garbled his account of the Cathars immediately preceding this anecdote.[8] But we may infer from him at least that there was some examination, and that no full, blanket permission to preach was then given to the group. The Laon chronicler says that Pope Alexander III embraced Valdes, 'approving his vow of voluntary poverty, but forbidding preaching by either himself or his followers unless welcomed by the local priests'.[9] Local clergy were not welcoming, and so the pope's decision in practice was the near-equivalent of total refusal.

The approval of the vow of poverty coupled with the grave caution about preaching are characteristic of the traditional attitude. The practice of a dedicated way of life, in or on the margins of monasticism, was applauded; preaching remained the proper function of the clergy. Map's account recalls another facet of the situation – the clergy's fear of the consequences of any breach of their exclusive position. After describing the way of life of the Waldensians – going about two by two, barefoot, clad in woollen garments, owning nothing, holding all things common like the apostles, naked, following a naked Christ – he added the sharp observation, 'They are making their first moves now in the humblest manner because they cannot launch an attack. If we admit them, we shall be driven out.'[10]

The following year Valdes and his followers were still in the Church. The papal legate Henri de Marcy, a leading Cistercian who had become the principal in high-level attempts to check the growth of Catharism in the Midi, presided over a diocesan council at Lyons in which Valdes assented to a profession of orthodox

---

6    Selge, *Waldenser* I, pp. 22n., 23n. But there was debate within the clergy on lay preaching: see P. Buc, '*Vox clamantis in deserto*. Pierre le Chantre et la prédication laïque', *Revue Mabillon*, n.s. IV (1993), pp. 5–47; Rubellin, 'Au temps', p. 211.

7    Selge, *Waldenser* I, p. 23; see discussion, pp. 21–35; 243–59.

8    W. Map, *De nugis curialium*, ed. M. R. James (Oxford, 1914), pp. 60–2; tr. in *WEH*, pp. 202–4. I owe the interpn. to Professor C. N. L. Brooke.

9    *Chronicon universale*, ed. Waitz, p. 449, tr. in *WEH*, p. 203.

10    *De nugis*, in *WEH*, p. 204. Here the sending of the Seventy is plainly a pattern. The sandals worn by the preachers point in the same direction.

faith.[11] The great fear of authority, it would seem from this document, was that Waldensian enthusiasm would be infiltrated by the Cathar heresy. The profession was prophylactic, intended to alert Valdes to the dangers, and secure his specific rejection of a number of dualist tenets, taken either from twelfth-century experience in the field or derived from a profession of faith compiled in the fifth century and formerly used in the consecration of bishops under the Gallican rite. Other, non-dualist tenets, such as the Donatist rejection of sacraments administered by evil priests, common coin among quite varied twelfth-century groups, may well also have stemmed from experience of Cathars in the Midi. There was in addition a careful enumeration of the sacraments to be accepted, one or two other errors, probably unrelated to Catharism, to be repudiated, and a conclusion relating specifically to the Waldensians, in which Valdes declared his intention to renounce the world, to be poor and take no thought for the morrow, to accept neither gold nor silver, and to accept the precepts of the gospel as commands. It was a programme derived from the sending of the Seventy – but there was a total and significant silence on the right to preach. Valdes showed his will to obedience and orthodoxy by making the profession of faith; in return, as it were, he was able to state the intention of his group.

Trouble again came out of local conditions. At the end of the profession Valdes had repudiated unorthodox zealots who took the name of his association; perhaps he had not in the event been able to prevent their infiltration. Étienne de Bourbon, echoing the classic anti-heresy text of 2 Timothy, chapter 3, sourly describes the indiscriminate preaching which aroused hostility, of those 'stupid and uneducated' persons 'men and women alike' who 'wandered through the villages, entered homes, preached in the squares and even in the churches'.[12] John of Canterbury, archbishop of Lyons, possibly after a vain attempt to bring them under control through the appointment of a provost, prohibited their preaching; they refused, and were excommunicated and driven from the lands where the archbishop held temporal power.[13]

For the disobedience a number of factors were responsible. One, to judge by later Waldensian writing, was the sense that Valdes had a direct mission from God; another was the state of the Church, and feeling against unworthy clergy;

---

11   Text by Dondaine in *AFP* xvi (1946), pp. 231–2, Selge, *Waldenser* ii, pp. 3–6, Gonnet, in *EFV*, pp. 31–6; analysis in C. Thouzellier, *Catharisme et Valdéisme en Languedoc*, 2nd edn (1969), pp. 27–36 (deep analysis of contemporary controversial literature), tr. *WEH*, pp. 204–8; dating: p. 709, n. 1. Either 1180 or 1181 is possible. Gonnet (*Les Vaudois*, ed. Audisio, p. 11) notes that Valdes's early actions recorded in Anonymous of Laon correspond to the *propositum*, vital at the end of a profession of faith.

12   Lecoy de la Marche, *Anecdotes*, p. 291; *WEH*, p. 209; Patschovsky, 'The literacy of Waldensianism', *BHL*, pp. 112–36 at p. 129.

13   Also known as Bellesmains: see P. Pouzet, *L'anglais dit John Bellesmains* (Lyon, 1927), pp. 7–9. Rubellin, 'Au temps', believes that his succession, ending period of favour under Guichard, led to trouble, see G. G. Merlo, 'Frammenti di storiografia e storia delle origini valdesi', *RHR* ccxvii (2000), pp. 21–37, with criticisms; M. Rubellin, 'Guichard de Pontigny et Valdes à Lyon: la rencontre de deux idéaux réformateurs', Ibid., pp. 39–58 (continues hypothesis). Events: Selge, *Waldenser*, i, pp. 76, 84, 184–5, 254–9; texts, Russell, *Dissent*, pp. 41–53. Did Alan of Lille's polemic exaggerate heretical views? (Cameron, *Waldenses*, p. 26).

another may well have been the ambiguous language of the profession of faith, in which Valdes declared his resolve to follow the precepts of the gospel as commands. Had not the Saviour enjoined his disciples to preach, in the same passage in which they were told to take neither gold nor silver, to carry neither scrip nor staff? The disciples, whom the Waldensians imitated, had been told to preach the gospel to every creature, and Peter before the Sanhedrin had appealed to a higher obligation when he said that one should obey God rather than men. Fidelity to Scripture and the divine call seemed to require preaching. So the association was carried into schism.

Similar forces were at work among the Humiliati of northern Italy.[14] Like other penitential associations, they aimed to lead a purer ethical life in the world in accord with the gospels without renouncing marriage. In reaction to the commercial life of Italy, free from the temptations of usury, they earned their bread in a number of Lombard towns by simple manual work, largely in the wool industry. As a sign of their humility they wore garments of undyed wool, and received their name either because of their way of life or their dress. A strict and literal interpretation of the gospels led them to reject oaths as well as lies, and the practice of litigation. Though a few individual, leading figures were well-connected citizens, most Humiliati stemmed from a social level well below that, although they were not, as Zanoni once alleged, members of the proletariat: they included clergy. They repudiated the accumulation of wealth, and gave away all superfluity in alms.[15]

The impulse to apostolic life here had another outlet, which did not include wandering begging, but did include a demand to preach and the wish to exercise a ministry with the direction of souls. First of all the orthodox groups in the Church, they seem to have hit on the idea of preaching to refute heresy, while themselves following an interpretation of the gospels and apostolic life no less strict than that of the leading heretics.[16] Once again there was an attempt to cross the line which divided the practice of a better moral life, whether in or out of monasticism, from the right to a cure of souls; and it received the same rebuff as had the Waldensians. Alexander III heard and rejected their request to be allowed to preach.

The Waldensians and the Humiliati came under consideration at Verona in 1184. In one sense, the legislation which issued as a by-product of the reconciliation between pope and emperor after their long disputes represented a step forward in the Church's battle against heresy. The bull *Ad abolendam*, which involved the active co-operation of the emperor Frederick Barbarossa, is the first attempt in the whole century to try to deal with the challenge of heresy from a supra-national point of view. Hitherto the onus of action had lain heavily on the individual bishop, exercising his duty as successor of the apostles to act as

14   B. Bolton, 'Innocent III's treatment of the Humiliati', in *SCH* VIII, pp. 73–82; F. Andrews, *The Early Humiliati* (1999) supersedes older work.
15   B. Bolton, 'The poverty of the Humiliati', *Poverty in the Middle Ages*, ed. D. Flood, FFor XXVII (1975), pp. 52–9.
16   *RB*, p. 65.

guardian of orthodoxy and to repress heresy, little aided from above. He had reacted to the presence of heresy in his diocese in very different ways, according to his own predilections.[17] Some bishops were quite inactive; others who did act were uncertain what procedure to follow. In the case of the peasant brothers suspect of heresy at Bucy-le-Long, discussed above, the bishop of Soissons had first applied the primitive procedure of the ordeal by water, found that one of his suspects failed the test and, uncertain what to do next, went off to seek advice; while he was away the mob burst into the prison and burnt the suspects.[18] A council at Rheims in 1157 had specifically mentioned a duty of the laity to aid the bishop in reporting cases of heresy, but still no detailed procedure was laid down.[19]

The papacy gave vacillating direction. In the case of Flemish townsmen accused of heresy who came to appeal to Alexander III, the pope first attempted to send them back with letters to the archbishop of Rheims from whom they had appealed and, then, when they demurred, decided to confer further with the archbishop, Louis VII of France and others. His letter to the archbishop urged restraint rather than strictness, but offered no direction as to how that prelate was to set about establishing whether or not the townsmen really were heretics.[20]

The one locality which concerned the popes over generations, and where they repeatedly exhorted against heresy, was Languedoc – and not only its heartland (where the problem ultimately became acute) but Gascony and Provence as well.[21] From the time of the Council of Toulouse in 1119, a scattering of provincial councils under papal presidency warned against the presence of heresy, and urged local secular leaders not to give heretics protection. Evidently it was the toleration of heresy by lords which created anxiety.

*Ad abolendam* attempted more than provincial legislation for the Midi, for it surveyed the field of heresy generally, not merely in the south of France, and it attempted to invigorate and systematize the bishops' pursuit of heresy.[22] It dealt seriously with heresy in Italy, the place of origin of a good proportion of the sects condemned. In the Church at large all exemption from the bishops' jurisdiction in matters of heresy was abolished; the bishop or his representatives were required to visit the parishes where heresy was believed to exist once or twice a year, and impose oaths on local inhabitants who would then declare any knowledge they might have of heresy in the locality. Secular authorities were to assist

17 Ibid., pp. 51–2; also Maisonneuve, *Etudes*, ch. 2; C. Thouzellier, 'La répression de l'hérésie et les débuts de l'Inquisition', *Histoire de l'église*, ed. A. Fliche, V. Martin, x (Paris, 1950), pp. 291–340.
18 Above, p. 56; defending, Moore argues (*SCH* xxi, p. 49), the right of community judgement in the ordeal.
19 Maisonneuve, *Etudes*, pp. 108–11.
20 *RB*, pp. 55–7.
21 Ibid., pp. 52–5; on definition of Languedoc, see below, p. 90, n. 62. The county of Provence lay in imperial territory.
22 Mansi, xxii, cols 476–8; Maisonneuve, *Etudes*, pp. 151–6. On the changing attitude to repression of heresy 1179–84, see R. Manselli, 'De la "persuasio" à la "coercitio"', in *CF* vi, pp. 175–97; discussion, A. Kolmer, *Ad Capiendas Vulpes* (1982) (precise investigation of development of techniques of repression, investigation in Languedoc), p. 29, n. 21.

this inquisition under pain of penalties both secular and ecclesiastical. Maximum publicity was to be given by higher ecclesiastics to these regulations.

These decisions failed, however, to sway the situation to the Church's advantage. Discovery of heresy was still dependent on the accidents of popular denunciations – effective enough where there was general feeling against heresy, as in northern France, of little use in areas such as the regions of Languedoc or northern Italy, where there was more inertia or toleration. Procedure for proving or disproving the existence of heresy in formal trial remained primitive: it still included the oath and the ordeal, and did not impose the appropriate solution, i.e. the interrogation of suspects by experienced theologians. The bull of Lucius III reorganized the episcopal inquisition, but provided no means for ensuring that bishops in fact observed their duty to maintain it. Finally, and most deleteriously, *Ad abolendam* offered no solution to the problem of recognition and classification of heresy. A series of groups were named and anathematized – 'the Cathars and the Patarenes, and those who falsely call themselves the Humiliati or Poor of Lyons, the Passagini, the Josephini, the Arnoldists...';[23] the only distinction made was that between those who preached without authority and those who preached actual error. The Waldensians and Humiliati were in the first category – linked in the Latin by *vel*, not necessarily because they had joined forces, but because, in an abusive word-play, they are linked together as liars, falsely taking to themselves the name of 'the humble' or 'the poor' without justification for the title.[24] For the author of the document, neither the humility nor the poverty could be genuine, because it was unaccompanied by a saving obedience to the Church's authority; in a common anathema they are lumped together with the profound heresy of the Cathars, to which they were bitterly opposed. The faithful are merely informed how heretics may be recognized by their unauthorized preaching, by their errors against the sacraments, or by declarations made by the bishops. This is a crude labelling technique; we have no word about the inner core of false doctrine that has led the sectaries into their denials of the sacraments or their preaching, and no encouragement to the churchmen who might wish to distinguish more subtly between the recalcitrant and those who could be led more gently back to the Church.

So *Ad abolendam* completed the rejection of the Waldensians. There followed an equivocal phase, in which the edict was only partially effective.[25] In practice, Waldensianism as an enemy took second or third place to the Cathars, and the general inefficiency of repression helped to preserve them. The penalty of expulsion, often the most serious punishment applied, did no more than disseminate

---

23   Mansi, XXII, col. 477. On Passagians, see *WEH*, pp. 173–85, Manselli, 'I Passagini', *BISLAM* LXXV (1963), pp. 189–210; on Josephini, *WEH*, p. 31.

24   *RB*, p. 67, n. 120, comments: pp. 68–9; Selge, *Waldenser* I, p. 177, n. 151.

25   For this phase and examples below, Thouzellier, *Catharisme et Valdéisme*, pp. 50–1, 133–8; Selge, *Waldenser* I, pp. 131n, 279–81, 287, 290–1; M. H. Vicaire, *Saint Dominic* (1964) (trans. of 1957 French, K. Pond), p. 75; Innocent III, *Epistolae* xii, 17 (*PL* CCXVI, col. 29f.); P. Montanari, 'Valdesi a Milano tra XIIe XIII secolo', *RHR* CCXVII (2000), pp. 59–74; Id., 'Milano "Fovea haereticorum": le fonti di un' immagine', *Vite di eretici e storie di frati*, ed. M. Benedetti *et al.* (1998), pp. 62–8; *MLC*, p. 95.

their influence more widely. The sequel to the decisions of 1184 was, moreover, muffled. In Languedoc the archbishop of Narbonne, Bernard-Gaucelin, made an enquiry into Waldensian beliefs and issued a condemnation, probably between 1185 and 1187. But it was not effective. The populace approved their moral life; some lower clergy regarded them as auxiliaries and were sympathetic. Their preachers moved about freely, and were even invited to participate in debates which allowed expression to heretical and orthodox points of view. Only in Montpellier, where Count William VIII was hostile, does there seem to have been effective counteraction. In Aragon, Alfonso II in 1194 and Pedro II in 1198 issued edicts against Waldensians, the latter imposing the death penalty for obstinacy. Perhaps these edicts were aimed as much at conditions in the fiefs of the kings of Aragon on the French side of the Pyrenees as in the kingdom itself: in neither area do they appear seriously to have handicapped the preachers. To the north of Languedoc in Lorraine and in the border lands between France and the Empire, Waldensian missions gained success, although in Toul in 1192 the bishop ordered the rounding-up of 'Wadoys'. In Metz at the end of the century the authorities were so ill-informed that, when they came across laymen reading the Scriptures in unauthorized gatherings, they failed to realize that they were Waldensians. In Italy the inability of the hierarchy to get on top of heresy in the cities meant that the Waldensians shared in the general atmosphere of liberty. Only in the period 1196–1206, for example, was the archbishop of Milan able to enforce the destruction of a school that they had long held undisturbed in the city. In 1209 almost a hundred of them were ready to seek reconciliation, but wished to retain the meadow on which the school had been built; Innocent III's response, while avoiding any suggestion of bribery, was sympathetic. The possibility existed of a major recruitment to Catholicism and there were warm relations between the papacy and the commune at a time not long before Otto, then the papal candidate for the Empire, was crowned. By contrast, in 1212 when the commune was hostile to the troops of the new papal candidate, Frederick Hohenstaufen, Innocent called the city a 'fovea haereticorum'.

Toleration aided the Humiliati, who spread in the cities, sometimes also in the *contado* where some of their groups had originated. They appealed to industrial workers and artisans or to peasants lately come to the towns; their workshops and houses were usually found in the *faubourgs* where artisans lived. Attitudes to them were equivocal: condemned for unauthorized preaching, they still received support from bishops and were given legacies. It was an intensely local movement; different houses had different histories. Active hostility was rare, and 'may have been particularly linked to the area of Verona'.[26]

The Waldensians, spreading through the zeal to preach the gospel, their mission expedited rather than hampered by the expulsion from Lyons following the excommunication by Archbishop John, found a home in the anticlerical atmosphere of Lombardy and became more radical in consequence.[27]

26    Above, p. 74, n. 14. Andrews, *Humiliati*, p. 248 (an important revision).
27    Selge, *Waldenser* I, pp. 259–63, 284–8.

? Liège *1202/3*

Mainz *1233*

*Main*

? Trier *1231*

Regensburg c.*1262*

? Schwäbisch Hall *1243*

Metz *1199/1200*

*Danube*

Toul *1192*

Strasburg *1211/2*

Jonvelle c.*1218*

*Rhine*

*Inn*

Besançon *1248*

*Rhône*

Dongo

Bergamo *1218*

Gruaro

Lyon *1177*

? Seregno

Vienne *1198*

Legnano

Verona *1199*

Milan *b.1206*

Cerea *b.1203*

Pavia

Ronco

Turin *1210*

Valence c.*1235*

Pinerolo *1220?*

Piacenza c.*1192/7*

*Po*

Montélimar

Modena

Bollène

Embrun *1198*

Genoa

Faenza *1206*

Bagnols

Orange

Sisteron

Carpentras

Avignon

Florence *1206*

Nîmes c.*1204*

Antibes

Arles *1198*

Aix *1198*

? Ramatuelle

0        250 miles

0        400 km

Rome *1179*

○ Places of origin of Waldensians          ‡ Seat of Archbishop
● Places of residence of Waldensians     † Seat of Bishop
*1206* Earliest dated evidence of the appearance of Waldensians before 1218
*1237* Earliest dated evidence of the appearance of Waldensians after 1218

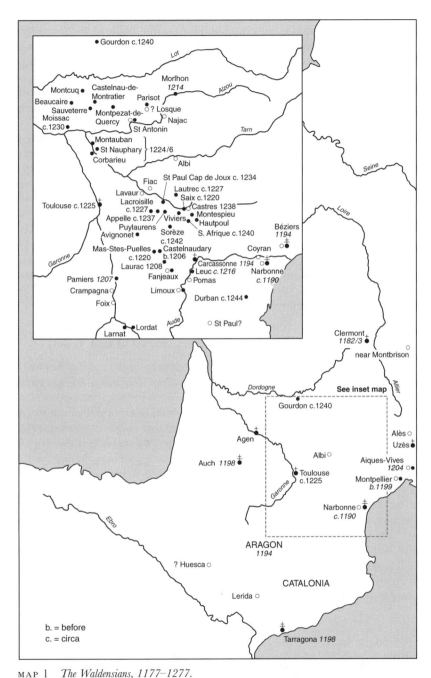

MAP 1 *The Waldensians, 1177–1277.*

*Source*: Map by J. V. Fearns, from Herder's *Atlas zur Kirchengeschichte* (Freiburg-im-Breisgau, 1970), no. 56B.

*Note*: The Waldensians of Austria, detected in an inquisition of *c.*1266, will be found on Map 4.

In Languedoc they seem to have been attracted by the frailty of the hierarchy's control of the religious scene, which enabled them to preach without interference in many places, and showed themselves eager to take advantage of the opportunity to show both the injustice of their excommunication and the orthodoxy of their beliefs by preaching against the Cathars and opposing them in debates. From Lyons they passed over to north-east France and into the German-speaking regions on the Rhine and beyond.[28]

Their appeal at first cut across class divisions. In the early days, companions of Valdes are described as giving up their goods and bestowing them on the poor, a fact which shows they were of some substance. Laymen formed a majority, but there were also fugitive monks and nuns, and some priests and *litterati*. Some support came from higher ranks in society, though it was less than the Cathars enjoyed; members of the class of *ministeriales*, lesser nobility in the service of the Empire, were noticed, for example, as adherents in the diocese of Metz.[29] The influence which preaching had on women was observed with a hostile eye by Catholic writers. Women thought suitable had the right to preach on terms of equality with the men, which may well have made the movement seem attractive to certain temperaments, dissatisfied with the circumscribed opportunities for religious service for women within orthodoxy.[30]

### The Development of Waldensian Organization and Tenets

No rule for the new association has come down to us from the hand of Valdes or his contemporaries, but the regulations of the Poor Catholics, the group of reconciled Waldensians who carried on their way of life with the approval of the Church in the early thirteenth century, combined with incidental references by both Waldensians and their opponents, are sufficient to provide a reconstruction of the life of the group as it developed over the decades following *Ad abolendam*.[31] The leaders in the movement were the preachers, known as the *pauperes spiritu, fratres, sorores*, and later in Lombardy and German-speaking lands, *magistri, magistrae*, 'apostles', 'lords' (*Herren*); they travelled two by two in accord with the gospel texts, wearing simple, apostolic dress, at first apparently barefoot, but seen in sandals of a particular sort that came to serve as a sign of their special status. The granting of the right to wear the sandals accompanied the right to preach. Catholic writers sometimes called them the *Insabbatati* (from the word *sabot*) because of this.[32] Like Valdes, they had to renounce the world and give up their goods before they could become preachers. But though authentically part of the twelfth-century movement of wandering preachers, poverty did not have the

---

28   Ibid., pp. 288–93.
29   *RB*, pp. 161–4, Selge, *Waldenser* I, pp. 266–9, Böhmer, in *RPTK* xx, col. 809. G. Koch, *Frauenfrage und Ketzertum im Mittelalter* (1962). I express here my regret at Dr Koch's tragically early death.
30   Koch, *Frauenfrage*, pp. 158–9.
31   Böhmer, in *RPTK* xx, cols 811–12; survey of life and ideas on cols 811–19.
32   Ibid., cols 806, 812, 813; Selge, *Waldenser* I, p. 270, n. 118.

same passionate force among them that it had had among the hermits of western France, or that it was to have in the future among the Franciscans. Valdes, after making a similar break with the world of property as St Francis of Assisi, and influenced like him by the tension between the Christian conscience and the business world, thereafter did not feel the same need to strive perpetually for the highest possible form of renunciation.[33] Austerity rather than destitution was the keynote of the Waldensians.

Preaching consisted of simple exhortation, the call to repentance, and the criticism of sins, both in the individual and in the Church, together with the repetition of many texts of Scripture, learned by heart in the schools of the movement, often in astonishing quantities.[34] The training necessary for the preacher, which on the French side of the Alps came later to be some five or six years, and on the Lombard side one or two,[35] was particularly devoted to the direct study and memorization of the bare text of Scripture in vernacular translation. Only after selection and training, together with the renunciation of goods and of marriage, could the preacher begin his mission. Thus, in a sense, he was as marked off from the rest of society as any Catholic priest. The difference was that in the association no episcopal ordination was considered necessary; women might be granted the right to preach; and no distinction was made between those who happened to be in priest's orders and the others who were laymen.

Preaching helped to recruit more members for the office of preacher. Moved by exhortations, the hearer might then receive spiritual counsel to go and undo the injustices that he had committed and from this he might progress to the status of the 'recently converted', who in a kind of novitiate were tested and instructed in preparation for mission.[36] Others remained in the world, and were known as 'friends' (*amici*), who supported the preachers by their alms and participated in the study of the vernacular Scriptures. Their task was to see to the bodily needs of the preachers, to collect a kind of tax among the supporters, later known as the *talea* in Italy, and to maintain the schools of the association, generally held in private houses.[37] Like the preachers, their knowledge of the Bible was often remarkable. Children began to learn the gospels and the epistles. It was not unknown for an illiterate supporter to know forty Sunday gospels by heart, and in Austria in the thirteenth century a relatively objective Catholic observer, the Passau Anonymous, recorded the case of a member who knew all the book of Job by heart.[38]

Attitudes of churchmen towards vernacular translations (in so far as they were to be used by the common people) tended to be hostile partly because of the use

---

33  For my dissent from Selge on the poverty issue, see *LMH*, 1st edn, pp. 353–5.
34  Böhmer, in *RPTK* xx, col. 814.
35  Ibid., col. 812.
36  Preaching in Selge, *Waldenser* I, pp. 95–127, 142–7; relation to confession (using Durand of Huesca), pp. 95–8.
37  Böhmer, in *RPTK* xx, cols 815, 829–30 (assuming later practice reflected earlier; evidence of the *talea* Ibid., col. 830).
38  Ibid., col. 815 and references; on Passau Anonymous, see below, p. 166.

made of them in practice by heretical preachers. When the bishop of Metz wrote to Innocent III in 1199 denouncing laymen and women who had commissioned vernacular translations of Scripture and relied on them for debating about their contents in secret gatherings and for preaching, the pope was slow to authorize repression.

His chief concern lay with the unauthorized preaching. He asked the bishop to find out about the author of the translation, his intention and the quality of faith of those who used it – and about their attitude to the papacy and the Church. His reply to the bishop's renewed complaint that some of them had been disobedient to Innocent's requirements, alleging that they owed obedience only to God, was to commission three Cistercian abbots to go to Metz to investigate further and correct the laity where necessary. It is not known what happened, though a later Cistercian chronicle speaks of abbots burning translations in Metz. It was a likely outcome.

Clearly Innocent was suspicious of an over-hasty bishop and anxious not to extinguish enthusiasm. He said that the 'desire for understanding the Holy Scriptures and a zeal for preaching what is in the Scriptures is something not to be reprimanded but rather to be encouraged', and it is significant that at the end of his pontificate, when he drew up constitutions for the fourth Lateran Council of 1215, he did not include in them any blanket prohibition of translations of Scripture. Nevertheless he also explained that 'the secret mysteries of the faith ought not . . . to be explained to all men in all places . . . For such is the depth of divine Scripture, that not only the simple and illiterate but even the prudent and learned are not fully sufficient to try to understand it.'[39] Here lay the nub of the matter. The study of Scripture demanded training and skill; the use of it formed a part of the Church's teaching and could not be divorced from it. If the use of translations came to be associated with teaching hostile to, or contemptuous of the priesthood, as was the case in Metz, then the translations were likely to be casualties. Repression of translations as well as of heretical preachers was the simple disciplinary solution, especially when local prelates had narrow horizons.

Scripture was to be mediated, as it were, to the faithful through authorized preachers; the bare text was not to be put into the hands of anyone who might misuse and misunderstand it. The Waldensians naturally rejected this viewpoint and were inclined to think that the authorities and the learned created needless obfuscation. They stressed the literal understanding of the text and the direct fulfilment in their own lives of Christ's demands.

There was a gradual slide deeper into heresy; as the original moderation of Valdes and the Lyons group was breached, the Waldensians spread and developed their teaching in fresh circumstances, and the split from the Church took a psychological toll. The process can be traced in the years between *Ad*

---

39  *Epistolae* (*PL* CCXIV, cols 695–9); work on this by M. Deanesly, *The Lollard Bible* (1920), p. 31, superseded by L. E. Boyle, 'Innocent III and vernacular versions of Scripture', *SCH* Subsidia IV, pp. 97–107. See Böhmer, in RPTK XX, col. 815.

*abolendam* and 1205, the time at which the French and Lombard wings of the movement divided.

Valdes's own influence was always exerted in favour of moderation, with an eye to the ultimate reconciliation with Rome that he seems never finally to have ruled out. He was supported by some of the clerical converts, for whom Durand of Huesca, the former priest, active in Languedoc against the Cathars, is the best spokesman. His *Liber antiheresis*, composed in the late 1180s or early 1190s, a handbook designed to equip former clergy who read Latin for controversy with both Catholics and Cathars, is proof of the surviving will to orthodoxy in some sections some years after the condemnation of *Ad abolendam*. It is also proof of the calibre of Durand with his power of argument and sophisticated – sometimes too sophisticated – Latin.[40]

Durand was fighting a battle on two fronts: against the orthodox controversialists, who objected that the Waldensians had no right to preach, and that they parasitically lived off their hearers when they ought to have earned their bread by their labour; and against the Cathars, with their own claim to observe the apostolic life, who objected that the Waldensians were not members of the Church because, unlike themselves, they did not have the orders of bishops, priests and deacons. In justifying Waldensians and arming his readers for attack on the weak points of Catharism, its dualism and the lack of austerity of its believer class, Durand keeps free of heresy for most of the time. The root of the matter, of course, was the right to preach, even after authority had prohibited it, and the appeal which Durand makes to God's call to Valdes as justifying it. Here there was a direct challenge to Church authority. But Durand, a practical controversialist with a missionary aim, does not use the issues as a springboard for a developed heretical theology. He does slip into Pelagianism in his eagerness to refute Cathar teaching on predestination but as a whole, the simple biblically based piety of the *Liber antiheresis* is orthodox.[41]

Some made more radical inferences from the common Waldensian thesis of the prime responsibility of the individual for his destiny, and denied Catholic belief in the value of prayers for the dead, or went farther and rejected purgatory altogether. Others, setting out from the Waldensian desire for fidelity to the texts of the gospels, argued that the sayings of Jesus, such as His injunction, 'swear not at all', were to be taken literally, and that in consequence of this principle, all lies were to be treated as mortal sins, and oaths and shedding of blood forbidden in all circumstances. One group in Languedoc carried rigorism so far that they claimed that, as true disciples of Christ, they alone could baptize where neither the Cathars nor the Catholic clergy could. Valdes repudiated them about 1200,

---

40   Above, p. 70, n. 2; dating: Selge, *Waldenser* II, pp. xvii–xviii; purpose, Ibid., I, p. 45; Thouzellier, *Catharisme et Valdéisme*, pp. 60, 271. The name is Durand of Huesca (Aragon) and not Osca (Ibid., pp. 213–14 of 2nd edn, correcting theory of Dossat). Analysis, Cameron, *Waldenses*, pp. 26–30.

41   Prologue to *Liber*, Selge, *Waldenser* II, 8; discussion, Ibid., I, ch. I; for Durand on predestination, see Thouzellier, *Catharisme et Valdéisme*, p. 75; K. V. Selge, 'Discussions sur l'apostolicité entre Vaudois, Catholiques, et Cathares', *CF* II, pp. 143–62.

whereupon they seem to have formed themselves into a Church of their own, with a hierarchy of bishop, priests and deacons.[42]

There were many pressures working against early orthodoxy. Awareness of the moral need of the Church, which was a mainspring of the movement, easily inclined preachers to move on from a criticism of fallen clergy to a rejection of their sacraments. The study of the vernacular Scriptures could rouse fresh questions about contemporary belief in the minds of idealists. Initially, Scripture-reading was buttressed and restrained by a concomitant study of the Church Fathers – Valdes's initial stock of translations included patristic texts[43] – but there were many simple men in the association, and the battle with the hierarchy over the legitimacy of their preaching constantly led Waldensians to appeal to the text of Scripture. From this the way led to a more clearly Biblicist attitude, in which whatever was not justified in the text of Scripture alone was not legitimate. The battle with the Cathars also tended to move them away from orthodoxy because it put pressure on them, as they wrestled for the souls of the people, not to seem less faithful to the words of Scripture than their opponents and not to appear mere collaborators with the stained Catholic Church. The Cathars wholly rejected lies, oaths and the shedding of blood: could the Waldensians afford to seem less Biblicist on these issues than the Cathars were? The stress on doing penance in the movement led to an increased use of confession which could hardly be met by clergy accustomed to hearing confessions at most once a year. Low estimates of the character of the Catholic priesthood also inhibited recourse to them, and so confession to laymen within the Waldensian circle emerged as a substitute. A similar motive, of concern for the pastoral needs of their adherents, led the Waldensians to celebrate the eucharist themselves in regions where it was not readily available from the hands of Catholic priests.[44] When the former Waldensian, Bernard Prim, was received back into the Church in 1210, it was conceded that honourable motives were at work among Waldensians who did this.[45] But the move was dangerous because it opened the way to a rival Church and organization, with its own 'pure' sacraments, in contrast to the 'impure' ones of the sinful priests in the Church.

Spontaneous moves farther from the Roman Church were aided by the geographical diffusion of the movement away from its original nucleus. More radical views emerge among the Waldensians found at Metz in 1199. Though not yet formally Donatist, they are highly critical of the clergy, and tend to be exclusive in their attitudes to their own preachers and translations: they give the impression of a group on the verge of forming a counter-church.[46] The Waldensians who crossed the Alps to Italy grew more extreme. Ardizzo's report

42  For this paragraph, see Selge, *Waldenser* i, ch. 2; comment by Grundmann in *DA* xxiv (1968), pp. 572–3.
43  Étienne de Bourbon in Lecoy de la Marche, *Anecdotes*, p. 290; Selge, *Waldenser* i, p. 152, n. 73.
44  Selge, *Waldenser* i, pp. 155–7 (reaction to Cathars), 146–9 (confession), 159–63 (eucharist).
45  Ibid., p. 159; Innocent iii, *Epistolae* xiii, 94 (*PL* ccxvi, col. 291); on Prim, see Thouzellier, *Catharisme et Valdéisme*, pp. 232–7, 262–7; Cameron, *Waldenses*, pp. 55–7.
46  *PL* ccxiv, cols 695–9 (above, p. 82, n. 39); Selge, *Waldenser* i, pp. 290–3.

on them in Piacenza in the last decade of the century describes how they broke up marriages in gaining recruits, took nuns from nunneries, and taught that only with them was salvation to be found.[47] The Humiliati affected the newcomers in another way, influencing them to adopt their own static life of manual labour, even for preachers, in place of the primitive wandering. To Valdes this was quite unacceptable: the gospel texts were mandatory for the preacher class, who were obliged to live from their hearers rather than by their own efforts.

Another source of dissension lay in the Lombard group's selection of ministers for the duty of administering the sacraments, in contrast to the purely temporary *ad hoc* arrangements normal on the French side of the Alps. The decision had a symbolic importance: where Valdes still thought in terms of reconciliation with Rome, and he and those like him saw a Waldensian administration of the sacraments as merely an occasional bowing to necessity, the Lombards wanted to make a permanent arrangement, and were indifferent to the effects that this might have on their relations with Rome.

A third factor precipitating crisis was the election of John de Ronco as provost, opposed bitterly by Valdes on the grounds that the only leader of the association could be Christ. Personalities played some part. The Lombards detected despotic tendencies in Valdes; John de Ronco seems to have been a raw personality, and a later report from the Catholic controversialist Salvo Burci accused him of being unlettered.[48] The election brought about a split in 1205; despite attempts at reunion, it was never healed, and the Waldensians for the rest of the Middle Ages remained divided into the Lyonist group, who remained faithful to Valdes, and the Poor Lombards,[49] as they were called, with their stronghold in northern Italy. After 1205 the latter drew away still further, and became more explicitly Donatist.

The Italian split was one element in a general process of alienation of Waldensians from the Church. From the first refusal of the prohibition of preaching at Lyons in the early 1180s there had been a gradual decline from schism to heresy proper. The authorities had had the worst of both worlds, for prohibition had not greatly inhibited the spread of the movement yet it had contributed to its deterioration. The hope of reconciliation could not be deferred too long; even ineffective persecution increased Waldensian hostility to the Church; the breach from Catholic instruction and aid inevitably opened the way to popular heresies inside the movement. A natural impression is that the papacy and the bishops had wholly underestimated the strength of feeling which lay behind the Waldensian demands, and that a heresy had emerged largely out of the attitudes of the Church.

47   Letter of Ardizzo, bishop of Piacenza, ed. A. Dondaine, in 'Durand de Huesca et la polémique anti-Cathare', *AFP* xxix (1959), pp. 273–4.
48   *WEH*, p. 273.
49   For the causes of the split, see Selge, *Waldenser* i, pp. 172–88; for prime source, see below, pp. 101–2.

## The Speronists

While the Waldensians slipped out of orthodoxy into the world of the sects, another heretical group was forming in Lombardy, the Speronists.[50] They resemble the Waldensians in one thing: they were a group founded by a layman – something for which we have no earlier precedent, if we except the followers of Eon de l'Étoile as too like a robber band to be properly discussed.

Speroni was a jurist, a one-time friend of the great legal authority Vacarius, to whose refutation of Speroni's heresy we owe nearly all our information about the sect. Consul in Piacenza in 1164, 1165 and 1171, Speroni between the years 1177 and 1185 fomented a movement against the Church which lasted fifty years. Piacenza was and remained its centre. A probable starting-point can be seen in Speroni's involvement in the long conflict over the rights of the monastery of S. Giulia in Piacenza, in which he and other protagonists of Piacenza met papal opposition.

The heresy represented an extreme rejection of all Church authority, which spread well in Piacenza because the anticlerical spirit of the town favoured any movement of opposition to the Church. Priesthood itself was jettisoned. Here Speroni differed in approach from Arnold of Brescia, whose denial of the place of the priesthood sprang from a rejection of their vices: because they had sinned so deeply, their acts had lost validity; and because the Roman Church had become involved in property, it had lost its right to confer sacramental powers. Speroni was much more radical. No doubt his views were born out of a reaction against a power-loving priesthood, but his understanding of religion left no place for a priesthood *ab initio* and on principle. They simply had no function left, for Speroni condemned all the sacraments – especially baptism, the mass and penance – as their stupid inventions. All formal acts of worship and exterior observances represented an idolatrous materialization of spiritual religion; they were quite simply an obstacle. Arnoldists, or followers of the wandering preachers, might well have broken into overt acts of violence – Petrobrusians, for example, felt so deeply about the distortions of the contemporary Church that they rejected them in dramatic scenes, burning crosses or eating meat ostentatiously at forbidden times. For the Speronists all this was unnecessary. Their members had already the consciousness of union with the Word; in Speroni's phrases, they had the Holy Spirit, the Spirit of Jesus and of wisdom, and were in union of faith and love with Jesus. They could therefore quietly attend mass while their minds were elsewhere, pursuing the interior calm and justice that lay at the heart of their beliefs, *alieno mente*.

The centre of their religion was a kind of interior baptism, a spiritual communion with God. It was not an ascetic movement, and had nothing in common with

50   Ilarino da Milano, *L'Eresia di Ugo Speroni, Studi e Testi* CXV (1945); analysis of heresy and Vacarius's polemic: text, pp. 483–583; see esp. on Speroni (pp. 37–75) reconstruction of core of heresy (pp. 411–22); place on Italian scene (pp. 423–69); extract in *WEH*, pp. 152–8.

the twelfth-century striving after apostolic life[51] – on the contrary, Speroni and his followers rejected ascetic practices, the good works and moral activity of the individual, in favour of a total devotion to interior sanctification. All that mattered was the inner life of the individual. Speroni denied that there was original sin, but argued for two categories of humanity, the predestined and the foreknown. The foreknown were doomed to damnation; by contrast the predestined soul remained holy even when, from the point of view of exterior justice, it was leading a life of sin.

Such a theology could hardly be the basis of an effective organization, and Speroni had no predilection for preaching. Yet his following lasted. One major reason, we may assume, was the Speronists' consciousness of their predestination. Speroni's liking was for a ministry of the written word, and we may suspect that he drew a following from the better educated. Certainly they outlasted his death, though they never became a dynamic feature on the Italian scene. The *Liber supra stella*, written by Salvo Burci in 1235, also a citizen of Piacenza, is evidence that some fifty years later they were still in existence.[52]

## The Crisis Areas

The Speronists were odd men out in their century, but not in their locality. Lombardy, and to a lesser extent, central Italy in these decades was rapidly attaining the distinction of being the land of heresy *par excellence*, rivalled only by Languedoc. The causes were embedded in the development, economic, social and political, of all those regions where the semi-independent commune had established itself as a determining factor. A burgeoning economic life, in advance of developments anywhere else in Europe, put everything into the melting pot. There was an extraordinary mobility of classes, with peasants from the *contado* moving into the towns or transferring from one part of the *contado* to another, lords from the countryside coming into the towns and joining in the social struggles within them, while fortunes were made from commerce and industry. New classes of artisans, notaries and petty businessmen were formed, and the communes defied outside authority and started to battle for control of their own regions. Social change and mobility, Violante has suggested, made men ready to break with tradition in religion and opened their minds to unorthodox ideas.[53] The vivid economic life of Italy fostered reaction against the business world and the practice of usury bound up with it, and led some idealists into the heretical groups who practised poverty, or stimulated them into violent reaction against a hierarchy who officially denounced usury and were leaders of a Church based on a gospel which called for renunciation,

51   Ilarino da Milano, *Eresia*, p. 435.
52   Ilarino da Milano, 'Il "Liber supra stella" del piacentino Salvo Burci contro i Catari e altre correnti ereticali', *Aevum* xvi (1942), pp. 272–319; xvii (1943), pp. 90–146; xix (1945), pp. 218–341; see his *Eresia*, p. 42.
53   *HS*, pp. 171–98; Italian background in Volpe, *Movimenti religiosi*; attempted refutation by Morghen in *Medioevo Cristiano*, pp. 204–81; see also *MLC*, pp. 60–86.

yet were themselves deeply involved in moneymaking. The continuance of a lay educational tradition in Italy, and the intellectual agility sustained by the commercial life and political intensity within the communes, opened the way to protests against a bureaucratic Church with a limited place for its laity, and aided the growth of heretical groups which gave a place to the laity for preaching, Scripture reading and spiritual direction. The same agility and the questing spirit which accompanied it was also a seed-ground for those elements of plain disbelief which intertwined with other causes of dissent to create heresy. Orthodox enthusiasms, like the flight to eremitism or the increase of itinerant preachers, blended with economic forces to create a flux which shook the power of traditional ecclesiastical forms and organization to hold the faithful. Exchanges of view were facilitated by the heterogeneous character of the travellers, not so much on the great international routes, but on the lesser roads where the pace was less hot, and lower clergy, pedlars, itinerant artisans and pilgrims were thrown into informal contact.[54] The geographical position of Italy and the opening of routes through commerce facilitated both the entry of missionaries and the flight of refugees from persecution elsewhere. Movement itself created a psychological climate in which it was easier to step outside orthodoxy.

The politics of communal struggles aided heresy because they weakened the authority of the natural guardians of faith, the bishops, and confused the context between orthodoxy and heresy with the battle for independence of the communes from episcopal and papal power. The investiture controversies had destroyed the control of the bishop over his town. He remained a considerable figure because of his high birth and connections with ruling families, as well as the lands and rights of his bishopric; but his interest had become only one political force among a series of others, and he had no power any more to ensure that the rule of faith was maintained and heresies put down by force. So heretical groups might be tolerated in communes, not because they had a hold on a major portion of the populace, but because they demonstrated independence from episcopal control.

Similar effects flowed from the popes' struggle against the temporal claims of the emperors in Italy. There was a natural alliance between heretics and the Ghibellines, the factions which existed in the cities based on local and family groupings and interests, but owning a general allegiance to the Empire. Heresy was a stick with which imperial supporters could beat the papacy, disliked for its political rather than its religious claims. Ghibellinism, then, provided the favourable milieu in which heretics could swim. At the same time the efforts which popes made to raise money, levy troops and exert pressure in these contests made them easy targets for the classic contrast drawn by the preacher between a worldly and wealthy Church involved in the infighting of Italian politics and the simple band of apostles gathered round Jesus or depicted in action in the Acts of the Apostles.[55] Too often the clergy in Italy appeared in the guise of politicians, tax gatherers or warriors rather than as pastors. It is the political involvement of

54   Violante, *La Pataria milanese* I (1955), pp. 103–25.
55   Volpe, *Movimenti religiosi*, pp. 38–48, Morghen, *Medioevo Cristiano*, pp. 275–81.

the popes in Italy which explains the apparent paradox that in the Middle Ages heresy flourished most readily in lands that lay closest to the seat of the papacy.

An upward movement in the graph of heresy over all Western Europe, placed by Wakefield about mid-century,[56] was followed in the 1160s by an intense struggle between Alexander III and the emperor Frederick Barbarossa over Italy. This had the effect of distracting the popes from the problem of heresy, and of delaying attempts to grapple with it. *Ad abolendam* followed on the reconciliation of pope and emperor and was a first fruit of the new peace. While the contest was on, there was much destruction in Italy; the fighting and schism in the papacy fomented by Barbarossa disrupted religious life, and contributed to the weakness of ecclesiastical authority on which Italian heresy flourished. Most suggestive is the transmutation which took place in the term 'Patarene' between its origin in the eleventh century, as a term for supporters of the orthodox if radical reform in Milan favoured by the papacy, and its reappearance in the third Lateran Council of 1179, and then in *Ad abolendam*, long after the Pataria had died away, as a technical term for Italian heretics, most often applied to the Cathars.[57] It was an indication of the loss by later twelfth-century popes of the leadership of popular religious sentiment, now tending to flow out of the Church rather than into it.

Two examples, one of partial success, the other of defeat for the forces of orthodoxy in the last decades of the century, may suffice to show how the situation then lay in Italy. In Milan St Galdinus, consecrated archbishop in exile during Barbarossa's wars, began in 1167 to restore the fortunes of his see and, towards the end of his pontificate, to preach against the Cathars who were then spreading in the city.[58] His *Vita* attributes much success to his efforts, and to the effects of his campaign we may perhaps assign the conversion of the heretical teacher Bonacursus, who proceeded in his *Manifestatio* to describe the heresy he had left.[59] The significant feature of the *Vita* is the vagueness with which the heresy is mentioned, a sign that at this time Catholics were not very well informed about their enemy, and the fact that St Galdinus had no other weapon but exhortation. Evidently he could not coerce the citizens to drop Catharism. He checked the rise of heresy, but only temporarily. In the first decade of the thirteenth century James of Vitry said, with a moralist's exaggeration, that Milan was a pit of heretics.[60] In fact they were minorities, divided and disputing among themselves, but they were energetic, and each group seems to have had more supporters there than anywhere else.

The other example is that of Orvieto, where Catharism first appeared a little after mid-century, to make but modest progress till about 1170, when the arrival

56  *WEH*, p. 28.
57  See above, p. 44, n. 4; for heretical nomenclature, see Thouzellier, *Hérésie et hérétiques*; and on Patarines, pp. 204–21.
58  *Acta sanctorum*, 18 April, II, p. 591; *WEH*, p. 151.
59  Ilarino da Milano, 'La "Manifestatio heresis catarorum"', *Aevum* XII (1938), pp. 281–333; *WEH*, pp. 170–3.
60  *Lettres de Jacques de Vitry*, ed. R. B. C. Huygens (Leiden, 1960), pp. 72–3; comment: G. G. Merlo, *Valdesi e Valdismi Medievali* (1984), I, p. 18.

of two preachers from Florence began to raise the temperature. In the end a territorial dispute with the papacy caused Innocent III to put Orvieto under interdict; the bishop withdrew, Catharism made inroads in his absence. Innocent's action had an effect opposite to the one intended: while the city still lay under the ban, an heretical teacher from Viterbo began to preach and drew many after him.[61] Orvieto yielded to interdict, but when the pope sent in an impetuous member of the Roman senatorial nobility, Pietro Parenzo, to restore order and repress heresy, he was assassinated. In the reaction and the proliferation of miracles which followed on instant popular veneration of the dead Pietro, Catharism went underground. But it still survived, and the story had lessons, *mutatis mutandis*, for the treatment of heresy in all the Italy of the communes. Catharism and the evangelical heresies, some of which had been in part stimulated into existence by the menace of the Cathars, had made a place for themselves within many of the towns. Responsibility for their progress or repression lay heavily with the laity, as the case of Orvieto shows. The popes and the bishops could not count on support to put them down. This loss of authority over heresy and the evident failure of *Ad abolendam* produced in Italy a state very like crisis by the end of the century.

In the other major area of disquiet, Languedoc, the conditions which fostered heresy were unlike those in Italy,[62] though the end result in the emergence of small but tenacious heretical minorities, and a loss of power by churchmen to control them, was much the same. The resistant forces were not primarily the towns, which were smaller than those of northern Italy and lacked their independence, but elements of the petty nobility in the countryside. St Gilles and Toulouse had international trade connections, and there were common linguistic and cultural links along the Mediterranean littoral into northern Italy; yet commerce in the Midi was smaller in scale than in Lombardy. Industry produced for a regional market, by and large, and was stable. The flux in social classes which followed on the exceptional economic vitality of Italy, as well as the intellectual agility and the higher standards of lay education, were missing.

The precondition for the success of heresy in the affected regions of Languedoc was the chronic political anarchy caused by the gradual decomposition of the authority of the counts of Toulouse since the time of the journey to the first crusade of Count Raymond IV,[63] and the disequilibrium created by the rival, undecided claims to suzerainty of three powers, the kings of France, the kings of England and the counts of Barcelona, followed by their heirs the kings of Aragon. Local

---

61 J. M. Henderson, 'Piety and heresy in medieval Orvieto: the religious life of the laity c.1150–1350' (PhD, Univ. Edinburgh 1990); C. Lansing, *Power and Purity* (1998), pp. 23–42 (combines analysis of Orvietan Catharism with *aperçus* on Italian Cathars; helpful intro. to Italian research (notes, biblio., appendices); role of scepticism, pp. 81–105; Florence, 71–6; over-estimates role of politics and arbitrary nature of decisions on heresy; gender discussions made difficult by frailty of Italian evidence, but see comparison of Italy and Languedoc, pp. 118–20).
62 W. L. Wakefield, *Heresy, Crusade and Inquisition in Southern France* (1974) (*WHC*) (concise survey with translations).
63 Background of politics, Barber, *Cathars* (below, p. 115 n. 1); M. Costen, *The Cathars* (1997) (see esp. analysis of society and geography).

conditions also militated against the establishment of any one overriding political authority; the existence of partible inheritance by females created a fatal subdivision of rights in land, and hampered the raising of armies by feudal means. Mercenaries were widely employed in consequence; and churchmen, denouncing the spread of heresy, simultaneously deplored the ravages of these *routiers*.[64] Chronic war disrupted Church life and handicapped bishops who might be interested in an active oversight of the rural parishes where heresy first established itself. It also created a condition of lawlessness, with plundering of Church property by secular lords and much petty friction, which tended to devalue the influence of churchmen in purely religious matters, and correspondingly increase the popularity of a profoundly anticlerical heresy which rejected all Church authority. Conversely, the effect of Cathar missionaries in diminishing the size of tolls illicitly exacted by mountain lords from merchants using a trade route to the sea, and restraining the anarchy inflamed by such lords' adultery with their neighbours' wives, raised the prestige of the heresy and brought recruits below the mountain lands, according to an ancient tradition emanating from Pisan merchants. Disorder inhibited the great local lords when the call came to put down heresy: they lacked the power to do so, and in the uncertain conditions could not afford to alienate any subjects. Research has uncovered another factor. Nobility who gave their support to the Cistercians, anticipating none the less that their patronage would exert a certain control in traditional ways, were alienated by the Cistercian constitution, which eliminated family influence. They turned to the Cathar perfect.

The petty nobility in the rural areas enjoyed a large measure of independence from their suzerains, but no very secure economic position. The subdivision of inheritance led to the appearance of large numbers of knights, with resources insufficient to support them and little outlet but in waging of war. Usurpation of tithes by these men was widespread. Rural clergy were poor for this reason, and heavily dependent on local nobles; the latter had a commitment against doing justice to the legitimate claims of churchmen, and a predilection for anticlerical heresy which taught that the payment of tithes could not rightly be demanded by the Church from the laity. As in Italy, anticlericalism formed the favourable ambience for heresy proper, but it was an anticlericalism focused more closely on local rights and less concerned with high political claims. Within this anticlerical atmosphere, men in the early stages were more often patrons, fautors of heresy or fringe members, the women the true converts. As they joined the ranks of Cathar perfect or gave wholehearted support to their preachers, the heresy began to settle in. In a second generation more menfolk made the renunciations demanded for admission to the leading class of perfect or, at least, became believers; under the umbrella of noble protection the heresy was preached to lower classes. Both then

---

64 A. Vauchez, 'Les origines de l'hérésie Cathare en Languedoc d'après un sermon de l'archevêque de Pise, Frederico Visconti (1277)', *Società, istituzioni, spiritualità: studi in onore di Cinzio Violante* II (1994), pp. 1023–36; Griffe, *Débuts*, pp. 7–14, 117–24; M.-H. Vicaire, '"L'affaire de paix et de foix" du Midi de la France', *CF* IV, pp. 102–27; J. D. Gordon, 'The laity and the Catholic Church in Cathar Languedoc' (DPhil, Univ. Oxford, 1992).

and earlier the heresy made its impact in some of the towns, especially Toulouse, where it secured some men of influence, though the surest support for it always remained in the countryside.[65]

The clergy of the Midi lacked the will, the ability and the resources to put effective obstacles in the way of the heretical preachers.[66] The higher clergy were also affected by the disorders, and were often not on good terms with their secular counterparts. They had their share of unworthy prelates – the archbishop of Narbonne from 1190 to 1212 was an ineffectual absentee – and the best of them were competent rather than inspiring. Before Fulk of Toulouse (appointed in 1206), who launched a drive with aristocratic support against both heresy and usury, none of them was able to inspire the laity in their charge to fervour against the heresy. Clergy most in contact with the heretics were hampered by poverty which, because it was not voluntary, had no spiritual benefit, and was merely a handicap. As far as we know, the lower clergy were no worse morally, than, say, the lower clergy of Normandy, where there was no heresy;[67] but they were poorly educated and demoralized by their treatment at the hands of the laity. They made a feeble showing in contrast to the dedicated ascetics who represented the heresy, and they lived in a region not distinguished for the quality of Catholic intellectual development.[68]

The Midi's achievement in the cultural sphere lay in the study of Roman law and its troubadour literature, sponsored by the courts of leading aristocrats and especially by noblewomen. It was not heretical, though it did share in the prevailing anticlerical atmosphere; its influence was confined to a small class, and it was irrelevant to the heresy question.[69] In the religious sphere the land was underdeveloped: it lacked the schools which gave lustre to northern France and provided the sinews for intellectual defence against heresy and, though there had been orthodox preaching missions and a special association with the crusading ideal, no major reforms had affected Church life. As elsewhere, a demand for apostolic life in poor wandering preaching was met, not by the orthodox, but by heretics.

One feature of the region was its toleration of different views and races. Jews were well treated,[70] so were heretics; Waldensians as well as Cathars moved freely.[71] Given the inability of local forces to contain the situation, intervention

---

65    Griffe, *Débuts*, ch. 7 (comment, p. 182, n. 14). Koch, *Frauenfrage*, ch. 1, s. 1, overstresses towns and textile workers (but pp. 26–8 presages Griffe's hypothesis; see discussion of motivation, p. 31); J. H. Mundy, *Europe in the High Middle Ages* (London, 1973), pp. 534–49, is perceptive.

66    Y. Dossat, 'Le clergé méridional à la veille de la croisade albigeoise', *RHL* 1 (1944), pp. 263–78, 'La répression de l'hérésie par les évêques', *CF* vi, pp. 217–51; H. Vidal, *Episcopatus et pouvoir épiscopal à Béziers* (Montpellier, 1951); R. W. Emery, *Heresy and Inquisition in Narbonne* (1941); on learning, see *CF* v; *WHC*, ch. 4 (surveys Church; discussion of numbers of heretics, pp. 68–71); on relation of reform to heresy, cf. Griffe, *Débuts*, pp. 16–19. See below, p. 105, n. 22.

67    J. R. Strayer, *The Albigensian Crusades* (New York, 1971), p. 18; Strayer is outdated on heresy.

68    Bibliography in P. Ourliac, 'La société languedocienne du xiiie siècle et le droit romain', *CF* vi, pp. 199–216.

69    D. Zorzi, *Valori religiosi nella Letteratura provenzale* (Milan, 1954); Koch, *Frauenfrage*, pp. 139–44.

70    B. Smalley, reviewing the 2nd edn of Thouzellier, *Catharisme et Valdéisme* (*JEH* xxi (1970), pp. 184–6).

71    Above, p. 80.

from outside the Midi might well seem the only answer; it was attempted, following an appeal to Louis VII of France and a letter to the Cistercians sent by Raymond V, count of Toulouse, in 1177, but it was not pressed home, and the results were superficial.[72] A projected expedition by the kings of France and England came to nothing. A legatine mission scored some success by securing condemnation of a rich heretic, Pierre Maurand, in Toulouse and bringing two leaders of heresy, one probably the Cathar bishop of Toulouse, to a public discussion in the city. But the two came under safe conduct, and left freely at the end, excommunicate but not otherwise punished.[73] In 1181 an armed exped-ition to Lavaur put pressure on the Trencavel viscount of Béziers, implicated with heresy, and enforced the handing over of the two heretics who had gone free in 1178. They duly confessed.[74] But such short-term expeditions only scratched the problem, and were handicapped by lack of local knowledge.

There was a vicious circle here. Churchmen in the Midi were not tackling the problem; churchmen outside could not well understand the area. More lay below the surface, probably, than the legates understood. Raymond V's appeal may be interpreted as an attempt to call in fresh forces in the ancient quarrel with the viscounts of Béziers.[75] There is a suspicion that Maurand's emergence as the major suspect in Toulouse owed something to social tensions there and his own successful career in business.[76]

The legates did what they could. Of Henri de Marcy, the conscientious Cistercian who was member of the first mission and leader of the second, one could not reasonably expect that he be another Bernard of Clairvaux. He did not greatly like the Midi, and turned down an offer of the bishopric of Toulouse.[77] After he left the scene this phase of intervention ended. Alexander III especially had given attention to the problem after the easing of the crisis with the Empire. From the fall of Jerusalem in 1187, however, the papacy was preoccupied elsewhere. For the cure of the affected region of Languedoc, probably some lever was needed against the aristocrats who declined to use force against heresy; what was certainly necessary was prolonged preaching by churchmen who knew the language and the locality, and this the region did not have.

In the absence of fresh intervention, the situation grew worse rather than better. Not all of the south was seriously affected. The heresy noticed in Gascony did not become a problem. The Mediterranean seaboard was scantily affected.

---

72 Gervase of Canterbury, *Chronicon*, ed. W. Stubbs, LXXIII, 1 (RS) (London, 1879), pp. 270–1; date of Raymond's appeal, Thouzellier, *Catharisme et Valdéisme*, 2nd edn, p. 19, n. 23; letters, *PL* CCIV, cols 235–42; CXCIX cols 1120–4.

73 Sources, tr. of Roger of Hoveden, *WEH*, pp. 194–200; similar text tr., *MBPH*, pp. 113–16.

74 Narrative 1173–81, Griffe, *Débuts*, chs 4 and 5; on Lavaur, see pp. 126–32.

75 *WHC*, p. 83.

76 J. H. Mundy, *Liberty and Political Power in Toulouse, 1050–1230* (1954), pp. 60–2 (links between heresy and social tension, pp. 74–84); his *Europe*, p. 304; and his *The Repression of Catharism at Toulouse* (1985), pp. 12–13; survey on early history of repression, pp. 7–26; P. Hordern, in *EHR* CIII (1988), pp. 477–8, suspends judgement on Mundy's early datings.

77 Griffe, *Débuts*, pp. 113–14, 137–9; for Cistercian attitudes, B. M. Kienzle, *Cistercians, Heresy and Crusade in Occitania, 1145–1229* (2000).

The crucial region lay, rather, to the west and inland, in the eastern Toulousain, the Carcassès and the eastern Albigeois and in their leading towns, within, but not co-terminous with, the holdings of certain great men of the region, the counts of Toulouse, the Trencavel viscounts of Albi, Béziers and Carcassonne and the counts of Foix, unable or unwilling to repress the heresy.[78] In certain places within these lands, by the end of the century the Cathars had come near to displacing the Catholic Church, rendering parish clergy impotent, preventing the administration of the sacraments and securing in practice a right of open preaching for themselves. In Toulouse and other towns they were a known but unmolested minority, and included men of influence. The leading aristocracy were still not effective persecutors and Raymond vi, who succeeded his father as count of Toulouse in 1194, was more equivocal in his attitude to heresy than his predecessor.[79] In many *castra*, the fortified settlements of the countryside, the Cathars' leading class was installed in houses, directing men and women in austere lives, preaching and giving counsel, even receiving the payments normally due to the parish clergy. Waldensians, officially under the ban of the Church, were in practice little hampered.

## Conclusion

To survey the regions of Italy and Languedoc, where the Church's authority to impose submission to its doctrines had broken down, makes a fitting conclusion to a chapter on heresy in the twelfth century, because it is a story of lost opportunities and of only partially successful repression: by the end of the century the balance in the battle between heretical minorities and ecclesiastical authority had definitely swung against the Church. One should be chary of giving literal credence to the preachers and reformers who so loudly proclaimed the sins and weakness of the Church; the medieval Church retained great vitality together with its scandals and defects, and was ever capable of comprehending in one organization extremes of devotion and of wickedness. Nowhere could one justly speak of a mass apostasy, and only the ambiguous character of the anticlerical ambience in which heresy proper moved could lead one to think it was likely to happen. The will to heresy has to be distinguished from faint-hearted orthodoxy and a desire to impede any increase in the secular power of the Church; and the number of committed heretics, by all indications, was still not very great.

None the less an anxious situation did exist, the more so because the hierarchy seemed not to have ideas for meeting the challenge. The tragedy had been that so much enthusiasm had already slipped away, condemned to the twilight world of the sects. With few exceptions, the heretical groups of the century were still not mounting a profound doctrinal challenge to the Church. Their appeal was emphatically to Christian life, and they drew converts above all because of the

78  Griffe, *Débuts*, pp. 176–7 (see also map on endpapers).
79  Ibid., p. 207.

attractive power of the earnest and dedicated lives of many of their teachers and the force of their exhortation to moral living in their hearers.

No doubt because of the utterly changed circumstances in which the heresies of the high Middle Ages expanded as contrasted with those of the late Roman world, we miss the intellectual heresy based on the teaching of some distinguished mind that formed the stuff of the classical heresies condemned in the early centuries. The intellectual appeal of the heretical leaders in the twelfth century is very limited and, though they are often men in orders, they do not include anyone of strong academic background. The common ground between many of them was the appeal to an apostolic life based on wandering preaching in poverty and, where this was practised, crowds could be drawn to listen and follow.

Sometimes it seems almost a matter of chance whether the following collected will remain orthodox or form a sect. Instruction was not adequate to guard the faithful against deviations of belief, and the situation remained fluid. Leaders of heretical groups were not always clear themselves where their ideas were leading them. In these circumstances, the decisions of authority were particularly potent: elements within the dissident religious movements were susceptible to a recall to the Church, provided outlets could be found for their enthusiasms. The desire to hear preaching and to preach was a recurrent theme. So was the yearning for simplicity, sometimes an illusory simplicity of the romanticized early Church and an impatience with sophisticated explanations. Certain texts from the gospels struck their leaders, and demanded a direct and literal observance. There was a will to understand directly what lay in the gospels. Asceticism had an appeal *per se*, irrespective of the motivation and the doctrinal substructure. Anticlericalism was generally the stimulus for heresy, as well as being its protection. The most common heretical tenets were concerned with the powers of the priesthood and the demands of conscience – with the validity of sacraments administered by unworthy clergy and the value of infant baptism, as opposed to the willing acceptance of belief by the adult. Involved with the deviations from orthodoxy were social tensions hinted at rather than clearly revealed in the sources, associated with the lack of outlets for religious women, struggles for power in the towns, poverty and wealth.

That reform in the lives of the clergy would have taken much of the sting out of twelfth-century heresy is a commonplace. Part of the difficulty lay in the rising expectations of the laity and the stimulus imparted by Gregorian reforms. The corollary of the way of thinking that laid such stress on the sacred character of the priest's office was that the priest's life must be worthy of so high a calling. The solution, given the problems of the recruitment or supervision of clergy, their training, and the standards of the higher clergy in many areas, remained bafflingly difficult.

What was clear was, that to meet the challenge of heresy, it would not be enough to maintain the old ways. On the lowest level, the episcopal inquisition was not adequate for the searching out of offenders, and its operations were too dependent on the energy, or lack of it, of the individual diocesan. Understanding of the tenets of the heretics, though it had grown through the century, especially with the appearance of full-scale summaries of unorthodox beliefs after 1160, still had far to go. Parts of Languedoc and much of northern and central Italy plainly presented peculiar difficulties because of the widespread fautorship and patronage of heresy. At a higher level, the demands and enthusiasms of the popular movement for preaching and the apostolic life, though they conflicted with much precedent and canon law and upset interested parties, were not of themselves heretical at all. Doors closed at Lyons and Verona could be reopened. More could be done to separate off misled enthusiasm from the recalcitrant elements, to bring into focus the alien inspiration of Catharism, and draw away from it adherents unaware of the implications of dualism. The lines between heresy and orthodoxy altogether could be drawn more clearly.

There was not much time. The sects had grown since the beginning of the century in cohesion and durability. In the early decades they barely outlast the deaths of their founders, and are obviously profoundly dependent on the force of the individual charismatic personality. Then Catharism develops, a supranational heresy, no longer nearly so dependent for its existence on individual personalities, important though they may be, and capable of lasting because of its developed ritual and organization and the dogmatic envelope it gave to dissent. As the century wore on, the evangelical heresies seem also to last better, and Waldensianism appears, the culmination of the previous wandering preacher movements, strengthened by the novel element of vernacular translations of Scripture.

By the end of the century there was more heresy, it was more firmly embedded, and two crisis areas had emerged. It was this sombre scene which confronted the young Pope Innocent III on his elevation to the papacy in 1198.

*Part III*

---

Heresy and the Church

# 6

# The Counter-Attack: Innocent III to Innocent IV

With the advent of Innocent III the papacy was for the first time occupied by a churchman who made the treatment of heresy and the religious movement associated with it one of the prime occupations of his pontificate.[1] In the previous century Alexander III and Lucius III had both taken steps to deal with the problem; but in comparison to Innocent's subtle handling of the difficulties their solutions appear fumbling and incomplete. Moreover, Innocent was followed by three popes, Honorius III, Gregory IX and Innocent IV, who all gave attention to the counter-attack on heresy. The work of two saints, Dominic and Francis, and the emergence of the orders of mendicant friars, encouraged by Innocent and aided by his successors, had a powerful effect on thirteenth-century religious life, and provided trained personnel to preach against heresy and to pursue its recalcitrant adherents. More study of heresy and the application of scholastic methods to its refutation brought forth fruit in treatises and handbooks that classified heretical tenets, and made clearer where precisely the boundary between heresy and orthodoxy lay. Northern Europe laid the foundations for the move forward. Paris masters combined intellectual activity with action to instruct the priesthood, and arm them against heretics. They preached, wrote treatises, acted as expert witnesses in trials; crusade to the Holy Land, crusade against heretics, counter-preaching, exhortation to reception of the sacraments, explanations of the mass, the use of logic and disputation formed an ensemble designed to raise standards and protect the Church and its laity. Paris-educated men were drawn to the friars, and the traditions of reforming schoolmen thus contributed directly to the mendicant advance. Cistercians, certain northern bishops and the masters have been underestimated in the white light of publicity attending the dramatic events in Languedoc which unfolded under Innocent.[2] Under Gregory

---

1 *RB*, pp. 70–156; comment by E. Jordan in *RHE* XXXII (1936), pp. 968–72. Cf. A. C. Shannon, *The Popes and Heresy in the Thirteenth Century* (Villanova, PA, 1949); B. Bolton, *Innocent III* (1995) (coll. articles); *Pope Innocent III and His World*, ed. J. C. Moore (Aldershot, 1999).
2 *BK*, pp. 6–21; J. Bird, 'The construction of orthodoxy', *Trials*, ed. P. Biller, C. Bruschi; Id., 'Heresy, crusade and reform in the circle of Peter the Chanter, c.1187–c.1240' (DPhil, Univ. Oxford, 2001);

IX use of the overriding authority of the papacy brought into being inquisitors to supply the deficiencies of the episcopal prosecution of heresy, and to give new energy to the tracking and examining of offenders. By the mid thirteenth century the guiding principles of the Church's counteraction were settled, and most of the machinery requisite for repression was in action, not to be altered in essentials for the rest of the Middle Ages.

Innocent set out principles for future action. His approach was two-sided: he offered to enthusiasts who had strayed a means of returning to the Church, and diminished the dangers in the movement for wandering preaching in poverty by welcoming this form of apostolic life under safeguards within the Church; and at the same time he attempted to make the use of force against fautors and obstinate heretics more effective. His metaphor was that of the farmer who distinguishes carefully between wheat and tares in his field, taking precautions against uprooting the one with the other.[3] Proper handling of the heresy problem demanded precise and careful examination of what heretics believed and, above all, of their attitudes to authority. If they were willing to submit, then arrangements might be made to meet the needs of enthusiasts wherever they did not conflict directly with orthodox doctrine. If they were recalcitrant, then every kind of measure might be employed to bring them to justice and force those who patronized them to relinquish their support.

Innocent explored all the resources of canon law to find a place for popular religious associations that had hitherto lain on the margin of orthodoxy or beyond, welcoming their representatives to the curia and obtaining from them *proposita*, short statements of intent, tending to stabilize their position. Humiliati who wished for recognition were accepted, and given regulations that allowed the continuance of three branches with separate ways of life: one clerical, a second consisting of laymen and women living in communities, and a third consisting of married men living with their families, all according to existing legal norms. The structure itself may well have originated among the Humiliati themselves.[4] A careful explanation showed them that there were legitimate occasions when oaths had to be sworn, but they were allowed to avoid any that were not strictly necessary, and to retain other special features of their apostolic way of life as they had observed them while under the ban of the Church. The wholesale refusal of the right to preach that had helped the Humiliati into heresy after the third Lateran Council was breached with a fine distinction: members of the third, the married group, who were 'wise in faith and expert in religion', might preach, provided that they confined themselves to moral exhortation and eschewed the preaching of doctrine – that was properly the province of the clergy.[5]

---

I am indebted to the generosity of Dr Bird. See also C. Muessig, 'Les Sermons de Jacques de Vitry sur les Cathares', *CF* XXXII, pp. 69–83.
3   *PL* CCXIV, cols 788–9, p. 74, n. 5. Cp. *PL* CCXV, cols 1246–8; and Bolton, in *SCH* IX, p. 86.
4   M. Maccarrone, 'Riforma e sviluppo della vita religiosa con Innocenzo III', *RSCI* XVI (1962), pp. 29–72; Bolton, 'Innocent III's treatment', p. 78; Andrews, *Humiliati*.
5   Tiraboschi, *Vetera monumenta* II, pp. 133–4; *RB*, p. 81, n. 24, tr. of phrase, Bolton, 'Innocent III's treatment', p. 77. B. Bolton, *The Medieval Reformation* (1983) (concise, wide-ranging survey; Humiliati:

Durand of Huesca, converted after a colloquy with the representatives of orthodoxy at Pamiers in 1207, was given, together with the colleagues who came over with him, the right to lead a life of wandering preaching without property, engaging in mission against heresy, exactly as he had done while a Waldensian, provided that he accepted Catholic authority and repudiated errors such as Donatism, which had been current among some Waldensians. He and his group were given the technical status of penitents in the Church, living under three vows of poverty, chastity and obedience, and styled 'the Catholic poor'.[6] Bernard Prim, also a Waldensian from Languedoc who came over in 1210, was given similarly sympathetic treatment. As with Durand's group, the basis for his reconciliation with the Church was the profession of faith which Henri de Marcy had imposed on Valdes, with the addition of certain points on the sacraments and the repudiation of the right of women to preach.[7] The important difference with the case of Valdes was that, the repudiation of errors once completed, preaching was permitted. Durand and Prim, after they had submitted, were allowed to continue essentially the same way of life as poor wandering preachers.

These decisions in effect detached a small group of moderates from the movement of Waldensian preachers and rescued many Humiliati for the Church. For a moment it might well have seemed that Innocent's policy was going to have more far-reaching effects, as a hundred Waldensian preachers in Italy after Durand's conversion asked, under conditions, for acceptance by the Church;[8] but we do not know what happened to them, and after 1212 we hear no more of such requests. Innocent's sympathetic approach could only work if reconciling moves came from the Waldensians themselves: the bulk of the movement made no further approaches to Rome, but attempted to recover unity amongst themselves.

At first, in the aftermath of the Waldensian split of 1205,[9] the situation remained confused. Donatist views gained ground amongst the Poor Lombards, who were in a strong majority in Italy; yet members of the Lyonist wing, who were faithful to the tradition of Valdes, did not disappear altogether. A reaction amongst some of the Italian membership in the direction of moderation took place after a council of the Lombards in the period 1208–9, when a hen upset the chalice as John de Ronco celebrated the eucharist, and women trampled on the spilt wine. There was a split. Some indignant brothers declared, in reaction against such disorder, that the sacrament should only be administered by Roman priests.[10]

pp. 63–6); K. V. Selge, 'Humiliaten', *TRE* xv, pp. 691–6. On poverty as the mark of the 'new man' in the twelfth century, see B. Bolton, '*Paupertas Christi*: old wealth and new poverty in the twelfth century', *SCH* xiv, pp. 95–103.

6  *EFV*, pp. 129–36; *WEH*, pp. 222–6, Selge, *Waldenser* i, pp. 193–225; Thouzellier, *Catharisme et Valdéisme*, 2nd edn, pp. 215–26; for status, cf. Maccarrone, in *RSCI* xvi (1962), pp. 29–72.

7  *EFV*, pp. 136–40; Thouzellier, *Catharisme et Valdéisme*, pp. 232–7; Selge, *Waldenser* i, pp. 188–93.

8  Selge, *Waldenser* i, pp. 204–5. Pou y Marti argues for a disturbing effect of Poor Catholics in Catalonia in H. E. Lee, M. Reeves, G. Silano, ed., *Western Mediterranean Prophecy* (1989).

9  Above, p. 85.

10  Selge, *Waldenser* i, p. 307.

Contacts between Lombards and Lyonists over the Alps were not totally severed. In time the deaths of John de Ronco and Valdes appeared to remove personal obstacles to reunion, and a last attempt, possibly emanating from the Waldensians then feeling the effects of persecution in Languedoc, was made to bring the two wings together. Six representatives from each side met in conference near Bergamo in 1218 to thrash out their differences. The Lyonists were ready to make generous concessions on the issues which had kept them apart, allowing provosts and ministers for the sacrament to be appointed for life if the Lombards insisted, and dropping Valdes's rigid opposition to their arrangements on manual labour. The conference broke on the Lombards' Donatism, and the issue, subordinate but of high emotional significance, of the salvation of Valdes and his companion Vivet. The Lyonists insisted that they were in paradise; the Lombards answered coldly that they would be if they had satisfied God for their sins before their deaths. Eucharistic beliefs formed the doctrinal breaking-point, the Lombards making merit, not office, the crucial question for the validity of the sacrament and, in our source for the conference, a letter of information to adherents of the Poor Lombards in Germany, massing authorities in Scripture and the Fathers for their point of view, their opponents standing on the Catholic belief that the sacrament was valid only if the celebrant were a priest, whatever his life might be.[11]

Two rival traditions had evolved. The Lyonist wing supporting Valdes in 1218 had still not broken irrevocably with the Church. They stood firm on the belief that their preachers had a direct mission from God, and they rejected the Church's excommunication. They did not press on, as the Lombards did, to subject all practices of the Church to stern examination in the light of Scripture and the pattern of the early Church. If critical of the Roman hierarchy and priesthood, they had still not unchurched them. The Lombards had, and pressed the others to do the same.

The wings never came together again after the failure at Bergamo, though some sporadic and not wholly hostile relations between them continued, aided perhaps by the fact that the missionary endeavours of the two wings tended to lie in different regions.[12] The moderates did not return to the Church, and voluntary reconciliations, such as those of Durand and Prim, are not recorded again; instead, persecution encouraged more out-and-out opposition. The chance of reunion with the Church seemed to have disappeared.

The success of the Waldensian groups who returned to the Church was partial. Prim's group brought to the service of the Church an apostolate based on a poor life, with exhortation and some recourse to manual labour; the Poor Catholics under Durand pursued a more learned mission, with a hospital at Elne in Roussillon which also formed a centre for the production of antiheretical

---

11   *EFV*, pp. 169–83, tr. *WEH*, pp. 278–89; Selge, *Waldenser* I, pp. 305–12, Böhmer, in *RPTK* xx, cols 810–11. I accept Germany as the destination, on the evidence of the title subsequently added to the document. Text in A. Patschovsky, K. V. Selge, ed., *Quellen zur Geschichte der Waldenser*, pp. 20–43; see Biller, *Waldenses*, p. 120, Cameron, *Waldenses*, pp. 43–5; dissident view on Germans, p. 98.
12   Böhmer, *RPTK* xx, col. 811.

writings. The hospital had fifty beds and catered for 'those in distress, the poor, the sick, abandoned children, poor women in childbirth and the provision of clothing in winter'. There was a division of function between those who preached and the converted laity who looked after the sick.[13] Durand, a precise polemicist who painstakingly followed the convolutions of developing dualist doctrine and over-matched his opponents in knowledge of Scripture, worked on, growing in stature between his Waldensian *Liber antiheresis* and his Catholic *Contra Manicheos*. His revision of Peter of Capua's *Alphabetum* shows him to have been in the forefront of new ideas for aiding preachers.[14] Both groups had the advantage over heretics of realizing in their own persons the apostolic life of poor preaching; but they were unable to break down the hostility of the bishops or to gain a major popular success, and in the perspective of thirteenth-century Church history they appear as imperfect sketches of the successful mendicant orders. The reconciled Humiliati earned the praise of James of Vitry in 1216 for their preaching against heresy in Milan; he knew of some 150 houses of theirs.[15] Their success was of its time; the Humiliati remained exclusively Italian, and they did not go on to form an order of first-class importance. The breakthrough for the harnessing of the apostolic life of poor, wandering preaching to the mission of the Church came only when two saints were able to make use of the fertile climate of opinion and Innocent's will to experiment.

In Languedoc in 1206, when a mission of Cistercians, earnest but hampered by official status and entourage, failed to make progress in a preaching drive, the Castilian bishop Diego of Osma with his subprior Dominic hit on the idea of preaching in poverty on terms of equality with their enemies the Cathars. It proved a winning formula: a preaching campaign was held in 1206–7. Diego died in December 1207, and peaceful preaching, though hindered by the growing tensions which ended in the Albigensian Crusade, was, long term, the way forward against Catharism. Dominic had a universal zeal for souls and a will to preach to all; circumstances gave him a special role in the battle against Cathars. Encouraged and aided by Innocent, he established himself in Cathar country, and fostered a house founded at Prouille for women and girls rescued from the Cathars.[16] In 1215 he moved to Toulouse; in 1216–17 he obtained recognition for his order of preachers, known to history as Dominican friars – in effect a special development of the way of life of the Augustinian canons to whom

---

13  Elne, in Roussillon, then ruled by the kings of Aragon, diocese in province of Narbonne. On the school, Thouzellier, *Catharisme et Valdéisme*, pp. 269–84; for quotation and hospital, Biller, '*Curate Infirmos*', *SCH* xix, p. 60; *Waldenses*, p. 53.

14  *Liber*, text: Selge, *Waldenser* ii; analysis: Thouzellier, pp. 60–79, implications: Selge, *Waldenser* i, ch. i; *Contra Manicheos*, in Thouzellier, *Une Somme anti-Cathare* (1964); analysis, Thouzellier, *Catharisme et Valdéisme*, pp. 303–73 (authorities cited, pp. 375–424). Pioneer study, A. Dondaine, 'Durand de Huesca et la polémique anti-Cathare', *AFP* xxix (1959), pp. 228–76. R. H. and M. A. Rouse, 'The Schools and the Waldensians: a new work of Durand of Huesca', in S. Waugh, P. Diehl, ed., *Christendom*, pp. 86–103.

15  *Lettres*, ed. R. Huygens (Leiden, 1960), p. 73 ('CL congregationes conventuales').

16  Vicaire, *St Dominic*; *CF* i; J. Guiraud, *Cartulaire de Notre Dame de Prouille*, i–ii (1907). M-H. Vicaire, *Dominique et ses prêcheurs* (Paris and Fribourg, 1977).

Dominic belonged. Circumstances in the Midi gave a bias towards defence of its faith against heresy; in Italy all the emphasis in the early days was on the need for preaching pure and simple. Meeting a widespread demand, the Dominicans rapidly grew into a large international order.[17] They affected the whole religious landscape, through preaching, entering the universities and playing a major part in the development of scholasticism, bringing their piety and zeal to bear on the towns short of pastoral care, where heresy found adherents, and deploying against Cathars and Waldensians the silent but most effective argument of their own observance of apostolic life. Determined papal support, good planning by Dominic and his successors, and the Languedoc emergency all helped the young order to avoid suffocation by conservatism, though opposition by the secular clergy to the rights of the friars to preach, to hear confessions and to intervene in the parishes long remained a factor in Church life.

Five years before the fourth Lateran Council, at which St Dominic's plans were discussed, St Francis of Assisi, with eleven companions, asked at Rome for confirmation of a way of life of the most extreme poverty blended with preaching based on the gospels, especially the account of the sending of the Seventy.[18] Francis's first rule consisted largely of texts, and was not based on an existing rule at all; moreover, the renunciations he asked for seemed beyond human powers. The pope seems to have hesitated, but was persuaded by the argument that to turn down Francis's request would be tantamount to saying that the gospel itself could not be observed. He met the request by the unprecedented course of giving Francis's way of life an oral confirmation; a right to preach was granted to Francis, and through him to his followers, on terms resembling those given to the Humiliati. The group, at first a lay association, was allowed to preach penance – to engage in moral exhortation rather than the preaching of doctrine that was reserved to clergy. Rapid growth in numbers, contemporary needs and papal policies soon turned them into a great international order of friars, clerical and often learned, with full rights of preaching, and many resemblances to the Dominicans.

St Francis himself hardly referred to heresy at all. His Testament has an observation on binding suspect members of the order so as to bring them safely to the cardinal protector. Etienne de Bourbon records a meeting with a heretic who complained to him of the misdeeds of a concubinary priest. Francis's response was simply to kiss the priest's hand in token of reverence for his office.[19] Preaching for him was a spontaneous overflow of the interior life; unlike

---

17   For introduction, C. H. Lawrence, *The Friars* (London and New York, 1994); S. Tugwell, 'Notes on the life of St Dominic', *AFP* LXVI (1996), pp. 5–200, *AFP* LXVIII (1998), pp. 5–116, with important corrections on Dominic's attitude to the mission in the Midi and to preaching against heresy; in 1219 he thought of moving Prouille's nuns to San Sisto, Rome (*AFP* LXVI, pp. 10–16); plans for an Italian campaign against heresy in 1220 are probably Ugolino's, not his (Ibid., p. 46); see discussion of possible missions to unbelievers (*AFP* LXVIII); summaries, Ibid., pp. 66, 84; Diego and preaching, pp. 40–2.

18   Matt. 10: 7–13. See below, ch. 11.

19   L. Lemmens, *Testimonia Minora* (Quaracchi, 1926), pp. 93–4; K. Esser, 'Franziskus von Assisi und die Katharer seiner Zeit', *AFH* LI (1958), pp. 225–64.

Dominic, he had no aim of confuting heresy specifically, but thought of his order as auxiliaries to the priesthood, preaching penance and thereby, no doubt, recalling men from error. Circumstances changed this, and the Franciscans came to play an important part directly against heresy through preaching, the intellectual refutation of error, the writing of treatises, and a full apostolate in the towns, made more effective through the institution of the third order. But their most distinctive contribution lay in the revolution they helped to bring about in popular piety through their stress on the incidents of Christ's life and His sufferings, and their acceptance of the created world and joy in nature. It was the indirect answer to Cathar rejection of the world and their non-human Jesus.[20]

In the problem area of Languedoc, the centres of heresy once discerned, Innocent characteristically began seeking solutions at two levels simultaneously. One was the fostering of religious revival through preaching, as shown in his advice to his Cistercian legates 'to proceed in such a way that the simplicity of your attitude is clear to the eyes of all',[21] and in his encouragement of the mission of Diego and St Dominic; the other was the application of pressure to the unwilling episcopate of the region and the leading nobles who would not put heresy down. The second came to dominate the first after his legate, Pierre de Castelnau, was assassinated in 1208 in circumstances which threw suspicion on Count Raymond VI of Toulouse. Innocent called a crusade, and north French barons responded. At the end of the pontificate Raymond stood dispossessed of nearly all his holdings apart from those in Provence, and the bulk of the episcopate had been deposed. War drew local patriotism and interests into hostility to crusaders and defence of the cause of heresy. At the outset local sentiment cast the Trencavels as natural enemies of the crusade, it has been argued, because of their hostility to the Cistercians, and their fall excited less opposition than it might have done because of suspicion that they had complicity with Peter of Aragon's ambitions in the area. But as the crusade proceeded other landholders reacted with hostility as their own rights were threatened. The terrain gave refuge to mountain lords accustomed to independence. Too many of the North French served only for the forty days requisite to secure the crusade indulgence.[22]

20   E. Delaruelle, 'L'influence de saint François d'Assise sur la piété populaire', *Relazioni* III, pp. 449–66; Manselli, *Eresia*, p. 270.

21   *PL* CCXV, col. 360; tr. Vicaire, *St Dominic*, p. 87.

22   *BC*, pp. 120–40 (see esp. for Simon de Montfort, with novel analysis of his effects on Cathar survival; a shrewd survey with a masterly ch. 2 on the reasons for Cathar success in Languedoc); *CF* IV (ideas); *WHC*, ch. 6; B. Hamilton, *The Albigensian Crusade* (1974) (Hist. Assocn. G. 85); J. Sumption, *The Albigensian Crusade* (1978) (vivid; ch. 2 outdated); M. Costen, *The Cathars and the Albigensian Crusade* (1997) (social context); M. Roquebert, *L'Epopée Cathare*, I: *L'Invasion* (1970), II: *La Dépossession* (1977), III: *Les Lys et la Croix* (1986), IV: *Mourir à Montségur* (1989), V: *Les Cathares ... 1244–1329* (1998) (gripping narrative with understanding of personalities); for chronicles see Peter des Vaux de Cernay, trans. W. A. and M. D. Sibly, *The History of the Albigensian Crusade* (1998) (intro. illuminating diplomacy, full notes, appendices; see esp. pp. 313–20 on Innocent and crusade); *Chronica Magistri Guillelmi de Podio Laurentii*, ed., trans. J. Duvernoy (Paris, 1976); *The Song of the Cathar Wars*, ed., trans. J. Shirley (Aldershot, 1996); E. Graham-Leigh, 'The Trencavel Viscounts of Carcassonne, Béziers, Albi and Razès and the Albigensian Crusade' (PhD, Univ. London, 2000).

Innocent gave a full legal justification for the crusade, based especially on his own decretal of 1199, *Vergentis in senium*, with its assimilation of heresy to the crime in Roman law of *lèse-majesté*, with draconian secular penalties; but he was unable to keep control once the crusade was launched, or to maintain canonical procedure. The lands of Raymond VI were confiscated without any trial taking place. The war had its own momentum. Ferocity on the southern side excited ferocity from the crusaders.[23] The champion of the Church, Simon de Montfort, was a fine general who lacked the gifts of a politician. Innocent was not master of the spirits he had conjured up.

In the long term the crusade helped to create a new political situation dominated by the north French, in which effective persecution became possible. But there were side-effects. Crusade was a blunt instrument. The bishop of Bremen called a crusade in 1234 against the *Stedinger*, peasants who opposed his rule and refused tithes, as though they were heretics, and in so doing showed how easily the mechanism could be corrupted.[24] It will always be open to doubt whether such an application of force to the situation in Languedoc was required, and whether Innocent, distant from the scene, was misled on the true character and extent of heresy in the Midi, especially by the authoritarian Pierre de Castelnau. Not many years were given to preaching. Dominic had few helpers and only the one religious house at Prouille in the early days.

The active pontificate of Innocent III left a body of case-law, precedent and legislation for dealing with heresy which supplemented and improved, but did not fundamentally change, the episcopal inquisition as prescribed by *Ad abolendam*. The influence of the bishops was weighty at the council and tended to conservatism. Exhortation, the use of legates with overriding powers – even deposition of unworthy bishops, as in Languedoc – gingered up episcopal prosecution of heresy, or alternatively tempered its crudities. Outside the Patrimony, Innocent knew well how Ghibelline traditions, anticlericalism, local disputes and the spirit of civic independence hampered ecclesiastical authority: he never pushed matters to extremes but exhorted, aided bishops, appealed to civic pride and did what he could to secure the incorporation of anti-heresy legislation into municipal statutes as a springboard to more effective action in the future.[25] At the end, in the fourth Lateran Council canons summed up existing legislation, and a dogmatic constitution, mainly anti-Cathar and based closely on the profession of faith presented by Henri de Marcy to Valdes, gave a concise picture of the errors to be suppressed. The pope's own use of procedure *per inquisitionem*, in which the responsible judge carried on both investigation and judgement, and started an inquiry on the basis of

23   Maisonneuve, *Etudes*, pp. 156–8; R. Foreville, 'Innocent III et la Croisade des Albigeois', *CF*IV, pp. 184–217; Kolmer, *Vulpes*, pp. 35–41; a war 'far beyond the normal conventions', M. Barber in his 'The Albigensian Crusades: wars like any other?', *Mélanges* for Jean Richard, ed. B. Kedar et al. (forthcoming).
24   Grundmann, *Ketzergeschichte*, p. 39; Lea, *Inquisition* III, pp. 182–6.
25   H. G. Walther, 'Ziel und Mittel päpstlicher Ketzerpolitik in der Lombardei und im Kirchenstaat', *Anfänge der Inquisition*, ed. P. Segl (1993), pp. 103–30; L. Kolmer, 'Christus als beleidigte Majestät: von der lex "Quisquis" (397) bis zur Dekretale "Vergentis" (1199)', *Papsttum, Kirche und Recht*, ed. K. Mordek (1991), pp. 1–13; D. M. Webb, 'The Pope and the cities: anticlericalism and heresy in Innocent III's Italy', *SCH* Subsidia IX, pp. 135–52 (clear analysis).

mere *fama*, was part of his passionate will to correct the abuses of churchmen.[26] Simplicity of procedure aimed at short-circuiting the delays of the accusatorial process, and the use of *fama* at breaking through barriers of secrecy in clerical corporations. But, though its aim was to detect simony and moral failing, not heresy, the utility of the procedure was manifest for heresy cases. Innocent's moral investigations marked a stage on the road to the development of the inquisition commissions of Gregory IX.[27]

An intellectual heresy, the trinitarian views of a Calabrian abbot, Joachim of Fiore, was also condemned at the council, albeit with a stress on Joachim's own submission to the papacy in his lifetime.[28] Joachim's error was contained in a *libellus*, now lost, in which he attacked the trinitarian teaching of Peter Lombard, author of the authoritative textbook, the 'Sentences', and a leading influence at the Paris theological school, to which Innocent himself had belonged. Joachim's own major literary activity, in which he applied traditional methods of exegesis to Scripture in order to understand the patterns of history and to foresee the future, was not condemned, although, amongst much that was orthodox, it contained a potentially subversive notion of a coming third age of the Holy Spirit, that would in some sense supersede the arrangements of the present Age of the Son.[29] A group of supporters of Amaury of Bène, a Paris master who died in about 1206, had been condemned in 1210, some to death, others to perpetual imprisonment; another master, Godin, was burnt about two years later.[30] Amaury's corpse was exhumed from consecrated ground; the sect was virtually annihilated.

Amaury, a brilliant speculator, had been influenced in a pantheistic direction by his reading of John Scotus Eriguena, the ninth-century theologian, and elements in his teaching had created scandal during his lifetime. His followers, often intellectuals themselves, seem to have taken his views further. They were accused of holding an amalgam of heretical beliefs, pantheist, antinomian, gnostic, libertine. A bowdlerization of the *Pater Noster* was attributed to them,

---

26   Pope's attitude, B. Bolton, '"A show with a meaning": Innocent III's approach to the Fourth Lateran Council, 1215', *Medieval History* I (1991), pp. 53–67; Id., *Innocent III*, no. XI.

27   Mansi XXII, col. 982, *EFV*, pp. 158–63; trans. *DTC* I, pp. 653–6; Innocent's policy, Kolmer, *Vulpes*, pp. 35–63; W. Trusen, 'Von den Anfängen des Inquisitionsprozesses zum Verfahren bei der *Inquisitio haereticae pravitatis*', *Anfänge* ed. Segl, pp. 39–76.

28   Mansi, XXII, cols 982–6, M. Reeves, *The Influence of Prophecy in the Later Middle Ages* (1969) (the fundamental study of Joachim and his influence), pp. 28–36; B. McGinn, *The Calabrian Abbot* (1985) (valuable in relating Joachim to the body of Christian exegesis and apocalyptic; summary on historical context, pp. 1–47); extracts: B. McGinn, *Visions of the End* (1979), pp. 126–41; K. V. Selge, 'L'origine delle opere di Gioacchino dà Fiore', *L'Attesa della fine dei tempi nel medioevo*, ed. O. Capitanei, J. Miethke (1990), pp. 87–130 (establishes sequence of works).

29   Definitive exposition is in Reeves, *Prophecy*, pp. 16–27, 135–44; illuminating analysis, Id., 'The *Liber Figurarum* of Joachim of Fiore', *MRS* II (1950), pp. 57–81; M. W. Bloomfield, 'Recent scholarship on Joachim of Fiore and his influence', *Prophecy and Millenarianism*, ed. A. Williams, M. W. Bloomfield (1980), pp. 21–52 at p. 27, notes how Joachim gives the New Testament 'an inner future spiritual dimension'.

30   *RB*, pp. 355–73, M. Th. d'Alverny, 'Un fragment du procès des Amauriciens', *AHDLMA* XXVI (1951), pp. 325–36, sources tr. in *WEH*, pp. 258–63. Bène (sometimes Bènes or Bena) was a parish in the diocese of Chartres. All previous work is superseded by G. Dickson, 'The burning of the Amalricians', *JEH* XL (1989), pp. 347–69; Id., *Religious Enthusiasm*, ch. 3.

designed to play down phrases awkward to their tenets.[31] They were said to believe in their own sinlessness and to have rejected the sacraments – which was all the more troubling to ecclesiastical authority then concerned with the sacramental life of the Church and anxious to popularize the practice of confession. By denying or trivializing sin, they obviated the need for penance.[32] The crisis of Amaury's death and the loss of his leadership seems to have galvanized them into becoming an active missionary sect. Perhaps at the same time, they became convinced that an Age of the Spirit was at hand, of which they were the forerunners, when all men would become 'spiritual', as they were: it sounds like a crude version of Joachim's Age of the Spirit.[33]

The pantheistic views of Amaury were condemned in the same canon of the council as Joachim's trinitarian exposition; on some other occasion in the pontificate Ortlieb of Strasburg was also condemned for having taught that man must keep himself from all external things and only follow the Spirit in him,[34] and in 1210 a work of David Dinant imbued with pantheism was also burnt. From the evidence we have there appears to have been some efflorescence of 'spiritualizing' heresy cut short under Innocent. Of Joachim, however, more was to be heard.[35]

Innocent's successor, Honorius III, at once less resolute and less original, nevertheless continued to build up antiheretical legislation by ensuring that laws on the duties of secular powers to repress heresy and aid Church authorities were made part of secular codes. The Emperor Frederick II made such laws part of imperial legislation – it was originally his *quid pro quo* for coronation by the pope – and made burning the punishment for the recalcitrant.[36]

But the major innovation came under Gregory IX when, after some experiments with various procedures and after realizing the inadequacies of episcopal inquisitions, he resorted to special agents equipped with full powers from the papacy to hunt out heretics. In 1231 he empowered the Dominican prior of Regensburg to launch a campaign – in which, none the less, key powers of hearing evidence and judging heretics were left in other hands. In 1233 the Dominican Robert le Bougre was given powers both to preach and to examine and condemn, a prelude to a wide-ranging campaign in France and the Empire, and in the same year within Languedoc similar powers to denounce and examine were given to Dominicans appointed by provincials for the task. Such special agents showed themselves so much more efficient than the bishops that their

---

31  D'Alverny, *AHDLMA* xxvi. We may detect a pantheistic note in it, the replacement of material bread by vague needs, the transformation of Evil into accidental evils.

32  A point made by Dickson, *JEH* xl, p. 361; p. 355 corrects d'Alverny on intellectual level.

33  Grundmann's judgement in *RB*, p. 365, and *Ketzergeschichte*, p. 43. I follow Dickson's judgement (above, n. 30) on the likely link between the aftermath of Amaury's death and the development of the idea of the new age.

34  W. Preger, *Geschichte der deutschen Mystik* i (Leipzig, 1874), p. 468, 1. 78. On Ortliebians, see A. Fössel, *Die Ortlieber* (1993). See Leff, *Heresy* ii, p. 309; on all these episodes, cf. Grundmann, *Ketzergeschichte*, pp. 41–2.

35  Below, pp. 213–25.

36  Maisonneuve, *Etudes*, pp. 243–57.

inquisition became the normal means of extirpating heresy. The episcopal inquisition tended in most lands affected by heresy to become of secondary significance. So the papal inquisition of the Middle Ages was born.[37]

It was the last move required to implement all the existing laws against heresy. The agents so appointed supplied the deficiencies of the bishops, for they were appointed for the one purpose of putting down heresy, and were not distracted by other business. Their commissions to act as inquisitors were of long duration; appointees could thus build up knowledge and gain a professional's expertise. Most commonly Dominicans were appointed to the office by arrangement with their superiors: they brought to the task the dedication of men under vows belonging to a highly trained order with a special vocation against heresy. Franciscans, more rarely appointed, had similar dedication. Continuity of record was established. Each inquisitor kept registers, with the depositions of suspects, which could be handed on to his successors or used as a basis for further inquiries at a later date. Manuscripts were skilfully laid out in an innovatory way to allow speedy retrieval of names and confessions. The records were a threat to everyone who had once been interrogated, and even to the relatives and descendants of suspects, against whom a record of conviction or complicity could be invoked. With such data at his disposal a medieval inquisitor had resources comparable to that of a modern police officer, ever ready to check and cross-check information. One full confession by a heretic of wide acquaintance could uncover a multiplicity of leads to his fellows; the practice of granting a period of grace at the beginning of an inquisition in which punishments were waived for those who gave information, and the insistence that only full confession of all available facts gave proof of repentance were calculated to produce a free flow of incriminating details. Inquisitors could link up actions against heresy in different lands, and try to prevent the escape of refugees; flight at an early stage of proceedings or while awaiting trial remained one of the few effective means of avoiding successful prosecution.

As the customs and procedures of the inquisitors developed, so in time a class of writing often known as 'inquisitors' handbooks' came into existence, assembling past experience on heretics and their beliefs, and giving information on the customs inquisitors used and the regulations under which they worked.[38] In Languedoc a working knowledge of Catharism under a few simple heads had

---

37   Y. Dossat, *Les Crises de l'inquisition toulousaine* (1959), ch. 5; Lea, *Inquisition* I, ch. 7 *et passim* (still of value, repr. with intro. by W. Ullman, H. C. Lea, *The Inquisition of the Middle Ages* (London, 1963)); B. Hamilton, *The Medieval Inquisition* (1981) (surveys assumptions; see esp. pp. 49–59 on relationship of confessor and inquisitor); lit., Kolmer, *Vulpes*, pp. 13–22; J. B. Given, *Inquisition and Medieval Society* (1997) (inquisitors' techniques as control mechanisms; sociological analysis with excellent statistics, focusing on Languedoc 1275–1325).
38   A. Dondaine, 'Le manuel de l'inquisiteur (1230–1330)', *AFP* XVII (1947), pp. 85–194, *GK*, pp. 21–7. Polemical literature (see below, pp. 196–7) in Dondaine, 'Nouvelles sources de l'histoire doctrinale du Néo-Manichéisme au Moyen Age', *RSPT* XXVIII (1939), pp. 465–88; W. L. Wakefield, 'Notes on some antiheretical writings of the thirteenth century', *FS* XXVII (1967), pp. 285–321 (demonstrates extent of casual plagiarizing). On origins and working of the inquisition, see P. Segl, ed., *Die Anfänge der Inquisition im Mittelalter* (1993) (conference articles). T. Scharff, 'Schrift zur Kontrolle – Kontrolle der Schrift. Italienische und französische Inquisitoren-Handbücher der 13. und frühen 14. Jahrhunderts', *DA* LIV (1998), pp. 547–84 (importance of written word for inquisitors' success).

become the common knowledge of clergy habitually in contact with the heretics, and this knowledge passed over to the thirteenth-century inquisitors; in Italy, ever more sophisticated, inquisitors tended to have a more speculative interest in the origins and nature of the heresies they were dealing with. There was in any case a general rise in the number and standards of the treatises which described and refuted heresy, a product of the new scholasticism and of the concern of churchmen over the problem; these contributed to the pool of information available to the inquisition; in turn, further treatises were also influenced by the habits of mind of the inquisitors themselves.

The inquisitor was the heir to the body of legislation against heretics and their supporters which reached back to *Ad abolendam* as well as to the enactments passed after 1231 in his favour. It was a formidable structure. Ecclesiastical law on heresy was keeping pace with developments in civil law, where there was also a strong trend to the use of the inquisitorial rather than the accusatorial procedure. That procedure was ideally suited for the uncovering of heresy, which was an elusive crime. Under it any suspect could be summoned and put under oath to declare his participation in forbidden rites and meetings, his contacts with heretics, or any relevant information at all about his beliefs and his movements; from 1252 by a decision of Innocent IV, who improved the detailed workings of the inquisition, torture might be used on him.[39] It was intended that the instruments should be applied by the secular power, and not the inquisitor's staff; but four years after Innocent's bull his successor, Alexander IV, permitted inquisitors to evade the restriction. The subject could thus be compelled to incriminate himself. Heavy penalties compelled suspects or witnesses to appear and to answer; others enforced the aid of the secular power, whenever required, to ensure his attendance and to assist with, or be responsible for his or her punishment if convicted. Rights to the property of convicted heretics also helped to secure the willing support of the secular power. Fautorship of heresy was a grave crime, and penalties could be incurred by a mere obstruction of the inquisitor in his duty.

In the determination that nothing should stand in the way of speedy and efficient action against heresy, the checks designed in canon law to ensure fair trial, the validity of evidence, and the impartiality of the judge were all set aside. Depositions were accepted from classes of witnesses normally debarred in canon law and defendants were commonly not told the names of witnesses who testified against them. In the last resort the inquisitor, who combined the role of judge and of priest dealing with a penitent, held near-unfettered powers over the suspects who came before him. At his discretion – and the scrutiny of his sentences required under the regulations tended to be slight and formal – was an array of penalties stretching from fines, pilgrimages, beatings, and the wearing of yellow crosses on the clothing, to imprisonment up to and including life and burning, as well as sentences of confiscation, destruction of dwellings, and attendant

---

39  Maisonneuve, *Etudes*, p. 312; E. Peters, *Torture* (1985), pp. 64–5; Id., 'Destruction of the flesh – salvation of the spirit: the paradoxes of torture in medieval Christian society', *The Devil*, ed. A. Ferreiro (1998), pp. 131–48.

disqualifications from office-holding affecting descendants. The priest in the confessional would impose penance in accordance with the guidance of the confessors' manuals and his judgement of circumstances and culpability: this flexibility carried over into the exercise of the inquisitors' office and the penances or penalties exacted were in consequence much more finely tuned than those imposed by secular judges. Moreover, the penances were commonly adjusted over time so that sentences of imprisonment were lifted and commuted perhaps to wearing crosses; in effect, a form of parole system was in operation and continued in effect even after the penance had been completed, for the 'penitent' remained a known name and it was understood could conceivably still have further penances imposed.

Imprisonment could be used to intimidate: delays before the hearing or between one hearing and the next loosened tongues through the effects of boredom, uncertainty, detachment from family and the incurring of debts through the costs of imprisonment. After conviction, there was a sharp distinction between an open form of imprisonment with the right of free circulation and a strict form of confinement to a cell, low diet and, perhaps, shackling; transference from one form to another was possible, according to the prisoner's behaviour and willingness to give information. The wearing of crosses was no light penalty. Its size was precisely decreed and it could never be left off: it commonly humiliated the wearer and made it harder to get employment. From the sentence-book of the experienced early fourteenth-century inquisitor, Bernard Gui, it has been calculated that of 118 such sentences, the shortest period of wearing was just under one year, the longest over thirteen.

The yellow cross was part of the grand theatre of developed inquisitorial proceedings – yellow for the convicted, red tongues for false witnesses, a public beating by a priest at church, walking on pilgrimage to denoted shrines, above all, the *sermo generalis* in which sentences were promulgated or commuted in the presence of an assembly of the faithful, with churchmen and the lay power. Mercy was shown as sentences were reduced; the faith proclaimed by a sermon including an explanation of the heresy condemned; heretics turned publicly into penitents; the obdurate condemned or, in the contemporary phrase, 'relaxed to the secular arm'. The breach of the faith implicit in heresy was healed in a ceremony – order was restored in a great demonstration of authority, carefully orchestrated on lines laid down in handbooks.[40]

If the clergy and secular authorities did give wholehearted support to the inquisition, and its agents were given time to conduct thorough and repeated investigations, it was difficult to see that, armed with these powers, they could fail to eliminate a popular heresy.

The innovations of these decades permanently altered the circumstances under which the Church met the challenge of heresy. The initiative passed to the

---

40   See Lea, *Inquisition* I, chs 12, 13; Dossat, *Crises*, pp. 247–68; articles in *CF* VI. Given, *Inquisition*, pp. 52–90; comment, p. 65; see also *CF* XVI; G. G. Merlo, 'Il *Sermo generalis* dell' inquisitore: una sacra rappresentazione anomala,' Benedetti *et al.*, *Vite*, pp. 203–20.

Church. The enclaves of orthodox Europe, where in practice heresy had enjoyed a measure of toleration through ecclesiastical inertia or the anticlericalism of the secular power, were gradually eliminated. The decisions taken early in the century marked an end for the view, still sporadically expressed earlier on, that gave precedence to peaceful conversion and counter-preaching over repression. It was accepted that force was the correct answer, to be applied vigorously, and an apparatus was now in existence that legitimized its use and defined the offences against which it was to be employed. The phase of uncertainty that had characterized the eleventh and twelfth centuries now finally came to an end.

The counteraction of the Church affected the manifestations of heresy. In place of the open preaching and agitation of the twelfth century, we meet more secret missionizing and underground conspiracy. The emergence of the friars met for a time the demand for poverty and wandering preaching in an orthodox context. James of Vitry in his Life of Marie of Oignies popularized an ascetic way of life, wholly orthodox and committed to the sacraments. The development of theology and the diffusion of information about heresy enabled the seeker after truth to know better where he stood. The distinction between heretical sects and Catholic orders grew clearer.

Yet all was not progress: counter-attack against heresy was not the same thing as fundamental reform. Innocent III had always stressed the intimate connection between heresy and the failings of the clergy, and in some ways it was easier to welcome innovations in the religious life and to legislate for more efficient repression of heresy than to make reform prevail against deep-seated abuses or deficiencies in the Church. Grave problems connected with the numbers, selection and training of the clergy remained. The difficulty of the wealth of the Church continued, and was basic. The reforms initiated at the fourth Lateran Council had but limited success; response to legislation varied widely in different lands, stretching all the way from the English Church, where the council was the prelude to something of a golden age with a plethora of scholars and saints on the episcopal bench, to the churches of Spain, obsessed with the crusade in the Iberian peninsula, where the effect was non-existent. Innocent's own will to experiment with forms of dedicated life met an apparent check in canon thirteen of the council, which forbade new religious orders. Although its meaning was less restrictive than has been assumed,[41] nevertheless, given episcopal conservatism and the decisions of later popes and councils, the net effect was to make it harder for the Church to accept fresh religious movements in the future, and Innocent's immediate notion of communities of clergy for preaching and ministry under the direction of bishops was stillborn.

In the political sphere, Innocent's design for a settlement of the old problem of papal–imperial relations and the security of papal lands in Italy failed to hold: a subsequent struggle for power with Frederick II overshadowed the pontificates of Gregory IX and Innocent IV, began to tarnish a traditional focus for lay piety

---

41   Leff, *Heresy* I, p. 15, needs to be modified by Maccarrone, in *RSCI* XVI (1962), pp. 29–72; on James of Vitry, Jessalyn Bird, above, p. 99, n. 2.

through the misuse of crusades launched against the Hohenstaufen, and led the very popes who did much to raise the efficiency of prosecution of heresy, as we have seen, to restrain their agents wherever disturbances caused by the pursuit of heretics led to the risk of losing allies against Frederick.

The heavy conflict with the Cathars was not brought to a successful conclusion until the early fourteenth century.[42] Friars, inquisition, lay confraternities, the development of Catholic piety, and rising standards of education, together with the internal dissensions of the heretics, combined to bring them down, but only after great efforts had been expended. The Waldensians, though by and large less pressed than the Cathars, came under heavy fire in the lands of their origin on each side of the Alps, but compensated in some degree for their losses by wide extension of missions in German-speaking lands to the east and by finding refuge from persecution, both geographically and psychologically, through the erection of a camouflage of subterfuge.[43] These heretics lasted beyond the thirteenth century into the age of the Reformation. Cathars and Waldensians, the most notable of the surviving twelfth-century heretics, now demand separate treatment, and will be discussed in chapters of their own, with the intention of showing both the attractions of their life and beliefs that gave them vitality and drew in recruits, and also how each of the heresies fared under the stiffer pressures of a resurgent Catholicism.

New developments in Church life did not, however, bring a final solution to the problem of heresy. Reform by means of centralization and the growth of canon law raised standards in the Church; but, carried on against a background of inadequate communications and central bureaucracy, coupled with the strain of papal taxation and the Italian conflicts, it created simultaneously a ground swell of opposition, the potential seedbed of heresy. Above all, stress on law, when it was unfertilized by religious sentiment, aided the growth of formalism. It was no chance that 'spiritualizing' heresies, with varied roots but having in common a claim that their adherents were more 'spiritual' than their fellows, and a desire for escape from the routine of the medieval Church, its hierarchy and sacraments, grew more common as the thirteenth century wore on. What is noteworthy is that the heresies sprang more commonly from inner circles of Church life, and were not the heresies of 'outsiders', as were those of the Cathars and Waldensians.[44]

The very instruments of the Catholic resurgence that won back the initiative for the Church began to create heresy. The Franciscan friars, subjected to great pressures in their swift development from a small brotherhood to a large and powerful order with a leading intellectual role, fell into difficulties, growing in

---

42  Below, pp. 137–57.
43  Below, ch. 8.
44  For Cathars, below, pp. 121–9; Waldensians, above, p. 80; see also ch. 8 *passim*. There were few clergy among the Cathars, and hardly any of high rank. From the later thirteenth century Waldensianism is pre-eminently the religion of the small man; for orthodox Church life, see R. N. Swanson, *Religion and Devotion in Europe c.1215–c.1515* (Cambridge, 1995).

intensity from the time of the Council of Lyons in 1274 and issuing, first, in internal rebellion and then in true heresy, which was spread to the laity through the third order.[45] The inquisition's techniques, directed by the papacy and higher churchmen, could and did make heresy where none existed, imposing beliefs on victims who did not hold them, or, through interrogations under torture, exaggerating and distorting the unorthodox views they in fact held. So some disquieting features in lay mysticism and the views of a few deviant individuals, handled with prejudice, were blown up into the supposed heresy of the Free Spirit in the early fourteenth century.[46]

How these new heresies came into existence or were artificially created will be discussed after an analysis of the position of the Cathars and Waldensians.

45   Below, ch. 11.
46   Below, pp. 199–207.

# 7

# The Cathars

Catharism appeared to be the most powerful heresy of the thirteenth century.[1] Reaction against it by leading churchmen helped to change patterns of Church life. More than any other group, the Cathar heretics inspired alarm and hostility, and they stimulated the development of the inquisition; not only bishops, but also popular movements that were themselves under suspicion, the Waldensians and the Humiliati, felt the need to check their influence. A description has already been given of the factors in twelfth-century popular religion that favoured the rise of Catharism, and of the means whereby their early teachers found a platform for spreading their beliefs, blending their ascetic life with an existing movement for wandering preaching in poverty. A narrative account of twelfth-century heresy has described, in effect, the external reasons for the growth of the heresy of Catharism. It should now be balanced by an analytic account, intended to examine more closely internal reasons for its success, taking evidence without strict attention to chronology from varying points in time after the end of the first missionary phase in the early 1160s. Italy and Languedoc will be the prime sources for examples, since they were the regions where Catharism was most

1 Lambert, *Cathars* (*MLC*) (comprehensive); M. Barber, *The Cathars* (*BC*) (clear-sighted survey, distinguished by understanding of chronicles, terrain and nobles); Stoyanov, *The Other God* (inc. Catharism in survey of dualism); M. Loos, *Dualist Heresy in the Middle Ages* (helpful on Slav aspects, unduly bland on Cathar internal history); Borst, *Katharer* (*BK*) (classic, with historiography to 1950, reference sections on belief and practice: exaggerates effects of Nicetas) (trans. C. Roy, *Les Cathares* (1974); Id., *Barbaren, Ketzer, Artisten* (Munich, 1988) (trans. E. Hansen, *Medieval Worlds* (1991)); J. Duvernoy, *Le Catharisme* I: *La Religion des Cathares* (*JDR*); review, C. Thouzellier, *RHR* CXCIII (1978), pp. 218–25 (rejects hypothesis on origins), II: *L'Histoire des Cathares* (1979) (*JDH*), see esp. part 3 on Midi (knowledge of MSS, terrain), succinct survey on Italy, pp. 165–92 (sympathetic to Catharism, more suspicious than Borst of orthodox sources); A. Brenon, *Le Vrai Visage du Catharisme* (1988) (crisp, popular account, in sympathy with Duvernoy interpn.); G. Rottenwöhrer, *Katharismus* IV, 1–3 (*GRK*), *Glaube und Theologie der Katharer* (1993) (definitive study of doctrine); M. Roquebert, *La Religion Cathare. Le Bien, Le Mal et le Salut dans l'hérésie médiévale* (Paris, 2001) (thoughtful, well-written account including sympathetic analysis of *Liber de duobus principibus*, and relating problem of origin of evil to the twentieth century; opens horizons in his wide bibliography; insufficiently aware of weaknesses of R. Nelli as exposed in *GRK* IV).

strongly established and where evidence is readily available; though it should not be forgotten that Cathars were apparently well represented in Germany until the persecutions there in the 1220s and 1230s and that Northern France had a bishopric in the twelfth century.

## THE APPEAL OF CATHARISM

### The Status of the 'Perfect' and the Rites of the Sect

Any attempt to explain the attractions of Catharism must take the 'perfect' as a central theme. Numerically, these men and women, the adepts, were a small elite. Although in the time of prosperity for the Cathars in parts of Languedoc, when whole families became deeply committed and young adolescents adopted the status, there would be quite heavy concentrations of the perfect, as for example at Mirepoix, where there were said to be fifty houses of them,[2] it was still true that the perfect were few in comparison with the other classes of adherents, the believers and the more loosely attached sympathizers. On this small body of the perfect in normal health the drawing power of the movement depended and, when they fell both in numbers and in calibre, it was doomed.

Entry to the status was conferred by the ceremony known as the *consolamentum*,[3] which derived from the rite whereby the Bogomils admitted their adepts.[4] A first part of the ritual, the delivery of the prayer, possibly once corresponding to the *baptisma* of the Byzantine Bogomils, granted the candidate the right to say the Lord's Prayer, the rank and file supporter, being still in the domain of Satan, having no right to call his God 'Father' at all. A second part of the ritual (or separate rite),[5] corresponding to the Byzantine *teleiosis*, forgave the candidate's sins, and did away with the consequences for him or her of the fall of the angels from heaven and their imprisonment in bodies by Satan. At the Fall, it was believed, the angel that formed

---

2   Griffe, *Le Languedoc cathare de 1190 à 1210* (1971), p. 150. 'usque ad quinquaginta' – a rhetorical phrase.

3   *MLC*, pp. 33, 141–5, 189–94; *BK*, pp. 190–202; Rottenwöhrer, *Katharismus* I (in 2), II (in 2) (1982) (*GRK*) (full scholarly text of rituals, sources, criticisms of Church); dating of Latin ritual, *GRK* IV (1), pp. 35–42, doctrine, pp. 42–67, correction of Borst, p. 63; *consolamentum* (Latin), A. Dondaine, *Un Traité neo-manichéen du XIIIe siècle* (1939), pp. 151–65; Provençal, L. Clédat, *Le Nouveau Testament* (1887), pp. ix–xxvi; M. R. Harris, 'Prolégomènes à l'histoire textuelle du Rituel Cathare occitan', *Heresis* VI (1986), pp. 5–14; comparison, Dondaine, *Traité*, pp. 34–49; with other rites, *WEH*, pp. 465–96; origins, Hamilton, 'Wisdom from the East'; G. Schmitz- Valkenberg, *Grundlehren katharischen Sekten* (Munich, Paderborn and Vienna, 1971) (concentrates on Moneta of Cremona); Y. Hagman, 'Catharism, a medieval echo of Manichaeism or of primitive Christianity?' (PhD, Univ. Lund, 1988) (esp. rituals); history of dualism, G. Rottenwöhrer, *Unde Malum* (Bad Honnef, 1986); terminology *re* perfect, M.-H. Vicaire in A. Brenon, N. Gouzy, ed., *Christianisme médiéval* (1989), pp. 165–6; M. D. Lambert, 'Catharism as a reform movement', ed. Šmahel (1998), pp. 23–39; A. Brenon, *Le Dico des Cathares* (2000) (simple encyclopedia for reference).

4   Above, p. 63, n. 41; *LMH*, 1st edn, pp. 12–23.

5   *WEH*, pp. 465, 776, n. 4.

the soul of a man had left behind his spirit in heaven; with the *consolamentum* soul and spirit were reunited, and the soul passed out of the power of Satan.

The preliminaries to attaining the status were usually arduous. The candidate had to be approved by other perfect and have shown fitness to undertake the life by a year's probation, in which he fulfilled the fasts of the perfect on every Monday, Wednesday and Friday as well as during three penitential seasons – all on bread and water – and at all times observed the prohibition of the products of coition: meat, milk, eggs, cheese. In effect both candidate and perfect observed the dietary regime, made more rigorous by days and weeks of bread and water, of the modern vegan who declines any aid to life from the animal kingdom at all. The one exception to the rigour of this rule was the consumption of fish, which the Cathars, in common with many orthodox, believed to be the product, not of coition, but of water itself.[6] Naturally all sexual contact was forbidden and, especially in the last days of the movement, even the most harmless physical contact between man and woman was rigorously excluded.[7] If married, a candidate had to abandon his or her partner; if not, lifelong celibacy was the rule.

Sexuality formed part of Satan's creation. The angels imprisoned were sexless; in one of the most affecting of the dualist myths they wept when they found that the bodies in which Satan had thrust them were sexually differentiated.[8]

Once having received the *consolamentum* – or, in the contemporary phrase, 'having been consoled' – the newly fledged perfect faced a lifetime of rigid observance of the precepts of his life, made more exacting than the analogous life of the most ascetic orders in Catholicism by the incongruity with Cathar theology of any device for meeting lapses, such as the Catholic confession, contrition and penance. Every month the perfect of a community or locality held a meeting for the public confession of sins amongst themselves, the *apparellamentum*;[9] but this was reserved for minor faults, such as failure to say the requisite number of *Pater Nosters*, and was an occasion for mutual encouragement in the tense battle for perfection in their way of life. It was not used for breaches of the code of abstinence which formed the backbone of Cathar morality. These all ranked the same: it was equally serious, say, to fall by eating an egg as to indulge in theft or commit a murder;[10] any breach of the code involved the sinner once more in Satan's world, and lost him the *consolamentum*. It is not quite clear what did happen in the early days to one who had lapsed. Later a form was used for re-consoling a sinner; but it was a ceremony held in private, without the presence of the mass of supporters, and it was only allowed after substantial penance.[11] Standards were long maintained. Pseudo-Capelli, an anonymous controversialist from Milan, carries conviction

6   *BK*, p. 184; training, D. Müller, *Frauen vor der Inquisition* (1996), pp. 72–5.
7   Koch, *Frauenfrage*, pp. 108–9.
8   *Le Livre secret*, ed. E. Bozóky (1980); *WEH*, pp. 458–65 at p. 460 (Reitzenstein edn).
9   *WEH*, p. 466; *BK*, pp. 199–200.
10  Sacconi's *Summa* ii; Dondaine, *Traité*, pp. 64–78, D. Kniewald, in *Rad Jugoslavenske akademije znanosti i umjetnosti* CCLXX (1949), p. 104ff.; *WEH*, pp. 329–46 at p. 320; *MBPH*, pp. 132–45.
11  *BK*, pp. 178–96.

when he describes the short shrift given to a fornicating perfect: either he was ejected, or only re-consoled after a heavy penance.[12]

Breach of the code entailed loss of the *consolamentum* both for the sinner and for all those who had in turn been consoled by the sinning perfect. One fall could entail a chain-reaction. Sacconi, the Dominican inquisitor and former Cathar perfect who wrote a classic *Summa* on Cathars and Waldensians, comments, 'all Cathars labour under very great doubt and danger of soul'.[13] The reason was that no one could tell if a minister of the *consolamentum* had committed a secret sin. There was, in consequence, much anxious re-consoling as rumours of faults of these men reached their followers. All in all, the perfect in the heyday of Catharism walked a tightrope, carefully, even obsessively, maintaining a way of life that was intended as far as possible to eliminate outlets for the natural instincts, taking care not to eat the forbidden grease, ensuring that the proper gulf was maintained between the sexes, repeating over and over his chains of *Pater Nosters*, the prayer of the sect.

Yet this harsh way of life had its attractions. There was the sense of common endeavour among the perfect of a community. Capelli writes of the spirit which prevailed among the deacons of the sect in Italy and the Cathars who came to their hospices 'linked to each other by a bond of affection'.[14] There was, too, the appeal of being able to carry the burden; the analogy is with the monks of the Egyptian desert, competing like athletes of Christ in their austerities. There was the appeal of exclusiveness itself. Only the *consolamentum* saved; it was the sole means of escape from Satan's power. The perfect had received it, and, provided that he could maintain his footing on the tightrope and the minister who had given it to him did not lapse, he was assured of his return at death to heaven, or at least of progress on the chain of being towards it. How deeply the *consolamentum* was valued is revealed in a surviving MS of the ritual used in Italy, together with the major Cathar treatise the *Liber de duobus principibus*, on which one Italian perfect wrote three lines in cipher recording his own consoling, probably in November 1254; it was one of the great events of his life.[15]

In the world, moreover, there were immediate compensations. The perfect, except in time of persecution, seem never to have been withdrawn from society. If he held office he was continually on the move, preaching, administering the *consolamentum*, encouraging his fellow perfect. Thinness and pallor through fasting, the black robe put on at the *consolamentum*, were the outward signs and the uniform of his state of perfection; they revealed him publicly as it were for the admiration of all. If he or she did not hold office, then a house would be their normal seat, where sympathizers would visit them, for at least as long as the time of security for the perfect lasted. Their struggle for perfection was played out against a background of public respect and adoration; even in the underground years after the inquisition had got a hold, as perfect moved about secretly,

12   *WEH*, pp. 301–6 at p. 305.
13   Dondaine, *Traité*, pp. 69–70; *WEH*, pp. 329–46 at p. 336.
14   *WEH*, p. 303.
15   C. Thouzellier, *Livre des deux Principes* (1973), pp. 29–32; *MLC*, pp. 189–90.

they were still sustained by the devotion of a believer class who saw in them a race of restored angels, the one tangible presence of the divine in Satan's world.

Ritual and instructions for daily living brought perfect and adherents into contact on terms which highlighted the status of the former. The *melioramentum*, the greeting to the perfect which was often the first overt sign of involvement in Catharism and which the inquisition called 'adoration', conveyed the gulf between the categories and the aspiration of the adherent to be one day consoled. It was supposed to be given on all occasions of meeting, at services, or on entry to a house of perfect. Threefold genuflections and greetings to the perfect with replies culminated in the exchange – from the adherent, 'Pray God for me, a sinner, that he may make me a good Christian and lead me to a good end', and from the perfect, 'May God be prayed that he may make you a good Christian.'[16] This had special meaning; to be a good Christian, or a Christian at all, in Cathar belief was to become a perfect. To come to a good end was to die in possession of the *consolamentum*, not having forfeited it by lapse. In the exchange and the genuflection perfect and adherent reminded each other of their status, the one waiting, not yet freed from Satan, the other outside his power, in a unique position.

The breaking of bread, the ceremony preceding a meal, again gave the key-role to the perfect. The senior present held bread, wrapped in a white cloth, while the *Pater Noster* was said, blessed it and distributed it to all. Variously explained as an allegory recalling the supersubstantial bread of the Cathar version of the *Pater Noster* or as an imitation of the Catholic *eulogia*, a distribution of blessed bread, the act served to bring perfect and adherents together.[17] The bread was a reminder to the rank and file of the presence of the perfect; in time of persecution the fragments of the blessed bread were carefully preserved by adherents for later use.

Instructions for the saying of the *Pater Noster* kept the gulf between adherent and perfect. The Provençal ritual, one of the two texts of their ceremonies to emanate from the Cathars, refuses all place to the rank and file adherent: 'The office … of saying the Prayer should not be confided to a layman', it says.[18] Their role was quite passive; they would merely listen as the perfect said the *Pater Noster*. So the formal ceremonies supported the perfect in his way of life: entry to the status was hard, and preserving it inviolate harder still; but the conscious-ness of a unique position in mankind, reinforced by the attention of the outer supporters of his sect, would often hold him to his austerities. Belief reinforced resolution. The believer class could do nothing for themselves. Being still in the power of Satan, they could not pray; the perfect alone could pray for them, interceding for their salvation, a high responsibility giving additional purpose to their existence and providing an unceasing occupation, which may well have been underestimated by historians. A significant number

---

16   *BK*, p. 198; preaching is under-investigated: see J. H. Arnold, 'The preaching of the Cathars', *Medieval Monastic Preaching*, ed. C. Muessig (1998), pp. 183–205.
17   *BK*, p. 201 (*eulogia*); Manselli, *Eresia* (allegory).
18   *WEH*, p. 491, Clédat, *Nouveau Testament*, p. xxi.

of perfect, at least in the heyday of the movement, refused recantation and faced the fire. There was a logic in this. Perseverance brought near certainty of salvation, an end to the conflict with the body and its desires and to rebirth into Satan's world. 'The Cathars', it has been said, 'did not fear death, they feared life.'[19]

The appeal of the position of an adherent in the sect was of a quite different type. The great majority of the ordinary sympathizers would never go forward to receive the *consolamentum* in full health and so endure the *abstinentia*, the period of probation, or the restrictions of the perfect's life, though these were features which attracted them to the sect in the first place. Their attachment to Catharism was marked by attendance at sermons and by the performance of the *melioramentum*. A little deeper attachment might involve attendance at the breaking of bread and a more active share in the maintenance of the perfect.

The status of believer was something more. It is still not clear whether a formal ceremony was needed to attain the status. The Provençal ritual speaks of a believer who has had the Prayer administered to him, and the rite which precedes the administration of the *consolamentum* proper is styled the ministration of the Prayer. Was the believer, the *credens* of the inquisition sources, one who had passed through special training and had the right to say the *Pater Noster* though he had not yet received the *consolamentum* and was not one of the perfect, or was he or she simply a heavily involved supporter of the sect?[20] In the dark days for Catharism the inquisition classed believers according to their functions: of collectors, for the expenses of the perfect, of receivers, who gave them refuge, or of the guides, for the perfect making their way over the country in secrecy.[21] The matter is not clear.

But whatever the truth of the position with regard to the believer, it is apparent that all who were not perfect, whether fringe sympathizer or committed believer, had very limited functions in the sect, and could not have more so long as they were still attached to Satan's creation. In practice they seem to have lived in no way greatly different from their orthodox contemporaries, were married, engaged in war, and worked in various ways for their living. Logically, however, Catharism had no morality for them at all so long as they remained without the *consolamentum*. From this probably sprang the assumption of most Catholic polemicists that their morals were low, especially that they tended to sexual depravity and had usurers among them, who were unrestrained by Cathar teaching. Accusations of sexual failings tend to be commonplace abuse; evidence about usury is more equivocal. There may have been point in Fulk of Toulouse's drive against both heresy and usury in Toulouse, and investigation of the evidence for confiscations for heresy affecting Toulouse families has shown a significant minority of the patrician and wealthy class there were involved in

---

19   B. Hamilton, 'The Cathars and Christian perfection', *SCH* Subsidia XI, pp. 5–23 (illuminating comparison of Cathar and Catholic attitudes).

20   Clédat, *Nouveau Testament*, pp. xi, xxi; *WEH*, pp. 485, 491.

21   Y. Dossat, 'Les Cathares d'après les documents de l'inquisition', *CF* III, pp. 71–104 at p. 89; R. Nelli, *La vie quotidienne des Cathares* (1969). See P. Biller, 'Cathar peacemaking', *Christianity and Community*, ed. S. Ditchfield (2001).

Catharism. There does not seem to have been much appeal to the poor in the city. In general, some Cathars did retain wealth even as perfect. On the other hand, the practice of usury straddled the religious divide and leading business-men were often firmly orthodox.[22]

All accusations of sexual depravity in the Middle Ages need to be treated with care. Like any other group whose activities were secret, Cathars tended to be the butt of accusations that meetings were occasions for orgies, even when, in the case of the perfect, it seems least probable. So, *mutatis mutandis*, with the adherents. No doubt it was logical for them, sharing Cathar beliefs, to regard any sexual activity that did not issue in procreation as at least one stage better than bringing more souls into the power of Satan through childbirth: whether in fact they acted on their assumption on this point has yet to be proved. They may well have lived like the Catholics – or better.

One action was crucial for all categories of adherents: the reception of the *consolamentum*. The Provençal ritual, a late thirteenth-century text as it stands, includes a formula for consoling the sick.[23] The ministers are to inquire how the candidate has behaved to the Church and whether he owes it money; he is to be clothed and helped to sit up in bed. The rites of the delivery of the Prayer and the laying-on of hands are there, but shortened and run together; all that the sick man or woman has to do is to make the responses and promise abstinence; the absolute minimum is to be conscious enough to say the *Pater Noster*. It became part of the art of the ministers of the sect to time the administration well, so that the candidate could speak, but death would soon follow. If there was recovery, the Provençal ritual required another administration of the *consolamentum*. For the dying the austerities they promised were of little moment; the reward in escape from Satan was no less great than that of the perfect who were consoled in full health. Many more received the *consolamentum* in this way than through the ceremony reserved for those who had passed through the period of probation. The austerities of the way of life of the perfect were so great that it could never have been undertaken by the mass of the membership, and the deathbed *consolamentum* was the solution to the problem.

## The Social Context

Certain social factors intertwined with the religious influences to keep the elite in being and to draw in sympathizers. These can most easily be studied in Languedoc[24]

---

22   Compare *BK*, pp. 105–6 and R. W. Emery's review, *Speculum* XXIX (1954), pp. 537–8. See J. H. Mundy, *The Repression* (1985) on class of adherents, pp. 54–61, usury, p. 58 and compare his *Liberty and Political Power in Toulouse* (1954); sexual accusations, *WEH*, pp. 46–7, Manselli, *Eresia*, p. 201, *BK*, pp. 180–3, below, pp. 142–3.
23   Clédat, *Nouveau Testament*, pp. xxii–xxvi; *WEH*, pp. 492–4; Dossat, 'Les Cathares' at p. 83.
24   Griffe, *Languedoc, passim*; Roquebert, *L'Epopée Cathare* I. M. D. Lambert, 'The motives of the Cathars: some reflections', *SCH* XV, pp. 45–59; A. Cazenave, 'Hérésie et société', in *Christianisme*, ed. Brenon, Gouzy, pp. 7–61, suggests occitanian interactions between heresy and society (see esp. pp. 22, 34, 52–3; note A. Vauchez, p. 61). Brenon, p. 60, notes relevance of a 'familiarité' and 'solidarité' in occitanian feudal caste, aiding oral diffusion. A. Brenon, 'Les Cathares: bons

because there a systematic investigation by the inquisition from the fourth decade of the thirteenth century onwards elicited series of confessions from most of the key affected areas which go right back to the decades before the Albigensian Crusade when the heresy settled in. Italy is more problematical because really effective action by the inquisition came so much later in most cities, and thus the evidence does not relate in the same way to the time of the implanting of heresy in the last thirty years of the twelfth century. Moreover, the history of heresy in Italy tends to be more disparate. Each city has its own story.[25] Nevertheless, certain generalizations emerge for Italy and may be used as points of contrast.

In Languedoc favour by the rural nobility provided the matrix for Catharism. In the first generation of the implantation period men were more often the patrons, while their womenfolk seem to have been drawn towards the position of perfect in rather larger numbers. In the Niort family,[26] for example, the men began as patrons, and took to the *consolamentum* only in the course of the thirteenth century. A comparatively small number of supporters and actual perfect high in the social categories gave prestige to the movement; lesser nobility were thickly involved, and all classes participated. Certain areas of the country-side were most heavily affected but there was no gulf between town and country and movements of population carried heresy from one to the other and vice versa. Family influence is the most important single social factor, and here the initial impact of the Cathar missionaries on women in the *castra* of the countryside was decisive. Inquisition records build up a vivid picture of houses of women perfect, often only with a mere handful of inmates, but densely distributed across the affected regions in many of the villages where candidates for the *consolamentum* were trained, sermons were delivered to any of the locality who were willing to hear and common meals were held. From them the deacons and officers of the sect went out on their pastoral duties. A widow might receive the *consolamentum* and then be joined by others in her own house, which thus became a natural centre for the sect, or a single woman might be aided by her family; in other cases women left their husbands to undergo the probation. A good example of a noble lady setting up as a perfect is the case of Blanche de Laurac, whose brother Sicard had been one of the major figures in the rural nobility.[27] She received the *consolamentum*, and made her home a house of perfect; one son and four daughters were brought up in heresy, three daughters marrying and thus diffusing Cathar-ism at the adherents' level; another became a perfect and the son, after first supporting Simon de Montfort, went to defend his sister at Lavaur and was hanged for breaking faith with the crusaders. Blanche's grandson remembered

---

Chrétiens et hérétiques', *Christianisme*, ed. Brenon, Gouzy, pp. 115–70 (with debate) argues that interpretations by Dondaine and Borst are outdated (p. 121); I do not agree. But she conveys the nature of the appeal of Catharism, esp. in the Midi. On class, *CF* xxxiv, pp. 243–5.

25  E. Dupré-Theseider, 'Gli eretici nel mondo comunale Italiano', *BSSV* lxxiii (1963), pp. 3–23.

26  W. L. Wakefield, 'The family of Niort in the Albigensian Crusade and before the inquisition', *Names* xviii (1970), pp. 97–117, 286–303; prosecution: Kolmer, *Vulpes*, pp. 82–104.

27  Griffe, *Languedoc*, pp. 109–13; Roquebert, *Epopée*, i, p. 114; J. Duvernoy, *Heresis* xxix (1999), pp. 145–6, corrects *MLC*, p. 77 on Blanche.

living with her and eating bread blessed by the perfect. In about the year 1200 almost all the population of Laurac turned out to hear preaching and give the *melioramentum* to the perfect.

Houses of men perfect were formed in the same way, as in the case of the knight Pierre Raymond de Cuq, who was consoled in his house at Auriac and lived there with other men perfect.[28] But, although the houses for men were also of some importance, one may suspect that the quiet diffusion and implanting of heresy in families was naturally a woman's work, and that men perfect played their most effective role as the mobile ministers of the sect, bishops, bishops' auxiliaries, deacons, preaching, visiting, administering the *consolamentum* and, above all, calling on the dying to administer their *consolamentum*, which came to take the place of the Catholic extreme unction.[29] A territorial basis existed for their organization. Bishops took titles in an impudent imitation of Catholicism, but in Languedoc resided at rural places where they were sure of the protection of the local nobility, and not in the towns of their title. The *filius maior* and the *filius minor* were vicars of the bishops, and succeeded them at their deaths; deacons had their spheres of influence and regular residences. But all these ministers must often have been on the move. Officers had financial muscle. Donations, special collections and bequests buoyed up the Cathar economy, at least until persecution began to bite.

Noble or humble, a perfect lived cheaply, for the way of life demanded so little expenditure. But whereas the noble woman could live on her own money, together with gifts of adherents or family, those lower in society had to work, and so some houses of perfect engaged in cottage industry or trade: at Mirepoix they had a shoemaker's shop, at Les Cassès and Montmaur they made shirts and footwear.[30] Heretical influence was then diffused at the place of work or, as in the case of Pierre de Gramazie, who went to work in his childhood in workshops owned by the heretics at Fanjeaux, imbibed with apprenticeship.[31] A lord would expect his servants and dependants to share in and serve his ideology: Jourdain de Roquefort's bayles, his miller Guillaume Guibert, actively supported the perfect, doubtless because their master wished it. When another of Jourdain's men, Pierre Grimaud, pleaded before the inquisitors that he had acted virtually under compulsion ('quasi coactus'), he nevertheless found his excuse rejected and was sentenced to life imprisonment. Sometimes protection of the perfect out of duty could lead to personal commitment as in the case of Guillaume Garnier, who for years looked after the Lamothe sisters on the orders of the Auriol family of Lanta. His duty over, he fled to Montségur, served as a sergeant in its defence and at its fall chose to be consoled and face death rather than leave in freedom.

---

28  Griffe, *Languedoc*, p. 99.
29  Dossat, 'Les Cathares', correcting J. Guiraud, *Histoire de l'Inquisition* (1935), esp. i, ch. 7.
30  Griffe, *Languedoc*, p. 189; Cordes, Koch, *Frauenfrage*, p. 18n; A. Roach, 'The Cathar economy', *RMS* xii (1980), pp. 51–71.
31  Griffe, *Languedoc*, p. 189; status of weaving, *FK*, p. 95; combination of work and instruction seen as corner-stone in L. Kaelber, *Schools of Asceticism* (1998) (reasoned analysis of sociology of heresy), pp. 196–216.

The influence of heretics on children helped to make Catharism part of the background of life; Bernard Mir remembered as a child going in to a house of perfect at Saint-Martin-la-Lande and being given nuts to eat and taught to bend his knees to ask for a blessing, so being trained in the *melioramentum*. The strength of the personality of Garsen of Le Mas, a matriarch of the stamp of Blanche de Laurac, ensured that the devotion of the ruling family over years helped to induce a quarter, or perhaps a third, of the population to support the faith in the years before 1245.[32] Hospitality made contacts. At Puylaurens the mother of Sicard de Puylaurens lived with two of her sisters and another noble lady, all perfect, and men and women came and ate fruit from their hands. Families tolerated widely different views. In the Arrufat family at Castelnaudary the head of the household left his wife free to welcome both Cathars and Waldensians. Pelfort de Rabastens, lord of the settlement there, had a mother and sister who had been consoled. A witness described the easy contact between the family and its heretical members, as Pelfort's wife visited the heretic ladies; yet the same noble house produced Raymond de Rabastens, archdeacon of Agen and, briefly, bishop of Toulouse.

In a few places Cathar influence reached a peak. At Cambiac, for example, the curé complained that he considered all his parishioners bar four to be Cathar believers, at Caraman, Lanta and Verfeil about 1215 few died without the *consolamentum*, although as well as the heavily affected villages there were others where Cathars were a minority. Fanjeaux had a distinguished pedigree. Here in 1204 Esclarmonde, widowed sister of the Count of Foix, was consoled; it was long the residence of a leading perfect, Guilhabert of Castres, subsequently bishop of Toulouse; it made a remarkable recovery as the tide of war in the 1220s turned against the crusaders.[33]

The perfect often enough occupied in practice the position of the Roman clergy, being exempt from certain impositions and receiving goods at the death of their faithful. The creation of an atmosphere in which adherence to heresy was nothing abnormal, in which custom reinforced devotion, was a considerable achievement, and its effects were long lasting.

We may ask how far non-religious factors were at work in producing this result. Koch, the East German Marxist historian, put his finger on one factor when he described the social and economic forces influencing the women in Languedoc.[34] Koch put down casual meetings of the perfect and other women as if they were houses of *perfectae* and consequently exaggerated their number, but he was right to point out that these houses with their simplicity, openness and low costs occupied the place of beguinages elsewhere in Western Europe, providing places for

32  Griffe, *Languedoc*, pp. 125–6; W. L. Wakefield, 'Heretics and inquisitors: the case of Le Mas-Saintes-Puelles', *CH* LXIX (1983), pp. 209–26; Müller, *Frauen*, pp. 101–2; Roquebert, *Epopée*, V, *Les Cathares*, pp. 147–66.
33  Villages, Griffe, *Languedoc*, pp. 65–8, 95, 122–3; M. Roquebert, 'Un exemple de Catharisme ordinaire: Fanjeaux', *EO*, pp. 169–211; numbers, *WHC*, pp. 68–70.
34  *Frauenfrage*, chs 1–3; motives, pp. 14, 31; correction of Koch, Hanssler, *Katharismus in Südfrankreich* (1991), pp. 92–109; P. Segl, 'Die religiöse Frauenbewegung in Südfrankreich zwischen Häresie und Orthodoxie', *Religiöse Frauenbewegung*, ed. P. Dinzelbacher, D. R. Bauer (1988), pp. 91–116.

widows and other single women. Poor girls were left with perfect women. Jordan of Saxony, the Dominican, complained of the way in which parents put daughters into these houses of the perfect to be supported – and so, inevitably, to be drawn into heresy. It was a natural consequence of the acceptance of Catharism in certain localities. There were factors more specific to Languedoc. For the nobility, Roman laws of inheritance gave a place to women that they did not have in many other parts of Europe, and so made it easier for widows and heiresses to set up houses of the perfect. The life of the perfect might give meaning to a woman's existence, just because of its rigid duties of prayer and fasting; so might the use of her residence as a focus for missionary work and hospitality.

In ritual and status, Catharism offered certain advantages to women not to be found in Catholicism. No position in Catholicism, not even that of abbess, offered the status which accrued to a woman who received the *consolamentum*. The woman perfect, no less than the man, possessed the Spirit. If she was debarred by her sex from holding office and could never be deacon or bishop, she took precedence in any gathering over all supporters who were not perfect, whether man or woman. If no man perfect was present, she would lead the prayers. She was entitled to the *melioramentum* from all. It would seem that members of the nobility tended to avoid giving it to a woman, but no doubt those lower in the social scale did not.

Status might attract; the teaching about marriage and procreation on the other hand might, and sometimes did, repel women. The wife of William Viguier of Cambiac resisted her husband's pressure to make her an adherent because she had reacted against the Cathar teaching that pregnancy was from the devil. A mother, Sybil Peter of Arques in the days of Pierre Autier's revival, was told by a perfect not to feed her sick infant daughter Jacoba any more after she had been given the *consolamentum*, but when the perfect and her husband had left, she gave Jacoba the breast, to the subsequent anger of her husband. Humanity prevailed over Cathar belief. Careful statistical analysis from the inquisition evidence of the proportion of women adherents of Languedocian Catharism has thrown up the fact that men were more often *credentes* than women. That does not seem to be the position in Waldensianism. It may be that, for many women,[35] the utter denial of the value of carnal affection and family life which, masked as it often was in the day-to-day contacts between perfect and

---

35  P. Biller, 'The common woman in the Western Church in the thirteenth and early fourteenth centuries', *SCH* xxvii, pp. 127–57; *Registre d'Inquisition de Jacques Fournier* ii, ed. J. Duvernoy (1965) (*JF*), pp. 414–15; R. Abels, E. Harrison, 'The participation of women in Languedocian Catharism', *MS* xli (1979), pp. 215–51; J. H. Mundy, 'Le mariage et les femmes à Toulouse au temps des Cathares', *Annales* (1987), pp. 117–34; Id., *Men and Women at Toulouse in the Age of the Cathars* (1990), pp. 43–4 (underestimates role of *perfectae* houses); M. Barber, 'Women and Catharism', *RMS* iii (1977), pp. 45–62; A. Brenon, *Les Femmes Cathares* (1992) (inquisition evidence, vivid), review, M. D. Lambert, *Cristianesimo nella Storia* xv (1994), pp. 212–16; see also Brenon, 'Le Catharisme dans la famille', Id., *Les Archipels Cathares* (2000), pp. 205–26; *MLC*, pp. 148–52; A. Fössel, A. Hettinger, *Klosterfrauen, Beginen, Ketzerinnen* (2000) (survey, originals trans., fine biblio.); Müller, *Frauen*, pp. 56–129 (examines types of *perfectae* and *credentes*); *CF* xxiii; P. Biller, 'Cathars and material women', *Medieval Theology*, ed. P. Biller, A. J. Minnis (1997), pp. 61–107 (historiography in depth and inquisition evidence); Id., 'The earliest heretical English women', *Medieval Women*, ed. J. Wogan-Browne *et al.* (Turnhout, 2000), pp. 363–76.

supporters, none the less lay at the heart of Cathar teaching, worked against the movement.

There were varieties of response to Cathar teaching. Sometimes a religious passion is the only possible explanation for a woman maintaining the perfect's life, as in the case of Furneria, wife of Guillaume-Roger de Mirepoix, who apparently left her husband to live in a house of perfect women, went to Lavelanet, returned to take her daughter away, induced her to be consoled and finally fled before the crusaders to the fortress of Montségur. On the other hand, a recurrent pattern reveals immature young girls, consoled out of idealism and family influence, staying a few years then leaving and taking a husband.[36]

In Italy family links were still of crucial importance, though all our early generalizations are weakened by a lack of broad-based evidence for the years of initial infiltration. Certainly there Catharism had a less firmly territorial base. Whereas in Languedoc the historian can draw a line on the map – say from Marmande in the Agenais in the north down to the foothills of the Pyrenees in the south, and from Toulouse in the west to Béziers in the east – and be sure that he has included much the greatest part of the heretical activity in the Midi, and that all the heaviest concentrations within the outline are directly contiguous to each other,[37] in Italy Catharism had its supporters scattered in a multitude of cities, especially Milan, Piacenza, Cremona, Brescia, Bergamo, Vicenza, Verona, Ferrara, Rimini, Florence and Orvieto, in the countryside and along the routes which led from southern France to Lombardy.[38] Bishops, deacons and supporters kept in touch with each other through the network of communications established in the developed areas in the north and centre where Catharism largely settled, but the nexus was, in geographical terms, much looser than in Languedoc. Bishoprics, which in Languedoc were delimited territorially, in Italy generally were not. Instead, the dividing lines were differences of belief, which sprang out of Italian contentiousness and ingenuity and the greater proximity of Italy to the cradles of dualism in the East.[39] Personalities counted for more, and disputes were exacerbated by them. Bishops and deacons ruled adherents scattered over sprawling territories, with duplicate organizations at enmity with each other exercising oversight in the same cities.

Mobility was a keynote of the lives of many of those involved in Catharism, more so in Italy than in Languedoc. The merchant class, of greater weight because of the Italian economic development, was of its nature given to travel. Catharism had a hold amongst them and, to judge by the statistics of the goods confiscated by the inquisition in the course of the thirteenth century, some wealthy individuals were found among them.[40] Many of the lesser men in the sect, the artisans and pedlars, were also forced to travel by the nature of their

---

36   Griffe, *Languedoc*, pp. 148–9; Biller, 'Cathars and material women', pp. 97–8.
37   Griffe, *Languedoc*, pp. 18–22.
38   Dupré-Theseider, 'Gli eretici' at p. 11; survey of Italian Catharism, *MLC*, pp. 81–6, 92–7, 171–214, decline, 212–96.
39   Below, pp. 137–43.
40   Dupré-Theseider, 'Gli eretici', p. 17n.

occupation, and weavers and other cloth and leather workers were often enough footloose people.[41] There were significant links in the late thirteenth century between Catharism and the trade of pursemaking at Bologna.[42] The workers travelled from house to house and town to town making and selling their wares and at the same time making heretical contacts. Inns, workshops and mills were casual meeting places for supporters. At Modena certain mills were known in the late twelfth century as 'the mills of the Patarenes' (which by this time meant Cathars).[43] In other cases certain houses were known to be safe refuges for perfect who travelled about on their pastoral duties. Armanno Pungilupo of Ferrara said that signs were used which made it possible to recognize houses of the Cathars. Evidence given to the inquisitors provides us with glimpses of the blend of family influence and upbringing, casual contact and proselytism in which heresy existed, much on the lines of Languedoc. In Ferrara, for example, a maker of sacks had brought up his son and daughter to be supporters of the sect; they received instructions at home and in a neighbouring house, and were visited by a number of perfect. Aristocratic dwellings in the *contado* of various cities formed safe hiding-places for leading Cathars under pressure in the cities.[44]

In Orvieto the charged relationship with the papacy, ever conscious of the town's strategic importance by the road to Florence and the resulting frictions, was a seed-ground for heresy, coupled with a toleration which shrugged off sporadic attempts at repression and provided a shield for the religious appeal of the Cathars to exert its pull. Cathars survived the Parenzo affair, were strong enough to fire the Dominican convent and wound an inquisitor in 1240, and were only uprooted by an inquisition in 1268–9 which condemned 88 persons, living and dead, including members of the civic elite, lesser merchants, money-lenders and furriers. Amadeo Lupicini, whose body was exhumed, had been rector of the commune in 1266: it is hard to believe that his faith remained unknown to contemporaries. Networks of adherence based on family and occupation had held together over decades. Clientage was not important: networks were held by horizontal rather than vertical links. The leading class was a group of new and rising families, often interconnected, who benefited from the rise of the popolo. A committed follower, Stradigotto the furrier, was a guildsman with contacts through trade to the nobility and fellow furriers, one of whom he persuaded to go and listen to a perfect preaching and take salt fish to others in hiding. Bellapratu, widow of another furrier whose house had been demolished for heresy, leaving her in possession of the site in dowry rights, gave it to her son in return for necessities, probably as a means of evading confiscation should she

41   C. Violante, 'Hérésies urbaines et hérésies rurales en Italie du 11e au 13e siècle', in *HS*, pp. 171–98, s. 3.
42   L. Paolini, *L'Eresia* 1.
43   Dupré-Theseider, 'Gli eretici', p. 16.
44   Violante, 'Hérésies urbaines', p. 186 (Pungilupo; the sack-maker); for Orvieto, *MLC*, pp. 274–8; Henderson, 'Piety', pp. 70 (Lupicini), 61–4, 74 (Rainerio), 117 (rich and poor); Lansing, *Power* (rightly stresses horizontal linkage), pp. 66–71, 78 (furriers), 10, 66–7, 71 (Stradigotto), 9, 43–56, 60–6 (new families and popolo).

be convicted for heresy – as indeed she was in 1268. Such adherents were shrewd operators. But a full range of inhabitants were touched by the heresy, from the rich nobleman Domino Rainerio, who visited the perfect for counsel, to a household servant, and from a merchant consul to a cobbler.

Aristocratic patronage was important – the support, based on hostility to the Church, of Ezzelino da Romano and the marquis Oberto Pelavicino, for example, was of great value for the spread of Catharism in the regions of the March of Treviso and the Po valley that they controlled[45] – and developed into deeper involvement in a number of cases, such as those of Stefano Confalonieri in Milan,[46] Conrado da Venosta in the Valtellina,[47] and the Uberti of Florence.[48] But the carrying class, as it were, of Italian Catharism seems to have been the artisans and lesser traders. Two modern authorities, Violante and Dupré-Theseider, concur in this generalization. Although Cathars did exist among the major bourgeoisie, by and large the leading businessmen tended, as in Languedoc, to be conventional in religion. Members of the *arti minori*, minor commercial operators and artisans, were those most persuaded by Catharism, and the reserve areas of support in the cities seem to have been the suburban areas between the old walls and the new ring, built to accommodate the population growth of the twelfth and thirteenth centuries. Here the Humiliati and the friars installed themselves, and here, above all, the battle was fought out between heresy and orthodoxy in the thirteenth century.[49] The most insecure and dependent were not members in any great numbers; both perfect and adherent tend to be those who had at least a small competence. The unskilled labourers and the flotsam and jetsam of the cities were not numerically significant. Nor were peasants. Whereas in Languedoc the peasants were early drawn in, albeit in small numbers, by the patronage of the rural nobility, and then became more and more important later in the history of the sect, in Italy this class was missing from the membership, or from the records, throughout.[50] Evidence from the Austrian region, which includes Ivo of Narbonne's story of his wanderings and his long stay in Wiener Neustadt in what was then Styria, and the attacks of the Austrian poet Stricker on specifically Cathar errors, leaves no doubt that Catharism had a presence in this frontier province. Evidence is lacking, however, about the heretics' social background. The most that one can say is that the disturbances in Austria in the first half of the thirteenth century gave a good opportunity for heresy to grow there.[51]

The sect developed some intellectual appeal. Ivo of Narbonne reveals the existence of university aspirations; Alan of Lille knew Cathars who were capable

---

45   Guiraud, *Inquisition* II, pp. 447–51, 472–3, 534–8, 543, 545–50.
46   For the organizer of the plot against St Peter Martyr, see Guiraud, *Inquisition* II, pp. 496–8, 542–3, and Violante, 'Hérésies urbaines', p. 181 (note survey of Catharism in cities, pp. 179–84).
47   Violante, 'Hérésies urbaines', p. 181; see Manselli, 'Les hérétiques dans la société italienne du 13e siècle', in *HS*, pp. 199–202.
48   See J. N. Stephens, 'Heresy in medieval and Renaissance Florence', *PP* LIV (1972), pp. 25–60.
49   A. Murray, 'Piety and impiety in thirteenth-century Italy', in *SCH* VIII, pp. 83–106 at p. 86.
50   Violante, 'Hérésies urbaines', pp. 184–5.
51   P. Segl, *Ketzer in Österreich* (1984).

of using scholastic logic; Dominic's work implies that there was a challenge to be met by preaching and reason. Italy presented the greater menace, for Catharism had freedom to evolve over a much longer period of time; intellectual development was cut short by crusade and repression in Languedoc. Polemicists modified traditional assumptions about heretics as *illiterati* in the light of experience.[52]

One may ask how far it was the status of the perfect which appealed to the artisan and to those of lower class generally. The Cathar conception of perfection, attained through a set of tangible measures of abstinence and by repetition of prayers, appealed to the individual's sense of achievement.[53] Ascetic life was not, as in an informed Catholicism, a means to perfection; it was the sole means of salvation. The Cathar teacher could say without reserve to his neophyte, 'Do this; receive the *consolamentum* and you will be saved.' It was a part of the strength of the movement's appeal. How far did the rise in status, achieved by the individual's own efforts at self-mortification, entitling him to the *melioramentum* from members of all social classes and to a veneration from all adherents, appeal to those whose occupation kept them low in the social scale? Was this a factor which helped to hold to the way of life the apostles of Cathar Italy, Mark the gravedigger and his humble companions?

## Teaching

In all areas methods of missioning followed the pattern of the Bogomils: there was a pedagogic progression from the generalities, which seemed to blend easily into the contemporary religious environment, to the inner mysteries, reserved for the perfect or for believers of long standing.[54] The approach, natural to all sects of a gnostic character, had the effect of concealing the profoundly heretical nature of Catharism from the neophyte until he was sufficiently detached from the influence of orthodox belief.

Much proselytism was done informally, and in this all the perfect and believers played their part. Formal preaching, whether in houses, on ritual occasions or in the days of prosperity openly in public places in Italian cities and the villages of Languedoc, was more commonly a duty of those who held office in the sect.

But because of the overriding importance of the class of the perfect, from whose number alone the officers could be chosen, no duty was ever reserved entirely to these officers, and rank and file perfect sometimes preached – women among them, though never so much as Waldensian women preachers – their most likely audience being a gathering of adherents, not other perfect.

The nature of these sermons can be gleaned from chronicle and other accounts, from extant Cathar treatises, and to some extent from the text of the

---

52  Cazenave in *Christianisme*, ed. Brenon, Gouzy, pp. 51–2; use of Scripture and Cathar beliefs: Brenon, *Visage*, pp. 58–72; L. Paolini, 'Italian Catharism and written culture', *BHL*, pp. 83–103.
53  E. Werner, reviewing Borst, in *Byzantinoslavica* XVI (1955), pp. 135–44.
54  Manselli, *Eresia*, pp. 223–31.

rituals. Two principal objectives in the open preaching seem to have been to detach casual sympathizers from the influence of the Church, by playing on the sins of the clergy in contrast to the standards set down for Christian living in the gospels and epistles, and by using a particular Cathar exegesis of Scripture, together with unwelcome natural phenomena, to inculcate the belief that the visible world was evil; thunder, earthquakes, the existence of worms, toads and fleas, for example, were cited to show that the world could not have been the work of a good God.[55] Many of the world-renouncing texts of Scripture were pressed into service to show how the teaching of Christ and his apostles rejected material things. No attention was paid to the rules of exegesis: texts were wrenched out of context, and no hint was given of the precise meaning of 'the world' to the New Testament writers.[56] But the audience for a Cathar sermon would not be familiar with the rules of exegesis, and they would hear what would seem to them an exhortation by good men based on the words of the founder of Christianity and of his followers. Preaching was heavily larded with texts – at least, this seems a fair inference from the surviving Cathar treatises, a good part of which consist of scriptural references and quotations.

The leadership staked a claim to be part of the world of books and learning. At Le Mas in 1235, the Cathars promised a boy who herded cattle that they would make him a good scholar if he came to them; no doubt they hoped to train him as a perfect but his mother foiled them. At Labécède about 1236–7 a scribe and notary read the text of the Passion to a gathering in a knight's hall after which one of the perfect expounded its meaning, demonstrating at one and the same time the calibre of adherent which Catharism could attract and its ability to handle Scripture with all the solemnity of a priest in his church. At a solemn moment in the ritual a gospel book or New Testament was placed on the head of the candidate; both were also used in consoling the dying. Books and learning and possession of the Gospel gave prestige in a society of limited literacy.[57]

Much Cathar exhortation was, of itself, wholly orthodox and dwelt on the need for patience under persecution, a moral life and fidelity to Christ. Outwardly, the perfect were not readily to be distinguished from good monks or nuns. In a *cause célèbre* which dragged on until 1301 Armanno Pungilupo, of ascetic reputation, who had been buried with honour in the cathedral of Ferrara

55   R. Manselli, 'Eglises et théologies Cathares', *CF* III, pp. 129–76 (psychological insight) at p. 169.

56   C. Thouzellier, *Un Traité Cathare* (1961); *WEH*, pp. 498–500; P. Jiménez-Sanchez, 'Le "traité cathare anonyme"': un recueil d'autorités à l'usage des prédicateurs cathares?', *Heresis* XXXI (1999), pp. 73–100 (origins in pre-crusade polemics, important revision).

57   P. Biller, 'The Cathars of Languedoc and written materials', *BHL*, pp. 61–82. See (1) Thouzellier, *Traité*; (2) *Liber de duobus principiis*, ed. Dondaine, *Traité* (1939); Thouzellier, *Livre des deux principes*; *WEH*, pp. 511–91; (3) *A Vindication of the Church of God* and gloss of *Pater Noster*. T. Venckeleer, 'Un recueil cathare: le manuscrit A.6.10 de la collection vaudoise de Dublin', *RBPH* XXXVIII (1960), pp. 820–31; XXXIX (1961), pp. 762–85, trans. *WEH*, pp. 592–606; *Vindication* as catechism, A. Brenon, 'La Parole Cathare', *Actes du VIII colloque Jean Boisset* (1995), pp. 99–121; intro. to Italian translation, F. Zambon, *La cena segreta* (1997); revision by E. Riparelli, *Heresis* XXIV (2001), pp. 77–129.

in 1269, was finally proved to have been guilty of heresy and posthumously condemned.[58] Near Toulouse in 1234 when an old woman near her end desired the *consolamentum* the Catholic bishop got wind of it: he came in and spoke to her of the contempt of the world and of earthly things. Hearing him, she believed he was a Cathar, and confessed her heresy. The bishop had her burned.[59]

At a number of points orthodoxy and Catharism converged, and the likeness readily deceived the unwary. Some dualist teaching on Satan would have sounded like Catholic doctrine. The *consolamentum* administered to the dying must have seemed like Catholic extreme unction. In orthodoxy, it was not unusual for a dying man to be carried to a monastery before his end, and there take the habit: the practice of taking the dying to a house of perfect, which occurred in Languedoc, would have appeared much the same. The language of orthodox ascetic writers, discussing the nature of the world or the inferiority of the female sex, often came quite close to dualism. Even the practice of the perfect of saying chains of *Pater Nosters* was not unknown to thirteenth-century piety. The perfect honestly thought that they were the only true Christians, that the clergy were servants of Satan's Church; and that Cathar teaching presented a stream of pure underground Christianity, often persecuted, but always surviving and reaching back to the days of the apostles.[60] By a strange chance the rite of the *consolamentum* that appears in the thirteenth-century texts does seem to have been based on a rite for baptism and on practices connected with the catechumenate much earlier than the contemporary Catholic rites of baptism or ordination.[61] The adherent who witnessed these ceremonies was exposed to much that was wholly edifying and orthodox. Little wonder that many in the days of the growth of the sect were deceived.

One other element in proselytism is at first sight surprising in a sect whose inner mysteries made considerable demands on the credulity of followers. This was the appeal to raw scepticism. We have seen this in action in the Rhineland, where Cathars appealed to materialist arguments to deny orthodox views of the mass.[62] Heresy did not create this scepticism, which was of spontaneous growth,[63] but it latched on to it to deny this or that doctrine or practice of the Church. Catharism benefited from doubts cast on the validity of the Church's teaching, just as Bogomilism had done.

Introduction to the hidden revelation of Catharism came after the neophyte had received a grounding in dualism, and through rites and practices had had impressed upon him the vital importance of the *consolamentum*. The period of *abstinentia* before receiving the *consolamentum* was also a period of instruction when, if not earlier, the candidate was given more specific information on

---

58   G. Zanella, *Itinerari ereticali* (1986); *MLC*, pp. 280–3.
59   Dossat, 'Les Cathares', pp. 101–2.
60   Dondaine, *Traité*, p. 159 ll. 22–4; *WEH*, p. 477; see Lambert, 'Catharism as a reform movement', *Häresie*, ed. Šmahel, pp. 23–39.
61   Guiraud, *Cartulaire* I, pp. clxi–clxv; *Inquisition* I, ch. 4.
62   Above, p. 66.
63   Murray, 'Piety and impiety'; Dossat, 'Les Cathares', p. 78; cf. English Lollardy (below, pp. 301–5).

positive beliefs of the sect and acquainted with their mythology. Doctrines held in the inner circle of the perfect were sometimes denied altogether, as in the response of two perfect to Bernard de Montesquieu of Puylaurens in 1273, who was told, contrary to fact, that they did not believe that the devil created man's body.[64] For most candidates, entry on the *abstinentia* would have brought an end to this concealment: they could then feel the attractions of the secret revelation, placed, they would believe, in the position of the apostles, to whom Christ had said, 'it is given unto you to know the mysteries of the kingdom of heaven'.[65]

These secrets were concerned pre-eminently with finding explanations for the presence of good in a world which the neophyte had already been taught to regard as evil. How had the soul, which was the work of a good God, found its way into a body created by Satan? Many of the answers given by teachers in the sect followed, with variations, the pattern of the Bogomils.[66] Satan was a good angel, or a son of God, who fell and carried other angels with him, then created the visible world and with it bodies into which he beguiled the fallen angels.

A second set of explanations, however, was based on quite different assumptions: that there was an evil God, co-eternal and of equal powers with the good God, and that the Fall and imprisonment of the angels in bodies was caused by an invasion of heaven, which captured good angels and imprisoned them in bodies of the evil creation against their will. In this version the evil principle and his creation would never come to an end, although the good angels would be released from their prison; in the older Bogomil version, as in orthodoxy, Satan in the end was subject to the power of God; his evil creation would in the Last Days be consumed. The crucial difference between these views – the first moderate dualist, the second radical dualist – lay in the status of evil: did it originate with a fallen spirit or an eternal evil principle? Both views evolved in Balkan and Byzantine dualism, and were then transferred to Western soil. The first was the dualism described in Bulgaria by Cosmas the Priest and, with variations, in Byzantium by Euthymius of Peribleptos and Zigabenus;[67] the exact origins of the second view are still obscure, and all that we know with certainty is that it was brought into the West from Constantinople by Nicetas, the most influential of medieval dualist missionaries, in the late 1160s or a little afterwards.

Despite their profound differences, both views rested on the same conviction of the utter incompatibility of the body and soul. Both set the struggle between matter and spirit, good and evil, on which the candidate for the *consolamentum* was already engaged, within a cosmic frame. Belief in the truth of Cathar teaching

---

64   Dossat, 'Les Cathares', p. 38.
65   Matt. 13: 11.
66   *BK*, pp. 143–56; myths discussed in H. Söderberg, *La Religion des Cathares* (1949); Manselli, 'Eglises et théologies cathares' (sketch with psychological insight).
67   Above, p. 63, n. 41; *LMH*, 1st edn, pp. 10–23; on psychology of dualism, see *FK*, pp. 149–50, and *GRK* IV (3), pp. 277–383 (perceptive overall summary). A. Greco, *Mitologia Catara* (2000), clarifies psychology of myth-makers; myths are essential to dualism.

rested on personal experience of this struggle, and the exemplification of it in the perfect; the myths came to add colour and literary force, to give a sense of space to the daily struggle of the candidate or perfect, and to provide fantastic narratives for the adherents.

## The Stories

The raw material for the stories about the Fall and its consequences derived from a mixture of scriptural reminiscence, names and anecdotes, with much apocryphal matter, part from Jewish apocalyptic literature, part from ancient extra-canonical Christian legends still circulating in the Middle Ages, combined with the sheer imaginative power of certain teachers. Legendary material played a considerable part in medieval popular religion; thus the use of apocryphal material was nothing strange in itself. Scriptural fragments, incorporated arbitrarily to authenticate the stories, maintained contact with the central Christian tradition. The Apocalypse was a storehouse of images; the story of war in heaven and the fall of Satan[68] was familiar in the orthodox tradition. The teacher embroidered further on these themes with a dualistic bias. One direct importation was the *Interrogation of John*, or Secret Supper, brought from the Bogomils in Bulgaria who composed it to Nazarius, bishop of the Italian church of Concorezzo, about 1190.[69]

What the stories have in common, whether exemplifying moderate or radical dualism, is literary force, a tendency to gross materialization, an interest in sexual themes, and a strong vein of fantasy. The *Interrogation of John*, describing how Satan solved the problem of inducing Adam and Eve, angels imprisoned in clay bodies, to have sexual intercourse, depicts him planting a bed of reeds in paradise, making a serpent of his own saliva, then entering the serpent and emerging from the reeds to have intercourse with Eve with its tail.[70] The story echoes part of the narrative of Genesis, but embellishes it with some powerful carnal imagery.

The same literary quality and free play of storytelling emerges from stories of the Fall current in a last phase of Catharism in Languedoc. In these[71] Satan stood outside the gate of heaven for thirty-two years hoping to entice the good angels; once inside, he tempted them with the greater joys he said he had to offer in his own kingdom, including a most beautiful woman. Curious to see a woman, something quite unknown to them, the angels fell into Satan's trap, were inflamed with lust, and in crowds followed him out of heaven, until God closed the gap through which they fell. Satan then created a heaven of glass for them; but God broke it and the angels found themselves despoiled of their splendour, and deceived. They repented, and sang songs of Sion; to take away memories of their past, Satan shut them up in human bodies.

68  Rev. 12: 7–9.
69  Bozóky, *Livre*, p. 26; *WEH*, p. 465; P. Biller, 'The Cathars of Languedoc'.
70  Bozóky, *Livre*, p. 60; *WEH*, p. 460.
71  Summary by Söderberg, *Religion*, p. 73, based on versions as related to inquisition ed. Döllinger (*Beiträge* II, pp. 149–51, 173, 176, 186, 203–5, 213–15, etc.).

In some accounts the battle between Satan and his seduced angels and the forces of the good God in heaven took pride of place;[72] there were vivid descriptions of the flow of blood, the destruction of the seduced angels' bodies, and the fall of their souls from heaven. The sufferings of the children of Israel in Psalm 78 were taken as an allegory of this battle.

Sometimes a wild fantasy takes charge, as in the explanation, cited by St Peter Martyr and probably derived from an Italian group, of the Cathar prohibition of flesh-eating.[73] Beasts and birds, it was said, were of human flesh – the foetuses of pregnant women which fell from heaven on to the earth after they had miscarried during the battle between the forces of God and Satan. The prohibition of eating their flesh thus amounted to a prohibition of cannibalism.

Together with the stories of the Fall in all their variations, there was a vision of heaven not substantially different from that of orthodox popular religion, but sharpened by the utter contrast in dualist belief between earth and the heaven of the good. We have an example of its consolatory power in the case of a perfect from Languedoc related by a witness before the inquisition at Pamiers in 1321, who had been troubled by doubts about Catharism, and was rewarded by a vision, in which he mounted on the shoulder of an angel through the seven heavens to the presence of the Father, who asked him whence he had come. 'From the land of tribulations', was the answer. He wanted to stay, but the Father told him that he could not do so, 'since flesh born of corruption could not remain there', but must descend to the land of tribulations and preach the faith. The vision was of a southerner's heaven. He saw 'great brilliance, many angels, beautiful groves and singing birds . . . most moderate temperatures'.[74] The model for his journey through the heavens was an *apocryphon* of the early Christian centuries, the *Vision of Isaiah*, much used by the Bogomils. Such images were an especial aid in persecution, which was made more tolerable by the certainty of entry to heaven, provided only that a valid *consolamentum* was retained.

The stories obviously played a major role in Catharism, for members of the sect devoted much attention to retailing them and weaving new ones out of the mass of available material; a kaleidoscope of these poetic narratives, continuously developing through the history of the sect, has been bequeathed to us. Variations are accounted for by the different nuances of dualism, stretching all the way from the frail Satan of the Bulgarian *apocryphon*, the *Interrogation of John* (which influenced the moderates), powerless to act except at the will of the Father,[75] to the external evil principle of the Italian teacher John of Lugio.[76] Adjustments in the stories met the needs of different schools of dualism, developed within the Cathar movement by leading personalities.

72   *BK*, pp. 145–6; See Biller, 'Cathars and material women', pp. 90–6.
73   T. Kaeppeli, 'Une somme contre les hérétiques de S. Pierre Martyr(?)', *AFP* xvii (1947), pp. 295–335 at p. 330; Manselli, *Eresia*, pp. 226–7.
74   Döllinger, *Beiträge* ii, pp. 166–7; *WEH*, pp. 456–8. See Vaillant, reviewing Kniewald, in *RES* xlii (1963), pp. 109–21.
75   Bozóky, *Livre*; *WEH*, p. 459.
76   Below, p. 143.

Flexibility of myth was also a consequence of the sovereign power of the perfect in the field of religious belief. Inventiveness in the teacher was apparently prized. The language of the stories was that of revelation: Cathars listened to a teacher expounding mysteries that he knew, which were guaranteed by his personality and status, and which they were disposed to accept. The stories evidently met an emotional need – for legendary narrative *per se*; for an expression, it may be, of disgust with organic life registered in the sequences of coarse imagery of the stories; for a transposed sexuality, for an outlet for poetic imagination. Most simply, they met the needs of those who lacked much logical and critical sense, who were satisfied with the flimsy, partial argumentation of Cathars handling sacred texts, and who loved good stories.[77]

The liking for myths was the common possession of radical and moderate dualists alike; but radicals differed so much from all the schools of moderates that it is reasonable to assume that the attractions of Catharism were for them somewhat different, requiring a little separate treatment.[78] Radicals were dualists who were prepared to rewrite the traditional tenets of Bogomilism in order to iron out the logical contradiction they saw in the appearance of good in an evil world. Moderates, they believed, did not solve the problem of the origins of evil by their stories of the fall of Satan and his ordering of the world on the basis of an initial creation by God, but only pushed it, so to speak, one stage further back. The dilemma remained: how was evil compatible with the creation of a good God? To satisfy themselves, they postulated two creations, wholly distinct and equally eternal, and bravely followed out the consequences of their belief – two heavens, two earths, for example, or a life of Christ in another world, judgement already passed, Hell identified *tout court* with this earth. There were still confusions, and all was affected by the atmosphere of uncritical myth-making characteristic of the whole movement. The pressures of Catholic teaching and polemic showed up their contradictions, and led them deeper into difficulties, especially on the nature of Christ.[79] But in so far as the radicals were faithful to their principles, there were important differences of psychology and belief between them and the moderates. Radicals had to be determinists. Evil is not born of an act of free will, as the moderates and the orthodox believed. Satan, no longer the officer of God who sins by pride, is the agent of the evil God who penetrates the good creation. The good angels are incapable of sin; Satan deceives or forces them.[80] If radicals still made use of the myth of the seduction of the angels, this was an illogicality, inherited from moderate Bogomilism.

The appropriate myth for the radicals is that of battle in heaven and conquest by Satan. Captured in Satan's bodies, radicals could not tell whether they were the angels conquered by Satan but bound to return to the good creation, or the

---

77  See Manselli's comments (*Eresia*, pp. 212–13).
78  *BK*, pp. 143–74 (fundamental), Manselli, 'Eglises', 129–76.
79  See Dondaine, introduction to *Traité* and extracts from John of Lugio in *WEH*, pp. 511–91; *BK*, p. 122.
80  *CF* III, p. 147; on role of devil in popular expositions on confession, A. E. Bernstein, 'Teaching and preaching confession in thirteenth century Paris', *The Devil*, ed. Ferreiro, pp. 111–30.

devils of the evil creation who would stay below in the Hell which was earthly existence; only at death would they know. Yet, as is common in such cases, this did not prevent their enthusiastic adherents from sacrificing themselves and clinging zealously to their *consolamentum*. Unconsoled, the angel trapped in the body of a sympathizer moved on in a chain of existence. Souls wandered from body to body, stretching back to humble creatures and forward to distinguished and noble men, till they arrived at a body of a perfect. If indeed the soul was an angel, then in possession of the valid *consolamentum* after death, it returned at once to the heaven of the good creation. A sympathizer, on the other hand, was in effect rewarded by a step up in the chain; he would next be incarnate in a more attractive being. So, as a stimulant, transmigration of souls had a similar function to the orthodox doctrine of purgatory; penance must yet be done, but there was ultimate hope. Cathars speculated with pleasure on their previous incarnations. In Languedoc a perfect related how he had been a horse, and conveniently found a shoe by the road that he said he had cast in his previous life.[81]

For an evil life, however, there was the penalty of slipping back on the chain to a lower creature. For the devils there was the prospect of endless punishment in different bodies as the evil God and his servant Satan imposed through sexuality their penalty of life on earth. It was a picture of stark force, more gaunt and at the same time more logical than that of the moderates.[82]

It is obvious how deeply Catharism distorted Christian belief, for all the appeal to the Scriptures, made more effective by the vernacular translations kept by the perfect, for all the Christian language of their ritual and the texts which decked their mythology. As Guiraud long ago pointed out,[83] the true affinities of the perfect lay with the ascetic teachers of the East, the bonzes and fakirs of China or India, the adepts of the Orphic mysteries, or the teachers of Gnosticism. Cathar belief, just like Bogomilism, to which it was heir, upset the structure of sacramental life in favour of one rite of supreme importance, the *consolamentum*; replaced a Christian morality by a compulsory asceticism, which made faults consist rather in a soiling by matter than an act of will;[84] eliminated redemption by refusing to admit the saving power of the crucifixion; and rejected the Trinity in favour of a subordination of two persons to the Father. Cathars could not admit that Christ was God – an angel, perhaps, or a son of God, but still not equal with the Father. Nor could they logically admit that he was man, with a body like that of other men. So the hinge of Christian belief, the incarnation, was destroyed. Radical dualism went still further in its destruction of the pillars of Christian belief, and can hardly be regarded even as extreme Christian heresy. With its belief in two gods and two creations, it might almost be described as another religion altogether.

Yet these distortions of Christian belief would not necessarily repel the uninstructed Catholics, who largely formed the audiences of heretical preachers; the

---

81   *CF*, III, p. 142.
82   Emotions best conveyed by Manselli, 'Eglises', pp. 129–76.
83   *Cartulaire* I, pp. ccxxii–ccxxiii.
84   As in Bogomilism; see Puech–Vaillant, p. 261.

divergences from orthodoxy in all probability would not be apparent to them. The positive drawing power of the heresy lay above all in the life of the perfect and the status of the *consolamentum*; we have seen how the allure of these two drew sympathizers into the heresy or, less reputably, kept them in a kind of vacuum waiting for a deathbed *consolamentum*, and how the social context in Languedoc and Italy supported a heretical church organization. Dogmatic instruction followed on a process of assimilation of the sympathizer to the heretic's way of life, which excited his zeal and interest while detaching him from the residual influence of the Church, damned from the start as the Church of Satan. Myths entranced those of poetic imagination and limited critical sense. As churchmen generally complained, a committed Cathar had great immunity to the preaching and teaching which pointed out the difficulties and contradictions of his position. So Cathars were made and retained for their faith.

### Divisions and Decline

The fall of Catharism was as dramatic as its rise. From appearing to be a major threat to the Church in the early thirteenth century, it sank to a small, persecuted minority and disappeared altogether in the course of the fourteenth. To account for this we need to bring together the history of the Western Church and the internal development of the sect itself. To some extent this will mean holding up the members of the sect to another kind of mirror to that employed in the previous section in order to show, in place of their attractions, the defects and weaknesses of their position. It will also mean a shift in emphasis amongst the sources, making greater use of Catholic anti-Cathar treatises and summaries in addition to the information from chronicles, inquisitors' interrogations and the works and rituals of the sectaries chiefly used above.

We should look first at the history of organizational and doctrinal dispute within Catharism, which followed speedily on its emergence in the West.

Missionaries, refugees or traders, the dualists of the East who carried their beliefs into the heart of Catholic Europe and began the Cathar movement, also carried with them the religious and personal conflicts which beset them at home.[85] The enterprise which built up Catharism reached the records in the West in the 1140s; in the 1160s Nicetas, bishop of a radical dualist Church in Constantinople, arrived in Lombardy to confront Mark the gravedigger and the youthful Cathar mission, thus sowing the seed of dissensions there which ended only when the inquisition destroyed the Cathar Churches of Italy. Two sources inform us of the encounter. One is the work of a Catholic observer in Lombardy writing before 1214–15, who had access to details of the doctrinal history of the Italian Cathars,[86] the other is the account of Anselm of Alessandria written some fifty years later, reflecting the tradition of the sect, which reached him in his

---

85   For Eastern dualists, see above, p. 63; D. Obolensky, *The Bogomils* (Cambridge, 1948); Puech–Vaillant (esp. for nuances of dualism).
86   *DHC*; *WEH*, pp. 159–67; *MBPH*, pp. 122–7.

capacity as inquisitor, no doubt via interrogations.[87] Differing in detail, they agree in the importance they attach to Nicetas's visit.

The message of Nicetas to Mark and his friends was quite simple: the Church order on which they based their status was faulty. The earlier source makes extensive use of the Catholic term *ordo*,[88] which seems to mean the authentic tradition both of the *consolamentum* and of the orders of bishop and deacon in the organization, on the analogy of the apostolic succession in the Catholic Church. It was of profound importance, for without the true order Mark's *consolamentum* and that of his group was void, and they were lost. Mark heard the stranger from Constantinople with attention, and decided to accept his order, that of Dragowitsa[89] or Drugonthia, in place of his own, which was that of Bulgaria. The Lombard group were reconsoled, and Mark received the gratification of episcopal orders from the hands of Nicetas, so becoming the first Cathar bishop of Italy.

More was involved in the reconsoling than a change of order. Subsequent history suggests that with the order came the doctrines of radical dualism. The location of Dragowitsa (probably the original of Drugonthia and other forms) is obscure: the name may possibly have derived from the river Dragovitsa in the region of Philippopolis in Thrace, long a stronghold of the Paulicians. Bulgaria is clear enough. This was the cradle of Bogomilism, and its order represented the traditional, early Bogomil belief described in Cosmas and the moderate dualism of the mission phase of Cathar history before Nicetas.[90]

From Italy, Nicetas and Mark passed on to Languedoc. The journey is not mentioned in Italian sources, but the presence of both men is attested in the Cathar record of a great council held at St Félix de Caraman, a village in the Lauragais in 1167.[91] The record as we have it, which begins with the liturgical formula 'in diebus illis' customary in introducing historical passages read at mass, may well have come from a historical record of Cathar history of the kind which might have been used in the education of the perfect. In summary form it commemorates a mighty gathering, crucial for the history of the Cathars, attended by the chiefs of the movement in the Midi, a 'great multitude' of all their followers and the leader from northern France, Robert de Spernone. The north

87   *TDH*; *WEH*, pp. 167–70, see also pp. 361–73; *MBPH*, pp. 145–54.
88   Compare *DHC*, *AFP* xix (1949), pp. 306–10 with *TDH*, *AFP* xx (1950), p. 309; for diaconate, *TDH* in *AFP* xx p. 309 1.2, 'factus est Marchus diaconus'; for vicars of bishops, *filius maior, filius minor*, *BK*, p. 211.
89   Identification (hypothetical), F. Šanjek, 'Le rassemblement de St Félix de Caraman et les églises Cathares au xiie siècle', *RHE* lxvii (1972), pp. 767–99.
90   'Dragonthia' (*DHC*), 'Drugontia' (*JDH*), 'Drogometia' (acts of council of S. Félix) (Act. Fel.), below, n. 91; 'Dugunthia' (Sacconi; see Dondaine, *Traité*, p. 70), taken as corruption of Dragowitsa. On Bulgaria, Stoyanov, *Other God*, chs 4, 5.
91   Earlier work superseded by B. Hamilton, 'The Cathar Council of S. Félix reconsidered', *AFP* xlviii (1978), pp. 23–53, which slays an old dragon. It is, he believes, a succinct and composite record of (1) an historical account of the Council, (2) Nicetas's sermon, (3) an agreement of 1223 on boundaries between their bishoprics of Carcassonne and Toulouse. J. L. Biget in a *table ronde*, 'Evangélisme et hérésie', *CF* xxxiv, pp. 223–47, argues (p. 247) that the Council did not take place; J. Duvernoy comments 'Oh! là là'. So do I.

MAP 2  *Dualist Churches and the spread of dissension.*

suffered more persecution than the south, but it had been the source of dualist missions both to southern France and to Lombardy. The gathering covered the lands of Cathar evangelizing in the West. All listened to Nicetas and, we must assume, his attack on the legitimacy of the order of Bulgaria, to which they had hitherto belonged, and were reconsoled under the order of Dragowitsa, including Robert, leader of the mother church.[92]

Only one Cathar bishopric then existed for the Midi, which had the title of Albi, and lay near the site of the open debate of 1165 between Cathar and Catholic representatives at Lombers. Its bishop, Sicard Cellerier, was reconsoled and reconsecrated. His bishopric had most to lose by a subdivision and reorganization which Nicetas proposed to the growing membership in the south, and it was to the Church of Toulouse that Nicetas addressed a sermon, briefly summarized in the record after the description of the great council at St Félix. Nicetas, after referring generally to the customs of the Cathar Churches, went on to speak of the tranquillity, which, he said, prevailed among the dualist churches of Byzantium and the Balkans, and of the virtues of a territorial delimitation between dioceses. The implication was plain: that the Cathars of the south where the heresy was growing should divide up the lands where they had their strength into episcopal units. This they did. In addition to the bishopric at Albi, three more were set up for Toulouse, Carcassonne and, by a plausible modern hypothesis, Agen,[93] with the north French leader as bishop of their Church. After candidates had been elected, they all received their episcopal orders from the hand of Nicetas. In his sermon he had listed the churches of the East, starting with the *Ecclesia Romanae*, Nicetas's own, the New Rome of Constantinople, Drogometia (= Druguntia), Melenguia, the Church of the Milinguii in the Peloponnese, Bulgaria and Dalmatia (elsewhere called Sclavonia). They echoed the churches of Asia of the Apocalypse. With Mark from Lombardy and Robert de Spernone for northern France, the three new bishops in the Midi and Sicard Cellerier at Toulouse, the Cathars of the West had their bishoprics and a symbolism was complete.

No word was said in the text of doctrine but the sporadic evidence of the teaching of the Cathars after this date shows that they were radical dualists accepting the two-god doctrine.[94] Boundaries were settled but an international

---

92  *JDH*, p. 219 argues Nicetas did not disturb doctrinal unity; see also *Christianisme*, ed. Brenon, Gouzy, pp. 159–62 and illuminating art. by A. Brenon, 'Les Cathares; bons Chrétiens', Ibid., pp. 115–55. Both believe that a unity imparted by the common rite of *consolamentum* mattered more than doctrinal divisions. This is untenable in the light of purely Cathar evidence of dissensions based on dualism, epitomized in the *Liber de duobus principibus*. See *GRK* iv (1); fresh analysis, P. Jiménez-Sanchez, 'Relire la Charte de Niquinta, (1) Origine et problématique de la charte', *Heresis* xxii (1994), pp. 1–26, (2) 'Sens et portée de la charte', *Heresis* xxiii (1995), pp. 1–28. B. Hamilton, 'Catholic perceptions of East European dualism in the twelfth and thirteenth centuries', Id., *Crusaders, Cathars*, no. xv, traces spasmodic Catholic interest in origins.

93  Hamilton, *AFP* xlviii (1978), pp. 35–6, preferred to Jiménez-Sanchez, in *Heresis* xxiii, pp. 15–20 (spirited case for Val d'Aran); on Albi, M. Becamel, 'Le Catharisme dans le diocèse d'Albi', *CF* iii, pp. 237–52; dating, *GRK* iii, pp. 517–22; see *MLC*, pp. 45–59.

94  *MLC*, pp. 53–9; *GRK* iv (2).

gathering of this calibre is unlikely to have been held solely to do this: doctrine and *ordo* were also in question. Nicetas returned to the East, having achieved a notable victory for his Church and teaching.[95]

After some years another visitor from the East arrived in Italy with disquieting news. Petracius of the Church of Bulgaria came to tell the Lombard Cathars that Simon, who had administered the *consolamentum* to Nicetas (presumably somewhere in the East), had been guilty of moral lapses, including suspect contact with a woman.[96] If this minister of the *consolamentum* fell, so did all he had consoled; and again the Lombard dualists were lost.

This time there was no unified response: some supported Petracius, others vacillated. Accounts differ a little:[97] in Anselm of Alessandria the coming of Petracius shortly preceded the death of Mark, the first bishop, and the succession of Judeus (John the Jew). When Judeus took office, Nicholas of the March, ambitious to be bishop himself, raised a fresh doubt: had Mark himself made a good end? Were the orders of Judeus valid? For the anonymous writer of the early thirteenth century, it was simply Petracius's story that troubled the consciences of the Lombards and resulted in the formation of two parties: that for Judeus and that against him, led by a certain Peter of Florence.

The Cathars yet felt their need of unity, and after a time sought advice from a Cathar bishop outside Italy, who recommended reconciliation by election and the drawing of lots: each party should choose a candidate from the other, and chance should then decide between them.[98] At Mosio, between Mantua and Cremona, they held a council, and Garattus emerged as the bishop accepted by all. But, according to the anonymous writer, just as Garattus was preparing to go in search of an undoubted *consolamentum* from the Church of Bulgaria and collection was being made for his expenses, he was discovered in reprehensible circumstances with a woman.[99] With that, all attempt at unity foundered.

Now others were despatched to find a foolproof *consolamentum*. From the Church of Bagnolo, with its centre in or near Mantua, Caloiannes went to the Church of Sclavonia, a group of moderate dualists in the predominantly Catholic coastal strip of Dalmatia converted to heresy by merchants trading from Constantinople;[100] from Vicenza Nicholas went to the same destination. Judeus, who had humbly resigned office before Mosio to create unity, was next persuaded to take office again as bishop of the Church based on Mark's birthplace at Concorezzo near Milan and to go himself to Bulgaria as a necessary preliminary to

95   *BK*, pp. 98, 108, 142; Borst sees Nicetas's journeys as fatal to Catharism.
96   *DHC* in *AFP* xix (1949), p. 306.
97   Compare *DHC* (Ibid.) to *TDH* in *AFP* xx (1950), p. 309; *DHC* is nearer events.
98   *DHC* in *AFP* xix (1949), p. 306, l. 22 to p. 307, l. 3. Emissaries are sent to a bishop 'ultra montes', who recommends the successful candidate to go to Bulgaria, i.e. to a moderate dualist Church. If Languedoc is radical dualist, who can this be?, asks R. I. Moore (*AM* lxxxv (1973), p. 87); Hamilton (*AFP* xlviii (1978), p. 73) argues for the bishop of Northern France, source of mission to Italy, whose Church had reverted to moderate dualism.
99   'garattus... duobus testibus astantibus, reprehensibilis, causa unius mulieris, habitus est' (*DHC*, in *AFP* xix, p. 307, ll. 35–6).
100  Identification of Sclavonia in *TDH* (*AFP* xx, p. 308, ll. 11–14).

get a valid order. Garattus, though at first subdued, remained a force to be reckoned with and later on seems to have made his own pilgrimage to Bulgaria. From the same misty land came the Bogomil *apocryphon*, the *Interrogation of John*, brought to Nazarius of the Church of Concorezzo.[101] Other Churches came into existence at Florence and the Val del Spoleto; here and probably elsewhere local patriotism played a part.

Thus on the ruins of Mark's original mission there emerged six separate Cathar Churches in Italy, with competing adherents scattered widely, but generally linked together by common belief and order; map 2 shows the distribution of their geographical centres as well as the journeys which fostered or accompanied their growth, from East to West the fateful movements of Nicetas and Petracius, from West to East the quest of Western Cathars for the authentic *consolamentum*.

Accounts of the Italian conflicts are retailed to us by hostile witnesses who were not displeased at the discomfiture of the heretics. It is difficult to know what to make of the sexual scandals which punctuate this history. Libertinism was an element in Gnostic heresy; from the tenet that all matter is evil and contact with it, including sexual relations, is to be condemned, it is possible to adopt another position, that for the elect, who have freed themselves from the taint of matter, it has become wholly indifferent whether they engage in sexual relations or not. They are, so to speak, beyond sin, and the rules which must be observed by neophytes no longer apply to them. This was the teaching of the Byzantine heresy of the Messalians, who believed that their initiates, after training and self-denial and the expulsion of the demon in every man's heart, could indulge or not as they pleased, wholly without sin in either case.[102] But there is little sign of libertinism on principle in the Cathars, to judge by the testimony of the inquisition or the evidence of the response of congregations at this stage to news of the fall of this or that perfect. Philip, bishop of Desenzano, was said by Anselm of Alessandria to have disseminated the maxim that there was no sin for man or woman below the girdle, and to have gained followers on the strength of it.[103] The story may have been slander. More significant was the statement of Sacconi from his own experience that perfect regretted not having taken more advantage of the sexual freedom of the believer before they received the *consolamentum*.[104] In the last resort, however, we need assume no more than the commonsense view, that some perfect did fall, as did many among the Catholic clergy, and that the hypersensitivity and rigidity of the Cathars over the *consolamentum* tended to exaggerate any genuine failing, and may even have led to the invention of others. The libertine in the days of vitality of the sect was very much the exception.[105]

---

101   Above, p. 133, n. 69; *JDR*, p. 108, n. 15 (corrects historians).
102   Obolensky, *Bogomils*, pp. 48–52.
103   *TDH*, in *AFP* xx, p. 310, ll. 3–4; cited as hearsay ('dicitur').
104   Dondaine, *Traité*, p. 66.
105   See pseudo-Capelli's evidence, above, pp. 117–18.

Personal conflicts, anxiety over the *consolamentum* and local patriotism all made the Italians a prey to dissensions imported from the East. Their intellectual activity perpetuated the doctrinal divisions and created others; differences of belief continued a disunity, in contrast to the relative stability of the territorially based and less speculative Church of Languedoc.[106] Dossat finds only one instance of an adherent in Languedoc refusing contact with another because of a doctrinal difference.[107]

In Italy the doctrinal quarrels continued after the disintegration into separate Churches, fed by the struggles of leading perfect against each other, and by the pressures of rational reflection or of the example and polemic of the orthodox. The most profound division was that which lay between the radical dualists of Desenzano and the moderates; the Churches which accepted the order of Sclavonia occupied a middle ground between them and the traditional Bogomilism of Bulgaria. Especially significant are the efforts in the thirteenth century of two Cathars on opposite wings of the movement to put their beliefs on a more rational footing. Desiderius, *filius maior* of the Church of Concorezzo, tried to do away with the influence of the *apocrypha*, and taught that the texts of Scripture on marriage were to be interpreted literally for the adherents of the sect, so providing them with a conventional sexual framework.[108] He acknowledged that Christ did have a human body. John of Lugio, probably originally of the Church of Desenzano, and his followers took the opposite view and taught that dualism of the moderate kind could not be defended, any more than Catholicism, and that the only logical answer to the problem of evil was a thoroughgoing radical dualism, given philosophical justification in the Book of Two Principles from their school, the most considerable intellectual achievement of any Cathar. Yet it was a sign that Italian Cathars were beginning to feel the force of Catholic polemic.[109]

The evidence suggests that the Cathars began with a stress on evangelical life in the twelfth century, and came in time to devote more and more attention to dualist beliefs, which at first had remained in the background. Catholic counter-attack constantly stressed dualism, aiming to show the wavering faithful that Catharism, so far from being a movement of reform and asceticism, was in

---

106   B. Hamilton accepts a conversion to radical dualism after the visit of Nicetas, and believes that there was an attempt by Bartholomew of Carcassonne in the aftermath of the Albigensian Crusade to win back ground for the moderate dualists in the diocese of Agen, but that this was short-lived (*AFP* XLVIII (1978), pp. 44–8). A. Brenon, 'Les Cathares', pp. 161–2, argues against a conversion of the Cathar leadership in Languedoc to radical dualism at the hands of Nicetas, citing the abjurations of moderate dualism by Raimon de Baimiac and his *socius* after the capture of Lavaur, and accepts, rather, a gradual move to radical dualism as a result of logical reflection (see also pp. 131–40). See also Brenon, *Archipels*.

107   *CF* III, 79.

108   *TDH*, in *AFP* XX, pp. 310–12, tr. in *WEH*, pp. 362–4; *MBPH*, p. 149. *BK*, p. 122.

109   *GRK* IV (1), pp. 211–79, supersedes all others. A. Reltgen, 'Dissidences et contradictions en Italie', *Christianisme*, ed. Brenon, Gouzy, pp. 89–109 (debate, pp. 110–13), discusses Cathar innovations as sign of weakness in face of vitality of Catholics in thirteenth century; see esp. pp. 92–4, 104–9. See also Zanella, *Itinerari eretical*i, pp. 29–45. *GRK* IV (2) shows *Diprinzipialismus* (preferred term for radical dualism) was dominant in Languedoc.

fact a heresy which denied fundamental doctrines of Christianity: their polemic forced the Cathars to think more about their dualism, and drew it out of the shadows.[110]

Both John of Lugio and Desiderius were attempting in their different ways to update Catharism in response to new needs and more effective attacks. Neither could impart a new direction to the heresy, though both attracted followers. Desiderius battled against his bishop Nazarius, a weaver of fantasies of the old school, and split the Church of Concorezzo; John of Lugio could not move older adherents but did reach some members of the younger generation of Cathars. The majority of the Italian Cathars were not deeply interested: they liked their *apocrypha* and their myths, for all their internal contradictions.[111] But where Desiderius and John of Lugio and their disciples had been impelled to rethink their position by the force of a revived and better informed Catholicism, we may assume others outside Catharism had been influenced against the movement altogether. Orthodox polemic and the preaching and argument based on it would not necessarily detach existing adherents[112] but it warned others against being drawn into heresy. Borst is surely right to see in the work of these two a symptom of decline.

Meanwhile, repression of heresy, first in Languedoc, then in Italy, grew more effective. The political situation decided the extent to which legislation against heresy was actually effective. In Languedoc, Innocent III's crusade at first threw the Cathars into disarray and scattered their communities. Numbers of perfect were killed as a by-product of operations, but the organization re-formed and continued to work, albeit with diminished numbers. In 1225, indeed, they held a council at Pieusse and decided to set up a new diocese at Razès.[113] The brutalities of the crusade inhibited the work of re-conversion of Bishop Fulk of Toulouse and St Dominic. Civic patriotism in Toulouse and the attitudes of the Midi generally, with its traditional toleration and penchant for political balancing, weakened the cause of orthodoxy. But the ending of warfare and the surrender of the count of Toulouse at the Treaty of Paris in 1229 opened the way to effective persecution. It descended like a storm on the minority of leading families and their supporters in Toulouse who had been involved in Catharism; between 1229 and 1237 the backbone of heresy in the city was broken; from mid-century Toulouse ceased to be significant in the history of Catharism. The Council of Toulouse in 1229 set the scene for persecution, systematizing existing canonical decisions, giving confirmation to a pre-existing development in the Midi of the synodal witnesses of the *Ad abolendam* era into a form of police specializing in heresy and fore-shadowing the mass investigations by inquisitors proper by its injunctions to the gathering of oaths of fidelity to the Church and the making of full lists of parishioners. A network for supervision was to be created, that would easily throw into focus any deviation from Catholic observance. Bailiffs were to be

---

110   Vicaire, 'Les Cathares', *CF* III, pp. 105–28.
111   Manselli (*Eresia*, p. 272 and n. 41) preferred to Dondaine, 'La hiérarchie', *AFP* xx, p. 274.
112   Implied in Manselli, *Eresia*, ch. 9; compare Vicaire, 'Les Cathares', pp. 122–3.
113   But note Wakefield's comment, *WEH*, p. 132.

St Lieux-les-Lavaur

Agout

0          10 miles
0          16 km

**Lavaur**

Girou

**Lavaur**   Places of origin of heretics
sentenced March–July 1246

• Massac

St Sauveur •

**St Paul-** •
**Cap-de-Joux**   Guitalens

• Gauré   Veilhes •

**Drémil** •    Saussens   Maurens
Valesvilles •     • **Cambon**     Saix •
St Anatoly •        Viviers-les
**Lanta** •   **Prunet**     • Puylaurens   Montagnes

Saune

Vendinelle

• Ste Foy d'Aigrefeuille     • Montespieu

**Odars** •   • Préserville   **Auriac** •

Fourquevaux    Nogaret
Tarabel
Labastide-de-Beauvoir   **Cambiac**   St Julia
**Montgiscard**   • Varennes    • **Montégut**
Maurémont   • Maurens
Bazièҫe   **Goudourville**   **St Germier**   • **Roumens**
Villenouvelle •   • Trebons • **Juzes**   • St Félix
   • Montgaillard    • Dreuilhe

**Montesquieu** •   **Lavelanet**   **• Les Cassés** • Vaudreuille

Gardouch •   **Barelles**   • Folcarde   **• St Paulet** • La Pomarède
Renneville •   Pechbertier   **• Montmaur**   • Labécède
**Avignonet**   Montferrand
Lagarde •   **Airoux**   • Issel   • Verdun
**Beauteville**       • Villemagne
St Michel-de-Lanès •   **• Baraigne**

**• Gibel**   Cumiès •   **Le Mas-**   **• Castelnaudary**
**Saintes-Puelles**   **St Martin-la-Lande**
Lasbordes •
**• Villeneuve-**   **• Villepinte**
**Montauriol**   **la-Comtal**   **• Pexiora**
Mireval- •   Fresquel
Peyrefitte •   Lauragais
Mayreville •   **• Bram**
**• Laurac**   **• Villesiscle**

Hers mort

Hers vif

Ariège

Generville •
**Gaja-la-Selve** •   • Cazalrenoux
     **• Fanjeaux**
Vixiège
Barsa
Blazens •   • Plaigne

MAP 3   *Inquisition versus Catharism: the enquiries of 1245–6.*
*Source*: Adapted from Y. Dossat, *Les Crises de l'inquisition toulousaine au* XIII*e siècle (1233–1273)* (Bordeaux, 1959), pp. 228–9.

coerced into cooperation.[114] It was not wholly effective, for Count Raymond VII in the 1230s was still acting equivocally and his servants gave only partial support to repression. The first commissions of Gregory IX to Dominicans to exercise authority in 1233 put into action some of the most formidable instruments of repression; but they were not all at once successful. The Dominicans were even driven out of Toulouse for a time in 1235, and in 1238 Gregory IX, who wished to detach Raymond from support of Frederick II, met the count's wishes and virtually suspended the tribunal based on Toulouse for three years. But time favoured repression, and a mechanism for pursuing heresy grew in efficiency.

In the country the years 1240 to 1243 were the turning-point.[115] Peter Seila, Dominican, former companion of St Dominic, who had campaigned earlier as inquisitor in Quercy with moderate success, achieved much more in a second inquisition of 1241–2, in which more suspects availed themselves of the time of grace at the opening of inquiries to make their confessions of heresy. Fear had grown of the reality of punishment to follow conviction. The tide had begun to turn. Two vain revolts showed the southern nobles that they would never regain independence by force; and the killing of a party of inquisitors at Avignonet aroused determination to scotch the heresy. The murder had been organized from Montségur, a castle in the foothills of the Pyrenees long a refuge for perfect and their supporters; an army under a royal seneschal besieged and took it and in March 1244 handed over to the Church two hundred or more perfect, including the bishops of Toulouse and Razès. The Cathars of the south never recovered from the loss of so many of the elite. At the same time Raymond abandoned his policy of equivocal support, and began to persecute. In 1249, with less discrimination than the inquisitors, he burnt eighty suspects at Agen in one day. His successor Alphonse of Poitiers, brother of King Louis IX and a cold zealot, was unusually energetic in persecution.[116]

In fact, for the majority of the southern higher nobility, the Cathars had always been negotiable. The wars had been fought over the control of the south, not over heresy, and Raymond VII was characteristic of most of the higher nobility in being ready to throw the heretics over when it was politically expedient to do so. Once the struggle for control of Languedoc was decided, the heretics found few important defenders. There were great conspiracies, both of silence and of action, including a plot to steal inquisition records at Carcassonne and the murder of inquisitors' assistants at Caunes.[117] Nevertheless, from 1243, the writing was on the wall.

114    On persecution in Toulouse, see Mundy, *Repression*; on Council of Toulouse, see Kolmer, *Vulpes*, pp. 64–78.

115    *WHC*, ch. 10; Dossat, *Crises*, pp. 271–5.

116    Seila: Kolmer, *Vulpes*, pp. 150–62; *BC*, pp. 150–8; Roquebert, *Epopée* IV; Id., 'Montségur, refuge ou quartier général?', *PC*, pp. 159–92.

117    J. L. Biget, 'L'extinction du Catharisme urbain: les points chauds de la répression', *CF* XX, pp. 305–40; W. L. Wakefield, 'Friar Ferrier, inquisition at Caunes and escapes from prison at Carcassonne', *CHR* LVIII (1972), pp. 220–37; Given, *Inquisition*, pp. 100–10; A. Friedlander, 'Les agents du roi', *CF* XX, pp. 199–220.

Why, given the final defeat of the indigenous baronage of Languedoc, this should have been so may be illustrated by examining the inquisitors of the region at the top of their form in the inquiries of Bernard de Caux and his aides in the region of the Lauragais and the neighbourhood of Lavaur in 1245–6.[118] In these investigations 5,471 persons in two archdeaconries were interrogated. Suspects brought to light were to an overwhelming degree Cathars; only forty-one references are to be found to Waldensians. Questions were of the police-court type, concerned with the external acts such as adoration, which revealed complicity with heresy; only marginally did they deal with belief. Each adult in the communities shown on map 3 was compelled to answer. If a suspect broke down under interrogation, others would follow; lies were uncovered by cross-checking. Pacts of secrecy were uncovered. Five more inquiries were launched in this region. In 1260 the record of the original investigation was recopied.

TABLE 1    *Sentences of Bernard de Caux, 1246*

| Community | Prison | Crosses and other penances | Community | Prison | Crosses and other penances |
|---|---|---|---|---|---|
| Airoux | 0 | 1 | Le Mas-Saintes-Puelles | 0 | 8 |
| Auriac | 0 | 4 | Les Cassés | 1 | 3 |
| Avignonet | 0 | 11 | Montauriol | 0 | 1 |
| Baraigne | 0 | 3 | Montégut | 0 | 3 |
| Barelles | 3 | 3 | Montesquieu-Lauragais | 0 | 7 |
| Beauteville | 0 | 2 | Montgiscard | 1 | 4 |
| Bram | 0 | 3 | Montmaur | 0 | 2 |
| Cambiac | 1 | 4 | Odars | 0 | 1 |
| Cambon | 0 | 4 | Pexiora | 0 | 5 |
| Castelnaudary | 0 | 8 | Prunet | 0 | 1 |
| Drémil | 0 | 1 | Roumens | 1 | 4 |
| Fanjeaux | 3 | 25 | Saint-Germier | 0 | 1 |
| Gaja-le-Selve | 0 | 1 | Saint-Julia | 0 | 1 |
| Gibel | 0 | 1 | Saint Martin-la-Lande | 7 | 19 |
| Goudourville | 1 | 2 | Saint-Paul-Cap-de-Joux | 0 | 1 |
| Juzes | 0 | 2 | Saint-Paulet | 1 | 1 |
| Lanta | 0 | 1 | Villeneuve-la-Comtal | 0 | 7 |
| Laurac | 2 | 28 | Villepinte | 0 | 3 |
| Lavaur | 1 | 5 | Villesiscle | 0 | 3 |
| Lavelanet | 1 | 0 | | | |

*Source*: From Y. Dossat, *Les Crises de l'inquisition toulousaine au XIIIe siècle (1233–1273)* (Bordeaux, 1959), pp. 258–90.

118    Dossat, *Crises*, chs 2, 3; Id., 'Les Vaudois méridionaux d'après les documents de l'inquisition', *CF* II, pp. 207–26 at p. 212; M. G. Pegg, *The Corruption of Angels* (2001) will re-examine MS 609 (hypotheses on value of the record; doubts on alleged dualism of the interrogated; this is speculative but he includes an unusually vivid recreation of contemporary emotions, and fine historiography); see also Abels–Harrison, 'The participation', at pp. 220–5.

The table of sentences, derived from the close study of Dossat, covers those pronounced by Bernard de Caux between 18 March and 22 July 1246, and gives us as fair a picture of the extent of heresy in this region in 1245–6 as we are likely to get. As Dossat warns, it is still not wholly accurate as a picture of heresy uncovered in these enquiries, as the manuscripts on which he based the table are not necessarily comprehensive, but it is unlikely to be gravely misleading. Heretics were a minority, but a tenacious one, and they were widespread, as the thirty-nine localities in the table shows. A wide, if rather thin, scattering seems a fair inference, although we may notice some concentration in the south-west corner of the region, in, for example, Fanjeaux, Laurac and St Martin-la-Lande.

However, tenacity on the part of the heretics was matched by tenacity on the part of the inquisitors. The sequence of enquiries shows that in this region the connections with heresy of the whole population were searched out by blanket interrogation, then rechecked over the years, gradually rooting out the guilty. Sentencing was not unusually harsh. The table lists 207 sentences; twenty-three were of imprisonment, and the rest consisted of lighter penalties, such as compulsory pilgrimages or crosses worn on the clothing. Burning was not included in the records Dossat surveys, but we know from other evidence that its incidence was quite light.[119] The essence of the method was persistence and long memory: terror was maintained as much by the threat as by the reality of prison or fire. The haphazard nature of inquisitorial proceedings, dependent on political support, affected by the zeal and personalities of inquisitors and subject to inefficiencies in enforcing verdicts, should not blind us to its long-term effectiveness. Roquebert's volume on the end of Catharism demonstrates how, decade by decade, inquisitors hunted down, removed, demoralized or drove into exile the perfect. A small inquisitional elite confronted a small heretical elite and over many years beat them. Economic pressures reinforced and followed on from the work of the inquisitors. A document issued by Philip III of France in 1229[120] granted amnesty to some 278 citizens of Toulouse and returned confiscated property: the offences for which confiscation was enforced are not specified, but must be assumed to relate to heresy, rebellion and associated acts, and give a glimpse of the scale of pressure brought to bear on those who resisted Church and monarchy. These leading citizens had been crucial patrons of heresy.

Rural Catharism was weakened by the effects of the phase of speedy persecution in Toulouse after the peace of 1229. There and elsewhere the friars had some success in raising standards. Peter Seila was able to influence the patriciate; he was more than an efficient inquisitor. At best, the friars could provide examples of idealism to rival the *perfecti*, and the growing practice of auricular confession gave a new vitality to orthodox spiritual life. Recruitment to the Dominicans from the

---

119   *WHC*, pp. 184–5, 193 n. 10; effects of inquisitional efficiency, Hanssler, *Katharismus*, pp. 196–220; A. Cazenave, 'La résistance Cathare de la défaite à l'exil', *Histoire et Clandestinité. Colloque de Paris* (Mai 1977), *Revue du Vivarais* ed. M. Tilloy *et al.* (Albi, n.d.), pp. 357–52; Id., 'La chasse aux Cathares', *L'Histoire* LVI (1983), pp. 22–31; I emphasize inquisition more than B. Hamilton, 'The legacy of Charles Schmidt to the study of Christian dualism', *JMH* XXIV (1998), pp. 191–214 at pp. 209–10.
120   Mundy, *Repression*; Roquebert, *Epopée* V, *Cathares*, pp. 341–5.

Midi rose. In Toulouse the extent of charitable foundations and activities witness to an orthodox conscience at work. In the country the problem of standards and training of local clergy remained. Force and persuasion worked together to undermine heresy. Bitterness over the cruelties of repression and the defeat of a traditional leadership worked negatively; the eventual victory of the north and the monarchy offered new opportunities.

Despite the major short-term effects of the crusade, demographic expansion and increasing prosperity helped to create a climate of acceptance. Grievances about the Church's financial exactions mattered less in an era of economic advance. Northern conquest, with its bitter fruit for some, offered new posts to others. Monarchy played a part in reconciliation: Louis IX linked traditional ideals of chivalry with the ardent defence of orthodoxy and offered outlets for Southern nobles, once Cathar defenders, in crusading to the East: Philip III's amnesty pointed in the same direction.[121] Signs of the decline of Catharism manifested themselves. Already in 1226 Arnaude de Lamothe, *perfecta*, with her mother and sister, had found herself compelled to start moving from safe house to safe house in Toulouse before being taken to the countryside where she became a hunted fugitive, was given the *melioramentum*, supported with necessities by the faithful. Her sister died while they were living in a subterranean hide in part of the forest at Lanta. Isolation compelled her to take the rare and bold decision of consoling a young girl brought to her by a supporter to be her companion. Well before her capture in 1243, the traditional role of the *perfecta* had been closed to her.

Some time after the fall of Montségur it became clear that fewer women were being consoled, either because fewer came forward or because the male perfect believed the life had become too dangerous for them. Meanwhile Dominic's foundation at Prouille grew, mustering fifty nuns about mid-century. Chances of proselytism lessened as houses for the perfect, male or female, were abandoned for secrecy in towns or huts and cabins in the countryside. More turncoats emerged, confessing and betraying, some becoming double agents: Arnaud Pradier, a deacon married to a former *perfecta*, was kept in the Château Narbonnais in Toulouse, no doubt for his own security and for the utility of his long experience in the ways of the Cathars. A straw in the wind is the opening in the Carcassès of a register for converted perfect; others emigrated. By about 1250 Sacconi, perhaps as a former perfect and an inquisitor exaggerating success, calculated that the old Cathar Churches of Toulouse, Albi and Carcassonne had fewer than 200 perfect between them.[122]

Still there was adaptation to circumstances. Under pressure, leaders authorized the perfect to shed blood; the *convenenza*, a pact between a perfect who would

---

121  P. Wolff, 'Role de l'essor économique dans le ralliement social et religieux', *CF* xx, pp. 243–55; E. Griffe, *Les Cathares et l'Inquisition* (1980), pp. 121–6; A. Peal, 'Olivier de Termes and the Occitanian nobility in the thirteenth century', *RMS* xii (1986), pp. 109–29; J. H. Mundy, 'Charity and social work in Toulouse, 1100–1250', *Traditio* xxii (1966), pp. 203–87; *BC*, pp. 141–75 (clear-headed analysis).

122  *MLC*, pp. 215–29; Arnaude de Lamothe, Ibid., pp. 137–8, 169–70, Koch, *Frauenfrage*, pp. 186–200 (partial text), Brenon, *Femmes*, pp. 13–58 (dramatized); women under persecution, Brenon,

administer the *consolamentum* and a candidate, to be fulfilled at a moment of necessity when death was at hand and the candidate could no longer speak, was evolved to meet the more desperate circumstances.[123] Networks of supporters passed information to the hidden perfect about those near death who wished to be consoled. Bread blessed by the perfect was kept as safeguard. Navarre of Belleval near Caraman concealed a piece in a trunk, believing that at the moment of death, it would have as much value as the presence of a perfect.[124]

Exiles from Lombardy still returned to console and comfort. Guillaume Prunel was one such, glimpsed intermittently in the Southern Albigeois, the Cabardès and Toulouse between *c.*1258 and 1283, who, though illiterate, was in contact with nobles, even relatives of clergy. His contemporary, Pagès, had the distinction of being protected by a North Frenchman, Robert of Sens, in high office under the crown. Inquisitions in the last quarter of the century unmasked prominent citizens from South and North in Carcassonne and Albi, who had established a *modus vivendi* in which they attended mass but quietly supported surviving perfect, gave them the *melioramentum* and were consoled at death.[125] The evidence suggests that, despite a more effective competition from orthodoxy and hammer blows from inquisitors and bishops, the old faith could still hold sway.

The last revival of Languedocian Catharism proves the point.[126] It was led by a notary from Ax, Pierre Autier, who left the mountain land of Foix in 1295 to be trained in Lombardy and returned as a perfect to campaign in 1299, mustering for mission no more than a maximum of sixteen perfect. After long evasion of the forces of repression, and missions which stretched south as far as the ancient heartlands of the heresy in the Lauragais and Toulouse, Autier was captured and burnt in 1309, not long survived by his devoted son and assistant, Jacques. By 1310 the movement had been decimated. The effective time span of the revival was a decade. The least reputable perfect of the group, Guillaume Bélibaste, who had once killed a man and cohabited with a mistress, lingered on with a few followers in Aragon, but was betrayed and burnt in 1321.

Autier was a commanding personality, capable of travelling in late middle age regularly over several of what are now the departments of modern France, adapting to secrecy and night movement, a man of iron resolution with an

*Femmes*, ch. 20 to end; role of *perfectae*, Koch, *Frauenfrage*, chs 4, 9, Dossat, 'Les Cathares', p. 74; bishop's inquiries, J. Paul, 'La procédure inquisitionale à Carcassonne au milieu du XIIIe siècle', *CF* XXIX, pp. 361–96; Pradier, *JDH*, p. 301; emigration to Italy, E. Dupré-Theseider, 'Le Catharisme languedocien et l'Italie', *CF* III, pp. 299–316; Sacconi, Dondaine, *Traité*, p. 70, *WEH*, p. 337.

123  Dossat, 'L'évolution des rituels cathares', *Revue de Synthèse*, n.s. XXII–XXIII (1948), pp. 27–30.

124  Brenon, *Femmes*, pp. 280–1.

125  Hanssler, *Katharismus*, pp. 115–28; *JDH*, p. 310; numbers, Hanssler, pp. 66–74, 222–3; Pagès, *JDH*, pp. 310–11; Friedlander, 'Les agents du roi'; see also Biget, 'L'extinction du Catharisme urbain'; Griffe, *Inquisition*, pp. 136–70, plot at Carcassonne, pp. 152–8; *BC*, pp. 171–201; Roquebert, *Epopée* V, *Cathares*, pp. 205–329, 369–444 (rich narrative).

126  *MLC*, pp. 230–71; J. Duvernoy, 'Le Catharisme en Languedoc au début du XIVe siècle', *CF* XX, pp. 27–56 (excellent); A. Pales-Gobilliard, *L'Inquisiteur Geoffrey d'Ablis* (1984) (register in French and Latin; valuable intro.); *Le Registre d'Inquisition de Jacques Fournier*, trans. J. Duvernoy I–III (1978) (*JFD*) (order of text rearranged, full annotations); Griffe, *Inquisition*, chs 8, 9; Koch, *Frauenfrage*, pp. 82, 87–8; Roquebert, *Epopée*, V, pp. 445–99.

unusual capacity for playing on a potential convert's doubts and wishes, a professional man working in a semi-literate society. Jacques, his proud father once said, 'could preach like an angel'.[127] Pierre's brother Guillaume, a gentler and slighter personality, none the less worked diligently with his wife to carry out death-bed consolings, now the principal task of the perfect.

The counts of Foix had a long tradition of complicity and Roger Bernard III had employed Pierre as notary. A dispute over tithes on *carnalagia* embroiled the Cistercian bishop of Pamiers, Jacques Fournier, with his laity and exacerbated a pre-existing anticlericalism. None the less, facing them all was a developed inquisitional technique handled by the level-headed Geoffrey d'Ablis and, in a final clearing operation, by that most tenacious enquirer, Fournier himself. The investigation sparked off by the success of Autier's little group of mixed talent – Prades Tavernier was crude and unlettered – uncovered Catharism in 125 localities involving a minimum of one thousand persons – more in reality as some records have not survived.

Contact with the Autiers' group, their friends and aides, runs like a thread through the confessions. Plainly in their short heyday this small band had a remarkable missionary success, showing that Catharism remained in potential a dangerous enemy.

The nucleus of the revival lay in the Sabartès, in which Autier's home at Ax lay, a remote, poor and mountainous land to the south and west of Foix, together with the neighbouring Pays d'Alion; the adherents were mainly humble people, artisans, peasants, minor traders. Still, the perfect were at pains to convert the wealthier and more skilled and had some success in doing so. Most significant of all, Autier and his friends made converts and contacts well to the south in more prosperous lands where the Catholic counter-attack and the forces of repression had been sporadically in action since 1229. There were still embers of Catharism to be blown on.

The pioneer historian J. M. Vidal was deceived by the slanted selection of sources transcribed by Döllinger into believing that the Catharism of the revival was decadent, polluted by folklore elements.[128] This was not true of the protagonists. There had always been individuality in Cathar teaching and the Autier group differed among themselves without tension. They taught within the Languedocian tradition of radical dualism and observed established Cathar practices. Pierre was punctilious in his observance of correct forms: he would not supervise the *apparellamentum* because he was not a deacon. The usual novitiate with residential training had to be abandoned, but the prohibitions and celibacy remained in full force. Pierre once told a *perfecta* that she would forfeit her status if she were to be touched on the naked skin by a man, and encouraged the dying, once consoled, to pass securely from life, taking no food, merely stilling thirst

127  *JF* II, p. 406.
128  'Les derniers ministres de l'Albigéisme en Languedoc: leurs doctrines', *RQH* LXXIX (1906), pp. 57–107, 'Doctrine et morale des derniers ministres albigeois', LXXXV (1909), pp. 357–409, LXXXVI (1909), pp. 5–48; *GRK* IV (2) supersedes all else; see summary, pp. 406–12.

pangs with water, in order to remove any possibility of forfeiting paradise, by, perhaps through chance or misunderstanding, taking meat or failing to say the *Pater Noster*. This was the *endura*, bluntly stigmatized as suicide by Fournier. There were a few scanty precedents for it before Autier, but he encouraged and formalized it. It was the one element of innovation in his campaign: in all other respects he kept the old faith.

The Autier brothers appear and disappear in the recollections of the inhabitants of the village of Montaillou, high in the Sabartès region in the south of the lands of Foix.[129] Catharism probably came nearer to taking over an entire locality in this remote hamlet than anywhere else, and the investigation of d'Ablis in 1308–9 and then, more spectacularly, of Jacques Fournier, subsequently Pope Benedict XII, provide an unusual richness of evidence for so small a place. Catharism entered by family relationship. Guillaume Autier was son-in-law to Arnaud Benet of Ax, whose brother Guillaume was head of a household in Montaillou. It was fostered by a strange circumstance in which two brothers, Bernard Clergue, the bayle, representing lay power, and Pierre Clergue, the priest, were sympathetic to Catharism and secretly fostered it. Pierre, a passionate and vengeful village Napoleon, used his authority to blackmail any Catholic opposition. Outwardly diligent, saying mass, hearing confessions, attending synods, he was a determined lecher who held Cathar beliefs and, behind a facade of Catholicism, favoured the heresy.

The perfect came and went secretly and mysteriously. They seemed to the inhabitants a race apart, not exacting as orthodox clergy often seemed to be, but living simply and earning their own way. Celibacy, abstinence from meat and extensive fasting gave them status: 'They follow the path of the apostles Peter and Paul', one inhabitant said. They had a social function helping to integrate a poor, divided society. Catholicism revolved round the Church building; Catharism round the household, the *domus* or *ostal*. Here the perfect or their committed followers set to work, instructing informally, talking by the fire, addressing small gatherings, exercising a talent for the storytelling in which the great myths of Catharism could be entertainingly brought over to a peasant audience. Illiterate though they were, the villagers were not lacking in interest in the issues of life, death and the hereafter. Heresy moved from household to household and descended in families. Interrelation and the fear of consequences inhibited denunciation.

The Catholicism of the village was that of a pre-Gregorian world, unreflective, syncretistic and wholly untouched by changes in the life of the Church at large. Friars did not come up to these heights. Side by side with the Catharism and Catholicism was the force of paganism, folklore and scepticism. On the whole this worked more for Catharism than against it, providing the basis for a crude

---

129   E. Le Roy Ladurie, *Montaillou* (1975), to be read in conjunction with L. E. Boyle, 'Montaillou revisited: *mentalité* and methodology', *Pathways to Medieval Peasants*, ed. J. A. Raftis (1981), pp. 119–40 (witty, penetrating critique); M. Benad, *Domus und Religion in Montaillou* (1990); H. C. Stoodt, *Katharismus im Untergrund* (1997); *endura*, *MLC*, pp. 239–44; Kaelber, *Schools*, pp. 218–21; magic and inheritance from past, A. Murrary, 'Missionaries and magic in Dark Age Europe', *PP* CXXXVI (1992), pp. 186–205.

materialism about the mass, leading readily to cynicism about the orthodox doctrine of creation. Catholicism lacked potency: baptism was customary but it had a predominantly social function. There was little genuine hostility to the heresy.

Here, as elsewhere, where Catharism scored most was at the deathbed: the *consolamentum* gave an assurance of salvation. The Cathar leadership was tolerant of the failings of rank and file members; rigid themselves, with rare exceptions, over sexual matters, they appeared to be, or perhaps had to be, complacent about the activities of villagers who were relatively untouched by Catholic teaching and were driven most of all by care for the family and the security and prosperity of the *domus*. It was an evil world, and sexual activity of any kind was diabolical; but all sins, however deadly, could be forgiven in a moment by the laying-on of hands and the dying promises of renunciation in the *consolamentum*. The reward was instant and unqualified by the pains of the Catholic purgatory – a paradise in which 'each soul will have as much joy and happiness as any other; and all will be one'. So long as the perfect remained in action and sustained their own renunciations the appeal of deathbed consoling kept its power; but the perfect were physically vulnerable, and in Geoffrey d'Ablis, 'a soul without feebleness', they met their match. Catharism disappears from the records from 1329.

The turn of the Italians to suffer persecution came later. When Ivo of Narbonne, fleeing from what he claimed to be an unjust heresy charge, wandered amongst the Cathars of northern Italy in 1214, he found a remarkable degree of freedom and vitality among them, at ease in Como, Milan, Gemona in Friuli and elsewhere, living well, spreading their faith among the merchants at fairs and sending adherents to study logic or theology at Paris, with the aim of overthrowing Catholicism from an inner knowledge.[130] While the Churches of Languedoc crumbled, Italy was a relatively safe place of refuge; during the siege of Montségur a Cathar bishop in Cremona sent through a fraternal letter to the bishop of Toulouse with an offer of asylum, which he refused. Guides and hospices by the way facilitated the emigration of heretics from Languedoc, probably for the sake of secrecy from Beaucaire, where cloth fairs cloaked strangers, via the valleys of Durance and Var over the Col di Tenda to Cuneo (Coni), known as 'nest of heretics', at the foot of the Maritime Alps.[131] A trickle of perfect came back on return missions to give pastoral care or the *consolamentum* to the fragments of the Churches of Languedoc, and at Asti, the greatest of the exiles, Autier, received his ordination. For years, a hierarchy in exile survived. Vivent, a successor to Betrand Marty, bishop of Toulouse who died at Montségur, lived at the bastide of Guardia-Lombarda near Naples; later in the century Bernard Oliba presided over a house of perfect at Sirmione at the southern end of Lake Garda. Believers in exile immersed themselves in the economic life of Italy. Pierre de Bauville, involved in the Avignonet killings, lived by trading for over thirty years in Italy before being

---

130   Manselli, *Eresia*, p. 221; Ivo of Narbonne, *WEH*, pp. 185–7; authenticity: Segl, *Österreich*, pp. 76–111.
131   Dupré-Theseider, 'Le Catharisme languedocien'; *CF* III, pp. 164–8; M. Barber, 'Moving Cathars: the Italian connection in the thirteenth century', *Library of Mediterranean History* (forthcoming); Coni in Döllinger, p. 38.

betrayed to inquisitors on a visit to his daughter in his native village in 1277. Others lived by baking, beltmaking and weaving. Sacconi noted that the remains of the North French Church, amounting to some 150 perfect in mid-century, had found refuge in Verona and Lombardy generally.[132] Their security there, far greater than in their homeland, was still based on no firm foundations since Cathars were tolerated, not so much for their own sake, as for the sake of city autonomy or because of anticlerical feeling.

Local sentiment was volatile. As we have seen, Catholic reaction in Orvieto brought Pietro Parenzo into power; his assassination instantly aroused popular feeling in sympathy. Yet in 1240, the Dominican convent in the city was sacked.[133] Though the Dominicans had long been installed and there had been action against heresy in Piacenza, a preaching visit in 1233 of the distinguished Dominican Roland of Cremona with experience of Catharism in Languedoc sparked off a reaction. Designed to stir a tepid authority into more positive action, his visit may well have seemed a provocation. He was attacked and one of his companions killed.[134] Florence was seat of a Cathar bishopric, yet it also produced so vast an audience for the Dominican preacher, Peter of Verona, that at the height of his power Peter asked for the piazza to be enlarged to accommodate the crowds. This did not prevent the commune, under the leadership of a hostile *podestà*, in 1245 turning against the inquisitor Ruggero Calcagni's attempt to bring Cathars to heel, and worsting his supporters, including members of the Society of Faith founded by Peter, in a pitched battle. Ghibellinism, support for Frederick II's intervention for the *podestà*, and the will to civic independence smothered anti-Cathar feeling. Peter turned inquisitor, and, known to history as Peter the Martyr, was assassinated in 1252 on the road to Milan; his funeral was the occasion for an immense demonstration in his favour and a spontaneous cult developed. Yet seven years later, there was protest against his successor Sacconi.[135]

So matters swung to and fro. What generally preserved the quasi-immunity of the heretics in the first half of the century was the struggle between Frederick II and the popes. Having secured the promulgation of antiheretical legislation by Frederick II and built up a corpus of law against heresy, the popes were unwilling to exert great pressure on the cities to implement this legislation for fear of losing allies. Suspicion in the communes of central authority was at first enough to prevent general acceptance of statutes of support for the introduction of the inquisition, and the popes lacked the leverage to insist. Frederick's own attitude was opportunist. The reality of his concern was shown by his inaction towards heresy in the Regno: to take effective action would have meant introducing the

132    Barber, 'Moving Cathars'; A. Roach, 'The relationship of the Italian and Southern French Cathars' (DPhil, Univ. Oxford, 1989); Sacconi in Dondaine, *Traité*, p. 70; *WEH*, p. 337.

133    Above, pp. 89–90, Lansing, *Power*, pp. 57–8.

134    C. Bruschi, 'Il *Liber Suprastella* (1235), fonte antiereticali piacentina. L'ambiente ed il motivo di produzione', *Archivio Storico per le Province Parmensi*, 4th ser. XLIX (1997), pp. 405–27 at p. 422.

135    *MLC*, pp. 177–8, 182–3, 212–13; Lansing, *Power*, pp. 71–6, 101–2 (hypothesis on civic independence and anti-material Cathar sentiment, p. 76); G. G. Merlo, 'Pietro di Verona – San Pietro Martire', *Culto di Santi*, ed. S. Boesch Gajono, L. Sebastiani (1984), pp. 471–88.

friars to his kingdom, and he was unwilling to do this on political grounds. But he noticed the reluctance of Gregory IX to press the heresy issue so long as his own political requirements made it inconvenient, and used this as a point of criticism in his propaganda.

The Cathars used any support that they could find. A natural conjunction of interest brought them into alliance with the Ghibellines. But the heretics never formed an independent force anywhere in communal politics; they generally tended to receive favour in times of interdict, but they were pawns in a political battle, and when the Ghibelline forces lost they were without support.

Until 1250 the association with Ghibellinism carried the heretics into a blind alley. While Frederick lived, relative security remained. They were not free of the risk of legal proceedings by any means; but they still had numerical strength. Sacconi, trying to reckon up the strength of the various Churches, assessed Concorezzo, the moderate dualists, as greatest with 1,500 perfect; below that came Desenzano with 500 and a series of smaller ones at lower figures: Bagnolo at 200, Florence, Val del Spoleto and Vicenza at 100. The organization outlasted Sacconi, and the lists of bishops for the various Churches go on without interruption into the 1280s.[136]

Nevertheless, the death of Frederick II and the decline of the imperial party in Italy, the victories of the papal champion Charles of Anjou against Frederick's successors, and the success of conservative Guelf parties in the cities tilted the balance against the dualists. Charles of Anjou's system had no room for the heretics; the popes, released from the anxiety over allies, could press the case for persecution. Patrons died: in Verona Oberto Pelavicino was succeeded by the Scaligeri, who were no longer willing to assist heresy.[137] One by one, in a halting sequence which lasted through the rest of the century, cities allowed thorough inquisitorial proceedings. Flight to protectors in the *contado*, movement to other cities, and concealment delayed but could not prevent decline. In Florence a stage in this downward movement is marked by the numbers of perfect who submitted in the inquisition held in 1282 by brother Salomone da Lucca.[138] At Sirmione by Lake Garda an expedition captured 178 perfect, who were burnt in Verona in 1278, and dealt a terrible blow to the Church of Desenzano.[139] The repression still did not go easily; traditional suspicion of the inquisition remained, and some Cathars struck back – in the Valtellina an inquisitor was murdered, Parma sacked its Dominican convent in 1279[140] – but by the end of the century even Milan, the ancient capital of heresy, had been brought to order. The last major series of trials were held in Bologna from 1291 to 1309.[141] The city lacked a resident hierarchy and contained believers of limited education and under-

136  *BK*, pp. 231–9; H. M. Schaller, 'Die Frömmigkeit Friedrichs II', *DA* LI (1995), pp. 493–513 (definitive on thought; actions); Manselli, *Eresia*, pp. 283–4.
137  *MLC*, pp. 272–96.
138  Manselli, *Eresia*, p. 218.
139  Guiraud, *Inquisition* II, p. 573.
140  Ibid., pp. 573, 575.
141  Paolini, *L'Eresia* I; Lansing, *Power*, pp. 151–7; *MLC*, pp. 283–7.

standing. The burning of Bompietro, long in the faith, caused a riot, not because of a sympathy for heresy but because the inquisitor denied him the sacrament at the point of death.[142] Cathar history hereafter is that of a remnant. In Italy, as in Languedoc, repression removed the most committed of the Cathars; it acted as sanatoria once did in the struggle against tuberculosis, by removing foci of infection. The ardent perfect were taken out of circulation. Missionary endeavour diminished. Fear deterred recruits.

Weight must be given to peaceful countermeasures, especially in Italy. Inquisitors were not necessarily only policemen. St Peter Martyr was a leader in the movement for setting up Catholic confraternities to deepen faith and erect barriers against heresy.[143] The Lombard Alleluia of 1233 and the flagellants of 1260 were popular movements of penance and revival, hostile to heresy. The intellectual level was higher than in Languedoc, and it is fair to assume therefore that the intellectual attack on heresy and the effect of the conflicts in Catharism mattered more. Police action was requisite to cut down the recalcitrant. But at the same time a general change in the atmosphere and a revived Catholicism inhibited the flow of recruits on the earlier scale; so the heresy was squeezed into its ultimate oblivion. One can speculate about economic factors, and argue that improvements in conditions drew men's minds from a creed which so relentlessly preached that the world was utterly in the power of Satan; but too many in easy circumstances participated in the heresy, and men's motives for adherence to a religious group are generally too complex for any simple correlation between poverty, injustice and Cathar recruitment, or between economic improvement and Cathar decline, to carry conviction. Catharism was in any case eclectic, a religion that absorbed ideas and practices sponge-like from various quarters, and so catered for varied needs, somewhat at the expense of consistency. Knowledge was expanding in the thirteenth century and, with the development of universities and of medical schools and the expansion of travel, horizons widened. Catharism could not keep up. Two developments on the Catholic side, however, were of especial importance for the change of outlook that inhibited this particular heresy.[144] One was the popularity of a new piety, associated especially with the Franciscans, which focused attention on the incidents of Christ's life. The Christmas crib, the vivid preaching about Christ's life, the devotions centred on the crucifixion which led the worshipper to participate in the sufferings of Jesus were the enemy of the dualistic faith. For most adherents the Cathar Christ was a wraith or a visiting angel and not a man; he was venerated above all as the distant founder of a pure Church. He could not survive against the competition of the Catholic Christ, man and God, as realized in the piety of the thirteenth century. The pastoral mission of the friars as preachers and confessors together with the development of confraternities for laymen and women who remained in the world brought a good Christian life within the range of the many – it was no longer reserved for the dedicated few who received the *consolamentum*.

142   *MLC*, pp. 285–6.
143   Intro. to classic work of G. G. Meersemann on confraternities, Vauchez, *Laics*; *MLC*, pp. 175–80.
144   Above, pp. 104–5.

Finally the appearance of Joachimism on the thirteenth-century scene contributed to popular religious feeling a set of myths that rivalled in their appeal the myths of the Cathars, and yet were more optimistic in tone.[145] As in Cathar eschatology, there was to be a profound struggle with evil, but it would issue in a state of bliss here on earth, a foretaste, after spiritual warfare, of the pleasures of paradise. For those who had taste for such things, these myths were more positive: dualist myths of creation and the End faded in competition with them. All was not gain for the Catholics; there were dangers in Joachimism, and heresies fed on it.[146] But it was another factor against Catharism. In a word, Italian dualism was in part eradicated by force and in part simply outgrown.

145   Manselli, *Eresia*, pp. 270, 331; Id., 'Evangelisme et mythe dans la foi cathare', *Heresis* v (1985), pp. 9–17; bibliography and obituary: Ibid., pp. 5–24 and xii (1989), pp. 79–86 (by J. Duvernoy).
146   Below, pp. 218–30; comment in Hamilton, *Crusade*, pp. 31–2.

# 8

# The Waldensians after the Conference of Bergamo

## The Lyonists in France

On 9 August 1319, just a little more than a century since the Conference at Bergamo had sought in vain to reunite the Lyonist and Poor Lombard wings of the Waldensian movement, Raymond de Sainte Foy, or de Costa, a Lyonist deacon, stood before Jacques Fournier, bishop of Pamiers. Though sitting with the Dominican representative of the inquisitor at Carcassonne, Fournier held the reins. He was no ordinary interrogator but an unusually conscientious bishop, determined to sift the beliefs and actions of his suspects so as to provide a just penance (or punishment), and by reasoning recall them to Catholicism. Raymond, who had studied in the Franciscan school at Montpellier, knew grammar, and some theology and had a deep knowledge of Scripture, was no mean representative of Valdes's moderate, reformist wing of the Waldensians and a dignified defendant. As the interrogation unfolded over many days, it revealed the thought-world of the Lyonists and the effects of repression, brought on by the Church's panic over Catharism.[1]

Raymond, captured with books and writings, his old nurse and a carpenter and wife of the same belief, had come from his native diocese of Vienne, probably to set up a *hospitium* and look for other Waldensian families in the town and neighbourhood; like other Lyonists in clerical office, he was firm in the view that

---

1  Underground Waldensianism surveyed, Audisio, trans. C. Davison, *Waldensian Dissent*, pp. 26–160 (esp. ch. 5 on life in hiding); Cameron, *Waldenses*, pp. 26–160 (under geog. headings); P. Biller, *The Waldenses 1170–1530* (2001) (coll. articles, illuminating on inner life, some unpublished, most notably 'The *Liber Electorum*', pp. 207–24); historiography, Id., 'The Waldenses in the fourteenth and fifteenth centuries: the current state of knowledge', Ibid., pp. 1–23; later pubns., Id., 'The Waldenses 1300–1500', *RHR* ccxvii (2000), pp. 75–99; J. F. Gilmont, 'Sources et critiques des sources', *Vaudois*, ed. Audisio, pp. 105–13; A. Patschovsky, 'The literacy of Waldensianism'; S. K. Treesh, 'Europe's peasant heretics: the Waldensians 1375–1550' (PhD, Univ. Rutgers, 1988) (esp. German Waldensians); M. Schneider, *Europäisches Waldensertum im 13. und 14. Jahrhundert* (1981) (teaching and orgn.); G. G. Merlo, *Valdesi e Valdismi Medievali: itinerari e proposte di ricerca* (1984) (essays stressing discontinuities), *Valdesi e Valdismi*: ii: *Identità valdesi nella storia e nella storiografia* (1991) (esp. historiography).

he should not work with his hands, the carpenter providing income and the women care.[2] The interrogation hit an obstacle at the outset: Raymond refused to take the oath, saying he had once suffered an epileptic fit while doing so and ten years previously had been urged in the confessional in his former diocese not to swear. He admitted he was a deacon, but left obscure the bishop who ordained him. Taxed with the possession of a parchment roll, apparently an appeal to the king, he claimed he had found it in the road. Evasion was a condition of survival.

Having established with the curia that he had the right to judge the case, Fournier applied his usual technique for recalcitrant cases. He left Raymond in prison. In December, Raymond asked to be questioned on the articles of faith and the seven sacraments, and declared his orthodoxy; but still refused to take an oath. On 2 January 1320, he threw aside concealments, thinking only thereafter of shielding his companions and the Waldensians he had left behind in the diocese of Vienne, consequently declining to give names, dates and places which could identify individuals.

To the bishop's evident interest, he described, with much scriptural buttressing, the shadow, parallel organization of the Lyonists he knew, which supplemented and sometimes, while remaining astonishingly close to Catholicism, supplanted it. There were three orders – the equivalent of bishop, the *majoralis*, priest and deacon, ordained by the laying-on of hands on the scriptural pattern. The *majoralis* was elected and had powers of discipline and leadership. He celebrated mass at Easter – a rite which Raymond said he had never witnessed – and on Maundy Thursday, in a ceremony reserved only for those in orders, washed companions' feet and blessed bread, fish and wine in a commemorative meal. Priests were not enabled to say mass but heard confessions – plainly an important feature of Waldensian life – in simplicity, hearing the penitent's sins, then exhorting, pinpointing sins with scriptural texts, seeking true contrition, imposing penances, firmly eschewing the Catholic direct absolution but praying to God to forgive the penitent.

Ordination to the diaconate required a novitiate of five or six years, with examination of conduct and scriptural instruction; they had no right to hear confession or carry the Host, but as in Acts, their duties were to provide for the material needs of the Church. Candidacy was expected to spring from a 'good, believing family', not true of Raymond who was converted to Waldensianism by a 'companion' who visited him while studying at Montpellier. As all the brothers, deacons maintained vows of poverty, chastity and obedience with strictness, said a version of the Hours, and observed the Church's calendar.

There were no individual possessions: Raymond referred to his organization as the poor of Christ, and the brothers as the 'perfect', alluding to Christ's injunction to the rich young man: 'If thou wouldst be perfect, go, sell all thou hast.'

<hr />

2   *JFD* I, pp. 55–150; P. Paravy, *De la Chrétienté romaine à la Réforme en Dauphiné* II (1993) (classic Gallic analysis of religion in Grenoble and Embrun dioceses; definitive), pp. 922–46; Raymond and Sisters, P. Biller, 'The preaching of the Waldensian Sisters', *Waldenses*, pp. 125–58; K. Utz Tremp, ' "Parmi les hérétiques": la Vierge Marie dans l'inquisition de l'évêque Jacques Fournier de Pamiers (1317–1326)', *Marie. Le Cult de la Vierge*, ed. D. Iogna-Prat *et al.* (1996), pp. 533–60.

Stress was laid on creating the conditions of true celibacy: the brothers were not to touch women or allow them to kiss their hand and were not to sleep in the same room as them except under grave necessity of concealment. A widower would not be considered for orders because he had become accustomed to the 'work of the flesh' and might consequently find celibacy too hard. Of necessity, open preaching had disappeared and was replaced by expositions of Scripture behind closed doors.

There was still an itinerant ministry with the poverty characteristic of the sending of the Seventy in Matthew 10, but without public preaching. Raymond had travelled in Italy with a *majoralis*, Jean Lorrain, for whom he retained great affection. The carpenter's wife also remembered Jean with admiration, since he refused her proffered gift of money, claiming he did not carry any; when she checked, she found his purse empty. The calibre of life and scriptural knowledge of the *majoralis* none the less had only limited opportunity to draw recruits since he was compelled, for fear of capture, to move incognito, travelling to and confirming existing Waldensian families in their beliefs but rarely speaking to non-Waldensians. The bishop asked Raymond if the *majoralis* had recruited in Italy. Raymond said No: it is likely to have been an honest answer. Earlier interrogations had shown how fruitful casual meetings could be: the meeting of Raymond and his instructor seems to have been an informal affair, though he declined details, for he feared betrayal. The carpenter met the *majoralis* in a house in Toulouse and was instructed there; his wife, wanting to meet him, came across him at the door of the Franciscan convent in Montpellier. But the scale of such contacts remained small. In effect, the Waldensians had become an unrecognized order of itinerant friars, carefully selected, living and travelling in secrecy, sustaining the use of the vernacular Scriptures, maintaining a disciplined and moral life yet unable to break out, preach and recruit openly.

Raymond insisted on the orthodoxy of his movement and, though he accepted the rightfulness of the execution of Cathars if unrepentant, believed it to be a mortal sin for the Church to put Waldensians to death for their beliefs. He and his fellows felt they constituted a reform movement waiting for permission to carry on their duties openly, hoping it would be effective in reawakening the reality of belief and conduct through the study of Scripture and in deepening the spiritual life through the confessional. The bishop pressed Raymond on Donatism. He was quite firm that moral failings in either his own brotherhood or the Catholic priesthood in no way rendered their sacraments invalid. His Waldensians accepted Catholic baptism and confirmation. The extreme rarity of the celebration of mass by the *majoralis* makes it likely that they had no objection to rank and file attending a Catholic mass and Raymond recorded no doctrinal division on this between them and the Catholics.

The question arises: given the high degree of acceptance of Catholicism, what was it which led the Waldensian brothers to remain outside the Church and continue in their awkward, concealed and potentially dangerous lives? The bishop's probing on the issue of authority clarified this: it lay in fidelity to Scripture, in the vernacular versions which buoyed up and sustained. Asked about the *majoralis*'s right to preach or send brothers to preach, Raymond gave his answer: he held this power from God and required no other authority. Vestments at mass were not a necessity, they provided solemnity; the crucial element lay in the use of the chalice, bread, wine and water and the repeating of the Saviour's words at the Last Supper. The sacrament of penance was accepted; Raymond believed it to have been instituted by Christ. But it was dominated by reference to Scripture and the removal of absolution by the priest was a significant change.

Collision came when Raymond was asked to accept oath-taking and belief in purgatory. Fournier wrestled with him, giving texts and precedents. He was unmoved. Against all else, he cited Matthew 5: 34, 'Swear not at all', and would not bend. He argued purgatory had no scriptural warrant and was not persuaded by citation from the Apocrypha (2 Maccabees 12: 43, 46) to the contrary. The classic text, from Peter's reply to the Sanhedrin in Acts 5: 29, 'We ought to obey God rather than men', backed Raymond's refusal to follow the common practice of Church and society and use the judicial oath – in other words, Raymond's Waldensian group followed Church doctrine and practice in most matters, because they thought it consonant with Scripture; in cases where they believed it was not, Scripture and not the Church was the decisive authority. This was the crux of the matter.

The bishop assembled a list of the errors of which Raymond was guilty, cited authorities, exhorted him to return to obedience to the Church, to reveal all his Waldensian complices, to abjure and to take an oath, promising to provide further elucidation of points at issue and allowing Raymond an extra day to consider his reply. In vain – Raymond retracted minor points, remained obdurate on most and was burnt. His companions suffered also, the old nurse with him, the other two later, almost certainly because Huguette, the wife, was pregnant.

The case roused strong emotions. It was said that the bishop wept. Guillaume Autast of Ornolac said it would have been better if the bishop had been burnt. Berenger Escoulan expressed himself forcibly in taverns and, hearing that after the bands securing Raymond's hands fell away in the fire he was seen clasping them in prayer, said he was a martyr. Before the bishop, he briskly withdrew, but still received a penance, probably a year's imprisonment.[3]

The response of Waldensians to effective persecution emerges from Fournier's trials as evasion, secrecy and flight. This is in vivid contrast to the days of freedom in Quercy some eighty years earlier, especially in Montauban, where an easygoing tolerance outlived even the major events of crusade,[4] enabling them to preach, heal and engage in missionary work with impunity. Their freedom may well have led casual supporters, patients or witnesses to sermons genuinely to

3  *JFD* I, pp. 154–6; Merlo, *Valdesi* I, pp. 86–92; K. Utz Tremp, 'Waldenser und Wiedergänger. Das Fegefeuer im Inquisitionsregister des Bischofs Jacques Fournier von Pamiers', *Himmel, Hölle, Fegefeuer* (1994), pp. 125–34, clarifies delay in burning.
4  Y. Dossat, 'Les Vaudois méridionaux d'après les documents de l'inquisition', *CF* II, pp. 207–26; Id., 'De Vaudès à Saint-François à Montauban', *CF* VIII, pp. 403–13; Schneider, *Europäisches Waldensertum*, pp. 8–29.

think that the preachers were not heretics. Montauban was the only place in Southern France where the Waldensians had more supporters than the Cathars, where they possessed a cemetery and a school and were in demand for their medical services. In Peter Seila's inquisition in Quercy from 1241, no fewer than seventy-three persons from Montauban, including Cathars, are recorded asking for medical help from them;[5] possibly there was a hospital.

In Quercy generally, the brothers tended the sick in accordance with Christ's injunction in the sending of the Seventy, sometimes staying with the patient. Rewards were commonly in kind: 'She gave them wine', one witness recalled, 'since they would not accept money.'[6] One name, Pierre de Valz, recurs in depositions because of both his preaching and his medical work: he was 'loved like an angel of God'.[7] A wisp of Cathar influence from the administration of the *consolamentum* may lie behind the laying of the Gospel of John on a patient's head by two Waldensian women.[8]

Women preached and there were houses of Waldensian sisters in Montcuq and Beaucaire, living a common life in celibacy: their role within the movement in general has been underestimated. Here and elsewhere they were, in effect, nuns, the counterpart of the male celibate preacher class, the *Meister, fratres* or *barbi*, with a role in some respects comparable to the second order amongst the friars. The contemplative element in Waldensian literature may well have been designed with them in mind.[9]

In Montauban, Waldensians were for years integrated into a community which tolerated both them and the Cathars and into the 1220s permitted preaching in public places. Disputations – apparently arranged by the rank and file[10] – took place between adherents of the two movements. Even in the hairdressers a customer might find himself the object of a Waldensian exhortation. There are examples of manual work undertaken without charge in a spirit of simple helpfulness. Support reached across classes. The Carbonel family, of sufficient rank to produce consuls, was deeply involved; its scion, Jacques, having received Waldensian instruction as a child, attended their eucharist and meetings and was a witness at disputations.[11] The adherence of great families, together with the slow pick-up of persecution and the preoccupation of ecclesiastical authority with the Cathars in the contested lands of Languedoc, helps to explain the toleration of Waldensians in Montauban and Quercy generally.

It did not last. Seila dealt with supporters rather than the core of preachers in Waldensianism or perfect in Catharism, and penanced relatively lightly adherents who came forward during the time of grace: nevertheless, his activities heralded decline. Enthusiastic support for wandering Waldensians could easily

5  Dossat, 'De Vaudès', p. 405.
6  P. Biller, '*Curate Infirmos*: the medieval Waldensian practice of medicine', *Waldenses*, pp. 49–67 at p. 57.
7  Ibid., p. 58.
8  Patschovsky–Selge, *Quellen*, p. 63; Biller, p. 58 n. 48.
9  Biller, 'The preaching', pp. 125–58.
10  Schneider's comment, *Europäisches Waldensertum*, p. 22.
11  Dossat, 'De Vaudès', pp. 408–12.

be transferred to the Franciscans and this clearly happened. Members of pro-Waldensian families were benefactors to the Franciscan convent in Montauban. Their representatives were present when the Poor Clares were put in possession of an endowment given by Alphonse of Poitiers in 1270, those of pro-Cathar families were not. Thus both inquisition and peaceful competition ended the glory days of the Waldensians.

As more effective persecution developed, itineracy for the preacher class, sometimes with disguise, became a matter of survival. Etienne de Bourbon, once an inquisitor, described a Waldensian preacher who carried with him the trappings of various crafts by which he could transform himself, like Proteus,[12] pilgrim, cobbler, harvester and the like – all activities likely to involve travel. All tasks, the manual labour and medical service, which had been open in Montauban for preachers and supporters to undertake together, had to be given up. The penumbra of casual support faded and the contact between the supporters proper, the *credentes*, and their preacher class became tighter as dangers grew: the heart of the movement came to be the act of confession behind closed doors with the associated exhortation and instruction. Close-knit family groups tended to become the carriers of belief, instructing their children in the home circle, intermarrying with other Waldensian families, maintaining a 'nicodemism' of conformity with the Catholic life around them, but valuing intensely the visits of their preachers and the opportunity given to examine their consciences and receive moral and scriptural instruction.

The persecution of Waldensian suspects from Gascony, originally migrants from Burgundy, launched by the inquisition at Toulouse about 1310 confirms this picture of their way of life.[13] The home was the focus. Families often produced preachers, trained especially in knowledge of Scripture, who ministered to related families, eating with them and giving them little gifts, gloves, needles or knives, mementoes, tokens of gratitude, sometimes, no doubt, part of the apparatus of disguise. There was much rote learning, an outlet for the illiterate, or semi-literate, and for preachers a possible means of evading the unwelcome attention that could be drawn to them if they carried books.[14] The naked text of Scripture remained a major force behind the movement; on visits, following a meal, the preacher would kneel and pray for a long time, often repeating a series of *Pater Nosters*.

The 'Burgundians', in the same tradition as Raymond de Sainte Foy, had remained faithful to Valdes, were not Donatist in attitude and never unchurched the Catholics because of the moral faults of their clergy. As Cameron points out, 'It was the authority of a persecuting Church, not its moral stature or its sacramental services, which the heretics denied'.[15] The persecutions appear to have been effective even though they touched supporters rather than their preachers.

12   *WEH*, p. 210.
13   Cameron, *Waldenses*, pp. 78–87, to which I am indebted for detailed analysis; map, p. 79.
14   Cameron's comment, p. 84.
15   Ibid., p. 85.

Lyonists faded. They had never been strong in the lands directly affected by the crusade. They were more numerous in Lorraine and Burgundy and on the fringes rather than in the heartlands of Catharism, in Quercy and Rouergue (where in an isolated atrocity the crusaders burnt seven Waldensians at Morlhon) rather than in Toulouse, Albi and the surrounding countryside. The great inquiry of 1245–6 in the Lauragais and neighbourhood of Lavaur produced evidence of very few Waldensians among the 5,471 persons interrogated.[16]

Bernard Gui, a very active inquisitor based in Toulouse in the early decades of the fourteenth century and author of the widely used *Practica inquisitionis*, uncovered Cathars and Beguins but only small batches of Waldensians. He played his part in the rounding up of the 'Burgundians', vulnerable as they were because of their family-based religion. They had brought their beliefs with them in migration and the conditions of life made diffusion of them difficult beyond intersecting family circles. Once authority broke into the families, Waldensianism fragmented and, having failed to make converts among their indigenous neighbours, faded.

Its adherents never bowed to persecution, they adapted to it. The retreat to the family, the evolution of the skilled, resolute, wandering preacher prepared to face the hard life of the guerilla in the battle for souls, the focus on confession and the adaptation of open preaching to the household was a success; the determined few stayed in being. But they were scattered indeed. The information elicited from two wandering preachers captured in 1492 in the fastnesses of the Alps, at Oulx, beyond the Col de Montgenèvre, provides a means of measuring the extent of the diaspora at the end of the Middle Ages: they had been on tour in France and had visited scattered families in a wide swathe of locations, Ardèche, Velay, Auvergne, Burgundy, the Lyonnais, the Valentinois, survivors in small numbers, too few to make a springboard for revival or a revivification of the free preaching of Valdes's day.[17] In mountain lands in the Haut-Dauphiné Waldensians kept redoubts till the Reformation; below in the kingdom of France, with the exception of Provence, they were a frail remnant.

### Italy and the German-Speaking Lands

Poor Lombards were more successful in gaining recruits long term than Lyonists, probably because their more radical challenge to the Church was a better inspiration to resistance and mission as persecution deepened. Born of a fusion between Waldensianism from France and the anticlerical ferment of northern Italy, they shared in the anarchic vitality of the Lombard plain.[18] This atmos-

---

16  Conclusion of Pegg, *Corruption*.
17  See G. Audisio, *Les Vaudois du Luberon* (1984) (reconstruction of life of most secret group, with reflections on *barbi* and adherents); summary, Audisio, *Vaudois*, ed. Audisio, p. 83. On Gui and captured Waldensians, see now P. Biller 'The Waldenses in Bernard Gui's Liber Sententiarum', *Trials*, ed. Biller, Bruschi; generally, 'Fat Christian and Old Peter: ideals and compromises among the medieval Waldensians', *Pragmatic Utopias*, ed. R. Horrox, S. Rees-Jones (2001).
18  Merlo, *Valdesi* I, p. 11; varieties of Waldensianism, pp. 143–5; Lyonists and Poor Lombards existed side by side in Italy.

phere ensured that they retained hostile attitudes to the Roman Church, the Whore of the Apocalypse, which view was only reinforced as the Italian cities, one by one, accepted a duty of repression. Catharism, however, was the major target and it is likely that Waldensianism came off more lightly. Its history in the thirteenth century remains obscure; the reason may lie in the absence of heresy trials rather than the accidents of the survival of documents.

Writing probably somewhere between the third and fifth decades of the fourteenth century, a Waldensian author looked back from the epoch of persecution in which he wrote to an earlier age of prosperity, following Valdes's preaching; he wrote from an Italian perspective and was evidently not informed about the wave of inquisition activity in Austria, for example. He did not see the thirteenth century as an age of persecution. Nearer his own day, persecution began to bite and he alludes to explusions from one region to another.[19] The movement faded in Lombardy but gained support in certain Alpine villages and the south of Italy. Waldensianism grew strong in Calabria, whither Charles the Lame, king of Naples 1285–1309, called in textile workers from the north, all unconsciously drawing it into his kingdom. There was also emigration to Apulia. As late as 1532 a Waldensian under interrogation saw Apulia and Calabria as lands of freedom.[20] There was displacement but not total loss.

In German-speaking lands there was positive and striking expansion. Waldensianism had a long history in the Empire: even in Valdes's time the language barrier had been surmounted. The first impetus seems to have come from the frontier with French-speaking regions and presumably from Lyonists. By the time of the Conference of Bergamo, however, the Germans stood on the Poor Lombard side,[21] and it was their Waldensianism which won new territory. The Waldensian cause was aided by the long battle between the papacy and the Hohenstaufen, with its interdicts, excommunications and political appointments. 'In times of interdict heretics rejoice' was a contemporary verdict.[22]

Popular unrest in Schwäbisch-Hall, based on support for Frederick, played into the hands of the Waldensians since Frederick's party rejected the interdict imposed by pro-papal clergy, declaring their exercise of office null because of their sins – an ideal sentiment for the adherents of the Donatist Poor Lombard wing. Prelates appointed for political reasons were unlikely to pursue heretics and though in his short career of less than two years as heresy-hunter till his death in 1233, the fanatic Conrad of Marburg killed many, he was indiscriminate in his judgements.[23] In preaching tours across German-speaking lands, Berthold of

19   Biller, 'The *Liber*', pp. 207–24 at pp. 207–8, 219–22.
20   Calabria and other immigrant communities best in Cameron, *Waldenses*, pp. 200–6; Gonnet–Molnár, *Les Vaudois*, p. 142.
21   See above, p. 102.
22   Segl, 'Berthold von Regensburg', p. 122, citing Patschovsky–Selge, p. 91; H. Haupt, 'Waldensertum und Inquisition im südöstlichen Deutschland bis zur Mitte des 14. Jahrhunderts', *DZG* II (1889), pp. 285–330, 337–411 (still valuable); R. Kieckhefer, *The Repression of Heresy in Medieval Germany* (1979) (institutional study, sidelights on beguines and Waldensians; omits Austria).
23   P. Segl, 'Conrad von Marburg, Inquisitor', *Neue Deutsche Biographie* XII (1980), pp. 544–6; see A. Patschovsky, *DA* XXXVII (1981), pp. 641–93; *MLC*, pp. 118–22.

Regensburg was aware of a Waldensian presence, which he repeatedly denounced in revealing detail.[24]

Germany was a springboard into the frontier province of Austria. A good source, the Passau Anonymous, a secular priest or Dominican, author of a compilation on Jews, heretics and Antichrist dating from the second half of the thirteenth century, gives us a detailed picture of their life based on his experiences of an inquisition conducted there in about 1266.[25] The forty-two place-names the Anonymous describes as bearing heresy are scattered over villages, farms and market towns in Lower Austria, roughly following today's railway line. The inquiry plainly extended only to the Austrian side of the Danube. It is not likely that the river was a barrier to the passage of heresy; rather, that Austria's ruler, Ottokar II, was the instigator of the investigations, and that they therefore dealt only with heretics in his territories.[26]

The Anonymous says very little on the social origins of heretics. He mentions only Henry the glovemaker of Theben, the modern Devin at the confluence of the Danube and the March, who frankly informed the clergy as he was led to execution at some unknown date, that they in turn could expect death at the hands of the Waldensians if ever they came to power.[27] A hierarchy appears little in evidence. The Anonymous mentions a bishop at Anzbach; a certain Neumeister burnt in 1315 in Vienna or at Himberg, near Vienna on its southern side, claimed to have been a bishop of the Waldensians for over fifty years, and may have been the same man.[28] The term may spring from the minds of inquisitors, labelling a leader of the Waldensians in the manner usual in orthodoxy: his authority may well have been more a matter of *regimen* than *ordo*.

A special feature of the heretics described by the Passau Anonymous was the absence of distinctive ranks. All were obliged to preach, women as well as men, and children were expected to take part in instruction. Ten places underlined are described as *scholae* – the instructional centres where formal teaching was given and the Scripture learnt, in a fashion similar to the English Lollards of the fifteenth century. Sacraments were of the simplest. Catholic priests were criticized for imposing heavy penances; these Waldensians, by contrast, remitted sin by the laying-on of hands, citing the words of Christ to the woman taken in adultery: 'Go and sin no more.' They spoke of daily communion, and rejected the rites of the mass: their communion service is likely to have been, above all, an expression of the fraternal solidarity of these Waldensian groups. The words of consecration could, they said, be spoken as well by a woman as by a man.[29]

24   Segl, 'Berthold', passim.
25   M. Nickson, 'The "Pseudo-Reinerius" treatise: the final stage of a thirteenth century work on heresy from the diocese of Passau', *AHDLMA* xxxiv (1967), pp. 255–314; A. Patschovsky, *Der Passauer Anonymus* (1968).
26   Segl, *Ketzer in Österreich* (definitive analysis; see on Anonymous and spread of heresy, pp. 165–233).
27   Ibid., p. 248.
28   Ibid., p. 315.
29   Solidarity: Schneider, p. 124; Segl, *Österreich*, p. 204 (consecration by women), *scholae*, pp. 193–4.

MAP 4     *The Waldensians in Austria: the inquisition of c.1266.*
*Source:* Adapted from M. Nickson, *Archives d'histoire doctrinale et littéraire du moyen âge* XXXIV (1967), p. 279.

The Passau Anonymous met with more than one type of Waldensian. The *Runcarii* he alludes to were clearly the heirs of John de Ronco, the leader of the Lombard split in Valdes's movement, and may be taken as a synonym for the Poor Lombards.[30] Lyonists were present as well, but the vigour of the attacks on the Church which he reports suggests a Lombard predominance.

He explains, directly or by implication, the reasons for the durability of the movement. They lay pre-eminently in the faults of the clergy, which form a strange blend of ignorance and superstition, personal, especially sexual, laxity, and excessive claims for themselves and their parishes; the flavour is rustic and backward, with some pseudo-miracles being claimed and parishioners being told that to go to another church would be adultery. The Host was sometimes dropped, the wine spilled and the confessional abused in a large number of ways. This miscellaneous, sometimes contradictory, list of ecclesiastical abuses shows the roots of Waldensianism amongst simple people: it lay in the contrast between a run of the

30   Segl, *Österreich*, pp. 218–19, correcting *LMH*, 1st edn.

mill, not too well instructed clergy with their human failings, and the cells of the Waldensian movement, studying the Scripture, a devoted underground elite.[31]

The Anonymous is uninhibited in his description of the tenacity of the heretics. 'All Leonists [i.e. Lyonists],' he says, 'men and women, adult and child, learn and teach unweariedly by day and night, the workman devotes the day to his work, the night to religious instruction; so that little time remains over for prayer; the newly converted after a few days seek others to draw into the sect.'[32] The Anonymous recalled the case of a Waldensian who swam the river Ibbs on a winter's night to make a convert; he noticed, too, that they taught in leper houses. *Scole leprosorum* were held in the village of Neuhofen. A curious passage described the Waldensian approaching wealthier potential converts in the guise of the travelling salesman selling pretty things, rings, scarves and the like, and then, when the customer asked if he had other items for sale, replying that he had much more valuable gems – but would need to be assured that he would not be betrayed to the clergy. There would follow a recitation of some gripping scene from Scripture – the Annunciation, John's account of the Last Supper, or Paul's exhortation in the twelfth chapter of Romans, 'Be not conformed to this world.' Such devices were designed to take the neophyte into a reading-circle.[33]

The basis of the vernacular Scriptures was important, because of the potency of Scripture itself, and the opportunity for direct instruction and self-instruction through the plain text afforded by the Waldensian system for the laity in contrast to their passive role at orthodox services.

Oral instruction was a religious outlet open to all, whether intelligent, partially educated or totally ignorant, and it kept knowledge of the text of Scripture in being. Donatism and Biblicism had prevailed and there was greater hostility to the Church, as witnessed in the threats to the clergy that they would have their tithes and possessions removed and be reduced to day work.

Much of the core of Waldensian belief lay in a cutting away of what were seen to be the excrescences of orthodox belief in purgatory, in images, in pilgrimages; in an insistence on moral life; and in the literal observance of the texts of Scripture. They would not take oaths; they would not lie; they would not accept judgements of blood – a belief which had the more poignancy when executions of heretics took place. What they heard of the Scriptures, no doubt initially from orthodox instruction, was to be observed to the letter and not glossed away. The Anonymous said they could be detected just because they were better than their neighbours.

Investigations in 1311 and 1313–15 based on Steyer, Krems and elsewhere (including Vienna) showed that the heresy had stayed alive in Lower Austria. Depositions give a hint as to how it was done: through secrecy and by attending services to ward off suspicion. Perjury, one said, was not a sin; another had little

31    Segl, *Österreich*, pp. 233–70; Id., 'Ketzer im Mittelalter', *'Ketzer' – Dissidenten – 'Volksschädlinge'*, ed. S. Krimm, U. Triller (1999), pp. 25–48 at pp. 39–48.
32    Nickson, 'The "Pseudo-Reinerius"'.
33    Segl, *Österreich*, p. 198.

vernacular phrases to murmur to himself at mass, denying what was done. 'Es ist gelogen was man singet' ('It is a lie what one sings'). Membership at all levels was distinguished by much rote knowledge of the Scriptures in the vernacular. The Church was vehemently attacked. The sacrament of the altar was an artificial god, 'der gemacht got', and the friars 'Kirchphaffen'. A burgher of Krems, Ulrich Woller, put on a public spectacle for his guests, using his children to pillory the sacrament of marriage, himself ostentatiously breaching the Catholic observance of Good Friday.[34]

A 'master of the heretics', like his predecessors in 1266, forswore the penances of the priests and simply enjoined his penitents to kiss the earth – an action linked to popular superstition, which led the orthodox in south Germany and Austria when they were in need of the last rites and no priest was available, to use earth instead of holy oil.[35] Witnesses said that they had sixteen, or in another account, twelve, apostles who travelled great distances to care for the believers, and that two of them would go every year to paradise to receive from Elias and Enoch the power of binding and loosing.[36] A woman called Gysla, when her interrogators asked if she was a virgin, said she was a virgin above ground but not below it – a belief apparently shared by others of the accused.[37] It is as if a curtain twitched back, then closed again, reveals in Austria a coarse, resolutely anti-Church movement, capable of rousing heroic resistance and still trained in scriptural knowledge, embedded, however, in a local vernacular culture with idiosyncratic and superstitious elements.

Waldensianism prospered in Bohemia and farther east. But it met powerful counter-attack. Fournier as cardinal advised John XXII and as his successor, Benedict XII, encouraged repression; Dauphiné came under increased pressure.[38] It is reasonable therefore to think that inquisitorial activity in Bohemia owed impetus to the papacy too. Fragments of the record of an inquisition conducted by the Dominican friar Gallus of Neuhaus (Jindřichův Hradec) between 1335 and c. 1353 reveal astonishing figures for heretics, chiefly Waldensians, interrogated and punished.[39] The fragments that remain witness by implication to an inquisition working over years, achieving numbers of interrogations, condemnations and burnings at a level comparable only with those of the classic tribunals of Languedoc. When Neumeister, the Waldensian bishop, was burnt in Austria in 1315, he told his enemies that the number of believers in Bohemia and Moravia was 'immeasurable'.[40]

They were German speakers and their appearance in Bohemia was the fruit of colonization, mission and flight from persecution by German speakers flowing

---

34    Ibid., pp. 324–41.
35    Ibid., pp. 305–7.
36    Ibid., pp. 314, 328; M. Erbstösser, *Sozialreligiöse Strömungen im späten Mittelalter* (1970) (Marxist summary on Flagellants, Waldensians, Free Spirit; illuminating on masters), pp. 147–53.
37    Segl, *Österreich*, pp. 309, 330.
38    Paravy, *Chrétienté*, II, pp. 947–8.
39    *Quellen zur böhmischen Inquisition im 14. Jahrhundert*, ed. A. Patschovsky (1979).
40    Ibid., pp. 18–24; Neumeister, p. 21 n. 33; quoting *Annales Matseenses* ('numerus infinitus').

over the frontier from Austria into southern Bohemia. They formed a dense network of relations and friends, above all in the villages but in towns as well, in Prague, Hradec Králové, České Budějovice, Jindřichův Hradec and, in Moravia, in Brno and Znojmo. Of Prachatice, close on the frontier with Austria, it was said that a majority of the population were Waldensians. They moved readily between town and village, to marry, to live with relations or for economic reasons. Most of the accused in Gallus's inquisitions were peasants or craftsmen, but close inspection of their situation in the villages shows them to be either in a leading role or at least of middle rank, the prosperous rather than the downtrodden, including village magistrates and heads of households with servants. Their Waldensianism was the self-confident protest of the tolerably prosperous and capable against an orthodox Church they believed, not without reason, to be neglectful. Perhaps those who migrated to improve their lot were psychologically more open to self-improvement via the open Scriptures.[41] It is likely that a nucleus of Waldensians had existed in Bohemia for about a hundred years before the earliest of the hearings noted in the extant Gallus inquisition protocols. The settlement Gallus uncovered was too thick to have arisen over a short period of time.[42] Discovery of fragments of the record dating from 1389–95 of hearings of two Waldensian women from Komotau, distant from the well-known Waldensian nuclei in southern Bohemia, demonstrates that there was a Waldensian presence in and near the German-speaking town at the end of the century, despite the fierce proceedings of inquisitors such as Gallus of Neuhaus.

Research elsewhere fills out the picture of an underground Waldensian network spread out across Germany and the colonized German-speaking lands to the east. Their presence has been confirmed in Trier and Heidelberg. They have long been known to have been widespread in Upper Germany. Whole districts of Brandenburg and Pomerania had substantial Waldensian populations and their presence in Schweidnitz has been investigated. R. E. Lerner notes that 'it now seems likely that there were more German-speaking Waldensians in the fourteenth century than there were heretics of any sort whatever from any other language group'.[43]

Pressure of persecution affected Waldensian thinking. The *Liber Electorum*, a poignant treatise of just over one thousand words, which survives in Latin and an Occitan version derived from Languedoc, bears witness to the consolation which in hard times they found in history.[44] Internal evidence suggests it was put together by a Waldensian brother in Italy between *c.*1335 and the 1350s, aware

---

41    Suggestion of M. Erbstösser, 'Strukturen der Waldenser in Deutschland im 14. Jahrhundert', *Mentalität und Gesellschaft*, ed. S. Tanz (1993), pp. 95–106 at p. 106; see Patschovsky, *Quellen*, p. 69.
42    Distribution, Patschovsky, *Quellen*, pp. 71–87; persecution and origins, pp. 81–2 correcting earlier views in his *Die Anfänge einer ständigen Inquisition in Böhmen* (1975), p. 45.
43    Rapports, xvi *Congrès International des Sciences Historiques* (1985), i, pp. 360–2; A. Patschovsky, 'Waldenserverfolgung in Schweidnitz 1315', *DA* xxxvi (1980), pp. 137–76; on Komotau, I. Hlaváček, 'Zur böhmischen Inquisition und Häresiebekämpfung um das Jahr 1400', *Häresie*, ed. Šmahel, pp. 109–31; role of German-speaking Waldensians may have been underestimated (p. 111 n. 4).
44    Biller, 'The *Liber*', pp. 207–24; 'Medieval Waldensians' construction of the past', *Waldenses*, pp. 191–206; Döllinger, *Beiträge* ii, pp. 352–5.

of the terror brought by the inquisitors and seeking to comfort by identifying the Waldensians with the Elect, the faithful, who rejected the Donation of Constantine and retained the poverty which the Church had lived in before the disastrous imperial gift.

Periods of light alternated with periods of darkness; three hundred years till Constantine, eight hundred in which a majority succumbed and evil grew while a minority, the Elect, remained faithful; then two hundred years during which Valdes was converted and people willingly heard him and his successors, when many were converted and there were great councils of 700 or 1,000 participants; then a great persecution which raged still in the author's time, who recalled the prophecy of Jeremiah 33: 18, 'Neither shall the priests and levites want a man before me to offer burnt-offerings...' The prophecy, he reminded his readers, spoke of one man to carry out God's will: the remnant to survive might be small, but survive it would. The moon signified the Church; its waxing and waning was a symbol of the phases of light and darkness in its history. The Church, he assured them, would rise mightily again.

The author wrote good Latin, was aware of the rules of composition, knew his Scripture and was probably using the *Glossa Ordinaria* and Peter Lombard. In its extreme brevity and staccato phrasing, the text was designed for memorization, and was indeed so used. It recalled Scripture, having echoes of the epistles and Acts. The author had his eye on Italy: he depicted Valdes as preaching there successfully and, in a curious twist, gave him a friend in the curia, a cardinal from Apulia (who none the less failed to win him acceptance). A phase of success and prosperity without persecution could fit thirteenth-century Piedmont, but not Austria where there were prosecutions.

But the text travelled over the Alps and was a central point in a Latin polemic between, on the one hand, faithful Waldensians of St Peter in der Au in Austria, supported and encouraged by Italian masters, and, on the other, German-speaking ex-Waldensian masters, who had converted to Catholicism.[45] Waldensians had evidently retained links between German speakers and Italian masters who in a crisis helped each other. Convert masters attacked the *Liber Electorum*: the surviving masters on both sides of the Alps defended it. It claimed that Valdes was a priest called Peter 'from a certain region called Waldis'. This was unhistorical and blurred the central issue behind Valdes's break with the Church – the right of laymen to preach. Peter was the leader of the apostles who defied the Sanhedrin, putting obedience to God above obedience to man. This was a kind of counter-claim to the papacy as successor to Peter, stigmatized in the more radical Poor Lombard tradition as 'heresiarcha'.

For all its moving appeal to scriptural precedent and call to fidelity and prayer, the *Liber* bore the scars of effective polemic from the Catholic side. Waldensians had obviously become susceptible to the hostile query: 'Where were you before Valdes?' and the story of the remnant who rejected the Donation is an attempt born of oral tradition to meet that query – an attempt which lacked proof, as the

45   Döllinger, Beiträge ıı, pp. 355–62; convert masters' arguments, Cameron, *Waldenses*, pp. 118–25.

Dioceses of Prague, Olomouc, Breslau
Archbishopric
Bishopric
Castle
ZNOJMO Place of inquisitorial hearing
Divec Place of residence of heretics or suspects
Počatky Place of origin and (voluntary or involuntary) place of temporary residence of heretics or suspects
Place of origin and temporary residence not certainly identified
Waldensians
Beguines or beghards
Suspects without precise adherence
Sites not certainly identified
Place included for orientation

1. Ober-Groschum (Horni Chrášt'any)
2. Unter-Groschum (Dolni Chrášt'any)
3. Klein-Groschum (Malý Chrášt'any)

0                     90 km

MAP 5   *Heretics in Bohemia and Moravia in the fourteenth century: the inquisition of Prague and Olomouc.*
*Source*: Adapted from *Quellen zur böhmischen Inquisition im 14 Jahrhundert*, ed. A. Patschovsky (Weimar, 1979).

opposition did not fail to point out, contrasting the shadowy heirs of the rejection with the historical line of popes. One of the convert masters, Johannes Leser, who wrote a letter in his own defence in 1368 followed by a treatise on the superiority of the Catholic position, reproached the Waldensians with their failure to administer all the sacraments: 'woe to those who wish or presume to be physicians and do not have the medicines to cure wounds'.[46] The Lombards may once have wished to make themselves a counter-Church; in practice this had proved impossible and believers had to depend in part on the ministrations of Catholic priests.

Argument had plainly skewed in directions favourable to the Catholic side; on authority, precedent and the sacraments. Simple followers, who believed their confessors went to paradise for instruction, would not be influenced by this trend; some masters, by contrast, evidently were and the debate of the 1360s was a herald of decline. It seems reasonable to link defections of German-speaking masters later in the same century to a loss of conviction about the status of the Waldensians based on the type of argument that emerged in the polemic of the 1360s. A list dating from the last decade of the century provides names of twenty masters, nineteen of whom went over to Catholicism. Five of them subsequently entered the priesthood and one a monastery. The losses were peculiarly grievous in view of the vital role the masters exercised in the movement.[47] They were the dedicated few, the celibates who travelled about the country, hearing confessions, using books, instructing the faithful – in a word, carrying out the work of an underground priesthood, effective because of their high moral standards. The faith of the rank and file was the more shaken when the preacher class, whom they venerated, defected, and, in some cases, set about missionizing amongst their former supporters. Moreover, the preachers had a wide-ranging knowledge of the location of their flock and inquisition procedures were such as to encourage, indeed demand, full disclosure of information as a sign of repentance of the sin of heresy.

The consciousness of a high level of danger and the bitterness of abandoned supporters is revealed when Waldensians murdered defectors. Four of the listed masters are said to have been assassinated. It was in crass contradiction to the doctrine repeatedly taught by the masters, the birth of which goes back to the early days of Waldensianism, when reactions against the effects of warfare, massacres of Jews, crusades and the harshness of judicial execution of thieves in times of famine issued in an absolute prohibition of killing under all circumstances.[48] In the Reformation epoch Waldensians were still uneasy about the use of force by the State; but a question by Waldensians to Oecolampadius in 1530 presupposes that there had been acceptance in the past of the legitimacy of putting defectors to death.

---

46   Cameron, *Waldenses*, p. 123 (quoting Biller's unpublished thesis, DPhil, Univ. Oxford, 1977).
47   Kieckhefer, *Repression*, p. 58.
48   P. Biller, 'Medieval Waldensian abhorrence of killing pre-*c.*1400', *Waldenses*, pp. 81–95.

The phase of defections merges into a series of large-scale campaigns against Waldensians in southern and eastern German towns in the years 1389–1401, probably sparked off by major informers. The major impetus seems to have come from three itinerant inquisitors, Martin of Amberg, Peter Zwicker and Henry Angermeier, who used episcopal authority when they needed it.[49] Zwicker, a Celestinian, was one of the great inquisitors, known to have been active in the field against Waldensians from 1391 to 1404 in a swathe of German-speaking territories stretching from the Baltic littoral into Austria and Hungary, and distinguished by his flexibility, his close engagement with the actual views of the Waldensians and the persuasive skill which he used against them in his treatise *Cum dormirent homines*. He deployed the same arguments as the controversialists of the 1360s via pungent, homely debating points, which no doubt he also used in sermons and interrogations, criticizing, for example, Waldensian Donatism, saying, 'A rose glows just as much in the hands of an emperor as of a polluted woman'.[50]

Zwicker's quality can be seen in the record of his attention to the Waldensian network in Brandenburg and Pomerania. He used a range of questions, more extensive than was customary, comprising seventy articles. He and his team were very thorough and the answers they elicited enable us to see with clarity the spectrum of Waldensian belief and practice in the field, not schematized, as is often the case in inquisitors' handbooks. Zwicker's penitents were generally small people, drawn from over 120 villages and small towns in Brandenburg and Pomerania. Some had wealth, with their own farms and households; most were of modest rank. No nobles or businessmen were involved. This Waldensianism had deep roots. An adherent who was over eighty said that his parents were born into the movement; a woman over ninety said she had been born into it too.[51]

Rank and file in these prosecutions lacked the capacity to give a justification for their beliefs, which stretched all the way from a borderline position between Waldensianism and Catholicism to wholesale polemic against the Church. The cult of Our Lady was one of the strongest links to orthodox piety. The leadership taught that prayer should only be addressed to God and not to the Virgin, who would thereby be disturbed in the fullness of her heavenly joy; but supporters were reluctant to give up accustomed ways and would pray for her intercession, at least in times of need. One adherent said that a person who died when on pilgrimage would be damned; yet another Waldensian woman went as a pilgrim to Rome, Aachen and Wilsnack. A majority rejected prayers for the dead and one with a characteristic pungency of denunciation said it was as senseless to pray

---

49   Kieckhefer, *Repression*, pp. 58–9.
50   Cameron, *Waldenses*, p. 143 from Gretser's edn of Zwicker; characterization, pp. 139–44; P. Biller, 'The anti-Waldensian treatise *Cum dormirent homines* of 1395 and its author', *Waldenses*, pp. 237–69; Id., 'Waldenses in German-speaking areas in the later fourteenth century: the view of an inquisitor', Ibid., pp. 271–90; D. Kurze, 'Zur Ketzergeschichte der Mark Brandenburg und Pommerns vornehmlich im 14. Jahrhundert', *JGMO* XVI–XVII (1968) (excellent trial analysis), pp. 50–94, see esp. pp. 71, 76, 88, 89; Leff, *Heresy* II, pp. 478–80.
51   Treesh, p. 82.

for the dead as to give fodder to a dead horse. For them there were only two ways, to heaven or to hell; purgatory did not exist. Mechtold of Groten Wubiser said that purgatory had been invented by priests to feed their avarice. Yet others did pray for the dead – whether, as Kurze notes, out of hazy conviction, custom, friendship or out of reluctance to stand against the parish priest. Some rejected wholesale the sacraments and apparatus of the Church, vestments, chants, bells, organs, hierarchy and relics; but baptism was accepted, some arguing that rainwater was as effective as holy water, others using it, falling in with custom or not wanting to make themselves conspicuous.[52] A widow in Brandenburg had no belief in the efficacy of holy water but admitted that she threw palms on to the fire during storms like other people.[53] In these ways Catholic custom and the environment of friends and neighbours modified Waldensian practice, as did a natural eclecticism and failure of logic.

The oath was firmly rejected; it was even said that one who swore an oath could not go to heaven. But it was understood that it might be needful to take an oath when in danger of death. Persecution and the need to establish their distinctive role led them easily to believe that only Waldensians could be saved; but that harsh view was mitigated in some cases by the positive sentiment of a membership deeply concerned with the pursuit of a moral life for good works, whoever performed them and whatever the background belief.[54]

What held these Waldensians together was the mobile preacher, coming in secrecy and by night, known only by Christian name, to exhort, instruct and, above all, to hear confessions. Fifteen of them are identifiable in Zwicker's record – Klaus of Brandenburg, Conrad of Saxony, Gottfried of Hungary, Nicholas of Solothurn, Nicholas of Vienna and so on – men who came remarkable distances to care for their people. These Waldensians, like their fellows in Austria, believed that the confessors went to paradise periodically to hear God's voice or to obtain power from him.[55] The evidence suggests that their educational standards were lower than those of a generation earlier. They were of humble background, artisans, sons of artisans and peasants, serving a country movement.[56] They were held in reverence, partly because of their anonymity, their very occasional visits and their evident devotion to their task – a bond of somewhat different character from that which existed between the Cathar perfect and their *credentes*, who usually knew them personally. They came on average once a year, alone or with a pupil, to visit their believers who led them from place to place secretly and cared for them with food, money and necessities. A majority of those who made their confessions to the masters did not receive them in their own houses; they came regularly to a limited number of hosts and it becomes apparent that there was a leading class of believers responsible for organizing these visits, collecting

52   *Quellen zur Ketzergeschichte Brandenburgs und Pommerns*, ed. D. Kurze (1975), p. 201; Treesh, p. 45.
53   Kieckhefer, *Repression*, pp. 62–3; palms, *Quellen*, ed. Kurze, pp. 140–1; Treesh, p. 46.
54   Kurze, 'Zur Ketzergeschichte', pp. 83–7.
55   Ibid., pp. 77–8, 81, 82–3; see Biller, 'The 1391 lists of Waldensian *magistri*: three further manuscripts', *Waldenses*, pp. 233–6.
56   Cameron, *Waldenses*, p. 127; Erbstösser, *Strömungen*, pp. 123, 127–9.

money or gifts which could be sold, acting as guides. It was on these that survival rested.[57] Mostly Waldensianism was an inheritance: in the records of the Mark of Brandenburg analysed by Kurze, 112 out of 176 interrogated were brought in by parents; 26 had only one Waldensian parent and 38 had not been influenced by their families.[58] The movement still had an independent missionary attraction, probably via the leading class of believers. Clearly attitudes to penance differed in different regions and at different times. In the long run the austere watchfulness of the confessor over his own life might well be reflected in the rigour of the penances he imposed.[59]

Effective as Zwicker was, he had no heirs with the same energy and ability.[60] His vigorous prosecutions make a caesura in the history of German Waldensianism, but not an end. He seriously damaged the leading class of masters but could not eliminate the substratum of the most committed believers who held the movement together. They were accustomed to abjure, to lie low and live to fight another day. Inquisitions in Brandenburg in 1458 revealed the same villages and the same families to be affected by Waldensianism as in Zwicker's time; and in 1480, they were still there.[61]

What changed the situation was the Hussite revolution. From the 1420s onwards, German Waldensians began to emigrate to the freedom of the Hussite lands.[62] Those still *in situ* felt an affinity with the Taborites, the radical Hussite wing, and later with the select, rigorous and pacifist *Unitas Fratrum*. News of Hussite success encouraged the Waldensians, but among Catholics it created fear of a Waldensian fifth column and stimulated inquisitions.

A Waldensian master, Friedrich Reiser, child of a believer in Donauwörth, tried to build unity between Waldensians and Taborites.[63] His first dream had been to bring together German and Italian Waldensians, and he set about learning the requisite languages, only to be required by his wealthy lay backer, Hans von Plauen of Nuremburg, to desist and concentrate on ministry in Germany. He roamed German-speaking lands, seeking to replace the work of lost masters by his own energies. Attracted to Tabor, he moved residence and was ordained a Taborite priest, subsequently taking the title 'bishop of the faithful in the Roman Church who scorn the Donation of Constantine'[64] – an indication of the passionate wish for a poor Church which he brought with him from his Waldensian past.

57  Comment of Erbstösser, 'Strukturen', pp. 99–101.
58  Kurze, 'Zur Ketzergeschichte', p. 90.
59  P. Biller, '*Multum ieiunantes et se castigantes*: medieval Waldensian asceticism', *Waldenses*, pp. 69–79.
60  Treesh, p. 87.
61  Ibid., p. 109; Kurze, *Quellen*, pp. 288–314.
62  F. Šmahel, 'Crypto et semi-vaudois dans la Bohème hussite', *RHR* CCXVII (2000), pp. 101–20, freedom, p. 101.
63  Treesh, pp. 65–6, 121, 158–62, historiography, p. 173; Cameron, *Waldenses*, pp. 147–50; H. Köpstein, 'Über den deutschen Hussiten Friedrich Reiser', *ZG* VII (1959), pp. 1068–82; F. Machilek, 'Deutsche Hussiten', *Jan Hus*, ed. F. Seibt (1997) (major conference on Hus and Hussitism), pp. 267–82 (wide-ranging survey).
64  Trans. Cameron, *Waldenses*, p. 148.

He began to ordain priests: to his projected unified Church, he brought the Hussite practice of communion in both kinds. In 1450, with the Taborites, he launched a more systematic attempt at unification. Regular meetings were held, followers gained and missionaries inspired. But the achievement was limited.[65] Not all Waldensians accepted Reiser, the Taborites were distracted by their own struggles and were not the same force after their defeat at Lipany. The Hussite movement was predominantly Czech-speaking and there were tensions between Germans and Czechs. Moreover, repression was still strong enough to pick off leaders: one of his lieutenants, Matthäus Hagen, was burnt in Berlin in 1457, Reiser himself captured and burnt in Strasburg in 1458 and his successor, Stephen of Basle, in Vienna in 1467.

Certainly, Reiser and his fellows made an impact. At a trial of peasants in 1462 in the neighbourhood of Zwickau, Margaret of Meissen revealed traditional Waldensian teaching combined with the new eucharistic practice of communion in both kinds.[66] The trend, however, was to seek refuge in Bohemia and Moravia and to unite with the *Unitas Fratrum* – a formal letter to them requesting acceptance of immigrants survives. A group of refugees who retained their individuality after moving to Fulnek and Landskron in Moravia was still traceable in 1603.[67]

Waldensianism in German-speaking lands was not confined to the countryside; towns had significant numbers of believers. The *De Vita et Actibus*, an account of Waldensian life and teaching written in Languedoc for inquisitional use *c.*1300, pragmatic and factual, barely touched by the classic prejudices, describes in detail the custom of Waldensians north and south of the Alps of holding annual general chapters in Lombardy or Provence, most commonly Lombardy, to which three or four representatives from Germany came with a 'clericus' or other interpreter, using pilgimage to Rome as camouflage, in which they conferred on the state of their movement, making decisions on the destination of money collections, especially for the necessities in food and clothing of the *sandaliati* – the masters – and for the hospices. Masters who were not wholly committed to the movement were not included, nor were the young apprentice masters; the celibate Sisters, even the experienced and mature, did not take part and the believer class were not represented at all. An oligarchy of experienced masters held together a loose federation.[68] Waldensianism was capable of spanning serious linguistic and geographical barriers; believers were sufficiently attached to the whole to be willing, not only to support visiting masters, but also to donate to collections for transmis-

65  Following emphasis of Treesh, ch. 4, Cameron, *Waldenses*, pp. 144–50, Biller, *Waldenses*, p. 7, Audisio, *Dissent*, p. 84 in preference to Molnár in Gonnet–Molnár, pp. 211–82 on Hussite-Waldensian 'International'. A dream was not realized.

66  Treesh, pp. 162–3.

67  Ibid., p. 166; Kurze, *Quellen*, pp. 319–20, 327.

68  P. Biller, 'The *De Vita et Actibus de Lugduno*', *Waldenses*, pp. 225–31; Döllinger, *Beiträge* II, pp. 92–7; the Sisters lived in hospices, sometimes little all-women groups or with two or three male masters, passing themselves off as wives or sisters to ward off suspicion; they appear to be nuns, running the hospices and providing food. There is no suggestion of libertinism.

sion across the Alps, and organization was strong enough to gather a war chest. The author added that the greater part of the money was brought from Germany.

Examination of records of inquisitions held in towns shows why German donors had such a major role; here were located the most prosperous of the believers anywhere.[69] Hans von Plauen plainly had a stranglehold on Friedrich Reiser; Fribourg believers in the fifteenth century included representatives of two leading firms, the Struders and the Praroman-Bonvisins, and the prosperous Mossus family; some Berne Waldensians were in the governing echelons of the town. Urban investigations c.1400 and later reveal the presence of, in Biller's summary, 'a sprinkling of the nobility...a heavy representation of families of citizen status, characteristically holding high office and of considerable wealth, principally based on cloth and hide trading'.[70] Evidence of the Waldensians of the towns before this date is fragmentary but sufficient to establish their presence. Probably Waldensian and trading links ran together as in the case of the Mossus of Fribourg and Zur Bircken of Strasburg in 1356.[71] By the time that investigations of heretics became effective in Fribourg in 1429–30 the links to Italy had gone, though one believer, Conrad Wasen, was aware of co-religionists there. Fribourg lay at the outer limit of German-speaking territory, which doubtless explains the lateness of investigation, and its visiting masters came from Germany and Bohemia, disguised as merchants in grey or dark blue, pretending they had come for business purposes. Greda 'mit der Nase' was remembered as saying, 'Come, come, the Good People have arrived'.[72] The fact that one witness believed there were seventy-two 'disciples of God', who came two by two, shows the continuing influence of Matthew 10.[73]

Berne had investigated its Waldensians in 1399 and expelled over 130 of them, handing over to Fribourg details of relevant suspects. Serious inquiry was warded off as the accused found compurgators and were acquitted. But it was not the end of the matter. Proceedings again took place in 1429, prelude to the major investigation in 1430, probably sparked off by a fear of the Hussites gaining a hold via the Waldensians. Twenty of those acquitted in 1399 were found guilty. The editor of the extant trial records, Kathrin Utz Tremp, believes that Waldensians had 'gained in structure and perspective' between 1399 and 1430 and attributes this increase in strength to the effects of the Hussites and their victories.[74] Another suspect, Richard of Maggenberg, a rich peasant from the countryside near Fribourg, who had escaped in 1399 was brought to trial in 1437.

69   P. Biller, 'German money and medieval heresy: the wealth of the German Waldenses', *Waldenses*, pp. 111–23; Id., '*Thesaurus absconditus*: the treasure of the medieval Waldensians', Ibid., pp. 97–110.
70   Biller, 'German money', p. 117.
71   Biller's suggestion, Ibid., pp. 117–18.
72   K. U. Tremp, 'Les Vaudois de Fribourg (1399–1430): état de la recherche', *RHR* CCXVII (2000), pp. 121–38; *Quellen zur Geschichte der Waldenser von Freiburg im Uechtland (1399–1439)*, ed. K. U. Tremp (2000); Id., 'Multum abhorrerem confiteri homini laico', *Pfaffen und Laien – ein mittelalterliches Antagonismus* (Freiburger Colloquium 1996), ed. E. C. Lutz, E. Tremp (1999), pp. 153–89 (colours, p. 177); Wasen, Treesh, p. 66; Good People, Ibid., p. 25.
73   Tremp, 'Multum abhorrerem', p. 178; my comment.
74   'Les Vaudois', p. 127.

The terms 'vaudois' and 'vauderie' were now being applied to sorcerers as well as Waldensians and the proceedings of 1429, imperfectly recorded, were directed against country people, especially women, and may well have been concerned with sorcery rather than heresy. The poison of accusations of libertinism and diabolism boosted by the actions of the fanatic Conrad of Marburg and by the issue of *Vox in Rama* in 1233 by Gregory IX, based on Conrad's wild imaginings, had its effect. A casual conversation between two women repeated in 1430 shows how the slander had penetrated society. Greda Lappen said that the preachers of the Waldensians preached secretly in corners; Greda Otschina stoutly claimed they were good preachers, 'as good as ours'. 'Why, then, do they kiss the cat under the tail?' No evidence from Fribourg corroborates this.[75]

Belief in the efficacy of prayers for the dead was of long standing in the Catholic world, as was their rejection by the Waldensians, but the growth in importance of the doctrine of purgatory in the late Middle Ages had the effect of intensifying Waldensian hostility. In Fribourg it was a key issue. Wills of known Waldensians and sympathizers omit anniversary masses in favour of donations to the poor: there is a clear analogy here to the wills of Lollard sympathizers in England.[76] With confession the difference was slight. The masters who came from afar were valued for their personal merit; one witness, expressing her distaste as a Catholic for the Waldensian practice of confessing to a layman, was given the classic reply, that the confessors were 'good and holy people' who stood in the place of the Apostles of God. What may have been new was the awareness that the Waldensian masters were only 'laymen', a view which even reached a child, Heinzli, who, when sent by his mother with the wine containers to his uncle's house, looked at the master there who expected to hear his confession, said 'You are no priest' and ran off – a possible sign of the efficacy of Catholic propaganda.[77]

The Waldensianism of German towns, which now disappears from the records, remained the classic Waldensianism of the underground in belief and practice, with a certain radicalism. Suspicion of church music led to some discreet boycotting of collections for a new organ in the parish church of St Nicholas in 1426–7.[78] What most distinguishes Fribourg is the degree to which the heresy had penetrated its most prosperous, governing levels. Twenty-four of the sixty-one male Waldensians were merchants, including eminent ones, the firm of Praroman-Bonvisin being almost exclusively Waldensian.

The Strasburg trials of *c.*1400 revealed some fifty Waldensian believers, multi-generational, including servants; several families traded in cloth and skins, others were lower in the social scale. They were protected by Blumstein of the lesser nobility, who threatened potential witnesses, and the Zur Bircken family, whose house was often used as a meeting place, was deeply implicated. There were nine

---

75　Treesh, p. 47, quoting G. Ochsenbein, *Aus dem schweitzerische Volksleben* (1881), p. 328.
76　See Tremp, 'Waldenser und Wiedergänger'; Id., 'Les Vaudois': below, pp. 277, 393.
77　Tremp, 'Waldenser und Wiedergänger', p. 131; Id., 'Multum abhorrerem', p. 185.
78　K. U. Tremp, 'Es ist gelogen was man singet', *Freiburger Geschichtsblätter* LXXVII (2000), pp. 27–49; Id., 'Les Vaudois', p. 156.

'schools', homes in which 'one prayed and confessed, heard preachings from great books and was instructed in all articles of the unbelief'.[79] Perhaps as the first stage in the selection process, believers appear to have put forward candidates for training; one such would lie on the floor in the centre of all believers, then, accepted, he would be raised, take a vow of celibacy, poverty and fidelity to Waldensian beliefs and, in ceremonial fashion, be greeted by each believer in turn, saying 'dear master, you are welcome'. One powerful witness, Die Alte zum Hirtze, a housewife who showed evidence of reading and leadership, was concerned to emphasize that they had women masters as well as men and the same procedure was followed.[80] The believers were wealthy enough to carry out the grim purpose of raising £50 to pay for the murder of a renegade master; but they were unable to influence events long-term and, as we have seen, were unable to prevent the capture and burning of Friedrich Reiser.

The ultimate fate of urban Waldensians is obscure. Despite their financial weight and the muscle that gave the movement, the towns were never centres. Masters mostly came from a distance and from relatively small places. Treesh is inclined to postulate a fundamental distinction between the resilience of village and small-town Waldensianism and its lack of durability in towns in the competitive conditions of the fifteenth century.[81] The heresy in larger towns was a victim, in part, of its own success; it had climbed into the ruling class, which, although when serious investigations threatened, was generally able to shield itself, avoid the harshest punishments and pay fines, had no depth of commitment comparable to that of country believers. Humbler members appear to have followed their leaders into renunciation. In contrast to the countryside, where the battle was straightforward between devoted visiting confessors and a local priesthood of low competence, these towns offered much on the Catholic side to distract the laity from Waldensian sympathies, such as the Beguin movement, the friars and the confraternities.

Attention in Fribourg switched to the pursuit of witchcraft; Berne, having banished Waldensians, did not feature on Reiser's list; the Reformer Oecolampadius, who talked with representatives from Piedmontese Waldensians, had no idea that Waldensians had once been in Basle; Martin Bucer had a similar experience in Strasburg. This looks like inner failure rather than a yielding to the *force majeure* of inquisitors.

## The Redoubts

On the Italian and French slopes of the Alps, the highlands of Piedmont and Haut Dauphiné shared a dialect, a common culture and way of life. Mountain valleys were refuges: the terrain and the problems of ecclesiastical and political

---

79    Biller, 'German money', pp. 113–15; Treesh, p. 73.
80    Treesh, pp. 25–6; P. Biller, 'The preaching', pp. 125–58, comment by Merlo, *RHR* CCXVII (2000), pp. 36–7.
81    Treesh, pp. 120–8.

authority at these heights drew refugees from territories where persecution was more effective: they were also lands where missionary enterprise had successes, in a defensible territory where Waldensian families could put down roots. The poverty and simplicity of the itinerant preacher was naturally attractive to poor shepherds and peasants struggling to make a living in a harsh environment. The parish clergy, working their land with scant external financial aid, lacked stimulus or training. Among their Catholic neighbours, Waldensians practised endogamy, maintaining, as elsewhere, a Waldensianism of the household accompanied by attendance at mass and reception of the sacraments.[82]

Both sides of the Alps were affected by the determination of the Avignon popes, especially after Fournier's experience, to put Waldensianism down. Catharism had been eliminated; Waldensianism was the major surviving enemy. Thus repression developed in both regions in the fourteenth century, though with important differences. The deep poverty and isolation of the Piedmontese valleys gave a feeling of distinctiveness as contrasted with the life of the plains. Inquisitors revealed some hundreds of suspects but secular authority was seldom zealous in support for fear of disturbing the local population. There were killings. In 1335 the parish priest of Angrogna, suspected of being an informer, was murdered in the square after mass; inquisitors were assassinated.[83] Waldensianism was contaminated. Piedmont formed a crucible for a Cathar–Waldensian syncretism which co-existed with the dominant strand of plain Waldensianism.[84] So we meet, beside the denials of purgatory and the invocation of the saints, the rejection of oaths, Donatism and the belief in the superiority of confession to their own preachers, an idiosyncratic logic that Christ was not true God since God could not die,[85] Cathar teaching on dualism and the *endura*, and, allegedly, the acceptance of sexual licence. We meet the extraordinary figure of Giacomo Bech, interrogated in 1388, who apparently had in his time been an adherent of the *fraticelli*, the Waldensians and the Cathars of the mitigated dualist variety;[86] and Giovanni Freyria, who confessed in the preceding year to having adored the sun and moon, saying the *Pater Noster* and *Ave Maria*.[87] We also meet the hoary old *canard* in the interrogations of 1387–8 and 1451 of the secret sexual orgy, begun after one of the preacher class, the *barbi*, put out the light, saying, 'Qui ama, si tegna!'[88]

The first known source in the medieval West for stories of heretics participating in indiscriminate sexual intercourse in the dark is the account of the Orléans

---

82   Paravy, *Chrétienté* II, pp. 947–67; Id., 'Waldensians in the Dauphiné (1400–1530): from dissidence in texts to dissidence in practice', *BHL*, pp. 160–75; mission to mountains, p. 162.

83   Paravy, *Chrétienté* II, p. 959.

84   G. G. Merlo, *Eretici e inquisitori* (1977) (*ME*) (analysis of heretical environment, stimulating, sometimes controversial, hypotheses); G. Gonnet, 'Casi di sincretismo ereticale in Piemonte nei secoli XIV e XV', *BSSV* CVIII (1960), pp. 3–36; *MLC*, pp. 290–6.

85   Gonnet, 'Casi', p. 19.

86   *ME*, pp. 93–4; confession, G. Amati, 'Processus contra Valdenses in Lombardia Superiori, anno 1387', *ASI*, 3rd ser. I (1865), pp. 3–52, II (1865), pp. 3–61 at pp. 50–61.

87   *ME*, pp. 31, 41.

88   Ibid., p. 33.

heresy of 1022 by the monk Paul of St Père de Chartres.[89] Such practices were attributed to heretics in the twelfth century by Guibert de Nogent[90] and Walter Map;[91] Gregory IX's *Vox in Rama* described heretics of his day who so indulged,[92] and interrogators elicited confessions about orgies at various times from Templars and rebellious Franciscans. A starting-point for the attribution of libertinism to the Waldensians may well lie in a phrase sometimes used at the end of a service: 'let him who has grasped (the meaning) retain it'. The congregation who had listened to the preaching would meditate in darkness for a few minutes before leaving.[93] Later medieval Waldensianism had to operate in darkness and secrecy and so came, willy nilly, to conform to the classic controversialist's picture of the insidious heretic. From darkness and secrecy to the slander of the secret orgy was an easy step. *Vox in Rama* was based on the fantasies of Conrad of Marburg about the doings of German heretics; receiving papal confirmation gave Conrad's poisonous stories a vogue they might not otherwise have had and helped to popularize accusations of libertinism. The story of the secret orgy, sometimes blended with fantasies about the sacrifice of a baby, has a startlingly long history, investigated by Norman Cohn,[94] reaching back to slanders of the early Christians by Minucius Felix, as table 2 demonstrates.

The story, it is clear, could be applied to any unpopular movement, and in the fourteenth century the Waldensians were losing ground in public opinion. The story of libertinism is on all fours with a popular slander also in vogue, of a hidden Waldensian treasure that gave the lie to their claims of leading a poor, apostolic life.[95] The most perceptive inquisitors rejected such stories. Zwicker refused belief in the legend of the hidden treasure. Pseudo-David of Augsburg, though he would give credence to doubtful tales about *barbi*, refused orgy stories. By contrast, the inquisitors in the Valleys were not of the highest calibre, and believed in stories of libertinism. Torture and pressures of interrogation forced out confessions, with elements of fantasy. Moreover, though many of those who came before them had indeed been involved in heresy, they were often fringe members.[96] What Merlo calls 'heretical syncretisms' floated about the Valleys. In Chieri part of the local aristocracy were under a Cathar-dualist influence; in the Valleys and in land immediately below them Waldensianism was stronger. Folklore played a part just as it did amongst the Cathars of Montaillou.

---

89    Above, pp. 16, 18–19.

90    Guibert de Nogent, *Histoire de sa vie (1053–1124)*, ed. G. Bourgin (Paris, 1907) III, xvii, pp. 212–13; orgies, M. Barber, 'Propaganda in the Middle Ages: the charges against the Templars', *NMS* XVII (1973), pp. 42–57 at pp. 45–8.

91    *De nugis*, ed. James, I, xxx, p. 47.

92    Trans. Barber, 'Propaganda', pp. 45–6; E. Peters, *The Magician, the Witch and the Law* (1978), pp. 156–7; *MLC*, pp. 121–2.

93    N. Cohn, *Europe's Inner Demons* (1975) (powerful analysis of fantasies, witch cult and slanders of Waldensians); see esp. pp. 32–42; alleged libertinism among Franciscans, pp. 42–54.

94    *Demons*, chs 1–5.

95    Biller, 'Thesaurus absconditus'.

96    Criticisms, K. V. Selge, reviewing Merlo, *Eretici*, *HZ* CCXXXI, pp. 445–7.

TABLE 2    *Accusations of libertinism*

| Author and date | Target | Reports |
|---|---|---|
| Minucius Felix first century | Christians | Worship of donkey's head; orgy; killing of baby |
| St Augustine | Manichees; the Elect class | Orgy |
| Paul of St Père de Chartres eleventh century | Heretics at Orléans | Orgy; viaticum from ashes of dead baby |
| Guibert de Nogent twelfth century | Heretics at Soissons | Baby killed by being passed from hand to hand |
| Walter Map twelfth century | Heretics | Worship of black cat; orgy |
| Gregory IX: *Vox in Rama* 1233 | Heretics in Germany | Worship of Lucifer in various guises; orgy |
| Nicholas Eymeric: *Directorium Inquisitorum* 1368 | Waldensians | 'in the dark it is lawful for any man to mate with any woman' |
| Antonio di Setto 1387–8 | Waldensians in the Alps | Drinking toad excrement; worship of Lucifer; orgy |
| St John Capistrano (source for Flavio Biondo) 1449 | Fraticelli burned at Fabriano | Orgy; baby roasted |

One of the most frequent tenets was the denial of purgatory, based on the standard Waldensian teaching that there were only two paths to follow, one of which led to heaven and the other to hell. The accused, however, sometimes said that purgatory existed 'in this world'. The oddities of this phase of Waldensianism can in part be attributed to the confusions of certain lay leaders resident in the villages, passing on what they had learned from travelling *barbi* and adding stray scepticisms and idiosyncratic views of their own.[97] Catharism and Waldensianism had once been mortal enemies; but the perfect and the *barbi* and *Meister*, celibate, devoted, wandering, had superficially something in common and to some degree they melded together. Individual cases exist of the giving of the *melioramentum*, of a Cathar greeting, of a leader engaging in a ceremony based on the Cathar perfect's blessing of bread.[98] In sum, here more than anywhere else in the long Waldensian history, we can justly speak, with Merlo, of 'Waldensianisms' – special circles of

---

97   See Cameron, *Waldenses*, ch. 7.
98   Examples, *MLC*, pp. 290–6.

followers, perhaps bound to a charismatic leader, extending or distorting the nucleus of well-established doctrine and practice.

But the idiosyncrasies and contaminations disappear: when the Waldensians of those same valleys welcomed first the representatives of the *Unitas Fratrum* and then later the Reformers of the sixteenth century, the visitors found that the *barbi* had been marked by their long underground existence and they denounced their nicodemism, but they did not meet the odd, amorphous syncretisms thrown up by these inquisitors. Based as they so often were on individuals and their eloquence, perhaps Cathar strays, we may conclude that contaminated circles lapsed as the leaders died or were laid by the heels by inquisitors and that in time, the main stream of Waldensian teaching was recovered.

From Piedmont came a substantial reinforcement for the shattered movement in France – at least in purely numerical terms – as Waldensians blended quietly with waves of emigration from the overcrowded Valleys between 1460 and the 1520s and settled, often as small landed proprietors, in the Luberon and other parts of Provence.[99] They kept possessions in their ancestral Valleys and returned occasionally for business and personal reasons.

It is hard to believe that the Catholic clergy of the lands of immigration were unaware of their presence; but, as elsewhere, inertia and perhaps humanitarian considerations led them to turn a blind eye. The Waldensians were careful to do nothing to make themselves conspicuous. In many things they did as their Catholic neighbours did. They paid tithes, they participated in observances which implied the existence of purgatory (whatever their private reservations) and they took oaths. Their faith was the faith of a household, just as Catharism had been in the Sabartès. Secrecy was maintained by a careful marriage policy. Waldensians married Waldensians and passed on their faith to their children. The same Christian names recur and recur over the years. Comparison of their wills with those of a predominantly Catholic settlement at Cucuron shows that the Waldensian families were inclined to make more gifts to the poor than the Catholics did – a survival, it may well be, of the stress on poverty and charitable activities going back to Valdes himself.[100] Commemoration of their dead took a more sober form in their bequests than in those of the Catholics. They tended to omit the additional commemorative masses which Catholics founded and made less use of the cross, holy water and torches at burials.[101] At Lourmarin, where there was a substantial Waldensian presence, the records of the parish priest reveal a full observance of Sundays and days of obligation.[102] The Waldensians were contributing without reservation to the support of their Catholic priest, yet at the same time maintaining in secrecy their inner life through contact with wandering preachers, taking what Audisio refers to as a 'homeopathic antidote' to the Catholic observance they followed so fully.

---

99   Audisio, *Luberon*, masterpiece of reconstruction, using refractory material.
100  Ibid., p. 270.
101  Ibid., p. 215.
102  Ibid., p. 220; see Treesh, pp. 6–7, Erbstösser, *Strömungen*, p. 142 on tacit acceptance of Waldensians in various places.

The eccentricities within the Piedmontese valleys are not matched in Provence or Haut-Dauphiné. In the latter region the movement was much more homogenous, concentrated in a small number of mountain villages carved by tributaries of the Durance, La Vallouise, the valleys of L'Argentière, Freissinières and the Italian Valcluson and capable of sustaining a social organization to stand up to the forces of repression.[103] These Waldensians suffered stiff persecution in the fourteenth century, with executions, confiscations, destruction of houses, issuing in waves of emigration to places of safety and freedom. Franciscan inquisitors continued a work of investigation and penancing, inducing abjurations but not conversions – or not on any scale. At risk of his life, St Vincent Ferrier went up to the valleys to preach, but with little effect.[104] They still held their nuclei and in Freissinières there was a time when the heretics were the majority.

Two developments in the later fifteenth century marked out the Haut-Dauphiné wing: one was the ability of their leaders to draw on legal proceedings to ward off the effects of the actions of inquisitors, to make use of the hostility between Louis XI and Jehan Baile, Archbishop of Embrun, and conflict between the jurisdictions of Paris and Grenoble; the other, intertwined with the first, was the emergence of a lay leadership within the local communities deputizing for the wandering masters, organizing resistance and making collections. Certain families predominated; but as one was reduced by the effects of repression, another emerged to take its place.

Defensive, legal action by the communities was rudely interrupted by an anachronistic, crude and brutal crusade in 1487–8, permitted by the pope, who gave the crusade indulgence, and inspired by Albert Cattaneo, an Italian churchman who wished to eliminate Waldensianism on both sides of the Alps, working hand in hand with the Archbishop of Embrun. Cattaneo was never able to mobilize Piedmontese authority to work in unison with the forces of repression on the other side. A Dominican inquisition, sometimes ineffective, was responsible in Piedmont, Franciscans, working with the archbishop, on the other side. A truly unified assault was the one action which might have eliminated Alpine Waldensianism, but it was never undertaken. The communities on both sides remained in touch with each other, providing refuges and preachers: Piedmontese *barbi* sometimes went over to minister to the Dauphinois. The crusade issued in both heroism and atrocity; it killed 160 Waldensians and renewed confiscations, abjurations and flights to freedom in Provence or Piedmont.[105]

The long-term result was unprecedented. The crusade failed to intimidate its survivors. Aided by some of the refugees, lay leaders took advantage of the inequities of Cattaneo, of royal concern and of a changing climate of opinion and succeeded after many years of striving in winning a rehabilitation from the Conseil Royal in 1509, which declared that the ostensibly Waldensian communities had been unjustly subjected to anti-heresy proceedings and that confisca-

103   Paravy, *Chrétienté* II, p. 959; see map, p. 957.
104   Ibid., pp. 969–70; K. U. Tremp, 'Hérétiques ou usuriers? Les Fribourgois face à Saint Vincent Ferrier', *Memoire Dominicaine* VII (1995), pp. 117–37.
105   Paravy, *Chrétienté* II, ch. xix; Cameron, *Waldenses*, pp. 176–200, esp. pp. 185–7.

tions were void. Royal interest lay in maintaining peace and security over Montgenèvre, one of the principal passes to Italy; rehabilitation may have seemed a means to that end.[106]

The nicodemism of the Waldensians stood them in good stead: in the series of proceedings which led up to the verdict of 1509, Catholic witnesses, even priests, testified to their good life and observance of the feasts and fasts of Catholicism. A distinction in the verdict was drawn between the heretical *barbi*, 'pseudo-apostles', deceiving the simple, and the lay members. Non-Waldensians preferred to testify in their favour and bring peace, doubtless influenced by memories of the blatant rapacity shown in the crusade and its subsequent confiscations.

The Waldensianism of Haut-Dauphiné was not substantially different from that uncovered by Zwicker: visiting preachers came to exhort and hear confessions, sometimes in houses, sometimes in fields; their flocks held traditional Waldensian views, with the possible exception of a softening of attitudes towards the swearing of oaths, with an admixture of not wholly logical attachment to some Catholic practices. Their moral calibre was high – there were convincing refutations of slanderous allegations of libertinism – and, as elsewhere, neighbours preferred to wink at their distinctive practices and beliefs.[107]

Alpine Waldensianism survived because of its territory and the disunities of its enemies, the will to peace of its neighbours and, in the Haut-Dauphiné, the quality of its lay leadership. Communities lasted to meet up with the Reform and generally accept Calvinism. But they left behind a remarkable testimony to their beliefs in what Paravy wisely describes, not as a Waldensian literature so much as a Waldensian library.[108] This working library was of a character adapted to its membership, with a predominantly ethical and scriptural cast. Vernacular texts were written in an Alpine dialect. Some two hundred dialect sermons and a collection of poems are extant, which together comprise a compendium of belief. They were designed to be memorized, to act as a support for faith in a largely illiterate membership, though there were also Latin texts. Despite the vicissitudes of their history, Waldensians retained men of some learning in their preacher class, who understood the medieval clerical tradition, which they adapted for the use of simpler colleagues and the benefit of all adherents. Their Latin provided a lingua franca for contact between the Italian- and the German-speaking wings.

---

106  Cameron, *Waldenses*, p. 200.
107  Paravy, 'Waldensians in the Dauphiné', p. 165; crusade, Id., *Chrétienté* II, pp. 977–96; G. Audisio, 'Famille, religion, sexualité dans une secte: les Pauvres de Lyon (xve–xvie siècles)', *RHR* IV (1992), pp. 427–57 discusses, first, confessions and family influence, then argues for *some* libertinism among believers, following analysis of defendants' statements. Not all, he believes, betray inquisitorial pressures. But orgy stories are often slanderous (table 2), witnesses in all interrogations can suffer from aberrations, Titus 1: 15 is unlikely to stand against St Paul's attacks on libertinism, the Free Spirit (p. 456) did not exist. Weight of evidence is against his view.
108  Paravy, *Chrétienté*, pp. 1085–1149, illuminated further, P. Biller, 'The oral and the written', *Waldenses*, pp. 159–67, Id., 'The *topos* and reality of the heretic as *illiteratus*', *Waldenses*, pp. 169–90; older research, Gonnet–Molnár, pp. 319–69; contrast to teaching of Reformers, Cameron, *Waldenses*, pp. 223–5; A. Brenon, 'The Waldensian books', *BHL*, pp. 137–59; Id., 'La réponse des hérétiques: les recueils des sermons vaudois de la fin du Moyen Age', Id., *Archipels*, pp. 311–17.

A Latin confessor's tract bears witness to the importance of penance among them. A bestiary is a good example of their willingness to adapt from the clerical tradition: Jaco, who translated it into dialect for some of his pupils, simplified it, no doubt for its use by preachers, and omitted material on heresy and Mary.[109] Masters were thus taking *exempla* from nature, following an earlier orthodox tradition which was displaced in some degree in later medieval piety as the cult of saints developed and *exempla* were more often drawn from saints' lives – largely alien material for Waldensians. A bestiary fitted the agricultural world. It moralized on creation and was a natural choice for a missionary elite working amongst peasant adherents with their animals round them.

Scripture held a dominant place: it was 'the unique norm of teaching and living' and to it appeal on all disputed questions was made. Vernacular translations were a nodal point for the instruction and rote learning which mattered so much to adherents. Waldensian literature proper, or literature taken over by the Waldensians, served the purpose of opening or explaining the Scriptures and of confirming the membership in their ethical life. One of the best-known pieces, the *Nobla leycon*, was a poem of about 1400,[110] which gives a survey of the whole Bible under the headings of the three laws of God: the law of nature, the law of Moses and the law of Christ. At its centre lies the little flock, faithful in adversity.

There was also simple catechetical material such as the seven articles of faith and orthodox extracts, such as a collection of sentences from the Fathers, and a work of Augustine on the virtues and vices, called the 'Thirty Stages'. These witness to a Patristic strand in the movement which went back to the founder. One poem is influenced by a work of the future Innocent III on the contempt of the world. This type of reading matter was not heretical at all and reveals no trace of syncretism or corruption through the underground existence of the movement. What does betray the clandestine existence of Waldensians are the tiny books, even as small as $2.5 \times 2.5$ inches, adapted for rapid concealment in the clothing of *barbi* threatened with discovery. The extant poems give a conspectus of Waldensian belief: they were mnemonics, designed to be supports for faith in predominantly illiterate congregations.

The masters clearly had a scriptorium and a sufficiency of men able to select, adapt and manage that part of the orthodox tradition which they found suitable, and were, of necessity, used to having work recopied to replace what was lost through wear and tear and the depredations of inquisitorial activity. The Hussite revolution evidently fascinated. Treatises emanating from it, Hussite, Taborite, works of Luke of Prague, were copied without omission or alteration, although parts of this material stood in clear contradiction to their own predominantly Catholic, medieval tradition.

So Waldensianism survived in its highlands supported to the last by a network of families, running over the Alps, linking up Piedmont and Haut-Dauphiné to the Luberon and associated areas; it was these families who gave sons for training

---

109   *Bestiario Valdese*, ed. E. M. Raugei, *Biblioteca dell' 'Archivum Romanicum'*, ser. I vol. CLXXV.
110   Biller's dating, '*Curate Infirmos*', p. 62.

as *barbi*. Candidates would be put through two or three years' probation and taught to read and write. Peasants' sons were being recruited to speak to peasants: it was part of the movement's strength and gave it the distinction of being the one medieval heresy which had the peasantry as its carrying class.

Scarred by long pressure, Waldensianism survived where Catharism had failed. It never suffered the profound divisions about belief which led to the strange and bitter denominationalism of Italian Catharism. The conflict between Lyonists and Poor Lombards, which the Conference at Bergamo tried to heal, was never resolved but it mattered less as time passed. There were indeed 'Waldensianisms', but they existed without major tension and they were mostly – and characteristically – Italian in origin. Inevitably many an individual Waldensian had his own version of faith, which one of the conscientious inquisitors not content with routine interrogation would elucidate: such interrogations produced a survey of belief not easily attainable in any other way, with the doubts, hesitations and illogicalities characteristic of present-day investigations into the beliefs of church members. Different individuals had their own compromises with the Catholicism surrounding them and with customs which pleased, even if incompatible with the core of Waldensianism.

The word itself, none the less, had its own power – that of the naked text, learnt as the first literature by a young man taught to read in order to master his vernacular Bible to become one of the *barbi*. Third World experience shows the powerful effects of what is first presented to an adult illiterate reading for himself. This inspired the *barbi*, already children of their household religion, and armed them for their dangerous, wandering years. They in the end were the most important factor in outlasting persecution, with the naked text of Scripture studied, learnt by rote, and the practice of confession. Cathars were exotics: their dualisms were oddities which failed in the face of a higher quality of pastoral care and preaching. Cathars managed texts with ingenuity; but the Bible or New Testament was used by them above all as a sacred object, to be placed on the head of a candidate in their most vital rite. Waldensianism stood closer to the main stream of Western Christianity and contrived by a narrow margin to outlive the popular slanders and the efficient but sporadic inquisitions to which they were subjected. Neighbours and, we may strongly suspect, parish priests were not inclined to betray them: repression came from outside.

Organization *per se* was not crucial.[111] It was not the office and the chapters as described, for example, by Bernard Gui in his handbook which kept them in being. Much of this fell away through time and persecution, leaving the simplest of structures at the end – the family, leading lay adherents, chapters for the Romance Waldensians linking the Alpine and Italian remnants and, above all, the *barbi*. It was these who mattered most. It was their tenacity and mobility in visiting their flocks which kept their movement alive till the Reformation.

111   Argument for organization, Leff, *Heresy* II, pp. 463–4.

# 9

# Tension and Insecurity: Gregory x to John xxii

While the Cathars were being put down by persecution and by peaceful competition from the Church, the popes faced grave problems, not directly connected with doctrinal unorthodoxy.[1] At first the search for security and independence in Italy lay at the heart of their troubles; they had fought for years to defend themselves against the menace of the Hohenstaufen dynasty holding simultaneously the Empire and the Regno, and threatening them in Rome. Under Innocent IV every means, fair and foul, was used to defeat Frederick II, and no small part of the papacy's reputation and sacral quality was sacrificed in the process. Later, in order to prevent Frederick's heirs again menacing the papacy's independence, a papal champion, Charles of Anjou, was employed to take and to defend the Regno. As we have seen, Charles's success had effect throughout the peninsula, and incidentally helped to create the conditions for the determined persecution of Cathars in Lombardy. The papacy achieved a major victory through the Angevin alliance, and eliminated the Hohenstaufen – only to find the power and ambitions of Charles, brother of Louis IX of France, and the strength of the Capetian dynasty to which Charles belonged profoundly disquieting.

The conflict with the Hohenstaufen had important side-effects: it tended to debase papal policy, and the search for a rival champion helped to create parties within the college of cardinals and to increase tensions between national groups. When in turn the dangers of Charles's power became apparent, one of the policies adopted was that of attempting to build up the papal states in central Italy as partial counterbalances by means of nepotistic appointments.[2] Successive

---

1   B. Moeller, *Spätmittelalter: Die Kirche in ihrer Geschichte*, ed. K. D. Schmidt, E. Wolf, II, pt 1 (Göttingen, 1966) (exposition from 1250); F. Rapp, *L'Eglise et la vie religieuse en Occident à la fin du Moyen Age* (Paris, 1971) (from 1303); reflections in R. W. Southern, *Western Society and the Church in the Middle Ages* (Harmondsworth, 1966). See J. K. Hyde, *Society and Politics in Medieval Italy* (London, 1973), and G. Barraclough, *The Medieval Papacy* (London, 1968); F. Oakley, *The Western Church in the Later Middle Ages* (Ithaca, NY, and London, 1979); R. N. Swanson, *Religion and Devotion in Europe c.1215–c.1515* (Cambridge, 1995); heresy, pp. 272–5; scepticism, pp. 329–40.
2   Hyde, *Society*, p. 130.

popes sought security through promoting relatives; but pontificates were short, and the relatives of one pope might well be the enemies of another. The policy brought no long-term security and damaged papal reputations.

Charles's decline was due, not to papal policy, but to the effects of his misgovernment. A revolt in Sicily in 1282, aided by intrigue and bribes from his foreign enemies, gravely weakened his position. The Angevin menace was thereafter effectively removed, but the popes did not jettison the Angevin alliance. Instead, they backed the attempts of Charles and his heir to regain the island of Sicily and, over a period of two decades after the revolt of the Sicilian Vespers, committed papal money and prestige to the Angevin cause, declaring expeditions against their opponents to be crusades. In the end, despite these efforts, defeat had to be accepted at the Peace of Caltabellotta, to which the pope assented in 1303.

This was one beneficent event in the pontificate of Boniface VIII, a first-rate canon lawyer and capable diplomat who was also a gross nepotist and ruthless power politician. Under his highly controversial rule, a dispute with the king of France, Philip IV, escalated into a major conflict. Shortly after Boniface had issued the bull *Unam Sanctam* in 1302, the most extreme statement of the temporal claims of the papacy, he was attacked by Philip's servants in his residence at Anagni, and died shortly afterwards of shock. His fate and his doubtful reputation overshadowed the following two pontificates, for Philip used the threat of a charge of heresy against Boniface as a means of applying pressure. Clement V, elected after the short pontificate of Boniface's immediate successor, Gascon-born, settled at Avignon, partly because of his personal predilections, partly because of the convenience of being close at hand for negotiations with Philip. The temporary residence of the papacy there lasted, with one short interruption, until 1377. Temperamentally reluctant to take firm action, Clement, however he might manoeuvre, in the end felt himself compelled to accept Philip's will. At the Council of Vienne in 1312 he suppressed the order of Templars, earlier convicted of wholly imaginary offences at the instigation of Philip, who needed their goods in order to satisfy pressing economic needs. As if to underline the changed position of the clergy *vis-à-vis* the laity, the same council discussed the encroachments of the laity on ecclesiastical goods and jurisdictions without finding any effective defence against them. It was a melancholy contrast to Innocent's fourth Lateran Council a century earlier.

After a prolonged vacancy, John XXII was elected to succeed Clement in 1316. As trenchant as Clement had been vacillating, he at once set about restoring the papal position, and in an eighteen-year pontificate, aided by the waning of France's strength after the death of Philip IV, went far towards recreating independence. In place of his predecessor's debts he built up an unprecedented surplus. The curia was reorganized, and once again the papacy came to occupy a central position in international diplomacy; all spheres felt the impress of the pope's personality – energetic, authoritarian, inflexible. On issues of faith and heresy, his instinct was to back authority, to define and condemn, and to give work to the inquisition. The pontificate was marked by a series of definitions and proceedings aimed at suspect theologians and sectaries. Authoritarian methods roused opposition. Obstinate determination to make his own will prevail over the choice of emperor aroused a conflict with Lewis of Bavaria, who gave protection to Franciscan rebels and heretics as a weapon against the pope, and John failed to bring him down. At the end, lacking the suppleness of Innocent III and the essential aid of powerful reform movements within the Church and religious orders, he had been unable to stimulate profound or long-lasting changes to the benefit of the Church, and the methods whereby he rebuilt the papal position alienated opinion.

Over the clergy, in contrast to the laity, the papacy exerted an ever-increasing control during these difficult years. Centralization continued apace within the Church, and canonists erected a structure of thought which drew out the implications of the doctrine of the 'fullness of power' inherent in the papal office. A major impetus to centralization was, however, fiscal. Costly wars and foreign policy, and expanding bureaucracy, demanded money and the growing papal power within the Church was more often directed towards stopgap solutions of immediate problems than the needs of reform. In form and theory, the place of the papacy within the Church expanded; in reality, popes suffered from a chronic insecurity and inability to match means to ends.

A changing society was becoming less amenable to papal leadership. Damaged by the papacy's own misuse, the attractions of the crusading ideal waned. One stage in its decay was reached by the time that Gregory X, a sincere crusading pope, summoned the Council of Lyons of 1274. It was intended to heal the schism with the Greek Church, counter Charles of Anjou's designs on Byzantium, and act as a launching platform for an expedition to the Holy Land. Gregory's investigations at the time of the council revealed how far interest in crusades had waned; a traditional link between papacy and laity was gradually eroding.

The Empire was far less significant than it once had been: power had passed to the national kingdoms. The events of the pontificates of Boniface VIII and Clement V showed the difficulties which popes had in coming to terms with the shift in temporal power that had taken place.

Educational standards amongst the laity were rising, and new directions in lay piety were beginning to make themselves felt. The mystical way, formerly the preserve of the monastery or nunnery, was being opened to the laity and to the secular clergy, with the aid of the friars and their spirituality. It reflected a developing trend towards individualism in later medieval piety, not of itself hostile to the Church and the sacraments – indeed eucharistic fervour might be a feature of the pursuit of the mystical way – but stressing the soul's experience of God rather than the Church's mediation.

No movement arose on the scale of the Cistercians in the twelfth century or the friars in the early thirteenth to rouse the energies of the devout and give backing to any papal reforming designs; reform impulses were still there, but they found expression in piecemeal, local movements or in the lives of dedicated individuals. The Franciscans, so long a support of the papacy, showed signs of strain; at the Council of Lyons earlier dissensions dating back to St Francis's lifetime began to emerge again in a form so acute as eventually to demand prolonged papal investigation.

Complexity, bureaucracy and worldliness produced a reaction. The popes faced difficulties that were not susceptible of swift, personalized solutions; but their position was rarely considered with sympathy, and from the early years of the fourteenth century we may detect something of the sense of betrayal which Leff rightly distinguishes as characteristic of late medieval opinion about Church leadership.[3]

Abuse of the inquisition's powers, the Free Spirit and the heresy associated with the Spiritual Franciscans, to be discussed in the following chapters, have to be set against this background of centralization, political pressure and change in the years between the Council of Lyons and the death of John XXII in 1334, affecting both the men and women accused of heresy and their repressors.

3   *Heresy* I, p. 29.

# 10

# Inquisition and Abuse

## The Problem of the Inquisition

The papal inquisition was founded by Gregory IX, building on the foundations of his predecessors, and the extraordinarily wide powers of investigation and punishment which accrued to inquisitors were granted in order to make an end of heresies already condemned by the Church, most notably Catharism.[1] Naturally new sects and heresies that arose fell within its purview and, equally naturally, the influence of those who were given inquisitional powers tended to be directed towards the tightening of the Church's law on heresy, in favour of condemnation rather than toleration of doubtful beliefs and practices. The desire of the inquisitor was for clear-cut condemnations and lists of erroneous beliefs that could be incorporated in handbooks and used as a basis for action in the field; his instinct was to widen the scope of his authority and to bring more activities into his sphere. So, for example, inquisitors attempted to bring sorcery under their jurisdiction after application to Alexander IV, whose ambiguous declaration that they might only do so if 'manifest heresy' were involved was used as a starting-point for an ultimate, if long delayed, assumption of authority in this sphere.[2] Churchmen who shared the inquisition mentality were inclined to see heretical tendencies in movements and groups in the Church of which they disapproved. Bishops within their dioceses exercised wide powers and, if zealous, could give scope to their suspicions on the same lines as the inquisitors. The untrammelled power of the inquisitor, the high penalties exacted or exactable for heresy and the opportunities in some cases of enrichment of interested parties in the wake of convictions made it inevitable that the unscrupulous would seek to take advantage of heresy charges to advance their own power, to ruin rivals or to feather their own nests. Unjust accusations of heresy were not new, and there

---

1  Bibliography, E. van der Vekené, *Bibliographie der Inquisition: ein Versuch* (1963); *WHC*; orientation, B. Hamilton, *The Medieval Inquisition* (1981).
2  Lea, *Inquisition* III, p. 434; see J. B. Russell, *Witchcraft in the Middle Ages* (Ithaca, NY, and London, 1972); *WEH*, p. 251.

is little doubt that zealots with no pertinacious will to unorthodoxy were killed or ruined in the twelfth century, before the development of more advanced techniques of detection and judgement. Confusion, then a major factor, was no longer so prevalent in the late thirteenth century; the new feature was the international character of persecution and its greater sophistication. On the one hand, the development of antiheretical treatises, bulls of definition and inquisitorial handbooks helped to dispel the old ignorance; on the other, if prejudice did once enter into these sources, they were disseminated much more widely, and the new character of persecution made possible what had not existed earlier – the manufacture of a whole artificial or semi-artificial heresy.

At the lowest level the office of inquisitor exposed its holder to temptation: it was the other side of the coin in the new efficiency of persecution which flowed from the commissions and legislation of Gregory IX and his successors. *Inquisitio* as a legal process confounded in one and the same person the offices of prosecutor and judge. There was also a blurring between the coercion implicit in a penal system and the healing of the soul which lay at the heart of the voluntary system of confession followed by the performance of penance. The secrecy of proceedings, the wide powers of arrest and imprisonment, the lack of any obligation to inform the accused of charges against him or to name witnesses, the absence of defending counsel, and the extreme difficulty of appealing against decisions meant that the preservation of justice rested to a large extent on the integrity of the individual who conducted a case. Using a commission of Gregory IX, Conrad of Marburg created a reign of terror in Germany in which innocent as well as guilty perished; an imaginary sect of Luciferans, alleged devil-worshippers, was the fruit of Conrad's wilful interrogations and misunderstanding. Robert le Bougre, also under Gregory IX, was guilty of arbitrary and doubtful acts through his passion for putting down heresy.[3]

There were other examples. That friars in office could be bribed or invent rackets was not just slander put about by heretics; inadequacies of supervision, the ease of working up accusations based on casual expressions of scepticism, the ill-defined offence of 'impeding' the inquisition, the weight given to mere *fama*, the ill report of a suspect's orthodoxy in a neighbourhood, opened the way to corruption, aided by the complaisance of governments. Inquisition verdicts could not be implemented without the lay power, since it received a share in the profits of confiscation. It is probably no accident that cases of malpractice grew as the prime target of inquisitors, Catharism, crumbled. Institutions seek fields of activity; inquisitors were inclined to accept artificial heresy and magnify the true. Some succumbed to financial temptation. Because of the benefits accruing, the lay power soon learned to manipulate inquisitorial proceedings. Doubtful

---

3  On Conrad, *MLC*, pp. 118–22, with lit.; for Robert, Ibid., pp. 122–5, but note that Jordan of Saxony gives clear confirmation that he fell and came to a bad end, and that M. D. Chapotin, *Histoire des Dominicains de la Province de France* (Rouen, 1898), p. 223 is evidence that he was, in effect, still acting as inquisitor in April 1244. I owe these points to Rev. Dr S. Tugwell. For definition of an inquisitor, Segl, *Anfänge, passim*.

practices thus existed in plurality with dedicated inquisitors[4] – and bishops – who continued the drive against genuine heresy after Catharism had faded.

Servants of the office of inquisitor were casually selected and employed and not closely supervised: notaries and others could seize opportunities opened by the wide, arbitrary nature of the inquisitorial procedure to enrich themselves, smear enemies and exercise power. Menet de Robercourt, notary to the Carcassonne inquisitor in the 1320s, by brutal handling after arrest, in effect killed off a sick priest of Montpellier, later proved innocent, let himself be bribed to pressurize witnesses to revoke testimony against a converted Jew, having them tortured to do so, and set in motion a false heresy accusation against a consul of Albi who had complained about him. His career of crime was checked by Jacques Fournier, who as Benedict XII ordered an investigation. The case was extreme, but not unparalleled.

By contrast, especially in the early days, inquisitors were often zealous, hard-working bureaucrats, exercising a dangerous task, inclined, perhaps, to cut corners in eagerness to get to grips with heresy, yet not gravely unfair to suspects. Some, however, yielded to the temptation of the office. In the March of Treviso in the last forty years of the thirteenth century, a small group of Franciscans held inquisitorial office and were with reason accused by Boniface VIII of manipulating their position for gain. Other such cases occurred in Tuscany in the fourteenth century: one genial rogue, Mino of San Quirino, accumulated a fortune by insinuating false or trivial accusations, then suppressing them for bribes, till he was uncovered by an emissary of John XXII.[5]

The most important danger, however, lay in misunderstanding and unconscious distortion, either through over-sophisticated questioning or over-rigid adherence to some preconceived pattern of heresy derived from treatise or handbook, then imposed by forceful interrogation on a cowed suspect. Bernard Gui, who completed his manual about 1322–3, gives us an example of the dangers of over-sophistication in his section on tricks of the Waldensians, in turn taken from a thirteenth-century work attributed to David of Augsburg.[6] The inquisitor questions his suspect on the articles of faith. He replies briskly, 'I firmly believe.' The inquisitor asks him about transubstantiation. He replies, 'Ought I not to believe this?' The inquisitor responds, 'I am not asking if you ought to believe it, but if in fact you do', and gets in turn the reply, 'I believe all that you and other good doctors order me to believe.' The inquisitor believes this is an evasion, and goes on, 'Those good doctors which you are willing to believe

---

4   For early inquisitor of integrity, Y. Dossat, 'Une figure d'inquisiteur: Bernard de Caux', *CF* VI, pp. 253–72; confusion of penance and punishment, Hamilton, *Inquisition*, pp. 49–59; Lea, *Inquisition* I, chs 7–14, is still of value.

5   A. Murray, 'The medieval inquisition: an instrument of secular politics?', *Peritia* V (1986), pp. 161–200. Id., 'The Epicureans', *Intellectuals and Writers in Fourteenth Century Europe*, ed. P. Boitani, A. Torti (Tübingen, Cambridge, 1986); see also C. Bruschi, 'An early inquiry into an inquisition (1330)', *Trials*, ed. Biller, Bruschi. Murray, together with continuing work on medieval suicide, will issue a new volume of essays.

6   *Manuel*, ed. Mollat, I, p. 67; on authorship, Dondaine, in *AFP* XVII (1947), pp. 93–4, 180–3; *BK*, pp. 22, 25; Patschovsky, *Passauer Anonymus*, pp. 135–6; *Bernard Gui et son monde, CF* XVI (1981).

are the masters of your sect. If I think as they do, you will believe both me and them; if not, not.' So the two continue to wrestle until the wily Waldensian is finally broken down on the sensitive issue of oath-taking.

No doubt life underground did produce the Waldensian heretic experienced in such evasions; but inquisitors would also meet simple Catholics, untrained on the limits of heresy and orthodoxy, nervously attempting to ingratiate themselves, and falling deeper in the mire. Behind interrogation lay torture, to be applied at the will of the inquisitor. Confinement, fear and detachment from family and friends worked like torture. Either could be used in such a way as to compel incriminating answers. The danger of a vicious circle was obvious, for inquisitors believed that in heresy they were fighting the work of the devil and were inclined to think that suspects were more subtle than they really were. Force, and the threat of force, could produce the guilty answers they felt they ought to be getting. The classic example is witchcraft, whose apparent popularity owed so much to the interest of inquisitors.[7]

More subtle distortion might spring from the use of leading questions based on handbooks' summaries of heretical tenets, obliterating an individual's personal variations of belief. In examining Cathars, for example, inquisitors commonly flattened out, J. H. Arnold notes, 'the myriad individual relationships between laity and *perfecti*' and did so out of a fundamental working assumption that the *illiterati* 'could not be engaged in "belief" in any complex fashion'. Heresies changed, and handbooks did not necessarily keep pace with them; they tended to be based on a stereotype, and did not take adequate account of variations within heretical groups in different areas and times. Or the ethics of heretics might be slandered, and their tenets confused with those of other, more extreme heresies.[8]

Each set of records of proceedings and testimony needs to be examined closely, in order to see whether the inquisitor or the bishop's officers have, through their

---

7 Lea, *Inquisition* III, p. 50; approach tends to differ from Russell, *Witchcraft*. Earlier work, H. C. Lea, *Materials toward a History of Witchcraft*, ed. A. C. Howland (Philadelphia, 1939, repr. 1957); J. Hansen, *Quellen und Untersuchungen zur Geschichte des Hexenwahns* (Bonn, 1901). P. Segl, 'Der Hexenhammer – eine Quelle der Alltags – und Mentalitätengeschichte', *Mentalität*, ed. Tanz, pp. 127–54; K. Blauert, *Frühe Hexenverfolgungen, Ketzer, Zauberei und Hexenprozesse des 15. Jahrhunderts* (Hamburg, 1989); *Der Hexenhammer. Entstehung und Umfeld des Malleus Maleficarum von 1487*, ed. P. Segl (Cologne and Vienna, 1988); A. Kors, E. Peters, *Witchcraft in Europe 1100–1700. A Documentary History* (Philadelphia, 1972, 2nd edn 2001); see *Witchcraft in America*, ed. M. Dimunation, E. Peters (website: access original witchcraft material: Primary Source Media); R. Kieckhefer, *European Witch Trials: Their Foundation in Popular and Learned Culture 1300–1500* (London, 1976); for tensions of later Middle Ages, P. Dinzelbacher, *Angst im Mittelalter* (Paderborn, Munich, Vienna, Zurich, 1996); case of slander, P. Segl, 'Angst in Pamiers in Sommer 1321', *Angst und Politik in der europäischen Geschichte*, ed. F. Bosbach *et al.* (Dettelbach, 2000), pp. 67–84.
8 J. H. Arnold, 'The historian as inquisitor. The ethics of interrogatory "subaltern voices"', *Rethinking History* II: 3 (1998), pp. 379–86; Id., 'Inquisition, texts and discourse', *Trials*, ed. Biller, Bruschi; Id., '"A man takes an ox by the horn and a peasant by the tongue": literacy, orality and inquisition in medieval Languedoc', *Literacy and Learning in the Middle Ages*, ed. S. Rees-Jones, F. Riddy, C. Cross (2001) (problems of establishing evidence from inquisition sources in the light of Foucault and anthropology generally); forthcoming, *Inquisition and Power* (Philadelphia, 2001); on confession generally and the interaction between confessor and penitent, see *Handling Sin. Confession in the Middle Ages*, ed. P. Biller, A. J. Minnis (York, 1998).

questioning, provided a fair and accurate picture of heresy or a heretical group. Sometimes there are signs of distortion of testimony or blind repetition of predetermined sentiments; sometimes idiosyncratic replies by suspects and the flavour of many-faceted heresy as it appears in real life will assure us of the substantial accuracy of what we read; sometimes the signs are that the beliefs of a group have remained fairly static, and our records are doing substantial justice to the accused.

In the higher ranks of churchmen manipulation of heresy charges occurred. A grey area is revealed, for example, in the activities of Bernard de Castanet, bishop of Albi, who controlled the workings of the inquisition in his city, damping them down as long as the heresy-infected leading bourgeoisie were on his side in battles of jurisdiction against the king, unleashing them in a famous set of trials of 1299–1300, after leading citizens had broken the alliance, and had come to work with royal officials against his interests.[9]

The development of papalist canon law in the thirteenth century tended to reinforce autocracy, and to encourage the inclination to equate heresy with disobedience to the pope, in the temporal sphere as much as in the spiritual; strangely enough, Frederick II's imperial legislation, *mutatis mutandis*, tended to confound heretics and political offenders in a similar fashion. The vague use of heresy charges ran hand in hand with the debasement of the crusade to attain political ends for the popes within Christendom, the accusations being a part of the propaganda against offending rulers and a justification for military action against them. So the Hohenstaufen were attacked in this way;[10] so Boniface VIII used the charge against his enemies in the Colonna family; so John XXII proclaimed his political enemies in Italy, the Visconti of Milan, the house of Este, the Ghibellines of Umbria, guilty of heresy, and declared the recalcitrant emperor Lewis of Bavaria to be a fautor.[11] As temporal opponents of the popes often favoured or tolerated heretics as pawns in their political game, or refused for reasons of security to allow the inquisition to operate in their lands, accusations of fautorship of heresy were not wholly baseless. But contemporaries recognized that it was concern, not about unorthodoxy, but about papal rights and the balance of power in Italy that motivated these charges. A debasement of the concept of heresy was implicit in this type of action.

The loose use of heresy charges could not be expected to remain a monopoly of churchmen, and Philip IV of France and his ministers made the most dramatic and unscrupulous use of them in the entire period in their actions against the Templars (1307–12). They had been preceded by charges against Boniface

9   J. L. Biget, 'Un procès d'inquisition à Albi en 1300', in *CF* VI, pp. 273–341; G. W. Davis, *The Inquisition at Albi 1299–1300* (1948). I accept Biget's viewpoint.

10   For this example and others, see Lea, *Inquisition* III, chs 4, 5; Grundmann bibliography in *HS*, pp. 448–50.

11   F. Bock, 'Studien zum politischen Inquisitionsprozess Johannes XXII', *Quellen und Forschungen aus italienischen Archiven und Bibliotheken* XXVI (1935–6), pp. 21–142; XXVII (1936–7), p. 109–34; 'Der Este-Prozess von 1321', *AFP* VII (1937), pp. 41–111, 'Processi di Giovanni XXII contro i Ghibellini italiani', *ADRSP* LXIII (1940), pp. 129–43.

VIII, a man of scant tact and of easy manners, whose insensitive actions and pungent remarks brought him many enemies, and provided a fund of disturbing statements that formed the pretext for charges of heresy and other malpractices brought by Philip the Fair and his servants.[12] The threat of a formal trial of Boniface acted as a blackmail on the insecure Clement v, and opened the way for the sudden assault on the Templars in 1307.[13] An advanced secular monarchy, already blooded in the contest of wills with Boniface VIII, made uninhibited use of inquisitional techniques in order to gain the Templars' wealth. The inquisitor of France was the king's confessor, and the bishops were solid in support of the monarchy's cause; the Templars were a rich, secretive body that seemed to have lost its *raison d'être* when the last foothold of the Christians in the Holy Land at Acre fell in 1291. Disappointment at the failure of Christendom to recover Jerusalem and the search for a scapegoat may have made some of Philip's subjects receptive to charges against the Templars; it does not seem that anyone outside France believed them. The Templars, it was said, imposed a denial of Christ and blasphemous rejection of the cross on their novices, required them to kiss their receptor's posterior, told them that homosexuality was lawful, adored an idol, and had the custom of not consecrating the Host when priests in the order celebrated mass. To this extraordinary farrago were added other variant tales – of eucharistic heresy, worshipping a cat, betraying the cause of Christendom to the Moslems, of laymen in the order hearing confessions and granting absolution, of unlawful gains and sinister secrecy in chapter meetings. Charges were skilfully selected to undermine popular confidence and had more than one echo of accusations customarily made against heretics.[14]

The vicious circle was operating with a set of accusations from tribunals directed by the episcopate and royal servants. Tortured or in other ways subjected to pressure, a sufficient number of Templars confessed, to provide 'evidence' for the case against them. The affair demonstrated that any string of accusations could be made effective, given the necessary zeal in interrogation and the employment of force.

## The Free Spirit and Heretical Mysticism

The Templar episode was the most naked case of the use of the machinery of persecution for pure slander; the treatment of the beguines, beghards and mystics in northern Europe was a more subtle case of misunderstanding, in which

---

12  T. S. R. Boase, *Boniface* VIII (London, 1933), pp. 355–79; articles in *HS* (Grundmann bibliography), p. 449, nos. 515–18.
13  Up-to-date account with literature in Barber, *NMS* XVII, pp. 42–57; see also M. Barber, *Trial of the Templars* (1978), the standard account; reflections, Id., 'The trial of the Templars revisited', *The Military Orders* II, ed. H. Nicholson (1998), pp. 329–42. P. Partner, *The Murdered Magicians: The Templars and their Myth* (1982).
14  Barber, *NMS* XVII, pp. 45–8, 54.

genuine grounds for disquiet combined with suspicious conservatism and the persecuting mentality to smear pious, unprotected groups.[15]

Beguines were religious women leading lives of chastity, generally grouped in convents, supporting themselves by manual work and engaging in prayer but without any fixed rule, organization or final vows.[16] In the north both *beguinus* and *beghard* as a term for a man was usual. The males frequently lived by begging, but resembled the much more numerous female beguines in leading a religious life without fixed organization. The terms, however, were used rather imprecisely.[17]

The beguine movement in the north was a spontaneous, local outgrowth of the urge to apostolic life which moved zealous Christians in the twelfth century and offered occupation for women, generally in comfortable circumstances, who could not expect to find a husband. One starting-point lay in the appeal of a charismatic preacher to women who wished to lead a holy life without necessarily entering a nunnery; so Lambert le Bègue (the stammerer), a humbly born parish priest and reformer in the diocese of Liège, who died in 1177, drew such a group of women whom he directed, and whose association is sometimes thought of as the first beguinage. Lambert was accused of heresy by a ruthless opposition, resentful of his fearless criticism of abuses: his letter of defence to Calixtus III shows how honesty and idiosyncrasy could give a handle to enemies.[18] The very institutional formlessness of the beguinages may have been an attraction, and their simplicity made foundation easy. Some beguines went on living devout lives of charitable service in their own homes or those of their parents; others entered loosely organized associations, which had a woman superior; others again were cloistered. They fitted naturally into urban life, met a need for women who could not find acceptance in established orders, and so continued an unobtrusive existence in large numbers in certain towns of Flanders, northern France and Germany. They also attracted devout women who preferred the role of the beguine on religious grounds to that of a nun, and women from poorer homes who could not afford the price of entry to a nunnery.

The beguine and beghard occupied an ambiguous position. Rigorous interpretation of canon thirteen of the fourth Lateran Council might put their position

15   H. Grundmann, 'Ketzerverhöre des Spätmittelalters als quellenkritisches Problem', *DA* xxi (1965), pp. 519–75 (fundamental reassessment of sources); R. E. Lerner, *The Heresy of the Free Spirit* (1972) (the standard critical account for northern lands); R. Guarnieri, 'Il movimento del Libero Spirito', *Archivio Italiano per la storia della pietà* iv (1965), pp. 351–708 (quarry for material, value for work on Porete's *Mirror*); J. C. Schmitt, *Mort d'une hérésie* (1978).

16   Background in E. W. McDonnell, *The Beguines and Beghards in Medieval Culture* (1954); reflections by Southern, *Western Society*, pp. 318–31. *RB* (pp. 170–318) discusses the problem of women and the religious life, and beguines (pp. 319–54), but see J. B. Freed, 'Urban development and the *cura monialium* in thirteenth-century Germany', *Viator* iii (1972), pp. 312–27); B. Bolton, 'Mulieres sanctae', *SCH* x, pp. 77–95.

17   Lerner, *Free Spirit*, pp. 35–7. The Beguins of southern France (below, pp. 225–32) form part of a different movement, linked closely to the Spiritual Franciscans, principally in the Franciscan province of Provence.

18   L. K. Little, *Religious Poverty and the Profit Economy in Medieval Europe* (1978), p. 129; *MBPH*, pp. 103–11.

in question. In status they lay somewhere between the orders and the parish clergy, subject to neither, and liable to be looked at askance by both.[19] Beghards formed a suspect penumbra to the mendicant orders. Mystical works stimulated the piety of these groups, often aided by confessors and directors from the mendicants and distinguished by a stress, in the style of the friars, on the incidents of the lives of Christ and Mary in the gospels. Because of their lack of established status and organization, they were vulnerable to the accusation of heresy, and popular suspicion seems to have given them their name, beguine being most probably a corruption of Albigensis, the term for a Cathar of southern France. Both beguines and beghards came to enjoy a strangely mixed reputation, sometimes the butt of accusations of sexual immorality on no good grounds, sometimes accused of the hypocritical feigning of virtue, but also praised and given patronage by churchmen of influence. James of Vitry gave them help;[20] Fulk, bishop of Toulouse, thought that beguines might be used as a bulwark against Cathar influence;[21] in the mid-thirteenth century Robert Grosseteste placed their way of life, poor but self-supporting through manual labour, on a higher level even than the mendicancy of the friars. They attracted devout women in considerable numbers, grew spontaneously as part of the evengelical movement of the thirteenth century and were certainly not frustrated would-be entrants to nunneries, though a persistence of suspicion about them led some to become nuns, and many beguinages to seek the protection of the friars.[22]

But by the time of the Council of Lyons in 1274, the earlier suspicion that had dogged them had again risen to the surface. It was a time of growing friction and tension in Church life, and beguines and beghards tended to be Aunt Sallies.[23] The mendicants, conscious of their waning popularity, struck out at groups close to them in their attitude yet precarious in status, and made them scapegoats; on the other side, forces hostile to the friars used them as stalking horses for attacks in reality directed against the friars. Self-interested hostility there had always been, in the resentment of relatives or would-be-husbands at the loss of their women to the beguine life. At the time of Lyons pamphlets appeared against the beguine movement; the Franciscan Gilbert of Tournai complained that beguines had unauthorized vernacular translations of the Scriptures containing heresies (which he did not specify), and that they read these in public places; Bruno of Olmütz proposed bluntly that they should be told to marry or enter one of the established orders. Canon thirteen of the fourth Lateran Council was reiterated and, by the decision of the council, became a barrier *tout court* to all new forms of religious life: no new order was to be founded, and those that had come into existence despite the canon were to be suppressed. Without leading to any direct action, this obviously made the situation of beguines and beghards more precarious. Nothing occurred in the following decades to refurbish their image. Instead,

19   Lerner, *Free Spirit*, ch. 2, is helpful.
20   McDonnell, *Beguines*, p. 20.
21   *RB*, p. 172.
22   Ibid., p. 322; A. Wilts, *Beginen im Bodenseeraum* (1994).
23   Lerner, *Free Spirit*, pp. 45–6.

synodal decrees in Germany witnessed to irritation at beghards as unauthorized preachers; arrests for heresy occurred at Colmar and Basle of both beguines and beghards in 1290; and the Franciscan chapter at Colmar, faced with a procession of 300 beghards begging for bread, warned their members against associating with these suspect competitors.

The beguines entered the crucial early decades of the fourteenth century vulnerable, their reputation damaged by accusations against their beliefs and behaviour, although they were not, as yet, the butt of any precise charge of heresy. The mystical movement generally had begun to occasion some suspicion: in an ill-recorded episode, the scholastic Albertus Magnus reported in the 1270s on a set of opinions emanating from the Swabian Ries that contained pantheistic and immoral beliefs – the outflow of speculation, it may be, on the state of mystical adepts.[24] But no evidence connects the mystics of the Ries with the beguines and the opinions, extant only as isolated fragments of testimony, are too inconsistent with each other and too unrelated to a historical or literary context to provide clear evidence of the reality of a heresy in Swabia at that date.

All that can be inferred safely from Albertus's judgement is that anxiety was stirring in the Church in his time about the pursuit of the mystical life. It was a consequence of a growing vogue for mystical reading in the vernacular, made possible by the greater leisure and resources of aristocracy and bourgeoisie and their higher educational standards, and an increased democratization of the mystical way. Once the province of the monk and nun, often in enclosed orders, the mystical way had become more accessible to those outside, to the beguine and to the pious layman. The possible dangers in the pursuit of mysticism, the absence of firm control through an institutional framework over those who now pursued it, and the very fact that profound theological matters were being presented in the vernacular, appeared as an anxiety to authority. The beguines heavily involved in the mystical movement were accused of harbouring a sect of heretical mystics, named as adherents of the Free Spirit.

Soon the popes began to concern themselves with antinomian heresy. In 1296 Boniface VIII issued a bull against a sect who prayed in the nude, and in 1311 Clement V was writing to the bishop of Cremona to require the uprooting of a sect of the Free Spirit of Italy, claiming freedom of action because of the inspiration of the Holy Spirit in them.[25] In 1307 an authoritarian archbishop of Cologne, Henry of Virneburg, included in decrees for his diocese, as well as complaints of a traditional style against beghards (of both sexes; he apparently preferred not to use the term beguine for the females) for defying the canons against new orders, preaching and interrupting friars' sermons, a charge of heretical mysticism. Then, between 1306 and 1308, a beguine named Marguerite Porete of Hainault, one of whose books had already been burnt by the bishop of Cambrai, was arrested for spreading heresy 'among simple people and beghards' through another book, and

---

24  Grundmann, *Ketzergeschichte*, pp. 45–6; Lerner, *Free Spirit*, pp. 13–19.
25  Lerner, *Free Spirit*, pp. 78–84 (also for Henry of Virneburg); L. Oliger, *De secta spiritus libertatis in Umbria saec.* XIV; *disquisitio et documenta* (1943) (accepts genuineness of accusations).

was sent to Paris. There she refused to respond to interrogation, and was convicted of heresy on the strength of some extracts taken from this book, submitted for judgement to a commission of theologians. Her earlier conviction meant that she was guilty of relapse, and she was burnt in Paris in 1310.

The charge was again heretical mysticism, but in this instance we have the heretic's own work with which to check the veracity of the accusations made against her. By chance, the treatise which caused her conviction and burning, the *Mirror of Simple Souls*, survived, to circulate anonymously in monasteries and nunneries, in the original and in translation, from the fourteenth century to the present.[26] So little obvious was the heresy in it that hardly any of its readers over the centuries questioned its orthodoxy; or if they did they came down eventually on the side of the *Mirror*, like the Middle English translator who felt some disquiet but concluded that it was written of 'high divine maters and of highe goostli felynges and kerningli and ful mystili it is spoken'.[27] Indeed it was, using an extensive vocabulary, and drawing on what was plainly deep personal experience to describe in dialogue form the progress of the soul through seven states of grace, the greater part of it being both traditional and edifying.

The danger lay in the fifth and sixth states, the highest that could be attained in this life, when the 'annihilated' or 'liberated' soul is unified with God. Here, in Lerner's judgement,[28] Marguerite Porete went beyond traditional masters, applying, for example, the similes used by St Bernard of Clairvaux for the state of the soul in paradise to its condition in an advanced mystical state here below. There were some extravagant thoughts: the soul, still in the body, is described as being united with the Trinity, or as finding God in itself without searching. There is much about the soul's farewell to the virtues, which could lead to misunderstanding by those who failed to observe Marguerite's reasons for saying it, that the virtues are always with the liberated soul in any case. Finally, there is something disquieting in Marguerite's description of the passivity of the liberated soul: it 'does not seek God by penance, nor by any sacrament of the Holy Church, nor by thought, words or works'.[29] Marguerite was aware of the dangers of *doubles mots*, and remarked that 'simple minds might misunderstand them at their peril'.[30] She was treating of esoteric matters, was both moving and elusive, and it was not a book for the many, although obviously designed for reading aloud in the vernacular. Two factors seems to have weighed in her condemnation: her pertinacity, shown in the repeated dissemination of her views and her refusal to respond to interrogation, and the alleged publicity given to the *Mirror*

26 Lerner, *Free Spirit*, pp. 68–78, text of *Mirror* ed. Guarnieri in *Archivio Italiano*, pp. 513–635; B. McGinn, *The Presence of God. A History of Western Mysticism* (1998), pp. 244–65 (lucid and penetrating). For the way in which suspicion came to play on the mystical language sometimes used in impeccable sources, see R. E. Lerner, 'The image of mixed liquids in late medieval mystical thought', *CH* xxx (1971), pp. 397–411.
27 Quoted, Lerner, *Free Spirit*, p. 74, from text, ed. M. Doiron, in *Archivio...pietà* v (1968), p. 247.
28 *Free Spirit*, pp. 200–8.
29 Ibid., p. 205; Lerner's translation from Guarnieri text on p. 586.
30 Lerner, *Free Spirit*, p. 208; Guarnieri text, pp. 533, 537.

among simple people. What might have been possible in an established nunnery, without publicity, appeared not to be allowed to a beguine who wanted to propagate her work. Her views were not fairly represented. The *Mirror* might seem doubtful on the passivity of the liberated soul and on its lack of any need for the sacraments, and presumptuous on the state of union with God in the fifth and sixth states; but it is not libertine. Porete's enemies argued that it was, quoting a phrase of the *Mirror* on the liberated soul, giving 'to nature, without remorse, all that it asks';[31] they omitted Porete's covering explanation, that in the liberated state nature 'does not demand anything prohibited'. A recent authority has argued that Marguerite remained silent because her book, in its dialogue between Love and Reason, which elucidates her controversial distinction between 'Holy Church the Great' and 'Holy Church the Less', had already met all possible objections against its orthodoxy.

Heresy, then, in this case, if it existed at all, was of a specialized character, concerned solely with the condition of mystical adepts at an advanced stage of perfection; there was no advocacy of libertinism and disregard of the moral law for anyone; and the accusations against Porete gave an unfair picture of her views. Doubts about her case are only reinforced when we realize that the inquisitor of France directing the final moves against her was also responsible for accusations against the Templars.

Hard on the heels both of the Porete case and of the statutes of the Council of Mainz in 1310, witnessing to a continuing concern in the Rhineland about beghards and heresy, came the decision of the general Council of Vienne in 1312, in *Ad nostrum*, that there was a heresy of the Free Spirit amongst the beguines and beghards of Germany;[32] it was called an 'abominable sect'. Beliefs were set out in eight clauses. All were concerned with the belief that those who had attained a lofty state of perfection, such as the adepts who reached the fifth and sixth states of the *Mirror of Simple Souls*, could then escape the trammels of ordinary men. The opinions that those in this category had become incapable of sinning or of surpassing their present state of grace, that they did not need to fast or pray since they had obtained such control over their senses that they could afford to them complete freedom, and that they were not subject to obedience, because 'where the spirit of the Lord is, there is liberty',[33] were all condemned.

---

31 Lerner, *Free Spirit*, p. 76; Guarnieri text, p. 527. D. Turner reassesses the position of the *Mirror* and gives reasons for the author's silence (see end of para.) in his *The Darkness of God: Negativity in Western Mysticism* (1995).

32 P. Fredericq, *Corpus documentorum inquisitionis haereticae pravitatis Neerlandicae* I (Ghent, 1889), n. 172, pp. 168–9, partial tr. in Leff, *Heresy* I, pp. 314–15 (Leff's exposition of the Free Spirit (ch. 4) cannot be recommended; see Grundmann, in *DA* XXIV (1968), pp. 284–6; Offler, in *EHR* LXXXIV (1969), pp. 572–6; Lerner, *Free Spirit*, p. 8). A Patschovsky, 'Strassburger Beginenverfolgungen im 14 Jahrhundert', *DA* XXX (1974), pp. 56–198 (clarification of beguine and beghard trials in Strasburg with new MS evidence); see p. 117, n. 153. He regards concern about heresy in the Rhineland episcopate as the major impetus leading to *Ad nostrum*; see also his warning about elements of genuine heresy in some Free Spirit accusations (pp. 98–9). For Council of Mainz, Patschovsky, *DA* XXX, pp. 96, 141–2. Professor B. Töpfer will argue that there is truth in some accusations.

33 2 Cor. 3: 17.

Five other clauses dealt with further consequences or aspects of the condition of sinless freedom, condemning the view that it was possible to attain final blessedness in this life; that the divine light of glory was not needed to enjoy the vision of God; that acts of virtue were only necessary for imperfect men, and that the perfect soul no longer needs them; that sexual intercourse was not a sin when nature demands it; that it was not necessary to rise at the elevation of the Host, since this meant descending from the heights of contemplation. The sect who held these views was to be rooted out.

But did such a sect ever exist? The surprising answer, after so much research has been carried out on a supposed heresy of the Free Spirit, is that in the medieval inquisitor's usual sense it did not. There was no organized sect at all, with a teaching programme hostile to the Church, like the Cathars or the later Waldensians. All that really existed were individual mystics in communication with like-minded friends and followers on an informal basis, some of whom wrote or said some dangerous or extravagant things. *Ad nostrum* took a set of these statements that looked heretical or immoral when quoted out of context, and wove together a heresy and a sect from them.[34]

The Council of Vienne took its decision in an atmosphere of intense hostility to the beguines. We know from another of the bulls decided on at Vienne, *Cum de quibusdam*, that the fathers of the council had seriously considered suppressing the beguines outright.[35] The bull opens by decreeing suppression, and draws back from doing so only in an escape clause at the end, the fruit either of Vienne's second thoughts or of a subsequent revision. The perils of beguines discussing high theological matters, disputing on the Trinity, the divine essence and the sacraments, were mentioned in the bull as ground for suppression.

On top of this general hostility arrived the reports of antinomian heresy abroad in the Church. Much of the documentation of the Council of Vienne has vanished, making exact reconstruction of the historical context of *Ad nostrum* impossible; but Marguerite Porete's *Mirror* gives us an essential clue as to how the council came to attribute antinomian heresy to the mystics, for there we have the opportunity to put side by side some of the charges against a mystical suspect and the actual statements from which they are derived. The *Mirror* was a quarry for certain suspect statements condemned in *Ad nostrum*: clause six of the bull, on the perfect soul having no need of the virtues, is derived from Porete's work but, significantly, without the justification that the fuller context of the statement in the *Mirror* would give. Other clauses on rising at the elevation of the Host, on attitudes to prayer and fasting, and to sexual intercourse, have analogies to statements in the *Mirror*, or can be derived from misunderstanding of statements

---

34   The central theme of Lerner, *Free Spirit*; compare Grundmann, in *DA* xxi (1965), pp. 519–75; contrast Leff, *Heresy* i, ch. 4 and M. Erbstösser and E. Werner, *Ideologische Probleme des mittelalterlichen Plebejertums* (1960), who offer differing explanations of the Free Spirit (see extract tr. by Russell, *Dissent*, pp. 143–7), but are alike in accepting the existence of a sect; discussion on these assumptions also in Erbstösser, *Strömungen*, pp. 84–119.

35   Fredericq, *Corpus* i, no. 171, pp. 167–8; partial tr. in McDonnell, *Beguines*, p. 524.

there.[36] Mystics, of whom Porete is a fair, though not distinguished, example, were describing rare states and treating great mysteries, that lay near the limits of ordinary language: they used paradoxical, even shocking, phrases in trying to convey their meaning. These were taken up, rawly and literally, by the council, and fashioned into a heresy.

Definitions in *Ad nostrum* helped to create heretics to match the bull. When it was issued early in John XXII's reign, it became part of the apparatus for fashioning interrogations by inquisitors and other churchmen who believed themselves to be on the trail of the Free Spirit. Faced with the suspect beghard or beguine, or what they believed to be a heretical mystic, they took him or her through the clauses of *Ad nostrum*, and in successful cases elicited the appropriate, self-convicting answers. Preliminary questions – Was the suspect 'free in spirit'? Did he believe he was sinless? – answered affirmatively, could open the way to a systematic interrogation based on the clauses of the bull, taken one by one. Answers as given by suspects in the records sometimes reproduce almost word for word the expositions of *Ad nostrum*.[37]

Testimony appeared to show that those who held the views condemned in *Ad nostrum* did practise libertinism. There were stories of orgies, of aberrant sexual practices, outrageous statements like that of Johann Hartmann in 1367, that the free in spirit could have intercourse with sister or mother, even on the altar.[38] It is all suspect; Hartmann was probably a verbal exhibitionist. Other testimony sprang from envious gossip, inquisitorial imagination, or distortion of the paradoxical statements of true mystics.[39] The accusations consort uneasily with the hard evidence of poor, ascetic lives among beguines and other followers of mysticism. Magnetic rogues of the Rasputin variety, combining libertinism and religion, cannot be excluded; but they were surely a small proportion of those interrogated. Similar scepticism should be applied to talk of other breaches of the ethical code, theft, murder, disobedience; such offences have not been proved.

What in fact did the Free Spirit amount to? For a century and a half after *Ad nostrum* cases of the heresy were turned up. Suspicion of the kind that issued in the bull played round other, greater figures. The leaders of the vernacular mystical movement had to exercise vigilance in their teaching to avoid the suggestion of complicity with the Free Spirit. Meister Eckhart himself fell victim of the same Henry of Virneburg who had launched accusations against the Cologne beguines; he was accused of heresy, and had twenty-eight propositions from his work condemned in 1329 after his death. Beguines and beghards went on suffering from suspicion; as a movement they were saved from total shipwreck by the hesitation in *Cum de quibusdam*, and in 1318 by John XXII's defence in *Racio recta* of 'good' beguines who led stable lives and did not dispute on high theo-

---

36   Lerner, *Free Spirit*, pp. 82–3.
37   Grundmann first brought out the vital relationship between *Ad nostrum* and the interrogations of suspects (*DA* XXI, pp. 519–75).
38   Testimony in Erbstösser and Werner, *Ideologische Probleme*, pp. 136–53, comment, Lerner, *Free Spirit*, pp. 135–9.
39   As above, pp. 203–4.

logical matters.[40] But the Free Spirit affair damaged them, and so long as the zeal against the Free Spirit lasted, which seemed to have been for about a century after *Ad nostrum*, they were at peril from investigations.

The beguine movement reached its term in the fourteenth century, after a remarkable efflorescence. In the middle of the century in Cologne there were 169 beguinages and 1,170 beguines: they still met an economic and religious need and were supported by the urban patriciate. In 1452, however, the number of beguinages had fallen to ninety-three and of beguines to 637. In Strasburg there were eighty-five in the fourteenth century; in 1538 they had fallen to seven. Heresy accusations dwindled generally in the fifteenth century but hostility did not; polemics against them on the grounds of idleness, hypocrisy and unjustified begging, never wholly absent, grew in number and intensity and took the place of accusations of heresy. There was a change in the climate of opinion; the negative image of the 'sturdy beggar' took hold; the patriciate, source for the crucial benefactions, turned away from them and beguines declined in number and esteem.[41]

Meanwhile, the Free Spirit investigations trawled up odd cases, usually in the towns of Germany. The sources in the north are resistant to much positive analysis. A thorough sceptical analysis on the lines of Lerner's work has yet to be undertaken for the supposed cases in the southern lands; an analysis may turn out to give different results from the north. But what peeps through the distortions seems to be this. There was a movement of radical mysticism, running *pari passu* with the writings of the best-known masters such as Eckhart, and feared by these masters. It was not libertinist or immoral, but went at least to the limits of orthodoxy in its views on the possibility of union with God in this life, and was indifferent, if not hostile, to the sacraments and to the mediating role of the Church. Apart from this core of somewhat perilous belief and practice was a miscellaneous assemblage of suspects, suggestible women liable to say what interrogators wanted, some eccentrics, even madmen who might have remained untroubled but for investigating zeal, some religious individualists, perhaps touched by mysticism but having odd views of their own – anti-sacerdotal for example, possibly Amaurian, or rigorist on sexual ethics. Free Spirit suspects were not necessarily beguines or beghards at all, and there was a good deal of slander.[42]

---

40   Fredericq, *Corpus* ii, no. 44, pp. 72–4, McDonnell, *Beguines*, p. 536; subsequent history, below, pp. 233–4; the literature on Eckhart is substantial, but for a short note see B. McGinn, in *Neoplatonism and Christian Thought*, ed. D. J. O'Meara (Norfolk, VA, 1990).

41   Schmitt, *Mort*, pp. 47, 148–51, 187–91, 203–4; discussion of terms: pp. 64–70; Małkaw case of 1391 as classic of multiple unjustified heresy accusations: p. 77.

42   See D. Müller, 'Les béguines', *Christianisme*, ed. Brenon, Gouzy, pp. 351–84; A. Vauchez, Ibid., pp. 385–6, stresses search for the divine in the fourteenth century and inspired women, radical but orthodox, consulted by male Church leaders; notes Boniface viii's *Periculosum*; for beguine survival and forced marriage, J. Duvernoy, Ibid., pp. 388–9.

# 11

# Spiritual Franciscans and Heretical Joachimites

## The Franciscan Problem

The origins of the Franciscan problem run back deep into the thirteenth century and are inseparable from the ideals and personality of St Francis himself.[1] Utterly dedicated to the ideal of poverty which he saw in Christ's commands in the gospels, above all in the account of the sending of the Seventy, Francis bequeathed to his followers the belief that the Franciscan way of life reincarnated that of Christ and the apostles. His way of living was extraordinarily hard, harder to bear than that of the most ascetic monastic orders, for Francis aimed to renounce not only individual but also common property, the normal background of collective security for even the most austere individual monk. Moreover, Francis intended that for many of his followers an extraordinarily harsh standard of poverty should be combined with a pastoral activity in the world. From early days the two objectives tended to run counter to each other; yet the very combination of harsh poverty and pastoral activity gave a spiritual force to the early Franciscans which drew in recruits at a prodigious rate whose presence and needs soon began to distort the original ideal. Troubles occurred in Francis's own lifetime: at the end, after years of semi-eremitical life in resignation from active government of the order, Francis dictated a last Testament in which he looked back with nostalgia to the simple early days of

---

1   M. D. Lambert, *Franciscan Poverty. . . . 1210–1323* (1961); heavily revised 2nd edn (1998) supersedes 1st; see on Italian version, P. Zerbi, 'Ancora sul problema storico della povertà Francescana', *RSCI* ii (1996), pp. 158–61. Leff, *Heresy* 1, pp. 51–255 (esp. helpful for intellectual aspect and bulls of John xxii), J. R. H. Moorman, *A History of the Franciscan Order from its Origins to the Year 1517* (Oxford, 1968) (comprehensive survey), R. B. Brooke, *Early Franciscan Government, Elias to Bonaventure* (1959) (constitutional history, personal insights); documents in H. Böhmer, *Analekten zur Geschichte des Franciscus von Assisi*, 3rd edn (1961); *Scripta Leonis et Angeli Sociorum S. Francisci*, ed. R. B. Brooke (1970) (see introduction), D. Knowles, *Religious Orders in England* i (Cambridge, 1948), ch. II (short introduction), R. B. Brooke, *The Coming of the Friars* (1975) (documents on early Franciscans, background of preachers and heretics, with comment). D. Nimmo, *Reform and Division in the Franciscan Order 1226–1538* (1987), introduction and pt I; D. Burr, *Olivi and Franciscan Poverty: The Origins of the Usus Pauper Controversy* (1989), ch. I (penetrating observations on Franciscanism); M. A. Habig, ed., *St Francis of Assisi: Omnibus of Sources* (Chicago, 1973) (all texts translated).

his brotherhood and, by implication or direct statement, condemned many of the developments then taking place which mitigated the old poverty and simplicity, and tended to give his order a privileged place within the Church.[2] It was his deathbed statement, and to this day it cannot be read without emotion. Constitutionally Francis had no right to bind his successors; yet he ordered this Testament to be kept with the rule and read with it, and his command, legally invalid as it was declared to be,[3] carried all the emotional weight of the dying speech of a beloved founder. More than any single document, the Testament was the stimulus to subsequent internal dissension.

The majority of friars were either not fully aware of the distinction between Francis's personal wishes and the existing way of life in the order, or felt that change was positively desirable. Transformation still retained a considerable degree of poverty, more than that of the older monastic orders; yet it enabled the order to fulfil a major role in the life of the Church which would have been impossible if the numbers and conditions of Francis's own time had continued unchanged. Papal policy favoured change, and a series of clarifications of the rule from the popes legitimized the process. How far this adaptation of the order's life was right or wise must always remain controversial; the historian of heresy must observe that the transformation, by deploying so much disinterested zeal in the service of the Church and diffusing Franciscan preaching and piety, went far to aid the defeat of Catharism.

Dissatisfaction with the transformation of the life of the order to fit the needs of a clerical body with a place in the universities, developed techniques of preaching, and privileges to take up all the duties of the secular clergy, and the mitigation of the old poverty which this entailed, found only occasional outlet, both in Francis's lifetime and for years afterwards. The nucleus for this disquiet lay in a body of simple early companions, generally with a taste for the eremitical life, who could not approve of the influx of learning and the great place which the Franciscans gained in the Church: these men handed on the traditions, filtered through their own minds, of Francis's life and sayings especially in the last years, and kept alive the memory of the Testament.

A transformation so great and so rapid imposed strains on tender consciences. Were the friars in fact being faithful to the literal words of the rule which they professed when they followed the mitigated way of life of the bulk of the order? Were they in fact in breach of their vow? Was it honourable to continue to claim the highest poverty and a peculiar fidelity to the life of Christ and the apostles, when in practice they used money, which Francis had forbidden, and enjoyed the fruits of property, which Francis had excluded? Such questions were disturbing, and not only to rigorists. The most passive plea for freedom to follow a primitive observance implied a criticism of the majority's way of life and, as the practitioners of *satyagraha* in Gandhi's campaign against the salt-tax found, passive

2   Text and analysis in K. Esser, *Das Testament des heiligen Franziskus von Assisi* (1949); K. (Cajetan) Esser, *Origins of the Franciscan Order* (Chicago, 1970).
3   By *Quo elongati* (*BF*, Epitome, pp. 229a–231b).

FIGURE 1    *The habit of St Francis of Assisi: an authentic relic preserved at the Sacro Convento in Assisi. The Spiritual Franciscans imitated its destitution, sometimes with extravagance.*
*Photograph*: Leonhard von Matt, Buochs/Switzerland

disobedience can stimulate violent response. Hence the ferocity of punishment with which recalcitrant rigorists were treated by some superiors, and the casual violence apparent, for example, in the burning of the Testament over the head of a friar by some exasperated minister.[4]

## The Disputes in the South of France

The dispute over the rightfulness of the observance of poverty in the order had all the makings of a profound conflict. Yet a true crisis did not begin to emerge until the time of the Council of Lyons in 1274 and the following years, the 1290s being the watershed. This was almost certainly due to the fact that friars in considerable numbers would not be moved, so long as the order did maintain the substance of its mitigated way of life. After 1274, though much zeal remained, the Franciscans had passed the peak of their early enthusiasm, and in various provinces were no longer keeping adequately even to the mitigated way of life. Worldliness rather than gross abuse was the problem, together with the difficulty of holding firmly to a rule glossed and 'clarified' in various ways; but it was enough to stimulate a more widespread call to return to an earlier standard. Italian provinces – Umbria, Tuscany and the March of Ancona – were affected, partly because a living tradition of Francis's wishes existed there, and partly because of the existence of a strong eremitical tradition which tended to rigour over poverty, and in the case of Tuscany because of the influence of one teacher, Petrus Johannis Olivi, a native of the south of France and for some years lector in Florence, and of his fervent supporter Ubertino da Casale.[5] In the Franciscan province of Provence, geographically wider than the title would imply and including a substantial part of the Midi, a special situation existed.[6] Subsequent history must lead us to conclude that ministers in that area were both relaxed in their attitudes to poverty and harsh in enforcing discipline. Abuse stimulated rigour, and the province became deeply divided between defenders of the *status quo* (and worse), generally called 'Conventuals', and the rigorist Spirituals.

The situation was made more complicated and more acute by the abilities of Olivi, a friar from the convent of Narbonne; he was the dominating mind among the Spirituals and, independently of the poverty issue, a thinker of the front rank at a time of unusual disturbance and confusion in the history of scholasticism.[7] His achievement for the Spirituals was to work out a doctrine of the *usus pauper*. This firmly associated sustained and serious infringements of austerity in the use of

---

4   Lambert, *Poverty*, p. 88.
5   On Olivi, see below, n. 9; on Ubertino, Godefroy, 'Ubertin de Casale', *DTC* xv, cols 2020–34, and, a fine sketch, L. Oliger, 'Spirituels', *DTC* xiv, cols 2522–49; G. L. Podestà, *Storia ed escatalogia in Ubertino da Casale* (Milan, 1980).
6   R. Manselli, *Spirituali e Beghini in Provenza* (1959); cf. his *La 'Lectura super Apocalipsim' di Pietro di Giovanni Olivi* (1955). D. Burr, *Olivi's Peaceable Kingdom* (1993) (lucid and definitive; alters Manselli's perspective).
7   Leff, *Heresy* i, pp. 100–62; Burr, *Olivi*, ch. 2, revises chronology; summary: p. 135, suggesting beginnings of conflict 'around 1279'. His hypothesis of link to *Correctorium* controversy with Dominicans, pp. 148–58, is illuminating. See P. J. Olivi, *De Usu Paupere*, ed. D. Burr (1992).

goods with breach of the vow of poverty; repeated and gross deviations without justification, so that the 'use' of goods by a friar was to be considered 'rich' rather than 'poor', involved the offender in mortal sin. Friars who became bishops could not be dispensed from this obligation to the 'poor use'. This doctrine focused the order's attention on their actual, day-to-day, observance as opposed to their formal (and often rather hollowly juridical) renunciation of property rights. The years of transformation had issued in a theory of Franciscan poverty whereby the order held no property at all, all rights over the goods they used being by a legal fiction retained by the papacy.[8] Earnest but moderate friars, of whom the greatest was St Bonaventure, minister-general 1257–74, were not satisfied with renunciation of property rights as summing up Franciscan poverty; they accepted the papal ownership, but still struggled against practical relaxation in the use of goods. At a time of deteriorating observance, the Olivi doctrine appeared to strengthen such earnest superiors.

But there were difficulties. No aspect of Franciscan life was so vulnerable to changes as day-to-day poverty; powers of dispensation and the discretion of superiors were needed if Franciscans were to maintain their duties in the world, and consciences were not to be overloaded. The *usus pauper* could be held unduly to infringe these rights of superiors. There were problems in assessing what were necessities and what were not. Controversy over the Franciscan life with the Dominicans created sensitivities. Dominicans were irked by the Franciscan claim to be observers of the highest evangelical perfection. Behind Olivi lay poverty fanatics; it was not clear what they might make of the *usus pauper* as an obligation, so there were some grounds for considering Olivi's doctrine as 'perilous', in the words of one censure.[9] Controversy grew over this issue, strengthened by the Spirituals' honest reaction to abuses in the province, and by the chance that Olivi was a bold speculative thinker who in his scholastic writing threw off views which, in part following the way which led to Ockham, alarmed some other Franciscans.[10] Conflict began as a dispute between Olivi and another Franciscan lector, 'brother Ar.', involved the province, then the minister-general. Often inferior minds did not grasp what Olivi as an academic thinker intended; his views on poverty and points of doubt in his scholastic writing became bound together in an internal struggle in which superiors and other scholastics pressed charges of heresy and error over almost two decades before his death in 1298, and thereafter till the Council of Vienne in 1312, without ever succeeding in pinning a definitive condemnation on him. Much of this was unfair: though at one stage rehabilitated and sent to Florence, Olivi in conse-

8   Lambert, *Poverty*, chs 3–6.
9   D. Laberge, 'Fr Petri Johannis Olivi, o.f.m.: tria scripta sui ipsius apologetica annorum 1283 et 1285', *AFH* xxviii (1935), pp. 115–55, 374–407; xxix (1936), pp. 98–141, 365–95; note esp. xxviii, p. 382, ll. 7–8; Burr, *Olivi*, pp. 67–8, 135–58 (helpful comments: pp. 144–5); Id., 'The persecution of Peter Olivi', *TAPS*, n.s. lxvi, pt 5 (1976); S. Piron, 'Petrus Johannis Olivi, epistola ad Fratrem R.', *AFH* xcl (1998), pp. 33–64.
10  Leff, *Heresy* i, pp. 107–11; but see also A. Maier, 'Zu einigen Problemen der Ockhamforschung', *AFH* xlvi (1953), pp. 174–81; Burr, *Olivi*, pp. 41, 44.

quence of the dissensions did not achieve the academic recognition which his talents deserved and ended his career as no more than lector in Narbonne. Academic controversy, with serious undertones springing from the state of the order and the nature of Olivi's influence, had much the same effect on a smaller scale as conflicts at Prague over Wyclif had in the early fifteenth century:[11] issues, too long undecided, roused bitterly divided parties, and turned an academic conflict into a popular fight. Dissension amongst the Franciscans of the first order easily spilled over into the lay world through the institution of the third order: in the Italian provinces this does not seem to have happened on any scale, but in the Midi tertiaries from the towns were drawn in.

One reason lay in the existence of a tradition blending veneration for poverty and Joachimite speculation in a lay circle which went back to Hugues de Digne, Olivi's religious ancestor in the area, who can be glimpsed in mid-century pondering Joachimite prophecy with laymen, notaries and others at Hyères.[12] Olivi himself had magnetic qualities, not fully discernible to us in his extant writings, and endured harassment with courage: he acted as a focus for the religious sentiments of tertiaries under the influence of Spiritual friars who met to hear mass, to be encouraged in their personal life by the hearing of sermons and vernacular treatises in which Spiritual beliefs played a great part, and who became convinced both that Olivi was a martyr to unjust persecution and that the conflicts about poverty in the order were the prelude to the Last Times. Without understanding the academic issues, these tertiaries or more casual sympathizers, known as Beguins, were quite clear in their minds about the practical issues of poverty under discussion, the pressure that Spiritual friars were under, and the heroic virtue of Olivi. Joachimism, misunderstood or adapted for the Franciscan situation, heightened the tension in these Spiritual-directed lay circles, and was the most dangerous single element in an amalgam of doctrines forming in the 1280s and 1290s in the heat of persecution and conflict in the Midi.

## Joachimism and the Development of Heresy

The exact nature of Olivi's influence and of his own thinking about the Last Times remains the most suspect and elusive aspect of his work. One great stimulus to his eschatological interest lay in Joachim of Fiore, the Calabrian prophetic writer who died in Innocent III's pontificate after a lifetime spent pondering the patterns of history discernible through meditation on the Scriptures.[13] Three popes, Lucius III, Urban III and Clement III, had encouraged him in his exegetical writing[14] and, though his influence received a blow in the

11    Below, pp. 317–22, 325–38.
12    Lambert, *Poverty*, p. 189. Burr, *Olivi*, pp. 18–24, 29–30, subtly analyses Hugues's position on poverty; Hugues cannot simply be classified as a Spiritual but his *Disputatio* provides evidence of tensions over poverty in the south of France and punishment of dissidents by superiors. See also J. Paul, 'Hugues de Digne', *CF* x, pp. 69–97.
13    Above, p. 107.
14    Reeves, *Prophecy*, p. 28.

condemnation of a trinitarian *libellus* at the fourth Lateran Council, his ideas on history and the future were quite uncondemned, and had great potency, directly and indirectly, throughout the thirteenth century.

Joachim's ideas on a coming third age of the Holy Spirit had a special appeal to members of religious orders. Ever scholarly, reluctant to fix precisely on a date for the end of the present order of things or to describe closely the conditions of life in the third age of the Spirit, Joachim none the less lived in a state of constant expectancy – 'I suspect all times and all places', he said – and through his writings bequeathed to the clerical world a persuasive set of metaphors, symbols and scriptural parallels for apocalyptic speculation.[15] His diagram of the sequence of history, produced by him personally or under his influence in the *Liber figurarum* (*c.* 1200), may better convey the nature of his appeal than a more detailed exposition.[16] In the centre is the trumpet of the Apocalypse ('I was in the Spirit . . . and heard behind me a great voice, as of a trumpet saying, "I am Alpha and Omega . . ." '[17] It speaks in the third age of the Holy Spirit, given below the trumpet as *tercius status*, and provides the spiritual understanding which characterizes the Age of the Spirit. The history of mankind is flowing into the state of illumination which is the culmination of life on earth. There is a *status* corresponding to the first person of the Trinity, beginning on the far left of the diagram with the *initiatio primi status* marked by Adam, characterized by married men; then a second *status* corresponding to the second person of the Trinity, beginning on the upper left of the diagram with the *initiatio secundi status* marked by the reign of Uzziah ('Ozias'), in which the prophet Isaiah appeared, and characterized by the clergy. Mankind is on the eve of the dawning of the third age, characterized by a new order of monks – the words *presens tempus* can be seen below the bell-joint of the trumpet, still in the age of the clarification of the Son (*clarificatio filii* in the diagram). The *status* are not rigidly divided; they are seen by Joachim rather as relay runners in a race: at one point the runner gets ready to hand over the baton and the two runners run along side by side before finally making the changeover.[18] A herald, as it were, of the third age had already appeared in St Benedict

---

15   I follow here Reeves, *Prophecy* (with full literature, cited above, p. 107, n. 28), and *MRS* II (1950), pp. 57–81, work which I admire. For the broad context, see R. W. Southern, 'Aspects of the European tradition of historical writing 3: History as prophecy', *TRHS*, 5th ser. XXII (1972), pp. 159–80, esp. pp. 173–7; orientation in H. Grundmann, *Studien über Joachim von Floris* (1927); *Neue Forschungen über Joachim von Floris* (1950); discussion in relation to heresy in Leff, *Heresy* I, pp. 68–83; reflections in F. Seibt, 'Utopie in Mittelalter', *HZ* CCVIII (1969), pp. 555–94; B. McGinn, 'Symbolism in the thought of Joachim of Fiore', in *Prophecy*, ed. Williams, Bloomfield, pp. 143–64 (notes originality in development of symbols of growth and the role assigned to papacy); extracts on angelic pope and from Bonaventure, Spirituals, in McGinn, *Visions*, pp. 186–238.

16   *Il libro delle figure dell' Abate Gioacchino da Fiore*, ed L. Tondelli, M. Reeves, B. Hirsch-Reich, 2nd edn (1953), II tavola 18ab; M. Reeves and B. Hirsch-Reich, *The Figurae of Joachim of Fiore* (1972), pl. 9, and discussion (note two versions), pp. 120–9; authenticity of *Liber figurarum*: pp. 75–98.

17   Rev. I: 10–11.

18   See introduction to *Il libro* I by L. Tondelli, pp. 86–9; Reeves, *Prophecy*, p. 138; Reeves and Hirsch-Reich, *Figurae*, pp. 122–3. Note Reeves's summary (*MRS* II, p. 77), 'The third *status* describes the emergence of a new plane of spiritual existence rather than the appearance of a new set of institutions.'

of Nursia, founder of monasticism; a new order of monks, yet to come, would characterize the third age, and would be agents of the new spiritual understanding.

Joachim did not exactly know what this order would be: in the phrase of his modern interpreter Marjorie Reeves, like Moses he viewed the promised land, but could not enter it himself.[19] To be a member of that new order had a powerful attraction, and it is little surprise that religious of various kinds after Joachim's day believed that the spiritual understanding of the new age was to be bestowed on their institution. The friars, with their consciousness of innovation, were natural candidates, and the legend grew that Joachim had in fact forecast not one order but two, and that he had sketched the habits of the two major orders, the Dominicans and the Franciscans.[20] But of all the groups to whom Joachim appealed, the Franciscans were affected most deeply.[21]

Some of the reasons for the attraction of Joachim's ideas can be glimpsed from the diagram. One is the perennial attraction of the approaching end, seen in the proximity of the bell of the trumpet to the culmination of history, to be seen beyond the line on the right of the trumpet. To the ever-fascinating task of attempting to calculate the time of the Last Things, Joachim brought distinction of mind and a method familiar to all Scripture students of the day. That the Old Testament provided parallels and prophecies of the New was a commonplace; Joachim's method involved extending this use of parallels, natural in a time in which the inner meaning, as opposed to the literal sense, of Scripture was of such dominant importance, to provide a key to the time after the New Testament. As there was a concordance between the pattern of events in the Old and New Testaments, so there would be a concordance between the events described in Scripture and those that took place after the writing of the New Testament, and Joachim worked indefatigably on traditional exegetical principles[22] to solve the riddle of the future.

The essence of the technique lay in recognizing the key events and personalities, in their numerical sequence, which provided the parallels, mapped out time and marked the approach to the end of the world. The number twelve, for example, fascinated Joachim. In his *Liber de Concordia* there is an extraordinary sequence of mentions. The Children's Crusade of 1212 had multiple causes, but it is likely that prophecy focusing on the double twelve, ultimately derived from Joachim, played a part. Moreover, his third *status* was to be the *status* of the *pueri*. Prophecy worked both ways: it could both engender and be engendered by revivalist enthusiasm. Prophecy is also infinitely flexible. As is familiar in such speculations, each disappointment in forecasting can readily be overcome; the basis of calculation may be altered, while the principle remains intact, and the reader of prophecies prepared for some new date.[23] So one such date, 1260, marked by an

19   *Prophecy*, p. 146.
20   Ibid., pp. 72–3.
21   Ibid., pp. 135–292.
22   Reeves stresses the basis of Joachim's thought in traditional exegesis; see e.g. *Prophecy*, pp. 10, 16–17.
23   Southern, 'Aspects', p. 177.

FIGURE 2 *The third age of the Spirit: the seven* etates *of the world; Oxford MS 255A fol. 8v*.
Reproduced by permission of the President and Fellows of Corpus Christi College, Oxford.

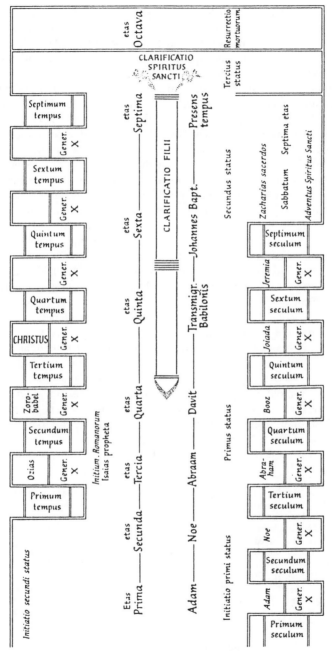

FIGURE 3    *The third age of the Spirit: the seven etates of the world.*
From *Il libro delle figure dell' Abate Gioacchino da Fiore*, ed. L. Tondelli, M. Reeves and B. Hirsch-Reich, 2nd edn (Turin, 1953), 11.

extraordinary outburst of flagellating penitential processions in Italy, spreading over the Alps to Germany and Poland, passed by with no supernatural event.[24] The focus of expectation moved on, and 1290 became the date, with subsequent transferences right through the Middle Ages, so long as Joachimite techniques remained as basis for prophecy.

The Franciscans' scriptural training and their preaching, with its taste for vivid symbolism and anecdote, opened the way for interest in Joachim's rich store of parallels and symbols; the high importance that all friars attached to Francis, and the early sense that something new, blessed by God, had appeared in the order, contributed to the spread of Joachimism in various forms and to the loose assimilation of the Franciscans by some writers to the role of the new order of the third age. An identification of Francis with the angel of the sixth seal in the Apocalypse, who in the Joachimite hypothesis was the herald of the new age, became a commonplace among Franciscan writers.[25] Attachment to Joachimism stretched all the way from a loose use of his symbols, as a kind of decorative *jeu d'esprit*, to a profound involvement in versions of his ideas which acted as a mainspring to religious life.

In the process Joachim's own views were remodelled. He had said very little about poverty for his new order in the third age; that aspect of religious life was crucial for Franciscans, and in their versions it became the decisive mark of the new order. Joachim had anticipated an intensification of persecutions as an immediate prelude to the dawning of the third age. There were to be two Antichrists, one shortly before the third age, the other at its end, as part of the persecutions which would herald the second coming and the end of human history.[26] The success of Islam under Saladin gave him one clue that his third age was not far off: it represented the requisite increase of pressure on the Church. But it was a characteristic of Joachim as an apocalyptic writer that he set the events of his own time in the full context of history, and so in the diagram of the dragon of the Apocalypse in the *Liber figurarum* (figure 4) Saladin features as one head in a sequence going back to Herod; the other, pseudo-Joachimite

24   G. Dickson, 'Prophecy and rationalism: Joachim of Fiore, Jewish messianism and the Children's Crusade of 1212', *Florensia* XIII–XIV (1999–2000), pp. 97–104; on 1260, Reeves, *Prophecy*, pp. 54–5; R. Manselli, 'L'Anno 1260 fu Anno Gioachimito?', *Movimento dei disciplinati* (1962), pp. 99–108; G. Dickson, 'The flagellants of 1260', *JMH* XV (1989), pp. 227–67; Id., *Religious Enthusiasm*, ch. 8, demonstrating that these flagellants, at first vigorously orthodox, were accused of heresy at a late stage and outside Italy. On Children's Crusade, chs 4, 5, note *pueri* as landless peasants who could not marry, ch. 4 p. 9, 'burned-over district', ch. 4 p. 12, kneeling sheep, ch. 5 p. 89.

25   Reeves, *Prophecy*, p. 176; S. Bihel, 'S. Franciscus, fuitne angelus sexti sigilli (Apoc. 7: 2)?', *Antonianum* II (1927), pp. 59–90; for changing patterns of pseudo-Joachimite literature and emergence of angelic pope, see H. E. Lee and M. Reeves, 'The School of Joachim of Fiore', in Lee *et al.*, ed., *Western Mediterranean Prophecy*, pp. 3–15; B. McGinn, *The Calabrian Abbot* (1985), ch. 7 (relates Joachim to Aquinas and Bonaventure). S. da Campagnola, *L'angelo del sesto sigillo e l'alter Christus* (1971); D. Burr, 'Bonaventura, Olivi and Franciscan eschatology', *Collectanea Franciscana* LIII (1983), pp. 23–40; R. E. Lerner, *The Feast of St Abraham: Medieval Millenarians and the Jews* (2000) (coll. articles).

26   Reeves, *Prophecy*, pp. 295–392; H. M. Schaller, 'Endzeiterwartung und Antichrist Vorstellungen im 13. Jahrhundert', in *Festschrift für Hermann Heimpel* (Max-Planck-Institut für Geschichte) II (1972), pp. 924–47.

diagram (figure 5) demonstrates both the process of adaptation and the diminishing of Joachimite prophecy to serve the preoccupations of one context in time.[27] The dragon in this example has turned into a bird of prey; the Holy Roman emperors assume a more important place on the side of evil, with both Henry I and Frederick II among the heads, the seventh, larger than all the rest, being that of Frederick. The text refers plainly to Frederick II and his heirs (*cum successione sua*) as Antichrist; the great struggle of the papacy with the Hohenstaufen is thus seen as the prelude to the coming of the third age. By contrast, the genuine Joachimite drawing leaves the last head anonymous – this is the Antichrist of Joachim's writings, yet to appear in history. The diagram gives only one mild form of adaptation – it may be allowed to stand for a wide variety of use and abuse of Joachimite ideas.

## Guglielma and Dolcino

Worse distortions of Joachim appeared outside the Franciscan order, in unlearned milieux where ideas were passed on from original Joachimite and pseudo-Joachimite texts, it would seem, by oral transmission. In Milan the bones of a certain Guglielma, who had died in 1281, were dug up and burned by the inquisition in 1300, when it appeared that a circle of her initiates in Milan revered her as an incarnation of the Holy Spirit.[28] The relatively harmless but simplistic idea of the angelic pope,[29] shortly to come to cleanse the Church, took on an unusual guise in the hands of this circle, who had come to believe that a woman from their midst, Manfreda de Pirovano, would be the pope, who would convert the Jews and Saracens and usher in a new age. She would be accompanied by women cardinals: all higher offices in the Church would be held by women. The existing gospels would be superseded by four new ones, written under the guidance of the Holy Spirit. Joachimite ideas, an interpretation of apostolic life and the effect of interdict and dispute in the Milanese Church on the administration of the sacraments, all fostered the growth of the movement.

Guglielma's heirs were not difficult to uproot; the Apostolic Brethren, however, founded by Gerard Segarelli in Parma in 1260, the year of the Flagellant outbreak and one of the key dates of Joachimite prophecy, were more resilient and had a surprisingly wide circle of influence.[30] Segarelli, according to Salimbene

---

27  *Il libro*, ed. Tondelli *et al.*, II, tavola 26, fig. 2; analysis in Reeves and Hirsch-Reich, *Figurae*, pp. 269, 274 (p. 147, for manifestation of Antichrist; index, for discussion of Antichrist and Gog and Magog).

28  Reeves, *Prophecy*, pp. 248–50; S. Wessley, 'The thirteenth-century Guglielmites: salvation through women', *SCH* Subsidia I, pp. 289–303; M. Benedetti, 'Il Culto di Santa Guglielma e gli Inquisitori', *Vite di eretici*, ed. Benedetti *et al.*, pp. 221–41.

29  F. Baethgen, *Der Engelpapst* (Halle, 1933); see B. Töpfer, *Das kommende Reich des Friedens* (Berlin, 1964) (survey of prophecies, esp. in twelfth and thirteenth centuries, subtly related to economic and political background; Marxist assumptions).

30  Reeves, *Prophecy*, pp. 242–8, with sources; Leff, *Heresy* I, pp. 191–5; I have made greatest use of Töpfer, *Reich*, pp. 280–324, illuminating in its comparisons of Dolcino's views with other prophecies.

FIGURE 4   *The seven-headed dragon; Oxford MS 255A, fol. 7r.*
Reproduced by permission of the President and Fellows of Corpus Christi College, Oxford.

FIGURE 5    *A debased dragon; MS Vat. Lat. 3822 fol. 5r. Reproduced by permission of the Vatican Library.*

the chronicler, had been refused admission to the Franciscans at Parma; a simple, unlearned man who must nevertheless have had some force of personality, he gathered a group who, like him, practised the most direct and literal imitation of the life of the apostles, to the embarrassment of the Franciscans, as Salimbene's hostility reveals. Quite literally, they lived for the day, begged only necessities of life which were consumed on the spot, had only one habit where the Franciscan rule allowed two, engaged in demonstrations whereby they stripped off their clothing and divided it afresh amongst themselves, so as to show their utter detachment from individual ownership, and called themselves, not *minores*, as the official order did, but *minimi*.[31] They lasted, and gained popular approbation, because they followed the Franciscan ideal with a rigour, even to excess and fetishism, in a way that the majority of the friars of the later thirteenth century did not. Parma supported them; the bishop in early years did not move against them. But the Council of Lyons in 1274 banned unauthorized orders; in 1285

---

31  Töpfer, *Reich*, pp. 284–6, 292. Töpfer notes that the term *apostoli* was used rather by outsiders than the group itself.

Honorius IV banned them explicitly; in the 1290s proceedings for heresy were taken against some members. Segarelli, first condemned to imprisonment, was burned in 1300. Inquisition proceedings of 1299 in Bologna give us a glimpse of a group, not as yet violently opposed to the Church[32] but justifying disobedience through their own attainment of the state of perfection of the primitive Church by the practice of poverty. Popes of the post-Constantinian Church (that had abandoned the poverty of the primitive Church), they argued, had no right to force them to give up their way of life.

With the replacement of Segarelli in the leadership by Dolcino, the bastard son of a priest from the diocese of Novara, who had picked up some learning, the sect grew more strongly heretical, and responded with violence to the pressures of the inquisition. Dolcino issued a manifesto in 1300, in which he claimed direct inspiration by the Holy Spirit for himself and a crucial role in the imminent coming of a new age for the Apostolics he led. Instead of the three *status* of the Joachimites he postulated four – one, of the patriarchs and prophets of the Old Testament, a second, initiated by Christ and the apostles and lasting till the time of Constantine, a third, just nearing its close, from Constantine, and a fourth, about to come, in which the true apostolic life of his group would prevail, and, side by side with the *status*, four *mutationes*, of which the fourth had been initiated by Gerard Segarelli. The conviction of the overriding value of the apostolic life, as observed by Dolcino's group in contrast to all others, led logically to the insertion in Joachim's scheme of a fourth *status* to accommodate it.[33] Even Francis's position is dimmed in comparison with that of the leaders of the Apostolics. He is not actually given the place of a 'forerunner' of the new *status*, shortly to come, and the way of life of the Apostolics, because of its stricter poverty, is taken as superior to that of St Francis and St Dominic. The fate foretold for the existing Church at the coming of the new age was dramatic: pope, prelates, clergy and monks, except for a repentant remnant, were to be exterminated within three years by a new emperor, Frederick, the king of Sicily, who had successfully defied papal and Angevin expeditions against him; then the holy pope would appear, and all the benefits of the new age would follow. This extravagant picture was rounded off by a passage in which Dolcino described a pattern of history in terms of the seven angels and seven Churches of the Apocalypse, in which Segarelli was the angel of Smyrna and he was the angel of Thyatira. In a second manifesto of December 1303 prophecies, unfulfilled, were brought up to date, and again in a manifesto at the end of 1304 which has not come down to us.

But there was no waning of confidence; some even alleged that Dolcino himself was to be the pope of the new age. He took to the mountains between Vercelli and Novara in 1304, and recruits followed him, both local peasants and Apostol-

---

32  Töpfer's interpretation.
33  Töpfer, *Reich*, p. 299, following R. Kestenberg-Gladstein, 'The "Third Reich": a fifteenth-century polemic against Joachimism and its background', *JWCI* xviii (1955), pp. 242–95 at p. 251.

ics from farther afield, who supported him in plundering raids and violent resistance of Church forces. Ghibelline leaders, with whom he had mysterious contacts,[34] may have emboldened him, and no doubt the inquisition's repression stimulated a violent response; the poverty of peasants near his mountain refuge made them susceptible to his teaching. But the rapid development under Dolcino of an extravagant but not profoundly dangerous movement[35] into a violent rebellion is pre-eminently a tribute to the heady influence, in appropriate hands, of pseudo-Joachimite ideas of the new age. It took more than one expedition and an application of the crusading indulgence before Dolcino was taken and burnt in 1307 and his following destroyed; even then adherents outlasted the leader and the failure of his prophecies.

In the Franciscan order itself, well before these events, one scandal, that of the Eternal Gospel in 1254, served to reveal the dangers of the third *status*. The question about Joachim's construction always was: What was the significance of the transition between the second and third *status*? Did it imply supersession of the present hierarchy and sacraments, in the same fashion as the coming of Christ and his founding of the Christian Church superseded the Synagogue and the Old Law? For Joachim this was never so. With talents rather poetic and artistic than dialectical, he saw the scriptural parallels and precedents in terms of a constantly moving kaleidoscope of images. The patterns of three, with their dangers, were always accompanied by patterns of two, standing for the two dispensations of the Law and Grace, of the two eons, before and after Christ, which would last to the end of time.[36] In the *Liber figurarum*, the words 'end of the New Testament' in diagrams are never associated with the transition from the second to the third *status*, only with the consummation of the orthodox patterns of twos. The changed conditions of life in the third *status* represented a fructification of trends in the second *status*, but not revolutionary institutional change. And yet, whatever Joachim's intentions, the whole tenor of his treatment of the third *status*, with its emphasis on 'spiritual men' and new spiritual understanding, tended easily to subvert faith in the present, visible order, with its hierarchy, laws and sacraments.

In 1254 a crude adaptation of Joachim by Gerard of Borgo San Donnino, who taught that Joachim's three principal works were the gospel of a new age, superseding the Old and New Testaments, revealed to all just what the dangers were.[37] His condemnation ended the phase of relatively carefree use of Joachim, and was followed by refutations of the three-age theory, but not the complete jettisoning of Joachimism. There was much more in Joachim than the three *status*, whose sinister potential had often not been recognized in early years, and various

---

34  Töpfer, *Reich*, pp. 314–16.
35  I have not been able to examine evidence of aberrant views on sexual activities; they are discussed by Töpfer (*Reich*, pp. 292–3).
36  Reeves, in *MRS* II, pp. 74–6. I find the description of Joachim as a poet helpful. See discussion of Joachim's orthodoxy by Reeves (*Prophecy*, pp. 126–32).
37  Lambert, *Poverty*, pp. 113–15; Reeves, *Prophecy*, pp. 59–70; B. Töpfer, 'Eine Handschrift des Evangelium aeternum des Gerardino von Borgo San Donnino', *ZG* VII (1960), pp. 156–63.

quite orthodox writers continued to make discriminating use of his symbols and categories. The Spirituals, however, held firmly to him, and wedded their doctrine of poverty to a version of Joachim's apocalyptic speculations, more subtle than that of the simple-minded Gerard, but still tending ultimately to the subversion of the contemporary Church.

No authentic text of Joachimite work has come down to us from the Spiritual Franciscans' leaders in mid-century, John of Parma and Hugues de Digne, but in Olivi's *Lectura super Apocalipsim* we have a major Joachimite text that gives us a clue to the nature of his influence in the south of France.[38] The work, completed late in life and, no doubt, the fruit of reflection on his sufferings and that of the Spirituals, adapts Joachim wholeheartedly to his own time. As in Joachim's own work, mankind was on the eve of great events, but they were seen pre-eminently in terms of current Franciscan history. It was St Francis who was the initiator of a new age, and his rule was its gospel; full spiritual understanding would come to Francis's true disciples (i.e. the Spirituals), but only after the persecutions of the carnal Church, made up of all the evil forces in the visible Church, and especially the enemies of poverty and the advocates of pagan learning, the false doctors. A deepening of suffering, and the falling away of many in the Church, would be followed by the joys of the new age, described in terms very like Joachim's. So the struggle between Spirituals and Conventuals in the south of France was invested with a cosmic significance. Joachim gave the groundwork for this scheme, but his fluctuating symbolisms had been given a precise, historical meaning. The dangers implicit in a third age were still there and intensified by being given a more definite historical setting. The problem, as with other Joachimites, lay in the relationship between a hypothetical new epoch shortly to dawn, and the institutions and laws of the contemporary Church and, although on this issue Olivi was careful, in controversy with his own sympathizers, to urge adherence to the commands of lawful authority in the Church and to distinguish in the *Lectura* between the carnal Church as a set of evil forces inside the Church and the visible Church as a whole, his teaching in the work very easily gave rise to revolt and heresy.

A similar subversive effect followed from the transposition of the Franciscan crisis, apparent here and elsewhere, into Joachimite terms. Spirituals, anxious about the undermining of the observance in the order through papal bulls and the glossing of the rule, harked back to Francis's Testament, called for literal observance and looked askance at papal 'clarification'. But what if the rule was

---

38   Manselli, *Lectura*; criticism in Leff, *Heresy* I, pp. 122–39, esp. p. 139. See E. Pásztor, 'Le polemiche sulla "Lectura super Apocalipsim" di Pietro di Giovanni Olivi fino all sua condanna', *BISIAM* LXX (1958), pp. 365–424; Cazenave, in *Christianisme*, ed. Brenon, Gouzy, p. 34, on Olivi's reference to sack of Béziers by crusaders as an event accompanying opening of sixth seal; see also p. 60. Survey by Lee and Reeves, 'Petrus Johannis Olivi', in *Prophecy*, ed. Lee *et al.*, pp. 17–26, stresses, against Manselli, *Lectura*, force of Joachimist influence on him (p. 19), notes he never equates Babylon and the Roman Church (p. 23) and calls his work 'the first major revision of Joachim's system' (p. 26). See *Peter of John Olivi on the Bible*, ed. D. Flood, G. Gál (New York, 1997), review D. Burr, *Speculum* LXXIV (1999), pp. 229–30; G. Barone, 'L'oeuvtre eschatologique de Pierre Jean Olieu et son influence. Un bilan historiographique', *CF* XXVII, pp. 49–61.

the gospel of a new epoch, and if Francis and his disciples, with the rule and the Testament, had taken the mantle of Christ as at the beginning of the Christian epoch? Was the rule in fact above all papal clarification and glossing? What if the persecutors of the Spirituals, their superiors and the false doctors were followers of Antichrist? Might not resistance *à l'outrance* to them be justifiable? Thoughts of this kind helped to raise a disciplinary dispute inside a religious order to the plane of doctrinal conflict. Moreover, Joachimism gave a purpose to the Spirituals' troubled lives. The sense of certainty of their victory gave them both courage and obstinacy, and helps to account for a certain extravagance and recklessness in their actions which tended to make the split between Spirituals and many of their superiors irreconcilable. So with the development from Joachim to Olivi: though heresy proper has not been reached, we stand on its verge. With the development of Joachimism and Spiritual ideas on poverty amongst simpler friars and Midi tertiaries behind Olivi we do reach heresy.

## The Beguins and Popular Heresy

In his *Lectura* Olivi inferred nothing more from the prophecies of approaching persecution than the necessity for the Spirituals to show patience in their sufferings. His comments on the Apocalypse were presented with caution, as possible but not certain interpretations of the future and, though he strongly developed Joachim's sentiment that the mystical Antichrist would be found within the Church and referred to the coming of a pseudo-pope, he never identified the carnal Church or Whore of Babylon with the Roman Church. In his popular works of edification, edited by Manselli,[39] he exhorts his followers to virtuous life on traditional lines of Franciscan piety; only mentions of the need for vigilance as the Last Times approach betray his special interests.

When a local adherent, the friar Matthew de Bosicis, who went to Rome in 1299 with five Beguins and thirteen women taking with him the works of Olivi, made a confession of faith at a date between 1299 and 1304, no doubt in consequence of the suspicion then spreading of the Spiritual movement, his words showed a simple adherence both to Olivi and his teaching and to wholly orthodox tenets on the need for obedience and the nature of the visible Church.[40] But was Matthew exercising 'economy' in his confession, and not revealing all his thoughts?[41] That there were

---

39   *Spirituali*, pp. 267–90. B. Tierney, *Origins of Papal Infallibility, 1150–1350* (1972), ch. 3, argues that Olivi's doctrine of infallibility was developed in order to meet the utterances of a pseudo-pope. His concern was to buttress the papal decrees already issued on the Franciscan way of life. For Olivi's views on the Apocalypse, see Burr, *Olivi*, pp. 173–83.

40   Tierney, *Origins*, pp. 42–6.

41   Compare the declaration of Cathars at Lombers 1165, above, p. 66; see M. D. Lambert, 'The Franciscan crisis under John xxii', *FS* xxxii (1972), pp. 123–43 at p. 131n. Manselli, in the tradition of Morghen, tends to stress the importance of the actions of ecclesiastical authority in 'creating' heresy in the province of Provence, especially after the burnings of 1318. To demonstrate this he must argue for the orthodoxy of Spirituals and Beguins there before the major persecutions of 1318 and the following years, when documentation is sparser and the point is very difficult to prove. Burr, *Kingdom* reassesses Olivi's work and explains why he alarmed authority.

grounds for disquiet in Olivi's oral contacts with his followers emerges from the ostensibly trivial point of the moment at which the spear pierced Christ on the cross. This occurred, Olivi said, before rather than after death; but that was not what the Vulgate text said. Olivi's ground for change, amongst other things, was the vision of a contemporary, which he alleged against Scripture. With the *usus pauper*, the spear-wound tenet was treated by followers as the teaching of a master, to be received with veneration. The affair gives us a glimpse of another more cloudy and visionary Olivi, not usually revealed in his writings.[42]

Authorities believed that his popular influence was baleful. Preoccupied with the prime battle over Olivi's scholastic views and the *usus pauper*, they did nevertheless periodically advert to the popular background in the province. In 1285 he was accused of being the head of a 'superstitious sect'; in 1290 Nicholas IV called for investigation of certain brothers 'who seemed to introduce schism into the province of Provence'; in 1299 a provincial council warned against extravagances; there was an investigation of his work on the Apocalypse, and a complaint about it in 1311.

The tragedy of the Spiritual movement was that its settlement was so long delayed. Treatment by the usual procedures of disciplinary action within the order could not work, because superiors who attempted to carry them out were self-interested and stained with abuses, especially in the Midi. There was yet too much idealism amongst the friars, and too much sympathy among outside sympathizers, churchmen and laymen, for a local repression to be carried out without complaint or publicity. The Spirituals, for all their faults, carried the authentic note of the passion for poverty; and this both united them to St Francis, and ever won them some hearts. At the same time, grounds for disquiet on doctrinal grounds did exist, both in Italy and in the Midi, in the influence of Joachimite thought, the rigidity and lack of balance of Spiritual views on poverty, and the exaggerated place that the rigorists gave to their heroes, above all to Olivi. So neither side could achieve victory for their views, which tended through combat to become more extreme; and as the disputes dragged on, first inside the order, then at the papal court and at the Council of Vienne, patience waned, and the Spirituals and Beguins became more deeply involved in Joachimite extravagance. Clement V, sympathetic but weak, never grasped the nettle: he removed some of the worst superiors from office, and stopped persecution, but did not make a viable settlement.[43] Then the whole landscape darkened for the Spirituals, as the chance of a double vacancy in both the papacy and the generalate from 1314 to 1316 removed central control, and allowed a resumption of persecution. The raising, then the dashing of hopes, and the renewal of persecution, was the stimulus to rank heresy; the identification of the carnal Church with the whole visible Church, that seemed to have turned against them, trans-

---

42    Lambert, *Poverty*, pp. 182–3; for all controversies, see chs 7, 8; fuller account, esp. valuable on Olivi's treatises and thought, Leff, *Heresy* I, pp. 100–63.
43    Leff, *Heresy* I, pp. 155–6, Lambert, *Poverty*, pp. 210–14; Manselli, *Spirituali*, p. 109, is interesting; comment, Burr, *Olivi*, pp. 193–4; see now S. Menache, *Clement V* (Cambridge, 1998).

formed individual popes and churchmen into the evil figures of Joachimite prophecy.

The distinctions in Olivi's work on the Apocalypse were finely drawn: it was not to be expected that untrained tertiaries would go on making them and stay within orthodoxy as they found Olivi's reputation attacked and heard of the cruelties of Conventual superiors. Olivi's death in 1298 did not help; equivocal as his teaching was, he did restrain the wilder spirits. Dead, his tenets became the centre for the *cultus* of an unauthorized saint, his death-day celebrated as a feast, pilgrimage to his tomb stimulating conversions to the Spiritual way, Joachimite interpretation turning him into the angel of the seventh seal, whose face shone as the sun.[44] Joachimism heightened expectations and stimulated a sense of crisis. Extravagance reached great heights: at the end of the chain of persecution, in 1325, a weaver, William Ademarii, a Beguin from Narbonne, told an inquisitor that Olivi had made a work on the Apocalypse that was admirable, and such that, if all the heads of men were reunited into one sole head, it could not have composed such a work if it had not been made by the Holy Ghost, and that it would convert the Saracens to the faith of the Roman Church – one of the events, in fact, that was to mark the start of a new epoch.[45]

Thus a popular heresy was in the process of formation in the Midi in the first two decades of the fourteenth century, fanning out from Spiritual friars to tertiaries under their influence to sympathetic secular clergy and lay patrons in the towns. The area affected abutted on, and to some degree corresponded with, old Cathar-infected regions, but the inspiration was quite different. Olivi and his followers were firm in their opposition to both the Cathars and the Waldensians, whom they saw as members of Antichrist, and there are hardly any signs of interpenetration of doctrine between Catharism and the Spiritual heresy.[46] Furthermore, the old centres of Catharism lay farther to the east, whereas the Spiritual heresy had its centres in two towns less important in Catharism and nearer the coast: Narbonne because of Olivi's memory, and Béziers because of the patronage of the devoted lay supporter Pierre Trancavel, and also because the two convents had been taken over by Spirituals during the interregnum in the papacy and generalate. The area of diffusion stretched at its maximum extent from the coastal line of Perpignan to Nice and, inland, from Toulouse to Avignon.[47] There was a thinner band of support over the Pyrenees, in more developed regions of the kingdom of Aragon. The core lay in the towns: workers in the country were not affected and neither was the layer of immigrant northern

---

44   Rev. 10: 1, from Catalan *De statibus ecclesie*, dated by Manselli to 1318 (*Spirituali*, pp. 164–7). It is fair to add that the general trend of Manselli's exposition (chs 2–4) differs from mine and, using esp. minor works of the Spirituals and supporters, stresses their relative orthodoxy before 1318 and the arbitrary nature of persecution. I have not been able to use *Franciscains d'Oc: Les Spirituels ca. 1208–1324, CF* x (1975).

45   Manselli, *Spirituali*, pp. 181–2; on literacy see R. E. Lerner, 'Writing and resistance among Beguins', *BHL*, pp. 186–204; on defender of Spirituals, *Processus Bernardi Delitiosi: The Trial of Fr. Bernard Délicieux*, ed. A. Friedlander, *TAPS* LXXXVI, pt 1 (1996).

46   Manselli, *Spirituali*, p. 264; for a possible exception, see p. 221.

47   Ibid, p. 256; for Cathars' sites, see above, p. 126.

Frenchmen, lay or clerical.[48] It was a Languedocian heresy, and may even have owed something to local feeling against authority. Towns backed the Spirituals and appealed on their behalf partly because they were opposed to the activity of the inquisition and its implications in secular politics, and adherents may well have been attracted by a movement which came to denounce wealthy upper clergy, because of their own experience of the clergy in Languedoc.

The Cathar crisis does not seem to have brought a major change in spiritual quality in the higher clergy; a more effective juridical activity can be observed, and the restoration of tithes opened the way to a major church-building pro- gramme in the century between 1250 and 1350, but this was not the same as spiritual revival.[49] Franciscan rigorists, in their obvious destitution, were not, in externals, wholly unlike the perfect; and the interrogations of the inquisition show how Beguins were attracted by the poor life of their leaders.[50] In each case, it was the ethics of the dedicated individual which formed a major appeal. Rich as well as poor laymen were involved but there were numbers of poor tradesmen of modest culture, butchers, weavers and the like, whose attitudes to the rich and powerful who, they believed, formed the carnal Church, were surely in part shaped by their social position and the gulf which separated them from the wealthy. Nevertheless the heresy sprang mainly from a religious motive: it was the belief of elite groups, devoted if unsubtle rank and file Franciscans, and dedicated laity. Numbers were fairly small – 120 members of the first order who took over the convents of Narbonne and Béziers, smaller numbers of friars in Italian provinces. When the inquisition set about destroying the popular base of the heresy in the Midi, they were working on groups linked by geography, family or individual personalities that did not usually number more than twenty and were often less. There was no popular involvement in terms of adherents or patrons on anything like the scale of Catharism.

Paradoxically, John XXII,[51] the dynamic administrator whose election in 1316 ended the long vacancy after Clement V, was at one and the same time respon- sible for cutting short the movement of Spirituals and Beguins and so safeguard- ing orthodoxy and for putting the finishing touches to the development of full- blown heresy within the movement. One hardly knows whether to wonder more at the energy and efficiency which John brought to the task of repression or the recklessness and haste which he demonstrated in his handling of the doctrinal problems of the Franciscans.

---

48   Ibid., pp. 258–63.
49   See J. H. Mundy, 'Charity and social work in Toulouse, 1100–1250', *Traditio* XXII (1966), pp. 203–87, esp. p. 206; *WHC*, p. 130 and n. For a case of the Church benefiting from an individual accused of heresy, see Wakefield, in *Names* XVIII (1970), pp. 294–5.
50   See Manselli's comments (*Spirituali*, chs 7, 8, *passim* (most valuable section)), and Leff, *Heresy* I, pp. 212–30.
51   For John and the Franciscans, see Leff, *Heresy* I, pp. 157–66, 206–11, 230–3, 238–55 (see characterization of John (pp. 206–7) and analysis of his terminology, using *Quia vir reprobus*); Lambert, *Poverty*, ch. 10, and 'The Franciscan crisis'; Tierney, *Origins*, ch. 5, is illuminating on the theory of papal power. Note his correction (p. 188) of Leff, *Heresy* I, pp. 241, 246, 249, on John and the key of knowledge. T. Turley, 'John XXII and the Franciscans: a reappraisal', *Popes, Teachers and Canon Law*, ed. J. R. Sweeney, S. Chodrow (1990), pp. 74–83.

For him, a native of Cahors, who had worked in regions neighbour to the Spirituals' catchment area in the south and came informed to the problem, the question was not whether the movement was dangerous or unorthodox but how it might most effectively be put down. Leading Spirituals who had patrons were removed from the scene without punishment, the rebellion in Narbonne and Béziers ended, Olivi's teaching on the Apocalypse again subjected to academic examination, recalcitrant Italians pursued. His neatest stroke was to take down the previous bull of clarification on the rule, Clement v's *Exivi de Paradiso*, extract two clauses, on the wearing of poor clothing and the prohibition of granaries and cellars, which Clement had concluded were points of obligation for the friars yet should be subject to the individual discretion of superiors, and to reiterate them in a bull of his own, *Quorumdam exigit*, insisting on the power of superiors to decide what was poverty (*vilitas*) in clothing and when it was right to have the security of food storage through using cellars and granaries.[52]

*Quorumdam* was used to sort sheep from goats. An inquisitor presented it to suspect friars and put to them two questions. Would they obey the precepts contained in *Quorumdam exigit?* Did they believe that the pope had the power to make such precepts as were contained in *Quorumdam exigit?* The questions touched on a nerve-centre, for to say 'yes' meant giving up the patched, dramatically poor habits that recalled Francis's dying words about his early life in the *Testament*, and served as a party badge and, against the tenor of the rule, allowing the foresight for the morrow, implied in the keeping of cellars and granaries. To return to obedience to superiors on these issues meant giving up the distinctive Spiritual position and admitting that, as John said, poverty was great but 'unity was greater';[53] to admit the pope's power of dispensation over the rule was to abandon the view, forged by the Spirituals in the battle over the observance, that the Franciscan rule, written under divine inspiration, was like the gospel and not subject to alteration by any human hand.

Four friars were obdurate in refusing assent and, after a high-ranking commission had reported that to refuse the papal right to make the precepts contained in *Quorumdam exigit* was tantamount to heresy, were burnt at Marseilles in May 1318.[54] Armed with *Quorumdam* and this decision, plus a bull which condemned unauthorized groups of friars and tertiaries (*fraticelli, fratres de paupere vita, bizzochi* or *beghini*),[55] the inquisition was equipped to roll up the movement in the south of France. Another bull, with a somewhat arbitrary list of errors, was issued primarily against Spirituals in Tuscany.[56] Meanwhile, a commission reported adversely – and with some injustice – on Olivi's work on the Apocalypse, and theologians condemned a more definitely heretical Catalan work on the ages of the Church. Olivi's *Lectura* was not definitively condemned until 1326; but his

---

52  *BF* v (Rome, 1898), no. 289, pp. 128–30.
53  Ibid., p. 130b.
54  For event and significance, see Manselli, *Spirituali*, pp. 150–78, 190.
55  *Sancta Romana* (*BF* v, no. 297, pp. 134–5).
56  *Gloriosam ecclesiam* (Ibid., no. 302, pp. 137–42).

tomb was destroyed early in the pontificate, and possession of his books was treated as incriminating.

Over some seven or eight years inquisitors destroyed the core of the heresy, catching the members of the first order who escaped the net spread by John and the Conventuals in 1317, moving against the patrons who helped fugitives and the Beguins who were the chief lay supporters. Condemnation to crosses, pilgrimages and burnings, and the usual pressures to produce recantations whittled support away, providing occasional small batches for the pyre, beside the Cathars and Waldensians, who still required attention in this region.[57] By 1326–7, when the inquisition laid by the heels Pierre Trancavel of Béziers and his daughter, who used his resources to aid refugees, and Bernardo Maurini, the secular priest of Narbonne who gave valuable exhortation and encouragement to the cause, the back of the movement was broken.[58] Thereafter, although there was still an aftermath in Languedoc, Catalonia, Majorca and the Western Mediterranean,[59] the Spirituals had lost their most significant territorial base.

So the crisis in the south ended. Yet John, who did most to destroy the movement, also played a part in pushing it deeper into heresy. The four friars who stood firm at Marseilles were regarded as martyrs, and interrogations after 1318 tell us of the shock that the news of the deaths gave to the fugitive friars and Beguins. Surely this blow was one of the persecutions that heralded the opening of the seventh seal of the Apocalypse and the new epoch in history? The decision against the rule, as they saw it, helped to confirm identification of John xxii with the mystical Antichrist who, it was prophesied, would strike against Francis and his true followers. When John, nothing if not thorough, turned his attention in 1322–3 to the contemporary doctrine of poverty of the whole Franciscan order, and made a dogmatic decision on the poverty of Christ and the apostles in an anti-Franciscan sense,[60] that only strengthened their conviction of his true position, as the enemy of the elect. Was not persecution the mark of those who would enter on the Sabbath age of quiet and contemplation? The ashes of those who burned were gathered up and venerated as relics. Gagliarda, wife of the notary Bernardo Fabri, confessed in a human touch that she had said over such relics kept at their home, 'If you are the bones of saints, help me.'[61] Others were firmer in their convictions. The *sermo generalis* before burning, at which the errors of the heretic were described and denounced, and the actual execution could and did have the effect sometimes of

57  See Bernard Gui's first-hand account in *Practica inquisitionis*, ed. C. Douais (1886); G. Mollat, *Manuel de l'inquisiteur* (1926) (abridged, with Fr. tr.); further materials in P. Limborch, *Historia Inquisitionis* (1692); account of sources in Manselli, *Spirituali*, ch. 1; J. B. Given, 'A medieval inquisitor at work: Bernard Gui, 3 March 1308 to 19 June 1323', *Portraits*, ed. S. K. Cohn Jr., S. A. Epstein (1990), pp. 207–32 at p. 232, notes how Beguins were more fiercely punished than Cathars; Id., 'The Béguins in Bernard Gui's *Liber Sententiarum*', *Trials*, ed. Biller, Bruschi.
58  Manselli, *Spirituali*, pp. 234–7.
59  For a discussion of Arnold of Vilanova, his influence, Beguins in Aragon and Catalonia, see Lee and Reeves, in *Prophecy*, ed. Lee *et al.*, pp. 27–88.
60  *Cum inter nonnullos* (*BF* v, no. 518, pp. 256–9); Lambert, *Poverty*, pp. 238–62; *Nicolaus Minorita Cronica*, ed. G. Gál, D. Flood (1996).
61  Manselli, *Spirituali*, p. 221, n. 3.

actually spreading heresy. At times of burnings the priest Peirotas was busy in the localities, using the occasion to exhort fellow believers, by the example of courage in martyrdom, to persevere in belief.[62] There was a chain-reaction, stiffening Beguins and others in their beliefs. The decisions of John strengthened the view that he was Antichrist, and precipitated discussion of the place of present events in the approach to the seventh age of the Church. Eschatological hopes made adherents more determined to be faithful to their beliefs; *Quorumdam exigit* decided them not to yield on habits and granaries; burnings provided more saints, nucleus of a spiritual Church opposed to the carnal Church of pope and prelates. But the effects could not last; the persistence of the inquisition soon swept the recalcitrant few away, and forced the others into recantation.

John's settlement was effective but undiscriminating. An artificiality hangs round the decisions in *Quorumdam exigit*, leaving the impression that heresy had come to consist in opposition to the orders of the pope. The authoritarian approach to problems of doctrine was characteristic of John. An impatient administrator, he produced a decision that provided a convenient basis for inquisition action. Later, when involved in controversy with the whole Franciscan order, he produced decisions about poverty that were careless, easily open to attack and which failed to grapple with the real issue – the place of poverty in the religious life and its relation to Christian perfection. There were curious cross-currents – Bertrand de la Tour, Franciscan cardinal, provided bullets for the pope to fire.[63] John's lack of care helped to cause another revolt of Franciscans, so that by the end of his reign there were not only *fraticelli de paupere vita*, the first-order heirs of the old Spirituals, but also *fraticelli de opinione*, former members of the official order, who opposed his decisions on the poverty of Christ.

Yet heresy there was, 'uncreated' as well as created, for a long incubation lay behind the views of the Beguins. John unwittingly stimulated certain excesses; but he did not bring the heresy as a whole into being.[64] Its essence lay in exaggeration. From earliest days poverty had been a prime occupation of the Franciscans, but it was transmuted by the simpler Spiritual friars and Beguins into the one crucial issue before the Church – a very different position from that of St Francis. The cumulative effect of the disputes, the repressions and the anxieties of rigorists about their views was to go far towards overturning the basis of Christian ethics,[65] and making it consist simply in renunciation of goods and destitution in daily living. Joachimism and the imminent expectation of cosmic change heightened the distortion. The intensified struggle between good and evil on the eve of the end of the world (or, as in Joachim's view, of the present epoch) tended to narrow down to the battle over the observance of poverty. A sectarianism made the writings of one devoted friar with a talent for speculative thinking

---

62    Ibid., pp. 218, 315–18.
63    P. Nold, 'Bertrand de la Tour and Franciscan poverty' (DPhil, Univ. Oxford, 1999; to be pub. in Oxford Historical Monographs).
64    There is a difference of emphasis between my judgement and that of Manselli and Leff.
65    Knowles, *Religious Orders* II, p. 93.

and a taste for the Apocalypse into a teacher on a par with Paul, or with the Four Doctors of the Church; and turned the Franciscan rule, on which a divine inspiration had played, into a writing that stood on a level with the gospels themselves. The battle over obedience, first in the order, then with the ecclesiastical superiors at large, led on to a viewpoint which rejected the whole visible Church, equated the pope with the mystical Antichrist, and waited confidently for the supersession of the hierarchy.

Earlier generations were inclined to shrug off dangers in prophecy. If they were false, events would prove them so.[66] The Midi heresy showed again the flaws in this view. Exaggerations of poverty showed up elements of unhealthy thinking in the whole Franciscan order, and through the Johannine crisis brought the Franciscans to their lowest ebb in the fourteenth century. It was a tragedy for the Church. The events of the early fourteenth century revealed how a popular heresy could emerge within the very citadel of the Church. It was the enemy within.

By the end of John xxii's pontificate in 1334 the roll-call of popular heresies and movements of religious dissent had swelled – the Apostolics, Dolcino's rebels, the extremist Spiritual Franciscans, and their outflow in the tertiaries and Beguins of southern France and the *fraticelli* of Italy, the heretical mystics, and the adherents of the Free Spirit in Germany, Silesia and Bohemia. The combative old man was busy to the last with the aftermath of his settlement of the problems of the Franciscans, writing at length in 1329 to refute the members of the order under the former minister-general Michael of Cesena, who could not accept his decisions on the poverty of Christ and had broken into revolt in the previous year,[67] then embroiling himself in his last years in a controversy over his own doctrine of the Beatific Vision,[68] first evolved in reaction against Olivi's treatment of the issue. The Vision affair, however, remained personal: no theological judgement was issued and John's successor, Benedict xii, sensibly regulated the matter in his bull *Benedictus Deus* of 1336.

Under Benedict the pace of activity died down. Time and periodic persecutions whittled away the heretics. Dolcino and the Apostolics had been a once-for-all outbreak. The Beguins of southern France had been exposed to intensive inquisition activity in the 1320s; they gave scant trouble afterwards. The intellectual Franciscans under Michael of Cesena, secure in their refuge with Lewis of Bavaria in Munich, having only an intellectual challenge and no popular appeal through austerity of life, faded with the deaths of their founders about mid-

---

66   This explains the long toleration of doubtful pseudo-Joachimite speculation. For normal use of prophecy in Middle Ages, see R. E. Lerner, *The Powers of Prophecy* (1983), summary: pp. 183–97; note comment, p. 194, on chiliastic beliefs as 'commonplace aids in coping with reality'. See also R. K. Emmerson, *Antichrist in the Middle Ages* (1981).

67   *Quia vir reprobus (BF* v, no. 820, pp. 408–49); Leff, *Heresy* I, pp. 238–55; B. Töpfer, 'Die Anschauungen des Papstes Johannes xxii über das Dominium in der Bulle "Quia Vir Reprobus"', in *Folia Diplomatica* (1971), pp. 295–306.

68   Knowles, *Religious Orders* I, pp. 248–52; Pásztor, in *BISIAM* lxx, pp. 365–424 and 'Una raccolta di sermoni di Giovanni xxii', *Bulletino dell' Archivio Paleografico Italiano*, n.s. ii–iii (1956–7), pp. 265–89; M. Dykmans, *Les Sermons de Jean* xxii *sur la vision béatifique* (1973).

century. In Italy, especially in the south, and in tiny groups elsewhere, the *fraticelli* who would not accept John's settlement and regarded him as a heretic continued an existence in the half-light.[69] Sectarian to the last, they disputed among themselves as to who would be the Saviour to usher in a new age. Most commonly, they unchurched all who gave obedience to John xxii and his successors, on the grounds that his decisions on poverty were heretical and the practices of the Church and Franciscan order unfaithful to Christ's precepts. But they advanced no new arguments, living on with the themes of their attack on John xxii unchanged, supported by a popular reverence for the austerities of their life. In Florence they had a particularly long influence.[70] It took the determination of the saints of the Franciscan Observance in the fifteenth century, Capistrano and James of the March, who blended a life of true poverty with orthodoxy, to roll up the last remnants of the rebellion. The last of them disappear from recorded history with a trial at Rome in 1466.

Prosecutions of supposed adherents of the Free Spirit fluctuated according to individual interests, and tended to run down as the vitality of the mystical movement in the beguinages faded. At Strasburg repeated persecutions are recorded, in 1317–19, 1365, 1368–9, 1374 and 1404.[71] In the first instance, in 1317, bishop John i was pursuing heresy, pre-eminently among the males, the beghards;[72] later, probably from the pontificate of Urban v in the sixth decade of the century, the curia, rather than the bishop, seems to have provided the major impetus; later still, an individual inquisitor had greatest weight. A strand of genuine heresy and disobedience cannot be discounted as a factor behind these persecutions, but one major recurring source of trouble lay in the resentments of the secular clergy in the city against the popular influence of mendicants who were intimately linked with the beguine movement.[73] Targets of the persecutions varied, including beghards, anticlericals and individualists, deviant mystics, beguines in convents, pious women, tertiaries: the effects of the troubles were to drive the beguine movement more than ever towards the mendicants, obviously for protection. Prejudice played a considerable role, and later persecutions produce less good evidence for doctrinal deviations.

In Germany, Silesia and Bohemia prosecutions were affected by the will of the ruler, being inhibited in Germany for the duration of the contest between John and Lewis of Bavaria, but supported in Silesia and Bohemia by the Margrave Charles, later king, and again given free scope in Germany when the pro-Church

---

69   Leff, *Heresy* i, pp. 230–8, documents ed. F. Ehrle, in *ALKG* iv, pp. 63–180, with discussion of term *fraticelli* (pp. 138–80). Summary by Oliger in *DTC* xiv, cols 2522–49; F. Vernet, Ibid., vi, cols 770–84, s.v.
70   Stephens 'Heresy in . . . Florence', pp. 36–53.
71   Patschovsky, 'Strassburger Beginenverfolgungen', pp. 56–198. Not all persecutions are well recorded; date of 1365 is a hypothesis (Ibid., p. 113). Summary (partially modified by Patschovsky) by Lerner (*Free Spirit*, pp. 85–105); see case of Małkaw (Ibid., pp. 101–3) for a classic case of slander.
72   Lerner, *Free Spirit*, p. 96; on decision of Council of Mainz 1310, see Ibid., pp. 141–2. On name of John i (incorrectly given as 'of Dürbheim' in Lerner, *Free Spirit*), Patschovsky, 'Strassburger Beginenverfolgungen', p. 94, n. 82.
73   See Patschovsky's summary ('Strassburger Beginenverfolgungen', pp. 116–18). Breaches of discipline play an important role, and the terms beguine and beghard are loose ones.

Charles reigned as Emperor Charles IV.[74] They revealed numbers of individual enthusiasts of varying orthodoxy, not necessarily adherents of the Free Spirit, together with Waldensians, the most resilient heretics of these regions. In an interesting case at Schweidnitz in Silesia the inhabitants of a beguinage were shown to be followers of a fiercely ascetic life, with much flagellation, fasting and hard work, believers in their superiority, despite outward humility, and despising church attendance, for which they were inclined to substitute their own prayers. Free Spirit beliefs in union with God did exist among them, but not libertinism, though they were accused of it.[75] The wave of persecution in the Empire led by Martin of Prague, Peter Zwicker and Eylard Schoenveld towards the end of the fourteenth century and in the early years of the fifteenth,[76] though mainly directed against the Waldensians, carried beguines, beghards and supposed heretical mystics into the inquisition's net, but by the time of the Council of Constance in 1414–18 the stream ran thinly. At the council, the beguines, shrunken in number, were defended against attack: *Ad nostrum's* influence had waned: few more cases turned up in the fifteenth century, although the pursuit of the mystical way still had its hazards. The last well-recorded case of Free Spirit heresy north of the Alps is that of Hans Becker of Mainz, burned in 1458.[77]

The heresies that emanated from the Franciscans, the mystics and the imaginations of churchmen were disquieting, not so much because they represented *per se* an important direct threat, but because they were symptomatic of failings in the late medieval Church.

Though the Spiritual Franciscans had some powerful patrons, notably in southern royal houses, their case was not one that of its nature would stimulate a serious revolt against the Church. The practice of poverty, rather than the whole structure of belief woven round the Spirituals' protest, formed the basis of their popularity. *Fraticelli* met a real need which orthodoxy did not. The tragedy of the disputes, so trenchantly resolved after 1316, was that they lost to the sects idealists who were sorely needed. Probably the heresy of the Languedocian Beguins and the *fraticelli* would not have come into existence if the order before the fourteenth century had been able to contain and give outlets to its zealots; after they had gone and the controversies had had their enervating effect, the order was the weaker, and the way to needful reform made harder by being associated with heresy.

Still less than the Franciscans were the adherents of the Free Spirit capable of mounting an assault on the established system. At worst, they were isolated, individual deviants: moreover, as we have seen, there was a great deal of artificiality about this heresy. What the Free Spirit episode did show was the inability of authority at the time of Vienne and afterwards to come to terms with the beguine

---

74  Lerner, *Free Spirit*, pp. 107, 131.
75  Ibid., pp. 112–19.
76  Ibid., pp. 145–6; for proceedings of Zwicker in Brandenburg and Pomerania, above, p. 175, n. 50.
77  Lerner, *Free Spirit*, pp. 177–81.

movement and to provide guidelines for its life, satisfactory to all parties in the Church. The cases after *Ad nostrum* also show us evidence of an anticlericalism both more widespread and more significant in the history of the Church than the Free Spirit.

# Part IV

## Evangelical Heresy in the Late Middle Ages

# 12

## Church and Society: Benedict XII to Eugenius IV

With the death of John XXII the most sustained effort of the popes at Avignon to recover their erstwhile power and independence came to an end; John's successors lacked his exceptional talents, and their problems grew.[1] The most significant legacy from John lay in the development of administration and the increased sophistication of papal fiscal machinery; under his successors the process of reserving benefices for papal provision went on developing, primarily for fiscal reasons; the volume of papal business grew, and itself created a demand for more finance. The popes, whether efficient or not, austere or luxurious, were caught in an inflationary spiral[2] in which their real power was in no way increased, while the activity of their officials grew and the opportunities for true reform, if anything, diminished. There was a quantity of self-interested protest at a high level about the growth of papal intervention and the 'sinful city' of Avignon, coexisting with what could fairly be called informal concordats[3] between the papacy and secular governments, with growing bureaucracies that needed rewards, hard-pressed for resources at a time of economic regression, and anxious to benefit from the treasures of the Church. A system had come into being, based on detailed compromises, which met the needs of various interests in Church and State, however much complaint was made about it; in practice, in the underlying alliance between Church and State, it was the State's power which was now uppermost.

At the same time, papal centralization and defects in its administration excited popular disapproval, reinforced by the feeling of the devout that the proper place for the popes was at the tombs of Peter and Paul. Within the college of cardinals there were signs of the growth of an oligarchy, seeking to assert the powers of electors and put shackles on individual popes. Much valuable day-to-day business transacted at the curia, and a certain sophistication within the bureaucracy could

1 See above, p. 190, n. 1; also M. E. Aston, *The Fifteenth Century: The Prospect of Europe* (London, 1968).
2 Southern, *Western Society*, p. 133.
3 I owe the phrase to Dr A. V. Antonovics.

not weigh in the scales against the general loss of prestige and leadership suffered at Avignon.

In 1378, shortly after the return from Avignon to Rome, disaster occurred. The conclave elected an unsuitable candidate, the aggressive and wilful Urban VI. A genuine reaction against the man they had chosen, combined with divisions among the cardinals, oligarchical sentiment and national feeling, created a schism. All existing problems were vastly accentuated. Thenceforward two popes existed, one with a seat at Avignon under Clement VII and his successors, and the other at Rome under Urban VI and his successors, excommunicating each other and their rivals' supporters, and deploying all available resources to unseat their opponents. Conflicts between states had helped to create the Great Schism, and now kept it in being; all the abuses for which the papacy had been held responsible in the past were sharply increased, as electors on the rival sides chose men of war and diplomacy rather than reformers, and the popes sacrificed all higher considerations to the search for victory.

Need stimulated response, and a conciliar movement developed, primarily in order to end the Great Schism, but secondarily, however, to reform papacy and Church, and in some cases to check a papal headship that appeared unworthy by leadership through general councils. The way to these objectives proved hard. At the Council of Pisa in 1409, the adherents of the conciliar party introduced a third claimant to the tiara, reigning as Alexander V, who was intended to end the conflict, but failed to obtain the withdrawal of his rivals. His existence only made matters worse, as did that of his successor, John XXIII, elected in 1410. Not till 1417 at the Council of Constance did one man, Martin V, emerge as a generally acceptable candidate. Weakened by the schism and by the advantages the kingdoms had gained during it, the papacy under Martin V trod warily and slowly regained ground. Both Martin and his successor, Eugenius IV, had to face tenacious resistance from supporters of the conciliar party, who wanted reform on their own terms, and they could only be said to have effectively outridden opposition from this quarter by about 1439, after Eugenius had succeeded in splitting the movement by transferring the Council of Basle first to Ferrara and then to Florence, and scoring the triumph of securing union between the Greek and Latin Churches.

Throughout the fourteenth century, the schism and the days of vitality of the conciliar movement, reform was constantly discussed, proposals put forward, and sermons preached, often in the most violent terms and by holders of high clerical office, denouncing abuses without bringing about any major reforming action. The need for reform tended to become a cliché. Naturally circumstances, especially after 1378, focused attention on the need for reform at the head. But how was it to be effected? Different voices recommended different means, and wished to carry measures of varying degrees of vigour. If there was to be reform in the head, should it not be in the members also? And yet bishops and cardinals were in various ways beneficiaries of the system to be reformed, and there were secular interests to be considered also. Meanwhile, the immediate need was to end the schism. After it was over, more profound reform remained on the agenda, as it had done on so many occasions in the past, but it tended to be driven into the background by the struggle between papalists and conciliarists, and so was never realized.

A concomitant, and to some degree a result, of these events, was a feeling of mistrust towards ecclesiastical institutions, especially those on a large scale; it was reinforced by the Great Schism, but is discernible earlier. It underlies the loss of vitality of the major orders, and helps to explain the earlier success of the beguine movement, till it was checked by official disapproval and the heresy accusations. While all the high-level disturbances in the leadership of the international Church continued, a popular religion blossomed in the towns, in the parish churches, and in the confraternities which became so popular, and which assembled various social groups for the practice of their religion. A great vogue existed for works of popular devotion in the vernacular, and there was some dissemination of scriptural versions in the form, not of the bare text of the original, but in compilations and meditations linked predominantly to the mystical movement of the late Middle Ages. The practice of pilgrimage flourished and the cult of saints developed, sometimes to extravagance. In the wealthy towns a merchant class spent heavily on the building and decoration of churches; preachers readily drew large crowds, and the individual prophetic figure characteristic of the time, the mystic or the reformer, attracted reverence.

Anticlericalism was the natural accompaniment to the major failures in leadership and to the abuses. It was not always the case that the state of the clergy was worse in the fourteenth and fifteenth centuries than it had been earlier, but their deficiencies were attracting a more impatient response from the laity.[4] The relationship between clergy and laity had undergone a change, due to the widening horizons, the spread of lay education and an increasing lay self-consciousness and independence which became apparent at about the turn of the thirteenth and fourteenth centuries north of the Alps. Italy had long been a special case because of the higher standards of education attained by the laity there in an earlier age. Congregations were less ready to accept a clerical leadership per se; they were more questioning, and their expectations were higher. A low opinion of the clergy was fostered in this period by elements in the clergy themselves, through denunciatory sermons; though one has to note the existence of a literary, satirical anticlerical tradition, of clerks making jokes about clerks, which is as old as Walter Map in the twelfth century.[5]

One difference between the late Middle Ages and earlier centuries was that anticlerical ideas were more likely to be put into effect in the latter period, and Erastianism was both more possible and more widespread. The clerical profession had always been a net holding all manner of fish, and it continued to be so; ordinations were on a considerable scale, and investigation of suitability merely

---

4  See Rapp, *L'Eglise et la vie religieuse* (Paris, 1971), ch. 9, and on Italy, D. Hay, *Italian Clergy and Italian Culture in the Fifteenth Century* (London, 1973); on German anticlericalism, see W. Eberhard in *HJB* CXIV (1994), pp. 349–80.

5  I owe comment to Professor C. N. L. Brooke.

formal; the bishop was generally a remote figure, appointed for political or social rather than religious reasons, unable, even if he willed, to break through the barriers of custom effectively to discipline or unite the clergy of his diocese; there were many avenues of promotion open to the talented priest, and a parochial post was not necessarily rewarding or attractive. It was at the level of the parish clergy, despite efforts at reform and some improvements, that the late medieval Church proved least effective, and it was here that some of the greatest stimuli to anticlericalism existed.

Extremism was a characteristic of the time. It links to political events and to economic troubles. The Hundred Years' War between England and France, which broke out in 1337, initiated a long sequence of conflicts, produced devastation over wide areas of France, and had a baleful effect on Church life; we have seen the part it played in the outbreak and continuation of the Great Schism. Secular governments had their own problems of authority, made worse by economic pressures and the effects of warfare. The Black Death in 1348–51 was a catastrophic event, removing more than a third of the population, and sparking off a great outburst of penitential flagellation, intended to assuage God's wrath and expiate the sins of the individual penitent; renewed visitations, though less disastrous, had important demographic effects and elicited similar, if not so violent, emotional responses.[6]

Processions of men, initially well organized, walking two by two, with a precise ritual to follow, of the saying of *Pater Nosters* and *Aves* and of flagellation accompanied by chants and songs, passed through Austria (probably their place of origin), Hungary, Germany, Bohemia, the Low Countries and Picardy, summoning the citizens of the towns to which they came to join them and scourging themselves in some public spot, generally the market-place.

The most striking feature lies in the strength of the emotions which lay behind these painful and repeated self-chosen penances, a reminder of the violence of feeling still latent in popular spirituality, comparable to the early crusade impulse, the Alleluia preachings in thirteenth-century Italy, or the outbreak of flagellation in 1260, coupled with the self-control often apparent in a movement that appears to be quite spontaneous, uncontrolled by any existing authority, and in the hands of the laity. The would-be flagellant took an oath to carry out his flagellation for thirty-three and a half days, recalling the years of Christ's earthly life, confessed to the masters of the movement, and undertook to pay his debts or make restitution for past wrongs. Within the procession he followed a strict ritual and obeyed the

---

6   E. Delaruelle, 'Les grands processions de pénitents de 1349 et 1399', *Il Movimento dei disciplinati nel settimo centenario del suo inizio* (1962), pp. 109–45 (on Netherlands, but with general references); G. Székely, 'Le mouvement des Flagellants au 14e siècle, son caractère et ses causes', in *HS*, pp. 229–38, Erbstösser, *Strömungen*, pp. 10–69 (Marxist analysis, with hypothesis of penetration of the movement in Thuringia by Free Spirit), R. Kieckhefer, 'Radical tendencies in the Flagellant movement of the mid-fourteenth century', *JMRS* IV (1974), pp. 157–76 (re-examination of sources, with critique of Erbstösser); English account in Leff, *Heresy* II, pp. 485–93. See J. V. Fearns's map and notes (*Atlas zur Kirchengeschichte*, ed. H. Jedin et al. (Freiburg im Breisgau, 1970), pp. 48, 65). For general comment, see R. E. Lerner, 'The Black Death and Western European eschatological mentalities', *American Historical Review* LXXXV (1981), pp. 533–52; F. Graus, *Pest-Geissler-Judenmorde. Das 14. Jahrhundert als Krisenzeit* (Göttingen, 1987); P. Dinzelbacher, *Angst im Mittelalter* (1996).

masters, flagellating twice a day in public and once at night; after the conclusion of the pilgrimage he promised to flagellate on Good Fridays for the rest of his life. Unbeneficed clergy joined, but the great bulk of penitents were laymen.

The attitudes of ecclesiastical authority varied. In the Low Countries, for example, the bishop of Thérouanne formally authorized them; at Tournai a rule which the Bruges flagellants had adopted was presented to the chapter; but the author of the *Annales Flandriae* thought that they were beghards, and attacked their belief that all sins would be remitted after their penance. The fear was of a lay movement without clerical control that had undertaken mass penance without authorization and without receiving the sacrament of penance from the priesthood. Moreover, there were extravagances. A Dominican preacher, for example, said that the blood of the flagellants was more precious than any since Christ's. In certain areas, notably Thuringia and Franconia, they tended to become more violent and anticlerical. Conceivably this was the case more often when their arrival preceded, rather than followed, the plague. Before the arrival of the Death, flagellation was one of the few outlets open to a fear-ridden population; after it had arrived, the worst could be seen, and there were practical tasks, such as burying the dead, available to dampen emotions.[7]

In the end, Clement VI condemned them in 1349. As the stimulus of mass mortality faded, so the movement waned, although there were recrudescences, in some cases associated with much more overt antisacerdotalism and heresy proper. The use of the scourge, long a traditional monastic discipline, had been taken up by the laity in a crisis on a mass scale, quite independently of the hierarchy, and by some of them turned into a kind of supreme sacrament.

The Death, a unique catastrophe for contemporaries, sparked off a religious response of unusual intensity; other long-term changes in the economy and society, still imperfectly understood, and the effects of warfare produced tensions and uprisings in town and country. The roots of these disturbances lay in the major changes in the Western economy which made themselves felt from almost the beginning of the fourteenth century in certain regions, affecting class relationships, the internal life of towns, and the condition of peasants. In towns a major factor lay in the rigidity of government by closed circles of wealthy bourgeois, directing affairs to their own profit, and arousing the hostility of artisans eager to share in the new wealth. Before the Death, the increase in town populations in advanced areas to an unprecedented size accentuated this hostility, as small groups of families were seen to regulate the destinies of so many; after the massive fall in population tension continued, as the rich in a contracted economy attempted to hold on to every source of wealth.

Troubles had begun in the late thirteenth century in the Low Countries, and continued during the following century; there were sporadic crises elsewhere and widespread disorder in Western Europe at various times between the spring of 1378 and the early months of 1383.[8] In France anger was turned against royal

---

7   Kieckhefer's hypothesis.
8   M. Mollat and P. Wolff, *The Popular Revolutions of the Late Middle Ages* (1973).

officials, tax collectors and moneyers; generally at the time of the Black Death the fear of mortality issued in pogroms of Jews, who were accused of responsibility for the epidemic; in England there were periodic xenophobic outbreaks.

In the countryside lords who were under heavy economic pressure attempted to enforce ancient rights over the peasants and, after the fall in population, to prevent free movement for better wages or conditions at a time of labour shortage. In France, one of the most violent peasant uprisings, the Jacquerie, took place in 1358; in England, the Peasants' Revolt of 1381 led to the death of Simon of Sudbury, archbishop of Canterbury; the mob attacked officials and destroyed records, and briefly held the south-east of the country in fear. A combination of grievances came to a head with the imposition of a poll tax for an unsuccessful war; the underlying factor was the irritation of a comparatively prosperous peasantry with out-of-date restrictions which lords were attempting to impose on them. Further visitations of the plague, on a smaller scale, in the later fourteenth century and in the fifteenth added to the tension of life, sometimes inducing flight to penance, as in the Flagellant episode. Man's mortality was unusually vivid in the years following 1348.

Thought was marked by a tendency to take issues to extremes, and by a mistrust of reason.[9] The great system-building of the thirteenth century was over. The synthesis between faith and reason of St Thomas Aquinas had fallen under heavy attack almost as soon as it was launched. The wholesale condemnation of theses, some of St Thomas, some of others, by Bishop Etienne Tempier of Paris in 1277 marked the turning-point; thereafter different groups of scholastics separated, debating among one another individual issues; the effect of the Tempier condemnations was first to create confusion, and, then, in the long run, to facilitate a division between the spheres of faith and reason.

New ideas appeared with great rapidity; Duns Scotus, the Scottish Franciscan who died in 1308, both subjected traditional Aristotelian and Augustinian views to effective criticism and launched forth on a structure of thought of his own, inventing novel technical terms to do so. William of Ockham, an English Franciscan who had his career in a university cut short when he joined Michael of Cesena's revolt against John XXII's decisions on poverty, was the fountain-head of a powerful current of thought often referred to, somewhat inaccurately, as nominalism. This school had in common with some thinkers of the eleventh and twelfth centuries a stress on the particular in the traditional debate about universals.[10] But discussion was being carried on in the fourteenth century in a quite different atmosphere from that of earlier centuries. Where Aquinas and other thirteenth-century thinkers had been concerned to demonstrate how far natural reason supported the truths of faith, the trend in Scotus, Ockham and other contemporaries was to stress the contingent and limited nature of man's know-

9   G. Leff, *Medieval Thought from St Augustine to Ockham* (Harmondsworth, 1958), pt 3; for debate on Ockhamism and its effects (with recent literature), Rapp, *L'Eglise*, pp. 332–46, and for more recent work by Leff, below, p. 249, n. 4.

10   For explanation, see Leff, *Thought*, pp. 104–14, 259–60; and on terminology, Rapp, *L'Eglise*, p. 337 and my comment below (p. 250, n. 8).

ledge. Ockham went farther than Scotus on this road; moreover, his expositions on the absolute freedom and overriding power of God, buttressed by a series of brilliant paradoxes, set a gulf between man and the unknowable God and appeared to sap the traditional bases of moral theology. Reason could not support faith, which rested on revelation and authority.

The separation thus effected had beneficial effects in one sphere, for it opened the way to advances in natural science; on the other hand, it undermined traditional supports for faith and moral behaviour, and issued in a fashion both for scepticism and for fideism; if reason could not support faith, it could be argued, then neither could it disprove it, and beliefs, even if they seemed improbable, could be accepted on external authority alone. How far Ockham has been adequately understood by modern writers, and how far he was responsible for some of the effects attributed to his teaching, is still the subject of debate; responsibility for some of the more extreme positions of fourteenth-century intellectuals may well lie with other, lesser contemporaries or successors of his. Whatever the ultimate origins of Ockhamism and the so-called nominalist school, it provoked a reaction against this *via moderna*, notably by Thomas Bradwardine, archbishop of Canterbury, who died in 1349, during the Black Death, reasserting traditional doctrine and in metaphysics taking up the opposite position to the Ockhamists, that of realism.[11] Characteristically, however, this reaction too was often marked by the extremism that we must expect of the age.

The more critical climate of opinion, the currents of thought stemming from Ockhamism in the earlier fourteenth century, and the weakening of clerical authority and prestige in the age of the Avignonese papacy and the Great Schism are essential background for the study of the evangelical heresies of the late Middle Ages, stemming from Wyclif, the English Lollards[12] and the Bohemian Hussites. The existence of so much high-level dissent, the reiteration at all levels of the need for reform, and the widespread doubt and uncertainty about the true nature of the Church and the authority of the pope gave opportunities and stimuli unknown to the heresies of the past. Wyclif, co-founder with his early preachers of the English Lollards and part-inspiration of the Bohemian Hussites, was one of the leading academic figures of his day; his progress into heresy in his last years, ignoring the verdict of authority, then deliberately disseminating his views, was something novel in a scholastic of his eminence. An academic could speak to academics, and sparks of Wyclifite heresy blew about in the university world, taking fire here and there among scholars, and passing from them more widely into society.

The widespread criticism of authority, the consciousness of abuse and the scandals of the schism both gave cover to and stimulated Wyclif's attacks. So

---

11    Leff, *Thought*, pp. 296–9; for explanation of realism and the reaction against scepticism, see below, pp. 250–1.
12    The best explanation of the origin of the name is in D. Kurze, 'Die festländischen Lollarden', *AKG* XLVII (1965), pp. 48–76; for first official use of it against English heresy by Bishop Wakefield in August 1387, see *A Calendar of Henry Wakefield Bishop of Worcester 1375–95*, ed. W. P. Marett, Worcester Historical Society, n.s. VII (1972), pp. 150–2. The term was used in Oxford against academics by Henry Crumpe in 1382.

his heresy gained, for a little time, a base in the university of Oxford, and, because of Wyclif's academic reputation, found its way to the university of Prague. Certain ideas of Wyclif on disendowment and clerical jurisdiction had a natural appeal to rulers and nobility – the potential was there to build upper-class patronage on a scale not achieved by any previous heresy. Heretical doctrine and practical politics could work together. Moreover, the heresies of Wyclif, the Lollards and the Bohemian preachers all lay within the main stream of Christian doctrine and appealed to discontents which were of common concern; the ground for support was wider than the appeal of the Spiritual Franciscans could be, and lacked the alien, exotic quality in Catharism, ultimately repugnant to informed Western Christians. Three factors – the initial base in universities, the potential for gaining upper-class support and the wide appeal of their teachings – made the new evangelical heretics more dangerous to the papacy and hierarchy than any earlier movement.

And yet, although Wyclif and his fellows gave expression, often in radical form, to widespread discontents, and worked within an existing intellectual and spiritual tradition, to which they were deeply indebted, their teachings and heresies only struck deep root in two countries, England and Bohemia. Wyclifite and Hussite heresies of various kinds were disseminated, and found some echoes, in Scotland, France, Poland, Hungary, Austria and other German-speaking lands, even in Dalmatia, but provoked no long-lasting response. Lands earlier moved by heresy were, on this occasion, not especially fertile. The machinery of repression moved against the heretics; Wyclif, Hus and the rest formed only a section amongst the many voices raised in favour of reform; there were still deep reserves of feeling behind orthodox doctrine and traditional practice; there was no printing to spread heresy rapidly from one country to the next; precisely the factors which built up Hussitism in the lands of the Bohemian crown acted to cut back support in neighbouring countries. So there was no breakthrough for the new heresies. But still the Wyclif affair and the rise of Lollardy was a major event in English Church history, and the long Hussite crisis formed a turning-point in the Bohemian lands.

# John Wyclif

## The English Church in the Fourteenth Century

England produced no significant heresy before the late fourteenth century. Orthodox movements, whether it was the developing interest in the canon law, the new monasticism of the twelfth century, or the orders of friars in the thirteenth, passed into England. Contacts with Europe culturally and ecclesiastically remained close. Commercial and economic links with the towns of Flanders, once a fertile ground for religious dissidence, remained active through the wool trade. Yet heresy from the Continent made no impact, and there was no native growth of it[1] before Wyclif fired an old store of combustible anticlericalism and untapped religious zeal in the late fourteenth century.

One reason for this lay in the tight-knit, close-governed nature of the English Church. By continental standards, the control of the ruler over the Church remained very close. The investiture controversy in England was a very brief one, and ended in a compromise that left the substance of power in the matter of appointment to high ecclesiastical office in the hands of the crown.

England was never the scene of the most spectacular scandals in appointments, which on the Continent were most often associated with areas of aristocratic dominance. Royal influence over episcopal appointments tended to be consistent with a fair standard, sometimes, indeed, a distinguished one, as the episcopate of the thirteenth century shows. Ecclesiastical abuse, that first stimulus to heresy, was not notably apparent in England before the fourteenth century. The Franciscans, whose decline on the Continent brought a new heresy to birth in the sect of the *fraticelli*, kept their purity and combined good life and learning longer in England than perhaps in any other province. Finally, the effective administration of the country kept a check on the ports, and care was taken to filter the ideas which might pass into the country. Cathars who came in from the Continent under Henry II, despite prelates' uncertainty, were caught and sentenced.[2] In

---

1  For the rare exceptions, see above, pp. 68–9, below, p. 393.
2  Above, p. 68.

1224 the first Franciscan missionaries were kept in Dover castle until they were able to prove their innocence of unorthodoxy.[3] Through the thirteenth century there is evident a care to supervise merchants from France and elsewhere who might be tainted with heresy.

By the latter half of the fourteenth century, the position of the Church had quietly and undramatically worsened. The episcopate was not unworthy, but it generally lacked the exceptional quality of the previous century. As in Europe generally, no new movement of note had arisen to fill the gap left by the decline of the friars as a source of the most disinterested zeal. There was still vitality in the religious scene, but it was a vitality that could easily lead away from orthodoxy. The English mystics, writing their treatises in the vernacular, making their own direct ascent to God, were no doubt read by few, but they may well be symptomatic of a wider feeling that was not fully content with the official channels of worship and organization. By the end of the century official sources were taking note of the existence of a new man, the literate layman; some action was taken to make a place for him, but not enough. The sermon literature of the time reveals the readiness of the churchmen to denounce abuses; it also reveals, by its repeated mention of abuses over the years, a failure to uproot them. Certain old failings remained throughout the later Middle Ages: an excess overall of clergy, an excess of ill-paid unbeneficed clergy who formed a re-servoir of discontent, a monasticism that could not be fairly called decadent but had ceased to be a motive force, a certain canonists' petrefaction in the machinery of the Church, too formal in its procedures easily to allow reform to be effective.

Against this background the period of war strain and ineffectual government which followed on the renewal of the Hundred Years' War in 1369 becomes significant. The failures in the French war and the taxation necessary to pursue campaigns that were in fact beyond the powers of the English kingdom created a cry for disendowment. The size of ecclesiastical endowments gave obvious occasion to this agitation; it was made popular by the desire of the Commons to do something to shift a burden of taxation that, ineptly imposed, helped to spark off the Peasants' Revolt in 1381. Unconnected with reforms as it was, the agitation against the Church gave special opportunities to radical preachers. It favoured the mendicants, with their old complaints against the endowed posses-sioners, and it gave a brief popular platform to John Wyclif. It favoured anticler-icalism, not specially strong in England, but at this time given an exceptional outlet by John of Gaunt and other soldiers and politicians. Ineffectual govern-ment in the dotage of Edward III and the minority of Richard II facilitated the rise of extremism and the struggles of factions, some of whom turned to attack the Church as part of their internal struggles.

When a native heresy appeared and was carried rapidly about England, the Church was unprepared. Lack of familiarity with heresy inside the country cut off English churchmen from the developments that had led to the rise of the papal

3   *Chronica de Lanercost*, ed. J. Stevenson (Edinburgh, 1839), p. 30.

inquisition on the Continent. The inquisition came to England only in the one exceptional case of the Templars, and, once the alarm was raised, the episcopate adopted cumbersome procedures in an attempt to stamp out the infection. Though they achieved the essential task of preventing Lollardy from coming to power, they had neither the experience nor the personnel to prevent a rapid expansion of adherents on the eve of the Peasant's Revolt, or to cut the movement off totally in the aftermath of Oldcastle's revolt early in the fifteenth century. Orthodoxy was never able fully to erase the effects of the agitation of the 1370s and the years immediately following, in which Wyclif's heretical ideas were formulated and the first Lollard preachers began to spread their message along the roads of England. But, before we examine the origins of Lollardy proper, it will be necessary first of all to outline Wyclif's career, and attempt some answer to the long controversial question: why and how did Wyclif come to hold his heretical views?

## The Development of Wyclif's Heresy

### Early career

No exact parallel to Wyclif's career can be found in the history of medieval heresies. His is a unique case of a university master turned heresiarch, who inspired a popular movement against the Church. A heresy charge was a recognized hazard in the intellectual contests of the Schools, and not necessarily of great import; deliberate defiance of the Church, such as Wyclif came to make in his last years, was another matter altogether. Two thinkers in the fourteenth century, Marsiglio of Padua and William of Ockham, had made such a defiance and developed lines of thought which show affinities to Wyclif's;[4] but neither is truly comparable. Ockham founded no movement – he joined the schism of Michael of Cesena and developed his views of the Church from the safety of Lewis of Bavaria's court at Munich, and his influence remained intellectual. The same is true of Marsiglio, an astonishingly secular-minded writer but a lone voice, political theorist rather than theologian, without a reputation or depth of learning like that of Wyclif. He too inspired no popular movement.

On the other side, the leaders or founders of popular heresies had not hitherto been men of intellectual standing. They had most frequently been preachers and agitators like Henry the Monk, Valdes or the dualist preachers of the twelfth century. Arnold of Brescia had an intellectual training, but his heresy owed all to his eloquence and powers of personal leadership.[5] Even Petrus Johannis Olivi offers no clear parallel, for, although he was of intellectual calibre to be mentioned in company with Wyclif and was the major inspiration of a popular

---

4  Leff, *Heresy* II, pp. 411–44 *passim*, and 'The changing pattern of thought in the earlier fourteenth century', *BJRL* XLIII (1961), pp. 354–72; see Offler's comment on Leff's treatment of Ockham (*EHR* LXXXIV (1969), p. 574).
5  Above, pp. 59–61.

heretical movement, he was in no sense the founder of the Spiritual Franciscans, which without him would certainly have existed, though they would have been less dangerous.[6]

Wyclif's heresy owed nothing to any pre-existing heretical movement. Its popular adherents, the English Lollards, came in the end to resemble the Waldensians, but they did so quite independently of any continental influence. They owed the germ of their beliefs, simplified and adapted as they were, to Wyclif himself. Wyclif's radical ideas were powerful enough to inspire a movement which outlasted persecution for over a hundred years, produced a literature of its own and a line of martyrs and devoted missionaries right up to the time of the Reformation, without their originator ever apparently having displayed any outstanding powers of personal leadership or even any very direct interest in the practicalities of building up a new religious group. The spontaneous incubation of so dangerous a heresy in intellectual authority, and the ambiguities of his relationship as a scholar with a movement of popular preachers, all lend special interest to the study of his life.

Wyclif was a product of the intellectual environment of Oxford, where by far the greater part of his life was passed, from the time of his entry to the university as a young man to his enforced departure at roughly fifty years of age in 1381.[7] His dabbling in politics in the 1370s took him away on occasional missions, and the last years of his life (after 1381) were spent in retirement in the rectory at Lutterworth. Otherwise he remained, in the usual and necessary fashion of the day, an absentee from the benefices whose revenues made possible his academic work at Oxford. His experience was very largely academic, and much less either pastoral or political.

Oxford marked him deeply, whether by direct influence or by provoking violent reactions. As a young man, he fell under the influence of the nominalism then fashionable, which had developed from the writings of William of Ockham and his school, and was marked by a mistrust of the power of reason to demonstrate the truths of faith.[8] Nominalism, and the scepticism and fideism which accompanied it, are fundamental for the understanding of the fourteenth-century intellectual scene, arousing deep conflicts, and opening the way for a series of radical or extremist thinkers to put forward their views. The anti-intellectual

---

6   Above, pp. 211–13.
7   K. B. McFarlane, *John Wycliffe and the Beginnings of English Nonconformity* (1952) (*MW*) (pungent reassessment of Wyclif and Lollardy by master of political history; partially outdated by his own and others' subsequent research); H. B. Workman, *John Wyclif* I–II (1926) (old-style compendium, weak on political side, eccentrically omitted from McFarlane); Leff, *Heresy* II, pp. 494–558 (penetrating assessment of thought); B. Smalley, 'The Bible and eternity: John Wyclif's dilemma', *JWCI* XXVII (1964), pp. 73–89 (illuminating); M. J. Wilks, '*Reformatio regni*: Wyclif and Hus as leaders of religious protest movements', *SCH* IX, pp. 109–30; J. I. Catto, 'Wyclif and Wycliffism at Oxford 1356–1430', *The History of the University of Oxford* II, *Late Medieval Oxford*, ed. J. I. Catto, R. Evans (1992), pp. 175–261 (adds perspective to Wyclif among friends and opponents; positive assessment, p. 218); historians, Biller, 'The historiography of medieval heresy', Id., *Waldenses*, pp. 36–9.
8   'Terminism' is felt by some historians to be a more accurate label. I have here used 'nominalism' simply because it is more familiar.

tone of moralists of the time and the development of the English school of mystics represent one kind of hostile reaction to this prevailing mode of thought;[9] the maturer Wyclif represents another reaction. In place of the distrust of reason introduced by the nominalists, he put forward, as Beryl Smalley shows, what he saw as a better way of reasoning.[10]

A strong reaction against nominalism at Oxford was, in itself, nothing new. Both Bradwardine and Fitzralph, for example, had earlier written against this school.[11] Like Wyclif they were Augustinians. The major thinker, Bradwardine, attacked the Ockhamist school not without effect, and probably some of the philosophical realism he had defended survived in the background. He and Fitzralph provide occasional parallels to Wyclif; he adapted one of his best known theses, on dominion and grace, from Fitzralph.[12] The work of Thomas Buckingham c.1350 shows that Bradwardine's great work against the nominalists, the *De causa Dei*, was still being discussed; this would make it natural for Wyclif to develop an interest in analogous problems. But when Wyclif's own metaphysical position had been fully formed and came under hostile criticism, no-one suggested that anyone else was responsible for it. His final position was too individual and idiosyncratic to have been borrowed: he had worked out an answer for himself, which differed drastically from the ideas of his youth.

From nominalism he swung round to the opposite extreme – to ultrarealism. Research has shown scattered through his writings, phrases in which he looks back on his past 'sophistries' in something of the same manner and tone that a spiritual writer might use in bewailing the sins of his youth.[13] The violence of the reaction was something analogous to a conversion, and he plainly had quasi-religious feelings about the philosophical position that he had come to adopt. Speaking of realism ('the knowledge of universals') he once said, 'A knowledge of universals is the pre-eminent step on the ladder of wisdom by which we search out hidden truth; and this, I believe, is the reason why God does not permit the school of universals utterly to fail.'[14] The element of personal conversion involved in the adoption of realism helps to explain the obstinacy with which he later clung to his metaphysics.

The intellectual environment of the Oxford in which he grew to maturity is a necessary background both for the high reputation he came to hold and for some of the idiosyncratic features of his thought. It is generally agreed that between

9   Smalley, 'The Bible', p. 73.
10   Ibid.; note comparison between Plotinus and Wyclif.
11   J. A. Robson, *Wyclif and the Oxford Schools* (1961), chs 2 and 3 (graceful introduction, fundamental for Wyclif's early philosophy).
12   A. Gwynn, *The English Austin Friars* (1940), pp. 35–59; K. Walsh, *A Fourteenth Century Scholar* (1981).
13   Robson, *Wyclif*, p. 145, more forcefully by B. Smalley reviewing Robson (*MA* xxx (1961), p. 202) and 'The Bible', pp. 77–81; another view in M. J. Wilks, 'The early Oxford Wyclif: papalist or nominalist', *SCH* v, pp. 69–98.
14   Smalley's translation ('The Bible', p. 81); text, Robson, *Wyclif*, p. 154, n. 1; see also Catto, 'Wyclif', pp. 192–3; he sees Wyclif's understanding of universals as transforming 'the academic logician and theologian into a great moral force' (p. 193).

*c.*1350 and 1370, the time of his initiation into academic studies, there was a lack of outstanding thinkers.[15] Wyclif spoke contemptuously of the thinkers of his age, and looked back behind them to Bradwardine and Fitzralph, as we have seen, and still further to Grosseteste in the thirteenth century.[16] At the time his metaphysic was formed, he needed the discipline of effective controversy to check the extremism to which he was naturally prone[17] and he did not get it. Because of this relative vacuum of leading figures, he seemed to overpower his contemporaries. Those who later became his enemies witness to the great effect he had. Thomas Netter of Walden, whose *Doctrinale* was the most effective reply to Wyclif's academic supporters, said that at first he was 'astounded by his sweeping assertions, by the authorities cited, and by the vehemence of his reasoning'.[18]

But most of all, he influenced contemporaries because, in contrast to the sceptics, he offered certainty of knowledge. The example of Scripture may be taken to illustrate this. Wyclif was troubled that the sceptics were criticizing Scripture. An important quotation came from Augustine's *De doctrina Christiana*, 'Faith will waver if the authority of Holy Scripture should fail. If faith wavers, then charity weakens.'[19] It was nominalism which he felt was undermining faith in Scripture; already, he believed, the supporters of nominalism were leading the laity into error.[20] His answer flowed from a metaphysic based on the indestructibility of universals. Scripture became a divine exemplar conceived in the mind of God before creation, and before the material Scriptures were written down. Because it was a divine idea, every word of it was true, and every part as authoritative as the other.[21]

It was a bold thesis, which at first might seem to bowl over the opposition. Yet the certainty was purchased at a high price, and the philosophical position Wyclif adopted had unorthodox implications, notably on the eucharist. John Kenningham, who was in debate with Wyclif in 1372–4, had seen that Wyclif's ultrarealism made impossible an acceptance of the orthodox doctrine of transubstantiation, with its concomitant annihilation of substance. As Wyclif moved from philosophical to doctrinal works, the awkward consequences of his metaphysics became ever more apparent. William Woodford, the Franciscan, early perceived his problem on the eucharist, and noted how he went on shifting his position over a period of time. Criticism probably caused him to shift his ground somewhat on Scripture also; in the *De veritate sacrae scripturae* he 'no longer sought to prove the literal sense to

---

15   Robson, *Wyclif*, pp. 97–112, S. H. Thomson, in *Speculum* XXXVIII (1963), pp. 497–9, J. M. Fletcher, in *HJ* LXI (1962–3), pp. 179–80.
16   B. Smalley, 'The biblical scholar', in *Robert Grosseteste*, ed. D. A. Callus (1955), esp. pp. 70, 83, 95–7; Robson, *Wyclif*, pp. 26–9, 186, Smalley, in *MA* XXX, pp. 202–3.
17   Leff, *Heresy* II, p. 500.
18   Robson's translation (*Wyclif*, pp. 203–4).
19   Smalley's translation, 'The Bible', p. 75; the original, Ibid., n. 10, and in Wyclif's *De veritate sacrae scripturae*, ed. R. Buddensieg (WS), I, pp. 157–389.
20   Smalley, 'The Bible', p. 77; the Middle English poem *Pearl* makes significant assumptions about the laity's interest in theology (Robson, *Wyclif*, p. 33).
21   Robson, *Wyclif*, pp. 163–4.

be true in every particular'. But the immense importance of Scripture in his thought remained unchanged.[22]

Political service was a tribute to his growing prestige as a theologian, and awareness in high places of his teaching on the desirability of disendowment and the necessity of reform of the Church by the State. He could be useful as a counterweight to more traditionalist academics.[23] In April 1374 he was presented to Lutterworth, at the time a benefice at the king's disposal.[24] In 1374 he was a diplomatic agent in negotiations with the papacy over a demand for financial contributions from the English clergy; in 1377 he gave an opinion in the government interest on the export of bullion to Avignon; and in 1378 he defended, in effect, the actions of royal servants in a *cause célèbre* on the violation of sanctuary.[25] But these episodes had an importance out of proportion to their intrinsic weight, for they secured to Wyclif the protection of great men, who headed off ecclesiastical authority's attempts to silence him. In two hearings, one in St Paul's in 1377, the other in Lambeth palace chapel in 1378, when the bishops tried to take action, the protection, first of John of Gaunt, then of the Black Prince's widow, was decisive.[26]

From about 1376 he emerged as a public figure, whose forum was no longer merely the university. His teaching on rightful lordship, in effect a theological justification of the disendowment of the secular clergy and the endowed orders, gave him political support and attracted the attention of the dissatisfied.[27] Agitation about the wealth of the clergy and the rights of the laity to remove it recurred in the 1370s. Augustinian friars raised the issue in 1371; a great council in 1373 probably discussed and rejected a papal demand for a subsidy; the commons in the Good Parliament of 1376 petitioned against papal taxation. Wyclif had a natural platform. His preaching carried his views outside the confines of Oxford: he began to head a movement of reform. Denunciation of clerical abuses was not new. Bishop Brinton of Rochester used comparable language. The fierce commonplaces of pulpit criticism may well have obscured the difference between men such as Brinton and Wyclif, who was fast becoming a revolutionary rather than a reformer. His strictures, moreover, did not spare high-placed laity. He repeatedly denounced warfare and booty and excoriated military men pursuing plunder as 'boys who hurt each other grievously to collect the wind-blown cherries'.[28]

---

22  Leff, *Heresy* II, pp. 500–12, making Kenningham affair basis for analysis. Note comment on Wyclif (p. 505), 'he had an inexhaustible supply of logical devices which hid an impoverished and inflexible mode of thought'. See Robson, *Wyclif*, pp. 162–70, Smalley, 'The Bible', pp. 86–7. Wyclif on Scripture, Leff, *Heresy* II, pp. 511–45, Id., 'The place of metaphysics in Wyclif's theology', *SCH* Subsidia V, p. 223; Catto, 'Wyclif', pp. 194–5, quotation on literal sense, p. 196.

23  *MW*, pp. 58–60; Catto, 'Wyclif', p. 199, n. 83 rejects Workman's evidence (I, p. 210) that Wyclif attended the 1371 Parliament.

24  Catto, 'Wyclif', p. 200.

25  Workman, *Wyclif* I, pp. 240–6, 302–4, 313–24; perspective, *MW*, chs 2, 3.

26  Workman, *Wyclif*, I, pp. 284–8, 307–9.

27  See below, pp. 258–9.

28  Catto, 'Wyclif', pp. 202–3, 208–9; quotation, p. 209 from Wyclif, *Sermones*, ed. J. Loserth, IV, p. 362.

The residual loyalty of Wyclif's former employers, together with the effect of the Great Schism on the freedom of papal action, preserved Wyclif from any personal judicial proceedings in the last years of his life, thus enabling him to produce his most radical treatises. Royal service coincided roughly with the time in which his interests turned to the doctrine of the Church. In the *Postilla super totam bibliam* (finished 1375–6), he can be seen stressing the poverty and humility of the early Church, and beginning to use Scripture as a standard of criticism for the Church of his own time. The need for poverty is again stressed, though still with moderation, in the *De civili dominio* (1376–8).[29] By the time we reach the *De ecclesia* (1378) Wyclif is defending a quite revolutionary doctrine of the Church which would overturn the established order.[30] This was the year of decision in his work as well as the year of the Great Schism.

When Wyclif put himself in the service of anticlerical politicians,[31] he could think, however unrealistically, that he was helping to hasten the time when the State would bring about the reform of the Church by force according to his own prescriptions. At the same time, the effects of this experience, together with the increasing pressure of controversy as the true nature of his views became apparent, helped to make him more bitter and violent. From 1378, the tone of his works tended to change for the worse; he was inclined to quote himself more, and abuse his enemies more violently; his theology becomes more radical, and his denunciations more repetitive. In December 1365 Archbishop Islip appointed Wyclif warden of Canterbury College, a quondam foundation for monks, which he had reformed to receive only seculars. A malign chance destroyed his prospects as warden when the only monk-archbishop of the century, Simon Langham, succeeded Islip and promptly returned the college to its former status. Wyclif and the secular fellows fought on till 1370 to reverse the decision; their failure makes understandable the violence of his later attacks on monks.[32]

Yet personal experience was no more than a contributory factor. His doctrine of the Church was closely allied to his metaphysics. An early citation may suggest how his view of the Church was influenced by his ultrarealism. He wrote, 'I consider that the Church ordains nothing, unless there is an underlying reason; on account of which there is rational cause that it *is* so before it be ordained by

29    B. Smalley, 'Wyclif's Postilla on the Old Testament and his Principium', in *Oxford Studies Presented to Daniel Callus* (Oxford, 1964), Oxford Historical Society, n.s. xvi, for 1959–60, pp. 253–97, and analysis in G. A. Benrath, *Wyclifs Bibelkommentar* (1966); Workman, *Wyclif* i, pp. 257–66; Leff, *Heresy* ii, pp. 529–30. See below, p. 260, n. 52.
30    Workman, *Wyclif* i, pp. 6–20; challenge of his ecclesiology best seen in Leff, *Heresy* ii, 516–45.
31    McFarlane (*MW*, p. 70) argued that Wyclif was acting as a 'clerical hireling' of his patron John of Gaunt by preaching in London in the autumn of 1376, stirring up public opinion against Gaunt's enemy William of Wykeham, then bishop of London. Walsingham is a chronicler hostile to Wyclif; his phrase about Wyclif 'running about from church to church' gives a basis for McFarlane's reconstruction. But six of his surviving sermons are placed in the autumn of 1376 by W. H. Mallard, 'Dating the *Sermones quadraginta* of John Wyclif', *MH* xvii (1966), pp. 86–105 at p. 99. They are concerned, not with Wykeham but with moral and spiritual instruction or renewal in the church. Benrath, *Bibel-kommentar*, p. 336, n. 137 notes this may cast doubt on McFarlane's interpn.
32    *MW*, pp. 27–30; Catto, 'Wyclif', pp. 187–8, noting that Wyclif's comments are 'at most ambiguous'.

man.'[33] So clearly did he have the archetypal reality of the Church before his eyes that he came to reject in its favour the visible Church of the fourteenth century.[34] Just as in the case of Scripture, the Church had existed from eternity; Wyclif denied the doctrine that it had come into being with the incarnation. In comparison with this eternal Church, the visible Church steadily lost authority in Wyclif's writings till it became in the end simply the dwelling of Antichrist. An adaptation of the Augustinian doctrine of predestination had the effect of voiding the visible Church of authority. Elect and foreknown were rigidly divided in this world. The elect were immune from the consequences of mortal sin: their grace of predestination stood, even with mortal sin. Conversely, the ministrations of the foreknown, however high they stood in the ecclesiastical hierarchy, were void of effect. The result was to remove the necessity of a priesthood, since every one of the elect was necessarily more priest than layman as a member of the Church.[35]

The heretical implications of Wyclif's doctrine need no underlining. Nor does the breach with traditional teaching in his doctrine of Scripture. He never made the text of the Bible alone the standard of judgement for all doctrine and conduct, for he always retained the need for an established interpreter – the Fathers – as a shield against heresy, above all Augustine.[36] But towards the end of his life, he did come to say that everything that was not in Scripture directly or by implication was Antichrist, and in practice Scripture more and more came to be an exclusive measuring-rod.

This attitude amounted to a radical innovation, for fourteenth-century theologians had not made a distinction between Scripture, tradition and the laws of the Church, which were understood to harmonize. Thomas Netter of Walden perceived this when he said, 'What chiefly fills me with dismay is that Wyclif in all his proofs halves the Christian faith: he accepts, so he pretends, the faith of Scripture; but beyond the written faith he disregards and sets aside that faith of the whole church which Christ and also Paul the Apostle handed down, though not in writing.'[37]

33   Smalley's translation is in 'The Bible', p. 83; text, amended by her, in footnote.
34   See esp. Leff, *Heresy* II, pp. 515–16; on the external factors in Wyclif's progression to heresy, see p. 499.
35   On the vital importance of metaphysics for Wyclif's view of the Church, see Leff, *Heresy* II, p. 511; analogous stress for doctrine of Scripture is in Benrath, *Bibelkommentar*, ch. 5; Leff, *SCH* Subsidia V, pp. 217–32, notes that 'there is an undeniable discontinuity in his intellectual development which cannot be explained simply by an appeal to intellectual criteria' and refers to the censure of articles from *De civili dominio* by the pope in 1377 as the 'immediately obvious candidate' among non-intellectual factors influencing the discontinuity (p. 218). He withdraws some earlier views in the light of the publication of Wyclif's *De Universalibus* but observes (p. 232) that while each of his positions was founded 'in contemporary attitudes or traditional doctrine', their ultimate effect was the 'rejection of traditional doctrine over the central truths concerning the nature of the Church, the role of the Bible, and the eucharist'. V. Herold, 'Wyklif als Reformer', *Jan Hus*, ed. F. Seibt (Munich, 1997), pp. 39–47 clarifies relation between Wyclif's philosophy and Hussitism and the reasons for Gerson's opposition to Hus (p. 47).
36   P. De Vooght, *Les Sources de la doctrine chrétienne* (1954) (a defence of Wyclif); M. Hurley, ' "Scriptura Sola": Wyclif and his critics', *Traditio* XVI (1960), pp. 275–352; reissued separately (New York, 1960) (corrects De Vooght); review by B. Smalley, in *EHR* LXXVIII (1963), pp. 161–2 (best short summary).
37   Quoted by Hurley, in *Traditio* XVI, p. 329. Note comment on Fitzralph and *sola scriptura* in K. Walsh, 'Preaching, pastoral care and *sola scriptura* in later medieval Ireland: Richard Fitzralph and the

As for the Church of Wyclif's day, by his death it had been stripped in his writings of all claim to belief. It had been stigmatized as the Church of Antichrist; the hierarchy had been rejected; the papacy, subjected to an historical analysis, had been shown to have no justification. Progressively from the *De potestate papae* in 1379 he attacked the papacy more fiercely till in the *Opus evangelicum* at the end of his life he identified the papacy, that is, the popes since the Donation of Constantine, and the Roman Church as Antichrist, 'a heinous conglomeration'. In detail, Scripture properly interpreted and described as 'God's law', had replaced canon law. Monastic life of every kind had been rejected as unfruitful: disendowment was to provide a basis for reforms, a class of preaching clergy. In an extraordinary demolition of the assumptions of the medieval Church, Wyclif took away the functions of monks and friars; the contemplative life and the monastic liturgy was useless.[38]

The indestructibility of universals and the consequences which Wyclif drew from it also involved him from early days in an inconsistency – he could not both accept transubstantiation and maintain his metaphysics. In Kenningham's time he had evaded the issue; it remained an unsolved question till 1379, when, with the publication of *De apostasia* and *De eucharistia*, he denied the doctrine held by the Church. It was a deeply emotional issue, one on which, it has been lately argued, Wyclif was influenced as much or more by scandal at contemporary eucharistic practice and its consequences as by his awkward philosophical position. He was not at ease in his teaching. He disliked what he interpreted as idolatry in the reaction to the elevation of the Host at mass or to the Corpus Christi processions, and he came to refer to transubstantiation as a 'harmful transaction'. It involved a doctrine marked by hypocrisy, postulating appearance without reality. He made clear his opposition to the annihilation of substance, but he arrived at no final definition of his own, even, it seems, altering his position in the very last years of his life. It was an emotional topic because he cared deeply about the sacrament.[39]

The eucharistic heresy had great historical importance because it led to the parting of the ways with the last of the Oxford supporters outside his own proto-Lollard group, and to his departure from Oxford. In mid-winter 1380–1, the chancellor, William Barton, one of Wyclif's opponents, summoned a commission

---

use of the Bible', *SCH* Subsidia iv, pp. 251–68. See also Id., 'Wyclif's legacy in Central Europe in the late fourteenth and early fifteenth centuries', *SCH* Subsidia v, pp. 397–417 at pp. 398–9.

38    On Antichrist, compare C. V. Bostick, *The Antichrist and the Lollards* (1998), pp. 60–73, and A. Patschovsky, 'Antichrist bei Wyclif', *Eschatologie und Hussitismus*, ed. A. Patschovsky, F. Šmahel (1996), pp. 83–98; 'heinous conglomeration', Bostick, p. 72; effects of Wyclif's position generally, Leff, *Heresy* ii, pp. 534–41, Workman, *Wyclif* ii, pp. 73–82, *MW*, p. 95; J. Renna, 'Wyclif's attacks on monks', *SCH* Subsidia v, pp. 267–80; W. Mallard, 'Clarity and dilemma – the *Forty Sermons* of John Wyclif', *Contemporary Reflections on the Medieval Christian Tradition*, ed. G. H. Shriver (1974), pp. 19–38 at pp. 34–7.

39    Robson, *Wyclif*, pp. 187–95; Leff, *Heresy* ii, pp. 549–57; M. E. Aston, 'John Wycliffe's Reformation reputation', *PP* xxx (1965), pp. 40–1, for contrast between Wyclif's views on the eucharist and the Reformers' notion of them; Crompton's summary in *JEH* xviii (1967), pp. 263–6; important discussion by Catto in *SCH* Subsidia iv, pp. 269–86. A. Kenny, 'Wyclif', *PBA* lxxvi (1990), pp. 91–113, discusses Wyclif's philosophy and the eucharist at pp. 102–4 (helpful quotations).

of twelve doctors, which by a narrow majority condemned his eucharistic views. There is no ground for thinking that the commission was packed or manipulated by outside ecclesiastical authority: it fairly represented a growing disquiet within the university about the development of Wyclif's views.[40] It mattered more than the condemnation of the theses on dominion and disendowment sent to Gregory XI at Avignon in 1377, for the beginning of the Great Schism in the following year eliminated the papacy's further interest, and on these issues Wyclif knew he could count on the support of his lay patrons as well as some academics. On the eucharist he lacked support. Disquiet about his eucharistic beliefs affected the Commons in the parliament of 1381 and alienated John of Gaunt. When in the *Confession* of May 1381 he reiterated his denial of transubstantiation he was defying both his fellows and some supporters. In the same year he withdrew from the university and retired to the rectory at Lutterworth. The eucharist controversy was not dampened; tension rose as Wyclif's views were promulgated in the vernacular by his followers to a wider audience. The doctrine of the mass was especially sensitive; orthodox vernacular instruction on the eucharist eschewed any resort to detailed explanation; the philosophical terms of scholastic debate on the subject, *transubstancio, substancia, accidens,* had not been translated. The convention was that such matters were not to be ventilated before the laity. Netter summed up the traditional view when he said, 'In the affairs of the faith, skilled spiritual men are said to understand: the rest of the people only simply to believe.' The alarm and hostility of authority was demonstrated by their moves to give publicity to the repudiation of Wyclif and confirmation of the doctrine of transubstantiation.[41]

## Wyclif and Lollardy

Wyclif had kept university supporters surprisingly late. There were a number of reasons why he should have had a strong influence. The most important has already been mentioned: in an age when the fashion in theology was doubt, he offered certainties. He was a bold dialectician and an able debater and a preacher of power, who attracted personal loyalty. He quoted Scripture more than contemporary commentators. His use of Scripture and the completion of his *Postilla super totam bibliam* in 1375–6 helped to bring back the Bible to the centre of studies. His anti-intellectual and Christocentric piety, the appeal for reform and the denunciation of abuses, all corresponded to strands of contemporary thinking, and could call forth suitable echoes.[42] For the arts faculty, in their conflicts

40  *MW,* pp. 97–9, corrects Workman, *Wyclif* II, pp. 140–8; note also Leff's summary (*Heresy* II, p. 554, n. 8) on Workman's treatment earlier (pp. 30–41) of Wyclif's eucharistic doctrine.
41  On the role of dominion theory, see Workman, *Wyclif* II, pp. 292–9; *MW,* pp. 79–81; for place of English Benedictines in stimulating papal intervention, see Knowles, *Religious Orders* II, pp. 98ff.; on eucharist and vernacular, see M. E. Aston, 'Wycliffe and the vernacular', *SCH* Subsidia v, pp. 281–330; quotation from Netter, p. 302 (*Doctrinale* II, cap. 44, col. 277); penetrating comments: pp. 299–300; publicity of followers in London: below, p. 268.
42  Benrath, *Bibelkommentar;* see De Vooght, *Sources,* pp. 168–200; Catto, 'Wyclif', pp. 218–19.

with law, he would gain popularity by his trenchant attacks on canon law.[43] His stress on the need for poverty in the Church and his attacks on the possessioner orders made him a natural ally of the friars, above all the Augustinians, who kept on terms with him longer than any other group. In 1377 four doctors from the mendicant friars were ready to defend Wyclif in St Paul's.[44] An Augustinian, Adam Stocton, described Wyclif on his copy of the *De potestate papae* as *venerabilis doctor*; only later was this crossed off in favour of *execrabilis seductor.*[45] It was only with the eucharistic heresy that he was abandoned by the friars.

Finally, Wyclif in his ultrarealism was in the van of a European movement of reaction against early fourteenth-century nominalism. This kept alive a respect for him independent of his late heresies, evidenced for us, for instance, in the acephalous and anonymous manuscripts in which his philosophical works were being collected in Oxford in the fifteenth century, or the reaction by university masters to Arundel's heavy-handed visitation in 1411; they were clearly not Wyclifites, but nevertheless valued university independence and thought Wyclif's views might still be at least the subject of argument.[46] He continued to influence subjects of debate and his philosophical views went on attracting attention. The reputation of Wyclif was accepted in some surprising quarters. Archbishop Arundel himself acknowledged the justice of the Lollard William Thorpe's remarks when he was standing trial in 1407. 'Sir,' Thorpe said, 'Master John Wycliffe was holden of full many men the greatest Clerk that they knew then living; and therewith he was named a passing ruely [virtuous] man, and an innocent in his living.' Arundel acknowledged that, 'Wyclif your author [founder] was a great Clerk', and that 'many men held him a perfect liver.'[47]

This reputation drew essential support for the heresy. As the condemnations of Wyclif's work became effective, particularly after the Blackfriars Council of 1382 and Courtenay's visitation of Oxford, the more superficial supporters in the university fell away.[48] But a distinguished and controversial career had gathered enough varied strands of patronage and interest for a residue of scholars to remain committed supporters. The existence of this circle was vital to the development of English Lollardy, for it provided the popularizers who mediated Wyclif's thought to a wider public.

Vital, too, were Wyclif's views on the relations between Church and State and the necessity for some measure of ecclesiastical disendowment, for it was obviously these which attracted the attention of great men, involved him in politics and gave him a wider public notoriety. Wyclif's remedy for the

---

43  J. Fines, 'Studies in the Lollard heresy' (unpublished PhD thesis, Univ. Sheffield, 1964), pp. 18–19. I am indebted to the author for generously allowing me to use his thesis.
44  Workman, *Wyclif* I, p. 286; *MW*, pp. 74–5.
45  Gwynn, *Austin Friars*, pp. 238–9.
46  Robson, *Wyclif*, pp. 240–6; review by J. M. Fletcher in *HJ* LXI (1962–3), pp. 179–80; E. F. Jacob, 'Reynold Pecock, Bishop of Chichester', *PBA* XXXVII (1951), pp. 121–53; J. Catto, 'Some English manuscripts of Wyclif's Latin works', *SCH* Subsidia V, pp. 353–9.
47  Quoted, *MW*, p. 35, from Thorpe's *Examinacion*. See below p. 268, n. 9. (*Testimony*, p. 40.)
48  *MW*, pp. 106–15; Workman, *Wyclif* II, pp. 246–93.

abuses of the Church lay in forcible reform by the secular power. The low moral standards of the Church were, he believed, caused by an excess of property – the State would help to bring about change by some measure of disappropriation. The clergy would be left a sufficiency. Tithes they might have, since they were permitted by the Old Testament; but even this concession was subject to good behaviour – they could be withheld by parishioners from a sinful clergy.[49]

As early as 1370–1 Wyclif had been expressing his ideas on possession; but it was not until the *De civili dominio* of 1376–8 that he put them in written form.[50] A doctrine of dominion and grace such as he developed there had a considerable lineage. It had once been used in an ultramontane sense by the Augustinian Giles of Rome, who had argued that dominion could only be justly held through the Roman Church; all outside it, heathen or excommunicate, forfeited thereby lawful rights of possession and authority. Fitzralph turned the argument against the friars, his *bêtes noires*, by arguing more generally that all rights of authority and possession derived from God, and were thus dependent on the holder being in a state of grace; the friars, who were not, thus did not justly exercise the rights which they held within the Church. Wyclif simply took over this argument, and developed it to cover the whole Church. It linked, of course, with his fierce attacks on clerical abuses: plainly many of the clergy were not in a state of grace, could not justly hold dominion, and might be deprived of their possessions. As a theory, it obviously commended itself to lay lords who, in a time of unsuccessful war and weak government finance, were seeking for some new means of financing the war effort. Wyclif attracted interest because of the virtually uninhibited place he gave to the secular power as disappropriators and reformers of the Church.

At first sight the theory of dominion and grace might seem to have dangerous and anarchical implications for lay lords as well as churchmen. Might they not also fail to be in the state of grace necessary to hold lawful dominion, and might they not also be open to disappropriation? In practice, that awkward conclusion did not have to be drawn: in the *De officio regis* (1379) Wyclif provided an answer in his thorough-going Erastianism. The king was God's vicar. He and secular lords could not lawfully be resisted. Even tyrants must be accepted. Sin did not invalidate their authority – only that of churchmen.[51]

It is now becoming clearer that the doctrine of dominion and grace, which became so famous in Wyclifian historiography, never had the importance that older writers tended to give it in the structure of Wyclif's thought. It was overshadowed by the much more fundamental attack on the authority of the visible

---

49  See M. E. Aston, 'Lollardy and sedition, 1381–1431', *PP* xvii (1960), pp. 1–44; Leff, *Heresy* ii, pp. 527–31; Smalley, 'The Bible', pp. 87–9. Wyclif's doctrine on the conditional nature of the clergy's right to tithes was among the Twenty-four Conclusions condemned in 1382; see Leff's comment (*Heresy* ii, p. 529).

50  *MW*, p. 60; Catto, 'Wyclif', pp. 198–208.

51  Description of *De officio regis* in Workman, *Wyclif* ii, pp. 20–30; on significance, see Leff, *Heresy* ii, pp. 543–5.

Church contained in Wyclif's predestinarian views and in the consequences he drew from them.[52] Yet its historical importance was considerable.

One of the first to be alarmed by Wyclif's views were the monks, a prime target in the attack on Church wealth. It was they who early engaged Wyclif in controversy on this subject, and it was they who sent propositions from the *De civili dominio* to Avignon to be censored by the pope in 1377.[53] Amongst the views which Gregory xi condemned were opinions which appeared to put all civil dominion into uncertainty, and thus affected lay lords as well.[54] When other controversialists took up their pen against Wyclif and the Lollards, they were naturally not slow to point out the dangers of anarchy for the secular power in the doctrine of dominion and grace; William Woodford the Franciscan, for example, argued that the upshot of Wyclif's views on dominion was that he legitimized a popular disappropriation of 'kings, dukes and their lay superiors whenever they habitually offended'.[55]

Wyclif seems to have been writing the *De blasphemia* as the Peasants' Revolt of 1381 took place: his mention of it in chapter 13 is followed by others deeply concerned with the event and full of anger at the churchmen, king and lords for allowing the state of affairs which led to the rebellion. The peasants did indeed set about disappropriation; Wyclif condemned them for excess and for executing the archbishop but argued that the removal of temporalities would have averted disaster. Contemporaries blamed Wyclif and his followers, and not only for their teaching about possessions; some saw a sinister coincidence in the fact that the feast of Corpus Christi was celebrated on 13 June, at a climactic point in the Rising, with rioting and murder in London and critical meetings taking place on 14 and 15 June. The rebels evidently chose the feast day for assembling their forces. Chroniclers were aware of Wyclif's eucharistic views; Walsingham saw the Revolt at Corpus Christi as God's punishment for eucharistic heresy. However unfairly, the revolt damaged Wyclif.[56] However, he never lost faith in lay lords as potential reformers and thus, somewhat oddly, at the end of his life combined a stark ecclesiastical egalitarianism with a profound belief in the just authority of the civil power. In his scheme of things, a sinful pope might be

---

52   I follow Leff, *Heresy* ii, pp. 546–9. He differs from M. J. Wilks, 'Predestination, property and power: Wyclif's theory of dominion and grace', *SCH* ii, pp. 220–36. Yet both dethrone dominion in the totality of Wyclif's thought. For the whole subject, B. Töpfer, *Urzustand und Sündenfall* (1999) (major work showing immense range of judgements on state of innocence and Fall and implications for property rights); one aspect, Id., '*Status innocentiae* und Staatsentstehung bei Thomas von Aquino und Wilhelm von Ockham', *Mittellateinisches Jahrbuch* xxxvi (2001), pp. 113–29; 'Die Wertung Töpfer's art....', *Häresie* ed. F. Šmahel, pp. 55–76, clarifies concepts; see also A. Hudson, *The Premature Reformation* (1988) (*HPR*), p. 360. M. J. Wilks, 'Wyclif and the great persecution', *SCH* x, pp. 41–63 (effects of delineation of the persecuted faithful).

53   Above, p. 257, n. 41.

54   Texts in Workman, *Wyclif* i, p. 293, n. 5; Lollard sources generally, *FZ*; origins, J. Crompton, 'Fasciculi Zizaniorum', *JEH* xii (1961), pp. 35–45, 155–66; Catto, 'Wyclif', p. 198.

55   Aston, 'Lollardy and sedition', p. 9.

56   *HPR*, pp. 66–72; A. Hudson, '*Poor preachers, poor men*: views of poverty in Wyclif and his followers', *Häresie*, ed. Šmahel, pp. 41–53; M. Aston, '"Corpus Christi and Corpus Regni": heresy and the Peasants' Revolt', *PP* cxliii (1994), pp. 3–47.

deposed, a sinful or tyrannous king not; the orders of society remained sacrosanct. In secular politics, Wyclif remained profoundly conservative; in ecclesiastical matters he became a near anarchist. This was unrealistic, for few would agree that the abuses of the late fourteenth century sprang so exclusively from the ecclesiastical side.[57]

Wyclif's ideas on disendowment drew him into political affairs, and seemed for a moment to open the way to reform on the lines he desired: in the event, the checks in Wyclif's writings against civil anarchy tended to be forgotten, as circumstances, the actions of some of his followers, the fortuitous event of the Peasants' Revolt, and the skill of his opponents all combined to give him and the movement he inspired the reputation of being political anarchists.[58]

Yet while Wyclif was losing support among the upper classes and in the universities, the movement of preachers was already getting under way; this carried his beliefs to a wider public, and partially compensated for these losses by embedding Lollardy among a section of the artisan class. Wyclif's connection with this process of evangelization is not well recorded. We know relatively little of his life once the breach with Oxford had been made. At Lutterworth he had as companion his secretary, John Purvey.[59] We can infer from the unbroken flow of controversial Latin treatises in his last years that he spent much of his time writing. These works break no new ground.[60]

A host of vernacular treatises was once attributed to him, and, although the majority must stem from the hands of his followers, a case still remains for some being written by him personally. His attitude towards the technical problems of translation was, in the words of a modern interpreter, 'amazingly nonchalant'.[61] A vernacular literature was a natural outflow from his ideas on the supremacy of Scripture, the necessity for the laity to set in hand reform, and his long-term pastoral concern. When wrestling with the grave problem of the eucharist, he showed a repeated concern for the way in which the laity regarded the mystery of the mass, and an impatience with the use of Latin terms which had no scriptural warrant to explain it. He threatened to publish his views to the people as early as 1380, and it is likely that he did so. Together with his followers, he broke a barrier on discussion of theology in the vernacular; Wyclifites, it has been pointed out, were responsible for an injection into the English language of technical terms hitherto unknown so as to deal with the doctrine of transubstantiation.

---

57  See Smalley's comment, in 'The Bible', p. 88.
58  Aston, 'Lollardy and sedition', p. 5.
59  M. Deanesly, *The Lollard Bible* (1920) (still best general survey on popular attitudes to Bible reading; ch. 9, pp. 225–51); pungent comment in *MW*, pp. 119–20, 152–3; correction is needed of Deanesly on treatises attributed to Purvey (see below, p. 268, n. 7); for Purvey's views, see *HPR*, pp. 159, 174, 242, 292, 301, 325, 327, 333, 340, 353, 355, 364, 385.
60  *MW,* p. 118; Workman, *Wyclif* II, p. 307; Smalley, 'The Bible', pp. 73–89.
61  *Select English Works of Wyclif,* ed. R. Arnold, I-III (Oxford, 1869–71); *The English Works of Wyclif hitherto Unprinted,* ed. F. D. Matthew (London, 1880), *EETS*, O.S. LXXIV; *Wyclif: Select English Writings,* ed. H. E. Winn (Oxford, 1929); attributions: M. Aston, '"Caim's Castles": poverty, politics and disendowment', *The Church, Politics and Patronage in the Fifteenth Century,* ed. R. B. Dobson (1984), pp. 45–81; 'Wycliffe and the vernacular', pp. 320–6; Aston on the *Wicket, PP* XXX (1965), p. 40 and n. 40,

He was not wholly consistent; in one of his last works, the *Opus evangelicum*, he issued a caveat against the ventilation of theological problems before the common people;[62] there is even a whisper of some kind of mild accommodation with authority at the end of his life. He repeatedly submitted his works to correction, more as a challenge to his opponents to pick holes if they could; at the end there was less defiance.[63] It did not matter: the crucial opening to the vernacular had been made. The greatest achievement of these years was the vernacular translation of the Bible. That, too, was a natural outcome of Wyclif's doctrinal position. If the visible Church had lost its authority to mediate salvation to the people, then the word of God, properly interpreted, was the one remaining certainty.[64] The novel relationship set up by Wyclif between Bible and Church demanded wider access to the Scriptures. If it was God's law, which should be asserted over the accretions of canon law that had usurped its place, then it should be known to those, clergy or laity, who had the duty of seeing that it was observed in England. The reform Wyclif envisaged was to take place on the basis of Scripture; it should then be known to the secular powers, who were to compel the clergy to reform, and to those elements among the existing clergy who were ready to heed the call to repent. Hence the phrases which occur in the *Opus evangelicum*, arguing that there was 'no man so rude a scholar but that he may learn the words of the gospel according to his simplicity',[65] or earlier, in the *De veritate sacrae scripturae*, that 'all Christians, especially secular lords, ought to know and defend the holy scriptures'.[66] He stresses the guidance of the Holy Spirit on those of good life, but not necessarily of much learning, who seek to understand.[67] In thoughts such as these lay a starting-point for later Lollard thinking.

---

shows how one Lollard work, which differs in its thinking from Wyclif, may yet have 'parallels from Wyclif's Latin works for certain of its arguments'. See A. Hudson, 'A Lollard compilation and the dissemination of Wyclifite thought', *JTS* xxiii (1972), pp. 65–81; Id., 'Wyclif and the English language', *Wyclif in His Times*, ed. A. Kenny (1986), pp. 67–104 (best gen. intro.); quotation on nonchalance, p. 90.

62   Smalley, in *MA* xxx (1961), p. 203, comparing *Johannis Wyclif De ente: librorum duorum excerpta*, ed. M. H. Dziewicki (WS, London, 1909), p. 131, with *Opus evangelicum*, ed. J. Loserth, i (WS, London, 1895), p. 367; original phraseology in Robson, *Wyclif*, p. 217; contrasted with Valdes in Deanesly, *Lollard Bible*, p. 245. On the practicability of Wyclif's position in his last year, note Smalley's comment: 'By that time he resembled a man who sets fire to a skyscraper and hopes that only the right people will notice.'

63   Aston, 'Wycliffe and the vernacular', pp. 325–8; on eucharist and vernacular, Ibid., pp. 291–330; note illuminating comment on authority's lack of comprehension of the menace of vernacular writings, as opposed to preaching, pp. 288–9; Hudson's view: p. 290, n. 22.

64   Leff, *Heresy* ii, ch. 7; see esp. p. 524. Kenny, 'Wyclif', argues (p. 106) for Wyclif's direct participation in translation; Aston, 'Wycliffe and the vernacular', p. 284, is cautious on Wyclif's responsibility.

65   Ed. J. Loserth, i, p. 92; tr. Deanesly, *Lollard Bible*, p. 246; H. Hargreaves, 'The Wycliffite Versions', *Cambridge History of the Bible* ii, ed. G. W. H. Lampe (1969), pp. 387–415; Id., 'The marginal glosses to the Wycliffite New Testament', *Studia Neophilologica* xxiii (1961), pp. 285–300; S. L. Fristedt, *The Wycliffe Bible* i (1953), ii (1969); *MS Bodley 959*, ed. C. Lindberg, i-iv (1959–73) discusses (vol. i) edn by J. Forshall, F. Madden, *The New Testament in English* (1879). I am indebted for refs to R. Rausch, *Abtrünnig im Glauben* (2000) (Lollard communications, excellent biblio.).

66   Ed. R. Buddensieg, i (WS, London, 1905), p. 136; tr. Deanesly, *Lollard Bible*, p. 243.

67   See esp. tr. from *De veritate sacrae scripturae* (Workman, *Wyclif* ii, p. 151).

The first translation, however, did not go so far. It was a painfully literal crib of the Vulgate, with past participles rendered direct into English and a Latin word-order imposed rigidly on the English sentence.[68] It was not intended for indiscriminate dissemination; one purpose may well have been to aid preachers who, basing themselves on the scriptural text on Wyclifite principles, would need to read out translations in their sermons. A translation of the whole Bible would give them a work of reference. Elements of Latin they might already possess; a crib to the Vulgate would be an ideal aid for them. More ambitiously, the translation could serve in a lord's household, where the newly literate upper-class laity might read the text and expound it to their subordinates.[69] The literalness of the version expressed a continuing reverence for the Vulgate; if the written Scripture expressed God's Word, then it might be dangerous to make free with the word sequence. Moreover, a rigid following of the Latin word-order facilitated the insertion of glosses phrase by phrase in a similar fashion to Richard Rolle's orthodox translation of the Psalter.[70]

Versions of the Bible for the laity were not wholly unprecedented. Certain vernacular versions existed in orthodox circles in various European countries, intended for the use only of rulers and the highest nobility. Wyclif cited them in defence of English translations. If Anne of Bohemia could have versions in Czech and German, he argued, then why were English versions to be judged heretical?[71] The precedent was only a partial one, for these Bibles circulated in a highly restricted milieu, where every check existed against misunderstandings of the text. They were expensive devotional toys. Even the first Wyclifite version would have had a wider diffusion. Copies were multiplied, and could be expected to pass freely into the hands of well-disposed laity at a level below that of the court circle. Moreover, the Early Version was gradually modified in the direction of a greater fluency. The translators worked methodically on, it seems, from Old Testament to New, and even the Early Version had gained in impact by the time that the New Testament was reached by a prolonged process of development as translators felt their way towards a more idiomatic rendering.[72]

In contrast to Rolle's Psalter, the Wyclifite version presented all who cared to read with a bare text, not merely of the psalms, which because of their use in worship presented a special case, but also of those parts of the Bible which

---

68   Compare the Vulgate of Gen. 1: 3 ('Dixitque deus, fiat lux, et facta est lux') with the translation in MS Bodley 959 ('And God said/be made light/And made is light') (spelling modernized) (Lindberg, MS *Bodley 959*; see p. 74) *HPR*, p. 242, rejects attempts to allocate authorship.

69   Deanesly, *Lollard Bible*, p. 245.

70   Ibid., pp. 144–7.

71   *De triplici vinculo amoris*, in *Polemical Works in Latin*, ed. R. Buddensieg, 1 (WS, London, 1883), p. 168; Deanesly, *Lollard Bible*, p. 248. See also M. J. Wilks, 'Misleading manuscripts: Wyclif and the non-Wycliffite Bible', *SCH* xi, pp. 147–61 at p. 155, n. 34. Anne's possession of a vernacular Bible does not imply Wycliffite sympathies: Rausch, *Abtrünnig*, p. 49, n. 197; see Rausch's discussion, pp. 29–40. K. Walsh, 'Lollardisch-hussitische Reformbestrebungen im Umkreis und Gefolgschaft der Luxemburgerin Anna, Königin von England (1382–94)', *Häresie*, ed. Šmahel, pp. 77–108 (finely detailed analysis).

72   *HPR*, pp. 238–40.

contained the most abstruse expositions of doctrine. Even in its clumsy early version, the Wyclifite translation had begun to break with medieval tradition which saw Scripture as a whole as a difficult text, to be assimilated by a trained clergy through the means of handbooks and expositions, and mediated to the faithful perhaps by gospel harmonies, but not under any circumstances to be placed raw in their hands without check and supervision.[73] The translation made vivid indeed Wyclif's innovation of separating Scripture from the whole body of tradition and the deposit of faith and making it stand starkly on its own. The early literal version was, of course, only a beginning: it had none of the driving force of the free translation which came out after Wyclif's death. But it was Wyclif's most important bequest to the Lollard movement.

On preaching, Wyclif's contribution to the rise of Lollardy is most ambiguous. Certainly the duty of preaching had a high place in his revolutionary concept of Church life, for it was the principal means of conveying the truths of Scripture to ordinary men. His late works are scattered with references to 'poor priests' who were to hear and spread true doctrine, and in one of his *Sermones quadraginta* we note Wyclif's feeling that he is speaking to members of a 'recognizable movement'.[74] But there is no evidence that Wyclif sent out priests himself. If he had been active in the development of preaching campaigns, then one would have expected Lutterworth to have been a centre of popular Lollardy. Yet it produced no single Lollard in all the record of heresy trials. Walsingham's picture of Wyclif sending out preachers in russet mantles is not confirmed by the other chronicler of early Lollardy, Henry Knighton, who shows Wyclif in a passive role, attracting acolytes by his academic reputation and his skill in disputation.[75] William Thorpe's account in the record of his trial conveys a similar picture when he speaks of those who 'commoned [communed] oft with him, and...loved so much his learning that they writ it, and busily enforced them to rule themselves thereafter'.[76] Walsingham wrote of ordinations of Lollards in Salisbury diocese, and there was indeed a case of a William Ramsbury being tonsured by a certain Thomas Fishburn, and invested with a russet habit to go and preach the heresy.[77] The chronicler assumed that Wyclif did the same. In fact, Wyclif was not the organizer of the heresy: his legacy to his followers lay in the realm of ideas.

That it was an explosive legacy will be apparent if one considers the doctrinal positions which Wyclif had reached in the course of his intellectual odyssey. He left the Lollards a set of ideas with all the potential to build an effective movement. His predestinarianism did away with the authority of the visible Church; his doctrine of Scripture armed his followers with an inexhaustible arsenal of criticism against it. He came near to a doctrine of the priesthood of all believers;

---

73   Deanesly, *Lollard Bible*, p. 239.
74   Mallard, 'Dating', p. 99.
75   *Knighton's Chronicle 1337–96*, ed. G. H. Martin (1995), p. 277; Workman (*Wyclif* ii, pp. 201 ff.) needs correction on the sending out of poor priests. McFarlane (*MW*, p. 101) brings good sense to bear.
76   Hudson, *Two Wycliffite Texts*, pp. 40–1.
77   Aston, 'Lollardy and sedition', p. 13. See below, p. 273, n. 23.

he did away with a hierarchy in the Church and, by his stress on the poor priests against the Caesarean clergy, appealed to a pre-existing cleft within the Church of his day. Finally, the literal translation of the Bible took the first step towards putting the bare text, with all its dangerous heresy-making potential, into the hands of any man who cared to read for himself or attend a Lollard conventicle.

# 14

## The English Lollards

### From Wyclif to Oldcastle's Revolt

#### *The early evangelists*

The reactions in Oxford to Wyclif's eucharistic heresy, the Peasants' Revolt and Courtenay's purge were all in their different ways blows to Wyclif's ideas and following, yet they were not fatal. Religious feeling, leaning in Wyclif's direction, obviously lay close to the surface and could easily be mobilized, while counteractions came a little too late. So Lollardy spread quickly, in Knighton's view, 'like the overwhelming multiplication of seedlings'.[1] He borrowed freely from William of St Amour's denunciations of the mendicants as false apostles and hypocrites, claiming the Lollards were true heralds of Antichrist with their russet clothing, labouring 'to change the Gospel of Christ into another', just as William had said the friars of the thirteenth century were turning the gospel into Gerard of San Donnino's Eternal Gospel.

A small group of academically trained men – proto-Lollards – mediated the master's late, radical ideas to the priesthood and to a wider audience. The best known are Nicholas Hereford, Philip Repton, John Aston and John Purvey. The first three had been attracted to Wyclif's ideas in Oxford; the fourth was evidently a man of education but details are lacking. Repton was an Austin canon; the others were secular clerks. All at one time recanted or submitted to ecclesiastical censure, and two (Hereford and Repton) finally abandoned support of Lollardy for ever. They were men who desired reform and had been swept away by Wyclifite ideas; counter-argument, more mature reflection and, perhaps, realization of the consequences of persistence in heresy detached them from their new beliefs. Even so, the

---

1 *Knighton's Chronicle*, ed. Martin, p. 244; Id., 'Knighton's Lollards', *Lollardy and the Gentry*, ed. Aston, Richmond (*LG*) (conference arts. of high calibre), pp. 28–40 (editors' misdeeds and Knighton's accuracy); M. Aston, 'Were the Lollards a sect?', *SCH* Subsidia xi, pp. 163–91, esp. p. 189; Fines, 'Studies', p. 33; C. Cross, *Church and People 1450–1660* (1976), esp. chs 1, 2 (penetrating survey); A. Hudson, 'Wycliffism in Oxford 1381–1411', *Wyclif in His Times*, ed. Kenny, pp. 67–84 and *HPR*, ch. 2 illuminate Oxford's role.

first enthusiasm had kept its hold for one, perhaps, two of them, who returned to Lollardy.

Hereford,[2] an Oxford master of arts, was believed by Knighton to have been the first leader of Lollardy, and there is evidence that he played a significant part in the writing of the first Bible.[3] It was he who preached the inflammatory sermon on Ascension Day 1382 at Oxford in the vernacular, openly advocating disendowment by the laity. He was a natural radical, who supposedly once preached a sermon arguing that Archbishop Sudbury, who was lynched in the Peasants' Revolt, had deserved his fate, and a man of curious optimism, who responded to Courtenay's excommunication of him by travelling to Rome to appeal to Urban VI in person. After escape from Rome and a period underground, he was arrested. Eventually he recanted some time before 1391, and not only recanted, but spoke against Lollardy.

Repton, the Austin canon of St-Mary-in-the-Fields, Leicester, recanted before Hereford, and rose to be abbot of his house and finally bishop of Lincoln, where he had to pursue Lollards. As bishop he worked hard as a reformer within the Church.[4] Lollardy for a time had seemed to him a key to reform; then he dropped it. But an underlying zeal remained.

Aston was originally of the diocese of Worcester. Like the rest, he recanted; but later he returned to Lollard evangelism, and seems to have died in the heresy about 1388.[5]

John Purvey,[6] probably of Lincoln diocese, was described by Knighton as the 'fourth heresiarch': he lived in the same house as Wyclif, he said, was intoxicated by his views and laboured to forward them. Netter, who refuted two of his works, called him the librarian of the Lollards, the disciple and the glossator of Wyclif, epithets compatible with a work of assemblage and propaganda rather than creativity. He appears later than the rest in the records and lasted longer in the movement. When he was finally laid by the heels and recanted in 1401, it was a heavy blow; put on probation by being given the benefice of West Hythe,

---

2   Workman, *Wyclif* II, pp. 131–7, Deanesly, *Lollard Bible*, pp. 232–6, 276, 377 (but with no sound evidence of Leicester canonry), *MW*, pp. 102, 107–12, 115, 118, 126–9, 137; *HPR*, pp. 70–3, 81, 111, 122, 161, 176–8, 200–1, 241–2, 283–4, 337–8, 365, 509–10.

3   Certain MSS of EV break off at Baruch 3: 20; Bodl. MS Douce 369, part I, gives Hereford as translator to that point; Cambr. Univ. Lib. MS Ee. i. 10 notes, 'Here endith the translacioun of Her. and now bigynneth the translacioun of J. and of othere men' (spelling slightly modernized). See Lindberg, *MS Bodley 959* v, pp. 90–7, who argues that the break was caused by Hereford's final recantation, not by his flight to Rome in 1382; contrast Deanesly, *Lollard Bible*, p. 254. MS Bodley 959 breaks off at the same point without comment. Fristedt (*Wycliffe Bible* II, p. xlvii) observes that the break 'simply marks the point at the bottom of the last recto column ... where the scribe waited for the ink to dry'. *HPR*, pp. 241–2, sees the evidence as weak and rejects attribution to Hereford as 'misguided'. S. Forde, 'Nicholas Hereford's Ascension Day sermons 1382', *MS* LI (1989), pp. 205–41.

4   Workman, *Wyclif* II, pp. 138, 162–3, 252, 282–9, 335–6; Deanesly, *Lollard Bible*, pp. 121–3; *MW*, pp. 102–3, 108–15; M. Archer, 'Philip Repington, bishop of Lincoln, and his cathedral chapter', *UBHJ* IV (1954), pp. 81–97; *HPR*, pp. 43–4 (Knighton's handling of the Repton affair), 70–3, 77, 79, 200–1, 283–4.

5   Workman, *Wyclif* II, pp. 138, 162–3, 252, 282–9, 335–6; Deanesly, *Lollard Bible*, pp. 135–6, 276, 445; *MW*, pp. 102, 109–11, 113–14, 122, 126–8; *HPR*, pp. 66, 70, 73, 77–8, 122, 200–1, 283–4.

6   Academic in contrast to the simpler Lollards: there is still no evidence that Purvey was at Oxford.

conveniently near Archbishop Arundel's castle of Saltwood, he held it for only three years before he resigned, driven back, it would seem, by his true feelings toward Lollard evangelism.

Recantations could not break the movement. Hereford had a career as an evangelist before and after the abortive journey to Rome. Repton had time to introduce Lollardy to Leicester and Brackley on the road between Oxford and Northampton. Aston preached in Bristol and Leicester. Hereford, Repton and Aston challenged Courtenay in 1382 by making public their eucharistic views in London by means of vernacular handbills and posters. Purvey was hardly molested in his long career as Lollard before trial and recantation. Enough was done to embed Lollardy in some key centres and to scatter converts and writings. Some places were likely to be unreceptive: Lincolnshire, for example, was too backward and conservative, but Leicester had major advantages for incipient Lollardy. It lay at a distance from the episcopal manors of the bishop of Lincoln, John Buckingham, who, conscientious and resident as he was, seems not to have entered Leicestershire at all after 1366. John of Gaunt had authority there and exercised local patronage in the Lollard interest; it had a superfluity of unbeneficed chaplains, who caused trouble; and it contained St Mary's Abbey, whose benefices gave ample scope for the preaching of Philip Repton.[7]

There were others, less notable but still academically trained, who took to evangelizing. The two best known are Richard Wyche, a priest of the diocese of Hereford, who was active during the late fourteenth century in the north, had contacts with Sir John Oldcastle, and was burnt in London in 1440 after a long career as an evangelist.[8] He would have been too young to know Wyclif personally, but he argued so skilfully with the assessors of the bishop of Durham, and was so familiar with Wyclif's views, that he must have had an academic background. William Thorpe, who travelled round England in a threadbare blue gown, preaching and talking with well-disposed clergy for nearly twenty years before he was brought before Archbishop Arundel in 1407, claimed to have known Wyclif personally, and talked of the master's career as an academic.[9]

Others still, like Thomas Brightwell, an Oxford man with prebends in Leicester, once associated with Wyclif's heresy but an early backslider, Thomas Hulman, rector of Kibworth Harcourt between 1380 and 1385, William James, a

---

7   All previous work is superseded by A. Hudson, 'John Purvey: a reconsideration of the evidence', *HLB*, pp. 85–110, with its devastating revelation, pp. 102–3, of the manner in which a mere guess at his authorship of LV and General Prologue passed into academic currency. Leff, *Heresy* II, pp. 578–83, analyses Lavenham's compilation. For Leicester's role and the effects of college patronage, A. K. McHardy, 'The dissemination of Wyclif's ideas', *SCH* Subsidia V, pp. 361–8.

8   F. D. Matthew, 'The trial of Richard Wyche', *EHR* V (1890), pp. 530–44; J. A. F. Thomson, *The Later Lollards 1414–1520* (1965) (*TLL*) (standard account of Lollard trials), pp. 15, 148–50, 177, 192; *MW*, p. 162; *HPR*, pp. 127, 160–1 (Wyche's trial and attitude to martyrdom), 164, 172, 190, 221–2 (trial evidence, 244, 274, 276, 284, 325, 341, 345, 357, 370, 373, 376, 378, 381–2); C. von Nolcken, 'Richard Wyche, a certain knight and the beginning of the end', *LG*, pp. 127–54; A. Hudson, 'Which Wyche? Framing of a Lollard heretic', *Trials*, ed. Biller, Bruschi; Id., 'Confession to God – confession to true men', *La Confession et les Confessions* (Paris, 1995), pp. 43–51.

9   *Testimony of William Thorpe, Two Wycliffite Texts*, ed. A. Hudson, *EETS* CCCI (1993), pp. 24–93; 'faction', *HPR*, pp. 220–1; historicity of *Testimony*, pp. xlv–liii.

marginal figure in the outbursts of Oxford Lollards in 1382, pursued and captured outside Oxford in 1395, are examples of lesser-known men who spread the word by the ordinary casual mechanisms of preaching or parochial life.

Behind the named individuals lies a penumbra of committed Oxford academics, whose existence is demonstrable by the mute evidence of a substantial class of scholarly vernacular material, designed to spread Lollardy outside the university through an instructed clergy, creating a revolution in doctrine and in Church–State relations by means of the written and spoken word.[10] As more is edited and analysed, it becomes clear that Courtenay's counter-measures of 1382 cut off some of the heads of heresy in Oxford and checked its open development but left many roots.

The translation of the Bible, in a set of versions stretching from the crudely literal crib of the Vulgate to an eloquent and idiomatic rendering, commanded the services of a whole sequence of scholars over years in what can only have been a tedious and demanding labour. There was an early work of removing the corruptions from versions of the Vulgate; a need to elucidate the text by using patristic commentary from the *Glossa Ordinaria*; creative work to be done in bending the vernacular for use in a biblical translation; finally, an immense task of writing, correcting and rewriting. The academic conscience can be seen at work in the mass of corrections in the text of the Early Version. The time-scale was considerable. The Early Version was in existence in Wyclif's lifetime, since he wrote of the utility of the translation of the gospels for the instruction of secular lords; the developments which came to term in the Late Version might well have been completed by 1395–7. Amongst the hidden group of scholars responsible for the translating were some capable of breaking the psychological barrier imposed by the literal text of the Vulgate as the word of God – a barrier never breached by Wyclif himself.

An individual voice of academic Lollardy in the period from Christmas 1389 to Easter 1390 was that of the author of the *Opus Arduum*, a Latin exposition on the Apocalypse, written by a man lying in prison for his views, who used scriptural exposition to denounce the evils of the friars and the persecution of the Lollards. He knew of the Lollard machinery of book production and wrote confidently of the replacement of works which the bishops had destroyed by others which were 'much stronger'; strangely, though he wrote from prison, he had access to the full apparatus of biblical academic commentary. The vigour of the denunciation of Urban VI and the oddity of a man condemned for heresy having facilities to write a heretical treatise make Nicholas Hereford, perhaps merely technically under restraint in the care of a pro-Lollard magnate, a possible author; an alternative candidate may have been an academic detained in the Franciscan house at Oxford, who would thereby have a library to use. Yet,

---

10 It is Professor A. Hudson's achievement to have demonstrated this. For early popularization, see *HPR*, pp. 103–10; *Wyclifite Bible*: pp. 108–9, 231–47; *Opus Arduum*: pp. 264–6, authorship: p. 266, n. 189; A. Hudson, 'A neglected Wycliffite text', *HLB*, pp. 43–65; for lesser Lollards, *HPR*, pp. 77, 78, 88–9.

whatever hypothesis is correct, the writer remains simply in the text the 'faithful preacher' and in this is characteristic of the majority of Lollard writers, who were determined on anonymity, and consciously so, for they were the elect, subsumed as individuals in the movement for reform. Under pressure, fearing introduction of the death penalty on the continental model and enjoining on himself and others the need for patience under persecution, the author was still, since he wrote in Latin, confident enough of his ability to appeal to an academic audience to whom he interpreted the Apocalypse in terms of Lollard reform, developing what is in effect a coded language for the events and personalities of his time. The eagle flying in the midst of heaven is a 'true *doctor evangelicus*', that is, Wyclif; the earthquake at the opening of the sixth seal is the earthquake in England at the time of the Blackfriars' Council of 1382; the seven angels with trumpets are the preachers against Antichrist, which, as in Wyclif, are the papacy and the hierarchy.

The Schism of 1378 and Despenser's failed crusade of 1383 are associated with Antichrist. Wyclif's eschatology is updated, given more precise references and deployed to encourage the author and his fellow Lollards in the midst of persecution with the assurance of their ultimately victorious role in the last struggle against Antichrist.[11]

The persecution of which the author of the *Opus Arduum* spoke was still a long way from destroying the intellectual leadership in Oxford and its writing-office. Between 1384 and 1396 it produced a working dictionary of theological, ethical and ecclesiastical learning arranged alphabetically under headings, forming a guide to Wyclifite thought. It is a substantial work – some 509 entries in the fullest version, the *Floretum*,[12] comprising approximately 3,000 pages of modern print – and makes full use of patristic and traditional commentary and of the canon law, subtly deployed so that it can be turned against the canon lawyers, the enemies of the Lollards. There are 180 passages of quotation from Wyclif's pastoral work. The appropriate entries are clearly heterodox; but much is not, and the whole is not notably polemical. It is designed to provide a preaching clergy without access to a major library with an adequate apparatus of learning. An intermediate version, with the same number of entries but reduced content, and a shorter one called the *Rosarium*, with 303 entries, together with one extant text of the early fifteenth century, Trinity College, Cambridge B14.50, combining the *Rosarium* in the vernacular with other Lollard material, including sermon notes, shows both how the authors adapted their material for different readers and how the working dictionary might be used in the field by a Lollard preacher. The *Floretum* was an academic project and its derivative commentary material implies use of a major library.

---

11   C. V. Bostick, *The Antichrist and the Lollards* (1998); A. Hudson, 'Lollardy and eschatology', *Eschatologie und Hussitismus*, ed. A. Patschovsky, F. Šmahel (1996), pp. 99–113.
12   A. Hudson, 'A Lollard compilation and the dissemination of Wycliffite thought', *HLB*, pp. 13–29, 'A Lollard compilation in England and Bohemia', pp. 32–42; partial summary, *HPR*, pp. 106–8, including changed estimate of length, p. 107, in contrast to *HLB*, p. 14.

Much the same might be said of the Glossed Gospels, vernacular commentaries, generally drawn directly from the standard, orthodox compilation, the *Catena Aurea* of Aquinas, but also implying consultation of original authorities.[13] The complexities of the MS tradition, comprehending long and short commentaries on different gospels and the lack of a uniform system of citation, are indications of multiple authorship, albeit, probably, under one directing mind. Groups of verses from the Early Version of the Wyclifite Bible are followed by a sequence of commentaries on them.

Yet another academic production of the years before 1400 – and one which exceeds all others bar the Wyclifite Bible – is the Lollard sermon-cycle,[14] a vernacular collection amounting in its fullest version to 294 sermons, designed for use in association with the liturgy and providing a complete set of sermons for epistle and gospel respectively on Sundays, for named saints (expurgated on Lollard principles, for the movement was very wary of post-biblical saints), for other unspecified saints and martyrs and for other weekdays. In all, there was provision for 120 weekday sermons. There were two major rearrangements of parts of the cycle, every sign of professionalism in rubrication and correction, and evidence that over forty different hands had been at work on the collection.

Translation was not simply drawn from the Wyclifite Bible, nor was exegesis derived from the Glossed Gospels. We have yet another substantial and independent academic work, based on a professional writing-office and meeting substantial production costs. Of the thirty-one extant MSS, about twenty are of such a size as to require a lectern to read from.

The content is demanding and allusive. Much is conventional and orthodox, but passages of fierce, anticlerical denunciation, especially of the religious orders, are also included. The authors appear not to have felt the need for the anecdotal aids characteristic of the orthodox preaching, which they denounced. Their assumption seems to have been that the Bible would speak for itself and that a sustained, rational exposition, without artifice, would carry the day with lay congregations.

Together, Wyclifite Bible, the Latin *Floretum*, the Glossed Gospels and the sermon-cycle provided the apparatus for a take-over of the English priesthood from within for Lollard, reform ideas – all carefully assembled by an industrious and capable academic leadership, confident that they could persuade their fellow clergy to open their churches to the vernacular Scriptures and to Lollard sermons, preached extensively, and on weekdays as well as Sundays.

It was not to be. One of the reasons why the Lollard leadership failed to make a breakthrough in their battle against the hierarchy of the day lay precisely in the

---

13  *HPR*, pp. 108, 248–59 ('part of an attempt to build up a library of materials...an effort... worthy of Oxford Wycliffism in the 1390s', pp. 148–9); extracts in A. Hudson, *Selections from English Wycliffite Writings* (1978), pp. 49–52, 60–4.

14  See extracts from English Wycliffite sermons in Hudson, *Selections*, pp. 52–4, 64–6, 168–70, 172–3; Id., '"Springing cockel in our clene corn": Lollard preaching in England around 1400', *Christendom and Its Discontents*, ed. Waugh, Diehl, pp. 132–47 (evidence of a copy left for a congregation to study, p. 136; sermons 'unrelievedly plain', p. 143).

uncompromising academic quality of their major productions. One is entitled to ask: how much use was ever made of the massive sermon collection, for example? And yet the existence of this quality of academic leadership, and of its learned propaganda which the bishops were not at first able fully to suppress helps to explain their alarms.

A second category of early Lollard evangelists consisted of chaplains, unbeneficed priests and lower clergy generally. Here Lollard tenets fell on fertile soil. They had little in common with a wealthy upper clergy. In the Peasants' Revolt the lower clergy were active as agitators and sometimes associated with the most violent episodes. Some may indeed already have been wandering anticlerical agitators, as John Ball had been for years before the revolt broke out. Doctrines which rejected a hierarchy in the Church, wished to redistribute Church wealth and sharply criticized the religious orders and the upper clergy, would find willing hearers in this category.[15] Chaplains were frequently the sons of craftsmen. As Lollardy put down roots among the craftsmen, so chaplains and the unbeneficed clergy would find themselves talking to their own kind. Their class and their economic background made them more effective and dangerous evangelists. Training was hardly thorough. They were thus open to the influence of new doctrines and, by lack of education, shielded from the academic treatises in which Wyclif's opponents sought to refute his views.[16] Lollardy thus both spread widely in the country and began to lose its academic basis.

The case of Swinderby at Leicester is a good example of the process.[17] The first seed was most likely planted by Philip Repton. It flowered in a nucleus round the chapel of St John the Baptist outside the walls of the town, where a chaplain called Waytestathe and a craftsman, William Smith, became active in preaching and the production of tracts. The most notable member of the group, however, was William Swinderby, who had had a career as a revivalist before Lollardy appeared on the scene, travelling round the country from a base in a cell at the abbey of St-Mary-in-the-Fields, or, John of Gaunt being his patron, living as a hermit in the woods outside the town. Lollardy gave him a congenial set of tenets to preach and he may well have been drawn to them by the early influence of Repton; to Lollardy he brought gifts of denunciation and rhetoric that remind us of Henry the Monk in the twelfth century, who, like Swinderby, came to heresy only after a previous career as an orthodox preacher.[18] Like him, he could rouse a town, using popular support at Easter 1382 to defy the bishop's inhibition against preaching and getting the mayor and twelve leading citizens to put their seals to a letter supporting his denials of heterodoxy. There is no doubt, however,

---

15   S. Justice, *Writing and Rebellion* (Berkeley, Los Angeles and London, 1994), analyses Ball's 'letters', Wyclif's role and the 'idiom of rural politics'.

16   Anti-Lollard academic work, *HPR*, pp. 45–58, 430–40. Popular antidotes are rarer; see Fines, 'Studies', p. 41, n. 3, p. 119; for anti-Lollard sermons of Henry v's reign, R. M. Haines, '"Wild Wittes and Wilfulness"', *SCH* viii, pp. 143–53; for parentage of chaplains, Deanesly, *Lollard Bible*, p. 189.

17   *MW*, pp. 103–5, 121–5, 127–36, 150, 174; A. Hudson, *DNB Missing Persons*; Martin, 'Knighton's Lollards', pp. 34–8.

18   Above, pp. 52–4.

of his Lollard commitment, despite the tendency of his accusers to attribute to him, ready made, the opinions condemned at the Blackfriars Council. Aston's appearance in the town may have been a spur to his heresy. The errors which he abjured before the bishop of Lincoln illustrate some of the tenets which appealed to Leicester citizens. He had taught, among other things, the rightfulness of parishioners withholding tithes from an incontinent parish priest, the illegitimacy of imprisonment for debt, or of a prelate excommunicating except where he knows the sinner to be already excommunicate by God. The priest in mortal sin who says mass 'rather commits idolatry than makes the body of God'.[19]

Swinderby was one of the most effective of all the evangelists. He planted heresy in Leicester and some of the market towns round about, then in Coventry, and finally in western Herefordshire, where the gentry gave him protection against the bishop. He almost certainly converted the young Oldcastle, the future military leader of Lollardy. Only in 1392 did his career come to an end, when he disappeared with a faithful companion into Wales.

Others, too, had considerable achievements. In the early fifteenth century William, the parish priest of Thaxted, nurtured a whole series of Lollard groups in Essex. In one circle at Colchester a Franciscan, John Brettenham, joined in the reading of tracts and translations.[20] Similarly, heresy in the north Midlands owed much to the chaplain William Ederick from Aston-on-Trent.[21] William Sawtry, the first Lollard to be burnt, had been a chaplain in Norfolk and had an unknown period of Lollard preaching behind him when he was first apprehended in 1399. He moved to London, where he became a parochial chaplain. The discovery of a judicial document linking him to the son of a Lollard squire, Thomas Comp-worth, suggests he was not as insignificant as sometimes supposed.[22] William Ramsbury is an interesting case of a Lollard layman being ordained by one of the sect and then wandering for four years before 1389, spreading his beliefs in the Salisbury diocese. He held some radical views, notably on marriage, with senti-ments that sound oddly like those attributed to the adherents of the Free Spirit; yet he had not emancipated himself from the mass, which he said according to the Sarum use with vestments, allowing himself a few omissions.[23]

*The laity*

A heresy which preached the equality of laity and priesthood might be expected to find lay evangelists also. William Smith was an example, often to be repeated in fifteenth-century Lollardy, of the self-taught craftsman disseminating heresy. A conversion to vegetarianism and teetotalism after he had been jilted was in turn

19   Swinderby's abjuration is in *FZ*, pp. 337–9; see *HPR*, pp. 73–7; influence of Aston, p. 77.
20   *MW*, pp. 173, 178.
21   Ibid., pp. 174–5, 178.
22   Ibid., pp. 150–2; A. K. McHardy, 'De Heretico Comburendo', *LG*, pp. 112–26 (detailed analysis with discoveries), Compworth, pp. 119–22.
23   A. Hudson, 'A Lollard mass', *JTS* xxiii (1972), pp. 407–19; influence from the Free Spirit is doubtful, and so is promiscuity.

followed by service to the Lollard group. For years he went barefoot. He taught himself to read and, when Swinderby had left the scene, continued with the activity of producing works based on Scripture and the Fathers, possibly copies of the Glossed Gospels. Practical issues of worship and religious practice rather than highly academic heresy took chief place: when he and his fellow Lollards of Leicester were denounced in 1389, the accusations related to lay preaching, indulgences, auricular confession, tithes and the veneration of images.[24] Doubtful views on transubstantiation may have been unjustly attributed to the Leicester group.[25] Smith's career was cut short by a visitation in 1389 from Courtenay, who saw to it that his Lollard works were surrendered and he did penance.

In Herefordshire, an esquire, Walter Brute, proud of his Welsh background, with some rhetorical gifts, a bias towards the Apocalypse, a striking capacity for writing Latin and using Scripture and canon law, was aide to Swinderby.[26] He taught that a layman held the keys of absolution as much as a priest and that women had the power to preach, to consecrate the eucharist and to absolve. Northampton harboured a Lollard group in 1392–3; Anna Palmer, an anchorite at St Peter's church, was described as principal receiver of Lollards, associated with six others including priests and laity. A major role seems to have been played by John Fox, the mayor. Here vanity and self-display were as much in evidence as righteous living, with William Northwold laying false claim to a doctorate of divinity, and preachers dressing themselves in hoods and gowns to which they had no right.[27]

Thomas Compworth, an esquire of Kidlington in Oxfordshire, is an uncommon example of a follower higher in society who was more than a mere fautor of heresy, having indulged in lay preaching and got himself into trouble by refusing tithes to the abbot of Osney.[28] In general, however, the laity were not public preachers. Their role was that of a supporting layer, encouraging their clergy and forming reading circles. Claydon, the prosperous tanner from London burnt in 1415, invited friends to join him in readings and brought his servants into the heresy.[29] Adherents in the stationers' trade were especially useful for the distribution of tracts. Included among the heretics denounced at Leicester in 1389 were a parchmener and a scrivener. Oldcastle had connections with the stationers' trade in London.[30]

An appeal to the individual to search out the truths of Scripture for himself was part of the drawing power of Lollardy: it was most effective for the self-taught, for those who had lately become literate and for those in a trade which required literacy.[31] The craftsmen and bourgeoisie who in Leicester, Northampton,

24  *MW* p. 140; *HPR*, pp. 74–7, hypothesis on Glossed Gospels, p. 76, n. 100.
25  *MW*, pp. 124, 131, 133.
26  Ibid., pp. 136–8; *HPR*, pp. 47–8, 99, 274, 291, 295, 298–9, 326–7 (opinions and rebuttals); see her 'Laicus litteratus: the paradox of Lollardy', *BHL*, pp. 222–36.
27  *MW*, pp. 140–4, *HPR*, pp. 78–80.
28  *MW* pp. 141, 143, 178.
29  *TLL*, pp. 140–2.
30  *MW*, pp. 163, 166.
31  Ibid., p. 180.

London and elsewhere took to Lollard doctrines were not necessarily poor men; through their skills they often finally acquired a competence, or sometimes even more. The successful among them would be aware that they had succeeded largely by their own efforts. For most of them the late fourteenth century was a period of prosperity. In Bristol and its hinterland, where the efforts of early preachers, Hereford, Aston and Purvey, bedded down Lollardy in the class of skilled artisans, the textile industry which supported many of them was doing well.

Craftsmen and lower clergy predominate among the Lollards; but there were exceptions. Swinderby in the Welsh March touched the gentry class; they protected him against the bishop of Hereford. From this area came Sir John Oldcastle, one of the converts of high rank, being a baron through marriage. There are other examples.

The most interesting of all is the group known as the Lollard knights.[32] Differing lists of names of men of gentle birth involved with heresy are given for us independently by two chroniclers, Knighton and Walsingham,[33] amounting to ten names in all. Walsingham called them 'the hooded knights' because they would not uncover in the presence of the Host. K. B. McFarlane, giving a verdict of 'not proven' on three of the ten cases, provides a detailed analysis of the lives of seven, all professional soldiers, all in the court circle, all in service to Richard II by the early 1380s. Several were linked either to the Black Prince or his widow. One knight of Lollard sympathies, Sir John Cheyne, may have been a lapsed priest.

Three demonstrably gave help to the movement. Sir John Montagu removed the images from his chapel at Shenley and harboured Lollard preachers. Sir Thomas Latimer made his seat at Braybrooke, in Northamptonshire, a Lollard centre, and was summoned before the council in 1388 at the time of the Merciless Parliament to answer for the possession of heretical books. That was a party move by the Appellants' faction, striking at a king's man by means of the heresy accusation. Latimer was not deterred. At Chipping Warden, a small market town in the same county of which he was lord, the bishop of Lincoln had extreme difficulty in getting a writ served in 1388–9 on a chaplain accused of Lollard preaching. Latimer even brought a suit before the king's justices against the bishop's summoner. At the time of Hereford's arrest in 1387, Sir William Nevill petitioned for the prisoner to be delivered to his keeping as constable of Nottingham castle, 'because of the honesty of his person' – a strange description of a Lollard preacher on the run.[34]

Sir John Clanvow, a great friend of Nevill, who died on an expedition with him near Constantinople, wrote in the last year of his life (1391) a vernacular religious treatise on the broad and narrow way, which reveals an ardent piety,

32   K. B. McFarlane, *Lancastrian Kings and Lollard Knights* (1972) (*MLK*) (posthumous pubn.); J. A. F. Thomson, 'Knightly piety', *LG*, pp. 94–111; *HPR*, pp. 90, 112–14, 119, 214–17, 430.
33   *Knighton*, ed. Martin, p. 294; *Thomae Walsingham historia Anglicana*, ed. H. T. Riley, II (RS), pp. 159, 216; *Chronicon Angliae* (RS), p. 377.
34   *MLK*, p. 199.

nourished by a contemplation of the sufferings of Christ and marked by a concern for preserving an ethical life amongst the temptations of the world. There is no breath of overt heresy in it, but it ignores the Church as an institution and the author openly declared an attachment to the movement.[35] Sir John Cheyne's name, partially erased, is in a French Bible now in the Bibliothèque Nationale in Paris, probably purchased on one of his diplomatic missions, and almost certainly the same Bible which featured in his son's will. Testamentary provisions of father and son witness to an active piety, but not necessarily a Lollard commitment.

Some knights may have been pre-eminently anticlerical: the proportion of professional soldiers and links to the Black Prince suggest that disendowment proposals as a means of raising war finance could have attracted army men. The interest of some knights in the lands of alien priories taken into the king's hands during the French wars may point in this direction.[36] But the group included men of culture, friendly with writers, owners of their works – which would have made them more formidable had their talents been fully employed in the service of Lollardy. But they were not. No great issue comparable to the breach of Hus's safe conduct, which roused the Bohemian nobility, emerged to move noble opinion; the potential menace to the Church dissipated over time.

J. A. F. Thomson has carried investigation of the knights further and has succeeded both in enlarging McFarlane's list of sympathizers and modifying his conclusions. McFarlane laid stress on the wills of certain men in the chroniclers' lists expressing a hatred of their flesh and repentance couched in strong terms. Latimer, Cheyne and Sir Lewis Clifford described themselves as 'false', 'traitors of God', and he inclined to think they were expressing regret for a heresy which they had abandoned. Wider investigation has not borne this out. Too many who had no conceivable Lollard commitments left wills with comparable phrases, and expressions of contempt for the body are found in European wills even more frequently. As McFarlane noted, Archbishop Arundel wrote a will of this type, in which he said he was a 'most useless and most lukewarm minister' and referred to his 'foetid and putrid cadaver'.[37]

Though the self-contempt style of will is no touchstone for Lollardy, it is none the less one indication of a strand of strong piety within the English ruling class, embracing a spectrum of views from true commitment to the incipient Lollard movement to a casual interest perfectly compatible with pilgrimages, crusades and the funding of masses for the departed. Views might well be radical yet not heretical,[38] though still capable over time of turning into heresy.

The wills of the Brokes, father and son, who had personal connections with the chroniclers' suspects and a marriage link to the Lollard Oldcastle, reveal a strand

---

35   *The Works of Sir John Clanvowe*, ed. V. J. Scattergood (1975), p. 70; *MLK*, p. 205; Thomson, 'Knightly piety', pp. 97, 105 (Clanvow's widow).
36   *MLK*, pp. 190–2.
37   *MLK*, p. 219; Thomson, 'Knightly piety', p. 105 (Arundel family tradition).
38   Thomson's distinction, art. cit., p. 96; see also Id., 'Orthodox religion and the origins of Lollardy', *History* LXXIV (1989), pp. 39–55.

of radicalism. Father Sir Thomas, who described himself as a wretched sinner, left charitable bequests to the poor – three hundred were to have meat and drink at his funeral – and is significantly silent about the clergy except for the two who were his executors. The son, briefly arrested on suspicion of heresy in 1414, also omits the regular clergy and has a similar self-contempt clause. But both wished to have three masses said at the time of burial.[39] Here was, perhaps, sympathy for the Lollard movement but not commitment.

Research has vindicated McFarlane in his belief that a Lollard interest existed amongst eminent royal servants and that there were more than appeared in Walsingham or Knighton. When he published his *Wyclif* in 1952, opening a new epoch in Lollard studies, McFarlane believed Protestant hagiography had romanticized Lollardy and that it had insufficient support among men of power to stand a chance of putting through reform. He moved away from that view through his subsequent work on Lollard knights but he exaggerated their coherence and inter-relationships. Lollard sympathy was looser, less logical and less consistent than he thought. It would seem that there was a penumbra of support among certain men of rank, which inhibited repression and gave a measure of support for Lollard evangelists and translators. For a time a window of opportunity existed.

### *The appeal of Lollardy*

Lollard tracts invited their readers, as it were, to teach themselves; implicit in the process was the direct relationship between the reader and the Holy Spirit, who would inspire those of good life.[40] Preaching remained the first means of gathering converts; the tracts and the vernacular Scriptures came second. They provided ammunition for the preachers, and confirmed the converts in their beliefs after they had joined the reading circles. After preaching came the informal dissemination of beliefs, at work, in taverns, in the family circle, through trade connections.

From an early period the Lollards were reproducing parts of the Bible in translation for instructional purposes: we have a glimpse of the process at Leicester in 1384, when William Smith was at work copying scriptural material.[41] But the Early Version, pedantic and unlovely, was an imperfect instrument for a popular movement. With the development from it of the graceful and free-flowing translation known as the Late Version the situation began to change. It was completed by about 1395–7;[42] the many extant MSS of it show that it met a real need in the population. The text could point the way to heresy; the epistles and gospels, for example, could be used to stress the contrast between the simplicity of the early Church and the formalism of the contemporary ecclesi-

---

39   Thomson, 'Knightly piety', pp. 102–4.
40   Deanesly, *Lollard Bible*, p. 269, Lollard tract, p. 452.
41   Ibid., p. 278.
42   Ibid., pp. 252–67; *HPR*, pp. 242–7.

astical scene,[43] and the readings, which came to form the staple activity of the sect, could draw out the absence of overt warrant in the scriptural text for such doctrines as purgatory or transubstantiation.

Lollardy's appeal to independent judgement has to be set against the background of ordinary Church life, where laity and clergy were set apart, and the laity still had a relatively passive role. Books of devotion, like the *Lay Folk's Mass Book*, assume that two sets of devotions will be proceeding simultaneously, one for priest, one for laity.[44] Orthodoxy, despite the issue of vernacular works of instruction and the development of a literature of devotion, had not fully adapted itself to the needs of an age of increasing literacy.

One of the most vital features of late medieval English religious life was its devotional movement. It is enshrined permanently for us in the apparatus of worship of the late medieval English parish church. This movement was not imposed from above – the records of the time allow us to see that the adornment of the parish church, using every device of the craftsman to heighten the sense of the numinous, was a popular matter, and that ordinary parishioners readily subscribed. The Lollards had no sympathy for this; Smith and Waytestathe at Leicester were accused of chopping up an image for firewood, and Smith of calling images of Our Lady at Walsingham and Lincoln 'the witch of Walsingham' and 'the witch of Lincoln'. St Catherine in the hands of Smith underwent a second martyrdom in a curious parody of the judicial ordeal: were she a true saint she would bleed, if not she would make an excellent fire.[45] Thorpe represents himself in his trial by Arundel as attacking all paintings and images in church, pleading against this the second commandment.[46] The Lollards disliked symbolism and mystery – it seemed to them merely to obscure essential truths. In this way, on a lower level, they were following the lines of Wyclif himself, who laid such stress on the rational approach to faith.

The rational approach in their hands often came to mean a minimal approach to credal statements. Wyclif's consubstantiation, based as it was on a philosophical realism, came to be accepted by them on the basis of mere common sense. The bread could still be seen after the words of consecration; therefore it was plain that the substance of bread still remained. Sometimes, we may deduce, Lollard preachers appealed to a pre-existing doubt about the more difficult doctrinal demands of the Church. Richard Wyche before the bishop of Durham represented himself as appealing to the laity who were onlookers to confirm his own 'minimal' approach to transubstantiation – he was too honest not to admit that in this instance they did not support him, but one sees the way in which he

43   See J. Fines, in *JEH* xiv (1963), p. 165; on reading, Rausch, *Abtrünnig im Glauben* pp. 15–18.
44   See *HPR*, pp. 390–445.
45   *MW*, p. 140, on the accusations; for the parody of the ordeal and the rest of the sentence, I quote the unpublished survey by R. M. Haines, 'The changing face of Lollardy', in Dalhousie History Seminar, Oct. 1986.
46   Hudson, *Two Wycliffite Texts*, pp. 56–61; comment, pp. 119–20. E. F. Jacob, *The Fifteenth Century* (Oxford, 1961), pp. 282–3. M. E. Aston will write on Lollards and the cross in the forthcoming *Wyclif and the Lollards: New Directions in Wycliffite Studies*, ed. J. C. Havens *et al.* (2001).

would as a preacher have approached the laity in this matter.[47] Lollardy provided an outlet for certain kinds of scepticism, about saints and their miracles, pilgrimages, wonder-working images and, above all, the central miracle of the mass.

Anticlericalism played a strong part. It must have been the most usual springboard into heresy, which commonly began in an alienation from the Church, caused by dissatisfaction with the clergy. The frequently expressed Donatist view that a state of sin in the celebrant invalidated the sacrament, or the plan of reform that would turn the clergy into salaried officials would have had little point if there had not been a dissatisfaction with the state of life of the clergy. When an approach was made to secular authority, Lollards were always ready to play their anticlerical card, appealing to the layman's suspicion of Church wealth, or, as in the Twelve Conclusions of 1395, attacking clerical celibacy.[48]

Lollardy often issued from an outraged Puritan conscience. Lollard writers and preachers could denounce the failings of the visible Church, often with considerable literary skill, because they had themselves felt them so deeply. In Purvey's tract a faint-hearted adherent is brought to full conversion by a sarcastic narration of the easygoing ways of the ordinary parishioner, enjoying his 'theatres, wrestlers, buckler-players . . . dancers and singers', dining and drinking by night and going to church afterwards, with the good ale rising into his brain and preventing him from noticing the false doctrine of the sermon.[49]

Lollards had a sharp consciousness of sin. Swinderby's appeal to the king's justices in parliament, with its references to the ghostly enemy and the approaching end, gives us some inkling of whence this preacher drew his power.[50] The *Lantern of Light* gives much space to a stern warning against sin in general. It is in the first instance a call to repentance.[51] The revivalist element in Lollardy could readily deceive the unequipped parishioner. Owst has long shown us how fiercely the sermon and devotional literature of the time could attack clerical abuses.[52] Lollard denunciation might at first sight be believed to correspond with the sermons of orthodoxy, and there is some evidence that this is what happened. Thomas Beeby, a Leicester mercer, in 1382 left money in his will both to Swinderby and to the Franciscans, who were then the firm enemies of Lollardy.[53] Thomas Netter noticed how the audiences of the Lollards were liable to doubt whether they really were heretics.[54]

The entry of Lollard ideas was the easier because of the existence of a desire for quite radical reform within orthodoxy. Chaucer, when he described the Parson in

47   *EHR* v (1890), p. 532.
48   *FZ*, pp. 360–9; on unchastity, no. 3 (p. 361).
49   Deanesly, *Lollard Bible*, p. 274.
50   *MW*, p. 133.
51   *The Lantern of Light*, ed. L. M. Swinburne (1917) (*EETS*, o.s. CLI). Ch. 13 is repr. from 1831 edn in *Medieval Culture and Society*, ed. D. Herlihy (London, New York, 1968), pp. 404–10; *HPR*, pp. 211–14.
52   E.g. G. R. Owst, *Preaching in Medieval England* (Cambridge, 1926), pp. 292–4; Fines, 'Studies', p. 21.
53   *MW*, pp. 124–5.
54   *Thomae Waldensis Carmelitae Anglici doctrinale fidei catholicae ecclesiae*, ed. F. Bonaventura Blanciotti, I (Venice, 1757), cols 20–1; Fines, 'Studies', p. 34, n. 2.

the General Prologue to the *Canterbury Tales*, making him so like Wyclif's blue-print and omitting (perhaps fortuitously, perhaps not) any mention of his saying mass or hearing confessions and drawing so black a picture of the monk, the friar and other ecclesiastical personalities, witnesses to the degree to which Lollard ideas in the years after the founder's death ran parallel to some widespread concerns about Church life.[55] *Dives and Pauper*, a popular manual for the laity, at least opened the question of the potential ill-effects of some popular devotions and admitted, for example, that men might use images simply to win money.[56] Lollards were aware of this and were anxious to link themselves with pre-existing popular religious literature. Certain MSS of the English Psalter and the *Ancren Riwle*, which were ascribed to the orthodox mystic Richard Rolle, have been subjected to Lollard interpolations, no doubt with the aim of suggesting that Lollardy was not a novelty, but that such views had earlier had the support of an accepted devotional author who himself wrote in the vernacular.[57] The inter-polated English version of the orthodox *Lay Folk's Catechism* served a straightfor-ward propagandizing purpose, and did it rather crudely, for the Lollard sections exist in strange proximity to Archbishop Thoresby's offer of indulgences to readers.[58] The sermon-cycle combined orthodox with Lollard instruction in the framework of the Church's liturgy. As late as 1401 biblical translation had not been condemned.[59]

### *The strands of belief*

Variety of belief in the early days was a consequence of the development of the preaching strata in the movement from the proto-Lollards of academic circles to the simpler chaplains and laymen, and it was implicit in a theology which urged every man to seek his own guidance in the open Scriptures. Gradually a more academic Lollardy faded, as it was no longer reinforced by graduate recruits, and the simpler Donatism and anticlericalism of the less-educated preachers took its place. Fundamental to the movement were the ideas of the relationship between Scripture and the Church which went back to Wyclif; but inevitably the initial nuances were lost. The need to do battle with opponents and press on with an aggressive missionizing may also have helped to radicalize Lollard thinking; this, Deanesly suggests, was the effect on the naturally scholarly and moderate Purvey, which helps to explain the discrepancies between his pre-1401 treatises[60] and the

---

55   *HPR*, pp. 390–4.
56   B. L. Manning, *The People's Faith in the Time of Wyclif* (Cambridge, 1919), p. 101; *HPR*, pp. 417–21.
57   Deanesly, *Lollard Bible*, p. 304; E. Colledge, '"The Recluse" – a Lollard interpolated version of the "Ancren Riwle"', *Review of English Studies* xv (1939), pp. 1–15, 129–45.
58   Ed. T. F. Simmons and H. E. Nolloth (1901) (*EETS*, o.s. cxviii) (see esp. pp. 102, 103, 106); Workman, *Wyclif* ii, pp. 158–60, correcting Nolloth.
59   Debate in 1401: *HPR*, p. 417.
60   Theses extracted therefrom by the Carmelite Lavenham in *FZ*, pp. 383–99; see Workman, *Wyclif* ii, pp. 165–7, Leff, *Heresy* ii, pp. 578–83, for analysis of relation to Wyclif's thought. But Leff is using Lavenham, not Purvey's confession.

errors he abjured in 1401,[61] and the tract *Sixteen points putten by bishops ordinarily upon men which they clepen Lollards*, written after 1401, when he was no longer under the same pressures.[62] Direct contradictions between different Lollard authors are not lacking. The Twelve Conclusions of 1395 was pacifist,[63] the *Lantern of Light* of 1409–15 accepted the necessity of 'righteous smiting'.[64] The *Lantern* contained no eucharistic heresy, and was altogether moderate on the sacraments;[65] yet both Sawtry (burned in 1401) and the tailor Badby (burned in 1410) went to the stake in part because of their rejection of transubstantiation.[66] The *Lantern* expressed no Donatist views; yet the evidence of enquiries of the period shows that this was a relatively frequent heresy.[67] Lollardy was initially as much a mood as a formal body of doctrines, and for a long time distinct strands of belief co-existed.

The doctrinal relation of Lollardy to Wyclif is complicated. The exigencies of evangelization meant that Wyclif's conclusions were adopted without the arguments that he used to reach them.[68] For many the philosophical background to his thinking soon faded, and the moral stress of Wyclif tended to assume the centre of the stage. No major Lollard treatise, it would seem, took up the implications of dominion by grace for civil possession, though it was treated in the sermon-cycle and occasional suspects had firm views on the point.[69] Most revealing of all is the change which Wyclif's eucharistic beliefs underwent in the hands of the Lollards. His positive views, as we have seen, can most fairly be said to have corresponded at the end of his life with consubstantiation; but the *Wicket*, put out under his name, much later, preached that the eucharist was a simple commemoration meal.[70] In this way Wyclif was simplified and at times distorted. Yet he could certainly have recognized some of the tenets of late Lollardy. The effect of his explosive ideas on Scripture and the body of the elect are traceable throughout Lollard history.

### The actions of authority

By sounding the alarm, condemning some Wyclifite tenets and taking action in Oxford, Courtenay checked the heresy though he could not entirely eliminate its

---

61   *FZ*, pp. 400–7; the first five topics of Lavenham's compilation appear as topics of the abjuration.
62   Text in Deanesly, *Lollard Bible*, pp. 462–7; dating follows Deanesly's hypothesis (pp. 461–2; discussion on pp. 284–5). Note difference between views on priesthood in Lavenham's treatise, pp. 387–9 (distinguished from Wyclif's by Leff, *Heresy* II, p. 580) and those in the *Sixteen points* (Deanesly, p. 465).
63   See *FZ*, pp. 366–7; discussion of texts in Workman, *Wyclif* II, p. 391, n. 2; H. S. Cronin, 'The Twelve Conclusions of the Lollards', *EHR* XXII (1907), pp. 292–304.
64   Ed. Swinburne, p. 99.
65   Ibid., pp. XV (introduction), 59.
66   *FZ*, pp. 410, 411; Foxe, *Acts and Monuments*, ed. S. R. Cattley, III (London, 1837), pp. 221–9, esp. p. 222 (Sawtry), pp. 235–9 (Badby); *MW*, pp. 150–2, 154–5; On Foxe, see below, p. 404, n. 66. On the Badby case, P. McNiven, *Heresy and Politics in the Reign of Henry IV* (1987). A Bristol link, fear of eucharistic heresy, and tension springing from the preparations for holding a Parliament in 1410 at Bristol are suggested as factors in the trial of Badby in M. Aston's review, *EHR* CV (1990), pp. 451–2.
67   Above, n. 51.
68   See Leff, *Heresy* II, p. 576.
69   *TLL*, pp. 29, 145; *HPR*, pp. 360–2.
70   Aston, in *PP* XXX (1965), pp. 37–8; also her 'Lollardy and the Reformation: survival or revival', *History* XLIX (1964), pp. 149–70.

intellectual basis.[71] The Peasants' Revolt of the previous year was a stroke of luck; the diffused belief that Lollards had some responsibility influenced the reactions of authority.[72] Its sequel was a statute restraining the activities of preachers.[73] Eucharistic heresy frightened off some supporters; the association between Lollardy and sedition helped the process. Hereford and Repton sought out Gaunt to protect them against Courtenay in 1382, but were met with a refusal. Sir Philip de la Vache may well have replaced him, but Gaunt's withdrawal was a heavy loss to the cause.[74]

Lollardy could have been pushed back earlier and more effectively if the bishops had matched Courtenay in vigour. Buckingham was slow in dealing with the Leicester outbreak, as was Trefnant, bishop of Hereford, with Walter Brute.[75] It is likely that the episcopate generally were aware of residual sympathy for Lollardy in high places, in the governing class to which they themselves belonged.[76] Moreover, concern for souls tended to outweigh the practical merits of draconian measures. England was slow to follow continental example. Torture was not used: time for reflection in an episcopal prison was usually effective enough. Burning was the ultimate deterrent: the English punishment of having the badge of a faggot sewn into a convicted heretic's clothing was a grim reminder of it, and Joan Clerk, compelled for her penance to set light to her father's pyre at Amersham about 1506, was subjected to a peculiarly repellent punishment. Yet burning was relatively rarely imposed. Stress was laid on the need to convert. Richard Wyche spent some three months in the bishop of Durham's prison, during which time he was subjected to six hearings before the bishop or his advisers, as well as two visits to him by individuals seeking to influence his mind, before the two formal sessions in which he was excommunicated and sent back to prison.[77] The rewards for recantation were generous: Purvey received a benefice after he had given in, and the anchoress Matilda at Leicester found that after she had been brought back to orthodoxy the archbishop offered indulgences to those who gave her gifts.[78]

Restraint helped to keep preachers in the field. William Taylor, the academic Lollard, is the classic example. He was cited twice by Arundel, in 1406 and 1410, and on both occasions did not appear. He was taken to court in the Worcester diocese in 1417, and in 1420 came before Archbishop Chichele, when he recanted. He was subsequently in trouble with the bishop of Worcester and came before Convocation in 1421 but was released; only in 1423 was he again

71    Courtenay's vital role was first noticed by McFarlane in his *Wycliffe*: Courtenay, not Wyclif, is the true hero of the book.
72    Above, pp. 260–1.
73    The most helpful article on this is Aston, 'Lollardy and sedition': I am much indebted to it. See also H. G. Richardson, 'Heresy and the lay power under Richard II', *EHR* LI (1936), pp. 1–28.
74    Workman, *Wyclif* II, p. 282; *MW*, p. 110; M. Aston, C. Richmond, Introduction, *LG*, p. 7.
75    *MW*, pp. 121–4, 135–7. For lack of zeal by Wakefield of Worcester, see *SCH* XI, pp. 143–4.
76    *MLK*, pp. 225–6. For Buckingham, see *SCH* IX, pp. 131–45.
77    Wyche's own account is in *EHR*, V (1890), pp. 530–44. There is no general evidence for torture, *TLL*, p. 230; on Joan Clerk, McSheffrey, *Gender* (below, p. 292, n. 112), p. 97.
78    Fines, 'Studies', p. 40.

apprehended and burnt.[79] Wyche is a similar example; his career as a missionary could have been brought to an end long before 1440 by keeping him under some surveillance.

The laity were most moved by the fear of rebellion, and action was most likely when their political interests were involved. Thus Courtenay pressed home his attack on Lollardy in the period of reaction which followed the Peasants' Revolt of 1381; the action of the Cambridge parliament of 1388, setting up new commissions of laymen as well as churchmen to deal with Lollardy, was in part an outcome of the Appellants' wish to maintain order in the secular as much as in the ecclesiastical sphere; the introduction of burning by the statute *De heretico comburendo* in 1401, a strangely hugger-mugger affair, was in part the child of the popular association of heresy with insurrection and of the anxieties of a usurper king. There may have been a fear of the danger of keeping obdurate heretics for life in insecure prisons.[80]

Attitudes of the laity were volatile. There was an enduring wish of some for instruction and edification in the vernacular, witnessed in the surviving MSS of the Late Version of the Lollard Bible. The total is such as to make plain that lay lords who were not members of the Lollard movement went on possessing and reading it. Arundel was attempting to meet this wish when he gave his blessing to the Carthusian Nicholas Love's English translation of a *Speculum vite Christi*, a compendium account of the life of Christ together with meditations and polemical thrusts at Lollard tenets: this was an orthodox presentation which avoided giving a naked text of Scripture without explanation or supplementation.[81] There was an unwillingness to betray preachers. The careers of the major evangelists, Thorpe, Wyche and Purvey, would have been impossible if the great majority of their hearers had not kept silent about their activities. In the Commons, a reluctance to put more power into the hands of churchmen warred against a recurring fear that State and property were being threatened by Lollardy.

Lollard attitudes to the secular power were also affected by the course of events. They had inherited from Wyclif the belief that the secular authorities should be the instrument to reform the Church,[82] and the last two decades of the fourteenth century saw a series of attempts to persuade the State to take action. Only after long disappointment did a section abandon persuasion in favour of a *coup d'état*. After the *coup* failed, the general tendency was to leave the reform of the Church in the hands of God, and wait quietly for better times. Wyclif himself constantly appealed to the State; Swinderby to the justices in parliament. Tracts were written with an eye to influencing the upper classes, and in 1395 a Lollard bill demanding reform was put on the doors of Westminster Hall and

79   *TLL*, pp. 24–6; Hudson, *Two Wycliffite Texts*, pp. xi–xxvi, 3–23.
80   Aston, 'Lollardy and sedition', pp. 32–3; McHardy, 'De Heretico Comburendo', p. 118.
81   M. Aston, 'Bishops and heresy: the defence of the faith', *The Church*, ed. Dobson, pp. 45–81; Id., *Faith and Fire* (1993) (coll. articles), pp. 73–93.
82   Wyclif's attitudes, Leff, *Heresy* II, pp. 543–5.

St Paul's when parliament was in session.[83] As late as 1410 a proposal came before parliament to disendow the possessioners; but it gained no support at all in the quarters where it mattered most – with the king and the prince of Wales.[84]

### Oldcastle's revolt

The immediate occasion for the resort to force by Lollardy was the imprisonment of their most distinguished secular leader, Sir John Oldcastle.[85] Oldcastle was, like some of the Lollard knights, a man who made his way through the profession of arms, rising from a modest family background in Herefordshire: there is a parallel between his military service to the future Henry v when prince of Wales and the service of some Lollard knights to the Black Prince. But times had changed. Henry v was a man of devout character, and a determined opponent of heresy. Awareness of this deterred knights sympathetic to Lollardy from going further; the king's actions towards Oldcastle demonstrated beyond doubt that he would not tolerate heresy. For a time Oldcastle's social status had kept him inviolate despite being twice brought before the Council to answer charges of heresy. But he was unable to withstand evidence of association with Lollard chaplains and distribution of their tracts, and was arrested in 1413. Henry's unwillingness in the last resort to protect his old companion in arms was a crucial blow to the hope that a nucleus of men in authority would back Lollard reform. As Thomson observes of the Lollard knights, 'They were king's men first and religious radicals second'.[86] At Oldcastle's trial in St Paul's he defied Arundel, declared his heresy on the eucharist and the Church, and was condemned. During the forty days respite which he was allowed by special grace of the king to reconsider his position, he was rescued from the Tower, and raised his followers in rebellion, no doubt to enforce a Lollard reform. It was a wild scheme. The plot was betrayed, and the rebels rounded up before they could inflict damage.

It should impress us that a prisoner on the run could rouse rebellion from scattered Lollard congregations and self-seekers scattered as far west as Bristol and as far north as Derby. Map 6 plots the results of McFarlane's researches into the judicial records of the investigations into the revolt.[87] A shrewd judge, he estimated that our picture of the extent of the rebellion may not be far from the truth, for the attempt at revolution, even including the assassination of the king, plainly roused both officials and the populace to counteraction.

---

83   Correction of Deanesly (*Lollard Bible*, p. 283) on 1395 episode, *MW*, p. 147; see Aston, 'Lollardy and Sedition', p. 17.
84   Aston, 'Lollardy and Sedition'. It is not necessarily of direct Lollard inspiration.
85   For what follows, see W. T. Waugh, 'Sir John Oldcastle', *EHR* xx (1905), pp. 434–56, 637–58; *MW*, pp. 160–83; his widow, *LG*, pp. 101–2.
86   Thomson, 'Knightly piety', p. 109.
87   It follows closely *MW*, pp. 172–80.

Rebellion was one result of the Lollard missionizing of the previous decades. Areas where the bishops had found Lollards to prosecute tend to coincide with those which sent men to join Oldcastle's last throw. Bristol, the old Lollard centre, sent the largest contingent, some forty craftsmen setting out under the leadership of six chaplains; the Leicestershire villages' participation reveals that, even if Leicester itself was not so deeply involved, the heresy was still embedded in the surrounding countryside. Yet some Lollard-influenced areas were mute on this occasion – Swinderby's old preaching-ground in Herefordshire and on the Welsh border generally, East Anglia, that we know to have given evidence of heretical activity, Oldcastle's area of influence in Kent.

Sometimes the depositions enable us to pick out a decisive leader who has roused a region. Such were William the chaplain of Thaxted, the evangelist of Essex; Walter Gilbert alias Kibworth, who had influenced both the Leicestershire villages near Kibworth Harcourt and the Derby area; and, in Derby and its surrounds, another chaplain, William Ederick; in Oxfordshire William Brown alias Davy, a glover of Woodstock. The patrons of heresy in higher classes also had their part to play – at Drayton Beauchamp in Buckinghamshire, the Cheynes; at Smeeton Westerby, among the Leicestershire villages, the most committed of the Lollard knights, Sir Thomas Latimer, its lord; in the lower valley of the Cherwell in Oxfordshire, Thomas Compworth.

Yet the map only presents a partial picture of the extent of Lollard sympathies in Henry v's reign. The total numbers involved were very small. Three hundred is a maximum. Some may well have declined Oldcastle's call on principle; others may not have been able to come in time, because of their geographical isolation from London. The rebellion attracted the seditious and adventurers who had no unorthodox religious affiliations, but were merely out for rewards, as in the case of the rich brewer of Dunstable who bought gilt spurs in anticipation of the knighthood that was to reward his participation. The proof of the participation of non-Lollards lies in the actions of government. Of those sentenced to be executed, a majority was condemned to be hanged. The bodies of the genuine Lollards were burnt after they had been hanged; this was an action adopted in only a small proportion of the total cases. Numbers of rebels and sympathizers were treated mercifully, and in these cases many were released after a term of imprisonment without being handed over to an ecclesiastical court – another indication that opportunists predominated over those of religious conviction. But the Lollards did participate: John Purvey was captured after the revolt and died in prison.

The revolt marked a turning-point in the relation between Lollardy and the State. It finally demonstrated to the country that the suspicion that heresy and sedition went together had good grounds and so condemned it to the underground existence of a small minority.[88]

---

88   See Aston, 'Lollardy and sedition', p. 35. On Purvey's capture and his library, see M. Jurkowski, 'New light on John Purvey', *EHR* cx (1995), pp. 1180–90.

**Inset A**

Leicester
Illston-on-the-Hill
Kibworth Harcourt
Shangton
Kibworth Beauchamp
Smeeton Westerby
Saddington
Market Harborough
Braybrooke

Dee
Trent
Chaddesden
Derby
Thulston
Littleover
Aston
Wilne
Tutbury
Belton-in-Charnwood
Loughborough
Sileby
Mountsorrel
A
Leicester
Market Harborough
Rothwell
Severn
Coventry
Newton
Kenilworth
Brixworth
Holcot
Baddesley Clinton
Pitsford
Chesterton
Daventry
Kingsthorpe
Northampton
Sutton
Worcester
Avon
Byfield
Wye
Banbury
Chenwell
Severn
Upper Heyford
Woodstock
Kirtlington
Handborough
Kidlington
Bladon
B
Thames
Oxford

**Inset B**

Drayton Beauchamp
Bovingdon
Chesham
Little Missenden
Chinnor
Latimer
Amersham
Chenies
Turville
Wycombe
Hambleden
Marlow
Henley

Wycombe
Henley

Bristol
Avon

White Lackington

0 ——— 50 miles
0 ——— 80 km

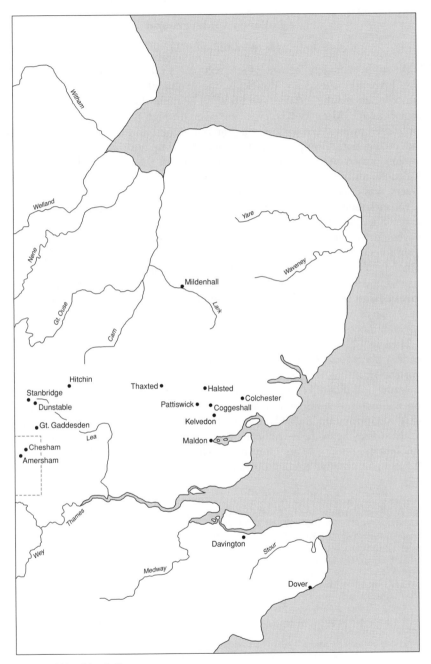

MAP 6  *Oldcastle's rebellion.*
*Source*: From K. B. McFarlane, *John Wycliffe and the Beginnings of English Nonconformity* (London, 1952).

## Lollardy Underground

*The prosecutions after 1414*[89]

In the surge of anxiety following the revolt plots were discovered linking Lollards with England's enemies – the Scots, the Welsh, the false Richard II – and emotions against the sectaries ran high.[90] The somewhat eccentric but orthodox English mystic, Margery Kempe, being taken through Beverley under arrest, was confronted by local housewives, who ran out of their houses shaking their distaffs and crying out, 'Brennith this fals heretyk'.[91] Because of the revolt, public opinion turned decisively against the Lollards. In this phase of high emotion, detection and prosecution had every assistance. Oldcastle, hidden by sympathizers, was none the less rounded up and executed.

Yet such intensity of feeling could not last. Groups of Lollards rode out the storm. Surviving pro-Lollard clergy and other evangelists helped to keep the movement in being. Secular interest waned; the impetus to detection passed back again to ecclesiastical authorities. In 1428 Archbishop Chichele was apparently calling for fair copies of prosecution records to be deposited at Lambeth, with a view to making persecution more effective by co-ordinating information.[92] Stiff drives against heresy launched in Canterbury and Norwich dioceses showed that the Lollards were still in existence, and in considerable numbers;[93] in the Norwich diocese 101 came before the courts between 1424 and 1431.[94]

Then in 1431 another revolt was launched, but feebly, in circumstances that made it almost a caricature of that in 1414; though it resembled the Oldcastle rebellion in aiming at disendowment and the removal of the king and aristocracy, its leaders, William Perkins, a former bailiff of Abingdon with a record of conviction for non-religious offences, and John Russell, former associate of Richard Gurmyn the Lollard baker, in the London textile industry, once engaged in false moneying, were insignificant and the action fizzled out in the scattering of handbills in London, an assembly at East Hendred to march on Abingdon abbey, and a similar abortive attempt on Salisbury cathedral.[95] Only in Coventry, where

---

89    *TLL* (comprehensive survey, based on bishops' registers); *Heresy Trials in the Diocese of Norwich 1428–31*, ed. N. Tanner (1977) (*HTN*); *Kent Heresy Proceedings 1511–12*, ed. N. Tanner (1997); *Trials of Coventry Lollards 1486–1522*, ed. S. McSheffrey, N. Tanner, (2001); J. Fines, 'Heresy trials in the diocese of Coventry and Lichfield, 1511–12', *JEH* XIV (1963), pp. 160–74 (best short account of a trial); I. Luxton, 'The Lichfield court book: a postscript', *BIHR* XLIV (1971), pp. 120–5. I am indebted to Fines, 'Studies' (analysis of Lollardy in select dioceses).

90    *TLL*, pp. 8–18; Aston, 'Lollardy and sedition', pp. 20–3.

91    *TLL*, p. 195.

92    Fines, 'Studies', appendix 2, and *EHR* LXXVIII, pp. 528–31.

93    For incidence of prosecutions, see table in *TLL*, pp. 237–8.

94    Fines, 'Studies', p. 245.

95    Fullest account by Aston, 'Lollardy and sedition', pp. 24–30 (note valuable footnotes); Mrs Aston kindly informs me she would now modify some of the views in her article. I have followed the approach of *TLL*, pp. 58–62, 102, 146–8, minimizing the affair. See Thomson's 'A Lollard rising in Kent, 1431 or 1438', *BIHR* XXXVII (1964), pp. 100–2.

there were executions, and in Leicester did something more serious occur. The link with Lollardy was tenuous.

Thereafter no violent movement labelled as Lollard again gathered support over even as wide an area as the 1431 plot had done. *Pari passu*, as far as our records are concerned, incidence of prosecutions drops away in the following decades. Apart from an action under Bishop Chedworth in the Chilterns in 1462–4, we meet few cases about mid-century.

Recorded prosecutions form a kind of parabola over the course of the fifteenth century – higher in number in the earlier decades, descending in the centre of the period, then rising again in a curve from 1486, when there was an important action in Coventry and Lichfield diocese, to the eve of the Reformation, when Protestantism from the Continent comes in to add another dimension to local heresy, and to complicate the task of the historian of Lollardy.

From 1486 prosecutions started to occur more frequently, and in certain areas they involved a greater number of abjurations – 74 in Coventry and Lichfield in 1511–12,[96] 96 in Salisbury diocese between 1491 and 1521, 300 in Lincoln between 1511 and 1521. The diocese of London, which included Essex as well as the capital, was strongly affected: a high figure may be given for the prosecutions there in 1511,[97] 50 for the prosecutions of Fitzjames in 1518, over 200 (when Protestantism from abroad was already in the field) between 1527 and 1532.[98] If the mid-century lull in our records corresponds to a real lull in prosecutions, we can reconstruct what happened. Pressure from the bishops lessened in the middle years, so Lollardy revived and made more converts; an increased tempo of prosecution was the response, which none the less failed to stamp out the heresy.[99] Still a small minority, Lollardy was a tough one. It survived to merge with the new Protestantism.

## The reasons for survival

Two reasons may be given for this survival, one linked to the English episcopate, the other to the qualities of the heresy and the nature of its adherents. Bishops, as we have seen on the Continent, tended to have a less sustained interest in the pursuit of heresy than inquisitors had; in England at this time they had multifarious duties and political commitments; some were absentees. Only a proportion of them took active steps against Lollardy. Moreover, the proceedings that they did take were not of the drastically efficient, repeated kind that could uproot a heretical group altogether.

96  Fines, in 'Heresy trials', p. 161.
97  For this estimate and the other figures, see Fines, 'Studies', p. 245. On episcopal approaches, Aston, 'Bishops and heresy'.
98  A. G. Dickens, *Lollards and Protestants* (1959), p. 8; Id., 'Heresy and the origins of English Protestantism', *Britain and the Netherlands* II, ed. J. S. Bromley, E. H. Kossman (1964), pp. 55–6; cf. *TLL*, pp. 137–8, 170–1.
99  Fines's hypothesis: 'Heresy trials', p. 160; support for a comparable view in J. F. Davis, 'Lollards, reformers and St Thomas of Canterbury', *UBHJ* IX (1963), pp. 1–15 at p. 6; verdict of 'not proven', *TLL*, p. 3; discussion in *HPR*, pp. 447–50.

The individual, truly thorough investigations occasionally recorded throw into relief the deficiencies of the majority of episcopal prosecutions. At Norwich Bishop Alnwick kept at his task from 1428 to 1431, ensured that the forceful leader of the East Anglian heresy, William White, was captured and burnt, and saw to it that eighteen of those who abjured were each given a copy of their abjuration to take home with them as a reminder of penalties that might occur for relapse. The Alnwick prosecutions formed part of a wider drive, involving Kent, Essex and Suffolk as well, spurred on by fears of England's heresy being reinforced by the Hussite movement in Bohemia. In 1427 Martin v had asked for the sentence of the Council of Constance to be carried out: the exhumation of Wyclif's bones in the following year was the response of the English episcopate to his request, and when, in 1428, convocation discussed procedures against heretics they also in the same session considered a subsidy for the crusade against Bohemia. Urgency was given to the moves against Lollards by the betrayal of preparations for a rebellion, nipped in the bud by Archbishop Chichele, Alnwick and other bishops.[100]

Other members of the episcopate did not proceed with the same thoroughness. One wonders whether the efficiency at Norwich is responsible for the fact that we hear no more of heresy there after Alnwick's action. In Coventry the well-conducted investigation of 1511–12 brought seventy-four before the court, of whom only forty-five were sufficiently deeply involved to be mentioned by name.[101] Coventry was a strong centre; but it also looks as if a thorough drive was uncovering the connections of heresy in a way that was not usual elsewhere.

For a series of prosecutions in England, our records give us only a trickle of abjurations, probably pruning some, but never all, of the branches of a local grouping, and so leaving a residue to grow again. Mercy as well as inefficiency kept heresy alive, maintaining an English distinction between relapse *vere* and *ficte*, which put off the final penalty and helped to keep missionaries in the field.[102] Heresy tended to be uncovered by chance. The routine of archidiaconal visitations of Kentish textile villages in the years before 1511 give no hint that there was heresy there at all; yet, when a drive was launched in 1511, it became clear that it was rife among them.[103] Perhaps the inclusion of heresy among the commissions of vicars-general at the end of the fifteenth century improved the situation; in general, however, the launching of prosecutions remained quite fitful and spasmodic.

---

100   Fines, 'Studies', pp. 74–9, 83–6, *TLL*, pp. 131–2; M. E. Aston, 'William White's Lollard followers', *CHR* LXVIII (1982), pp. 469–97 (shrewd analysis of teaching and structure of White's group), commenting on *HTN* (definitive edn); on Lollard geography, see R. G. Davies, 'Lollardy and locality', *TRHS* 6th ser. I (1991), pp. 191–212, who pleads against underestimates of Lollardy. N. Tanner, 'William White', *DNB* (forthcoming 2004); I am indebted to the author.

101   Fines, 'Heresy trials', p. 161; *TLL*, p. 109 shows there were more guilty than this; on the episcopate, a balanced statement by R. G. Davies, 'The episcopate', *Profession, Vocation and Culture in Later Medieval England*, ed. C. H. Clough (Liverpool, 1982), pp. 51–89.

102   Davis, 'Lollards', p. 6.

103   *TLL*, p. 190; on vicars-general and heresy, see Davis, 'Lollards', p. 3. *Kent Heresy Proceedings*, ed. Tanner.

The other factor preserving Lollardy was its appeal to the craftsman, the skilled artisan and his family who, the residual upper class support cut off, became the carrying class of the movement in its terminal phase. A Lollard community was above all a reading community, basing its common life on the public and private reading of the Scriptures and of Lollard tracts. At Coventry the sect came together for readings, either in twos, with a teacher helping a new convert, or in small groups.[104] In the East Anglian group Margery Baxter had her husband read aloud to her in bed at night 'from a book of the law of Christ'.[105] Lollard schools gave specific instruction, perhaps inculcating the aphorisms which conveyed beliefs to neophytes and illiterates.[106] The effects of the Lollard scares were to inhibit internal reform. Fear of the vernacular tended to check rather than foster the struggles of the medieval Church to raise the standards of the humble parish clergy. There is no evidence that Pecock's attempt at the use of reason in counter-argument had any effect. The answers of the Church to Lollardy tended to be the heating up 'of the fires of devotion'. Those features of the English Church to which the Lollard temperament objected were not changed, and it was never likely that they would be. Churchmen have been criticized for their negative attitudes to Lollardy yet, given the gulf between the Church and Lollard evangelists and their rejection of its teaching, it is hard to see how accommodation to Lollardy could ever have been possible.[107] Copying and distribution kept the Scriptures and the heretical literature in being, a jump ahead of authority, which tried but never succeeded in gathering it all in. The inner membership conducted their activities in an atmosphere of earnest study – which was exactly what would attract a type of recruit frequent among the skilled artisans. A reading sect had a natural appeal to a class in which literacy was incipient, and which included hard-working, independent people anxious to learn and to form judgements for themselves.

Conditions of work for the skilled man, who in order to gain an apprenticeship and earn a living was forced to move about, helped evangelization by person-to-person contact and kept loose links between the major Lollard areas; for example, John Jonson, the Birmingham cutler caught in 1511 in the ordinary course of pursuing his craft, had moved from his birthplace near York to London to be apprenticed, then migrated in turn to Coventry, Gloucester, Bristol, Taunton and other places, then to London, Maidstone and finally back to Coventry and Birmingham. Lollard meetings could easily be disguised as trade contacts.[108] In one interesting example, industry itself formed the matrix of heresy, when

---

104   Fines, 'Heresy trials', p. 166.
105   *TLL*, p. 130.
106   Fines's hypothesis ('Heresy trials', p. 167).
107   See review of *HPR* by R. M. Haines in *Canadian Journal of History* xxiv (1989), pp. 221–2. On the fires of devotion, see E. F. Jacob, 'Reynold Pecock, bishop of Chichester', *PBA* xxxvii (1951), pp. 121–53; on Pecock, R. M. Haines, 'Reginald Pecock: a tolerant man in an age of intolerance', *SCH* xxi (1984), pp. 125–37; aphorisms, sardonic on Church life: Fines, 'Heresy trials', p. 163.
108   Does this explain the prominence of skilled men in underground movements? See J. F. Davis, 'Lollard survival and the textile industry in the south-east of England', *SCH* iii, pp. 191–201 at p. 196. For Jonson, Fines, 'Heresy trials', p. 163.

Thomas Moon of Loddon, a glover, used his workplace to influence employees. There Lollardy passed from the laity to the clergy, as John Pert, a reader in the school built up at Loddon under Moon's influence, in turn initiated Hugh Pye, chaplain at Loddon.[109] Mobility imposed itself on a veteran evangelist, helping him to keep ahead of persecution, while at the same time possession of a skill helped him to move round the country. So James Willis the weaver, burnt in 1462, long eluded capture by changing his residence from one Lollard centre to another, from Bristol to London and finally to the Chilterns, confessing in Lent and taking communion at Easter, all the while instructing followers and keeping his copies of Lollard literature. William White used his position as parish chaplain at Tenterden to sustain a Lollard circle; by 1426 he had established himself as a leading figure in East Anglia.[110] A few dedicated men of this kind were a mainstay of the movement at the end, whose vitality rested on the determined missionary.

Lollard beliefs might descend in great secrecy, as in the Morden family at Chesham in the Chilterns, where Richard Ashford, son-in-law of John Morden, knew nothing of his father-in-law's hidden beliefs till the old man opened his heart to him on his deathbed, initiating Ashford in a heresy he retained till his capture in 1521.[111] In another case in Coventry, a daughter was brought by her mother to the heretical household of the Laudesdales to be read to from a large book; years later she brought her husband to the same house to receive instruction. In the home, at the fireside, with servants, talking to other women, influencing children, the Lollard housewife exerted her influence. Men travelled more, had better opportunities to cloak evangelism in occupational journeys and were more commonly the leaders in meetings, often enough held for men alone. Shannon McSheffrey draws attention to the way in which 'undistinguished tradesmen' achieved authority within Lollardy by force of personality. She argues that research has not corroborated the view that women in Lollardy achieved a status not available to them elsewhere, and were correspondingly attracted to the movement. Their role, she believes, was not so markedly different from that in society generally. Men led, although women clearly established niches for themselves as readers and reciters in the reading circles and certain women were of key importance, such as the widow Alice Rowley from the civic elite, active in Coventry, where an unusual number of women were literate or owned books; she rejects Luxton's view that a number of wealthier Lollards in Coventry remained undetected.[112]

---

109   Fines, 'Studies', p. 54.
110   *TLL*, pp. 34, 68–71, 152, 236n, 242 (Willis); for White, above n. 100.
111   Ibid., pp. 90–1.
112   Ibid., p. 110; Fines, 'Heresy trials', pp. 165–7, 171. S. McSheffrey, *Gender and Heresy* (1995) (see also for valuable detail on nature of Lollard meetings). C. Cross, 'Great reasoners in Scripture: the activities of women Lollards 1380–1530', *SCH* Subsidia I, pp. 359–80 lists cases; argues women were prone to conceal their literacy. Joan Collins and daughter in Burford, reciting the Scriptures, had a status unavailable in orthodoxy (p. 378); comment, C. Cross, *EHR* CXIII (1998), pp. 162–3; review, A. Hudson, *MA* LXV (1996), pp. 353–4.

Family affiliations kept the heresy going but leading personalities were needed to make converts in larger numbers and to efface the effects of anti-heresy drives. Occasionally we catch glimpses of these key men in action: for example, William White in East Anglia, instructing by vivid demonstration, employing a layman to celebrate the eucharist at Easter in place of himself, despite the fact that he was in orders, or quasi-ceremonially eating cold sausages with his followers on Good Friday to defy the Church's ordinance on fasting.

White's distinctive views can be traced repeatedly in the confessions of his followers. Even an individual turn of phrase, contrasting the dead wood in the making of images with the strength of the growing tree, recurs in the confessions. White's personality gave a special cast to the East Anglian group. Teaching travelled down from layer to layer, sometimes given a particular twist by the more independent-minded, even eccentric members. One theme did not survive the transition from teachers to lesser fry. White's doctrine that the eucharist was 'corpus Christi in memoria' did not take root: John Reve, glover of Beccles, for example, believed that it was simply material bread.

The number of cases in the ensemble of the trials in which an individual is mentioned provides a working guide to his or her importance in the diffusion of heresy. So the leading teachers emerge, as we might expect, as White himself, mentioned sixteen times, flanked by Hugh Pye, twelve times. Both were in orders. White had been a leader in Tenterden and he was aided by others who had also once been active in Kent. Below White and Pye came a class of missionaries and teachers in schools, some lay, some in orders, mentioned six times or less, shading down to three in the case of John Waddon, once in Kent, who was executed. Below this category came local supporters and those who gave hospitality to Lollards in their homes, mentioned between one and five times, including the redoubtable Margery Baxter with her pungent housewife's sayings. She is not to be underestimated. She worked in evangelizing with her husband, hid William White, whom she called 'a great saint in heaven', in her own home and sought converts herself. Joan Clyfland of Norwich remembered how she sat sewing by the fire in her husband's absence instructing both Joan and her two teenage servants using a question and answer technique.

Authority in the Alnwick prosecutions took care to preserve individual statements and did not force them into the mould of pre-existing interrogations; suspects, for their part, were, it has been suggested, astute enough in some cases to feign illiteracy in the hope of mitigating their guilt. White's sphere of influence seems to have lain mainly in the Waveney valley outside Norwich itself, which as far as extant and exploited records are concerned, remained remarkably untouched by heresy, its population faithfully supporting its numerous parish churches in traditional ways up to the Reformation.[113] What must have been a

---

113  N. Tanner, *The Church in Late Medieval Norwich* (Toronto, 1984); note comment by R. B. Dobson in *EHR* cii (1987), p. 478: 'the Reformation was possible in 1530 and not in 1370 because the late medieval Church had succeeded in stimulating the religious aspirations of its parishioners not too little, but too well'. The problem is twofold. (1) Norwich seems strangely immune from Lollardy. (2) It

personal charisma is now lost to us but implicit in results, in the case of Thomas Man, long resident in the Chilterns, who claimed that he and his wife had converted between 500 and 700 followers. No doubt he exaggerated, but there was a core of truth, for a witness at his second trial in 1518 said that he had instructed followers at Amersham, Billericay, Chelmsford, Stratford Langthorne, Uxbridge, Burnley, Burnham, Henley, Newbury and London, as well as in Suffolk and Norfolk.[114]

Whether the psychology of the convert was affected by the circumstances of his work it is now impossible to say. Where the records allow us to check occupations, they lie most frequently in the textile industry, this being the biggest employer of skilled workers in England.[115] Weavers as such are not specially prominent. As the master clothier emerged, employing his own labour and depressing the status of the once-independent worker to that of a wage-earner subject to dismissal, so circumstances of work for many deteriorated. The sources do not allow us to say whether many Lollards were seeking a psychological refuge from a disadvantageous economic position in an underground religion preaching religious equality;[116] we have no positive hint that this was so, though the possibility cannot be excluded. The number of prominent Lollards who had servants points against this view; more significant is the evidence that, broadly speaking, Lollardy survived in regions where it had already laid down support before 1414, at a time of greater prosperity for textile workers. A living tradition of Lollardy went on attracting recruits, whether work circumstances changed or not. The assumptions and outlook of the craftsman,[117] which made a minority susceptible to the Lollard mission, were what counted.

### Class structure and distribution

The attractions of Lollardy to the artisan class worked in two ways. On the one hand, they gave it endurance within the Scripture-reading circle after the disaster of 1414; on the other, they made it more difficult for the heresy ever again to climb higher in the social scale. Adaptation to the needs of artisan circles accompanied, and was a consequence of, the diminution of the academic leadership. Oxford had been purged originally by Courtenay, then again by Archbishop Arundel in 1411, and the doors to academic recruitment thereby closed. Academically trained men of an older generation who stayed in the field were

---

moved rapidly from a rich traditional Church life to Protestantism. On White and his following, see Aston, 'William White's Lollard followers', pp. 469–97 (note tabular analysis of structure, p. 481); 'cold sausages': Fines, 'Studies', p. 54; aphorisms as teaching aid: 'Heresy trials', pp. 166–7. See *HTN*, pp. 41, 43–51; I am indebted to Rev. Dr N. Tanner for use of his work on Lollard women (forthcoming, *DNB* 2004).

114  *TLL*, pp. 170–1, Dickens, 'Heresy and origins', p. 58.
115  Statistics in Davis, 'Lollard survival', pp. 191–201.
116  This forms one of the explanations of Lollard survival discussed by Davis, 'Lollard survival': see esp. pp. 198–201.
117  Dickens brings out the significance of artisan membership: see introduction to his *Lollards and Protestants*.

whittled away in time. Peter Payne, an academic latecomer of considerable talents, left for Bohemia after he had been cited for heresy in the reaction after Oldcastle;[118] his logic pupil, Ralph Mungyn, worked on till he was condemned to life imprisonment in 1428;[119] the veteran Wyche was burnt in 1440.[120] By mid-century, though occasional conversion from within the religious orders brought in trained men, leadership was in the hands of unbeneficed clergy, generally of limited learning, and laymen, self-taught or instructed in Lollard schools. These could speak to their own kind; but they could not compose, and so new Lollard texts did not emerge, the only exceptions in the present state of knowledge being the lost tracts of William White from the 1420s and Wyclif's *Wicket*, of uncertain, but possibly late fifteenth-century date.[121] Nor could they easily carry the heresy higher in the social scale. The association between Lollardy and sedition kept those of gentle blood away, and fresh recruits in that class were not made.[122] Wealthier business circles were touched in London, and the number of Lollards in this category had grown by the sixteenth century. The rich might help the poor through their common bond of belief: so the illiterate water-carrier, Robert Benet, who kept in his belt a translation of the Four Evangelists which he could not read, went for shelter in 1497 to the house of John Barret, a goldsmith of Cheapside. Richard Hunne, whose mysterious death after arrest for heresy in 1514 created an outcry, was of the Merchant Taylors: his conflicts with the Church may have owed something to his marriage to Anne Vincent. The connection is not quite clear, but if Anne's father was Thomas Vincent, then Hunne was the son-in-law of the devoted evangelist who taught Hacker his beliefs. In London the wealth and privileges of sections of the clergy were peculiarly obvious, and gave a hold to Lollardy. Most wanted to reform rather than undermine the position of the clergy, but there were perennial financial quarrels between the Church and the city, an ambience in which the religious dissidence could grow. On the eve of the Reformation there was 'a distinct heretical community' in the capital.[123] To a lesser degree the upper echelons of Coventry society were involved in heresy: richer men's interest can be glimpsed about the time of the 1511–12 trials.[124] The overall picture is of a sect able both to survive and to grow at a certain level of society, but not able to break much fresh ground, socially or intellectually.

118   Below, p. 367, Emden, *Biographical Register, Oxford.*
119   *TLL*, pp. 143–5.
120   Ibid., pp. 148–50.
121   Perspective given in Aston, 'Lollardy and the Reformation', and on *Wicket*, 'John Wyclif's Reformation reputation' at pp. 37–8; *HPR*, pp. 11, 203–4, 289, 451–2 (on content); on White's works see Fines, 'Studies', p. 52.
122   That is, in England; for Scotland, see below, p. 296.
123   S. Brigden, *London and the Reformation* (1989), pp. 66–7; the will to reform rather than undermine: p. 67; the distinct heretical community: p. 84; Dickens, 'Heresy and origins', pp. 54–6; for earlier cases in London, *TLL* pp. 85–6, 156–7 (I prefer 'rich' as translation of *locupletes* (p. 85n.)); background given in J. A. F. Thomson, 'Tithe disputes in later medieval London', *EHR* LXXVII (1963), pp. 1–17.
124   Luxton, 'The Lichfield court book', pp. 120–5. See also C. Cross, 'Popular piety and the records of the unestablished Churches 1460–1660', *SCH* XI, pp. 269–92; for Buckinghamshire, see below, pp. 394–5.

Map 7, which plots prosecutions for heresy between 1414 and 1522, illustrates this underground phase of Lollard history. Three inferences may be made from it. One is that Lollardy survived, broadly, in the same regions where it had lodged before 1414, and did not, it would seem, open up new ones. As Thomson has shown, Lollardy after 1414 was to be found in seven regional groupings, based in Kent, London, the Chilterns and the mid-Thames Valley, Bristol and the West Country, the Midlands, especially Coventry, Essex and East Anglia, with lesser clusters in Hampshire and the Forest of Dean. As far as we can see, it was a southern survival. We know that at the time of Richard Wyche's trial in 1403 a community existed in the Newcastle area.[125] So many northern registers for the period have disappeared that it is impossible to say whether it lived on or not, and whether heresy was so exclusively a southern phenomenon. Oldcastle's revolt, for reasons of geography if nothing else, had no northern participants; it too was a southern phenomenon, and its rebel-bearing regions correspond fairly broadly to those of Lollard survival after 1414: London, the Chilterns and mid-Thames Valley, Bristol, the Midlands and Essex all sent rebels to Oldcastle and produced heretics after that date. One oddity is Kent, almost blank for the rebellion, although Oldcastle should have had a local following through the Cobham estates he held there, and it was fertile for heresy later. The other is East Anglia, which contained heresy on some scale in the 1420s; it may be blank for the rebellion merely because of its isolation from London. In sum, however, there is a geographical correspondence between the rebellion and the post-1414 heresy. Scotland is a curiosity. Some thirty persons in the late fifteenth century in Kyle and Cunningham, Ayrshire, including gentry and members of the court circle, were accused of Lollardy; background information is lacking and it is hard to tell what basis there was for accusation.[126]

Within the seven regions prosecutions continued to be launched at varying intervals through the period; only in East Anglia do they come more or less to a stop. Persecution, in other words, was ineffective in eliminating heresy from at any rate six of the seven major regions.

Sometimes there are long periods between drives; the area of the Chilterns was only investigated vigorously on three occasions, by Chedworth in 1462–4, Smith in 1511, and Longland in 1521–2, yet it produced substantial hauls of heretics every time; from the well-documented prosecutions of 1462–4 and 1521–2 we can distinguish a number of places as fertile in heresy in the last prosecution as in the first, despite the intervening lapse of time.[127] Often individual towns and villages have but one or two prosecutions recorded. This, however, can be somewhat deceptive. Episcopal registers, the staple source of evidence, tend to give places of origin less profusely than the rarer heresy court books. So if we must use registers alone, our source may give us, for example, only a selection of

125    M. G. Snape, 'Some evidence of Lollard activity in the diocese of Durham in the early fifteenth century', *Archaeologia Aeliana*, 4th ser. xxxix (1961), pp. 355–61.
126    Kent, *MW*, p. 173; Scotland, *TLL*, pp. 204–7, *HPR*, pp. 126–7.
127    Fines, 'Studies', pp. 102–9, 157–205; *TLL*, ch. 3.

principal places and omit to mention lesser villages. The evidence, dependent as it is on the chances of detection and the survival of judicial records, is fragmentary and discontinuous.

Certain notorious centres of heresy emerge none the less from the evidence we have: London at the top of the list, partly because it was the focal point of a large diocese and refugees from elsewhere fled to anonymity there;[128] Bristol, with a striking continuity and evidence of survival in certain districts, especially the Redcliffe area;[129] Tenterden, the Kentish textile village where White probably laid down a tradition;[130] Coventry, active in heresy and in the revolt of 1431; the Chilterns, at a point of intersection of dioceses.[131]

Another inference to be drawn from the map is that prosecutions in the seven regions of survival were generally launched against individuals or groups involved in Lollardy rather than against anticlericals or isolated heretics unconnected with the movement.[132] Heresy drives give us for a moment, it is true, a glimpse of the religious sentiments in an area, not all of which fall neatly into the rival categories of Lollardy or orthodoxy. Endemic anticlericalism was the milieu in which Lollardy floated and a convert passed through personal contact with a committed member from anti-Church views of an uncoordinated kind into a deeper involvement. The laconic entries of the episcopal register do not always enable us to draw this line, which in reality must often have been ambiguous.

One criterion of high reliability does exist, however, and has been noticed on the map. When prosecutions record the presence of suspect vernacular books in a locality, we can feel a measure of confidence that we are on the trail of a Lollard reading-circle, for these books were most commonly the tracts and Scriptures of the heretics rather than innocent vernacular works of piety such as *Nicodemus* or *Dives and Pauper*. Records of the presence of these books are to be found in every one of the seven major regions in which Lollardy survived; in some they lie thickly, and prosecutions of suspects with books occur repeatedly over the years in the same places. True Lollardy formed the core of the cases in these regions up to the eve of the Reformation.

One further inference may be that Lollardy, by and large, survived in artisan circles, for the map demonstrates that the clusters of heresy-bearing localities lie in the areas of high population where industry had been developed. Only two regions significant in the development of the textile industry, York and the south

128  *TLL*, pp. 139, 155, 236.
129  Ibid., pp. 22, 25, 26, 28, 33, 34 (see also 35), 39, 44, 46, 47; compare entries for 1448 and 1511–12 (a group active *c.*1505–6) and note evidence of a continuity over half a century in the Redcliffe area; note also that the longest gap in prosecutions lies between 1457 and 1476, a time of general slackening of prosecution in England. Social composition in Bristol (according to Thomson) is as follows: 1420 two priests; 1423 one of the same priests (William Taylor); 1448 weaver (unnamed), smith; 1476 three men (no details); 1511–12 (a group active *c.*1505–6) carpetmaker, wiredrawer and others, no information for 1429, 1441, 1448 (case of William Fuer of Gloucester), 1457, 1499.
130  Ibid., pp. 173, 174, 175–6, 178 (somewhat tentatively), 180, 187–9.
131  Ibid., pp. 101 (John Grace, called a 'false prophet', but not a Lollard: see Aston, 'Lollardy and sedition', p. 14 and n. 70), 104–6, 107–16; for 1489 prosecution, see Fines, 'Studies', p. 129, and for 1511–12, 'Heresy trials', pp. 160–74.
132  For cases of individual heresy in the fourteenth century, see below, p. 303.

**Insert A**

Ashley Green •

Princes
Risborough      • Chesham
    • Missenden
Little Missenden      • Chesham Bois
Chinnor            • Amersham
    • Hughenden
Stoken-      • West Wycombe
church
    Wycombe    Penn      • Beaconsfield
Turville            Hedgerley      Harrow
Hambleden    Great Marlow            • Denham
    **Bisham** •    • **Cookham**            Uxbridge
**Henley**    Burnham    • Maidenhead            • **Iver**
    Abbey    • Dorney
        Bray      Chalvey
    Fifield
        Windsor •
        Ankerwick •

• Ashbourne

                                    *Trent*

            • Wiggington      • **Leicester**

    • Birmingham

        **Coventry** •

                    • Alcester
    • Worcester            *Avon*      • Byfield

**Almeley** •
    • **Eardisley**

                *Wye*

        • Staunton
Walford •    *Severn*    • Norton Underhill
    Micheldean •    • **Gloucester**    • Hasleton    Windrush
                                • Asthall      • Kidlington
        **Lydney**                Burford    Witney
    Aylburton •                Lechlade            Thame •
    Woolaston •        Buscot    • **Faringdon**
                    Coxwell •    W. Hendred    • **Steventon**
← Pembroke                    Wantage •    • Brightwell
                            • E.
                            Hendred
                    **Letcombe Basset** •    • **Henley**
                        Letcombe    **Wallingford**
Portishead •                Regis    Speen    Reading
    • **Bristol**                    • **Newbury**
            Turleigh    Broughton    **Hungerford**    Woodhay
            Bradford    Gifford
    **Bath** •        • **Devizes**    Marden    • Pewsey            **Dogmersfield**
Wrington •    Hinton    Keevil    • Wilsford    • Woodhay    Odiham •
    Norton St Philip    • Rode    Steeple    Chirton                Crondall •
    Holcombe        Ashton
    **Wells** •    Leigh    Beckington    • **Netheravon**    *Test*
            Marston
            Bigot

    **Taunton** •            Salisbury •        • Winchester
                                Meonstoke •

0 ┠──────────────── 50 miles
0 ┠──┬──┬──┬──┬──┬── 80 km

Wrington •    Heretics detected
**Taunton** •    Heretics with suspect English books

MAP 7 *Lollardy underground.*

Cotswolds, are either omitted or scantily represented; the gap in the former region may be due to *lacunae* in the surviving records, and in the latter to the lack of prosecuting zeal of the bishops of Worcester.

The map tends to underestimate the extent of the Lollard survival. No doubt, despite some sifting of the sources, the prosecutions still include some of mere sceptics, anticlericals and idiosyncratic heretics, but the exaggeration of the survival of true Lollardy which ensues must be more than offset by the contrary effects of defective source material. Many episcopal registers have been lost; others list no heresy, not because it did not exist, but because bishops and their officers did not detect, and perhaps were uninterested in pursuing it. There are curious blanks. Wales, into which Swinderby and Brute disappeared, has but two cases: of a priest and a layman at Pembroke in 1486 and 1488.[133] Was this due to absence of heresy, aided by the linguistic barrier over part of the region, or to ecclesiastical disorganization? One cannot say. The Welsh March is another puzzling area, for the region that included Oldcastle's seat and had once been Swinderby's campaigning ground might have been expected to have a later history of Lollardy, yet it is mute in the revolt of 1414 and has evidence of only two subsequent prosecutions: one at Almeley in Oldcastle's estates in 1433, and another at Eardisley in 1505,[134] both revealing the presence of suspect books. The border area was later of importance in the history of Nonconformity, and registers for crucial periods are missing: there is a presumption that there was more Lollardy in the March than the map reveals.

It must be emphasized that the map is simply a pictorial record of the evidence of prosecutions of Lollards and other religious dissidents in the extant registers and court books; used with care, it gives us a blurred outline of the heresy underground, but never the complete picture.

### Late Lollard beliefs

Life underground and the disillusionment of 1414, perhaps of 1431 also, largely stripped the sedition from Lollardy. Willy nilly, Lollards found themselves in some opposition to the State as it backed the demands on them of the Church, but they mostly gave up conspiracy. The Apocalypse comforted them. It was a tradition initiated by Wyclif, though his emphasis on State reform inhibited a full-scale dependence on cataclysmic divine intervention as a resolution of problems. Defendants in the Norwich trials of 1428–31 denounced the Pope as Antichrist.[135] In 1448 William Fuer expected war with the Catholics.[136] A group at Newbury uncovered in 1400–1 consoled themselves with the prospect of eschatological change.[137] Hacker, one of the great evangelists, was quoted as saying in

133   *TLL*, pp. 44–5. The priest was Irish.
134   Ibid., pp. 31–2, 48.
135   Bostick, *Antichrist*, p. 74, *HTN, passim*; see index.
136   *TLL*, p. 78.
137   Ibid., p. 36.

1520 that there should be a battle of priests and all the priests should be slain.[138] The Apocalypse was a book often enough owned by Lollards.

But there was no realistic prospect of a pro-Lollard war. The regional groupings existed without much knowledge of each other; no one man knew them all. Survival was the immediate concern.

Late Lollards were not very conscious of Wyclif; his distinctive ideas on dominion or predestination or the role of the secular ruler were generally lost to view;[139] but his legacy still helped them.[140] The concept of the Scriptures as a divine exemplar, existing before the creation, had worked on the minds of the early Lollards and clerical missionaries;[141] the effect of this belief in the final phase, however little ordinary followers could have grappled with the realist philosophy which underlay it, was to provide comfort in persecution. Its effect was to substitute for the authority of the Church the infallibility of Scripture;[142] Wyclif's doctrine of the Church acted in a similar fashion. The visible and hierarchical Church which persecuted the Lollards was the Church of Antichrist; the true Church became the congregation of true believers.

Investigatory procedure made Lollardy sound very negative. An interrogator subjected the suspect to a series of standard questions, negative replies on orthodox points being recorded to be used as the basis for convictions.[143] Three denials of Catholic belief and practice recur: on the veneration of images, on pilgrimages, and on the mass.[144] The basis for the denials often lay in a simple logic. John Morden of Chesham in Buckinghamshire, explaining his beliefs about the mass to his still orthodox son-in-law, said, 'Thou art deceived, for it can nothing profit thee; for it is but bread and wine; and so it is when the priest began with it at mass, and so it is when the mass is ended.'[145] Alice Rowley at Coventry seized on the priests' gain from mass offerings to call the service a 'pretty falsehood' of the priests which enabled them to buy the bread for the Hosts and then to sell it at a higher price.[146] In East Anglia Margery Baxter resorted to a coarse *reductio ad absurdum* to attack transubstantiation.[147]

Morden's statement on images was similar to his view of the mass. 'They are but stocks and stones', he said, 'for they cannot help themselves, how can they

---

138   Hudson, 'Lollardy and eschatology', *Eschatologie und Hussitismus*, ed. Šmahel, pp. 99–113 at p. 110, quoting Foxe IV, 234.

139   Comment in *HPR*, pp. 269–70.

140   For interesting notes on the reverse side of the picture – continuity in Lollardy from Wyclif – see Ibid., p. 472.

141   I am indebted to Professor M. Deanesly for this comment in a private letter; see also her view in *JEH* XVII (1966), p. 266.

142   *HPR*, p. 510: 'The Bible was the central pivot of the whole.'

143   *TLL*, pp. 224–6, 228–9; on Coventry, a typical case, see Fines, 'Heresy trials', pp. 169–71. For trial records, see A. Hudson, 'The examination of Lollards', *BIHR* XLVI (1973), pp. 145–59.

144   *TLL*, p. 91 (note comment, p. 126).

145   Ibid., p. 91, spelling modernized, as in later quotations.

146   Fines, 'Heresy trials', p. 166.

147   False gods eaten by the priests, who later 'Commestos emittunt per posteriora in sepibus turpiter fetentibus': *HTN*, p. 45.

help thee? And the worshipping of them is but idolatry.'[148] On images the appeal to the unvarnished text of Scripture was potent. John Burell, of the East Anglian Lollards, appealed to the decalogue to dismiss the medieval practice of veneration.[149] Dislike of pilgrimages was bound up with the attack on this veneration, since representations and relics of the saints were the customary goal of the pilgrim's journey. In East Anglia the crucifix was attacked in terms oddly reminiscent of the Bogomils; 'no more credence should be done to the crucifix', it was said, 'than to the gallows which thieves be hanged on.'[150] At Coventry the focus for discontent lay in a particular image of Our Lady.[151] Pilgrimage centres received sarcastic names: among the East Anglian group Canterbury became 'Cankerbury'.[152] James Willis disapproved of church music and bellringing; in East Anglia church bells were described as 'Antichrist's horns'.[153] There is a recurrent feeling that the Church's demands on the faithful were unnecessary, a mumbo jumbo dictated by the desire of priests to get money or gain their own ends. Pilgrimages were rejected on the grounds that they involved waste of money.[154]

Beyond the three best-known denials, different Lollards attacked various other sacraments. In East Anglia during Alnwick's prosecutions, and again in London in 1499, marriage as a ceremony was rejected as superfluous: the basis lay in the belief that the will of the two parties was sufficient, without the presence of priest or any formal ceremony.[155] Dislike of ceremonies and mortuary fees lay behind the rejection of the need for burial in consecrated ground, implicit in the statement of Thomas Whyte of Ringwold in Kent in 1473, that it was as good for his soul if his body were buried in a marsh as in a cemetery.[156] Objections to the practice of baptism by a priest in church were expressed by two men from Lydney in 1470, who said it could be done as well in a ditch as in a font.[157] This was an aphorism with a long history, for it is met in the confession of James Willis at his last trial in 1462, and in the confession of William Bull, the Dewsbury shearman, in 1543.[158] In a sense this was not heresy, but rather an objection to a canonical practice. A rejection of baptism altogether occurs in the East Anglian group, always one of the most radical, on the grounds that a child was redeemed in any case by Christ's blood;[159] rejection of sacraments or ceremonies of the Church was the message of the aphorisms of the sect, couched in terms that would be familiar to workers, in towns or on the land. For a Dewsbury shearman

148   *TLL*, p. 91.
149   Ibid., p. 126.
150   Fines, 'Studies', p. 63; *LMH*, 1st edn, p. 17.
151   *TLL*, pp. 104, 112.
152   Ibid., p. 126.
153   Ibid., p. 69; Fines, 'Studies', p. 63.
154   See Fines's comment ('Studies', p. 250).
155   *TLL*, pp. 127, 159.
156   Ibid., p. 183.
157   Ibid., p. 41.
158   Ibid., p. 69; Dickens, *Lollards and Protestants*, p. 48.
159   *TLL*, p. 127; Fines, 'Studies', p. 66.

the font was a 'stinking tarn';[160] for a Lollard at Steeple Ashton in Wiltshire in 1488 it would be better to be sprinkled with lake water than holy water if the priest was a sinner;[161] for another at Kevill (Keevil) in 1506, Ball the carpenter could make as good images as those which were worshipped.[162] The 'better than' or 'as good as' of these comparisons is characteristic of the wry, sardonic religious egalitarianism of the typical heretic.

The appeal to reason could have odd results. Beside the standard views, we meet now and again quite idiosyncratic beliefs, such as that of John Edward in the Newbury area, who believed that Our Lady conceived and bore another son after Christ's ascension; or that of John Wodeward of Wigginton, near Tamworth, who was against baptism because there was no baptism before the time of Christ.[163] Such ideas can hardly have been inculcated in the reading sessions of the movement. Sometimes the opening of the Scriptures led to the development of odd personal views; sometimes an eccentric parishioner was attracted to the Lollard circle. Or concern with heresy alerted authority to doctrinal deviations unconnected with Lollardy which existed under the recorded surface. Cathars had penetrated England, albeit at a low level; also some twelve cases of scepticism, idiosyncratic belief, perhaps mental unbalance, appear in published records between 1300 and 1370.[164] Then there was no need for a doctrinal alert; after Wyclif and the turn to active persecution, more of such casual cases might come to light.

The tone of Lollardy was sceptical, ironical, highly suspicious of emotion.[165] Persecution did not produce the state of exaltation which Manselli rightly distinguishes in the later stages of the proceedings against Olivi's followers.[166] Accusations of sexual immorality, frequently launched against continental heretics, were hardly ever made in England.

Pushed up against orthodox parish life and its ceremonies, which many of them dare not evade, and lacking strong intellectual leadership, it was natural that fifteenth-century Lollards should express their religious feelings in explosive negatives. We hear very little of rites of their own: occasional celebrations of the eucharist, some confessing to each other. Perhaps a ceremony lies behind the Coventry password, 'For we shall all drink of a cuppe'.[167] The customary

---

160 Dickens, *Lollards and Protestants*, p. 69.
161 *TLL*, p. 45.
162 Ibid., p. 83.
163 Ibid., pp. 76–7, 104. Comment, K. Thomas, *Religion and the Decline of Magic* (London, 1961), p. 168.
164 Fines's calculation, 'Studies', pp. 8–16. F. Makower, *The Constitutional History and Constitution of the Church of England* (London, 1895), pp. 183–94. Cases of Margaret Syward, I. J. Churchill, *Canterbury Administration* (London, 1933) I, pp. 313–14; Ralph Tremur, *Exeter Episcopal Registers: Register John de Grandisson*, ed. F. C. Hingeston-Randolph, II (London, 1897), pp. 1147–9, 1179–81.
165 *TLL*, p. 249.
166 Above, p. 227.
167 Aston, 'Lollardy and sedition', p. 13 and notes; Fines, 'Studies', p. 251 argues that most believed in the priesthood of all believers. Eucharistic beliefs, *TLL*, pp. 82n., 112, 246–7; Fines, 'Heresy trials', p. 167.

exchange between the evangelist Sweeting, meeting the carpenter Brewster for a reading group in the fields outside Chelsea, reads like an antiphon: 'James Brewster should say, "Now the Son of the living God help us"; unto whom William Sweeting again should answer, "Now Almighty God do so".'[168] Whatever Lollard rites did exist, they were not important. The strongest positive part of their life was the reading, the mutual exhortation and the earnest practice of the virtues. The core of their belief lay in the direct contact of the praying, reading adherent with God, based on Scripture and unencumbered by any sort of intermediaries. It was a simple, radical sort of belief, with a spiritualizing view of the sacraments.

Anticlericalism grew stronger. Recourse to the Fathers became less and less feasible; they may even be attacked. The more strictly academic and doctrinal concerns faded. *Scriptura sola* became the norm; the ethical concern, always important, became dominant. Lollardy had adapted to the circumstances of its followers. The swing in Lollard opinion, moving farther away from its founder as time went on, made similarities to Waldensians, especially of the more radical kind, ever more apparent, despite the lack of contact with them and the different origins of English Lollardy. Though Lollards had less explicit doctrine of their own than any other movement to set against the Church, and they lacked any formal distinction between preacher and rank and file, with the special obligations and celibacy of the preachers, yet they had in common with the Waldensians an ethical stress, an emphasis on word rather than sacrament, biblical translation, and an appeal to artisan membership. Both movements had the power to inspire a line of dedicated evangelists and pastors, more inclined to bow to persecution, so that they might live to fight another day, than many of the Cathar perfect, but quite as tenacious. On these few men both movements to a large degree rested. Other contributory factors in the survival are the relative leniency of the English tradition of persecution after the reaction to the Oldcastle revolt was spent, and the sporadic character of Waldensian persecution.

There is much to be said, however, for the view that both late Lollardy and Waldensianism of the Poor Lombard variety were the heresies of the Middle Ages *par excellence*, the perennial religion of the layman from lower classes, who painfully acquired some booklearning or learnt by rote passages of Scripture and passed on by word of mouth his anticlerical, Donatist views, mixed with an earthy scepticism about facets of Catholicism. Even in radical Hussitism, whose history, as we shall see, was so much briefer and more dynamic than that of the Lollards or Waldensians, we meet similar wry aphorisms. Long before Lollardy, the Dominican master-general Humbert de Romans, drawing on vast experience and writing *c.*1270–4, commented on elements of scepticism in his advice on sermons for casual occasions. Analysing the source for insight into the beliefs of the poor, A. Murray distinguishes 'sensuous indifference' and *accidia* as prime enemies of a conscientious friar. But Humbert also alludes to scepticism about

---

168   A. Hope, 'The lady and the bailiff: Lollardy among the gentry in Yorkist and early Tudor England', *LG*, pp. 250–77 at p. 265.

immortality, the fate of the dead and the resurrection of the body – a hardy perennial.[169] Perhaps the durability of both the English and the continental heresy was due in the last resort to its appeal to this submerged reasoning piety, the beliefs of laymen who had their own devotional life and their own doubts about individual points of doctrine. A Valdes or a Wyclif and his followers could appeal to these sentiments. But they did not call them into being, and, among the multifarious causes of heresy, this body of largely hidden sentiment has been one of the underestimated forces in medieval Church history.

169   A. Murray, 'Religion among the poor in thirteenth century France: the testimony of Humbert de Romans', *Traditio* xxx (1974), pp. 285–324.

# The Bohemian Reform Movement

## Introduction

At almost the same time that English Lollardy as a political force went down to defeat in Oldcastle's rebellion, a comparable movement of religious dissent, in part stimulated by Wyclif's writings, was shaking the bonds of the distant kingdom of Bohemia. The dramatic but desperate revolt of Oldcastle was the last throw of the native English movement; after it, as we have seen, a residue of Lollards lived on underground by dint of their own tenacity and by courtesy of the lack of determination in persecution of some members of the episcopate. In the sixteenth century they showed some fresh vitality. But as a political force, even in potential, they ceased to exist after Oldcastle's revolt. In Bohemia reform and heresy went a great deal farther. Disputes, in which Wyclif's name figures prominently, shook the university of Prague; agitation reached the Bohemian court and the international Church assembled at the Council of Constance. At the moment when Henry v's soldiers were hunting down Oldcastle's conspirators, many of the Bohemian nobles were displaying their solidarity with the cause of their native reform leader, Jan Hus. Four or five years later, when Lollardy was reduced to a few of the clergy and some hardy artisan circles in England, its basis in the nobility and merchant classes almost wholly vanished, Hussite supporters were intimidating their opponents and preparing to do battle for their beliefs.

All was not Wyclif in the Bohemian movement − indeed it would be a misnomer to describe Hussitism *tout court* as his child. Nevertheless his ideas played a significant part in the complex of factors underlying the Hussite movement, and some of the religious enthusiasts given free play by the events leading to the revolution shared the ideas of the English Lollards.

The most remarkable feature of Hussitism was its repudiation of the close control of the papacy in doctrinal matters, and its establishment, however briefly and imperfectly, of a measure of religious toleration.

For some seventeen years, between the Defenestration of Prague in 1419 and the acceptance of Sigismund at Jihlava in 1436, and to a lesser degree in the years of struggle before 1419, the older unity of doctrine and canon law in the West under the papacy was, first in practice, then in open defiance, broken in pieces in this one country, and a remarkable range of belief unfolded. The Hussites and their supporters went farther than any other popular religious movement labelled as heresy before the Reformation in shaking the old order, and for this reason demanded extended study. The history of their struggle, a failure in the end yet, relatively speaking, the most successful of them all, forms a natural conclusion to a study of the major heretical movements of the Middle Ages.

## The Setting[1]

Bohemia was a latecomer to the circle of advanced nations. Under the first Přemyslid rulers it had been hardly more than a frontier province, on the fringe of the Holy Roman Empire; then under the last rulers of the dynasty it advanced more rapidly, aided by the influx of colonists and the growth of the indigenous population, to achieve under the Luxemburgs, above all Charles IV (king, 1346–78), a remarkable flowering of economic, cultural and political life. Charles had been administrator of the country on behalf of his absentee father John; then from 1346 he ruled both as king in Bohemia and as Holy Roman emperor till his death in 1378, and sought to make the country a focal point in his revised conception of the old Empire. With his father, he succeeded in securing the elevation of the see of Prague to metropolitical status; in 1348 he founded the university of Prague as an intellectual centre and training ground for administrators within the Empire; by his addition of the New Town he added greatly to the size and economic significance of his capital; finally, by his summons to the Austrian Augustinian canon Waldhauser to come and preach in his lands, he gave impetus to an indigenous movement of Church reform, the platform from which emerged, after decades of agitation, the Hussite revolution of the fifteenth century.[2]

His own part in sponsoring reform and opening the way for Hussitism is equivocal. On the one hand, many features in Bohemian Church and intellectual life which aided the progress of the movement had their roots in, or were affected

1   F. Seibt, 'Die Zeit der Luxemburger und der hussitischen Revolution', *Handbuch der Geschichte der böhmischen Länder*, ed. K. Bosl, I (1967), pp. 351–536 (comprehensive, with bibliography; insufficiently known in England); F. Seibt, 'Bohemica, Probleme und Literatur seit 1945', *HZ*, Sonderheft IV (1970), esp. pp. 49–99 (introduction to post-war work on Bohemia, with comments; valuable for Czech literature). R. R. Betts, *Essays in Czech History* (1969), omitting ch. 3; H. Kaminsky, *A History of the Hussite Revolution* (1967) (fundamental and detailed study of history of ideas in relation to politics up to 1424, with distinguished knowledge of doctrinal sources); bibliography: pp. 551–3; on Charles IV: pp. 7–8. J. K. Zeman, *The Hussite Movement and the Reformation in Bohemia, Moravia and Slovakia (1350–1650)* (1977) (bibliography); F. Seibt, *Hussitenstudien* (1987) (collection of articles published elsewhere, distinguished by understanding of personal motives). Background in E. Werner, *Jan Hus* (1991), chs 1 and 2. Names are given in the Czech forms here, except where a German or anglicized form is likely to be more familiar to the English reader.

2   F. Seibt, *Karl IV* (1978), pp. 367–97 (classic, wide-ranging account); full bibliography: K. Walsh, 'Wyclif's legacy', p. 401, n. 14; T. Fudge, 'The state of Hussite historiography', *Mediaevistik* VII (1994), pp. 93–117.

by, the policies of his brilliant reign; on the other, his own piety, sincere as it was, remained relatively conventional. He, and the forerunners of Hussitism, whom he sometimes sponsored, did not favour heresy: he was the author of stern decrees against beghards and in favour of the inquisition. Religious feeling and economic interest combined to make him one of the great relic-collectors, and Prague a centre for saint cults and rich churches – features vividly attacked for their associated abuses by early preachers of the reform. The opening of Bohemia as a centre for the Empire involved also the opening of the Bohemian Church to the inroads of Avignonese fiscality, and appointment to high office became a matter of agreement between him and the popes.[3] His appointments to episcopal sees were generally wise, but biased in favour of his friends and servants; he secured the persons he wished, while the papacy was given exceptional opportunities to obtain cash and benefits from the kingdom.

The nobility were the losers by such arrangements. They were beneficiaries from the traditional *Eigenkirche*, with its heavy lay control, and in this distant area the *Eigenkirche* style of Church government lasted on well after its supersession in more advanced lands. Reform ideas on Gregorian lines were only beginning to make their impact in the thirteenth century, when free election was secured for the sees of Prague and Olomouc, and Andrew of Prague led his campaign for freedom from lay control. For a long time papal intervention was slight and hesitant: for the whole period 1221–1316 Jaroslav Eršil has uncovered only twelve papal provisions relating to Bohemia.[4]

It was the absence at the curia of the bishop of Prague, John of Dražice, between 1318 and 1329 that opened the way for the introduction of papal provisions on an extensive scale; when it came, it came with a rush. Under Charles, all bishoprics and an increasing number of abbacies fell within papal rights of provision – at least theoretically – while in ten years of Clement VI's pontificate 300 bulls sent to Bohemia were concerned with lesser benefices.[5] Many of these provisions concerned appointments of foreigners, especially Germans. There was a comparatively small gap in time between the old lay-controlled *Eigenkirche* and the late medieval type of informal concordat between pope and ruler for the distribution of office. This had important consequences, for the nobility retained a strong memory of their rights under the *Eigenkirche* and were, not wholly unjustly, inclined to see papal provisions as a system for rewarding foreigners. The course of events created a natural interest group, stronger than its opposite numbers in England, that had in practice seen rather

---

3  J. Eršil, 'Les rapports administratifs et financiers de la papauté avignonaise avec les pays de la couronne de Bohème entre 1352 et 1378', *Rozpravy československá Akademie Věd* LXIX (1959), p. 130 (summary of Czech article); R. E. Weltsch, *Archbishop John of Jenstein* (1968), pp. 40–9; role of nobility and patronage in J. M. Klassen, *The Nobility and the Making of the Hussite Revolution* (1978), pp. 27–34.

4  Eršil, 'Rapports', p. 131; for general background, F. Mildenberger, 'Die böhmischen Länder im Früh und Hochmittelalter', Bosl, *Handbuch* I, pp. 165–347. The background to the problems of John of Dražice is clarified in Patschovsky, *Anfänge*, pp. 30–43.

5  Eršil, 'Rapports', p. 132.

more of late medieval papalism at work at the financial level and rather less of reforming Gregorianism, and was ready to swing its support behind a movement which advocated disappropriation and an implicit return to the rights of lay patrons.[6] The whole issue, like most others in Bohemia, was complicated by the existence of an incipient division in language and culture between German and Czech peoples.[7]

Much of the early development of Bohemia was due to the entry of German colonists. The early Bohemian towns tended to be German-dominated, and the mining areas, especially centring on Kutná Hora (Kuttenberg) and Jihlava (Iglau), which brought so much wealth to the Bohemian crown, were largely in the hands of German immigrants. The indigenous Slav peoples at first followed a German lead, their peasants adopting the settlement rights of the Germans because they were so successful, and their nobility, through the clergy, adopting the knightly culture of the German-speaking lands. But by the turn of the fourteenth century the flow of German immigration had passed its peak,[8] and signs appeared of an increasing self-consciousness in the Czechs of the Bohemian lands, with a greater interest in their language. The number of translations begins sharply to increase: the knightly literature of the preceding era is translated from German, by the end of the thirteenth century a complete Czech psalter is in existence, there are creeds and prayers in Czech, and in the course of the fourteenth century a Czech translation of the *Historia scholastica* of Peter Comestor and a Czech life of Christ put together by a Dominican from the *Meditationes vitae Christi*.[9] First awareness of national and linguistic difference appeared among the clergy; it was complicated by the development of a local patriotism, supporting inhabitants of the kingdom, Czech or German, against inroads of foreigners.

Yet, wherever social tensions existed in fourteenth-century Bohemia, they could readily become associated with the linguistic distinction between Czech and German speakers, as in the case of the slow Czech penetration of towns, where Czech speakers might come to resent the dominance in local government of the wealthier Germans, or in the relations of Czech nobles with towns in their neighbourhood, where the national difference served to heighten class antagonism. In Church life the rising standards of the lower Czech nobility in education carried them more frequently into the ranks of the clergy, and caused resentment of the entrenchment of the Germans in high positions, the inevitable consequence of their earlier cultural lead. Under the Luxemburgs there were attempts to redress the balance, as in the founding of Roudnice (Raudnitz), a house of Augustinian canons for the sons of Czech-speaking parents, which became a centre for the vernacular religious tradition, or Charles IV's foundation of a house for Czech canons in the old imperial palace at Ingelheim, in the middle of a

---

6  Seibt, 'Die Zeit', p. 440.
7  K. Bittner, *Deutsche und Tschechen* (1936).
8  Seibt, 'Die Zeit', p. 416.
9  Ibid., pp. 458–60, E. Winter, *Frühhumanismus: Seine Entwicklung in Böhmen* (1964).

German cultural area.[10] What Charles wanted in Bohemia was a balance between races and languages; but he did not wholly succeed in getting it, and underlying antagonisms continued, witnessed for us by the abbot Ludolf of Sagan, who studied in Prague in the 1370s and spoke of the hostility of German and Czech as comparable to that between Jew and Samaritan.[11] Balance was harder to maintain after 1378, when the strong central direction of Charles was replaced by that of his son, Wenceslas IV (1378–1419), who, surrounded by grave political difficulties, was incapable of emulating his father's mastery of this problem, or indeed any other.

A third characteristic feature of the Bohemian kingdom lay in the existence from about 1350 of a movement described by Eduard Winter, its principal historian, as 'early humanism'. Its most striking, but also more superficial, feature was letter-writing in the new humanistic style and the literary contacts with Prague of Petrarch, who stayed in the capital, and of Cola di Rienzo. Of more lasting significance was the new piety referred to by Winter as a parallel and even forerunner of the better-known Netherlands *devotio moderna*. In Bohemia it was associated pre-eminently with the spread of houses of Augustinian canons, who arrived in Bohemia in 1350, and were favoured by two archbishops of Prague, by Charles IV and by a number of noble patrons. Their spirituality stressed the study of books, notably by Augustine and the Fathers, the inner religious life of the individual, typified for example in the influential constitutions of Roudnice by the division of the *dormitorium* into individual cells, and had a strong pastoral concern. Other religious houses contributed; the Cistercian Königsaal produced the devotional masterwork, the *Malogranatum*, translated during the century into both German and Czech, and the Premonstratensian house of Tepl played a part in biblical translation. As Seibt has warned us,[12] the influence of these new ideas affected only a thin upper layer of society; the Augustinian canons were no direct protagonists of the Hussite movement, but rather its opponents and, after the revolution, often its victims. Yet at least the *devotio moderna* of Bohemia helped to create in some influential circles the atmosphere of moral earnestness and a certain caution towards the formal and external machinery of traditional religious life that made a propitious climate of opinion for Hussitism.

Conflicts over the arbitrary and dangerous procedures of the inquisition, introduced as a permanent institution by John XXII in 1318, probably in the first instance through the fear of the heresy of the Free Spirit, contributed to instability in Church life. The strange affair of the Italian doctor and philosopher,

---

10   F. Seibt, *Hussitica: Zur Struktur einer Revolution* (1965) (essays often subtle and stimulating, based on textual analyses), see on nationalist issue: p. 62 (Roudnice), pp. 63–4 (Ingelheim); R. Kalivoda, 'Seibts "Hussitica" und die hussitische Revolution', *Historica* XIV (1967), pp. 225–46; E. Lemberg, *Geschichte des Nationalismus in Europa* (1950), p. 135–44.

11   Bittner, *Deutsche und Tschechen*, p. 11; see *Speculum* XLIV (1969), pp. 310–11; Fudge, *Ride* (below, p. 319, n. 42), pp. 216–18.

12   Seibt, 'Die Zeit', p. 447; note section on monasteries, pp. 444–9. I am indebted esp. to Seibt's survey for Bohemian background. On the Bible generally, see J. Kadlec, 'Die Bibel in mittelalterlichen Böhmen', *AHDLMA* XXXVI (1964), pp. 89–109, a study comparable to Deanesly, *Lollard Bible*; but see, on the effects of Scripture within Tabor, below, pp. 345–7, 351–4, 358–60.

Richardin of Pavia, whose book was condemned for Averroistic views, led to the suspension of bishop John of Dražice in 1315. Colda of Colditz, the Dominican who took office in 1318, clashed with secular authorities in Prague and with the Prague canon, Michael Folclini; he was threatened with death and twice had to leave the city. Gallus of Neuhaus interpreted his duties with a remarkable freedom: clashes took place over issues that could only in an arbitrary and artificial fashion be called heresy. Pope and bishop, apart from the early episode with John of Dražice, worked well enough together: it was the fear of an inquisitor's wide powers, the secrecy of witnesses and arbitrary condemnations, and anxiety for the security of traditional jurisdictions which threw up *ad hoc* alliances of judges, town governments and the secular clergy against the quasi-political activities of certain inquisitors, and created a ferment of opinion, damaging to Church authority.[13]

## The Beginnings of the Bohemian Reform Movement

Some of these characteristics may be seen in the preaching of Conrad Waldhauser,[14] who from 1363 worked as a freelance preacher supported by a benefice in Leitmeritz, then operated from the chief church of the Old Town of Prague. Charles's invitation to him to preach, and his position as his confessor and court chaplain, gave him official status from the outset. A keynote of his preaching was the denunciation of the abuses of the clergy, especially of simony. Religious orders were a special target because of their avarice and laxity; parents were even warned against putting their children into the novitiates of the mendicant orders because of their failings. Waldhauser disliked the abuse of relics: he attacked the passing off of a relic of St Barbara carried in procession in Prague as the saint's own, when its original, as he believed, could only be in Prussia. Denunciation of clerical abuse, a strong ethical stress, and radical social criticism were mingled with apocalyptic denunciations of the pseudo-prophets that deceived the people. Soon clerical opponents complained of him, and he was forced to go to answer them at Avignon, where he died in 1369. But before his career thus ended, he had established a circle of hearers among the Prague townspeople and students, and helped to set the tone for what was to follow.

His successor and convert, Jan Milič of Kroměříž, once a notary in the imperial chancellery, then a canon at the cathedral, had been led by Bible-reading and the preaching of Waldhauser to turn his back on his old life. After a year of solitude he became a poor preacher of repentance in 1364, based on the parish church of St Giles in Prague.[15] The style was reminiscent of the orthodox

---

13  Patschovsky, *Anfänge*, pp. 15–65, 78–80.
14  Leff, *Heresy* II, pp. 610–11; Seibt, 'Die Zeit', pp. 466–8.
15  P. De Vooght, *L'Hérésie de Jean Huss* (1960) (fundamental for theology of Hussites and opponents to 1415); see also his more detailed *Hussiana* (1960), pp. 7–21. Kaminsky, *Revolution*, pp. 5–55, repays study; J. M. Clifton-Everest, 'The eucharist in the Czech and German prayers of Milič z Kroměříže', *Bohemia* XXIII (1982), pp. 1–15; P. C. A. Morée, *Preaching in Fourteenth Century Bohemia. The Life and Ideas of Milicius de Chremsietr* (Slavkov, 1999).

wandering preachers of the twelfth century: we recognize the same fiery asceticism, the refusal of meat and wine, sleeping on the hard ground, long prayers and lack of rest, combined with a certain vein of eccentricity, demonstrated in his obsessive interest in the coming of Antichrist and his extraordinary denunciation of Charles IV, his journeyings to convince the pope of the evils confronting the Church, and finally his strong moral concern and his interest in the conversion of prostitutes, reminiscent of the activities of Henry the Monk. Success with his hearers gave him the opportunity to take over twenty-nine houses in the prostitutes' quarter of the city, which he renamed Jerusalem and turned into a house for reclaimed prostitutes together with a community of preachers living a common apostolic life. Success in preaching, the institution of a new kind of parish in Prague, fiery denunciation of the sins of the clergy on the lines of Waldhauser, perhaps the hint of the suspect beguine style of life being fostered in Jerusalem, led to his being compelled to answer accusations launched against him in 1373, and to go to Avignon to do so. After justifying himself, he died before he could return to Prague, and his enemies combined to destroy the experiment of Jerusalem.

De Vooght, with justice, calls him the father of the Czech reform,[16] for in him the movement took root in a native Bohemian. His preaching at St Giles, then at the Týn church in Prague, was in Latin and Czech – German he had to learn in order to reach another category of hearers. By the foundation of Jerusalem, however short-lived, he began the process of gathering a nucleus of the reform-minded around an institution within the capital, and, to judge by the twelve articles of complaint against him, such as the charge that he recommended daily communion to inmates at Jerusalem, and used the phrase *Sanctus est sacerdos*,[17] he pointed the way to future developments.

The third in the line of reformers in Prague was Matthias of Janov, the theoretician of the movement.[18] Milič had been no intellectual, but Matthias, his disciple, had studied in Paris (1375–81), to leave as a *magister artium*. In Prague he lived as a titular member of the cathedral chapter, supported by his patron Adalbertus Ranconis, then for the last five years of his life from 1389 with the aid of a benefice in Nova Ves outside Prague. With Matthias the reform movement gained its major written work, the *Regulae veteris et novi testamenti*, a set of twelve rules of conduct, four derived from the Old Testament and eight from the New, intended to defend the faithful from the insidious attacks of Antichrist, whose members Matthias saw as omnipresent in the body of the visible Church. The work was a loosely articulated set of treatises, designed to meet the emergency in which he believed the Church lay. By a return to the evangelical law found *par*

---

16   *Hérésie*: cf. pp. 14, 20–1.
17   Seibt, 'Die Zeit', p. 468, noting controversy on what he did in fact say; summary on sacramental reform, D. Holeton, ' "O felix Bohemia – O felix Constantia": the liturgical commemoration of Saint Jan Hus', *Hus*, ed. Seibt, pp. 385–97 at pp. 385–7.
18   Leff, *Heresy* II, pp. 612–19 is helpful; see De Vooght, *Hérésie*, pp. 21–35, Kaminsky, *Revolution*, pp. 14–23 (quotations but frail psychological interpretation).

*excellence* in Scripture and by the adoption of frequent communion, the Christian would be armed spiritually against the hypocrisy and formalism of existing Church life. Matthias continued the tradition of castigating the sins of the clergy and the religious orders while reinforcing the apocalyptic consciousness of his predecessors.

The work is overshadowed by the developments subsequent to the outbreak of the Great Schism, which seemed to be bringing the scourges of Antichrist within the Church to a climax. Attacks on clerical disorders had been common enough in Western Europe; in other countries, as in Bohemia, congregations who heard these attacks believed them, but did not act; then the shocking spectacle of two rival popes, at Rome and Avignon, excommunicating each other and their rival's supporters – with Christendom divided into two camps because of the papal schism, exacerbated by national disputes – gave a new urgency to consideration of the state of the Church. As the schism dragged on, its obvious damage to the Church greater than in earlier papal disputes of the kind, men became convinced of the need, not only to stop the conflict by restoring unity to the papacy, but also to see that abuses in the Church were ended. Circumstances focused attention on the popes as the source of troubles, for, in the need to get and keep supporters and money, both sides positively fostered abuse.

The outbreak and continuance of the schism is essential background for the understanding of the development of the Bohemian reform, for it stimulated the fight for change, and forced churchmen to think more about the nature of the Church and the papacy's place in it. It also weakened the authority of the papacy for dealing with doctrinal dissent, as the reform in Bohemia began to pass into heresy.

The situation was made more difficult after 1378 by the problems of Wenceslas as ruler.[19] His accession coincided with the outbreak of the schism; his character and circumstances meant that he could never be relied on to back the suppression of heresy (or what was labelled as heresy) in his kingdom. Charles had divided the Luxemburg inheritance among six relatives and, though Wenceslas had the lion's share in the kingdom of Bohemia, and was simultaneously king of the Romans, he was frequently troubled by the disputes and needs of the Luxemburg heirs, and unable either to use Bohemia as a firm support-point to develop his policies in the Empire or to rely on his powers in Germany, enfeebled by a long course of development outside his control, to aid him in Bohemia. In his kingdom he faced many troubles with his nobility, exacerbated by his relatives, especially by his brother Sigismund, and even had to endure imprisonment at the hands of his own subjects. He never secured coronation as emperor, and in 1400 he was deposed as king of the Romans and replaced by his rival Rupert of the Palatinate. All this, together with the complexities of the politics of the Great Schism, distracted him from Church affairs in Bohemia, leaving neither time nor inclination either to co-operate with reform or to help other churchmen put down the Bohemian movement. Wenceslas's problems had not fully unfolded at the time of Matthias's writing of his *Regulae*, but they are not irrelevant to it. Both the Church

19   Seibt, 'Die Zeit', pp. 473–94.

and Bohemia had entered on a time of troubles, and Matthias's work reflects this in the urgency of its writing.

A number of features were, admittedly, not wholly novel: his attack on the proliferation of regulations in canon law, and his yearning for a new simplicity, the implied appeal to an earlier, more primitive Church, the interest in distinguishing the true Christians from the members of Antichrist within the visible Church – all have parallels in a century of Church life confronted with problems calculated to stimulate theological thinking of this type. What, however, is most striking in Matthias of Janov is his insistence on the value of the eucharist. To it he devotes the great part of the first two and all of the fifth of a massive five-book work, and it inspires some of his most eloquent passages.[20] Just as the return to the Bible enables the faithful to find their way through the suffocating mass of regulations of human invention, so the practice of frequent, and preferably daily, communion enables them to avoid the distractions of needless formalism in worship, of false relics and miracles. It is this which sets off Matthias from other reformers of the time.[21]

The advocacy of frequent communion for the laity was the issue which attracted the hostile attention of authority. In 1388 and 1389 the decrees of the Prague synod against attacks on the veneration of images and against the receiving of communion more than once a month by the laity were aimed, among others, at Matthias's teaching. On both issues he recanted; but he was again in trouble in 1392, two years before his death. Such harassments hardly affected his influence, and, though disciplined by loss of his functions for six months, he suffered no major disabilities. His work was not heretical, but nevertheless, it enshrined in written form some of the essential views of Bohemian reformers. It was a preacher's exercise, and concerned with Christian practice rather than dogma; if the theology was correct, the whole trend was towards criticism of the actions of churchmen, and in the stress on the personal spiritual probity of the individual lay raw material for attacks on the Church and its leadership. The vehement attacks on abuses were now available in written form, and influential after Matthias's death, as well as in his lifetime.

Each of the major figures, Waldhauser, Milič and Matthias of Janov, had had to meet entrenched clerical opposition; none of them had allowed their course of action to be deflected by it. A proof of their influence with some of the laity lies in the case of Thomas of Štitné, the south Bohemian country gentleman who attended lectures at Prague university and issued a series of handbooks for family religion in the vernacular, quite orthodox and unoriginal, but inculcating the same wariness towards formalities and superstitions in popular religious life, the same caution about the calibre of life in the monastery, and the same stress on the Bible and frequent communion for the laity.[22]

20   Leff, *Heresy* II, p. 616.
21   As Kaminsky observes (*Revolution*, pp. 21–2).
22   M. Spinka, *John Hus* (1968), pp. 19–20 (by enthusiastic supporter of Hus, valuable for factual detail). On Thomas, contrast to English situation, *LG*, Intro., pp. 9–10.

The influence of the new ideas was reinforced by the foundation of the Bethlehem chapel in Prague, opened for sermons in the Czech vernacular in 1394 and seating 3,000 people.[23] Among the patrons was a German knight, Johannes von Mühleim, but it was predominantly a Czech enterprise: together with the burgomaster of the Old Town, three masters of the Bohemian nation at the university were to fill the preacher's benefice. Bethlehem was thus the successor to Milič's Jerusalem as a focal point for reform; the vernacular preaching for which it was founded helped to stress the Czech aspect of the movement.

Reform ideas were not confined to Bethlehem and the audiences of the popular preachers. They also made their way at university level[24] in the complaints of John of Dambach, a Dominican, pupil of Eckhart and teacher of theology in the early days of Prague, who contrasted the baleful effect of the interdict on Church life in Germany with Charles's relic-collecting at home – a theme characteristic of the dislike of Bohemian reformers of formalism at the expense of true pastoral care – and later in the theses of Henry Totting of Oyta and of his pupil Conrad of Soltau, who in 1377 expressed doubt about the administration of the sacraments by concubinaries. Henry of Bitterfeld, the German Dominican who held a chair at Prague, spoke for frequent communion, and expressed his unease about indulgences, helping to form a Prague tradition on which Hussites proper were to build.

Thus by the end of the century there was a breadth of base to the reform movement of the preachers in Prague, aided by the existence of the Bethlehem chapel and the popular support it brought, and some dissemination of innovating ideas in the university. Yet no parallel success was being achieved in the prime aim of the movement, the reform of the body of clergy in Bohemia.[25]

The wealth of the Bohemian Church fostered abuse. Superfluity in endowments attracted unworthy candidates for ordination, and inspired an unhealthy interest in Church goods on the part of the laity. It would also seem that there were simply too many clergy: Tomek calculated that in Prague towards the end of the century, a city of 35,000 to 40,000, there were 1,200 clergy, 200 of them at the cathedral.[26] There was not work enough for them to do, and a contemporary treatise complains of the plight of clergy who did not know how to live from the daily mass-stipend of a Prague *groschen*. So, added to the dangers of overendowment, Bohemia was saddled with a clerical proletariat, a source of dissension within the clerical body and of scandal to the laity. Surviving aristocratic influence had something to do with this: John IV of Dražice, bishop of Prague, the founder of Roudnice, struggled against the abuse of the *mercenarii*, priests paid only a portion of their stipend by aristocratic patrons who confiscated the remainder to their own use. Both the first archbishop of Prague, Ernest of Pardubice, John's successor and then, after him, Archbishop John Očko of

23  Spinka, *Hus*, pp. 47–51; Seibt, 'Die Zeit', p. 501; see his whole summary on Hus (pp. 500–6).
24  Seibt, 'Die Zeit', pp. 462–5.
25  Ibid., pp. 436–44; Weltsch, *Jenstein*.
26  Cited by Seibt, 'Die Zeit', p. 439; see De Vooght, *Hérésie*, pp. 99–101.

Vlašim were able to carry out administrative reforms in co-operation with the lay ruler; neither was able to make a substantial change in the situation. Between Avignonese centralism and the control of the royal power, the ecclesiastical head of the Bohemian Church had little room for manoeuvre and, although Charles IV was sympathetic to reform, he was not prepared to push it on to the detriment of a system of royal patronage that benefited his bureaucracy rather than Church interests.

Under Wenceslas hopes diminished. His archbishop, John of Jenstein, had a strong personal piety and an interest in reform, but lacked political finesse; under his regime friendly relations with the ruler broke down in the pressure of schism politics, as John remained firm on the Roman side, while Wenceslas veered, for his own ends, towards Avignonese interest. The archiepiscopate was disturbed by disputes, with Wenceslas in 1393 claiming what a modern writer has described as a return to the old proprietary system.[27] Personal conflict culminated in the same year in the murder of John of Pomuk, the archbishop's official; finally, John resigned. It was the tragedy of his generation that John of Jenstein could not make his way through these conflicts, for he had some contact with Matthias of Janov, wrote treatises himself, and was in touch with devotional currents of the time.[28] In the event, perhaps not wholly willingly, by supporting the attack on Matthias's advocacy of frequent lay communion, he ranged himself with the opposition and his own attempt at administrative reform, in the visitation of Prague in 1379–80, was checked by legal action and not resumed. Jenstein claimed that it was the first such major visitation, and it revealed that in no fewer than sixteen out of thirty-nine churches the incumbents gave cause for scandal.[29] After Jenstein, neither of his successors, his nephew Olbram ze Škworce (1396–1402) and Zbyněk Zajíc of Hasenburg (1402–11), showed themselves equal to the demands of their position.

Abuse thus continued, intensified by such scandalous arrangements as that arrived at between Wenceslas and the Roman pope, Boniface IX, in 1393 whereby a jubilee indulgence was granted to pilgrims visiting four churches in Prague as if they had visited Rome, and a half of their offerings at the Church of St Peter on Vyšehrad were granted to the king.[30] The result of the failure to reform was an impatience in some sections of the population with churchmen, and a new stridency among the reformers. Earlier preachers stressed individual piety and the Second Coming; reform was to come through spiritual renewal by holy men. Matthias lamented the schism, but did not propose constitutional mechanisms to end it, as members of the conciliar movement did.[31] Now that was beginning to change; the element of popular demonstration against ecclesiastical failings intensified; the use of force to institute necessary reform was becoming more prominent.

27    Weltsch, *Jenstein*, p. 72; see his ch. 2 generally (pp. 40–78).
28    Ibid., pp. 154–79.
29    Ibid., p. 162.
30    Ibid., p. 71.
31    I am indebted to Professor Seibt for discussion on this point.

## The Influence of Wyclif

A further novel factor was introduced by the appearance of Wyclifite ideas at the Charles University in Prague. Although his theology was not wholly unknown in early days – for Nicholas Biceps, a Prague professor, was arguing against Wyclif's eucharistic beliefs while Wyclif was still alive,[32] it was the philosophical works which first attracted attention. Marginal comments in manuscripts of Wyclif's philosophical works, which by a coincidence were copied by the young Hus, helping to earn his keep as a student, convey the atmosphere in which this interest in Wyclifite philosophy sprang up. One warns the reader that the treatise *De ideis* should not be recommended to *non intelligentibus*; another sounds a note of uneasy admiration: 'O Wycleff, Wycleff, more than one head you have turned.'[33] These two comments show members of the university reacting in a similar manner to the Oxford scholars who first heard Wyclif's ultrarealist philosophy. It was difficult, sometimes alarming, and it could bowl men over with its bold propositions.

Interest in the philosphical treatises soon led on to an interest in the theological; and in stages, aided by the visits of Bohemian scholars to England, Wyclif's more dangerous works arrived in Bohemia. Two of these scholars, bachelors of the university, seem to have established direct contact with English Lollards and to have stayed at Latimer's manor at Braybrooke. Together with the treatises, they took back with them a fragment of Wyclif's tomb. Thereafter, until Lollardy was forced irretrievably underground, the two movements in England and Bohemia remained in contact.[34]

Wyclif brought complications.[35] On the one hand, his works gave a much stronger intellectual framework to the ideas of reform that had long circulated in Bohemia, and, for those who accepted Wyclif's inspiration, it imparted a new aggressiveness to the drive for reform. At the university the entry of his thought ended the phase of disparate, even somewhat opportunistic, reform thinking, which coexisted in the last three decades of the century with the predominantly moral revivalist preaching associated with Waldhauser, Milič, Matthias of Janov and the priests at the Bethlehem chapel. On the other hand, it repelled some intellectuals who had been sympathetic to reform, and gave a new handle to its opponents inside Bohemia, who were able to tar reformers with Wyclif's heresy.

In contrast to England, local circumstances in Bohemia provided an additional reason for the popularity of Wyclif's writings. It lay in the hostility, mingled with envy, of the Czech masters for the Germans at the university of Prague. One of

---

32   D. Trapp, 'Clm 27034: unchristened nominalism and Wycliffite realism at Prague in 1381', *RTAM* XXIV (1957), pp. 320–60; background in F. Šmahel, '"Doctor evangelicus super omnes evangelistas": Wyclif's fortune in Hussite Bohemia', *BIHR* XLIII (1970), pp. 16–34 (succinct and illuminating). See also A. Hudson, 'Accessus ad auctorem'.

33   Šmahel, 'Doctor evangelicus', pp. 18–19 and 19, n. 2; incorrect attribution by Spinka (*Hus*, p. 38).

34   Šmahel, 'Doctor evangelicus', pp. 20, 25, for scholars' visits.

35   Seibt, 'Die Zeit', pp. 501–2; intellectual landscape in Šmahel, 'Doctor evangelicus'.

these manuscripts of Wyclif has in the margin the gloss, in another hand: 'Haha, Germans, haha, out, out.'[36] The manuscript is of a philosophical work: the comment expresses the pleasure of a Czech at finding a philosophical weapon against the prevailing nominalism of the German masters. Ultrarealism could bloom in Prague because it seemed to be an answer to the Ockhamist views of, probably, a majority of the teachers in the theological faculty, who hailed from German-speaking lands or sprang from the Germans within Bohemia.

In the first years of the university Czech students had been few in number. By Charles IV's foundation the university was divided, on the Parisian model, into four nations, described according to the points of the compass, as Bohemian, Polish (which in practice often meant German), Saxon, Bavarian.[37] At the outset the Czechs (who would be only a part of the Bohemian 'nation') formed an insignificant proportion. In time, internecine university disputes and the founding of new universities in German-speaking lands led to a fall in the proportions of Germans to Czechs overall. In the arts faculty during the 1380s 25 per cent of all graduates came from the Bohemian nation; by about 1400 the proportion had risen to 36 per cent. Where the Bohemian nation in early years had provided some 10 per cent of the deans in the faculty – an elective office – they were providing almost 40 per cent by the years 1391 to 1408. In theology their masters had not earlier been leading lights. As a body, they tended to adhere to a somewhat conservative Augustinian realist tradition, and to have some feelings of inferiority: to such Wyclif's ultrarealism, with its bold answers to Ockhamism, would appeal as a means of exalting their own intellectual position *vis-à-vis* the Germans. By reaction against this, Germans tended to be the initiators in attacks on the orthodoxy of Wyclif and those who defended him – though not exclusively, for there were cross-currents, not all Germans being nominalists, and some Czechs of a moderate realist position opposing the ultrarealism of the Wyclifites. Nevertheless, the Czech-German division added a new dimension to the study of Wyclif and controversy about him.

## Jan Hus

Just as Wyclif's teaching had begun seriously to affect the university, Jan Hus was appointed rector of the Bethlehem chapel. The new strands now discernible in the Bohemian reform movement all met in him: Wyclif, the stress on a Czech reform, the new urgency against abuse. His academic training brought him to Wyclif: he was a member, though not the most prominent, of the new radical generation of Czech masters to whom Wyclif initially appealed.[38] Other Czech

36   Cited by Šmahel, p. 20.
37   For these and following details, see Seibt, 'Die Zeit', pp. 449–57; also Bittner, *Deutsche und Tschechen*, pp. 102–6; on the university with bibliography, see Betts, *Essays*, pp. 13–28.
38   Early university career in Spinka, *Hus*, pp. 24–53; early theological work in De Vooght, *Hérésie*, pp. 54–64; note contrast of latter's judgement (*CV*VIII (1965), p. 236) and that of F. M. Bartoš (*CV*IX (1966), pp. 176–7); on his audience, F. Šmahel, 'Literacy and heresy in Hussite Bohemia', *BHL*, pp. 237–54 at p. 245; biblio., *Jan Hus*, ed. Seibt, pp. 419–500.

masters made the pace, and were deeper thinkers. Hus, in this resembling the older tradition of the fourteenth-century reformers, was first and foremost a preacher, agitator and spiritual writer. Some time before his ordination as priest in 1400, he underwent conversion and ceased to be, as he later confessed, a conventional clerical careerist.[39] He found himself at the Bethlehem chapel. Flajšhans, the editor of his sermons, estimates that he preached some 3,000 sermons during the twelve years of his service at Bethlehem, normally twice on every Sunday and saint's day, to overflowing congregations. Under him the Bethlehem chapel became the centre of the popular movement, as it had not been under his two predecessors, who had been distracted by other duties. By combining his preaching at the chapel with his position at the university he brought together the popular reform movement in the capital and the critical university masters.[40] The situation can be vividly reconstructed, for we have texts of his sermons, even down to notes for his own delivery, showing immediate emotional rapport with his audience:[41] 'and then, as the audience responds, speak against idolatry'; 'this is the judgement of the letter. And then amplify if the attitude of the people justifies it.'

The chapel was a large, plain building, a preaching-church somewhat in the style of the churches of the Franciscans. On the walls were pairs of pictures: the pope on horseback and in pomp, contrasted with Christ in poverty, carrying his cross; Constantine making his donation to the pope, contrasted with Christ, wearing a crown of thorns, before Pilate.[42] Sermons corresponded to the pictures – orthodox, but fiercely attacking the abuses of the modern Church, and repeating the contrast with the poverty and simplicity of the primitive Church. Hus never fell into the Donatist view, impugning the validity of the sacraments administered by the unworthy priest,[43] but, a deeply emotional man and a committed reformer, he was touched to the heart by the abuses that he saw around him, and he communicated this indignation to his congregation.[44] The effect of his preaching was enhanced by his own good life and obvious lack of personal ambition – he never wished for higher office than that of rector of Bethlehem, and his sermons and letters have running through them a thread of pastoral concern for all ranks of Prague society.[45]

39  Spinka, *Hus*, pp. 28, 43–6.
40  Ibid., p. 51; F. Seibt, 'Die hussitische Revolution', *Hussitenstudien*, pp. 79–96 (reflections of 1963, still helpful) at p. 81; Id., 'Jan Hus-Zwischen Zeiten, Völkern, Konfessionen', *Hus*, ed. Seibt, pp. 11–26 (balanced perspective and historiography).
41  Kaminsky, *Revolution*, p. 40, n. 124.
42  Spinka, *Hus*, pp. 48–9; T. A. Fudge, *The Magnificent Ride* (1998) (history with a Taborite interpn.; esp. helpful on Hussite propaganda, ch. 4; good biblio.), pp. 228–9, 232.
43  Leff, *Heresy* II, pp. 659–62; also his 'Wyclif and Hus: a doctrinal comparison', *BJRL* LX (1968), pp. 387–410.
44  See De Vooght's comment (*Hérésie*, pp. 71–4); also Kaminsky, *Revolution*, p. 40, and comment on De Vooght (Ibid., pp. 35–7).
45  *The Letters of John Hus*, tr. M. Spinka (1972), and *John Hus at the Council of Constance* (1965), Spinka's tr. of Peter of Mladoňovice's account of Hus's trial, with intro. (letters of Hus, pp. 237–98); for background, P. Brock, *The Political and Social Doctrines of the Unity of Czech Brethren* (1957), pp. 11–34; Weltsch, *Jenstein*, pp. 130–40.

The congregations at the Bethlehem chapel were Czech-speaking. Hus did not continue the practice of the earlier reformers, of speaking in both the Czech and the German vernacular; he spoke only Czech. He had been born among free peasants in an area of rich German settlement in southern Bohemia, and was conscious of the national and linguistic differences, so apparent in a nationally mixed area. He believed that the Czechs should be first in the offices of the kingdom of Bohemia, 'as are the French in the kingdom of France and the Germans in their own lands'. With the elements of Czech nationalism came also a consciousness of their special religious responsibility. He derived Bohemia from the Slav *Bôh* ('God'), called the kingdom *christianissimum*, and wrote of the *verny Chechy*, the faithful Czechs.[46] At Bethlehem he extended the range of his congregation, appealing to some artisans as well as the Czech-speaking middle class. A prominent part was played by Czech hymns. But he did not reach the German-speaking middle class of the capital, and his tenure of the rectorate of Bethlehem tended to aid the polarization, gradually taking place in the early fifteenth century, between Czech reformers and German opposition.

## The Attack on Wyclifites

This polarization was accelerated by the development of an attack on supporters of Wyclif by German masters, which began in 1403 with an appeal for action against Wyclif's works to the Prague diocesan authorities by Elias Hübner,[47] a Silesian Dominican from the university, continued with an attack on the Czech Wyclifite Stanislav of Znojmo's writing by John Štěkna, an *émigré* from Prague, and culminated in 1408 with an appeal to the curia by Ludolf Meistermann, a Saxon also from the university. Interest in Wyclif's philosophy often coexisted with membership of the reform movement, and attacks on him tended to be seen by reformers as covert attempts to stifle their movement. The fact that Germans were responsible for these attacks drew the Czechs together in defence, not necessarily of the substance of Wyclif's teaching, but of the right to read and teach him, whether or not they all as individuals shared Wyclif's views. In fact some certainly did not, and there was a spread of views from very moderate teachers who thought Wyclif could be used, to Stephen Pálec and to Stanislav of Znojmo, who actually taught the Wyclifite eucharistic doctrine of remanentism, thus denying transubstantiation, in his *De corpore Christi*. Both of these produced works so influenced by Wyclif that the Wyclif Society in the nineteenth century

---

46   On Hussitism and nationalism, subtle chapter in Seibt, *Hussitica*, pp. 58–124; on Hus, see pp. 87–9, 100. For Hus's stress on preaching rather than liturgy at Bethlehem, see E. Werner, 'Wort und Sakrament im Identitätsbewusstsein des tschechischen Frühreformators Jan Hus (um 1370–1415)', *Sitzungsberichte der Akademie der Wissenschaften der DDR, Gesellschaftswissenschaften* (1989), no. 13, pp. 3–26. His biography, *Jan Hus*, investigates Hus's thought and emotions; S. Bohemia and friends, M. Svatoš, 'Hussens Freunde', *Hus*, ed. Seibt, pp. 67–72. See also E. Werner, 'Das Altarsakrament in Religions-verständnis von Jan Hus', *Husitství*, ed. Pánek *et al.*, pp. 317–28.

47   For doctrinal disputes, De Vooght, *Hérésie*, pp. 75–118; Spinka, *Hus*, pp. 47–85.

thought that they were Wyclif's own.[48] Jerome of Prague was a passionate supporter who brought back from Oxford copies of Wyclif's *Dialogus* and *Trialogus* and engaged in an international agitation against abuses of the Church. But controversy should not be seen solely and crudely in terms of battle between German nominalists and Czech realists and there were Czechs such as Andrew of Brod, who did not defend the teaching of Wyclif in his last phase, and disliked the idea of remanentism spreading in Bohemia.[49]

The pro-Wyclif Czech party were lucky in that the archiepiscopate was then held by Zbyněk, a former soldier of high family, ill-equipped theologically yet sympathetic to reform, who was lenient to the Wyclifites, and took till 1408 to make up his mind that firm action against the spread of Wyclif's views was necessary. The contrast to Courtenay's resolution against Lollardy is obvious.[50] Zbyněk's benevolence delayed condemnation, for though the German masters were strong enough to secure a university decision against Wyclif, they needed the archbishop's backing to bring the Wyclifites down, and the prolonged debate on the issue, mediated to the populace by Czech students at the university, popularized radical tenets of Wyclif (or alleged tenets) in a way that nothing else could have done.

Hübner's original list of excerpts was an old one – the forty-five items included twenty-four from the English condemnation made at the Blackfriars Council of 1382, and the remaining twenty-one probably came from an earlier condemnation[51] – and he was attempting to argue that Wyclif had already been officially condemned, and that such condemnations should automatically be given effect in Bohemia. At the time this did not make much of an impression; but the excerpts were disseminated over the years in a way that Hübner and his colleagues never expected. They were cited out of their contexts, in short and pungent sentences that could not have been better adapted to act as the slogans of a popular movement.[52] They solved the problem of conveying ideas of Wyclif from the difficult setting of the master's prolix Latin treatises.

Such sentences as article 10 ('It is contrary to Scripture that churchmen should have possessions'), article 16 ('Temporal lords can at will take away temporal goods from the Church and possessioners who habitually offend') or article 14 ('Any deacon or priest can preach the word of God without the authority of the apostolic see and the Catholic bishop') had an immediate and subversive

---

48   On varying influence of Wyclif, De Vooght, *Hérésie*, pp. 85–92; on the sincerity of Hus's rejection of remanentism, Ibid., pp. 60–3, 96–7, 365–6, 473–4; *Hussiana*, pp. 263–91.

49   Kaminsky, *Revolution*, pp. 38, 113, n. 54; Spinka, *Hus*, p. 71; on Jerome of Prague, see Walsh, 'Wyclif's legacy', p. 406; nominalist-realist division, p. 405; F. Šmahel, 'Leben und Werk des Magisters Hieronymus von Prag', *Historica* XIII (1966), pp. 81–111; A. Strnad, 'Die Zeugen im Wiener Prozess gegen Hieronymus von Prag', *Husitství*, ed. Pánek *et al.*, pp. 331–67. Condemnation in Vienna was a stage on the way to his burning at Constance.

50   Above, pp. 281–2.

51   Kaminsky, *Revolution*, p. 24, n. 66.

52   Šmahel, 'Doctor evangelicus', p. 22, see also pp. 24–6. Text of 45 articles, M. Spinka, *John Hus' Concept of the Church* (1966) (useful summary, pro-Hus in tone), pp. 397–400; analysis in De Vooght, *Hérésie*, pp. 80–3.

significance. In effect, the excerpts thus collected were such as to void the hierarchical and sacramental system of the Church, open the way to a reduction to apostolic poverty, and put her in the hands of the royal power and the temporal lords. Powerful heresies were represented: article 4, denying sacramental validity to the acts of a bishop or priest in mortal sin, was pure Donatism; article 5 denied Christ's institution of the mass; article 37 said that the Roman Church was a synagogue of Satan. Two excerpts, articles 7 and 11, by undermining both absolution and excommunication, much weakened the position of priesthood and episcopate. Bandied to and fro, the articles containing such sentiments passed out of university circles.

Meanwhile, in the university Wyclif remained a centre of debate. The questions would always arise: How much of Wyclif was to be assimilated? Was it to be the philosophy only? The reforming sentiments and the political ideas? The remanentism and the doctrine of the Church? The Czechs at the university continued to maintain a common front despite their individual differences. When Zbyněk started to put real pressure on them in 1408, they responded by agreeing as a body to forbid any defence of the forty-five articles 'in their heretical, erroneous and objectionable sense',[53] an action which preserved by implication a right to read Wyclif, but explicitly condemned only these specific articles, leaving open the question of their rightful attribution to Wyclif.

Yet the writing was on the wall when, ten days earlier, the master Matthew of Knín was tried in the archbishop's court and subsequently had to abjure remanentism, and there is little doubt that a full uprooting of Wyclif in Bohemia would still have been possible if Zbyněk had been able to follow up his first actions of the spring of 1408. The curia had backed Meistermann when he made his appeal: this turned the affair into an issue of authority, and made up the archbishop's mind for him. Gone were the days of the synodal decrees against abuse and the invitations to Hus to preach;[54] pressure from abroad took Stanislav of Znojmo and Páleč away from Bohemia, to abandon Wyclif and become enemies of the movement they had once supported.[55] Implicated as they were in late Wyclifism, the Czech masters, as these events show, could yet have been deflected from defence of Wyclif, and popular dissemination of heresy could have been checked if Zbyněk had been able to keep up his counteraction.

What intervened was politics and the interests of Wenceslas in an emotional cause, which made it possible to build a party round the defence of reform, Jan Hus and the radical tenets of Wyclif, and created a new situation, without parallel in the history of Lollardy in England.

53   Tr. Spinka, *Hus*, p. 83.
54   On Zbyněk's early favour to reformers and his change of mind, see Spinka, *Hus*, pp. 66–7, 69–71, 79, 83–7; and on his attitude to authority, De Vooght, *Hérésie*, pp. 95–6, 101; see below, p. 323.
55   Events outlined in De Vooght, *Hérésie*, pp. 105–6; for subsequent views, see below, pp. 326–7, 329, 333, 338.

# Politics and Hussitism, 1409–1419

### The Decree of Kutná Hora

Schism politics interrupted Zbyněk's proceedings, and finally brought the effect-iveness of his archiepiscopate to an end. Tired of the contest between the rival popes, a group of cardinals renounced allegiance to their masters, and proposed the election of a compromise candidate who should rally churchmen of both sides to end the schism. But their candidate, the conciliar pope Alexander v, was unable to do this, and so the move merely created three popes instead of two.

At the time, however, the conciliar proposal drew Wenceslas's favour. An agile, wavering politician,[1] he saw a chance to regain the office of king of the Romans he had lost in 1400, and to confront his rival, Rupert of the Palatinate, by shifting from the Roman to the conciliar interest, demanding support for his claim against Rupert as his price for doing so. This affected the Wyclif case, for it created a rupture with Zbyněk, who in his soldierly fashion declined to break his oath to the Roman pope,[2] and suddenly made the Czech element in the Bohe-mian nation at the university seem a valuable source of support. To make his move to the council's party, Wenceslas needed the university on his side, and found that the German-dominated nations, Bavaria, Saxony, Poland, at the Charles University, obedient to Zbyněk and mindful of the benefices they might one day wish to have in German-speaking lands of the Roman obedience, declined to change allegiance, while the Czechs generally, hoping for conciliar support for their reform and less interested in the lands following Rome outside Bohemia, were ready to follow their king's plan. To get the university's vote, despite the hostile nations, Wenceslas simply changed the voting system of the nations by the decree of Kutná Hora (Kuttenberg) on 18 January 1409, which henceforth allowed the Bohemian nation three votes instead of one, and reduced

---

1  Characterization, with reassessment, in Seibt, 'Die Zeit', p. 477.
2  The oath is fundamental for Zbyněk's opposition to Wenceslas's decision for the conciliar party in January 1409; it is a good hypothesis that it also mattered in Zbyněk's turn against the reformers in 1408. See above, pp. 321–2.

the three foreign nations to one vote overall.[3] The Czechs were the majority in the Bohemian nation by that time, so Wenceslas got the change of allegiance he wanted. Kutná Hora and the secession of foreign masters and students to the number of seven or eight hundred, which followed their failure to reverse Wenceslas's decision, while it incidentally spread opposition to reform and to Wyclifism more widely in foreign universities, turned the Charles University into a regional university of a new pattern, and altered the balance of power broadly to the advantage of the reform party. Though not yet overall victors, the reformers had less opposition to conquer than before, since they no longer had to reckon with a concentration of opposition in the foreign nations. In the arts faculty Wyclif supporters now appeared to have a majority; in theology the situation was more complicated, since the philosophical ground of Wyclif's thinking was resisted by some Czech masters of the older tradition;[4] in any case the Bohemian nation included still the indigenous German masters, inclined against the reform party. Yet ground had been gained.

Most important was the realignment of political forces accompanying Kutná Hora. It had been won, in part, by skilful agitation under the direction of the lawyer John Jesenic[5] and the 'political intellectual' Jerome of Prague, the strange, stormy figure of the movement, a layman who was a theological teacher and a heavily committed realist.[6] Under their direction a link was forged between the ideas of the reform and the superior rights of the indigenous inhabitants of the kingdom. The association of this incipient feeling with Wyclif and reform was the distinctive feature of the Bohemian situation, which continued, despite vicissitudes, to hold and to grow in strength till older authorities broke down before it. The need to push Kutná Hora through helped the Bohemian reformers to become a political as well as an ecclesiastical party, allying with forces in the capital, and devising a propaganda that would appeal to native leaders. John Jesenic helped by creating a structure of theory, in part derived from Wyclif, justifying the supreme rights of the royal power in Bohemia in his work, the *Defensio mandatii*, thus influencing the king when he was uncertain whether to hold to his decision.[7] The notion of the Bohemian nation, chosen of God, faithful to its ideals, was launched by the Kutná Hora agitation.

In immediate terms, there was now a working alliance between king and reformers sufficient to prevent any legal action against the advocates of Wyclif, initiated abroad, from taking effect. The king hardly cared seriously one way or another about the cause of reform, but he was interested in scotching any foreign

3   Seibt, 'Die Zeit', pp. 490–1; Kaminsky, *Revolution*, pp. 56–75 (Kutná Hora and sequel, with insight into political motives); F. Seibt, 'Johannes Hus und der Abzug der deutschen Studenten aus Prag 1409', *AKG* xxxix (1957), pp. 63–80; analysis of decree in Seibt, *Hussitica*, pp. 65–7; *Hussitenstudien*, pp. 1–15.
4   See case of Blasius Vlk (Spinka, *Hus*, pp. 92–3).
5   Kaminsky, *Revolution*, illuminates this.
6   Betts, *Essays*, pp. 195–235; investigation of nationalism in Seibt, *Hussitica*, pp. 77–86; note summary on p. 86. See F. Šmahel, 'The idea of the "nation" in Hussite Bohemia', *Historica* xvi (1969), pp. 143–247; xvii (1969), pp. 93–197; F. Šmahel, 'Jan Hus – heretic or patriot', *History Today* xx (1990), pp. 27–33.
7   Kaminsky, *Revolution*, pp. 67–70. Leff, *Heresy* ii, pp. 628–9, on Kutná Hora, requires amplification.

moves on doctrine that might disturb the peace of his kingdom, and he was inclined for the moment to see Zbyněk as the source of these disturbances. He and his magnates found useful the pleas made for apostolic poverty and against ecclesiastical authority, but this was about as far as his positive interest in the reform cause went; nevertheless, uncertain as he was as a long-term Hussite ally, his attitude, coupled with the development of popular feeling, was quite sufficient to undermine Zbyněk's continued action against Wyclif supporters.

The archbishop called in Wyclif's works, excommunicated those who had held them, and proclaimed an interdict, without fundamentally altering the situation.[8] When he tried to bring the affair to a summary end by burning Wyclif's works in 1410, he encountered a popular agitation of university students and Prague citizens, who disrupted services, threatened priests, and invented a sarcastic ditty about the burning and Zbyněk's lack of theology. Popular opinion was influenced both ways, and the old theological battle over Wyclif came into the streets, with the opposition to Wyclif also taking to the pulpits, labelling the reform party Wyclifite,[9] and performing its parody of a reformer's mass. On the one hand, a party blocking the heresy case against Wyclif came into existence, blending learned university judgement, with its plea for free study of Wyclif and its varying mixtures of Wyclifite teaching and native reform, with political forces interested in Bohemian independence and royal power, supported at a much more uncivilized level by street agitation; on the other side were opponents, Czech and German, also capable of mounting popular agitation, with some strength in the capital but rather stronger in the provinces.

Hostility to his interdict finally forced Zbyněk out of office in July 1410; not long afterwards he died in exile. He was the last archbishop prepared to use all the canonical machinery to put down Wyclif's supporters. The king's physician, Albík of Uničov, his immediate successor, showed no eagerness in pursuit; Conrad of Vechta, archbishop from 1413, was equivocal in his attitude. In practice, a kind of Gallicanism,[10] facilitated by Wenceslas's policies, the enfeeblement of central authority in the Church, and Hussite pleas for the right of the kingdom to deal with its own affairs, was shielding Bohemia from the traditional pursuit of heresy. The tricky task of the pro-Wyclif party was to keep the king to this Gallican line.

### Jan Hus and Nicholas of Dresden

In the aftermath of the Kutná Hora affair Hus rose to the position which he held until his death as the principal symbolic figure at the head of the movement.[11] He

---

8   Events to death of Zbyněk, Spinka, *Hus*, pp. 100–20, 122–9; De Vooght, *Hérésie*, pp. 115–23, 128–43, 148–51; motives, Kaminsky, *Revolution*, pp. 70–5.

9   Seibt, *Hussitica*, pp. 10–14. *Hussitae* was first used at time of Council of Constance (Ibid., p. 11, n. 23). It was a term of abuse.

10   See Kaminsky, *Revolution*, p. 74; for Conrad, F. Seibt, 'Konrad von Vechta', *Hussitenstudien*, pp. 241–52.

11   Perspective by Seibt, 'Die Zeit', pp. 500–6. See text of complaints against him by Prague clergy in F. Palacký, *Documenta J. Hus vitam illustrantia* (1869), pp. 153–5; interesting comment in Leff, *Heresy* II, p. 627.

had not at first been a leader, but he had already become a target of the legal action against Wyclif's supporters; he was notorious to the conservatives because of the sharpness of his attacks on clerical abuse and, though his fame was most due to his popular oratory, he rose in intellectual pro-Wyclif circles as Páleč and Stanislav of Znojmo defected, and the departure of the foreign Germans gave chances for Czech scholars. In 1409 he was elected rector of the university. In 1410 he gained greater prominence through protesting against Zbyněk's burning of the books.

He was still not the most radical of the reform theologians; part of the case against him was that he provided a shield for preachers and agitators more clearly heretical than he was. This radical wing had certainly been in existence for some years; but its presence was felt more deeply because of the events of 1412.[12] In May an agent of John XXIII began to preach in Prague the crusade against Ladislas of Naples, and to offer indulgences to those who took the cross. The crusade was a mere instrument of schism politics, and the use of indulgences unusually cynical. The king, however, was in favour of the crusade and gained some of the proceeds. Hus's denunciation of the practices employed in the indulgences trade offended him and broke the alliance with the royal power.

The year 1412, however, both coincided with the emergence of more Waldensian-type popular heresy among the reforming party and gave new chances for radicalism. Typical of the popular demonstrations was the procession led by Voksa of Valdštejn, in which a student, dressed as a prostitute with bare breasts hung with a mock papal bull, mimicked the hawking of indulgences. Chests intended for indulgence money were smeared with mud; at the cathedral the treasure chest received a pronouncement addressed sardonically to the disciples of the evil demon Asmodeus, Belial and Mammon. Jerome of Prague found himself in his element, composing, if we may believe his enemies, popular Czech songs, slapping a Franciscan who disagreed with him, intervening in a quarrel between an exhibitor of relics at St Mary of the Snows and a Hussite bystander, and snatching a sword to put friars to flight.[13] In July preachers of the indulgences were interrupted by young men in their sermons at the cathedral, Týn and St James's churches. The royal wrath was aroused by the indulgence agitation, and the magistrates ordered three offenders to be beheaded. Crowds followed their corpses to the Bethlehem chapel, and clothes were dipped in their blood. The Hussite movement had gained its first martyrs.

Increasing violence on the Hussite side touched off counter violence from the conservatives. In the cathedral, priests beat protesters in the sanctuary; a crowd from neighbouring parishes assembled to storm the Bethlehem chapel; Páleč

---

12    Events described in Spinka, *Hus*, pp. 130–64, and theology of Hus and opponents in De Vooght, *Hérésie*, pp. 183–204; *Hussiana*, pp. 303–62; Walsh, 'Wyclif's legacy', pp. 400–1, notes widespread conviction inside and outside Bohemia, including the reformer Dietrich of Niem, that the crucial influence behind the movement was Wyclif.

13    Betts, *Essays*, pp. 216–18; Kaminsky, *Revolution*, pp. 88–9, esp. n. 129.

preached in Czech at the St Gall church, denouncing Wyclif as the greatest and most astute of heretics.[14]

Naturally, at a time of bitter feelings, the pressures of academic politics and of mass audiences gave prominence to the most exaggerated opinions among the debaters. Znojmo and Páleč evolved the notion of the *ecclesiasticum et misticum compositum*, with the pope its head and the cardinals its body, which appeared to shrink the Church to pope and cardinals only. The phrase used for the description of Scripture, a *res inanimata*, till it was vivified by the decisions of the Church, so defined, particularly distressed Hus. Hussite views on the Church were a response, in part, to an extremist doctrine of their opponents. Both sides reacted to each other.

Late in 1411 or early in 1412 the Hussite radicals were reinforced by the arrival in Prague of a party of Germans from Dresden, former teachers who had mingled a radical theology with the normal grammar and the arts; the later confession of a pupil reveals that in their Dresden school they had taught the rejection of oaths, the right of all priests to preach freely without further authorization, the disendowment of the Church, the rejection of obedience to the Roman hierarchy and of the papal headship, and the inclusion of all necessary belief within the Bible.[15] It sounds Waldensian, and it remains controversial whether the beliefs of this group represent an autonomous outgrowth of Waldensianism in an intellectual environment, or merely a case of German Wyclifism, possibly formed initially among students at Prague who left after Kutná Hora.

Installed in Prague, the Dresden group were a radical influence. Most important was the master Nicholas of Dresden, who composed the *Tabule veteris et novi coloris* some time before October 1412. They can most naturally be associated with the phase of street agitation in the time of the indulgences crisis, for their natural setting was plainly processional placards, conveying in a striking visual form the contrast between the Churches of the popes and of the apostles. Collections of authorities confront each other: on one side, the tables of the Old Colour, of the early Church; on the other, the tables of the New Colour, being texts and authorities which demonstrated the realities of the life of the papal Church as interpreted by Nicholas, forming a vivid and uninhibited attack on the whole apparatus of the law, hierarchy and endowment.

On the Prague streets the identification would have been plainer. A late Czech version of the *Tabule* illustrates the texts with pictures, and there is a high probability that the original was intended to be learned apparatus for a sequence of propaganda paintings, stretching from an early pattern of twos, contrasting Christ bearing his cross with the pope riding on a horse,[16] or Christ washing the feet of the disciples with the pope having his feet washed in the curia,[17] to the climax in which the Antichrist of Revelation is depicted in papal regalia

14   De Vooght, *Hérésie*, p. 219.
15   H. Kaminsky, 'Nicholas of Dresden and the Dresden School in Hussite Prague', *Master Nicholas of Dresden: The Old Color and the New*, ed. H. Kaminsky *et al.* (*TAPS*, n.s. LV, i) (1965), pp. 5–28, esp. pp. 6–7.
16   Table I (Ibid., p. 38); Kaminsky, *Revolution*, pp. 40–9; Fudge, *Ride*, pp. 226–8.
17   Kaminsky, *Master Nicholas*, table 8 (pp. 60–1).

surrounded by whores.[18] In Nicholas, we can see, the Hussite movement was passing from the theme of reform, however radical, within the existing framework of the Church, to an explicit rejection of it as the work of Antichrist.

Prague at this time gave special opportunities for men with a talent for street agitation. Before the end of the century it had attained the highest population figure for any city in central Europe.[19] Moreover, in the New Town of Charles IV there was an unusual concentration of manual workers: it was these men who formed the audiences for agitators such as Nicholas of Dresden and, later, Jan Želivský. F. Graus has produced calculations which suggest a high degree of poverty in Prague: 40 per cent of the population are classified by him as indigent.[20] Peasant immigration continually reinforced the *chudina*, the town poor dependent on casual labour; poverty coexisted with great wealth in the nobility and the patriciate, and class divisions reinforced the radical preachers' appeal. For the hungry and the underemployed, reiterated denunciations of an over-endowed Church and simoniacal benefice-holders from the ranks of the patriciate held a special appeal. For the preachers the issues doubtless remained theological; for their hearers social and economic factors came powerfully into play.

The New Town was also unusual because of its governmental position. The struggle of the artisans against the patriciate for a place in town governments, a general feature in Bohemian towns in the second half of the fourteenth century, could most easily be won by the workers in their guilds in the New Town because of their strong numerical position. These guilds gave support to the Hussite movement; the German chronicler Andrew of Ratisbon noticed their importance. Yet the guilds of the New Town could hold together only so long as the conflict with the patriciate demanded unity. An earlier united adherence to reform broke down and, as revolutionary doctrine emerged from what had been initially a more moderate movement, part of the New Town support went over to the conservatives.[21] There remained as a rank and file for radical preachers the less established middle class and the true poor.

Meanwhile, news from Prague as it reached the curia painted the situation in the darkest colours and led to further action. In July 1412, as part of the case launched against the best-known reform supporter, a major excommunication was pronounced against Hus by Cardinal Stefaneschi, technically for non-appearance. An interdict on Prague forced Hus out of the city.

Exile from Prague, which lasted till Hus finally left Bohemia for Constance, gave Hus the opportunity to put his thinking on to a firmer theoretical basis.

18  Table 9 (Ibid., p. 62); see heading ('What is said of the Antichrist applies to the Pope').
19  Seibt 'Die Zeit', p. 431.
20  Czech work, cited in J. Macek, 'Villes et campagnes dans le Hussitisme', *HS*, pp. 243–56 at pp. 245, 250, nn. 12, 13; F. Seibt, in *HZ*, Sonderheft IV, ed. W. Kienast, pp. 65–7; general background, M. Małowist, 'The problems of the inequality of economic development in Europe and the later Middle Ages', *EcHR*, 2nd ser. XIX (1966), pp. 15–28, esp. p. 21.
21  F. G. Heymann, *John Žižka and the Hussite Revolution* (1955) (detailed pro-Czech narrative from 1419), pp. 47–8.

Controversy over Wyclifite issues with his opponents tended to cohere round the fundamental question of the nature of the Church. Politically, the cause of Bohemian reform tended to move into a dangerous impasse,[22] with intransigent conservatives and reformers still locked in conflict, foreign churchmen anxious over Bohemian heresy, and the king, who summoned in vain a commission to reconcile differences, unable to bridge the gap between the parties. Hus's appeal to Christ from the Church was effective writing, but made no change in the situation.[23] Meanwhile, the rival protagonists – Stanislav of Znojmo and Páleč on the one side, Hus on the other – continued a passionate debate about the Church, to which Hus's De ecclesia, published by being read in the Bethlehem chapel early in June 1413, was the most significant contribution.[24] It was a full-scale answer to the doctrine of the Church implicit in the consilium of the conservative theologians at the synod of February. In contradiction to Páleč and Znojmo's notion of the ecclesiasticum et misticum compositum, Hus took as his starting-point the definition of the Church by Wyclif as 'the congregation of the predestinate'. Loserth long ago shook the early romantic tradition of Czech scholarship by demonstrating through simple textual comparison how deeply Hus plagiarized from Wyclif's writings;[25] his conclusion was that Hus was a puppet of Wyclif. Today, with a better understanding of the methods of scholasticism and a more realistic appreciation of Hus's intellectual powers, the discovery of widespread borrowing no longer shocks. Hus's relation to Wyclif was subtle. Wyclifian terminology was skilfully redeployed in the interests of a moderate and very largely orthodox theology.[26] Wyclif was valued as a reformer, while the full implications of his thought were not drawn out.[27]

Of course, such a proceeding was undertaken at the expense of fully systematic thought; but Hus was not a theological luminary of the first rank.[28] The structure of the De ecclesia makes this apparent. Part one was concerned with the nature of

22   Seibt, 'Die Zeit', p. 503.

23   De Vooght, Hérésie, pp. 224–9, discussion of appeal at Constance, p. 395, text tr. in Spinka, John Hus at the Council, pp. 237–40.

24   Context in De Vooght, Hérésie, pp. 245–88; on Hus's doctrine of the Church, see Hussiana, pp. 124–69; most detailed account in Spinka, Hus' Concept; on Hus as thinker and his fate, see Leff, Heresy II, pp. 657–85, and his acute observation in BJRL L (1968), pp. 387–410, stressing moral and practical character of his work. See F. Holeček, 'Hussens Auffassung von der Kirche', Seibt, Hus, pp. 183–91. For the text, see Magistri Johannis Hus tractatus De Ecclesia, ed. S. H. Thomson (Cambridge, 1956). A still usable translation is that of D. S. Schaff, De Ecclesia: The Church, by John Hus (1915).

25   J. Loserth, Huss und Wiclif (1884; 2nd edn, 1925. Engl. tr., London, 1884), written in six weeks (Thomson, in Speculum XXXVIII (1963), p. 118); see Kaminsky, Revolution, pp. 36–7; Šmahel, 'Doctor evangelicus' pp. 26–7.

26   A major theme of De Vooght, Hérésie: see esp. ch. 12; F. M. Bartoš, 'Apologie de M. Jean Huss contre son Apologiste', CV VIII (1965), pp. 65–74, controversy, Ibid., pp. 235–8, IX (1966), pp. 175–80; E. Werner, 'Der Kirchenbegriff bei Jan Hus, Jakoubek von Mies, Jan Želivský und den linken Taboriten', SDAB, Klasse für Philosophie (1967), x, pp. 5–73; on Hus, pp. 9–26; comment: Walsh, 'Wyclif's legacy', p. 400 – 'it is arguable that this intellectual sustenance was less essential for Hus himself than it was for Jerome of Prague'.

27   Leff (BJRL L (1968), pp. 387–410) brings a clear mind to bear.

28   Leff and De Vooght have been preferred on this to F. M. Bartoš (as revealed in CV VIII (1965), pp. 65–74).

the Church, and discusses Wyclif's definition; part two deals with practical issues. In the first part Hus commits himself to the Wyclifite definition of the Church as the body of all the predestined, which, understood as Wyclif intended it, was heresy; yet in the second he fails to draw out the implications of the definition. In Wyclif's writings his concept of the Church, with its vital distinction between the *presciti*,[29] foreknown to damnation, and the elect, logically led him to a denial of orthodox belief on the priesthood: no-one who was of the ranks of the *presciti* could be a true priest. In practice, priesthood in Wyclif's late writings has no obvious place. When we turn to part two of Hus's *De ecclesia*, we find he is ceasing to follow Wyclif: more at home in discussion of the practical issues confronting the Church, he veers towards the older and orthodox tradition in Matthias of Janov, of a distinction within the Church between the communion of the elect and the body of the faithful. The priesthood remains, even at the cost of logic. The turning back to Matthias is characteristic: it shows Hus in the last resort more the heir of the earlier Czech reformers than of the Wyclif he so venerated.[30]

In one issue his thought had moved during his career. In the *De ecclesia* he rejected the papacy as an institution of divine origin. The Petrine text referred only to Peter's confession of belief in the Son of God. The papacy, he believed, had originated with Constantine, and was dispensable. In his doctrine of the Church, therefore, Hus was unable to achieve the feat to which he attained elsewhere, of preserving Wyclif's words within a frame of orthodoxy: there, driven by his contemporary experience of the schism, he broke quite clearly with orthodoxy.[31]

Meanwhile, secure in aristocratic protection during his exile, he preached widely from his base in southern Bohemia, building up noble support in the countryside. When, in 1415, 452 of the nobility and gentry of Bohemia and Moravia put their seals to a protest to the Council of Constance against Hus's execution, a significant proportion of them, according to T. Č. Zelinka's calculations, sprang from this region, where Hus was active during his exile.[32] In this period he was at his most radical: 'he performed divine services, and preached at Kozí Hradek in a barn... he inveighed against the pope, bishops and canons, and constantly heaped abuse on the spiritual order'. The Czech chronicler goes on to describe activities at Kozí Hradek (sited immediately south of Tabor on map 8) of a more violent character. 'Here', he said, 'the priest Věněk began to baptize children in a fishpond, and to slander the chrism and holy oil and holy water.'[33] He was describing the beginning of Taborite radicalism in the countryside, a movement of which Hus could not have approved, but which he may have helped to stimulate by his rural sermons.

29   See Thomson's criticism of De Vooght's use of the term (*Speculum* xxxviii, pp. 116–21).
30   Leff, in *BJRL* L, p. 406.
31   De Vooght, *Hérésie*, pp. 466–8; W. Brandmüller, 'Hus vor dem Konzil', Seibt, *Hus*, pp. 235–42 (an intriguing article), goes farther in imputing heresy; Id., *Das Konzil von Konstanz 1414–1418*, 1 (Paderborn, Munich, Vienna, Zurich, 1991).
32   Spinka, *Hus*, p. 180.
33   Tr. by Kaminsky, *Revolution*, p. 165; on chronicler, see Ibid., n. 78.

## The Emergence of the Radicals

In the second decade of the fifteenth century the movement in the countryside rapidly took on a radical tinge: especially after the death of Hus and the introduction of Utraquism in 1415 as a Hussite Church began to form, parishes in the country were taken over by adherents of the reform, and radical priests inspired by the Hussite reform in Prague came out to conduct missions in the country. Some did not take benefices at all, and denounced those who did as 'priests of Pharaoh'.[34] These priests ostentatiously spurned all the apparatus of the late medieval Church, destroyed images, baptized, like Věněk, in ponds and streams, and celebrated mass in a 'purer', truncated liturgy in stables and barns. Their views were Donatist and anti-sacerdotal.

Spontaneously, this radical movement came to resemble post-1414 Lollardy, especially of the school of William White of Norwich,[35] or the Poor Lombard wing of the Waldensians.[36] To what extent the Hussite radicals were reinforced by a pre-existing underground Waldensianism in the countryside of southern Bohemia, finding an outlet as authority and the bonds of society were shaken by the Hussite movement, is uncertain.[37] The Waldensianism uncovered by the persecutions in fourteenth-century Bohemia and Moravia had in some instances a profound inner resilence, which enabled its determined members to survive persecution and the death of loved ones at the hands of inquisitors, to recover fully from the domestic disaster of confiscation of goods and still to continue evangelizing. Such members of the movement would have been receptive to radical Hussitism; but how far Waldensianism would have been able to leap the linguistic barrier between Czech and German remains uncertain.[38]

During Hus's exile, controversy made clear the impossibility of finding a formula to reconcile Hus with his opponents; Hus had become isolated from the king. In the capital the situation grew less favourable. The interdict imposed in 1412 represented perhaps the first success which the conservatives had had with public opinion since 1403. When in April 1413 Hus still lingered in Prague on one of his visits, and the parish clergy observed the interdict, there were disquieting signs that public opinion was being mobilized against him.[39] The king requested Hus to leave to avoid disturbances. His physical safety was still not in question, but the kingdom remained under pressure from abroad.

34  Ibid., p. 201; narration generally on pp. 132, 141–70 (clarification of radicals' origins is a major service of Kaminsky; see also his 'Hussite radicalism and the origins of Tabor, 1415–1418', *MH* x (1956), pp. 102–30).

35  Compare the radicals' sayings (Kaminsky, *Revolution*, pp. 166–7) with the Lollard aphorisms (above, pp. 302–3).

36  Above, pp. 82–5, 101–2.

37  Kaminsky, *Revolution*, pp. 171–9; Gonnet and Molnár, *Les Vaudois*, ch. 5; the crucial account, based on new evidence, Patschovsky, *Quellen zur Inquisition*, pp. 120–3.

38  Patschovsky, *Quellen*, pp. 35–6, discussing relatives of the smith, Henry of Jarosov nad Nezárkou, in southern Bohemia; discussion of the possible relevance of the search for a deeper, inner spiritual life, discernible in inquisition sources, p. 120.

39  De Vooght, *Hérésie*, pp. 262–3.

## Hus at Constance

An initiative, born of Luxemburg family affairs, seemed to break the impasse. Sigismund, the brother of Wenceslas and often his enemy, had in 1410 been elected king of the Romans, by implication in rivalry to Wenceslas who would not accept that he had been deposed from this position. In 1411 the two brothers sank their differences. Sigismund promised not to have himself crowned emperor so long as Wenceslas was alive. Then in 1414, if we can accept Bartoš's interpretation, the brothers struck another bargain.[40] Wenceslas agreed to the coronation of Sigismund on condition that Sigismund managed a settlement of his problem with Hus. The council which, largely through the initiative of Sigismund, had been summoned at Constance to settle the schism, offered a way out of the Hus issue. Hus should leave Bohemia to appear before the fathers of the council, thereby relieving Wenceslas of the external pressure on the kingdom, which he so much disliked.[41]

Probably neither of these lay rulers understood the intensity of feeling about Wyclifism. Hus hoped for more from the council than from the pope, and in optimistic moments believed that its members would join with him in reform. At Constance he had a sermon ready written but never delivered, calling on the council to put an end to the abuses.[42] He never completely trusted the safe conduct Sigismund offered – he wrote of the danger of death, and made his will before he left – but at the same time he was aware of the dangers to Bohemia if he stayed away from Constance. To go offered the chance of legitimizing the Bohemian movement and spreading it to the whole Church: bravely, and a little optimistically, he finally took the chance.[43]

When in October 1414 Hus left Bohemia on his journey to Constance, the movement for reform entered on a new phase. Long years of controversy within the kingdom had the effect that Hus, leaving for judgement at the curia, like Waldhauser and Milič before him, had behind him a much wider range of supporters and a much more thoroughly aroused public opinion.[44] A party that included clergy, skilful organizers, court officials and nobility followed with a passionate attention the twists and turns of a theological investigation which lasted from the end of the year, when Hus appeared first as an independent theologian freely come for learned discussion, to July 1415, when he was burnt as a heretic.[45] Stage by stage Hus's position worsened as, despite the initial com-

40   For all the complications, see Seibt, 'Die Zeit', pp. 476–93.
41   Bartoš, in *CV* viii (1965), pp. 69–70; Spinka, *Hus*, p. 222; on Hus's tactical error, Seibt, 'Hus' pp. 21–2.
42   Spinka, *Hus*, p. 226.
43   Seibt, 'Die Zeit', pp. 505–6, on safe conduct, p. 504 and n. 40; will in *Letters of John Hus*, tr. H. B. Workman and R. M. Pope (1904), pp. 149–51; see De Vooght, *Hérésie*, p. 316.
44   Seibt's comment ('Die Zeit', p. 504).
45   The best modern account is De Vooght, *Hérésie*, pp. 325–459; see also Spinka, *Hus*, pp. 219–90, comments in Kaminsky, *Revolution*, pp. 52–5, 125, 133, 136–61; correction in P. De Vooght, 'Jean Huss et ses juges', *Das Konzil von Konstanz*, ed. A. Franzen and W. Müller (1964), pp. 152–73.

promise when John XXIII left him freedom of movement in return for the promise not to preach or appear at the formal ceremonies of the council, he was arrested and the safe conduct disregarded. Then in March, after John had fled from Constance, he was taken to be held incommunicado in the castle of the bishop of Constance at Gottlieben and finally brought back to be exposed to tumultuous public hearings and condemned. Weeks of well-meaning pressure to secure recantation, always firmly refused, ended in the ceremonies of degradation and public burning.

This dark story was described in the *Relatio* of Peter of Mladoňovice, secretary to Hus's noble supporter, John of Chlum, who observed the course of events in Constance.[46] His work was the Passion of a martyr, forming the classic picture for public opinion in Bohemia, its story of the death in chapter 5 becoming a set text for reading on the national day of Hus's suffering, 6 July. Sigismund, failing to stand by his safe conduct, was overheard acceding to Hus's burning, and thus played Judas; a party of native Bohemians, headed by the inveterate Czech enemy Páleč, the legal expert Michael de Causis, John Nas, the Prague canon of a German family, and Bishop John the Iron of Litomyšl, stood in the place of the Scribes and Pharisees at the trial of Jesus, and called for a hostile judgement. Hus, referred to as 'the Master', bore his martyrdom with patient dignity. He understood that the following of Christ, a motif of his life, would lead to martyrdom. The story, if written with *parti pris* by one of his supporters, followed the facts of the case, reproducing documents and quoting the participants with the pungency of an eye-witness. Hus himself, apart from the stay at Gottlieben, was never held so close that he could not receive visitors and write letters. The simple letters of exhortation to his friends written at Constance came to form a part of the devotional literature of a saint, suited to strengthen the faith of simpler followers who could not follow the complexities of the debates during the trial. For the nobles, and for humbler followers, the issue of honour, centring on the safe conduct Sigismund had given, became a key factor; for it was something instantly comprehended by them, when theological complexities passed them by. Hus and his followers believed their master was to have the chance to explain the principles of the Bohemian reform at the council; the fathers at Constance had no such idea, and intended to investigate Hus like any other heretic. When it became clear that Hus was not going to receive anything other than the normal treatment of a heretic, the sense of shock and betrayal in Bohemia grew.

In October 1414 some leading nobles had written to Sigismund, drawing attention to Conrad of Vechta's certificate of Hus's orthodoxy, and urging him to ensure that Hus was not 'furtively abused, to the dishonour of our nationality and of the Bohemian land'.[47] That note, of the dishonouring of Bohemia by the council, continued to be struck. The nobles at home, informed by John of Chlum and his party and stimulated by a nucleus of committed Hussites, wrote letters of

46   Text in Spinka, *John Hus at the Council*, pp. 89–234.
47   Tr. Kaminsky, *Revolution*, p. 138; on term tr. as 'nationality', see Seibt, *Hussitica*, pp. 102–17. On the following of Christ to martyrdom, see Seibt, 'Hus', citing Werner, *Hus*; see esp. pp. 200–40.

protest to Sigismund.[48] Sigismund had to consider Bohemian opinion; the child-lessness of Wenceslas made it virtually certain that he would be the heir if anything occurred to remove Wenceslas from the throne. He was not prepared to commit himself à l'outrance to defend Hus from a council bent on prosecution of heresy; he did, however, use his influence to ensure that Hus was given a public hearing,[49] and Pierre d'Ailly, the cardinal and theologian who devoted himself to ending the schism, and the other directing forces of the council allowed Hus such hearings in order to satisfy Sigismund, despite the fact that by 7 June their own minds were made up against Hus. Major figures at the council were reformers – but not in the sense of Hus. The Wyclif connection damned him.

The hearings gained virtually nothing for Hus and his cause – the hearing of 7 June had to be adjourned because of disorder, and in two subsequent hearings Hus was interrupted too constantly to enable him to make an effective plea. Instead, they formed a part of the martyrdom: Peter headed his chapter on them in the *Relatio*, 'Here follow the so-called Hearings, but in Truth not Hearings but Jeerings and Vilifications.'[50] Towards the end, Sigismund became convinced that Hus was a heretic. Without following the theology with any attention, his interest then lay in urging Hus to recantation. Hus's scruples and his unwillingness to recant what he had not written Sigismund plainly did not understand. Then, when the final tragedy occurred and Hus was burnt, the resultant emotions in Bohemia blackened the council as an acceptable doctrinal authority, together with Sigismund as a ruler of honour, and fatally discredited the party of native Bohemians under Bishop John of Litomyšl, who had pressed for a condemnation and expected to go on to break the Hussites at home.

The protests of the nobility culminated in the letter of 2 September 1415 to the council, which baldly asserted that Hus was falsely burnt,[51] and amounted to a direct defiance of the proceedings of the council. In the eight copies which reached the council, 452 nobles of Bohemia and Moravia had put their seals to this defiance.[52] Such a rejection of an ecclesiastical decision on a matter of faith has no earlier parallel, certainly not in the patriotic support of an old Church, said to have been infected by heresy, in backward Bosnia,[53] or the mobilization of Languedocian patriotism and some religious feeling, part patronage, part true adherence, for the Cathars among the southern French baronage.[54] The actions of the council in 1415 had resulted in something new in the history of medieval

---

48   Spinka, *John Hus at the Council*, pp. 153–4, 158–61; on feeling behind letters, see Seibt, *Hussitica*, pp. 102–17; party organization, pp. 138–40; Klassen, *Nobility*, pp. 92–9; chs 7–8 gives analysis of noble attitudes to Hussitism. For survey, with penetrating comment, on Hussitism, see F. Šmahel, *La Revolution Hussite: Une anomalie historique* (1985); comment, F. Seibt, 'Eine historische Anomalie?', *Husitství*, ed. Pánek *et al.*, pp. 227–85.
49   De Vooght, *Hérésie*, pp. 335, 385–6.
50   Spinka, *John Hus at the Council*, p. 163; comment, Seibt, 'Hus', p. 23; on Sigismund, see *Sigismund von Luxemburg*, ed. J. Macek, E. Marosi, F. Seibt (Warendorf, 1994).
51   Kaminsky, *Revolution*, pp. 143, 144 n. 9.
52   For text and list of names, see Palacký, *Documenta*, pp. 580–90.
53   *MLC*, pp. 299–300.
54   Above, pp. 105–6.

FIGURE 6    *Hus led to execution, from a contemporary woodcut.*
*Photograph*: Bildarchiv der Österreichischen Nationalbibliothek. Reproduced by permission of Weidenfeld and Nicholson.

**Places where Hus lived**

▽ Sites of pilgrimages into the hills
(including the first Tabor near Bechyně)

★ The five cities of the prophecy

□ Towns belonging at various times to pro-Hussite alliances
(including both moderates and Taborite radicals)

Monastic houses attacked by the Hussites

⌐ Castles supporting Hussitism

MAP 8    *The Hussite movement in Bohemia and Moravia.*
*Source:* Adapted from *Atlas Československých Dějin* (Prague, 1965), no. 6B.

heresy. A deeply emotional issue, rapidly comprehensible to all, in which religious sentiment blended with the defence of the honour of Bohemia, had assembled a wide segment of the nobility in the defence of a cause now branded as heresy.

Such a mobilization of opinion at home, it will be noticed, would not have been possible if Hus had been induced to abjure. The protesters were aware that Hus died *non convictus et non confessus*;[55] had this not been the case, many who were not directly committed to the cause of reform would not have been brought to join the protest of 2 September, and Hus's own party would have been left in disarray.

To Cardinal d'Ailly, Hus was just another case of heresy.[56] A nominalist, he believed that realism had the eucharistic heresy of remanentism as a consequence, and was not impressed by Hus's denials. For the body of the council, the reputation of Hus in Bohemia was decisive; if they wavered in that view Páleč, John of Litomyšl and the rest were there to assure them.[57] Thus Hus's series of negative denials *nec tenui nec teneo* to the old Wyclifite forty-five articles made an impression, and his efforts at clarification had the result that the distorting forty-two articles of Páleč were finally whittled down to eleven; nevertheless, his own past defence of Wyclif dogged him. In part, the feeling of the council was comparable to that of inquisitors facing a simple heretic, who took the accused's denials for cunning evasions: repeatedly members of the council expressed the view that, though Hus might make sophistical denials, he continued to believe heresy with his heart. He was not allowed to examine the witnesses against him. While the extracting of articles from his works was supervised by the investigating commission with care, and did contain just, as well as unjust, attributions of doctrine, it was the testimony of witnesses that most obviously distorted Hus's views;[58] too many arrived at the council believing in Hus's guilt and the complexity of the evidence did not help them to shed their prejudice.

At the end, Hus refused to abjure, though to do so would have saved his life. He refused because of his utter unwillingness to abjure articles extracted from his works that he did believe and to recant articles that he claimed were not his own.[59] His courage helped to preserve the Bohemian movement. When on 31 August John of Litomyšl, following up the burning, received authorization to act against Hussites, he found a great barrier of sentiment interposed between Bohemia and the council decrees.

55   Seibt, 'Die Zeit', pp. 505–6.
56   Bartoš, in *CV* IX (1966), pp. 175–6; see also *CV* VIII (1965), pp. 72, 236; De Vooght, *Hérésie*, p. 389.
57   Kaminsky, *Revolution*, pp. 37–40, 52, Leff, *Heresy* II, p. 648.
58   De Vooght, *Hérésie*, pp. 334, 363, 388–90, 394, 410–11, 420–2.
59   See comments in M. Creighton, *A History of the Papacy from the Great Schism to the Sack of Rome*, II (London, 1899), ch. 5. Tr. of thirty articles on which Hus was condemned, Spinka, *John Hus at the Council*; comment: F. Seibt, 'Hus in Konstanz', *Hussitenstudien*, pp. 229–40.

## The Lay Chalice

Almost simultaneously the movement had acquired a symbol of its breach with the hierarchy assembled at Constance.[60] In the autumn of 1414 certain Hussites began to administer the chalice to the laity, and the practice spread. John complained to the council of irregularities accompanying the lay chalice; consecrated wine was carried about the country in flasks, and a woman who claimed the right of the laity to impose Utraquism snatched the chalice from the hands of a priest.[61] On 15 June 1415 the council prohibited the administration of the chalice to the laity. They admitted the facts of Christ's institution of the eucharist in both kinds and the precedent of the primitive Church, but argued that both the lay chalice and the reception of the eucharist after dinner had been discontinued for good reasons.[62] Hus had not initiated the chalice – 'Go slow, Kubo', he was supposed to have said to his friend Jakoubek before he left – realizing that it would complicate the situation for him at Constance. It was preaching that for him had the greatest significance; in the past he had not given close adherence to Matthias of Janov's teaching on the frequent communion of the laity; he observed that Jesus had begun to preach at the age of twelve, and at the age of thirty preached three years and several months long until his death, while he celebrated mass but once at the end of his time on earth. In the past he had noted, against the lay chalice, that the laity would not know how to communicate *pulchre*. None the less, when his own situation had darkened at the council and he had little to hope for, he rejected the council's decree because it was a decision which went against Scripture.[63]

Jakoubek, early defender of the lay chalice, spoke of the idea coming to him by *revelatio*, by which he meant the illumination which comes after prolonged consideration and study. Who exactly first raised the issue is still not clear. But it was a natural project to spring out of study of Matthias of Janov, who laid such stress on the importance of frequent communion, and to whom Jakoubek and others were so indebted. Over the centuries the laity had been excluded from the reception of the consecrated wine by a spontaneous development of the liturgy without any protest being made or the exclusion even being noticed: lack of interest in the issue was a natural concomitant of a situation in which the laity did not receive communion more than once a year.[64] Elsewhere in the fourteenth century, as in the case of the German mystical movement, stress on frequent communion did not lead to agitation for the restoration of the lay chalice. The Bohemian reform, however, was floated in an atmosphere of anticlericalism,

---

60   On introduction of chalice and controversy, Kaminsky, *Revolution*, pp. 98–126; F. Seibt, 'Die *Revelatio* des Jacobellus von Mies über die Kelchkommunion', *DA* xxii (1967), pp. 618–24. On Jakoubek generally, P. De Vooght, *Jacobellus de Stříbro († 1429)* (1972).

61   Kaminsky, *Revolution*, p. 132, and his section on 'The Utraquist victory' (pp. 126–36).

62   Ibid., p. 116.

63   Ibid., pp. 133–4; Werner in *Sitzungsberichte AWD* (1989) at p. 9; note Hus's treatment of eucharistic abuses, discussed pp. 6–8, and compare Catto on Wyclif's attitudes, *SCH* Subsidia iv, pp. 269–86.

64   D. Girgensohn, *Peter von Pulkau und die Wiedereinführung des Laienkelches* (1964).

which grew more intense in the early fifteenth century: in that atmosphere it is explicable that the withdrawal of the chalice should eventually have been seen as an unjust deprivation for which the clergy were responsible.

Paradoxically the council's decree against the chalice actually fostered its spread. The decree of 15 June was followed by Hus's burning on 6 July: the two decisions tended to be lumped together in the minds of the Bohemians and Moravians, and the emotional reaction against the one buttressed the other.

Once the idea was launched, pre-existing Hussite thinking about the Church was brought into play in its defence. The chalice, at first sight a minor issue of eucharistic practice, renewed the debate over the whole nature of the Church and its *magisterium*, which had developed over Hus's *De ecclesia* and had been important at Constance.[65] Both sides were agreed that the body and blood of Christ were contained wholly in either the wine or the bread after consecration, yet the withdrawal by custom, despite the words of institution by Christ in the Last Supper, raised the question: what were the limits of the Church's power of decision over scriptural precedents? The conservatives argued that the Church, having seen the benefits of communion in one kind, could rightly decide against the earlier precedents. For the Hussites that view was impossible, for the Church which decreed such alterations in early practice was the stained Church responsible for such evils in contemporary Christian life. They took their stand on such texts as John's, 'Except ye eat the flesh of the Son of Man and drink his blood, ye have no life in you.'[66]

The introduction of the chalice gained momentum as humbler members of the Hussite party among the clergy followed Jakoubek's lead, Hussite aristocrats sponsored the chalice, and local congregations eagerly responded. Passions were aroused. Prague, where the movement began, split into reformed congregations where the chalice was given, and traditional ones where it was not. In April 1415 the town councillors prohibited either side calling each other heretics.[67] Utraquism touched every attender at mass in an immediate fashion; it forced the ordinary man to think out his relation to the Hussite movement before he took the step of going over to a congregation where the chalice was administered. The erosion of discipline brought about by the earlier conflicts over Wyclifism now enfeebled attempts to suppress the movement.

In November 1415 a further attempt to use coercion had the effect of bringing the victory of Utraquism. Conrad of Vechta, the cautious and opportunist royal servant, was induced to impose an interdict on Prague on the grounds that it gave residence to John Jesenic, who had long been excommunicate. As the support for the lay chalice, apart from Christian of Prachatice, lay among the unbeneficed clergy, the interdict made possible a takeover on a revolutionary scale.[68] Those who refused the chalice found themselves restricted to the suburban churches, where the interdict had not been imposed. A lifting of the interdict only brought

65    Kaminsky, *Revolution*, pp. 108–26 *passim*.
66    John 6: 53.
67    Kaminsky, *Revolution*, pp. 156–7.
68    Ibid., pp. 157–61; note general comment by Seibt (*Hussitica*, p. 129).

the archbishop into difficulties with the council, still sitting at Constance; when it was reimposed in 1416 lasting damage had already been done to the conservative position.

Giving the chalice to the laity involved more than a mere liturgical change. Where, as in Prague, the crowd pressed for the lay chalice, or, as elsewhere in the country, the noble patrons of livings wanted it, benefice-holders were presented with an ultimatum: in the last resort, to accept the chalice or to leave.[69] The same process operated in Moravia, where the canons of Olomouc complained to the council of the barons who maintained Utraquist priests.[70] Such actions necessarily involved a breach of the legal structure which gave the clergy tenure of their livings and rights to tithes and alms, and left decisions over their discipline to the bishops and the procedures of the canon law. Introducing the lay chalice by force was an actual demonstration of the superior powers of the laity over their clergy, whether it was exercised in the name of the lay patrons or of a local congregation, perhaps loosely represented by a Utraquist crowd. Utraquism could thus appeal to patrons among the nobility who hoped to recover the wider powers of patrons that they had held under the *Eigenkirche* system.[71] Wyclif, Hus and the Czech reforming party had taught the need for a poor Church, and Hus in his Czech work on simony has spoken of the rights of lay patrons and their duties to ensure spiritual care of a benefice:[72] Utraquism offered the opportunity to secure all these things.

Failure of Utraquists to impose their will in the parish churches also affected the situation. It tended to result in the formation of *ad hoc* congregations, for whom Hussite priests celebrated mass, in the words of one complaint, 'in fields and on casks, in barns on no consecrated altar'.[73] Such arrangements might begin, *faute de mieux*, because a consecrated altar for Utraquist masses had been denied; they became demonstrations by the radical wing of the movement of their rejection of the apparatus of material aids to devotion and of the traditional ceremonial of the medieval Church. In congregations, Utraquism was one of a number of rejections, of the need for confession, for set forms of service, for law, even for priesthood with special powers.

Not all of these concomitants of Utraquism were desired by the nobility *en masse*; indeed, the Hussite league formed to defend Hussitism on 5 September 1415 by almost the same group of fifty-eight nobles who had sent the initial letter of protest about Hus's burning, never mentioned the lay chalice at all among the articles of their agreement.[74] The league stood for free preaching on Hussite lines

---

69   Kaminsky, *Revolution*, p. 160.
70   Ibid., p. 163.
71   Seibt, 'Die Zeit', pp. 512–13, early geographical distribution of Utraquists, p. 514; Kaminsky, *Revolution*, pp. 151–6.
72   Kaminsky, *Revolution*, pp. 152–3.
73   Tr. from letter of canons of Olomouc (Ibid., p. 163).
74   Tr. Ibid., pp. 144–5; on background, pp. 141–61; see still E. Denis, *Huss et la guerre des Hussites* (1878, 1930) (based on pioneer work of the great F. Palacký, yet has charm and perspective, and grows in value post 1415), pp. 177–9; J. Kejř, 'Zur Entstehungsgeschichte des Hussitentums', *Die Welt zur Zeit des Konstanzer Konzils. Vorträge und Forschungen* IX (1965), pp. 147–61.

without consideration for any technical issues of provision and appointment. The authority of bishops was not *per se* excluded: if accusations of error were made, the compact provided that a priest should be taken to his bishop for judgement, but that clause was subject to the important proviso that the error must be demonstrable by Holy Scripture and that, if the bishop attempted to punish a priest 'improperly, privately and without demonstration on the basis of Holy Scripture' the decision should be left in the hands of the university.

In effect, the league interposed a barrier between the kingdom and the operations of either the council or ecclesiastical authorities obedient to the council within the kingdom. The doctrinal authority of the international Church was replaced by that of the university,[75] and the jurisdiction of bishops made subject, in a way now characteristic of Hussite proceedings, to the private conscience of members of the league.

Nevertheless the league acted as a shield for the spread of the chalice, and inhibited the carrying out of hostile decrees of Constance through the vital years 1415–16. Citations to the council of all the 452 nobles who had put their names to the protest of September 1415, and proceedings against the magistrates and courtiers held responsible for allowing the spread of Utraquism were of no effect, since the league's membership was so weighty as to inhibit any Catholic reaction inside Bohemia from compelling obedience to these summons.[76]

The king remained passive. He carried neutrality towards the council almost beyond the limits of the possible. Alone of the kings of Western Europe, he sent no ambassadors to Constance. Probably his queen was more affected by the death of Hus than he was; his prevailing emotions seem to have been one of pique at the insult to his power, and suspicion of his brother's plans. Although he made no protest himself, he did nothing to prevent the protest letters of his nobility from being despatched. His whole position with regard to his nobility was weak. Aristocratic powers in Bohemia were a problem of long standing.[77]

Seen from one point of view the division of the country into factions based on religious differences was nothing more than a continuation of earlier baronial dissidence[78] and Wenceslas's response, doing nothing and declaring that there was no heresy in Bohemia, a natural course of action for a ruler who lacked effective weapons against his nobles. The council, however, was not sympathetic to Wenceslas's difficulties, and had in their hands the threat of a crusade, a fact which probably influenced Wenceslas to attempt to act against the Hussites late in 1416. The reaction did not achieve very much;[79] it neither diminished the use of the lay chalice, nor brought about a return of the ecclesiastical property that had been seized in previous years, and the king soon gave it up. From 6 July

---

75   See Kejř, *Die Welt*, p. 53.
76   Kaminsky, *Revolution*, pp. 149, 222–3; Denis, *Huss*, pp. 184–5.
77   Seibt, 'Die Zeit', pp. 476–7; Heymann, *Žižka*, pp. 24–8, 37; Klassen, *Nobility*, pp. 47–74.
78   Kaminsky, *Revolution*, pp. 147–8. Sigismund, who hoped to inherit Bohemia, was probably sincere in his appeals for unity at this time.
79   Ibid., pp. 223–7.

1416, one year after his death, Hus began to be commemorated in certain churches.

In the country, Čeněk of Vartemberk, meeting the threat of a stifling of the Utraquist priesthood in the long run by the refusal of the hierarchy to ordain men of Utraquist views, compelled a suffragan bishop in the Prague diocese to ordain at his castle of Lipnic his own candidates, all Hussite and tending to be radical in their theology.[80] The university, threatened in the winter, emerged from stress as the active doctrinal authority of a Hussite Church which the league of September 1415 had envisaged.[81] They settled their internal disputes by declaring on 10 March 1417 that the chalice was beneficial to the salvation of all.

### Radicals and Moderates within the Hussite Movement

Early in 1417 the university was engaged in defining its position towards its own Hussite radicals just as much as towards the council and its Catholic opponents. The gulf between the moderates of the stamp of Christian or Jesenic and the provincial radicals was already wide. The extremists, especially in the provinces, wanted drastic changes that entailed upsetting customary services. Rejecting purgatory involved the abolition of the chantries and the traditional masses for relatives and ancestors. Already a Czech version of the mass was in circulation, sponsored by Jakoubek;[82] provincial radicals wished to go beyond this and truncate the mass, turning it into a simple communion service with preaching closely based on the words of Scripture. They wanted to reject the intercession of saints. The radicals discussed in a letter of Christian of Prachatice to Wenceslas Koranda, a provincial preacher, advocated that 'dubious relics of the saints should be thrown out on dung heaps'.[83] Koranda was actively destroying images. If the radicals had their way, the moderate Utraquists would find customary patterns of Church life turned upside down. Moreover, there was an element of opposition to authority in the movement in the provinces: the driving-force came from certain lower clergy, but Christian also referred to unlearned laymen and women who were asserting their opinions.

The radicals were rejecting authority in the Church, whether of the bishop or of the university masters, in favour of the appeal to the text of Scripture. Their ideal was that of the gathered community centred on the chalice, using the power of magistrates to make the law of God prevail. From an attack on Hussite Church authority, there was an easy transition to the attack on secular authority, the rights of property, and the position of the nobility. Moderate Hussites, whose aims might be summed up in the desire for a measure of autonomy from the

---

80  Ibid., p. 242; Klassen, *Nobility*, ch. 6; on Hus and liturgy, D. Holeton, 'O felix Bohemia', Seibt, *Hus*, p. 390.

81  Full context, Kaminsky, *Revolution*, ch. 5, an account which supersedes earlier narratives of events in 1417–18.

82  Ibid., pp. 198, 257; cf. p. 194.

83  Tr. Ibid., p. 169. Note Kaminsky's reconstruction of the probable attitudes of Hussite lords to such actions (Ibid., pp. 228–9).

Roman Church and for the lay chalice, had every reason to be perturbed. The problem was not new in 1417. It followed from the cast of Hussite preaching before 1415, with its appeal to the law of Christ as overriding unjust decrees of the Church.[84]

Hussite theses opened the way to private judgement as the norm; the problem as the movement began to move sections of the populace was to know where to stop. At first the radicals, Nicholas of Dresden and Jakoubek, had worked together for the introduction of the lay chalice; probably in the autumn of 1415 they split, initially over the existence of purgatory. In the following year Nicholas left Prague and went to Meissen, where he was executed: Želivský, who took his place in 1418–19 as the radical preacher of the movement in Prague, believed that he had been pushed out by the university masters. Nicholas, in his sermon collection *Querite primum regnum*, was defending, in effect, Waldensian theses: he was rejecting all killing and oath-taking, and his discussion of the powers of the priesthood virtually eliminated the bishop. This was too much for the main body of Hussite masters, and for Jakoubek.[85]

Jakoubek's own position was unusual. As a leading radical among the masters and as the originator of the lay chalice, he held a certain responsibility for the extreme positions which were emerging in the provinces.[86] Clergy influenced by him went from Prague to preach in the country. Their violent destruction of images, so dangerous to unity, could find support in his writings; in 1414 in his *Sermo de confessione* he had rejected confession to a priest as inessential. A puritanical strain in his character, which led him to condemn singing and dancing, brought him closer to the radicals than to the moderate Prague leadership.

At the same time Jakoubek formed a part of the body of masters that were engaged in discussions intended to hold the often contradictory wings of the movement together. Because of his popularizing of the lay chalice, his simple and unworldly life, and his long connection with the reform party in the university, he occupied a position of leadership, and perhaps more than anyone helped to keep the wings together at a crucial stage.

The St Wenceslas synod of 28 September 1418 represented another attempt at a formula for unity, this time both more far-reaching and more inclined towards radicalism.[87] An assembly of masters and priests agreed on twenty-three articles, and laid down that in future no-one was to teach any novelty without first

84   See Werner, 'Der Kirchenbegriff', pp. 14–15, 21; A. Molnár, 'Hus et son appel à Jésus-Christ', *CV* VIII (1965), pp. 95–104; De Vooght, *Hérésie*, pp. 151–3, 173, 176, 208–9, 226–7, 395; *lex Christi* in Prague 1408: see pp. 89–92; for Jesenic on this issue, see Kaminsky, *Revolution*, pp. 63–4. On the use of the term *lex evangelica* in pre-Hussite Bohemia, see S. H. Thomson in *Speculum* XXXVIII (1963), pp. 116–21.

85   Želivský's evidence: Kaminsky, *Revolution*, p. 219; *Querite*: Ibid., pp. 207–13; death at Meissen: Kaminsky, 'Nicholas of Dresden', p. 12.

86   For this and Jakoubek generally, Kaminsky, *Revolution*, is fundamental: see esp. pp. 180–204, synopsis in his 'Hussite radicalism and the origins of Tabor', pp. 102–30; comments by De Vooght, in *RHE* LXIII (1968), pp. 543–7, with deserved praise, but with some doubt whether Kaminsky sometimes explains theological opinion too much by the background of events and politics.

87   Kaminsky, *Revolution*, pp. 259–64; comment on Czech liturgy, Holeton, 'O felix Bohemia', Seibt, *Hus*, p. 387.

submitting it for examination 'by the community of the brethren'. The articles rejected some key Waldensian-type theses, on the denial of purgatory, the refusal of the death penalty, Donatism and the right of laymen to consecrate at mass. The underlying principle of the extremists, that the explicit statements of Scripture constitute all that may be believed, was not allowed; yet, at the same time, the principle of the appeal to the primitive Church was preserved and, while a number of traditional Roman practices were allowed, they were suffered only under such qualifications as would still in fact allow for their abolition if the congregation so wished. The use of images, for example, was tolerated only if they were 'not wantonly or falsely adorned, in such a way as to seduce the eyes of communicants'[88] and provided it was not accompanied by outward acts of devotion, such as kneeling or the burning of candles. Latin was kept for the mass, but Czech was prescribed for the epistle and gospel, and all was subject to future change; ceremonies helpful to the law of God were to be kept 'unless something better is found'.[89] Infant communion, strongly disputed by John Jesenic and Simon of Tišnov, was allowed. The intention was to brake development on some issues, and to bring extremists under a Hussite synodal authority.

Unity among the Hussites from 1415 to 1418 was made easier by the rigid attitudes of the council. Having committed themselves in *Cum in nonnullis*, the fathers gave no sign thereafter till the end of the council in April 1418 that they were ready to negotiate the kind of compromise on the chalice that might have split moderate Hussites from extremists.[90] Those like Simon of Tišnov, who found the pace too hot, were offered no kind of halfway house between Hussitism as it was developing and complete submission to the other side. The election of Martin v as pope in November 1417, who had had earlier, hostile experience of the Hus case,[91] ensured the continuance of a firm line towards Bohemia. The project of a crusade was taken up again.[92] Early in 1419 the king determined on the only possible answer – the suppression of Hussitism. This, the last Catholic reaction of the reign, sparked off revolution.

## Tabor and Revolution

The king's major action was to decree the suppression of Utraquism in Prague and in the royal towns controlled by his officials. In the capital he yielded sufficiently to the entreaties of the magistrates and the burgomaster to allow three monastery churches to be left for the administration of the lay chalice. But

---

88    Kaminsky's tr. (*Revolution*, p. 261).
89    From Kaminsky's summary (Ibid., p. 260).
90    For conciliar attitudes, see Kejř, *Die Welt*, p. 60.
91    Spinka, *Hus*, p. 114.
92    For these and subsequent events, Denis, *Huss*, pp. 198–209 is still serviceable. Kaminsky, *Revolution*, pp. 266–96, blends narrative with analysis of motives of Želivský and incipient Taborites; his 'The Prague insurrection of 30 July 1419', *MH* xvii (1966), pp. 106–26, is the best account of the defenestration.

all the others, apart from Christian of Prachatice's church, were reoccupied by Catholic incumbents.

The Catholics celebrated their victory provocatively. Churches and altars were ceremoniously reconsecrated, Hussite clergy forbidden to use the side altars of churches, Utraquists thrust out of office, and absolution refused to the sick who would not renounce the chalice. Parish schools provided a point of conflict within the capital. The Utraquists did not give them up; the returned incumbents opposed to the chalice thereupon established their own in bell-towers and in buildings belonging to their parish. Pupils of the rival schools exchanged blows and, as adults joined in, affrays developed in which men were killed. The forces of moderate Hussitism felt unable to react against their king in his desperation. It was left to the radicals to fight the repression, and thus to save the whole movement from oblivion.

In the provinces, the sudden prohibition of Utraquism in the churches drove out the zealous congregations wherever the royal order was obeyed. Automatically, initiative passed to the radical clergy. In southern Bohemia, the traditional radical area, chronicles describe the assembling of deprived Utraquists at about Easter time, when under the old order the annual communion of the laity was due.[93] A hill, probably Němějice near the castle of Bechyně, became a gathering point at which Utraquist congregations received the chalice and listened to sermons, and was renamed Tabor after the site in Galilee where Christ took his disciples for the transfiguration;[94] it soon became the centre for a dramatic development of radical Hussitism. Persecution at this late stage fused scattered congregations and precipitated change. Tabor, from being an occasional meeting-place, became a settlement, with peasants from a distance abandoning their goods and setting off to the mountain for the services and the preaching; attempts by lords to prohibit their peasantry from attending helped to precipitate their flight. Other hills in southern Bohemia were taken as sites and given biblical names such as Horeb[95] and Olivet.[96] Congregations came together in great numbers in a kind of cycle of liturgical celebrations and open-air preaching missions, culminating in a meeting of 22 July which deeply impressed the chroniclers. They estimated the numbers present variously at forty and fifty thousand, and described contingents derived from the areas of Pilsen, Domažlice, Hradec Králové, Moravia and Prague.[97]

Preaching under the shadow of the imminent end of the lay chalice, a persecution which to the crowds at this time seemed to resemble those that presage the Last Things, aided the spread of chiliastic expectations. The renaming of Bohemian hills after the mountains in Scripture, as Molnár points

93    Tr. of sources in Kaminsky, *Revolution*, pp. 278–80.
94    Ibid., pp. 280–3 and notes. Fundamental Czech work on Tabor by J. Macek (Marxist) (reviewed, Seibt, 'Bohemica', p. 96 (and index s.v. Macek); discussed in Kaminsky, *Revolution*, pp. 149n., 172n., 285n., 287–8, 320n., 341–2, 352n., 393, 398, 403–4, 422).
95    Heymann, *Žižka*, pp. 131–3.
96    Kaminsky, *Revolution*, p. 288, n. 84.
97    Ibid., pp. 290–2.

out, would set up powerful echoes in the minds of the congregations – of the delivery of the Law to Moses on a mountain, of Christ's Sermon on the Mount, of the meeting of God and man in the transfiguration at Tabor.[98] Preaching and communion was followed by a meal, resembling the *agape* of the early Christians. Collections were taken to meet the costs of owners of fields damaged by the assemblies.[99] Food was shared equally, even to eggs and crusts of bread. Sermons were fiercely denunciatory of the clergy.[100] The climb up the hills intensified the feeling of withdrawal from a wicked world; a Taborite song stressed flight into mountains: 'Therefore do not resist evil,' it ran, 'but go out to the mountain, and here learn Truth; for so Christ commanded when he prophesied on the mountain and preached of the destruction of the temple.'[101] In a similar fashion the simple communism of the eating arrangements for poor peasants would mark the contrast between the charity of the mountain and the duties and obligations to their lords of the manorial world below from which they had come.[102]

In Prague the Taborite demonstrations in the countryside were paralleled by long processions of Utraquists to the churches where the lay chalice was still allowed. The king, on his way to mass, found himself surrounded by a crowd under the leadership of Nicholas of Hus, a petty nobleman of the radical party, demanding the re-granting of general permission for the lay chalice and infant communion;[103] he had Nicholas arrested. When the Utraquist councillors of the New Town intervened, he consented to banish him. Nicholas seems to have gone to agitate among the Taborites. Wenceslas dismissed the Utraquist councillors of the New Town on 6 July, replacing them by Catholics, who forcibly took over the remaining Utraquist parish schools, prohibited their processions, and probably imprisoned Utraquists.

At this juncture Jan Želivský, a former Premonstratensian who had abandoned his order and taken on the mantle of Nicholas of Dresden in Prague, took a hand in events.[104] There was much tension in the city as the king, characteristically moved by a personal episode in which he detected an insult to his power, seemed at long last to have decided to crush the Utraquists' movement. He was fearful of the Taborites: reports circulated that they were planning to depose him in favour of Nicholas of Hus. Želivský had arrived in Prague in about 1418, and had begun a career as a radical preacher based, in the days when Utraquism still flourished,

---

98    Tr. from Czech, Ibid., p. 283, n. 63. For A. Molnár's work, see Seibt, 'Bohemica', pp. 86, 91, 96, 97, 105. Original Czech form is Tábor.
99    Denis, *Huss*, p. 203.
100   Evidence of Lawrence of Březová (Kaminsky, *Revolution*, p. 284).
101   Tr. in Kaminsky, *Revolution*, p. 286.
102   Macek's reflection cited Ibid., p. 285.
103   Denis, *Huss*, pp. 203–4; for development of opinion on Nicholas, cf. Ibid., p. 224, Kaminsky, *Revolution*, pp. 410–12, Heymann, *Žižka*, p. 198; M. Polívka, 'Nicholas of Hus', *Historica* xxviii (1988), pp. 75–121.
104   For Želivský as theologian, see Molnár, in *CV* ii (1959), pp. 324–34; as politician and military leader, see Kaminsky, *Revolution*, Heymann, *Žižka* (see index). Kaminsky uses Molnár's edition of sermons to reconstruct events of 1419.

on the Church of St Stephen in the New Town. In the Catholic reaction early in 1419 he lost St Stephen; but was a preacher in one of the churches reserved for the Utraquists, Our Lady of the Snows. A large building, it housed a congregation of small artisans and poor people from the New Town. Želivský saw himself as their representative, describing himself in copies of his sermons there as 'Ž, preacher of the poor, unfortunate, miserable, oppressed'.[105] Powerful and eloquent preaching linked him intimately to his poor audiences. The Latin outlines for his vernacular sermons over a period from April to November 1419 survive, placing him in the radical tradition of Jakoubek, vividly contrasting Roman practice and the primitive Church, forceful in denunciation. A natural extremist, he was contemptuous of the university masters who had bowed to the king's will. The poor of his congregations helped to form the demonstrative processions of Utraquists in the capital; no doubt they sang the abusive songs about the rich lords and the clergy which have come down to us. The sermons dwell on the suffering of the true Christian, but not in any passive sense: suffering is linked with struggle.

On 30 July he used his congregation for a violent demonstration intended to destroy the new royal policy of suppressing the Utraquists.[106] After a sermon at Our Lady of the Snows, he took the consecrated Host in a monstrance, and led out his followers, some armed with pikes, swords and clubs, to his former church of St Stephen. Finding the Catholic priest had locked the doors against them, the congregation smashed them down and took over the building, which immediately was used for an Utraquist communion. From St Stephen, Želivský and the rest moved to the New Town hall, where they found a number of the Catholic Czech councillors of the king's appointment. They demanded from them the release of the Utraquists held by them in prison. When the councillors refused, the angry crowd broke in, and threw some thirteen of them from the windows into the street below, where those who survived the fall were killed. Želivský's men then took over the New Town hall, and summoned the residents to arms, electing four military captains and, later, new councillors to replace their victims. A force under the sub-chamberlain arrived at the town hall, but was too outnumbered to be able to restore the situation. The king, inflamed, yet persuaded of the need to compromise, was forced to confirm in office the New Town magistrates who had been thus intruded. Just over a fortnight later he died of apoplexy.

Inflammatory sermons, working on the imaginations of the poorest sections of the Prague population, had done their work. Želivský, however, was not only a scriptural preacher of great power, but was also a practical organizer and a politician. Kaminsky has given us attractive grounds for believing that the revolution of 30 July was a planned affair. Želivský planned a coup that would destroy the king's policy. His followers, if they broke out spontaneously against

---

105   Molnár, in *CV* II, p. 327.
106   Kaminsky, 'Hussite radicalism', pp. 106–26; *Revolution*, pp. 289–96. Seibt ('Die Zeit', p. 515) notes that it was a conflict between Czechs, Hussite and Catholic.

the councillors who shilly-shallied over delivering up the prisoners, were not so out of control as to loot the bodies of their victims;[107] the chains of office remained untouched on their corpses. The insurrectionaries proceeded at once to the business of electing captains and taking over control of the New Town. It is likely that Želivský did not stand alone but formed part of a conspiracy with members among the leaders of the Taborites.[108]

In a morning's action the radicals had gone far towards capturing Prague for their ideal. The death of Wenceslas spoiled the plan, but could not put back their cause. With the defenestration they had brought off a successful rebellion against their king, and had wrecked the Catholic reaction most dangerous to them. Reform in Bohemia, which entered on a new phase with the enactment of the decree of Kutná Hora in 1409, culminated in 1419 in a revolution against the established order in the name of religion.

---

107 Kaminsky, 'Hussite radicalism', p. 113.
108 Kaminsky's major hypothesis, attractive, not proved to the hilt. See also his attempt to relate the defenestration to Želivský's sermon (Ibid., pp. 120–6; *Revolution*, pp. 292–3).

# 17

# Success and Failure: From the Defenestration to the Agreement at Jihlava

### The Aftermath of Želivský's Coup

Wenceslas's death put the future of Hussitism into the melting-pot.[1] Sigismund, his brother, was the lawful heir, unacceptable to the radicals because of his record of complicity with the decisions of Constance, but still not wholly to be ruled out by the moderates. Moderate Hussites included in their ranks many attached to the principle of legitimacy, such as the university masters and the nobility, who would have found it difficult to reject Sigismund if only he had given some guarantees for a continued authorization of the lay chalice. Probably Ernest Denis was not wrong when he said that he could have taken the kingdom if he had moved at once. But he had other preoccupations, and the moment passed.

The Hussites united on a programme. At an assembly in late August or September, the barons and the towns set out their requirements.[2] They were,

---

1   F. M. Bartoš, *The Hussite Revolution 1424–37*, ed. J. M. Klassen, East European Monographs CCIII (1986) (abridged, poor tr. of *Husitská revoluce* I (last chapter) (1965), II (1966); narrative by master of Hussite history, sympathetic to Taborites and Orebites); Denis, *Huss*, p. 212; still well-balanced narrative of events, 1419–36; Ibid., pp. 211–454; to death of Žižka (1424), esp. for political and military aspects, cf. Heymann, *Žižka* (with final survey, 1424–36, pp. 456–83); lucid summaries in Creighton, *Papacy* II. Seibt, 'Die Zeit', pp. 494–536, gives outline to 1436 with full literature. Kaminsky, *Revolution*, pp. 296–494 (often used here), is esp. valuable on Tabor and ideology, but stops in 1424; for brief analysis, see his 'The religion of Hussite Tabor', in *The Czechoslovak Contribution to World Culture*, ed. M. Reichigl (1964), pp. 210–23. For concepts and nomenclature, Seibt, *Hussitica* (sections on just war, *jiazyk-linguagium*, *obec-communitas*); survey with perspective in F. Seibt, 'Die Hussitenzeit als Kulturepoche', *HZ* CXCVI (1962), pp. 21–62, sources tr. (esp. on radicals, Taborites) pp. 253–329; Peter Chelčický's teaching (pp. 333–443) in *Das hussitische Denken im Lichte seiner Quellen*, ed. R. Kalivoda and A. Kolesnyk (1969), introduction by Kalivoda; broad comparison, F. G. Heymann, 'The Hussite revolution and the German Peasants' War: an historical comparison', *MH*, n.s. I (1971), pp. 141–59; J. Kejř, *The Hussite Revolution* (1988).

2   Kaminsky, *Revolution*, pp. 296–8; for general problem of communities, Estates, see Seibt, *Hussitica*, pp. 125–82, and cf. K. Hrubý, 'Senior Communitas – eine revolutionäre Institution der prager hussitischen Bürgerschaft', *Bohemia* XIII (1972), pp. 19–43 (sociological approach).

in effect, the conditions of acceptance for Sigismund. Though Utraquism was not treated as a necessity for all, the lay chalice was to be authorized, the traditional reservation of the chalice to the priest and Utraquism coexisting, if necessary, in the same church. Simony, widely interpreted, was to be put down, and priests were not to hold civil office. Bishops were to ordain candidates for orders without discriminating between Catholics and Utraquists and neither side was to call the other heretics. Utraquists were asking, not for victory, but for peaceful coexistence. They intended to hold on to the gains of the past: the university was to remain the doctrinal authority; there was to be free preaching; papal decisions were to take effect in Bohemia only at the will of the king, council and barons. Yet there was still a desire for recognition within the international Church.

The nationalist demands were more far-reaching. The Czechs were to have the first voice in the kingdom. Judicial proceedings were to be held in the Czech language. Foreigners were not to take either civil or ecclesiastical office if capable Czechs were to be found to fill them. Thus, at the moment of crisis, the nationalist demands in Bohemia, which had grown contemporaneously with the religious, each supporting the other, reached their fullest expression. Other clauses reflected the interests of smaller groups. Prague had a special section of its own. The nobles had their particular interests; royal rights of taking escheats were to be restricted, Wenceslas's treasure was to be used in the interests of the kingdom, a hint that it should not be used to reward foreigners, such as the Germans and Hungarians of Sigismund's entourage, in preference to natives. The towns wanted an amnesty, the confirmation of their liberties, and laws against usurers and Jews.

### The Rise of the Military Tabor

One group was hardly catered for: the radicals. The death of Wenceslas had been followed by disturbances in Prague and other towns where they had a strong following. A crowd led by Jan Žižka, a professional soldier in the royal service, sacked the Carthusian house at Smíchov outside the capital;[3] the inmates, largely Germans, had to be put in custody at the Old Town hall for their own safety. Inside Prague brothels were destroyed by zealots. In the provinces the great assemblies on the hills for communion and preaching continued unabated. Unaided, the New Town radicals under Žižka and Želivský took the fortress of Vyšehrad; in November a group which included pilgrims from the provinces took royalist positions in the Small Side.

Despite their protestations, the assemblies were a political force, and were undergoing a transformation into a fighting one. Queen Sophie and Čeněk of Vartemberk at the head of the council of regency saw the danger, and took counter-measures. In November the first pitched battle between the rival sides

---

3 Heymann, *Žižka*, p. 69; background, ch. 4 generally; on Sigismund, J. K. Hoensch, *Kaiser Sigismund. Herrscher an der Schwelle zur Neuzeit* (Munich, 1996).

took place near Živhošť,[4] when a force of royalist nobility cut off a group from the south making their way to the November demonstration in Prague. In the capital the danger of a takeover by the radicals was more acute; but the combined forces of the New Town and the provincial zealots were unable to hold opinion on their side. The Vyšehrad was given up again to royalist troops, and the men from the provinces left Prague in disappointment, a mood which facilitated the swing to force.[5] Already at the 30 September assembly outside Prague, Wenceslas Koranda, leader of the Pilsen contingent, had said, 'The time to wander with the pilgrim's staff is over. Now we shall have to march, sword in hand.'[6] Koranda, with Nicholas of Hus, formed part of a small leading group engaged in the direction of the mass of pilgrims towards specific objectives, in the first instance political, then military.

Like the Waldensians, the radicals were initially believers in literal observance of the texts of the gospels prohibiting the shedding of blood; but even the Waldensians took up the sword in special circumstances, as for example, when their mountain refuges were attacked by troops under the inquisition.[7] There was an easy psychological transition from violent demonstrations, the image-breaking long usual in radical circles, the destruction of monasteries and brothels, on to the actual shedding of blood.

Preaching facilitated the process. In the winter of 1419–20, their leaders comforted the disillusioned with the prospect of the imminent end of the world. In a new coming of Christ their enemies would be destroyed; the remnant to be saved – which would come, of course, from the ranks of the radicals – were to flee to five cities in Bohemia,[8] where they would be saved from the wrath to come. Jakoubek and the main body of university masters reasoned against the radicals' use of texts and, in particular, against the necessity to flee to the cities of protection. On another side of the movement, Peter Chelčický, the yeoman of Waldensian views, stood apart from this development, and later wrote that he believed that the devil had deceived them into thinking that they were 'angels who had to eliminate all scandals from Christ's kingdom'.[9] Through all vicissitudes he clung to literal pacifism, and refused to have any contact with secular power. None the less, the prophets had their way. Lawrence of Březová describes how peasants sold up their holdings, even at a low price, and with their wives and families came to the radicals' centres, throwing their money into a common fund.[10] The end did not come, and the mood of imminent expectation passed, but not before it had played its part in setting up a confederation of like-minded radical communities.

---

4   Kaminsky, *Revolution*, p. 307.
5   Best described, Ibid., ch. 7.
6   Heymann, *Žižka*, p. 80; for analysis of political situation in September–October 1419, see Kaminsky, *Revolution*, pp. 301–6.
7   Lea, *Inquisition* ii, pp. 259–60, 267; see above, pp. 174, 186.
8   Kaminsky, *Revolution*, p. 311 ff.; Isa. 19: 18.
9   Ibid., p. 321 (tr. Kaminsky); for literature on Chelčický, see below, p. 374, n. 13.
10   Ibid., p. 331.

The five cities of the prophecy were all places where the radicals had made an early impact, and lay in western Bohemia: Pilsen, Saaz (Žatec), Louny, Slaný, Klatovy. Pilsen lay under the command of the fighting priest, Koranda, and was soon reinforced by Žižka, who brought a remarkable military expertise to canalize the energies of the dedicated men. Another area of refuge lay in south Bohemia, where Písek had a long tradition of extremism. Hradec Králové was yet another centre: here lay the rechristened Mount Horeb, with the Orebites under the priest Ambrose.[11] Both the southern and western centres were soon under attack. This intensified the religious emotions amongst the radical elect, but also led to losses. In a skirmish, Žižka for the first time demonstrated his skill in the use of artillery and war-wagons; but there was resistance to Koranda inside Pilsen, and disillusion when the projected date for an end of the world in mid-February 1420 passed. In March, after an armistice, Žižka and a party of the most determined followers left Pilsen to join the south Bohemian centre of resistance. There Písek seems to have fallen to the royalists, probably in February; but the zealots who had had to leave the town made a surprise attack before dawn on Ash Wednesday on another nearby town, Ústí-nad-Lužnicí, which they took.[12]

Finally, moved by the needs of defence, they left Ústí for the abandoned fortress of Hradiště, on a near-impregnable site formed by a peninsula, with water defences on three sides from the rivers Lužnice and Tismenice. Ústí was burnt, and contact with the old and normal life was cut off. A rigorous communism was set up, with the holding of private property being taken as a mortal sin. Fortifications were put up at great speed, and the population divided into four groups for military and political purposes under captains. From the fortress parties went out to subdue the surrounding countryside. To this society Žižka brought his soldiers and his military genius. The fortress was renamed Tabor. To the old pilgrimage Tabor near Bechyně, there had succeeded a new military Tabor.

Much as Cromwell was able to develop his military innovations in the intense religious atmosphere of the New Model Army, so Žižka used the religious exaltation of the inmates of Tabor to mould them into an unusually well disciplined fighting force. Among the Taborites the failure of the end of the world to occur as anticipated did not lead to a slackening of zeal: to the prediction of the imminent and catastrophic end there succeeded the notion that Christ had already come, but secretly as a thief in the night;[13] his public advent was yet to be. Meanwhile, it was a time of vengeance. After fighting would come the reward: the elect who had fled to the mountains would possess the goods of the wicked. The nature of Tabor inevitably drew only the most dedicated of radicals from their homes and normal way of life. In an atmosphere of feverish religious activity, novel ideas were thrown up very rapidly. A hostile witness describes the priests telling their followers of the

---

11 On these and all Hussite groupings against geographical background, Seibt, 'Die Zeit', pp. 518–27.
12 Events in Kaminsky, *Revolution*, pp. 329–36; military aspect in Heymann, *Žižka*, ch. 6.
13 Kaminsky, *Revolution*, p. 345.

wealth they would have when the millennium dawned: they would have an abundance of everything and would no longer have to pay rents to their lords.[14]

The violence of Tabor had religious roots; it also had a more practical cause, in the difficulties of supporting the zealots and their families; they needed the booty to be won in expeditions against their enemies. As the financial pressures made themselves felt, they were forced to impose the traditional lords' exaction of *holdy* on neighbouring peasants. This created disillusion; but the feeling of membership of the elect, the inspiration produced by the community in the fortress, the preachings, and the simple celebrations of the Utraquist communion, without regular altar, vestments or mass ritual, created a long-lasting momentum for Tabor that could ride out minor setbacks.[15]

Žižka's task was to improvise an army from the materials available to peasants.[16] Threshing-flails, consisting of swipples studded with iron spikes, initially had to serve in place of conventional weapons; as their worth became apparent, they were deliberately manufactured. Peasant carts made do as transport: soon Žižka adapted them as war-wagons. They were improved for defence purposes by adding boards to protect both their occupants and the wheels, and places were made for hand-guns. Shields were developed to close gaps between wagons. Žižka had had experience of warfare against the Teutonic Knights in a campaign on behalf of the king of Poland, and may there have learnt something of the use of wagons; but the extension of their use from transport to a whole system of mobile defence seems to have been his innovation. The great virtue of Žižka's war-wagons was that they enabled mobile columns to switch rapidly and effectively to defence against cavalry attack.

### Sigismund and the Battle of Vitkov Hill

Meanwhile negotiations continued, spurred by the moderate Utraquists' fear of the excesses of the Taborites.[17] At a diet at Brno in December 1419 the Estates swore obedience to Sigismund, and Prague asked for forgiveness for its rebelliousness. It seemed as if he would allow a policy of toleration for the lay chalice, provided that his wishes were respected on other matters. Quietly he appointed two Catholic nobles as steward and chamberlain, with control of royal castles and towns, to outflank Čeněk of Vartemberk. Again a successful entry as ruler to Bohemia seemed eminently possible. But Sigismund spoiled his chances by dropping the mask of compromise.

---

14   Tr. Ibid., p. 340 – surely significant for economic motivation. M. Polívka, 'Popular movement as an agent of the Hussite revolution in late medieval Bohemia', *History and Society*, ed. J. Purs, K. Herman (1985), pp. 261–85.

15   The atmosphere is reconstructed by Kaminsky in *The Czechoslovak Contribution*, ed. Reichigl, pp. 210–23; for the composite work on Tabor up to 1421, see F. Šmahel *et al.*, *Dějiny Tábora* i, pt i (České Budějovice, 1988), review: E. Werner, in *ZG* xxxviii (1990), pp. 457–9; wide-ranging discussion of the degree to which one may speak of revolution at Tabor and after by Šmahel, *Revolution*.

16   Heymann, *Žižka*, pp. 97–101.

17   Ibid., ch. 7; Denis, *Huss*, p. 233–7; Kaminsky, *Revolution*, pp. 361–5.

Another diet at Breslau assembled the magnates of the Empire; in the atmosphere of power there, the direct military solution of the Bohemian problem seemed attractive. There were still centres of Catholic dominance in the country. At Kutná Hora the German population was engaged in a wholesale elimination of Hussites who, as the town's executioner became overburdened, were thrown into the abandoned shafts of silver mines. In south Bohemia the Hussites had been unable to eliminate the opposition of Ulrich of Rosenberg (Rožmberk). In February Sigismund decided for an expedition, declared a crusade by Martin v. In Breslau he demonstrated his new attitude to Bohemian heresy by assenting to the burning of a Hussite merchant from Prague. As far as recalcitrant towns were concerned, he marked the contrast between him and his vacillating brother by quashing Wenceslas's mild response to a revolt of workers' corporations against the town council in Breslau.

In the winter and spring 1419–20 the university masters debated the issues of war and peace.[18] In February Žižka submitted this theme to the university – an interesting demonstration of links, however frail, which still held between different wings of the movement. A little earlier two priests, one in favour of the radicals, the other more conservative, debated publicly the righteousness of war; the dispute was referred to Jakoubek and Christian of Prachatice for judgement. They disliked the deductions being made by the provincial radicals from the imminence of the end of the world, but they allowed a right of resistance by Utraquist communities even against the will of the lords.

The necessities of the time were drawing university masters, as well as the Taborites, into the justification of revolution against the established order. In their discussions they moved, stage by stage, away from the traditional and much qualified support for Christian warfare to be found in Wyclif, and derived by him from Aquinas, to an acceptance of holy war, and even obligatory war, for the Bohemians who held to the cause of the chalice. Wyclif's exposition left no place for resistance against a lawful ruler; the Prague masters in their need boldly left him behind. As Seibt explains, their achievement was considerable.[19]

The crusade did what nothing else could do; it pushed into temporary unity the disparate forces of Hussitism.[20] In Prague, Old and New Town came together on 3 April 1420, and made an agreement setting up a form of military government under captains, with temporary powers overriding, though not superseding, those of the magistrates.[21] Želivský, who had been somewhat isolated during the phase of negotiation with Sigismund, regained influence. The citizens sent out a manifesto which struck the nationalist chord. Sigismund was to be repelled, as he had summoned a crusade and had called in the Germans, 'our natural enemies'. Responsibility for schism did not lie with the Czechs: the Church, a malicious

---

18  Kaminsky, *Revolution*, pp. 317–29; Seibt, *Hussitica*, ch. 2 (valuable for the intellectual origins of discussion).

19  Seibt, *Hussitica*, p. 55; note comment: pp. 53, 57.

20  Ibid., p. 17; note discussion of Hussites' lack of any self-devised term for all members of the reform movement, p. 14.

21  Kaminsky, *Revolution*, p. 368.

stepmother to them, had repelled them, despite the fact that they had only wanted to follow Christian law.[22] Čeněk, the weathercock of Hussitism, returning from Sigismund, joined the Prague citizens in their defiance, took over the Hradčany castle, and rallied the nobility. On 20 April the lords issued their manifesto, a formal *diffidatio* directed against Sigismund which enumerated his faults, from his complicity in the burning of Hus to the alienation of the Margravate of Brandenburg and the naming as bishop of Moravia of an 'enemy of the Slav race'.[23]

In both manifestos there was a similar theme of honour and nationality, defined in terms of language. The Czech keyword was *jazyk*, best translated as 'tongue'.[24] Its use links the manifestos of 1420 with the protests of the Bohemian and Moravian nobility in 1415. The later ones, which form a sequence of high rhetoric through the 1420s, almost certainly are the work of one hand, and reflect the interest of the Prague patriciate, university-educated, touched by humanism, and less orientated towards religion than secular concerns. Linguistic nationalism was a relatively sophisticated notion, but it was calculated to stir the emotions of Czechs far from university circles.[25]

As the crusaders made their way into the country, national feeling was reinforced by stories of martyrdom, the *passiones* of humble Hussites, of which the best-known is the burning together of parish priest, peasants and children who refused to recant at Arnoštovice in July 1420 by the troops of the duke of Austria.[26]

The manifesto of 3 April also included a formula for religious unity among the rival Hussite groups; modified, it reappeared on 20 April, and again on 27 May; decked with texts and authorities, it was translated and transmitted to Sigismund's army and to other towns. The formula became known as the Four Articles of Prague;[27] it was the minimum platform of Hussitism. The articles proclaimed Utraquism; the 'proper and free preaching of the word of God'; the necessity for all priests, from the pope downwards, to 'give up their pomp, avarice and improper lordship'; and for the Bohemian realm and nation to be cleansed both from public mortal sins and from slander. Different groups could read into it different meanings. The nobility on 20 April omitted the reference to public mortal sins; the radicals, on the contrary, saw the same fourth article as an invitation to a revolutionary upheaval in the country. But the lay chalice united all.

Yet for many radicals it formed only a preliminary to a wholesale revision of the mass, which stripped it down to the decisive scriptural texts, all translated into Czech, and it turned into a communion service bereft of traditional vestments and

---

22   Denis, *Huss*, pp. 238–9.
23   Ibid., p. 239.
24   Seibt, *Hussitica*, pp. 102–9.
25   In this and earlier sentences, I follow Seibt's research (*Hussitica*, ch. 3 (see p. 117); *HŽ* cxcvi (1962), pp. 21–62).
26   Denis, *Huss*, p. 248.
27   Kaminsky, *Revolution*, pp. 369–75, Heymann, *Žižka*, ch. 10.

ceremonial.[28] Where the most moderate were satisfied with the concession of the lay chalice, and perhaps the translation of epistle and gospel into the vernacular, others went further, and treated the first article as giving them the right also to administer the chalice to infants. Modifications of the articles in different versions reflected the tensions beneath the surface. But the articles served their purpose: evolved under the pressure of invasion, they held together moderates and radicals for a common defence. They represented a minimum of what all would accept. They lasted long because no better formula could be found to reconcile the irreconcilable.

In the city of Prague the new common actions of April and May and the stress on the national interests of the Czechs in the manifestos led to a major emigration of Germans and Catholics, not to be reversed.[29] Houses, gardens and possessions were confiscated and redistributed, the community thus claiming a wholly revolutionary right of disposal. In this way the appeal of the manifestos to a linguistic nationalism issued speedily in action, and the flight of the Germans and the ruin of the German-Catholic patriciate with the takeover by Czechs created interest-groups irretrievably committed to resistance. The emigration of the late spring and early summer could be paralleled elsewhere. The reform still retained a supra-racial significance, and a line-up of German Catholics inside and outside the kingdom versus Hussite Czechs was still far from automatic. Among the towns Pilsen, which unlike many Bohemian towns was exclusively administered in the Czech language, after a brief episode of radical dominance under Wenceslas Koranda, stayed faithful to the conservative side, while on the other side Saaz, a town of mixed linguistic usage with a strong German population, stayed with the Taborites.[30] Nevertheless, the events of 1420 had gone far to unite Czech interests with the chalice. Even at this late stage, moderate Hussites and nobility again tried to treat with Sigismund; but, being rejected, reunited with the Taborites, who entered Prague in May.

The city's chances of surviving siege were not high, for Sigismund commanded a great force, and royalists held the fortresses of the Hradčany and Vyšehrad on two sides of Prague.[31] The weakness of the royalist position lay in the difficulty of supplying such an army, and, more than all else, the problem of morale, with native Bohemian Catholics fighting uneasily at the side of Sigismund's foreign subjects from Germany and Hungary. The battle of Vitkov Hill decided the issue. It was not a full-scale engagement, and the losses to Sigismund's army were not high; his troops failed by the narrowest of margins to secure the ridge of the Vitkov in a strategic position on the north-east of the city. The balance was turned by Žižka's eye for crucial ground and the fighting qualities of his Taborites.

In defeat, Sigismund listened to the advice of his Bohemian nobility, had himself crowned in the cathedral, then moved away from the city to the security

28  Discussed, Kaminsky, *Revolution*, pp. 375–83.
29  Denis, *Huss*, p. 261.
30  Seibt, in *HZ* cxcvi (1962), pp. 21–62; *Hussitica*, pp. 95–6.
31  Heymann, *Žižka*, ch. 9, for military details.

of the Kutná Hora region, where he delayed through the rest of the summer and early autumn. Never wholehearted in military plans for long, he seems to have believed that his presence alone in the kingdom would in the end rally support for him as lawful ruler, and that the Hussites' unity would break down in internecine strife. But this was sadly to underestimate both the general suspicion of him as the betrayer of Hus, and the Czech national feeling against the Germans and Hungarians in his entourage. In November he came back too late to save the Vyšehrad fortress from going down to the assault of the Praguers, and in March 1421, after other conflicts, left Bohemia altogether with little accomplished. His hesitation and final departure were valuable to the Hussite cause, for they gave Žižka the chance later in 1420 and in 1421 to reduce towns and fortresses on the Catholic and royalist side, till Bohemia, though never wholly won for the chalice, formed a substantial bastion of Hussitism.[32]

### Húska, the Adamites and the End of Želivský

Military success formed a shield for debate and organizational moves in which the Hussite parties defined their positions and eliminated their extremists. In the flush of victory after Vitkov, the Taborites attempted to swing Prague to their views, presenting a programme of Twelve Points to the community, demanding either instant action on clauses of the Four Articles, such as the disappropriation of priests, or an interpretation of the clause on 'public sins', which would have imposed a puritanical regime on the city.[33] Their call for university masters to be subject to the 'divine law', which for the Taborites meant Scripture alone, would have destroyed the position of the university as the doctrinal authority of the Utraquists, and their demand that monasteries, 'unnecessary' churches, vestments and gold and silver chalices should be destroyed went far beyond the views of the moderate majority in the city. Destruction of the monastery at Zbraslav south of the city and desecration of the royal graves by a drunken contingent added disgust to the fear of Tabor of the moderates.[34] Repudiated, the Taborites left, and in September marked the doctrinal breach with Prague Hussitism by electing one of their preachers, Nicholas of Pelhřimov, as bishop. He was needed to ordain priests, to give status to Taborite preaching, and to organize it; the election marked a stage of definition within Tabor as well as against Prague, as the informal processes of the chiliast past gave way to more settled arrangements natural to a city-state, with dependent towns, craft industries developing, and peasants paying dues; by its disregard of apostolic succession, it also closed a door to reconciliation with the Utraquists.[35]

32    This point is clarified by Heymann (*Žižka*, pp. 170–2, 174–5, 181–2, 199–208, 217–19); on the significance of the events of 1420, see F. Seibt, 'Vom Vitkov bis zum Vyšehrad', *Hussitenstudien*, pp. 185–207 (note comment on Kaminsky, *Revolution*, at p. 197); on the literature of the Taborites, see A. Molnár, 'La letteratura Taborita', *RSLR* xviii (1982), pp. 3–23.
33    See tr. in Kaminsky, *Revolution*, pp. 376–7.
34    Heymann, *Žižka*, p. 168.
35    Kaminsky, *Revolution*, pp. 385–91.

As a settled church developed in the towns of the Taborite lordship and their dependent populations, so problems of discipline arose. Martin Húska, one of the most eloquent Taborites and an 'ordainer' of Nicholas as bishop, led a party within Tabor that denied a real presence in the eucharist, and taught that the bread and wine should not be received kneeling but informally, in quantity rather than sacramentally, in love-feasts reminiscent of the early Church.[36] The eucharist turned into a commemoration meal. Ardent as the Taborites were to strip down the mass to its scriptural components, abolishing all pomp, vestments and accretions to the liturgy, pleading against their moderate Utraquist opponents that Christ did not dress in a chasuble, they were not prepared to follow Húska's inferences from Scripture and reason. The eucharist was a highly sensitive issue among all Hussites, and the Taborites, radical as they were, were yet the heirs of Matthias of Janov and the fourteenth-century reform; although they had moved from transubstantiation, none the less they were believers in a real presence, and the belief was of great emotional importance. Martin deployed the rationalist argument that the physical body of Christ was in heaven, and could not be in the eucharist,[37] and, pleading the scriptural analogy of the Feeding of the Five Thousand, the people receiving seated on the ground, he contrasted the sacramental doses of wine and bread to the full banquet of the love-feast that he wished to introduce, while followers in the passionate fashion characteristic of Tabor proceeded to empty monstrances and trample on Hosts as a demonstration against traditional sacramental doctrine and practice.

Then Tabor exercised its authority to put down Húska's followers by force. As the new views evolved, Taborite leaders were engaged in discussion, centring on liturgical practice, with the moderate Utraquists of Prague, who had to be warned of the spread of the heresy, referred to as Pikartism, from Pikart, a corruption of Beghard, and a loose term of abuse for a heretic.[38] Húska, imprisoned, then released, finally taken in the summer of 1421, was burnt in August with the concurrence of both wings of Hussitism.

Húska went too far for the majority. Fragmentary references make possible a reconstruction of his teaching as based on a belief in the realization of the kingdom among his Taborite group, in a way that made the law of Grace unnecessary. Paul's strictures on the Corinthians' confusion of the eucharist with indulgent feasts did not apply in Húska's view; his group believed it was right to make the eucharist a love-feast, in Peter Chelčický's description, 'meeting in love on the holy day, being diligent in the word of God, feasting and filling themselves up ... and not growing thin on the little piece of bread of the popish and heretical supper'.[39] Chelčický found Húska's views drastic and disconcerting.

---

36  Subtle account, with full tr. of sources, Ibid., pp. 397–433.
37  Jakoubek's version (Ibid., p. 424). Compare rationalist arguments on transubstantiation (above, pp. 66, 278, 301).
38  Kaminsky, *Revolution*, pp. 407–18. On beghards, see above, pp. 199–207; Lerner, *Free Spirit*, pp. 36–44.
39  Tr. in Kaminsky, *Revolution*, p. 424. I follow Kaminsky's reconstruction of the development of Húska's views. Note criticism of Macek (Ibid., pp. 403–4). On Chelčický, below, pp. 374–5.

Martin, he said, was 'not humble or at all willing to suffer for Christ'.[40] He quotes him as believing in a new kingdom of the saints on earth, in which the good would not suffer, and saying, 'If Christians were always to have to suffer so, I would not want to be a servant of God.'

Lawrence of Březová reported that some of the group came to believe that, because the kingdom had been realized in them, ordinary laws no longer applied. A heretical opening for the Lord's prayer, 'Our Father who art in us', was attributed to them by their opponents;[41] a section of Húska's followers, it was said, went so far as to act as if they were in the state of innocence before the Fall, men and women going naked, on the argument that clothes were a consequence of the Fall, and having sexual intercourse if they willed, and saying that it was no sin.[42] This extreme development followed on ejection from Tabor – the Adamites, as they were called, formed a strange community, defending themselves against attack from the main body, and having to be crushed by Žižka, in battle, who had numbers of them burnt. Húska himself rejected the views of this group. Žižka, who sent a list of their evil doings to Prague,[43] believed that the community committed still worse acts, murder and sodomy included.

There is now no sure means of getting behind this testimony; one can note the undeniable fact that the group had aroused Žižka's ferocious anger, and the extraordinary hot-house atmosphere of Tabor in its early years, still, despite its greater anchoring in the economic world, relatively detached from ordinary living and dominated by the intense preaching of its priests and tireless discussion of Scripture. It was a setting in which every kind of dissident and novel belief was liable to come rapidly to life. Lawrence of Březová, the chronicler, attributed the start of the well-attested eucharistic heresy of Húska to the influence of a party of Pikarts and their families who first came to Prague as refugees in 1418.[44] The Pikarts are likely to be a red herring; in any case it is not necessary to call them in to explain the emergence of fresh heresy on the radical side in 1420–1. Taboritism itself was the great incubator of heresy. But the long tradition of sexual slander smearing doctrinal dissidents, the improbable nature of their naked romps in Bohemian weather at the relevant seasons and the high suspicion that *a priori* thinking, rather than true reportage, created the Adamites, makes slander the likeliest source of the accusations. Taborite innovation had reached its highwater mark at the destruction of the Adamites.[45]

Prague came to the fore in the months after the fall of the Vyšehrad in November 1420.[46] The original centre for reform and revolution, it gained

---

40   Ibid., p. 400.

41   Ibid., p. 427. Note the curious parallel with the Amalriciani (see above, pp. 107–8).

42   Report of Lawrence of Březová, tr. Kaminsky, *Revolution*, p. 430; *FRB* v, p. 475.

43   *FRB* v, pp. 517–20; tr. Kalivoda, *Das hussitische Denken*, pp. 327–9. Episode discussed by Lerner (*Free Spirit*, pp. 119–24).

44   *FRB* v, p. 431; discussed, Lerner, *Free Spirit*, pp. 121–3.

45   A. Patschovsky, 'Der taboritische Chiliasmus', *Häresie*, ed. Šmahel, pp. 169–95 is surely correct; Pikarts, pp. 177–80; climate, p. 184.

46   F. Seibt, 'Communitas primogenita: zur Prager Hegemonialpolitik in der hussitischen Revolution', *HJB* LXXXI (1962), pp. 80–100.

prestige from the military success won by its own forces, Tabor being sparsely represented at the assault; and in the spring it gathered under its hegemony a league of cities in mid- and western Bohemia. The adherence of Conrad of Vechta to the Four Articles in April 1421, after long wavering, was also a gain for Prague as well as for the cause of Hussitism generally.[47] His adherence ensured that there would be a sufficient flow of ordinations to eliminate the risk of priesthood in Bohemia gradually dying out, and it gave a cover of legitimacy to Hussitism, however much this was repudiated by Sigismund and the ecclesiastics in the outside world. But at Čáslav, where in June 1421 a diet declared its adherence to the Four Articles, again rejected Sigismund, and attempted to gain Silesia and Lusatia for the movement, the composition of the government of twenty members, set up as a kind of oligarchic substitute for a ruler, showed by the limited place it gave to Prague's representatives that the capital's bid for leadership would not succeed.[48] Nevertheless, its capture by the radical forces would still have meant a fundamental change in the balance within Bohemia, and the year of Prague's bid for hegemony as a city was also the year of Želivský's boldest attempt to bring both Old and New Town under his dictatorship.[49]

The accidental death of Nicholas of Hus late in 1420 gave an opening for leadership, and the takeover of German and Catholic houses by Želivský's adherents in the aftermath of the emigration of spring 1420 strengthened the radicals' voting power. After Čáslav he felt strong enough to sack the administrators of the Old Town and declare the union of New and Old. For some months the city was ruled under the dictatorship of one of his radical supporters. But it was an uneasy success; Želivský always had the crowd with him to push forward his measures, but also the long-term opposition of the propertied classes, the moderate Utraquists and the Prague patriciate against him working on his administrators, so that political radicals appointed by him lost the edge of their zeal in face of conservative pressure. What finally broke him was the defeat of the Prague forces at Most and his failure to bring victory in the field to the city's forces in the way that Žižka had done for the Taborites. In February 1422 John Hvězda, his dictator, lost office; in March Hvězda's more conservative successor had him executed. His courageous death brought a reaction from the manual workers that formed his support, yet fatally weakened his party: Prague thereafter could be usually reckoned as a pillar of the moderate party, in religion and politics.

The clash of classes and the inability of the artisans and poor to prevail against the wealthier in Prague were the main reasons for Želivský's fall. Religion also played a part, for Želivský believed in *scriptura sola* as the authority for Hussitism, and was constantly attempting to upset the doctrinal position of the university masters and subject it to the 'divine law', as the Taborites did, while his party came to treat the mass as a bare communion service, in the manner of Tabor.

---

47  Heymann, *Žižka*, pp. 220–1.
48  Ibid., ch. 14; Heymann, 'The national assembly of Čáslav', *MH* VIII (1954), pp. 32–55.
49  Kaminsky, *Revolution*, pp. 451–60; Heymann, *Žižka*, pp. 241–53, 266–7, 272–3, 278–80, 307–18.

Jakoubek and the university masters were firm against Želivský. 'Be diligent. Stop him,'[50] were Jakoubek's words to the magistrates, two days before Želivský's murder.

## The Major Parties

As Prague and Tabor thus cut down their dissidents, debate still continued between the moderate centre of Utraquism, based in the capital, and the radical force of Taboritism. While they talked, searching for a way to unity, their own differences tended to clarify.[51] Tabor's supporters debated their eucharistic beliefs, and settled on a common doctrine, that Christ's body and blood were contained in the bread and wine 'in a sacramental or figurative sense'.[52] This divided Tabor from the believers in transubstantiation or consubstantiation on the moderate Utraquist side. Controversy over mass vestments continued; as usual in such conflicts, it was the visible sign of difference that attracted most attention, intensified by the focus of all Hussites on the eucharist, the natural consequence of their tradition and of the adoption of the lay chalice. Taborite ritual was now of the simplest – consisting of a common recitation of the Lord's Prayer, then the words of Christ at the Last Supper, pronounced in the vernacular on an unconsecrated altar, perhaps a table, the eucharistic vessels being ordinary cups and plates, and the Church being bare of adornment. Priests wore no vestments, and were not distinguished from the laity. All received communion. Sermons, vernacular singing, and gospel-reading formed a part of what was a congregational service, with an emphasis very different from that of the traditional mass. When Taborites discussed the eucharistic celebrations of the Utraquist party, they attacked features of it as being useless to the people. The utility to the congregation is foremost. Fixed forms were inimical to the Taborite mode of life – readings of set portions of Scripture, for example, were dismissed because they would prevent the clergy from exposition 'according to the needs of the people and the time'.[53]

Divergences thus went so far between Utraquist and Taborite practice that it was difficult to see how any compromise formula could be worked out, though their representatives tried hard to do so. Moreover, beneath the liturgical differences lay a fundamental distinction of outlook which ran through all the issues dividing the parties. The Utraquists were reformers who desired changes where they saw a necessity for them; if there was not a positive reason for change in existing structures, on the whole they preferred to keep them. The Taborites were revolutionaries who insisted that all belief and practice must be brought to the touchstone of Scripture, the practice of the primitive Church, and common utility. It was *scriptura sola* at its starkest, set in the context of independent

---

50   Kaminsky, *Revolution*, p. 460.
51   Ibid., pp. 436–52, 460–81. For Tabor, I found Kaminsky's discussion in *The Czechoslovak Contribution*, pp. 210–23, esp. helpful.
52   Kaminsky, *Revolution*, p. 455.
53   Ibid., p. 470. See description of Taborite eucharist (Ibid., pp. 444–5).

communities of peasants and artisans, wielding political and military power. Under its impetus, a series of components of traditional Catholicism, purgatory, the intercessory role of the saints and of Mary, the sacrifice of the mass, went down to destruction, leaving a religion of stark contrasts, between heaven and hell, God and Antichrist, Scripture and the Babylon of Rome.

One other feature of Tabor, which sprang from the residue of the eschatological expectation in which it was born, was the belief, helpfully expounded by Kaminsky, that they were, not merely the imitators of the primitive Church, but that they in some way reincarnated that Church and possessed all its powers. This acceptance of a sovereign power of decision over all precedent and tradition emerges from Nicholas of Pelhřimov's discussion of the reliance to be placed on the Four Doctors and the Four Councils, a norm for the Utraquists. 'If by revelation...of Scripture', he said, 'God should today grant a more potent understanding to someone, that man would be more to be believed than those Doctors.'[54] Scriptura sola, the political independence and military power of the Taborite communities, and their belief in God's direct guidance on them, together made the Taborites one of the most dynamic movements of the Middle Ages. But it also made any form of accommodation with them extraordinarily hard.

Through the debates the two major parties were in fact drawing apart, for all the efforts at compromise. The effects of definition can be seen in the decisions of two synods, one held after the diet of Čáslav in 1421, the other almost a year later in 1422. The first, defining eucharistic belief in terms of the real presence, left open the way to compromise with Tabor; the second, by using the term 'corporeal substance', excluded their beliefs.[55] Within Tabor the departure of Žižka to join the Orebites removed an influence tending to restraint in religious matters; Tabor was allowed to become more radical, and compromise became yet more difficult.[56] Among the Utraquists the rise of John Příbram, a former adherent of Jakoubek, who still wanted the lay chalice, but in the context of reconciliation with Rome, and was prepared to cut away the other innovations of Hussitism to get an accommodation with the Church, sharpened the division with Tabor.[57] In 1422 and 1423 there were episodes of actual fighting between the two sides. The search for a substitute for Sigismund tended to weigh on the conservative side, for the candidate who arrived in Bohemia, Sigismund Korybut, nephew of Witold of Lithuania, first as governor-general for his uncle, then later as a claimant in his own right, favoured moderation in the reform.[58] His only chance, he came to see, of achieving acceptance in Europe as king in place of Sigismund was by making a reconciliation with the papacy, and so his influence was all on the side of

54 Ibid., p. 469.
55 Ibid., pp. 462–3.
56 Heymann, Žižka, pp. 354–6, 361–73.
57 Kaminsky, Revolution, p. 461.
58 Heymann, Žižka, ch. 20, Kaminsky, Revolution, pp. 460–2; below, p. 365; on the Slav background, see Denis, Huss, pp. 308–25; later career of Korybut in Heymann and Denis; Bartoš, Revolution, pp. 5–24.

Přibram's party. In any case, he was the candidate of the moderates, the nobles and bourgeois, who were uneasy at having no monarch. On the other side, Žižka originally tolerated Korybut. Tabor and the other radicals as a whole were indifferent, if not hostile, to monarchy.

It can be seen that almost every factor, the religious division, the conflict of class implicit behind it, and the differences in national policy, tended to keep Utraquists and Taborites apart. In favour of unity was the sense of common origin in the Bohemian reform, the symbol of the lay chalice, and the belief of many in both parties in the value of discussion. Tabor had a learned leadership, able and willing to engage in debate. There were experiments in toleration, but the Utraquists, though open to considerable deviation, were in the last resort unable to accept two such distinct sets of belief in Bohemia, while in Tabor there was too much that was irreconcilable. The gulf yawned.

One factor above all kept the two parties from civil war: the continuing pressure from the outside world. Sigismund had not given up the struggle when he withdrew in March 1421; he came again towards the end of the year with a formidable force, missed his chance of co-ordinating a two-pronged attack on the kingdom, but still had a numerical superiority over his opponents when Žižka soundly defeated him at Německý Brod early in 1422.[59] Vanquished, still attempting diplomatic moves against the Hussites, then distracted by his oriental schemes and the problem of the Turks, and not always on good terms with the imperial princes, he did not return for fourteen years to Bohemia. Nevertheless, there were other expeditions and pressures: still, if not so formidable, Martin V remained an unyielding opponent and Ulrich of Rosenberg's party among the nobility supported conservatism.[60]

Every crusade – and there were such expeditions, given the crusade indulgence, in 1420, 1421, 1422, 1427 and 1431, as well as lesser forays – pushed the parties into unity to repel the invader. Bohemia was a beleaguered country; alone, the moderates could not be sure of defending it; they had to sink their differences with the radicals to keep native independence and the lay chalice in being. And yet military action, decisive as it was, only staved off the problem of the future of Hussitism. What was to happen next? Both Tabor and the moderates wanted in their different ways to spread their views to the outside world; they could, together, defend the bastion of Bohemia against any army that the Catholics, often ill-led, were able to put against them, earning in the process such a reputation for Hussite troops that opposing forces sometimes dissolved at the mere sight of them; but they did not have anything like the same success in the peaceful process of disseminating their beliefs. From about 1423 at latest the support of Bohemia for Hussitism could be expected to hold; but there was no major fresh advance made after that date for the chalice, or for either of the two parties.

59   Heymann, *Žižka*, pp. 302–3; see Heymann, 'The crusades against the Hussites', *A History of the Crusades* III, ed. A. Hazard (Madison, 1975), pp. 586–646.
60   Seibt, 'Die Zeit', pp. 518–31, describes this period; list of crusades: p. 525; see map 8 above for Ulrich of Rosenberg's party.

## Attempts at Spreading Hussitism

One plan that foundered sprang from the moderates, aiming at a reconciliation with the Church on terms that would preserve the chalice and their reform. Alliance with Slav powers to the east on a platform of resistance to Germans seemed to offer the chance of replacing Sigismund, bringing in a diplomatic counterweight to the emperor, and perhaps spreading Hussitism. Hence embassies offered the crown to the Slav rulers, Wladislav Jagiello, king of Poland, and his cousin Witold, grand duke of Lithuania. There were factors for the scheme in the Slav resurgence, which had led to the defeat of the Teutonic order at Tannenberg in 1410. Czechs had aided Poles on that occasion, and there was some common Slav feeling to build on. Sparks of Hussitism had reached Poland through native students attending the Charles University; Jerome of Prague had once stayed at the court of Witold; the reactions of Sigismund and the fears of Polish bishops suggest that a field for missionary activity did exist in these Slav lands.[61] Wladislav, however, though he would have welcomed a chance to strike at Sigismund, had too much to lose by acceptance. Witold, more committed against Sigismund, eager to win a crown, and at times enticed by the vision of a grand pan-Slav realm, maintained his interest longer; but the papacy's influence was insistent, and he fell away in 1423. His nephew Sigismund Korybut, originally his emissary, offered himself as candidate in 1424, and in effect, became leader after the death of Žižka. But he brought only himself and a few followers, not the support of another State, for Witold disowned him; when in power the military success of a Žižka generally eluded him, and he entered on secret negotiations with Martin v. When discovered, he was imprisoned in 1427, and sent home in 1428.[62] The affair discredited for the time John Příbram and his party. The plans for Slav alliance had not worked.

Peaceful missionizing in German-speaking lands was another means of spreading Hussitism; it produced sparks of response but no conflagration, and did not change the outlook for the Bohemian cause. There were no major conversions to swing a ruler or a whole region to the chalice, only quiet underground missionizing on the pattern of the Waldensians by individuals who become known to us when they eventually fall into the hands of the inquisition.[63] Perhaps the most notable of them was Friedrich Reiser of Donauwörth, who received episcopal consecration at Tabor and was active for a long period in south Germany and Alsace till his burning in 1458; he was succeeded in office by Stephen of Basle for a further ten years. But nothing of great significance came of this work. The

61 Heymann, Žižka, pp. 30–1, Seibt, 'Die Zeit', p. 532; Denis, Huss, p. 309. Seibt, Hussitica, pp. 82–3 is interesting.
62 Heymann, Žižka, pp. 456–7, 460–1.
63 Seibt, 'Die Zeit', p. 532; Hussitica, pp. 94–5; H. Köpstein, 'Zu den Auswirkungen der hussitische-revolutionären Bewegung in Franken', Aus 500 Jahren deutsch-tschechoslowakische Geschichte, ed. K. Obermann, J. Polisensky (1958), pp. 16–20; H. Köpstein, 'Über den deutschen Hussiten Friedrich Reiser', ZG vii (1959), pp. 1068–82; above, pp. 177–8.

Hussites worked to spread their views in popular propaganda: the Four Articles were speedily translated and spread, and vernacular manifestos were dispatched to explain their movement. Saaz, the German-speaking area attached to Hussitism in northern Bohemia, was especially active in the field of written propaganda. But, without the rapid and effective dissemination of views made possible by the printing-press in the sixteenth century, the whole enterprise remained necessarily small-scale. Luther sold some 30,000 copies of his early works between 1517 and 1520; no comparable opportunity was available to the Hussites. Moreover, peaceful missionizing did not consort easily with military power, and the very success of the movement in Bohemia tended to work against its influence outside.[64] The decree of Kutná Hora, leading to the flight of German masters, created an interest block against Hussite theses in neighbouring universities; the flight of German Catholics later worked in the same direction. The association between the reform and Czech linguistic nationalism naturally weakened the international potential of Hussitism.

## The Offensive Expeditions

Peaceful missionary work then, did not, perhaps could not, be expected to bring victory to the cause. There remained military power and negotiation at the highest level with ecclesiastical authority, to secure recognition for the Bohemian movement that would give it immediate security from attack in its own lands, with the possibility of spreading in Europe later. From 1426 to 1433 Procop the Shaven, the Taborite priest from southern Bohemia, heir in military skills to Žižka, though not quite his equal, led expeditions into neighbouring lands, with the aim of extorting by force from the Church this official recognition.[65] 'We truly bear the burden of the war,' he said, 'only in order to bring about the recognition of these holy truths by the Church of God, and to live and see the blessing of peace and good days from which unity, brotherly love, moral reform and everything else will come.' Procop led radical forces, and a secondary aim was to maintain *élan* in groups, still radical in religion, that had lost their revolutionary zeal in social matters, and were in danger of earning the hatred of the peasants for their exactions. Action abroad brought booty and prestige without damaging Bohemia. The old magic in fighting still worked, and Procop won great victories, conquering Silesia, winning tribute from the Germans round about, and taking his army to the Baltic in support of Poland. His actions, the expeditions of the Orphans, the former Orebites, and the sufferings of the lands round Bohemia, coupled with the fears of churchmen that Hussitism might spread if the situation were not defused, led to negotiation.

---

64    This still seems a fair generalization, despite the evidence for German Hussitism given by Seibt, 'Die Zeit', pp. 524, 529–30 (with full references).
65    Heymann, *Žižka*, pp. 457–63; Bartoš, *Revolution*, chs 3–8; speech of Procop on war and peace: p. 101.

## Negotiation and Settlement

One more crusade was mounted, then repulsed at Domažlice in 1431. In 1433 long preliminary negotiation ended in the entry of a party of Bohemians on reasonable terms to Basle to treat with the fathers of the council. This included all the major groups, Procop himself, John Rokycana, the skilful and learned representative of what might be called the middle Utraquist group, anxious for acceptance by the Church, but only in a manner that would preserve the substance of their wishes; Nicholas of Pelhřimov for the Taborites, and Peter Payne for the Orphans.[66] Thus unity held as far as the negotiating table. On the other side, the leading spirit at the council, Cardinal Cesarini, who barely saved his life at Domažlice, had seen in practice the threat which Hussite power presented, and was convinced of the necessity to negotiate and to make reforms in the Church, more so than the hesitant pope, Eugenius IV, with whom the council was at odds.

Yet neither Cesarini nor his fellow members of the council intended that changes, even such as moderate Hussites wanted, should be imposed in the West; they desired to carry out reforms, indeed, on their own lines, but, most of all, to lead back the erring flock in Bohemia to the Church by gentle but temporary compromise and conciliation. Hussites cherished still the illusion that, if they were allowed to speak, the reasonableness of their case and the necessity for the lay chalice would be seen by ecclesiastical authority. It was an idea that reached back to Hus, in his undelivered sermon on the evils in the Church for the fathers at Constance; and it was still held at Basle, remarkably enough, by Procop the Shaven. That illusion was broken; still, the negotiators were realistic enough to insist on a foolproof safe conduct for their party, and they tried hard to secure an imposition of the lay chalice on all in Bohemia, Catholics as well as Utraquists, and so obviate the dangers of civil war.

Jakoubek, the finest of bridge-builders between the parties because of his personality and his role as the initiator of the chalice, had died in 1429: no-one could replace him. The economic decline of the Charles University had long dimmed the ardour of some university masters. The nobles mistrusted the military forces of the radicals, who had fought too long and now had too many mercenaries in their ranks. The negotiations did not stop their expeditions, still winning victories in 1431, 1432 and 1433, yet showing signs of indiscipline.[67]

In 1433 the radicals tried to eliminate Pilsen and its region of south-west Bohemia. Siege was opened in July.[68] The target was tempting because Pilsen and its *Landfriede* formed the last major support for Catholicism at a time when a

---

66 Denis, *Huss*, ch. 11; E. F. Jacob, 'The Bohemians at the Council of Basel, 1433', *Prague Essays*, ed. R. W. Seton-Watson (1948), pp. 81–123; Creighton, *Papacy* II, chs 5 and 6; on Rokycana, see Heymann, 'John Rokycana: Church reformer between Hus and Luther', *CH* XXVIII (1959), pp. 240–80; on Payne, see above, p. 295; Bartoš, *Revolution*, pp. 73–98.
67 For this phase, see Bartoš, *Revolution* (clear narrative by master of Hussite history, but with some lack of perspective on opponents of Hussitism), pp. 73–105.
68 Ibid., pp. 105–11.

series of other, external objectives had been closed to Hussite offensives by truce agreements, yet the decision to attack was fateful. It meant bringing the sufferings of war back again to Bohemia, and it exceeded the armies' powers. Opinion, influenced on the one side by the effect of army requisitions and on the other by the vision of peace aroused, yet not fulfilled, by the Basle negotiations, began to move against the fighting brotherhoods. The blockade, weakened by the introduction of provisions by the Taborite traitor Přibík of Klenové, dragged on; troubles broke out and Procop, removed from command by his captains, was replaced after a time by the unsatisfactory Čapek of Sány. While the brotherhoods were preoccupied in Pilsen, a conspiracy was hatched. The siege was broken off and on 30 May 1434 a confederation of conservative forces, including Hussite, Moravian and Catholic nobility and the Old Town of Prague, met the radicals, Taborites, Orphans and New Town under Procop in battle at Lipany and utterly defeated them.[69]

Curiously, smoke and wagon formation that had been so potent for the defeat of the crusading army at Ústí on the Elbe in 1425, was here cunningly turned against the Taborites and Orphans, who were lured out of their secure encampment and destroyed. Procop, who had so notably combined military leadership with the gifts of a statesman, was among the dead.

The battle marked the end of the military power of the radicals and opened the way to the acceptance of the Church's terms. The legates of the council had reported back that the lay chalice was one issue which would command wide support in the country; the council would have to make a concession of substance. In a confused scene in November 1433 at Prague, representatives of both sides accepted a version of the Four Articles known as the Compactata of Basle.[70] Lipany enabled this to become the basis of a final settlement, after yet more negotiation, at Jihlava, when in 1436 the Bohemians promised peace and were reconciled to the Church.

The settlement allowed the lay chalice for all who wished it, but did not declare it to be holy and salutary and did not impose it on the country. Division in Bohemia between Utraquists and Catholics thus remained. The council had merely granted permission for the chalice but had not encouraged it and had given no opening for the spread of the practice in the Church. The communion of infants, a valued Hussite practice, was not dealt with. The punishment of mortal sin was reserved to those 'whose office it is'; preaching was to be conducted by 'the priests of the Lord and by worthy deacons'.[71] Little here was to be seen of the radicals' zeal for righteousness in the kingdom, and the free preaching of lay men and women that they permitted. Priests were not to be owners of estates and they were to administer faithfully the property of the

69   Ibid., pp. 112–18.
70   Partial text in Denis, *Huss*, pp. 495–8; analysis: W. Eberhard, *Konfessionsbildung und Stände in Böhmen, 1478–1530* (1981), pp. 41–3; review article: R. Kalivoda, 'A new approach to the post Hussite development of Hussitism', *CV* xxvii (1984), pp. 73–90.
71   Heymann, *Žižka*, p. 471; on infant communion, D. R. Holeton, *La Communion des tout-petits enfants* (1989).

Church. The last clause came nearest to the most substantial effect of the Hussite revolution: the widespread transfer of Church and monastic lands to the laity, whose secure ownership was guaranteed by Sigismund fifteen days after the ceremony at Jihlava.

With the reconciliation with the Church came also the return of the legitimate ruler. In the last years of the negotiations Sigismund had played a skilful role, promising more privately to the Hussites than the representatives of Basle would concede, until in the end they accepted a weak settlement on the security of Sigismund's word. They were deceived; once back in power, Sigismund, in the short period before his death in 1437, initiated a Catholic reaction. Rokycana, elected archbishop of Prague by the Estates in 1437 with an eye to thus providing a Utraquist whose presence in the archiepiscopate should act as a guarantee of the security of the Compactata, was never confirmed in his office, and the province was ruled administratively into the sixteenth century.[72] The cathedral, on the castle side of the Vltava, occupied by a Catholic chapter, never received him; in the eyes of the papacy the see had remained vacant from the death of Conrad of Vechta.

The return of Sigismund marked the end of the classic phase of Hussite history. Between 1415 and 1436 the Hussites defied the Church and were the first declared heretics to beat off a Catholic crusade. In these years they changed entirely the basis of the economic life of the Church in Bohemia, produced a new kind of clergy, and forced high ecclesiastical authority to treat with them on equal terms. Inside their country they undermined the centralized power of the Luxemburg monarchy and produced a fighting force to terrorize Europe. Though they had no-one to match the powerful, if flawed, intellect of Wyclif, they mobilized a remarkable variety of interest and talent before 1419, and threw up a series of notable personalities, from Hus himself to Jakoubek, with his advocacy of the chalice and his leadership in the university, Nicholas of Dresden as a popular agitator, Želivský as priest-politician, Žižka and Procop as field commanders. Their fatal weakness lay in the cleft dividing the radical from the moderate wing of Hussitism. Radicals, through Želivský, made the revolution, and, through Žižka and the Taborites, defended it. Moderates could not do without them, yet could not in the long run live with them. Beside the fighting, there were also quite novel episodes of toleration, a will on both sides to widen the bounds of discussion, and a perennial, sometimes naïve yet refreshing belief in the potency of discussion in religious affairs.[73] In the end, the division of parties destroyed the pristine aims of the movement; war-weariness combined with the skills of Catholic representatives and of Sigismund to bring about a settlement unsatisfactory and insecure to the Bohemians.

---

72   G. H. Williams, *The Radical Reformation* (1962), pp. 209–10.

73   See Seibt, in *HZ* cxcvi (1962), pp. 21–62; for effects of Hussite revolution (esp. disendowment of Church), see E. Werner, 'Die hussitische Revolution: Revolutionsbegriff und Revolutionsergebnis im Spiegel marxistischer, insonderheit tschechoslovakischer Forschungen', *SSAWL* Phil-hist. Klasse cxxix (1989), pp. 5–38.

At Jihlava the Hussites were given a promise that future bishops would be ready to ordain Utraquist candidates to the priesthood. It was said that the Council of Basle would be sending letters to all Christian princes requiring them to accept the Utraquist Bohemians as good sons of the Church.[74] These steps were never taken, and the Hussites were not given the secure and lasting recognition for which they had fought and negotiated. Nor had they succeeded in spreading their reform outside the lands of the Bohemian crown.

And yet a letter of majesty issued by Sigismund early in 1436, a part of the price paid by him for his return to power, made arrangements to provide security for Utraquist priests and their parishes. Catholics, communicating under one kind, were confined to parishes where the practice of Utraquism had never existed. Parishes where communion had been given under both kinds were to continue their Utraquist tradition – in other words the decisive issue was not the will of the king, or the beliefs and practice of the priest, but the will of the congregation in the parish.[75] Amidst much that proved disappointing to the Utraquist cause, these decisions of Sigismund, forging a base for religious freedom and for the coexistence of Catholics and Utraquists, were potent for the future. They opened the way to a new phase of Utraquist history, in which the Bohemians fought, not so much for the right to spread, or even impose Utraquism in the Church at large, but for a measure of religious independence in their own country.

74   Eberhard, *Konfessionsbildung*, p. 43.
75   Ibid., p. 44.

# 18

# The *Unitas Fratrum* and the Development of Confessions

### The Emergence of George of Poděbrady

Rokycana's failure to achieve recognition was symbolic of the changes occuring within the Hussite movement. Tenacious, personally humble, capable of fiery preaching, he was a reformer rather than a confessional leader or a theologian of high calibre and to the end of his days looked for a reconciliation with the papacy which never came.[1] Utraquism had an emotional significance, a history and link to fighting Czech nationalism sufficient to maintain it in being, but its earlier supporters had never wished for a break with the Church and as they waited and manoeuvred for acceptance by a pope on terms acceptable to their tradition, something of the inner vitality of their movement began to fade.

The disorder in the country and the emergence of regional Landpeace associations facilitated the rise of a shrewd Czech nobleman, George of Poděbrady, who after the death of Albert of Austria, Sigismund's Habsburg son-in-law, succeeded in becoming governor of Bohemia, then regent to Albert's son Wladislav Posthumous and, finally, after Wladislav's premature death, king of Bohemia in 1458.[2] At the coronation the awkward problem of the status of Rokycana, unrecognized as archbishop of Prague, and his sacramental role, was resolved by securing the services of two Hungarian bishops who provided the vital episcopal presence while Catholic lords placed the crown on George's head and he swore an oath in secret to maintain obedience to the Roman Church and lead his people 'from errors, sects and heresies'. Fortunately, Charles IV's coronation *ordo*, which George followed, prescribed that the royal candidate should receive communion from the chalice, and the act satisfied the Utraquists. Thus, diplomatically, with mental reservations about the significance of the secret oath (for

---

1  F. G. Heymann, 'John Rokycana: Church reformer between Hus and Luther', pp. 240–80; F. Seibt, 'Das Zeitalter Georgs von Podiebrady', *Handbuch der Geschichte der böhmischen Länder*, ed. K. Bosl, I (1967), pp. 537–68 at pp. 555–6.
2  F. G. Heymann, *George of Bohemia, King of Heretics* (Princeton, 1965); Klassen, *Nobility*, p. 143, contrasts his fate with that of Čeněk of Vartemberk's dynasty.

George maintained that Utraquism, accepted by the Compactata, could not be regarded as heresy), a Hussite ruler, not even from the blood royal in descent from the Luxemburg dynasty, was accepted as king.[3]

George's native wit brought him recognition by Pius II and the Emperor Frederick III and enabled him at first to neutralize the persistent opposition of Catholic Breslau as a prelude to a blunt request to Pius for a permanent recognition of the chalice in 1462. It failed utterly, leading to a sentence against George personally by Paul II in 1465, a fostering of the rise of the Catholic League of the Green Mountain of opposition aristocrats within his lands and a struggle against his rule under a Catholic banner by Matthias of Hungary. George's qualities as a ruler, the papacy's wish to organize resistance to the Turks, used by George's diplomats to elaborate a scheme for international peace amongst princes (which would incidentally have preserved George's lands from ecclesiastical sanctions) and a subtle blend of force and diplomacy preserved his rule in all dangers.[4] But at his death in 1471 he did not feel strong enough to bequeath his kingdom to his son. Instead he passed the inheritance to the Catholic Wladislav II of Poland of the Jagiellon dynasty. The status of Utraquism within the kingdom was preserved but the opportunities for the spread of the chalice that had once appeared open through the election of a Hussite ruler passed away.

Utraquist attitudes to the papacy were marked by a strange blend of suspicion and optimism. Mistrust flared up, no doubt reinforced by the memories of years of battling against papal armies, when Cardinal Carvajal, entrusted with a mission of enquiry by Nicholas V in 1448, attempted to leave Prague in secrecy after he had encountered Hussite opposition to his views. He took with him – possibly accidentally – the original copy of the Compactata of Basle which he had been studying in his lodgings. A detachment of cavalry ensured that it was taken from him before he reached the frontier.[5] Much faith was placed in the Compactata, negotiated at a time when the pope had not finally broken with the council, and in certain ambiguous phrases about it contained in letters of Eugenius IV. It was not realized how much the fact that it was negotiated with the council in the first instance rather than the papacy weakened its effect, and how determined the post-Basle papacy was to liquidate the effects of conciliarism, including the agreement with the Utraquists.

As Aeneas Sylvius Piccolomini, Pius II in his younger days in 1451 had visited Bohemia on behalf of Frederick III and had talked sympathetically with George: it led George to hope for too much from Aeneas when he attained office. The trip to and from Bohemia included a detour to Tabor on the way home, where Aeneas looked on the gate with its shields, one of an angel carrying a chalice and the other of Jan Žižka, and debated theology with veteran Taborites and a Polish

---

3   Heymann, *George*, pp. 160–72.
4   Analysis of policy in Seibt, 'Das Zeitalter', pp. 539–52; see also Heymann, *George*, pp. 586–611, for survey, interesting on relationship between George's policy, Utraquism and the *Unitas*.
5   Heymann, *George*, pp. 36–40.

refugee theologian, John Gałka. The biblical knowledge of some Taborite women impressed him and he contrasted it to that of contemporary Italian priests, to their detriment. But his strongest impression was of the depth and variety of heresies which he encountered, and of the boldness of their defenders.[6] Behind the movement for the chalice lay a more profound doctrinal challenge to the Church. The most that he was prepared to allow for the Utraquists was a temporary concession of the chalice for those who had been accustomed to it, a concession which would be extinguished as an older generation died out. This was not what the Hussite armies had battled for.

Illusions about the possibilities of a papal acceptance were favoured by a certain intellectual isolation of the Utraquist leadership. George had scant formal education, no Latin and limited German: he and his servants, capable enough in their dealings with neighbouring princes, lacked insight into the papal curia and its assumptions. Rokycana's international contacts were restricted by his anomalous position. He tended to share the view of other Utraquist churchmen that, because the lay chalice was rightful, Church authority was in the end bound to concede it. The Compactata had demonstrated that concessions could be won from authority: it was a matter of time, patience and determination before permanent recognition was obtained. They did not see the truth, that though individual popes differed in the means which they favoured in dealing with the problem of Bohemia, all were set on the ultimate elimination of the lay chalice.

Reaction against the long wars and the casual violence associated with the breakdown of the brotherhoods, as well as George's need to establish his orthodoxy in the diplomatic struggle for his own recognition, created a pressure for order and respectability. As governor of Bohemia in 1452 he secured the surrender of Tabor, now a shadow of its former self, and imprisoned a recalcitrant few, including their bishop Nicholas of Pelhřimov. In 1461 he renewed the decree of Charles iv against heresy. In 1462 he put pressure on a convocation of clergy, both Catholic and Utraquist, to cease wrangling – a measure that was prudent in view of the political implications of religious tension within his lands, but marked a contrast with the early Hussite decades of vivid and informed debate among theologians.[7]

Circumstances, and George's policy, were combining to confirm the continuing existence of two recognized confessions, Catholic and Utraquist. George worked hard to see that they lived in peace with each other. A Hussite Latin gradual from the years 1450–60, commemorating the martyrdoms of Hus and of Jerome of Prague on Hus's death-day of 6 July, set in a liturgical context quite Roman and conservative, with a word-play on *constancia*, linking the site of the council which condemned Hus to his own fidelity to death, reflects the attitude of Utraquism of the time, cautious yet firm, waiting for recognition.[8]

---

6  H. Kaminsky, 'Pius Aeneas among the Taborites', *CH* xxviii (1959), pp. 281–309.
7  Heymann, *George*, pp. 60–3, 238–44, 290–1.
8  T. J. Talley, 'A Hussite Latin gradual of the xv century', *Bulletin of the General Theological Seminary* xlviii (1962), pp. 8–13; the whole context, D. Holeton, 'O felix Bohemia', pp. 390–7.

On the other side, as Seibt has observed, the Catholic Church in Bohemia and Moravia about this time took on some of the attributes of a Counter-Reformation, in Moravia organized round the bishopric of Olomouc and in Prague, in the absence of a recognized archbishop, led by the cathedral chapter and dean. In Moravia elements of a traditional structure of churches and monasteries survived and there were even new monastic foundations.[9] St John Capistrano's violent preaching against Utraquism in journeys between 1451 and 1454 had little effect in the heartlands of the movement but helped to renew Catholic support in Silesia, uneasy with the compromises of its leading class.[10]

Stability rather than mission was the keynote of Utraquism – a stability that was made more difficult by the effects of the non-recognition of Rokycana in a shortage of fresh ordinations to a priesthood serving those who accepted communion in both kinds. For Rokycana to ordain would weaken the Utraquists' case for papal recognition. Contact with the Greek Church to secure valid ordinations was not fruitful and the expedient use of Polish clergy, who were willing to leave their country and accept Utraquism for the sake of higher living standards, weakened fervour.[11] The royal subchamberlain, Vaněk Valečovsky, a moderate Utraquist, troubled by the politicization and deteriorating standards of the clergy of his confession, agitated in 1457 against their weaknesses.[12] On the wall of his house in the Old Town he had an allegory of the churches painted, reproaching the clergy on both sides. Horses were attached to both ends of a wagon, with rival coachmen, symbolizing the clergy both Catholic and Utraquist, whipping them up to pull in rival directions, while the passengers, frustrated in their search for salvation, fought among themselves.

## The Rise of the *Unitas Fratrum*

Dissatisfaction with the Utraquists led directly to the rise of a third religious force in Bohemia and Moravia. Peter Chelčický, identified by Bartoš as a yeoman farmer called Peter of Záhorka who had at first been attracted to the Taborites, separated himself from them because of their acceptance of the rightfulness of shedding blood. 'If power were supposed to be administered through Christ's faith by means of battles and punishments', he asked, 'why would Christ have abolished the Jewish Law and established a different, spiritual one?'[13] Chelčický

---

9   Seibt, 'Das Zeitalter', pp. 554–5.

10   Ibid., p. 555; Heymann, *George*, pp. 69–80, 119–20; criticism of J. Hofer: p. 69, n. 9; R. Rýšavý, 'Die erste Hussiten-mission des heiligen Johannes v. Capestrano in Mähren (1451)', *FS* xix (1932), pp. 225–55.

11   For the problems of the Church, see E. Denis, *Fin de l'indépendance Bohème* i: *Georges de Podiebrad. Les Jagellons* (1890); for its historiographical significance, see Eberhard, *Konfessionsbildung*, p. 19; the 1930 reissue of Denis: p. 21, n. 50; illuminating assessment, Eberhard, 'Ernest Denis, Konzeption der böhmischen Geschichte und ihre Funktion in der tschechischen Geschichtswissenschaft', *Frankreich und die böhmischen Länder im 19 und 20 Jahrhundert*, ed. F. Seibt, M. Neumüller (Munich, 1990), pp. 49–66.

12   Heymann, *George*, pp. 100–2.

13   Kaminsky, *Revolution*, p. 322; his relation to Tabor and the Waldensians, pp. 391–7; F. Seibt, 'Peter Chelčický', *Lebensbilder zur Geschichte der böhmischen Länder* i (Munich and Vienna, 1974),

was uncompromising, even rejecting the Hussite victory at the Vyšehrad over Sigismund in 1420 as a breach of the commandment against killing. He rejected life in towns and lived quietly on his estate, working with his hands and writing a series of ethical treatises in the vernacular, marked by colourful rustic metaphor, in which he denounced evils in Church and State with unswerving idealism, insisting on the duty of the Christian to have nothing to do with the exercise of political authority. Clergy and nobles alike were 'fat and gluttonous Baals'.[14] Observance of the exhortations of Christ in the Sermon on the Mount was a direct obligation. Like the Waldensians, he believed that poison entered the Church with Constantine; like them also, he rejected the use of oaths. Pope and emperor he compared in his best-known work, *The Net of Faith*, written about 1440, to great whales ripping through the net of faith spread by the apostolic fishermen in the fifth chapter of Luke to gather the elect, and so mangling it that only barely visible shreds of that original net, the primitive Church, remained. Withdrawal, humility, prayer, refusal of all power, judicial and military authority, and restoration of the way of life of the apostles was the only way open to the true Christian.

After so much warfare, diplomatic and high State action in the name of religion, it was little wonder that this ideal of radical separatism came to draw support. Chelčický stood apart from all the great events but maintained contacts with Hussite leaders. Despite a fundamental difference of views, Rokycana admired him, corresponded with him during his own exile from Prague, borrowed from one of his treatises in his eucharistic work and recommended him to his nephew Gregory and other devout men influenced by Chelčický's writings, who came together at the remote village of Kunwald in north-eastern Bohemia in 1457–8.[15] Close by, at the town of Zamberk, they found a Utraquist priest called Michael exhibiting the purity of life for which Gregory and his friends had searched for so long. Protection was given by Poděbrady who owned the estate of Litice where Kunwald lay. They called the members of the group brothers and sisters, practised community of goods on the apostolic pattern for priests and teachers, and some laymen, and attracted to their number peasants and simple craftsmen, working with their hands. The oath was utterly rejected, thus making it impossible to participate in judicial proceedings. Priests and lay preachers had no private property. The group followed Chelčický's stress on the sufficiency of Scripture and instructed the illiterate so as to make Scripture accessible to them.

---

pp. 49–61, repr. *Hussitenstudien*, pp. 209–16; Brock, *Czech Brethren*, ch. I; M. L. Wagner, *Petr Chelčický* (1983); A. Molnár, 'Bekenntnisse der böhmischen Reformation', *Jahrbuch für die Geschichte des Protestantismus in Österreich* XCVI (1980), pp. 310–32; H. Kaminsky, 'Peter Chelčický: treatises on Christianity and the social order', *Studies in Medieval and Renaissance History* I, ed. W. Bowsky (1964), pp. 106–79; analysis: pp. 107–36.

14  Wagner, *Chelčický*, p. 137; analysis of *Net of Faith*: pp. 132–47.

15  For further history of this group, see Brock, *Czech Brethren*; Wagner, *Chelčický*; R. Říčan, *Die Böhmischen Brüder: Ihr Ursprung und ihre Geschichte*, tr. B. Popelář (1961); note ch. 23 by A. Molnár on theology; J. T. Müller, *Geschichte der Böhmischen Brüder* I-III (1922–31) (standard work); Zeman, *Hussite Movement*, pp. 97–111; Denis, *Fin* I, pp. 281–366 (still a moving account despite its age and its underestimate of Utraquism).

Under Gregory's leadership communities formed elsewhere in rural isolation where the tenets of the movement with its utter rejection of civil obligations could more easily be observed. A high moral life was a prerequisite, with stiff penances for those who fell, and an ultimate penalty of expulsion, and so numbers remained low. Persecution, brought on by Poděbrady's need to ensure his position in relation to the papacy and ward off accusations of complacency to heresy, led to Gregory's imprisonment in Prague and some recantations. But Rokycana's sympathetic handling and the group's manifest lack of concern with politics helped to preserve them. The group, known as the Brethren of Christ's Gospel, later as the Unity of Brethren (*Unitas Fratrum*), began to define its position and in 1464 in a meeting in the Rychnov mountains worked out a set of distinctions important in subsequent history between the *substantialia* of the movement in belief, hope and love, the *ministerialia*, consisting in the word of God, the sacraments, the power of the keys, and the *accidentalia*, consisting in Church ordinances.

Gregory, disappointed in his search for a pure priesthood amongst the Armenians, the Greek Orthodox and the Waldensians, decided to provide them directly for his communities. In 1467, while the kingdom was distracted by the aftermath of Paul II's action against the king, the leadership came together secretly at Lhotka near Rychnov. On 26 March after prayer and fasting the sixty members of the assembly chose nine as suitable for ordination, prepared twelve pieces of paper, nine of them blank and three with the word *jest* ('he is'), on them and gave nine of the twelve, arbitrarily chosen, to the nine candidates. They wanted three to be ordained priest. Gregory, conscious of the importance of the decision, looked for an indication of God's will. Were they to have a priesthood of their own? The chance of the lots could have left all nine with blank slips in their hand; as it was three candidates unfolded slips with *jest* on them. 'God showed His wisdom and power in us', Gregory wrote.[16]

Michael the Utraquist priest then went to the oldest Waldensian *barba* in Bohemia and received ordination from him, on the supposition that the Waldensians had a fount of orders going back to the uncorrupted Church before Constantine. Finally Michael ordained the three himself, renounced his own orders, both Catholic and Waldensian, and asked for a new confirmation from Matthias, chosen on grounds of moral excellence as the chief of the three. When Gregory informed Rokycana, he condemned these moves.

There followed from 1468 to the death of Poděbrady a period of sharp persecution, even of executions, which did not break the movement. They were not economically vulnerable since most members supported themselves. Numbers were small and their lives simple. Gatherings for prayer took place in houses. It was easy to disperse and re-form. The *Unitas* members were tolerated by lords who valued their conscientious work on their estates: when, later, in 1481, Matthias of Hungary exiled them because they had given refuge to

16   Müller, *Brüder* I, p. 127; Říčan, *Brüder*, p. 29; note comment on implications for the future of the community and the concept of the episcopate.

Waldensians fleeing from persecution in Brandenburg, and brothers fled to Moldavia, a petition from Moravian lords persuaded Matthias to bring them back again. Others, touched by their simplicity and sincerity, gave them protection out of sympathy. A flow of pungent vernacular treatises defended their position and exposed failings among the Utraquists. A residual relationship subsisted with the official Utraquist Church: while Rokycana lived, Gregory did not wholly despair of a change of heart and in a seventh and last letter appealed to the archbishop to join them. In 1473 and 1478 the Brethren were allowed hearings by the Prague masters.

Recurrently, idealists brought up as Utraquists threw in their lot with them. When, for example, the priest Michael Polak, preaching in the Prague Old Town against laxities in his own Church, was imprisoned and died of torture in 1480, his suffering sparked off a reaction among students and teachers in Prague which carried them into the *Unitas*. The most distinguished of them, Luke of Prague, wrote later that Polak first made him feel 'the burdensome hunger after truth'; he read Chelčický, was moved by his uncompromising adherence to Scripture and finally joined the Brethren.[17] Luke, scholastically trained at the Charles University, with a knowledge of the classics and the Fathers, brought a depth of learning to the *Unitas* and, first as a junior to others, participated in major changes and then later as *de facto* leader and the *Unitas*'s principal theologian, buttressed and defended them.

By the 1480s tensions over justification by faith or by works had arisen, which had to be settled by a decision of the Inner Council: some feared an 'overgreat straitness', leading to the 'great evil of a vain religion...of trust in oneself'. Brethren entered towns and were embarrassed by the reproach of townsmen that they avoided civil obligations out of idleness. Some felt needlessly restricted by the *Unitas*'s regulations about commerce. In Litomyšl a growth in the number of adherents, facilitated by Bohus Kostka, member of a noble family early drawn to the *Unitas*, created special problems. Nobility, with rare exceptions such as the Kostka family, generally felt excluded from membership by the rigorous rejection of the oath and began to wish for entrance. At a synod at Brandýs in 1490 two such candidates participated in proceedings. The assembly, although recommending that members should not accept office as an alderman, judge or grand master of a guild or become a tavernkeeper or go to the wars, or take part in judicial proceedings involving judgements of blood, none the less permitted such things. 'If', they said, 'a Brother should be forced by the civil authority, against his conscience...he should submit...in whatever is not against God.'[18]

The ambiguous statement did not succeed in holding rival views in check; most moved on to dilute the inheritance of Chelčický and became known as the Major Party; a minority, often known as the Amosites from their leader Amos, a trader in wax, dissented and held to the old ways. In 1495 it was agreed by a majority that

---

17    See Říčan, *Brüder*, for a sympathetic account of Luke; in addition to A. Molnár's chapter in Říčan on theology: Gonnet and Molnár, *Les Vaudois*, pp. 276–80, on Luke and the Waldensians.
18    Brock, *Czech Brethren*, p. 128.

the writings of Chelčický and Gregory were of no absolute validity and should be disregarded if they did not correspond to the needs of the times. At Chlumec the split between the Brothers became final.[19] Luke altered the balance in the *Unitas's* theology between works and faith. The egalitarianism of Chelčický disappeared, as did outright prohibition of the oath, judicial office, certain forms of commerce. The *Unitas* forfeited something of its distinction. Yet it entered the sixteenth century a growing force, still earning admiration for its humility and ethical concern, and capable of riding out sporadic waves of slander and persecution.

### The Development of a Utraquist Party and the Agreement of Kutná Hora

The succession of the Catholic Jagiellon Prince Wladislav II in 1471 did not work to the benefit either of the kingdom or of Utraquism.[20] The damaging effects of the civil war and the battle against the claims of Matthias of Hungary continued until 1478, and were only brought to an end at the price of massive concessions to Matthias, and a settlement which roused the suspicions of the Utraquists. Former Catholic rebels were again taken into favour. Wladislav, leaning on their support rather than that of the Utraquists, looking for a reconciliation with the papacy and anxious to maintain his position in Hungary, showed himself hostile to the Utraquists. Some of the parishes, where the chalice had been guaranteed, slipped away from them under the pressure of the Catholic nobility.

In response the Utraquists organized and formed a party within the State as compensation for the loss of power at the centre of politics which they had enjoyed through the years of Poděbrady's rule, setting up a consistory of eight priests and four laymen with Wenceslas Koranda, the successor of Rokycana, at its head, forming a committee of three nobles, later called Defensores, to represent the Utraquist interest, reinforced by three further nobles and also creating an organization of deans to call decanal synods, oversee the affairs of the Utraquists in the localities and keep a wary eye on the activities of the *Unitas* and the Catholics.[21] Lamed as they were by the inability of Wenceslas Koranda to ordain priests, the consequence of the continuing failure of papal recognition, the Utraquists were in practice building a separate Church organization, carrying political power because of its ability to call crowds into action, to agitate and to move both towns and Utraquist nobility in a power complex against the king. These forces protected an Italian bishop who was brought into the country in 1482 to break the logjam of unfulfilled ordinations.

---

19   Discussion of theological issues in A. Molnár, 'Die kleine und die grosse Partei der Brüderunität', *CV* xxii (1979), pp. 239–48.
20   For this phase of Hussite history, Eberhard, *Konfessionsbildung*, is preferred to K. Richter, 'Die böhmischen Länder von 1471–1740', *Handbuch der Geschichte der böhmischen Länder* ii (1974), pp. 99–143; see Eberhard, pp. 9–40, for historiography and Czech literature; p. 37 for judgement on Richter (still a valuable quarry for facts); survey, with positive assessment of Utraquism, in F. G. Heymann, 'The Hussite-Utraquist Church in the fifteenth and sixteenth centuries', *ARG* lii (1961), pp. 1–26.
21   Eberhard, *Konfessionsbildung*, p. 50; for note of reassessment of Koranda by K. Krofta, see p. 21.

Prague, as before, was a keypoint. The king had used opportunities to put councillors in office who worked for a policy of Catholic restoration and declined to bring Prague into the Utraquist alliances which had sprung up to resist him. When these councillors went a step further and asked the Catholic party for protection for the capital, it was too much for the Utraquists, who rose in 1483, drove out or killed the councillors, even in some cases repeating the defenestration of 1419, and forbade communion in one kind altogether in Prague, thus actually prohibiting the dissemination of the agreed theological standpoint of the Compactata of Basle, that grace was conveyed as fully in communion under one kind as it was in both.[22] The Catholics were driven out, monasteries stormed and the death penalty decreed for any who engaged in secret negotiations with the king or the Catholic party in the kingdom. Wladislav, turning to the Catholic nobility for support, found they had no taste for a conflict with such determined opponents.

He was forced to negotiate. Prague assumed the leading role which it had held once before in the Hussite revolution. The king had to guarantee the freedom of the Utraquists' Italian bishop to exercise his office and to accept leaders of the rebellion as Prague councillors. At Kutná Hora in 1485 the two major religious forces in the kingdom, Catholics and Utraquists, united in a form of toleration.[23] It was agreed in an assembly of that year, confirming a decision of 1484, that both groups should keep the parishes which they held in Bohemia, those with the lay chalice, and those without, and should respect that dualism in peace for thirty-one years.

Neither side obtained all that they wanted. The Catholics had never given up the hope of restoring the religious status quo as it had been before Constance and the revolution of 1419, and so would have preferred but a short period of stabilization. Utraquists had wished for a permanent settlement, guaranteeing stability and equal treatment for them beside the Catholics for an indefinite period. Thirty-one years was a compromise between views that could not in the long run be reconciled. At the heart of the agreement lay the Compactata of Basle and the letter of majesty of Sigismund. These were again accepted. The rights of patrons were, however, effectively set aside by a decision of Kutná Hora, that the confessional affiliation of each community or parish church should

---

22    Eberhard's comment, *Konfessionsbildung*, p. 55; compare his note, p. 52, on the statement of the Utraquists earlier to the king, on papal confirmation of the Compactata, that it had already been confirmed by the higher power of the Basle Council and the Emperor Sigismund – a sign, he believes, of a greater intransigence and independence within Utraquism.

23    On Kutná Hora and its immediate consequences, Ibid., pp. 56–73; W. Eberhard, 'Toleranz als historischer Lernprozess der europäischen Kulture', *Akademische Monatsblatten, Zeitschrift des Kartellverbandes katholischen deutscher Studentenvereine* c (1988), pp. 2–7; general survey: J. K. Zeman, 'The rise of religious liberty in the Czech reformation', *Central European History* VI (1973), pp. 128–47; original survey of the Hussite revolution as a whole, R. Kalivoda, *Revolution und Ideologie: Der Hussitismus* (1976). A. Patschovsky, 'Toleranz in Mittelalter: Idee und Wirklichkeit', *Toleranz in Mittelalter, Vorträge und Forschungen* XLV, ed. A. Patschovsky, H. Zimmermann (1998), pp. 391–402 (wide-ranging analysis). F. Šmahel stresses tolerance in Bohemia as forced on by circumstances: 'Il movimento ussita', *Vita religiosa e identità politiche*, ed. S. Gensini (Pisa, 1998), pp. 527–48 at pp. 546–8.

remain undisturbed, irrespective of the views of the local lord. Conflict and fluctuation of confessional adherence through alienation of land was thus avoided. The individual gained his freedom: he was not to be compelled to follow the religion of his lord. The decree of toleration was a major achievement of the Hussite revolution, based in the last resort on a return to the dynamism of the years before the Compactata. Saaz (Žatec) bluntly asked three of its fellow towns which they were going to stand with, king or country.[24] Prague demanded the chalice as a necessity for the faithful and not merely as a tolerated ritual idiosyncrasy.[25] In face of this, the king and the conservative forces yielded, not least because some of the Catholic nobility had come to believe that the repression of heresy could not be allowed to take precedence over the interests of the country, and others, especially the most powerful, saw, via a settlement of the religious issue, an opening to a peaceful increase of their power within Bohemia.[26] Kutná Hora was accepted because of the exigencies of politics and the solidarity of the Utraquist Estates.

### The Utraquists and the *Unitas* in the Late Fifteenth and Early Sixteenth Centuries

One group, however, was excluded: toleration did not extend to the *Unitas*, and they remained subject to periodical persecution, which was sometimes aided by the Utraquists. They remained excluded when the decision of Kutná Hora was renewed in perpetuity in 1512. Utraquists were ambivalent about the Brethren; sensitive about accusations of heresy, they at times denounced and persecuted them, making clear to the outside world the gulf between them; at other times Utraquist lords quietly protected them, while some who had grown disillusioned with the long wait for papal recognition were inclined to make common cause with them and adopt some of their views. Wenceslas Koranda denounced both the Brethren and the supporters of Rome on various occasions, but in the 1490s, roused by fears of the activities of a wing of conservative Utraquists willing to move towards an accommodation with Rome, he directed his fire chiefly against the papal Church, sharpening criticism of their errors and stressing the issues on which the Utraquists differed, such as the lay chalice, the practice of infant communion and the use of Czech in the liturgy.[27] Voices were raised in favour of coming to agreement with the curia: the humanist Bohuslav Hassenstein of Lobkowitz argued that agreement could end Bohemia's isolation and improve its economic and cultural situation, and Wladislav favoured an ending of the conflict over Utraquism if it would bring aid for him from the curia against the Turkish

---

24   Eberhard, *Konfessionsbildung*, p. 58.
25   Ibid., p. 59.
26   W. Eberhard, 'Interessengegensätze und Landesgemeinde: die böhmischen Stände im nach-revolutionären Stabilisierungskonflikt', *Europa 1500*, ed. F. Seibt, W. Eberhard (1987), pp. 330–48 at pp. 335–6.
27   Eberhard, *Konfessionsbildung*, pp. 63–4; on Koranda's pluralist attitudes, see Heymann, 'The Hussite–Utraquist Church', p. 9.

threat to Hungary.[28] In reaction against such views, what has been described as a Left-Utraquist wing of the Church began to emerge.

The curia did not intend to make concessions of any importance: it continued a policy of stifling the Church by cutting off the opportunities to obtain episcopal ordination. Somehow the Utraquists none the less sustained their priesthood and their claim to the apostolic succession through bishops recognized by Rome. Yet there were strains. Partly because of this, the quality of the priests was uneven and there were abuses. The ecclesiastical position of Bohemia isolated the Charles University and, although it continued to train administrators and priests, a tendency grew for the best students to go abroad. It became provincial.[29] No first-class theologian on the Utraquist side came on the scene after the death of Koranda in 1519.

The more radical Utraquists were disinclined to wait for papal recognition and tended to abandon interest in the Compactata. Humanist and Utraquist Gregor Hrubý of Jelení translated Lorenzo Valla's exposure of the Donation of Constantine and Erasmus's *Encomium Moriae*. Wenceslas Písecký, formerly a master at the Charles University, defended Utraquism in Italy in 1510 and attacked Aeneas Sylvius Piccolomini's *History of Bohemia* as a source for the erroneous judgements passed on Bohemia as a place of heresy. The failure of yet further negotiations about the renewal of the archbishopric of Prague in 1512–13 led to a flurry of literary activity, within which a growing tendency to stress the foundation of Utraquism in Scripture was evident. From 1513 Jan Miruš was a parish priest in Prague, an effective preacher and a supporter of views that appear to have stood close to those once held by the priests of Tabor and by the *Unitas*.[30] The influence of the *Unitas* on the Utraquists grew as the Brethren attracted members higher in society.

Kutná Hora put the seal on the policy long followed by George of Poděbrady of achieving unity through the acceptance of two confessions, exercising mutual toleration, under the leadership of the monarchy. But it did not end the tensions within Bohemia. The Hussite revolution had changed the political and economic landscape. A massive disendowment of the Church had taken place.[31] The role of the clergy had changed and their authority and wealth had diminished. The monarchy had forfeited much of its economic power, which had passed to the nobility, and it had been forced into financial dependence on the Estates. Town leagues had played an important part in the revolution: towns now formed one of the Estates and were eager to sustain a political as well as an economic role. The Estates were capable of unified action; most often, they disputed or formed varied alliances according to shifting needs and policies, knights and towns tending to stand together against the nobility. The Estates in the fifteenth century had

---

28   Eberhard, *Konfessionsbildung*, p. 67 (Bohuslav), p. 64 (Wladislav).

29   Ibid., p. 102; Heymann, 'The Hussite–Utraquist Church', pp. 11–12.

30   Eberhard, *Konfessionsbildung*, pp. 103–5.

31   On its significance, E. Werner, *SSAWL* Phil-hist- Klasse cxxix (1989), pp. 5–38; Seibt, *Hussiten-studien*, p. 30; Šmahel, *Revolution*.

established their power, but it was necessarily an unstable authority which they wielded.[32]

The reigns of the two Jagiellon monarchs, Wladislav II and Lewis, who succeeded him in 1516, were marked by a weakness of central authority and by conflicts, both between the Estates and within them. Often these were primarily based on political and economic issues, but religious ones recurred and intertwined with the others. In the conflicts it was the Left-Utraquist wing, ingeniously and pertinaciously using political skills, who demonstrated that an inner vitality had still not left the Hussite movement.[33] The Left-Utraquists carried on their political struggle about office, decisions about parishes and representation of their viewpoint in external negotiations because they cared about the reform and the future of their Church. It was they above all who prevented the Catholicizing tendencies of the Jagiellons, the increasing political authority of the most powerful of the Catholic lords, and the minimalizing attitudes to the Compactata of the pro-Rome group within Utraquism from undermining the achievements of the past and ending the independence of their Church. When the teachings of Luther began to touch Bohemia, it was the *Unitas*, emancipating itself from a position at the margin of society, and the Left-Utraquists, looking behind 1433 and the attempt to accommodate with ecclesiastical authority to the independency of the Taborites, who were the most vital religious forces in the land.

32  Summary, Eberhard, *Konfessionsbildung*, pp. 113–16; discussion of positive features of Jagiellon epoch: Eberhard, in *Europa 1500*, ed. Seibt, Eberhard, pp. 345–8.
33  It is the principal service of Eberhard to have brought out the importance of Left-Utraquism; see also reflections on Kalivoda, W. Eberhard, 'Konflikt und Integration: die Dynamik in den Ergebnissen der Hussitenrevolution', *Studia Comenia et Historica* XXII (1992), pp. 31–56.

# Medieval Heresy and the Reformation

## Introduction

Politics, force and the power of new ideas in varying combinations in the sixteenth century created the Reformation. The unity of doctrine under the papacy for which medieval churchmen and laymen sacrificed so much, in time, labour and lives, broke down and Europe divided into Catholic and Protestant states, cities and regions, battling against each other in speech, writing and arms. The intentions of some of the groups condemned as heretics in the Middle Ages, Waldensians, Lollards and Hussites, appeared to have been achieved, at least in part, but by the hands of others. The power of the State, repeatedly used against dissidents by churchmen in the Middle Ages, was now used by Protestants in authority in their turn against the heirs of those churchmen. The easygoing religion of the majority in the medieval age gave way to a more disciplined and often more aggressive Catholicism, organizing its membership more coherently, attempting to put down the remnants of pagan folk religion and bringing new religious orders to birth.

The world changed. The heretics of the past disappeared, their remnants absorbed into the new Reformed Churches. Utraquism in Bohemia held for a time but faded out. The *Unitas Fratrum* lost its austerity and individuality.

The new Reformers looked on the religious dissidents of the past with mixed feelings. They recognized many affinities between their doctrines and their own, saw them as fellow warriors for the truth and valued them as courageous witnesses to the evangelical cause in earlier centuries. But they had reservations. Lollards and Waldensians, for example, were marked by their long underground existence and lacked an intellectually trained leading class. The Reformers, keen university minds, conscious of the rectitude of their message, did not feel that they had anything to learn from the heretics of the past. The heretics themselves were proud of their traditions and understandably reluctant to shed them at the requirement of their new and powerful cousins in belief. Hussites declined to be absorbed into the Lutheran Churches. In the Waldensian Valleys deep emotions were stirred, between a conservative and resilient peasant population of the mountains and freshly trained Calvinist pastors from the outside world, with the pastors feeling impatient with slow minds and with customs which seemed to them to be undesirable remnants of the medieval past.[1]

## The Waldensians

### The Italian Alps and the mission of Farel

News of the Swiss Reformation, of Berne and the charismatic preacher Guillaume Farel seems first to have stirred the Italian Valleys. The book always played a major role.[2] In 1526 one of the *barbi* called Martin, possibly Martin Gonin, came back from Switzerland and German-speaking lands bringing Reformation literature. Initiatives came from *barbi* who had international horizons, such as Georges Morel, probably originally from Embrun, fluent in Latin as well as French and Provençal, and Martin Gonin, linked to the printing trade.

Morel and another *barba*, Pierre Masson from Burgundy, went to question Reformers in 1530 on their beliefs. In Basle the Reformer Oecolampadius commented on Waldensian beliefs and practices set out by Morel in a Latin letter.[3] Morel put questions to Oecolampadius on practical issues of morality, 'like the reader of a confessional manual', as Cameron comments. They were questions no doubt drawn from Morel's experience as a confessor. Morel, well read in Luther and Erasmus, spoke none the less with enthusiasm of the simple Christocentric piety of his Waldensians and of the itinerant, disciplined life of the *barbi*, celibate and practising manual labour. He wrote: 'We are in agreement with you in everything. From the time of the apostles we have had in essentials an understanding of the faith which is yours. The only difference is that, through our own fault and through intellectual laziness, we have not grasped the sense of Scripture as correctly as you. That is why we have come to you for you to direct, instruct, edify and teach us.'[4] For Morel the driving force was respect for a superior scriptural learning. Oecolampadius's reply, based partly on Morel's description of Waldensian belief and practice, partly on his knowledge of the *Unitas*, whose views he assimilated to the Waldensians, was welcoming but lacking in understanding of their clandestine tradition and the outward conformity with Catholic practice, born of centuries of persecution. His ideal was of a settled Protestant parish system, manned by a residential married pastorate, supervising the faith and practice of their flock on the spot, and he looked askance at the wandering *barbi* with their underground instruction.[5]

1   E. Cameron, *The Reformation of the Heretics* (1984); discussions by G. Audisio and E. Cameron, 'Les Vaudois des Alpes: débat sur un ouvrage récent', *RHR* CCIII (1986), pp. 395–405, 405–9; J. F. Gilmont, 'Les Vaudois des Alpes: mythes et realités', *RHE* LXXXIII (1988), pp. 69–89.
2   Cameron, *Reformation*, pp. 129–66.
3   Gonnet and Molnár, *Les Vaudois*, pp. 298–304.
4   Ibid., p. 299; G. Gonnet, 'I rapporti tra i Valdesi franco-italiani e i riformatori d'oltralpe prima di Calvino', *Ginevra e l'Italia* (1959), pp. 1–63 at pp. 20–44; Cameron, *Waldenses*, p. 237.
5   Gonnet and Molnár, *Les Vaudois*, pp. 300–1.

Bucer, leader of the Reformed Churches in Switzerland and South Germany after the death of Zwingli, whom the two *barbi* consulted at Strasburg, rejected this nicodemism on similar grounds, although with more understanding of the manner in which it had evolved and of the dangers inherent in suddenly jettisoning it. He called the reception of the sacraments of the Catholics 'great infirmity' and rejected aspects of the disciplined practice of the Waldensians as savouring too much of a legalistic attitude, overly based on works rather than faith.[6]

Such a conflict of views was inevitable, given the origin of the Waldensians as a movement of ethical reform. They came to exclude a number of Catholic beliefs and practices, such as the doctrine of purgatory, the invocation of Our Lady and the saints, yet retained in their leadership a reformed priesthood, celibate like the Catholics, laying great stress on certain defined practices. No doubt the emphasis placed on the Scriptures, memorized in the vernacular, opened the way to the reception of new translations and Protestant interpretations, but there was much that was unfamiliar in the Reformed tradition, to be assimilated by their congregations only after prolonged discussion and instruction.

Bucer was unhappy about the Waldensian attitude to secular authority, and their rejection of oaths: his attitude to the Waldensian rejection of the Constantinian Church was on all fours with that which he proclaimed eleven years later to the *Unitas*: 'Religion is always built by the power of the Holy Spirit alone, and not by that of any creature. But the institutions and governments of cities are no less the work of this same Spirit which governs ecclesiastical institutions and ministries.' Bucer laid stress on the early Christian communities who were the recipients of St Paul's epistles and on Paul in the thirteenth chapter of Romans, with his insistence on obedience to terrestrial authority. 'If God wishes', Bucer wrote, 'he will raise the temporal power to be the minister of his flock, even against its will.'[7]

The mission of 1530 bore fruit and in a series of discussions and meetings the Valleys moved towards reception of the Reform, with the year 1532 marking a decisive stage in the turn towards sixteenth-century Protestantism. Traditionally, an assembly at the hamlet of Chanforan in the Val Angrogna marked the point in time when Waldensians accepted Calvinism. Farel dominated the events of that year, which committed the Waldensians to reform: the rank and file followed the lead of the *barbi*, without clearly understanding what they were doing. Two worlds collided. Farel was nearer to Calvin, whom he had brought in to reform Geneva, than he was to Luther. There was much in the Waldensian practice which he rejected. The *barbi* abandoned the fixed fasts, private confession, the laying-on of hands, the system of common property and the celibacy, Donatism, the stress on works and the literal interpretation of Scripture.[8] Not all agreed: some *barbi* wished

6  Ibid., pp. 301–4.
7  For this and the preceding quotation, see Ibid., p. 304.
8  G. Audisio, 'Pourquoi une Bible en Français pour les Vaudois?', *Olivétan, traducteur de la Bible*, ed. G. Casalis, B. Roussel (1987), pp. 117–34; Audisio, *Luberon*, pp. 181–2.

simply to stay with their ancient customs, others were mindful of the long contacts with the Hussite movement and the *Unitas*. Nevertheless, the attraction of the Reform carried the day. Behind Farel, a typical French Protestant leader with his driving energy and clarity of mind, lay the emotional force of the Calvinist type of dogmatic system built on Scripture, seductive for men whose lives had been devoted to the learning and exposition of Scripture. Farel, moreover, who sprang from Gap in Dauphiné, seems to have been able to speak to the Waldensians in their own language.[9]

He also persuaded the Waldensian leadership to subscribe the massive sum of 800 écus d'or to a new vernacular translation of the Bible – a historical curiosity, for the Picard Pierre Robert Olivétan, whom Farel sponsored and who came into the Valleys in the autumn of 1532, partly to spread the Reform, translated the Scriptures into French, a language not well known to the *barbi* or their people, their linguistic bond being an Alpine variant of the language of oc, not North French oeil. The learned Reformers had persuaded the Waldensians that their translations were defective, and had to be replaced. Olivétan's Bible was designed to have parallel translation into French, then being diffused under official auspices as a lingua franca in Provence, and into Latin, the language of the medieval Church and of a minority of *barbi*.[10]

Farel seems to have seen in the Waldensians an ideal instrument for making reality of his dream of a new standard translation underpinning the orthodoxy of the growing Protestant circles of French-speaking lands, based on the Hebrew and Greek and superseding the older work of Jacques Lefèvre of Etaples, which had been a translation of the Vulgate.[11] He had long been interested in a Protestant press, and from 1529 had been in collaboration with Pierre de Wingle, a Lyons printer who moved for security to Geneva, and then to Neuchâtel, won by Farel for the Reform in 1530. There in the Swiss Reformed stronghold Pierre de Wingle printed Olivétan's version in June 1535.

Farel's plan did not work out as he had hoped. Olivétan's massive folio was suited to public, formal meeting to hear the Word in a Protestant assembly rather than the secret consultation and undercover reading of the *barbi* in the house of an adherent, and the Waldensians were unsuited to providing a nucleus of reliable distributors. Selling a Bible was a task of a different order to the distribution of the tracts in the Protestant interest in which Farel and Pierre de Wingle had hitherto been engaged. Olivétan himself, a reticent man who habitually used a pseudonym, a translator rather than an exegete, who saw himself simply as an instrument for

9    For Farel see Audisio, *Luberon*, esp. ch. 5; Cameron, *Reformation*, pp. 168–70; G. Audisio, 'La fin des Vaudois (xvie siècle)?', *Les Vaudois*, ed. Audisio, pp. 77–99 at p. 90 (see also note on place and date of decision to accept the Reform, p. 91).

10    Audisio in *Olivétan*, ed. Casalis, Roussel, pp. 122–8; on the size of subscription, Cameron, *Reformation*, pp. 208–9; Audisio, in *Les Vaudois*, ed. Audisio, p. 92, comments on the purpose.

11    J. F. Gilmont, 'La publication de la Bible d'Olivétan: audaces et limites d'une enterprise de précurseurs', *Olivétan*, ed. Casalis, Roussel, pp. 31–7; also p. 137. Olivétan translated the Old Testament from the Hebrew; his New Testament version was a revision of Lefèvre's, using the Greek. Further details, Cameron, *Waldenses*, pp. 254–5.

the communication of God's word, was moved by his experience of the Waldensians, with whom he lived for much of the time between the autumn of 1532 and February 1535, when he dated his preface 'from the Alps' before leaving to oversee the work at Neuchâtel. In the preface he makes fun of the practice of writing elaborate, flattering dedications to influential patrons; instead he dedicates his work to 'the poor little Church of Jesus Christ', and writes with emphasis about the sufferings of the Waldensian communities.[12]

He was meeting the wishes of the Waldensians by providing them with a printed version, eliminating the scribal errors of MS production, and, again as they wished, unlocking the treasures of Hebrew and Greek; they received from him a push in the direction of Protestantism through his marginal comments. No doubt some bought the costly folio: Audisio has uncovered a case in 1540 of a family near Apt in Provence who had come originally from Piedmont and presumably took the translation with them when they migrated over the Alps.[13] As a whole, it did not sell well; there was some restiveness over the arrangements; for the rank and file little immediately changed. The *barbi* had their ancient Vaudois translations, minuscule in size, *aides-mémoire* for a text which through rote learning in their long training had already sunk into their minds.[14] The Olivétan text, like the decisions of 1532, was a portent of a new age, which many Waldensians were not yet ready to enter.

### The growth of Calvinist influence

A generation was needed before the Waldensian communities on both sides of the Alps could be grappled to the Reform. Two *barbi*, Daniel de Valence and Jean de Molines, struck out against the trend and set off in 1532 to Mladá Boleslav to alert the *Unitas* to what had been happening and to find out from personal contact whether they had sacrificed their earlier moral fervour, and their preachers had abandoned celibacy.[15] On the latter they satisfied themselves. Perhaps they had

---

12  Text in *Olivétan*, ed. Casalis, Roussel, pp. 169–76; comment on finances, Cameron, *Waldenses*, p. 255.
13  *Olivétan*, pp. 136–7.
14  G. Tourn, 'Sans nom ni lieu', Ibid., pp. 21–9, also pp. 135–6.
15  Gonnet and Molnár, *Les Vaudois*, pp. 311–18; Cameron, *Reformation*, p. 191, for a revision on Calvin's attitude. Earlier contacts: A. Molnár, 'Luc de Prague et les Vaudois d'Italie', *BSSV* LXX (1949), pp. 40–64. Treesh, pp. 234–49 rejects Cameron's view (*Waldenses*, pp. 240–83) that the Synod of Chanforan of 1532 is a myth. No 'epoch-making' decision was made then and there to accept Reform. On the site, and Monastier's error in placing a 1532 Synod there, see Cameron, *Reformation*, pp. 264–7; Treesh, pp. 236–7 reconciles geographical contradictions by noting that Chanforan is a meadow outside Il Serre, a town in Val Angrogna, a tributary valley to Val Luserne; different writers give different names, she argues, for what is in fact the same site. If nothing decisive took place in 1532, she asks (pp. 327–8), why did two dissident *barbi* set off to contact the *Unitas*? Behind the technical discussions lies a difference over the manner of reception of Reform: Treesh stresses the persuasiveness of Reformers and the Waldensians' initial will to contact them; Cameron, *Reformation*, p. 2 speaks of 'assaults on the integrity and self-consciousness of the Waldensian communities of the Alps'. But Treesh, Cameron and Audisio all agree on a long time-scale for *full* reception of the Reform.

hoped to enlist the authority of Luke of Prague in resistance to rapprochement with Farel and the Swiss, but he had been dead four years. Instead, the leaders of the *Unitas* wrote a letter to the Waldensians of the Valleys, advising them to be less precipitate and to prove the spirits, and recalling their long fidelity to their traditions. Dialogue was not prohibited – the *Unitas* itself under John Roh had been attentive to the new teachings – but the *Unitas*'s ancient confrères were reminded of the long-lasting links between the movements and warned that consolation was to be found 'in Jesus Christ alone'. But the Valleys in 1533 repudiated the initiative of the *barbi*. The decision marked the end of the years of sporadic contact and co-operation between Hussites and Waldensians: the Valleys lost their ecumenical links, and turned in more on themselves, a process which was accentuated when their Italian co-religionists in Calabria and Apulia were decimated in the persecutions of 1560. Swiss influence came to predominate.

In 1555 Calvin was fully in charge in Geneva. He valued the personal qualities of the Waldensians, but seems never to have wavered from the view that false doctrines were present among them, and that their teaching, especially on works, needed to be brought into accord with his own. In time Geneva-directed pastors came to displace the *barbi* altogether, and the process of thus uniting the Valleys to the Calvinist system began in 1555.[16] Thereafter a series of pastors was introduced, often at risk of their lives, to instruct, to diffuse literacy, to deal with idiosyncratic and undesirable local customs. It was recognized that the bringing in of the Protestant harvest in Piedmont was the most dangerous task a minister could undertake; there was also an inevitable gulf between such men as Scipione Lentolo, Neapolitan, trained in Venice, the product of the college at Geneva, minister at Angrogna from 1559, and his simple congregations of mountain people, whom he accused of 'excessive avarice and dedication to the things of this world' – probably a townsman's criticism of the cautious attitudes formed by the grinding poverty of many in these localities. Lentolo in his *History of the Great and Cruel Persecutions* began to write up Waldensian history. His work, and that of others, such as Girolamo Miolo, probably an ex-Dominican, linked by birth to the community of Waldensian exiles in Geneva, who wrote a subtle *Brief History* about 1587, steering a middle course between the crudities of inquisitorial propaganda and Calvinist unease about facets of old Waldensian belief and practice, demonstrated how times were changing, for histories are commonly written just as the phenomena they record are passing away.

In the later sixteenth century the Valleys abandoned their distinctive traits. They retained proudly their name, and their claim to a great antiquity of dissent from Catholicism, but in most other respects became indistinguishable from the expanding circle of Calvinist Churches. It is an historical curiosity that they retained the name Waldensian while their fellows in Dauphiné and Provence, who also accepted Calvinism, lost it.[17]

---

16    Cameron, *Reformation*, pp. 155–66.
17    G. Miolo, *Historia breve e vera de gl'affari dei Valdesi delle Valli*, ed. E. Balmas (1971); G. Audisio, 'Des Pauvres de Lyon aux Vaudois réformés', *RHR* ccxvii (2000), pp. 156–66 at p. 157.

## The Waldensians in the French Alps

In the Luberon, on the French side of the Alps, much the same process was at work. Here Lutherans and others began to penetrate the countryside and to alarm authority. The Waldensians, immigrants from the Italian side of the Alps, had lived for decades in a near-impenetrable nicodemism with their Catholic neighbours, outwardly conforming, albeit with reservations, carefully intermarrying and transmitting their religion secretly through households. Though they were in touch with their co-religionists and often still had lands for renting in the Waldensian mountains, they did nothing to excite persecution. Lutheran missionizing, the work of Farel, and the fear that both excited in ecclesiastical authority, coupled with the effects of a general impoverishment of the region, isolating the Waldensians, making them disliked as foreigners, undermined the atmosphere of discreet toleration. Quite suddenly, they came under heavy pressure. Jean de Roma, a Dominican from Bourges, noted by Farel as early as 1523 for his ferocious diligence against heretics, initiated proceedings against Lutherans in 1532 and 1533 which revealed the secret presence of Waldensians. The inquisitor through his interrogations came to believe in the existence of a conspiracy of Waldensian heretics, both structured and international, separate from the Lutherans, and dangerous.[18] Economic tensions and a growing suspicion of the aliens from Piedmont led local witnesses to denounce, where earlier they had remained silent. Jean was checked, and died of plague in the summer of 1533. But it was too late. The incoming of the Reform, Lutheran, Farelian, Calvinist, had changed the climate beyond recall; Waldensians, faced with the new beliefs, suffered, as in Piedmont, a crisis of identity and, after the massacre of Mérindol of 1545, when a French royal army devastated villages of the Waldensians and engaged in wholesale killing at Mérindol, came to make common cause with the new Protestants.

Religious fervour from the Catholics, passive suffering for their faith from the Waldensians, cannot provide us with a complete explanation of the tragedy of Mérindol. Waldensians fought. Attacks from Catholics brought reprisals; in Labrières the Waldensians fortified themselves and men of Mérindol pillaged a neighbouring abbey. Fear of breakdown of public order helped to unleash an army in 1545; pillaging by Catholics, quondam neighbours of the victims, can be explained less by hostility to heresy than by their will to recover the costs of maintaining a royal army in their midst.[19] But Mérindol and the other repressions achieved wide publicity and were a turning-point. After an uncertain intermediate phase, the underground Waldensians, pushed towards Protestantism by persecution, became Huguenots. Jean Rouet of Lourmarin married in a Catholic church in 1553 at Mérindol; in 1564 he had his son Joseph baptized in

---

18 Audisio, *Luberon*, p. 90; for a description of Jean de Roma, Cameron, *Reformation*, pp. 149–50.
19 Cameron, *Reformation*, pp. 151–4; review of Audisio, *Luberon*, in *JEH* xxxvii (1986), pp. 336–9; Audisio, *Luberon*, p. 370; on Dauphiné, P. Paravy in *BHL*, pp. 160–75.

the Calvinist church at Lourmarin.[20] Those who had married and had their children baptized in Catholic churches ceased to preserve the precarious symbiosis of the past: they turned instead to Calvin's congregations. Despite the years of persecution and silent protest, Waldensianism yet had something of compromise about it – part of the movement still looked back to the medieval past, whereas such an approach in the stern climate of the sixteenth century seemed wholly inappropriate. Perhaps, too, Audisio's theory has something to commend it – that the Waldensian attitude to poverty smelled of the thirteenth century, and the epoch of the mendicants. It was not compatible with the changing attitudes of the Reformation epoch, much more inclined to give a positive valuation to riches and see the hand of God in the work of the prospering Protestant tradesman.[21] The leadership of the movement lacked the training and equipment to take part in the great debates about doctrine characteristic of the new age. So Waldensianism disappeared in the Luberon as a separate entity, just as it did in Piedmont, but without even leaving its name behind. It was absorbed, traceable only in the unusual number of countrydwellers who were Huguenot in the lands in Provence where the Piedmontese Waldensian immigration had taken hold, an exception to the general rule that labourers on the land were Catholics, industrial workers Huguenots, in the Protestant nucleus in the massacre village of Mérindol, and in the survival of clusters of old Waldensian family names.

### Survivals outside the Alps

As in the Luberon, so in the other regions of Waldensian survival in France – the minorities disappear into the more powerful and numerous Reform movements. Apulia and Calabria are sometimes described as a kind of 'India' of sixteenth-century Catholicism, remote quasi-missionary provinces, where Waldensians found refuge from persecution and Waldensian communities long survived. Apulia's fate is ill recorded: whether through persecution or the pressure of resurgent Catholicism, the communities disappeared. In Calabria hostile attention was called to the Waldensians when they appealed for Protestant ministers in 1556; two came, only to be captured and executed, and in 1560-1 Catholic forces set about repressing them. Persecution decimated the Waldensians, and a successful Jesuit mission, following on the heels of persecution, reconverted the region. Waldensianism ceased to be a force in southern Italy.[22]

No consistent resistance was put up against Catholic revival in Italy. Gonnet, musing in 1983 on the reasons for the failure of the Reform to capture Italy, listed, together with the resurgent Catholicism of the Council of Trent, the work of the

20   Audisio, *Luberon*, p. 426.
21   Ibid., pp. 438–9; for a survey of the transition to Protestantism, see Audisio, in *Les Vaudois*, ed. Audisio, pp. 77–99, esp. pp. 95–6. For role of Waldensians in Protestant controversial writing, an illuminating exposition, Cameron, *Waldenses*, pp. 285–96.
22   Cameron, *Waldenses*, pp. 200–4. Merlo, *Valdesi* II, pp. 109–13, reviewing G. Audisio, *Le barbe et l'inquisiteur: Procès du barbe vaudois Pierre Griot par l'inquisiteur Jean de Roma (Apt, 1532)* (1979), notes how Griot saw Apulia and Calabria as a land of freedom. See Audisio, *Les Vaudois*, pp. 207–10.

Holy Office from 1542, the setting up of the *Index librorum prohibitorum* in 1559, Paul VI's iron resolution, the Bull *Licet ab initio* of 1562 and the tribunal of the inquisition which it put into action, a failure of will on the part of the supporters of Reformation in Italy, disorganized, over-individualistic, inclined to a pot-pourri of religion, philosophy and magic, and irresolute before persecution.[23] Italian Reformers, many of whom fled before the forces of repression, mattered more outside than inside Italy. The political confusion favoured the cause of the papacy: it was not in the interest of princes to support Protestantism. Gonnet wrote of an 'exhaustion of Reform', of a movement unquiet, even tumultuous and anarchistic which spoiled the opportunities which might otherwise have been open to intelligent, serious-minded groups (among whom he included the Waldensians) to change the course of Italian history. More recently, Welti confirms Gonnet's view of the lack of a geographical or doctrinal nucleus for the opposition to the Italian Church, and of the efficiency of its repression of dissent, notably of the potential of merchants carrying disturbing influences over trade-routes.[24] Menchi has written of the influence of Erasmus, who stirred a whole generation of young Italians with his educational works. Controversialists attacking Erasmus's religious teaching paradoxically roused a new interest in his works on this theme, hitherto neglected. A movement for change came into being, based initially on Erasmus's high educational reputation, widely diffusing his writings on religious freedom. The *De immensa misericordia Dei* was translated three times in the 1540s and 1550s. But the inquisition intervened, sharply checking this diffusion of subversive Erasmian views; here again, repression reigned.[25]

What is significant is that no modern writer on the Reformation has felt that Waldensianism had any noteworthy part to play in the success or otherwise of Reform in the peninsula; only Gonnet speaks a word of the 'might have been' of Waldensians, amongst other, quiet Protestant-orientated groups. Earlier persecution had pushed them to the margins.

The same generalization can be made about the French Reformation. Waldensians in France had been much reduced over the centuries. In Dauphiné they outlived a crusade. They continued in secrecy in Provence and the Comtat Venaissin. Immigration from Piedmont reinforced the numbers but did not modify their passive role, imposed by persecution. They transmitted their faith with resolution, but they did not missionize, or change the views of their Catholic neighbours.

Only in Germany does a question-mark about the deeper influence of Waldensianism remain. Böhmer long ago concluded from a dogmatic comparison

---

23   G. Gonnet, 'Sur les causes de la faillite en Italie des mouvements d'opposition à l'église officielle au moyen âge et au seizième siècle', *CV* xxxvi (1983), pp. 177–93.

24   Review of M. Welti, *Breve storia della riforma italiana* (1985), by R. Mackenzie in *JEH* xxxviii (1987), pp. 126–7. The classic account of the Italian Reform is in Delio Cantimori, 'The problem of heresy', *The Late Italian Renaissance, 1525–1630*, ed. E. Cochrane (1970), pp. 211–25 (tr. of article in *BSSV* lxxvi (1957), pp. 29–38).

25   Review by P. G. Bietenholz of S. S. Menchi, *Erasmo in Italia 1520–1580* (Turin, 1987), in *ARG* lxxx (1989), pp. 315–18.

that surviving congregations in Germany and Austria acted as a stimulus for the development of the Anabaptist groups well known in the early sixteenth century.[26] They had a considerable number of traits in common – the rejection of the oath, of war, of the holding of civic office. They shared an uncompromising rejection of the world. The rejection of infant baptism or the practice of ordaining the preacher may, it is said, have acted as a first step towards the rebaptizing characteristic of the movement. But these are only hypotheses still,[27] and there is too much uncertainty about the early Anabaptists to come to firm conclusions about their connection with the Waldensians, significant as they were in German-speaking lands.

## The Lollards

### The sixteenth-century movement

Unlike the Waldensians of France and Italy, the Lollards of England had not been pushed to the margins of society, and into mountain and frontier lands. The prosecutions of the sixteenth century show that they still existed in the regions singled out in Thomson's survey and were strong in the capital.[28] Persecution had lopped out a quondam leading class of trained clergy and eliminated the possibility of working a major change in England's religious beliefs by a process of academic-based education from above, using the vernacular, as Wyclif and the early founders had wished, but it had not destroyed the vitality of the movement.

The evidence of the courts suggests that recruitment was on the increase on the eve of the Reformation. Homespun evangelists in the Lollard style, repeatedly on the move, converting, carrying books, outwardly conforming, ready to recant, then slipping away to carry out what had plainly become for some a consuming task, helped to keep Bible-reading groups in being and gathered new recruits. John Hacker, the water-carrier, was known first in Hampshire and probably in Berkshire, and then resided in the Lollard locality of Coleman Street in London, making forays to the Chilterns, to Burford and the North Downs; subsequently he lived in Essex while keeping in touch with his fellow believers in London. Prosecution would not silence him: he abjured in 1521, but continued unabashed with his evangelizing until he was caught again in 1528. Hacker spoke effectively to his own kind: in London, for example, he was in contact with a bricklayer, a tallow-chandler, a saddler's wife, a haberdasher, a pointmaker and some tailors.[29]

---

26   *RPTK* xx, col. 832.
27   J. K. Zeman, 'Anabaptism: a replay of medieval themes or a prelude to the modern age?', *Mennonite Quarterly Review* (1976), pp. 259–71, puts weight on a spontaneous birth. Audisio, in *Les Vaudois*, ed. Audisio, pp. 81, 89, 96–7, notes our ignorance of the fate of the eastern wing of the Waldensians in Austria, Bohemia and lands further east in the sixteenth century and inclines to think that the Waldensian movement before the age of the Reformation had *de facto* divided into two, based on the barrier between the vernacular of the Alps and of the German-speaking lands, *barbi* and *Brüder*.
28   Above, pp. 295–300.
29   *HPR*, pp. 474–9. Hudson's whole chapter, 'The re-emergence of Reform', pp. 446–507, repays study, together with reference back to Aston, 'Lollardy and the Reformation'.

Family tradition remained a major factor. R. Lutton's investigations of Tenterden wills from families stretching over generations reveals a continuity of piety, not Lollard *per se*, but clearly a possible seed-ground for Lollard sympathies or recruitment. The Casteyn family produced seven wills stretching from 1473 to 1532 and covering four generations; it was one of the established families of Tenterden and its wills show, in Lutton's phrase, 'an extremity of orthodox piety which rendered its adherents particularly susceptible to Lollardy', with an earlier two generations making wills remarkably lacking in provision for conventional benefits for the dead and for cults centring on the parish church, obits, masses, lights, care of images, chantries; and two later generations, making less unconventional bequests, more attentive to the parish church yet focusing on the Jesus Mass, probably the mass of the Holy Name of Jesus, which became popular in the Weald in the early sixteenth century and may well be significant as a sign of dissatisfaction with the devotion to saints, so prominent in the past.

One Lollard emerged in the family; Stephen, a cutler, who abjured in 1511. He confessed that he learned to reject transubstantiation at the hands of William Carder, a fellow villager whom he met in Maidstone where he attended Lollard meetings. The story of Stephen's attraction to the movement is a typical one – trade probably took him to Maidstone, where from casual acquaintance, he was drawn into a house meeting, sitting by the fire of an evening and participating in denunciations of the mass and pilgrimages. Family tradition had made Carder a Lollard, for his mother had fled from Tenterden some forty years earlier to escape prosecution. He chose to return and evangelize, probably because Tenterden was a well-established Lollard centre. Stephen might well have been predisposed to conversation with Carder because of his family's evident wariness before orthodox late medieval religion.

Another family, the Pellonds, have comparable features in some wills, combining austerity towards orthodox religious custom with an emphasis on practical charity, two revealing an attachment to the Jesus Mass; they also produced a Lollard, William, penanced in 1511. Practical charity in preference to religious devotions was a perennial Lollard theme. William Baker remembered how, after a Lollard conversation, he decided not to make an offering to the Rood of Grace, but give to a poor man instead.[30]

The Lollard movement in its last phase adapted to its general loss of a clerical, trained leading class, and succeeded in putting the reading community in the centre of its life, with laymen and laywomen instructing, discussing, learning and evangelizing in different ways according to talent and opportunity, thus giving an impetus to small-scale growth. The movement had a deep suspicion of any form of clericalism; as, through circumstances of persecution, it became more and more heavily a lay movement, so its doctrine of the priesthood of all believers was lived out in practice within a web of house-churches and by casual, everyday

---

30  R. Lutton, 'Connections between Lollards, townsfolk and gentry in Tenterden in the late fifteenth and early sixteenth centuries', *LG*, pp. 199–228.

occupational meetings.[31] The lay teacher, supporter and missionary came into the forefront. He or she was naturally less vulnerable than the *barbi* of Waldensianism, leaders who made the decision in the interest of their own survival to maintain rather than to missionize, working through families in deep secrecy, keeping their movement alive in hard times but not expanding it. Lollardy, in its last phase, unlike Waldensianism, was not dependent on the ministrations of a select, trained few.

Though the vernacular mattered for the Waldensians, as it did for the Lollards, the scriptural and other texts were not at the centre in quite the same way. Lollardy was a religion of the book, and it had the resilience of a movement based on an underground literature, no longer growing, but copied, concealed, read out, and passed from hand to hand, still well able to stir the imagination, to console in adversity and to open simultaneously a world of literacy and of novel religious ideas. The records show its continuing potency.

A group of Buckinghamshire Lollards in the prosecutions of 1521–2 were described as sitting in Iver Court, the farm of a substantial Lollard, Robert Durdant, 'reading all the night in a book of scriptures'. Durdant invited guests to his daughter's wedding from Windsor, Amersham and London, who used the occasion to meet in a barn and listen to readings 'which they liked well'.

Buckinghamshire, an ancient Lollard site, gives proof that not all the heretics were of humble rank. John Phip of Hughenden was said to have burnt suspect books worth 100 marks to ward off prosecution.[32] Scrutiny of the Subsidy Rolls reveals that in Amersham, Great Marlow, Denham and Hughenden, Lollards were spread through the structure of society and by no means confined to the poorer levels.[33] Nor, in these few favoured localities, were they so small a minority. Over one quarter of those eligible to pay taxes in 1524–5 have been calculated to be Lollards, and of the total of Lollards that with good probability can be so labelled approximately 40 per cent were in the category paying from £4 to £9 and no less than 37 per cent in the category paying £10 and over. Men in these classes would hold authority, employ servants, bequeath inheritances by will and were able to exert pressure on dependants.

The state of Lollardy in Amersham showed what could be done by using wealth. Alice Saunders threatened a waverer with penalties if he left Lollardy, and when Thomas Houre abandoned his beliefs, saw to it that her husband dismissed him from his job, and that he even forfeited his post as holy-water clerk.[34] Lollards did not often wield that kind of influence, but research on adherents elsewhere, in Coventry and in Colchester, demonstrate the existence

31   *HPR*, pp. 449–51.
32   Cross, *Church and People* (sympathetic and imaginative account of late Lollardy), p. 35.
33   D. Plumb, 'The social and economic spread of rural Lollardy: a reappraisal', *SCH* xxiii, pp. 111–29; Id., 'The social and economic status of the later Lollards', *The World of Rural Dissenters*, ed. Spufford, pp. 103–31.
34   Plumb, in *World*, ed. Spufford, p. 121; for a characterization of the Buckinghamshire group, see Cross, *Church and People*, pp. 34–5.

of more patches of wealth among the membership than has hitherto been supposed. In Buckinghamshire there were Lollards of substantial and respectable families.

Ecclesiastical authority, sweeping into its net larger batches of suspects on the eve of the Reformation, occasionally burning, was not getting on top of the movement. Sentencing Lollards in Kent in 1511–12, Archbishop Warham carefully applied a gamut of penalties, relaxing five to the secular arm to be burned, using measures minatory and medicinal for the others, adapted to the guilt and circumstances of each, and, in a number of cases, allowing for a re-examination and remission of penalties. A trained canonist showed his calibre. But his measures fell short of uprooting the Kent communities.[35] The distribution of persecutions makes it highly probable that repression never eliminated nuclei in Lollard-influenced localities: even in East Anglia, so silent after the thorough persecution of Alnwick, it now seems that some at least lived on. The characteristics of English Lollardy, the ease of communications, the mobility and resilience of some missionaries and the special opportunities of the capital allowed it to survive and to some degree expand in London and in a swathe of localities in the south.[36]

TABLE 3    *Penances imposed on Kentish Lollards*

| |
|---|
| 33 carrying a faggot on a public occasion |
| 31 confinement to the parish or locality |
| 25 informing the archbishop of persons suspected of heresy and of books belonging to them |
| 17 wearing a badge with a faggot on it |
| 13 surrendering heretical books |
| 12 attending divine service in the parish church on Sundays and feast days |
| 10 recitation of the Lord's prayer, Hail Mary and creed |
| 9 fasting and/or abstinence in food |
| 7 imprisonment |
| 7 confession to a priest |
| 7 reception of the eucharist |
| 7 watching the execution of William Carder |
| 6 restrictions in dress |
| 3 offering a candle |
| 1 treating his wife well |

*Source:* N. Tanner, 'Penances imposed on Kentish Lollards by Archbishop Warham 1511–12', *Lollardy and the Gentry in the Later Middle Ages*, ed. M. Aston, C. Richmond (Stroud, 1997), pp. 229–49 at p. 235.

35    For Coventry, see above, pp. 289, 295, 297; for Colchester, J. C. Ward, 'The Reformation in Colchester, 1528–1558', *Essex Archaeology and History* xv (1983), pp. 84–95; *HPR*, p. 479; for Kent, N. Tanner, 'Penances imposed on Kentish Lollards by Archbishop Warham 1511–12', *LG*, pp. 229–49.

36    Cross, *Church and People*, pp. 36–7; *HPR*, pp. 446–7; on East Anglia, D. MacCulloch, *Suffolk and the Tudors* (1986), pp. 148–9.

*Lollardy and Protestantism*

The coming of continental Protestantism to England initially affected clergy and graduates primarily, and did so on a small scale, touching the universities, London and the east coast. Bishop Tunstall in a letter to Erasmus dismissed it as a reinforcement of Lollardy. 'It is no question of pernicious novelty,' he wrote, 'it is only that new arms are being added to the great crowd of Wycliffite heresies.'[37] Lutheran success in Germany could encourage the old Scripture-reading circles. Nicholas Field from London, presiding at a reading amongst Lollards in the Chilterns, was able to reinforce his point about the needlessness of the many traditional fasting days by referring to their elimination in Germany.[38] In an interesting case from Chesham an old Lollard, Thomas Harding, first convicted about 1506, prosecuted again after being informed on in 1532, was found to have under his floorboards such works of Tyndale as *The Obedience of a Christian Man* and *The Practice of Prelates*: at his trial he was convicted of a series of customary Lollard heretical beliefs, with a small admixture that was unquestionably Lutheran, derived, no doubt, from his reading of Tyndale. He had remained what he had for so long been – a determined Lollard, with views on images that were Lollard rather than Lutheran, for example, but quiet study had begun to carry him on in the direction of continental Protestantism.[39]

The old form of dissent could open the way to the new, and can be seen doing this in the case of John Tyball, of Steeple Bumstead in Essex, the articulate and persuasive lay convert to Lollardy, who succeeded in drawing Richard Fox, the incumbent of his parish, over to his opinions. Fox worked on the Augustinian friars of Clare in Suffolk. When one of their number, Thomas Topley, came into Fox's room, and found Wyclif's *Wicket* lying there, he read it and was moved by its exposition on the eucharist. 'I felt in my conscience a great wavering for the time that I did read upon it,' he said in his confession, 'and afterwards also, when I remembered it, it wounded my conscience very sore.'[40] Conversion was carried further by the preaching of Miles Coverdale, and the *Wicket*'s influence was accompanied and reinforced by Erasmus. Old Lollardy in this instance was a part of a complex of influences carrying some English circles into Protestantism and creating vital centres for the popular support of a Reform movement imposed, in stages, from above.

Tyball was unusual, consciously setting himself to make inroads into the clergy; the gulf, social and intellectual, between old Lollardy and new Lutheranism is manifest in the story of his journey to London with another Lollard to see Robert

37  A. G. Dickens, *The English Reformation*, 2nd edn (1989), p. 59. See esp. pp. 13–24, and his survey of Lollardy, pp. 46–60.
38  A. G. Dickens and Dorothy Carr, *The Reformation in England to the Accession of Elizabeth I* (1967), pp. 38–9.
39  *HPR*, pp. 505–7.
40  Foxe, *Acts and Monuments* v, pp. 39–40; *HPR*, p. 480; Cross, *Church and People*, pp. 40–1; comment by Aston, 'Lollardy and the Reformation', p. 162: 'Lollards might not actually make Protestants, but they could sow fertile seeds of doubt.'

Barnes, Lutheran, one-time prior of the Augustinian house in Cambridge and member of the White Horse circle of early Protestants. Tyball showed Barnes 'of certain old books that they had; as of Four Evangelists, and certain Epistles of Peter and Paul in English'. Barnes made little of Tyball's Lollard translations, which were, he said, not to be compared with Tyndale's New Testament, 'of more cleaner English', which he promptly sold to them for 3s 2d. He also met Tyball's request to write a letter to Richard Fox to confirm him in his views.[41]

The Late Version of the Lollard Bible, in its time a massive work of scholarship, was bound, as a translation of the Vulgate, to yield place to Tyndale, as a translator from the original languages – and, into the bargain, a master of English, the ultimate source of the literary triumph of the Authorized Version.[42]

Lutheranism did not always cohere with Lollardy. Luther disliked the moralism of the Epistle of James, the 'epistle of straw', to which the Lollards were drawn, and he did not share the Lollard hostility to the devotional apparatus of the late medieval Church, *tout court*, for all his attacks on abuses. His eucharistic beliefs were incompatible with those of the later Lollards.[43]

Ecclesiastical judges did not always know what to make of the differences between the two sets of beliefs. In the case of Thomas Bilney, who was made to recant by Tunstall in 1527, two interrogatories were available, one which was designed for a Lutheran offender, and was written in Latin, and another, written in English, designed for a Lollard and entered in the margin of the register. Against Bilney the Latin and Lutheran questions were used, and they may well have made him sound much more Lutheran than he was. The implicit assumption was that learned heresy would be Lutheran and that of the rank and file Lollard.

Bilney explained the development of his views in a letter to Tunstall as based on his personal experience of reading Erasmus's Latin version of the New Testament, probably soon after its publication in 1516, and especially of the sentence from I Timothy, 'It is a true saying and worthy of all men to be embraced, that Christ Jesus came into the world to save sinners.' This one sentence, he said, 'did so exhilarate my heart that immediately I felt a marvellous comfort and quietness'. He went on to say that he read Scripture anew, 'wherein I learned that all my travails, all my fasting and watching, all the redemption of masses and pardons, being done without trust in Christ...these, I say, I learned to be nothing else but even...a hasty and swift running out of the right way'.[44] Remorse at his recantation drove him out to preach again without authorization in Norwich Diocese, distributing Tyndale's New

41   Dickens and Carr, *Reformation*, pp. 35–6; J. Strype, *Ecclesiastical Memorials* (Oxford, 1822), I, pt 2, pp. 54–5.
42   *Tyndale's New Testament*, ed. D. Daniell (New Haven and London, 1989).
43   D. MacCulloch, *The Later Reformation in England, 1547–1603* (1990), pp. 67–8.
44   Dickens and Carr, *Reformation*, pp. 28–9; comment: Cross, *Church and People*, pp. 54–5; MacCulloch, *Suffolk*, p. 150, based on arguments of J. F. Davis, 'The trials of Thomas Bylney and the English Reformation', *Historical Journal* XXIV (1981), pp. 775–90; Id., *Heresy and Reformation in the Southeast of England* (1983), pp. 9–10; *HPR*, pp. 496–8.

Testament. He was burnt in 1531. Bilney was certainly not an orthodox Lutheran and J. F. Davis has given good reason for assuming that his judges in 1527 got it wrong; in fact his views then formed a personal amalgam of Lollard teaching, with its violent rejection of images and pilgrimages, and a reforming Cambridge Erasmianism.

Lollards, with their experience of underground book smuggling, aided the entry of Protestant books from abroad: Robert Necton, an importer of Tyndale's New Testament, was yet another of Hacker's contacts.[45] John Tewkesbury, a London haberdasher, burnt for heresy in 1531, also in Hacker's circle, read and sold both Wyclif's *Wicket* and Tyndale's *Obedience of a Christian Man and Wicked Mammon*.[46] Printing resurrected old Lollard texts, and gave them a wider audience; perhaps significantly, evidence suggests that the texts were being put out by publishers in a time-scale a little after the original continental works – and naturally the Lollards' texts are only a small proportion of the total flowing in from abroad. But they were there: Wyclif's *Wicket*, the General Prologue to the Late Version, Thorpe's *Trial*, the *Lantern of Light*, the *ABC Against the Clergy*. No doubt they were convenient material to feed a Protestant press, requiring neither translation for the English market nor any special preparation, and they served a Protestant purpose without mention of the name of Luther.[47] But they also met an ideological need. They demonstrated to the reading public that the battle against the conservative clergy was not a new one and that arguments like Purvey's on the rightfulness of biblical translation and that of the *ABC* on the evils of ecclesiastical lordship, had all been rehearsed before.

A twilight world was developing in the 1520s and 1530s in which Lollardy and Lutheranism, despite their differences, met and mingled. In London, certain wards and districts had a continuity of Lollard occupation; here, in the parish of St Sepulchre's, Oldcastle was concealed for a time after the failure of his rebellion in 1414, and in the same district John Claydon held his readings of the *Lantern of Light*. Hacker long had his base in Coleman Street, and one of his followers, John Stacy, a warden of the Bricklayers' Company, had a scriptorium there. A vicar of All Saints, Honey Lane, was a distributor of Protestant literature, and the pulpits of such churches as St Vedast, St Mary Woolchurch and St Mary Abchurch gave willing congregations to Reformed preachers.[48] Old and new supported each other. When the teaching of Zwingli reached England it is natural to assume that that, too, would combine with Lollardy and more easily

---

45    *HPR*, pp. 481–2.

46    Ibid., p. 477.

47    Ibid., pp. 491–2; perspective by Aston in 'Lollardy and the Reformation'. See A. Hudson, ' "No Newe Thyng": the printing of medieval texts in the early Reformation period', *HLB*, pp. 227–48. Powerful reassessment, E. Duffy, *The Stripping of the Altars* (New Haven and London, 1992); but note McSheffrey, *Gender*, p. 183, n. 140.

48    J. F. Davis, 'Lollardy and the Reformation in England', *ARG* LXXIII (1982), pp. 217–36 at pp. 224–5; Brigden, *London* (analysis of Londoners' reaction to Reformation, with sensitive re-creation of contemporary emotions); vivid depiction of Lollardy, pp. 86–106, see also pp. 411, 416–17; Stacy, p. 106.

and effectively, because Zwingli, like the Lollards, taught that the eucharist was a commemoration meal.[49]

What can be assumed is that Lollards would merge most naturally with teaching more radical than that of Luther, and that their affinities might be expected to lie with the Puritans rather than with the ultimate victor in the struggles about the English Reformation, the Church of England. So in Kent it can be no surprise to find a continuity of radical dissent in the same textile villages that had once been the haunt of William White in the fifteenth century. In 1511 Lollards were prosecuted in Benenden, Tenterden and Cranbrook; in 1539 a letter from Thomas Cromwell to Cranmer complained about the presence of sacramentaries in a number of localities, including Cranbrook; in 1556 John Philpot of Tenterden was tried for views which coincide with Lollardy rather than Lutheranism; under Elizabeth, Cranbrook became a well-known Puritan centre.[50] One of the intriguing examples is that of the Chilterns, where Nesta Evans has demonstrated a continuity of family names from Lollardy to Dissent, through the Reformation and beyond.[51]

### The role of Lollardy

Lollardy disappeared; but it did so by merger and osmosis, in ways that can now only be guessed at. An older view, that Lollardy played no part at all in the coming of the Reformation, which was brought about by the interplay of politics and the inflow of Protestantism from the Continent, is untenable; no-one would now argue that late Lollardy had lost all its capacity to move men, or that the success of Protestant enactments under Henry VIII and Edward VI was unrelated to the development of some public opinion in a Reform direction. What will long remain controversial is the degree to which popular views so moved, and the exact role of Lollardy in this peaceful change of opinion.[52]

The leading authority, A. G. Dickens, has described the heartland of the English Reformation before Elizabeth, where Protestant communities were most strongly developed, as 'a great crescent running from Norwich down to Hove and beyond'. Within that area there was a most intensive development in

49   MacCulloch, *Later Reformation*, gives a warning about the absence of evidence for contact between intellectuals of the Zwingli tradition and Lollards.

50   Davis, 'Lollardy and the Reformation', pp. 222–3.

51   N. Evans, 'The descent of the dissenters in the Chiltern hundreds', *The World of the Rural Dissenters*, ed. Spufford, pp. 288–308; review art., W. J. Sheils, *JEH* XLVIII (1997), pp. 121–31.

52   Debate on the role of Lollardy in the English Reformation forms part of a wider controversy over the part played by Protestant ideals in shaping opinion. A. G. Dickens, *The English Reformation* (London, 1964), following on the views in his *Lollards and Protestants*, long held the field. It has been challenged by C. Haigh, 'The recent historiography of the English Reformation', *The English Reformation Revisited*, ed. C. Haigh (1987), pp. 19–33 (see also introduction); for a powerful reply, see A. G. Dickens, 'The early expansion of Protestantism in England', *ARG* LXXVIII (1987), pp. 187–222; survey: R. O'Day, *The Debate on the English Reformation* (1986), esp. pp. 102–200; wise comment in M. E. Aston, *England's Iconoclasts* I (1988), p. 158: 'No adequate method has yet been found to test the plausible hypothesis that there was some continuity between pre- and post-Reformation dissent.'

Suffolk, Essex, London and Kent; a western offshoot ran up the Thames Valley into Oxfordshire and Berkshire, and thence into Gloucestershire and Wiltshire. The swathe of territory, although it includes the capital and east-coast ports, with Kent, which one would expect to be most readily open to continental influence, embraces, though it does not precisely comprehend, the traditional areas of Lollardy. It creates a presumption that there has been an interaction between the two. London, the underground capital of Lollardy, where authority found the maintenance of control particularly hard, was also a centre for Protestantism: here there was a long tradition of copying, and then of printing. Secret congregations could readily exist. St Nicholas, Cole Abbey and All Hallows, Honey Lane, were, for example, utterly diverse in attitudes, but they could quietly survive in close proximity.[53] This aided both old Lollardy and new Protestantism.

A comparison of Lollardy underground and of the burnings of the martyrs under Mary gives a broad but not very exact correspondence of areas of origin. The maps have a very different time-scale, the Lollard one, based on prosecutions, plotting the recorded incidence of Lollardy between 1414 and 1522, and the map of the Marian martyrs that of the place of origin and place of burning of those who suffered for their religious opinions in Mary's short rule; in fact in the three years and nine months from 3 February 1555 to the end of the reign.[54] The situation is confused by the differing attitudes of the gentry in various localities. There is, for example, a strong tally of martyrs in Sussex, but this may owe as much to the persecuting zeal of its gentry as to the depth of Protestant feeling.[55] Some turned a blind eye to the opinions of those in their area of authority, and were either sympathetic, or wanted no trouble; others responded earnestly to the policies of the government.

What must strike the observer is the new steadfastness of the victims of the burnings, and the rigour of the judges. Authority in England burnt but rarely before Mary's age. A figure has been cited of 544 trials between 1423 and 1522, issuing in only twenty-nine, possibly thirty-four, burnings.[56] Mary's judges burnt over 300 in a remarkably short space of time. The Protestant hagiographer, John Foxe, a generally careful recorder, listed 285 victims.[57] The Elizabethan historian John Strype gives figures for burning comparable to Foxe, ranged under counties, to a total of 288; A. G. Dickens has noted that a few cases are neither in Foxe nor Strype.[58]

Mary and her clerical advisers, reared in the traditions of the Spanish Counter-Reformation, were determined to extirpate heresy utterly. The bishops, faced

53   Brigden, *London*, p. 417; on the geographical distribution, see Dickens, *ARG* LXXVIII, p. 211.
54   For Lollardy underground, above pp. 296–300. For distribution of burnings and social analysis of victims, *LMH*, 1st edn, pp. 371–3.
55   M. J. Kitch, 'The Reformation in Sussex', *Studies in Sussex Church History*, ed. M. J. Kitch (Hassocks, 1981), p. 94; see discussion in O'Day, *Debate*, p. 154.
56   J. A. Guy, *Tudor England* (Oxford, 1988), p. 26 and reference given.
57   References in Lambert, as above, n. 54.
58   J. Strype, *Ecclesiastical Memorials* III, ii (Oxford, 1822), pp. 554–6; Dickens, *English Reformation* (1964 edn), pp. 264–72.

with offenders whose youth meant that their religious opinions had been formed after Henry's break with Rome, failed to notice an opportunity to allow mercy. These accused had been brought up when the Scriptures were freely available in the vernacular and Protestant views had begun to circulate. It could not be said that they had been instructed in the old faith, and then had wittingly turned their back on it – the assumption of medieval prosecutions.[59] This was a far cry from the slow-moving English bishops of the past, with their readiness to accept, and repeatedly accept abjuration. Before their judges the accused, gathered in organized churches of their own,[60] often humble men and women, resisted and defied their judges, where the Lollards of the past had preferred to suppress damaging evidence, to feign repentance and live to fight another day. Even those whose views suggest that they were in fact Lollards shared in the new attitudes, and went unhesitatingly to their deaths.

The impact on public opinion was all the greater because of the concentration of prosecutions and burnings within a small geographical area: 85 per cent of the burnings took place in London, south-east England and East Anglia.[61] Before the end there were signs of a stirring of opinion against authority. Restrictions were placed on those who could attend these spectacles – in itself a negation of the assumptions behind burning, that it should deter, and that it should be a public repudiation of heresy. Together with the unpopularity of Mary's Spanish marriage, and the failure of Pole and the government to revitalize the priesthood and, with rare exceptions, to counter Protestant propaganda, the burnings were a landmark in the slow change of sentiment amongst the mass of people who were neither zealous Catholics nor members of the new-formed Protestant communities.

Foxe, in his *Acts and Monuments*, popularly known as the *Book of Martyrs* by recording the sufferings of Mary's victims, gave a vital emotional underpinning to the Elizabethan Church.[62] In his first, English, edition of 1563 and in subsequent, improved versions published in his own lifetime, in 1570, 1576 and 1583, he showed himself scholarly and conscientious. Deeply committed to the Protestant cause, he none the less knew how a painstaking accumulation of detail carried conviction. The stories he related were of a type that all could understand and appreciate, of the courage of the humble before an unjust authority. The version of 1563 ran to over 1,800 pages, with more than fifty woodcuts and a calendar of martyrs and confessors. A truly Protestant history of the Church was in being, and capable of reaching a wide audience, through sales, only exceeded by the Bible, through readings, and through its use in the pulpit. It was the inevitable companion to the English Bible, and helped to secure the English Reformation.

---

59   P. Hughes, *Reformation in England* (London, 1953), ii, pp. 275–7; on the martyrs, see Dickens, *English Reformation*, pp. 293–301; sympathy for them: p. 297; role of women: p. 300.

60   P. Collinson, *The Elizabethan Puritan Movement* (London, 1967), p. 24; see Cross, *Church and People*, p. 113.

61   Guy, *Tudor England*, p. 238.

62   Analysis in O'Day, *Debate*, pp. 16–30; *John Foxe and the English Reformation*, ed. D. M. Loades (Aldershot, 1997).

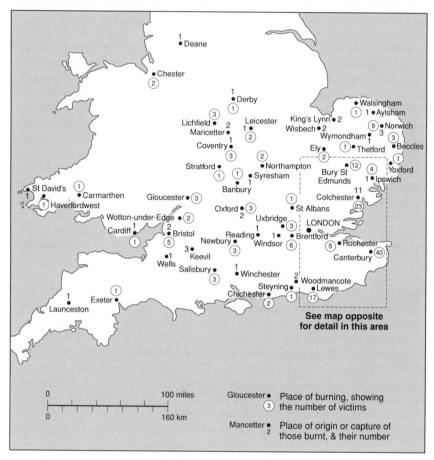

MAP 9A    *The Marian martyrs in England.*

Lollardy had a part to play. Foxe was influenced by the pioneer of Lollard history, John Bale, with whom he once shared lodgings. Bale, who published an account of Arundel's investigation of Oldcastle at Antwerp in 1544, saw the need to rewrite the history of the Church, and to displace in the public mind the Catholic martyr Becket by the Lollard Oldcastle. Foxe built on Bale's ideas.[63] He emphasized the Lollards from an early stage in the compiling of the *Martyrs* and its Latin forerunner, because their history was the answer to the gibe of the Catholic controversialist, where were you before Luther?

His was a providential history. For the first 300 years after the apostles, Foxe believed, the Church suffered; for another three it flourished; then declined for

63    L. P. Fairfield, 'John Bale and the development of Protestant hagiography in England', *JEH* XXIV (1973), pp. 146–60.

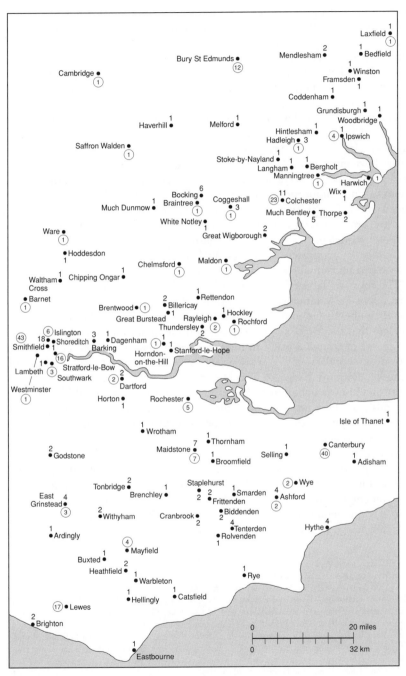

MAP 9B    *The Marian martyrs in England (detail).*

300 until about the year 1000. There followed the time of Antichrist, then in the sixteenth century the 'purging of the Church of God'.[64] The Lollards were witnesses for truth in England who grappled with Antichrist; the martyrs of Mary's reign were continuing the same struggle; Elizabeth was a second Deborah, called to battle for the truth. Foxe had borrowed from Wyclif and the Lollards the conception of a golden age of the Church, brought to an end by Rome and its clergy.

The reader who followed the story of Wyclif, his translation of the Bible, the attempted and failed reform, the persecution of the Lollards, then the intensity of Mary's attack across the pages of Foxe might not have realized, for all the detail which Foxe gives about their lives and beliefs, that Lollards were radical dissenters in a number of ways different from the adherents of Elizabeth's national Church. Foxe suppressed a little when he worked on the Waldensians for he glided over their rejection of all but two sacraments;[65] his account of the Marian martyrs omits reference to the separatists among them.[66] He wrote with a purpose, to defend an embattled English Church against its enemies, and to encourage its supporters, and presented the pre-history of Protestantism as a simple and unified whole.

The most signal service of Lollardy, it may be, was to provide Tudor and subsequent Protestants with a pre-history of heroes and martyrs before Luther. But they also had a more humdrum role, in preparing public opinion for the changes that they were no longer able to bring about themselves. They 'lacked the power of regeneration'[67] in consequence of long repression, but they could provide a secondary service, assisting the entry of Protestant ideas, and softening attitudes. Richard Flynte of Topcliffe in North Yorkshire, brought before the court in 1542 for failing to make his Easter confession, excused himself on the grounds that 'there was a saying in the country that a man might lift up his heart to God Almighty and need not be confessed at a priest'. When he was asked where he had heard this opinion, Flynte answered, perhaps honestly, that he did not know.[68]

The episode is a reminder that there was a diffused Lollardy, propagated outside the strict Scripture-reading circles, closely analogous to anticlericalism and sometimes fed from it, that sapped the foundations of traditional Catholicism. Flynte's sentiment, like that of Lollards within the country, was fundamentally subversive of medieval religion, and was a part of the ensemble of ideas

---

64   O'Day, *Debate*, p. 17.
65   Cameron, *Reformation*, p. 246.
66   J. W. Martin, *Religious Radicals in Tudor England* (1989), pp. 171–8; for Foxe's qualities as a historian, P. Collinson, 'Truth and legend: the veracity of John Foxe's Book of Martyrs', *Clio's Mirror: Historiography in Britain and the Netherlands*, ed. A. G. Duke, C. A. Tamse (1985), pp. 31–54, who comments (p. 35) that Foxe 'worked only a little more carelessly and a few shades more partially than would be tolerable in a modern doctoral thesis'. Note comments on style, pp. 48–9, and the intriguing transmutation of the contemporary Lollard view of William White as a saint into conventional sixteenth-century terms (such as a 'good and godly man'); *John Foxe*, ed. Loades.
67   Aston, 'Lollardy and the Reformation', p. 169.
68   Dickens, *Lollards and Protestants*, p. 48.

blowing to and fro, casually diffused, that helped to create the climate in which Reform ideas could grow and flourish. It is not easy to define, but the evidence for these views lies in the whole sequence of pithy and earthy Lollard aphorisms and negatives, displayed at trials, diffused in the readings of the movement, and quietly spread in society. They helped, with many other factors,[69] to bring down in England the medieval Church, which had persecuted the Lollards.

## The Utraquists and the *Unitas*

### Luther's encounters with Utraquism[70]

The young Luther shared the views of his German contemporaries on the dissidents in Bohemia. He rejected those who broke the unity of the Church and referred to the *Unitas Fratrum* as Pikhards. A volte-face over the Bohemians followed from his volte-face over the medieval Church. In the disputations at Leipzig in July 1519, Eck reproached him with defending the heretical views of Hus on the papacy, for which he was condemned at Constance. Luther at that time still rejected the Hussite movement as a schism but acknowledged the rightfulness of some of Hus's teaching. Then, when he read Hus's *De ecclesia*, he wrote: 'We are all Hussites without knowing it, and Paul and Augustine.'[71] As he was brought to a firm opposition to the papacy, so reservations about the Bohemians were dropped. In 1520 he had the *De ecclesia* printed and early in 1521 began to refer to Hus as a saint.[72]

---

69   O'Day, *Debate*, pp. 137–40; W. J. Sheils, *The English Reformation 1530–1570* (1989), pp. 7–9; R. Whiting, *The Blind Devotion of the People: Popular Religion and the English Reformation* (1989), though concentrating on the south-west, has comments of wider application – see esp. pp. 256, 266; and note p. 268, where he speaks of 'a Catholic collapse', but 'not necessarily or immediately a Protestant enthusiasm'. On late medieval piety, see C. Richmond, 'Religion and the fifteenth century English gentleman', *The Church, Politics and Patronage*, ed. Dobson (1984), p. 193–208, P. Heath, 'Urban piety in the later middle ages: the evidence of Hull wills', Ibid., pp. 209–34; interesting note on the evidence on survival of belief in purgatory, C. Burgess, ' "By Quick and by Dead": wills and pious provision in late medieval Bristol', *EHR* cii (1987), pp. 837–58. D. MacCulloch, reviewing J. F. Davis, *Heresy and Reformation in the South East of England* (1983), in *JEH* xxxv (1984), pp. 483–6, notes a piety 'vigorous and demonstrative but largely untouched by the austerity of the continental *devotio moderna*', which 'expressed itself in a highly materialistic form', and argues that the piety itself 'provoked a peculiarly English variety of reforming reaction just as much as the ideas of Wycliffe'.

70   W. Eberhard had originally thought of working on the theme of Luther in Bohemia 1520–1620 (*Konfessionsbildung*, p. 7), but discovered that: (a) basic groundwork had not been undertaken; (b) it was not easy to avoid analysing the theme one-sidedly, in terms of the one-way influence of the German Reformation on Bohemian neighbours. His two books, *Konfessionsbildung* and *Monarchie und Widerstand: Zur ständischen Oppositionsbildung im Herrschaftssystem Ferdinands I in Böhmen* (1985), concentrate on the development of the attitudes of the Bohemian Estates, parties within them and the interaction of politics and religion in the Bohemian confessions. They are concerned primarily with the political history of Utraquism, but none the less provide much information on religious history of Utraquists and *Unitas* and on the influx of Lutheranism. See also survey, Heymann, 'The Hussite–Utraquist Church', pp. 1–16.

71   *Les Vaudois*, ed. Gonnet and Molnár, pp. 284–90; citation: reference on p. 289.

72   S. H. Thomson, 'Luther and Bohemia', *ARG* xliv (1953), pp. 160–81 at p. 176; for Erasmus's influence, see A. Molnár, 'Erasmus und das Hussitentum', *CV* xxx (1987), pp. 185–97.

Luther was welcome to Utraquists who were disillusioned with the attempts at reunion with Rome. They valued him, not so much because of his doctrines *per se*, as because of his effective opposition to the papacy.[73] They do not seem at first to have differentiated clearly between him and Erasmus. The appearance of a protest movement in Germany, which had in consequence of the crusades in the fifteenth century for so long been the seat of the greatest hostility to the Hussite movement, was all the more poignant and exhilarating. It offered the opportunity to break out of the long isolation that had afflicted the Utraquist Church; contacts with Luther were thus speedily taken up by individual adherents of the Left-Utraquism which, on quite other grounds, had come into increasing prominence in Bohemian politics and in the churches of Prague before Luther's fateful change of heart. Such radicals as Jan Poduška, priest of the Tyn church, Wenceslas Roždalovský and, from 1522, Martin Hánek praised Luther, as did the popular lay preacher, the hermit Brother Matthew; the fact that such men obtained places in Prague and were tolerated is to be attributed to a growing strength of Left-Utraquism. The language barrier operated against a full and direct overspill from Lutheran strongpoints into Czech-speaking lands, such as occurred in northern and north-western Bohemia where inroads were made in the ranks of German-speaking Catholics. Knowledge of, and enthusiasm for Luther was at first mediated to Czech areas by individual preachers, influenced more profoundly in their beliefs by the tenets of the *Unitas* and recurrent Taborite-type attitudes to Scripture and the mass, but excited by a new star in the firmament of dissidence against Rome.[74]

Both sides were moved. Luther, when he got wind in 1522 of an attempt by Catholic clergy and conservative Utraquists to negotiate with Rome, come to an accommodation over the lay chalice and sacrifice the distinctive role of Utraquism, wrote a letter to the Estates designed to influence opinion against such a move, in which he praised Hus and Jerome of Prague and suggested a union of sentiment between like-minded Bohemians and Germans. The letter was successful – a tribute both to his reputation and to the growing force of the Left-Utraquist wing, who had been making progress since the removal of the conservative Administrator, Korambus, early in 1520. Politics aided confessional interests. The towns' representatives had long been drawn towards Left-Utraquism as part of their reaction against the policy of the Catholic higher nobility, bent on cutting back the towns' economic and constitutional gains.[75]

Gallus Cahera, a priest from Litoměřice, succeeded Poduška and Roždalovský, who died young of plague, as principal supporter of Luther in Bohemia after he had spent time with the master in Wittenberg. Luther formed a high opinion of him. It was his great error, for Cahera was an unstable egoist. When the Prague Council asked Luther in 1523 for his judgement on the thorny subject of

---

73   Eberhard, *Konfessionsbildung*, pp. 129, 147.
74   Ibid., pp. 127–31; Hánek: pp. 136–7.
75   Ibid., pp. 134–5; Korambus: p. 131; for general basis of development of parties, confessions, pp. 74–119 are illuminating; Thomson, *ARG* xliv, pp. 176–7.

maintaining the Utraquist priesthood, he replied in his *De instituendis ministris* recommending that a bishop be chosen from among the existing Utraquist priests who had been ordained under the Roman rite, to carry out the necessary ordinations, and gave Cahera's name as a suitable candidate. The Church shrank from the explicit breach involved in choosing their own bishop, although Cahera was made solitary Utraquist Administrator with wide powers, a quasi-bishop.[76]

How far radical views had spread among the Left-Utraquists is shown by the Candlemas Articles of January 1524 evolved by the Utraquists of Bohemia and Moravia, stressing the pure word of the law of Christ, its intelligibility and its precedence over all authorities, whether Church Fathers or Hussite teachers of the past.[77] The focus was on the two sacraments, holy communion and baptism, and there was a curious avoidance of the term 'sacerdos'. The articles spoke of servants, not priests, or of the 'clerus', and stressed the need for examination of conscience before reception of communion. The echo of Luther's voice was to be found in an article recommending the repression of Church feast days in the interest of putting down idleness, and in another on the role of the paterfamilias proclaiming the gospel within the family circle. The Candlemas Articles reveal the degree of influence being exerted on traditional Utraquism by the forces of the *Unitas* or of individual priests, such as Martin Hánek of Bethlehem, with Taborite-type views, and by Luther himself; and the existence, beside these strands, of a perennial Hussite concern for toleration of differing views within the Church. A clear division between Lutheranism and Utraquism lay in the Church's rejection of Luther's views on the marriage of the clergy and its lack of understanding of Lutheran solafideism.

In the same year as the Candlemas Articles, a reaction in Prague was initiated by the conservative master Pašek, exploiting the views of conservative food guilds and manipulating the organs of government, which lasted till 1528. Right-Utraquists and Catholics again co-operated and yet another initiative was launched for a reunion with Rome. Pressure was put on Hánek and the Utraquist radicals, and there were bannings and imprisonments as well as burnings of a Lutheran, an Anabaptist and supporters of a fringe group of the *Unitas*. Cahera, perhaps mindful of Luther's action against his own extremist Karlstadt, fell in with the reaction. Luther, who vainly appealed to him, was bitterly disappointed; the conservative Utraquists turned against Lutheranism and thereafter Luther grew more cautious in his dealings with the Utraquists.[78]

In 1526 the last of the Jagiellon rulers, King Lewis, drowned at the battle of Mohacs against the Turks. The Estates and the parties united on a candidate, Ferdinand I of the Habsburg dynasty. The decision was a tribute to the will of the parties, determined to avoid civil war and a crisis with neighbouring lands and to put the interests of the community first.

---

76 Eberhard, *Konfessionsbildung*, pp. 140–1, 165–71, supersedes all earlier work on Cahera.
77 Ibid., pp. 139–44 (fresh analysis).
78 Ibid., pp. 150–81; comment, Thomson, *ARG* XLIV, pp. 160–81 at p. 178.

The fact that there was tension between the pope and the Habsburgs encouraged some Hussites to be more willing to accept him; in doing so, they overlooked the warning implicit in Ferdinand's record of repression of Lutherans. Each party hoped for different concessions from the new monarch. Those who opposed the Regents, for example, who stood for the enlargement of the power of great nobles at the expense of monarchy, looked to a revival of central authority. It was another sign of the Hussite preoccupation with their own history and traditions and the secondary role played in their mind by Luther and his teaching.[79]

Ferdinand, an energetic ruler brought up in the world of Spanish Catholicism alien to the Bohemian tradition of liberty, gave sincere acceptance of the Compactata, but only in a narrow sense. Influenced by his confessor Fabri, subsequently bishop of Vienna, who stayed with him in Prague in 1528 and wrote a work pointing out the contradictions between Luther's teaching and the Hussite position and expressing a preference for the latter, Ferdinand followed a long-term policy of building an alliance between Catholics and conservative Utraquists so as to erect a barrier against the inroads of more radical dissidents, Lutherans, Left-Utraquists, members of the *Unitas*, Anabaptists.[80] By a skilled balancing policy he aimed to integrate the quarrelling parties and recover monarchical authority; in this he had a great measure of success over time and began the process of building the Habsburg absolutism which destroyed Hussitism in Bohemia.

## *Luther and the* Unitas

Luther as a young friar almost certainly gained his knowledge of the *Unitas* from the *Apologia* made in their defence by Luke of Prague to King Wladislav and printed in Latin at Nuremberg in 1511, and from the controversy which this unleashed with Jerome Dungersheim, professor at Leipzig. The detail of Luther's lectures on the Epistle to the Romans in 1516 make plain that he was, in his own mind, continuing a debate with the views of Luke.[81] When the decisive change in his attitude came after the clash with Eck, he felt the need for reconciliation. 'It is high time', he said in his appeal *An den christlichen Adel der deutschen Nation* of 1520, 'that we quite honestly and sincerely consider the case of the Bohemians, to unite them with us and us with them'.[82]

Relations with the *Unitas* were more difficult than with the Utraquists because of Luther's unease about their eucharistic teaching. Members of the *Unitas*,

---

79   Richter, in *Handbuch*, ed. Bosl, II, pp. 147–50; on issues in choice of Ferdinand, Eberhard, *Konfessionsbildung*, pp. 203–13, is helpful; Ferdinand did not stand on a right of inheritance and his succession was agreed in Bohemia.
80   Eberhard, *Konfessionsbildung*, pp. 245–8, noting, p. 246, the earlier existence of such a policy; for Ferdinand's brother, see F. Seibt, *Kaiser Karl V und die Reformation* (1990); on religion and the development of Estates, W. Eberhard, in *Crown, Church and Estates*, ed. R. J. W. Evans, T. V. Thomas (1991), pp. 23–47.
81   Thomson, *ARG* XLIV, p. 166.
82   Ibid., p. 172.

especially John Roh from Litomyšl who had been impressed by a reading of Luther's writings, took the initiative. Roh and a companion, Weisse, visited Luther in Wittenberg in 1522; Luke took up correspondence; Luther clarified his own position in his *Vom Anbeten des Sacraments* of 1523; further exchanges took place between Luke and Luther marked by a will to mutual understanding and by Luke's joy at the recognition of common ground. None the less, Luke was a theologian of calibre, not ready to give up the distinctive doctrines of the *Unitas*, long established, for which they had suffered persecution, and it was he who broke off the correspondence in 1523. Doctrines of the eucharist and justification divided them and contact had not been renewed when Luke died in 1528.[83]

The years 1530 to 1532 marked a turning-point in the history of the *Unitas*, as in the Synods a party of younger clergy, anxious to widen the appeal of the *Unitas* and open it to external influences, broke through the resistance of their elders.[84] In 1530 a number of nobles, who had been protectors, took the decision to accept baptism; the social and political significance of the *Unitas* began to increase. In 1525 it has been calculated that the numbers of adherents had climbed to about 150,000;[85] advance continued and recruits were won at the expense of the Utraquists. The appeal of Brother Vavřinec Krasonický was heard and the *Unitas* began to send candidates to university at Wittenberg. It was decided that the writings of Luke of Prague should have authority only in so far as they reflected that of Scripture. The views of John Roh on the desirability of opening contacts with Luther and the German Reformation prevailed. In 1532 the Synod chose John Augusta as one of the bishops; he was very young and had only been made priest the year before; he was a fine polemicist, a party chief, a preacher and man of both brilliant and dangerous qualities;[86] his powerful personality exerted a sway over the *Unitas* until his death in 1572. He believed in closer links with Lutheranism. At the time of the Synod, the leadership was asked for a written statement of belief to be shown to Margrave George of Brandenburg; written in Czech, it was translated by Weisse, the quondam companion of Roh in visits to Luther, into German with the title *Rechenschaft des Glaubens*. It showed very plainly the symbolic character of the *Unitas*'s belief on the eucharist, which clashed with Luther's doctrine of the Real Presence. The translation fell into the hands of Zwinglians, who were delighted with a statement in accord with their own views, and had it printed in Zurich as a means of reinforcing their own position *vis-à-vis* the Lutherans. A new German translation was made and sent to Luther who gave

83   Ibid., pp. 174–6; Richter, in *Handbuch*, ed. Bosl, II, p. 123; J. T. Müller, *Geschichte der böhmischen Brüder* I (1922), pp. 389–417; A. Molnár, 'Luther und die böhmischen Brüder', *CV* XXIV (1981), pp. 47–67; see also W. Eberhard, 'Bohemia, Moravia and Austria', *The Early Reformation in Europe*, ed. A. Pettegree (1992), pp. 23–48.
84   Eberhard, *Monarchie*, pp. 97–112.
85   Richter, in *Handbuch*, ed. Bosl, II, p. 117. For development of *Unitas*, see Eberhard, *Monarchie*, pp. 97–112.
86   Judgement of E. Denis, *Fin de l'indépendance bohème* II: *Les Premiers Habsbourgs* (1890) (the least durable part of his narrative, but still a vivid account), p. 100; see O. Odložilík, 'The Reformation leaders of the *Unitas Fratrum*', *CH* IX (1940), pp. 253–63.

it a foreword and had it printed in Wittenberg. Luther at this time wanted a united front against the Papists and valued the support of the Brothers. The *Rechenschaft* had many affinities with Luther; there was some movement in eucharistic doctrine towards the Lutheran position. A decision of 1532 had diminished the importance of the second baptism on entry to the *Unitas* and asserted the full validity of baptism of infants.[87]

But a gap between Luther and the *Unitas* remained; the *Unitas* had not accepted Lutheran justification theology. They retained a more explicitly ethical stress and a disciplinary mechanism within the Church, and they were unwilling to abandon celibacy. Luther went on publishing works of Hus and in 1538 issued a Latin version of the *Confessio* of the *Unitas*. He seemed, however, content to stop short of a formal link. He once said to representatives of the *Unitas*: 'Let us both, you Czechs and we Germans, be apostles. You labour there, as conditions demand and we will strive here as we are impelled.'[88]

The opening of links with Wittenberg and the German Reformation had its effects on Wenceslas Mitmánek.[89] Sent to Wittenberg in 1530 by the *Unitas*, he travelled widely, was influenced by Melanchthon and his concept of a True Church, invisible and not precisely delimited in its organization. On his return, he left the *Unitas* for Utraquism, soon rose to a position of influence, and argued more decisively than other Left-Utraquists for creating links with the *Unitas*, a policy which failed to win lasting support. The ferment of the German Reformation worked among the Utraquists in general, helping to induce among the Left wing an emphasis on the gospel, derived ultimately from German lands, which pushed into the background the earlier Taborite-type views of these circles on the eucharist, but never going so far as to create a unified Protestant Church in Bohemia.[90]

Augusta, child of pious Utraquist parents, retained links with Utraquist churchmen and was prepared to engage in vigorous polemic. He dreamed of a unity of church members, bringing together Utraquists, Lutherans and the *Unitas*. He spoke from a position of strength, for the *Unitas* was growing and was literarily active, unoppressed, as a select minority, with the problems of political and ecclesiastical management which fell on the Utraquists. But Augusta's efforts brought no wider union; they publicized the *Unitas* but also irritated the Left-Utraquists, whose position he criticized as illogical. In effect, the wider publicity given to the *Unitas*, its efforts at establishing contacts with the German Reformation and the crystallizing of its doctrines in a *Confessio* brought members to the status of being, in practice, a third confession within Bohemia, beside Rome and the Utraquists.

It was, however, a confession that had been given no legitimacy. The decree of toleration of Kutná Hora excluded them, and juridically if not in practice they remained in a state of exclusion. The aftermath of the Catholic victory over the

---

87  Thomson, in *ARG* XLIV, pp. 178–9; Eberhard, *Monarchie*, pp. 113–30.
88  Thomson, *ARG* XLIV, p. 179.
89  Eberhard, *Monarchie*, pp. 257–63.
90  Ibid., p. 310.

Schmalkaldic League at Mühlberg in 1547,[91] from which Ferdinand returned in anger to punish the Bohemians who had failed to follow his summons to the campaign, brought a sharp persecution on the *Unitas*. Augusta was put in prison for sixteen years. The Moravian lords, however, despite their religious allegiance, had generally not declined to obey Ferdinand's summons and his wrath did not fall on Moravia. There persecution was relatively ineffective; in consequence many of the Bohemian *Unitas* fled to Moravia, where the centre of gravity of the movement thereafter lay; others concealed themselves in Utraquism; others again moved farther afield into Poland; here and elsewhere the diaspora set in motion by Ferdinand gave the *Unitas* an international following.

### The policies of the Habsburgs

Meanwhile Ferdinand continued to strive to create a union between Rome and the conservative Utraquists and to bring vitality into his own Church in Bohemia, which had suffered, just as Utraquism had, from long conflicts, massive disendowment and shortage of priests. He had hopes that the Council of Trent would help in building a bridge between Utraquism and Catholicism but the definitions of Trent, fencing off Catholicism, worked rather in the opposite direction. Peace, he believed, would come to his realms if once the dissidents, Lutheran, *Unitas*, Anabaptists, could be excluded or driven into renunciation of their beliefs, and the Utraquists who stood close to Rome given the essential recognition of the lay chalice. An effective revival of Catholicism would have to wait, it was apparent, on the emergence of a new generation of clergy.

Ferdinand's invitation to Petrus Canisius and the Jesuits to settle in Prague led to the development of the Collegium Clementinum and the foundation of a new and more effective system of Catholic education which put up some bulwarks against the growth of Lutheranism and began to stem the outflow of the sons of nobles and wealthy bourgeois to German Protestant universities. But the Jesuits were more interested in the maintenance and deepening of Church life than in opening lines of communication with the Utraquists.

In the last decade of his reign, Ferdinand succeeded in gaining greater control over the official organs of the Utraquists – a facet of his will to develop the power of the monarch, and of his plan to ward off the influence of Left-Utraquists and bring the Right wing into a working union with Rome. However, he failed repeatedly in his attempts to persuade the papacy to permit the lay chalice. Finally, in 1564 Pius IV allowed it under conditions in the newly revived Archbishopric of Prague, in Olomouc and in some other dioceses. It was the last year of Ferdinand's life, and the measure should have crowned his endeavours to remove dissident Utraquism from his realms.[92]

---

91 For build-up of tension, Mühlberg and its aftermath, see Eberhard, *Monarchie*, pt III, pp. 335–501; effects on *Unitas*: Müller, *Brüder* II, pp. 199–238; Richter, in *Handbuch*, ed. Bosl, II, pp. 152–7.
92 For Ferdinand's policy and the response, see Richter, in *Handbuch*, ed. Bosl, II, pp. 158–61, 176–80.

In fact, it did not. It had come too late and what would have been a measure of prime importance in the fifteenth century had no significant effect in the conditions of 1564. Luther had followed Hussite precedent in adopting the lay chalice: old-style Utraquism was being outflanked.

Another link with the past disappeared as the Compactata was abandoned by general agreement under Maximilian in 1567.[93] It had come to be seen as no more than an instrument employed by the monarch to restrict the activities of Utraquists. It had never concerned the *Unitas*, and the inner development and radicalization of Left-Utraquism had outpaced it. In the third quarter of the century, Lutheranism grew apace despite the repressive policies of the Habsburgs, repeatedly moderated in practice by political necessity and pressures from abroad.

Lutheranism and the precedent of the Confession of Augsburg facilitated the agreement on doctrine enshrined in the Bohemian Confession of 1575.[94] It sprang from an initiative of the Estates, where the nobility of the *Unitas* and of the Utraquist allegiances could come to agreement more easily than their clergy. Maximilian and the Catholics opposed it, and that fact assisted the confessions in coming to agreement. The Augsburg Confession provided a basis, albeit modified by the tenets of Utraquists and the *Unitas*. The latter could hope for a measure of recognition, but they did not intend to give up their independent Church order. Maximilian was only willing to give oral approval; little in practice was gained.

Utraquism sank. It lost its popular links; clergy became demoralized; there were losses to Lutheranism; others, closer to Rome, took the final step and surrendered to the papacy. In 1587 and in 1591 groups of clergy, some of note with two Administrators among them, took an oath of obedience to the pope and the archbishop of Prague and renounced the distinctive practices and tenets of Hussitism.[95] A majority of Utraquist clergy continued their independence and the evangelical wing succeeded in making some improvements.[96] But the Church was not what it had been.

The sixteenth century was the epoch in which the *Unitas* flowered, overcoming the schism of the Amosites, gaining ground at the expense of Utraquism and responding to persecution by flight and fresh missionizing. With the aid of their protectors they made excellent use of the printing press.[97] A powerful vernacular hymnology emerged. It was decided that some control should be exerted over the hymns used by various congregations which circulated in hand-written versions and in 1561 an official hymnbook was printed, with a foreword noting how the writing of hymns had been stimulated by the age of persecution.

---

93    Heymann, 'The Hussite–Utraquist Church', p. 14; Richter, in *Handbuch*, ed. Bosl, II, p. 172.
94    Richter, in *Handbuch*, ed. Bosl, II, pp. 172–3.
95    Ibid., p. 174.
96    M. S. Fousek, 'Spiritual direction and discipline: a key to the flowering and decay of the 16th century Unitas Fratrum', *ARG* LXII (1961), pp. 207–25 at p. 208.
97    For inner history of *Unitas* and Blahoslav, see Müller, *Brüder* II, pp. 344–68; hymns and dating of Kralice Bible, Richter, in *Handbuch*, ed. Bosl, II, pp. 198–9.

John Blahoslav, who battled with Augusta over the rightfulness of pursuing learning within the *Unitas*, translated the New Testament into Czech from the Greek and was a mainspring behind the collective effort to produce the monument to original work with the Czech vernacular, the six-volume Kralice Bible with commentary, completed in 1588. Blahoslav contributed to the language itself: his Czech grammar was designed to purify the language rather than to serve the schools of the Brothers. He justified the project as a recreation for times when he was too tired to pursue theology. His disciple Orlik called him a 'precious jewel' of the *Unitas*.[98] With his death in 1571, and that of Augusta not long afterwards, there passed the generation of great bishops.

Successors were unable to resist decline. The practice of sending the most promising clergy for training at universities outside Bohemia exposed them certainly to wider horizons, but also to novel influences. At first they went to Lutheran universities, then, after Melanchthonian teachings had been eliminated, to Calvinist centres in Germany or in Switzerland.[99] Calvin's influence grew at the expense of their own independent tradition. Celibacy ceased to be obligatory for the clergy. The practice of private confesson was eroded. Its part had been vital in sustaining the ethical calibre of the *Unitas* from the time of Luke of Prague's *Directives to Priests*. For a time after his death, the authority of the *Directives* was weakened because of synodal decisions of 1531 and the impact of Lutheran ideas, but after a period of uncertainty both Augusta and Blahoslav recalled their followers to the heritage of Luke. Augusta's *Art of the Work of the Lord's Ministry*, written during his imprisonment, revived Luke's concept, albeit with warnings against overscrupulousness. A structure of probation, confession and examination of new members, with a catechumenate and a sequence of steps to be taken before admission to full membership maintained an exclusive Church on the principles of Peter Chelčický.[100] Its fruit in the standards of conduct of the members had been the major appeal of the *Unitas*. The practice of private confession was being vigorously defended against Calvinist objections in 1558; later, however, it faded out as the *Unitas* lost its sense of identity. Members, deprived of the rigour of the old discipline, went over to other Churches, in Poland to the Calvinists, in Bohemia and Moravia to the Utraquists.[101] The clergy, without the tool of confession, ceased to have an insight into the needs of the souls committed to them. Comenius, bishop in exile, mourning over the near-extinction of his Church, concluded in 1649 that the cause of it was not the enemies of the *Unitas*, the persecuting forces of the Habsburgs unleashed after the victory of the Catholics at the battle of the White Mountain in 1620, but the Brethren themselves. By abandoning the inner Church discipline bequeathed to them by Luke of Prague, they had destroyed themselves.[102] Certainly a 'hidden seed' survived as he had hoped it would, in Moravia, and crossed the borders to

98  Denis, *Fin* II, p. 257.
99  Fousek, *ARG* LXII, p. 209.
100  The central theme of Fousek's article.
101  Fousek, *ARG* LXII, p. 208.
102  Ibid., pp. 207–8, 222, 224.

Herrnhut in Saxony, where under the leadership of Count Zinzendorf in the eighteenth century, the Moravian Brethren entered on a new and yet more striking phase of their history. Yet in the late sixteenth and early seventeenth centuries they had come within a hair's breadth of foundering altogether.

In this it was like the other movements condemned as heretical by the medieval popes. Lollards, Waldensians, Utraquists, *Unitas* survived all manner of pressures to live on into the Reformation epoch. The Lollards contributed to the success of the English Reformation; but then they and the Waldensians were absorbed into sixteenth-century Protestantism. The Utraquists in the fifteenth century had achieved a measure of public recognition. They had become a force to be reckoned with for kings, popes and governments and continued to play a major role in the history of Bohemia and Moravia in the sixteenth century. But in time they changed character; the Compactata were abandoned and the lay chalice ceased to have its traditional importance; its most conservative clergy submitted to the papacy; Left-Utraquists both lost ground to Lutheranism and were, in the end, themselves profoundly influenced by Luther. Their independent existence ceased in the seventeenth century.

Thus medieval heresy merged into the Protestant Reformation.

# Heresy and Reform

Reform and heresy were twins. The Dark Ages and its fissiparous Churches, dominated by kings and aristocrats, repeatedly threatened by inner anarchy and external pressure of barbarians, produced very little heresy. The Christianity of the epoch gave security: it protected its adherents in life and offered them hope at death. This pre-Gregorian world 'enjoyed a secure understanding of the holy. It resided not in men but in places, objects and rituals under the custody of a priesthood whose value resided not in the ephemeral acknowledgement of personal virtue, but in the general recognition that it held the keys.'[1] Reform, and the stirrings of fresh intellectual life in the eleventh century, began to change those assumptions, and thus the rebirth of popular heresy took place just as new life emerged within orthodoxy. A revival in the schools of France, the reading of John Scotus Eriguena, a backlash from the tide of monastic renewal, the beginnings of lay literacy and the formation of new groupings in society are all variously responsible for short-lived incidents of heresy in the eleventh century.

On a small scale the Peace of God movement, fuelled by the will of both clergy and laity to escape the consequences of the breakdown of order in parts of France, roused a febrile enthusiasm, with high expectations of its leaders; disappointed, supporters readily turned to heresy.

On a much wider scale, the orthodox Gregorian reform of the eleventh century captured the energies of enthusiasts and engaged them in the struggle against abuses in monastic and ecclesiastical life. As these movements gained impetus, the incidents of heresy appeared to dry up for a time. But Leo IX, Gregory VII and the other heroes of the reform had let a genie out of its bottle. They had insisted on the sacred character of the priesthood and the necessity of lives matching the vocation of the clergy, and thus had put before the membership of the Church the notion of individual responsibility. They had demanded high ethical standards. These were ideals which inevitably could not be realized as a whole in the circumstances of the time and as something of the first impetus

---

1 Moore, *Origins*, p. 277.

of reform faded in the twelfth century, heretical groups reappeared, led by fiery, dissenting preachers of the calibre of Henry the Monk.

Reform within orthodoxy and heretical movements outside it interacted with each other. So the notion of individual responsibility touched the monks, turning them against the practice of accepting oblates, which in the Dark Ages had seemed wholly unexceptionable, and at the same time influenced the heretics against infant baptism. The most common heresies of the century shared by various groups were, firstly, that the unworthiness of the priest made the sacraments which he administered invalid and, secondly, that the baptism of infants, being administered before they could make any conscious decisions of their own, was worthless: these views had their starting-point in the general preoccupations of Church and society of the time.

Waldensianism became an international heretical movement but its lay founder never intended to break with the Church. Valdes showed his originality when he commissioned translations of Scripture and the Fathers. Refused the right to preach, he preferred in the last resort to follow the mission he believed he had received from God, rather than obey ecclesiastical authority. His movement was the only one condemned as heretical by the papacy to survive from the twelfth century into the age of the Reformation, mainly because of the courage and high ethical standards of its celibate leaders, the *barbi*, and of the manner in which they adapted to a life of secrecy and to the needs of a peasant following.

Catharism, by contrast, was the exotic intruder in the Western tradition, the child of Bulgarian and Byzantine Bogomilism, carrying into Latin Christendom the dualist doctrine that all matter is evil, with its destructive consequences for central doctrines of orthodoxy. It made its landfall in the West for reasons connected with the preoccupations of the Western Church, their adepts making an initial impact because their poor, wandering and hunted life so well reflected the life of the apostles sent out to preach, two by two, by Jesus in the gospels. An interpretation of the apostolic life, not as the settled life of the early Christian community in Jerusalem, but as poor wanderers on the lines of the sending of the Seventy, had not hitherto found a secure home within orthodoxy. Cathar preachers filled a gap.

Western churchmen were more hostile to Catharism than to any other heresy because it offered so profound a doctrinal challenge to Catholicism, was a complete counter-Church with distinct hierarchy and rites, and in some sense clearly represented a recrudescence of an ancient heresy. Manichaean in strict terms it was not, for Bogomil was not the heir of Mani, but churchmen were perfectly right none the less to see in it a dualist sect, whose inspiration had much in common with the heresy which had once attracted Augustine and had then been denounced by him.

Hostility was compounded by the West's lack of experience of heresy. The *tabula rasa* of the Dark Ages had left them ill-equipped to deal with it, and a sense of powerlessness persisted through the twelfth century as the menace of heresy increased. It only began to dissipate as Innocent III took measures against it, as the mendicant orders began their work and as Gregory IX began to issue wide-ranging commissions to investigate and condemn heretics. Although Dominic's original vocation was to a universal preaching, his order soon developed a special calling to preach against heresy and meet its appeal by counter-reason, and both his order and the sister order of the Franciscans provided dedicated men to serve as inquisitors. Preaching became more frequent and more effective. Catholic fraternities and Third Orders developed. Innocent's decree on annual confession began to bear fruit. In consequence, the weaknesses of Catharism were exposed and its heroic but vulnerable leading class, the *perfecti*, were hunted down. It disappeared, leaving not a wraith behind of its own influence and teaching.

It is hard to imagine Catharism establishing itself at any later stage in the history of the Western Church. It made converts when it did, above all, because of a lack of instruction of the laity, who had no adequate defence against eloquent and determined preachers using the texts of Scripture and the incidents of the gospels in the interest of a core of teaching that was profoundly heretical but not understood to be so by innocent auditors.

The records of investigation of heresy from the thirteenth century onwards provide us for the first time with something approaching an informal religious survey. We learn from them the opinions of many humble people, and can see how thin the veneer of Christianity could be, and how much doubt, materialism and paganism existed in the age of faith – the raw material for the detaching of Church members from a superficial Catholicism as a preliminary to entry to heresy. The positive achievements of the Latin Church in the epoch of the Cathars were real enough, but they affected in the main the upper layers of society, ever the best recorded. Moreover, achievement was patchy and regional, and frictions associated with the new relationship of clergy and laity that flowed from the reforms and with the wealth and privilege of individual clergy provided occasion for many disputes, feeding anticlericalism and creating a class of fautors, not heretics themselves, but willing to give protection to heretics as a stick to beat the churchmen with.

The Cathar experience left its legacy in a set of mechanisms designed to meet the problem of heresy, which remained in being for the rest of the Middle Ages. Legislation to enforce the backing of the secular power for repression was accepted by rulers. Capital punishment as the ultimate penalty for the obdurate became the norm. Most significantly, confiscation of goods, as Henry C. Lea long ago observed, was a penalty which provided a continued incentive to potential beneficiaries to pursue heretics and provide backing for their condemnation.

Alone, however, it does not explain the repeated successes of repressive action, which sprang from an underlying and commonly underestimated commitment to orthodoxy, based, it may be, on the recognition that authority was indivisible and that in the last resort the lay and ecclesiastical powers, despite their family quarrels, must support each other. Support might also spring from indignation at what was seen as an irreverent assault on the mystery of the mass, as in the case of Lollardy: when Wyclif crossed the Rubicon and rejected transubstantiation, much support fell away. It might be felt that churchmen had their own hobby-horses, were over-privileged and over-wealthy and that they made free with accusations of heresy for their own ends; yet denials of the core of Christian belief stirred opinion in most places and at most times. No doubt public opinion and clerical propaganda demonized heretics; in the late Middle Ages the Waldensians in particular were crudely caricatured, but the identification of heresy as the work of the devil made acceptance of such caricaturing easier and fostered the view that toleration of heresy would bring down the wrath of God on a locality.

The heretics of the late Middle Ages were more intimately associated with elite groups than Catharism had ever been, with its lack of substantial clerical support and its paucity of intellectuals. The heresy of the Beguins in the Franciscan province of Provence and the *fraticelli* in Italy in the early fourteenth century sprang out of the internal struggles of the Franciscan order over their observance of poverty, fanning out into the lay world through the institution of the Third Order, aided by the powerful and enigmatic personality of Petrus Johannis Olivi, a Janus figure looking, on the one hand, to the orthodox Franciscan tradition, an academic teacher of high quality, and on the other to cloudy, mystical circles of excitable laymen and women. Working on the mind of Olivi was the magnetic concept of a third *status* in history, shortly to open, bringing after tribulation a time of new happiness and blessing for mankind, the fruit of the meditations of Joachim of Fiore in the second half of the twelfth century. He released an idea of great potency in the Church, which, when mishandled and misunderstood, gave a spur to heresy and rebellion.

Crisis in the Beguin affair was induced by the intensity of the struggle over poverty among Franciscans and their followers, in which the whole balance of Christian ethics was threatened by an extravagant stress on voluntary poverty; John xxII, who had the shrewdness to see this, attempted to settle a theological conflict by essentially administrative means, so creating more storms. His Bulls give colour to the view that popes in the later Middle Ages by defining and condemning created 'new' heresies, giving fresh work to inquisitors and bishops' officers and ever diminishing the indeterminate territory in which differing views could be held without incurring condemnation.[2]

The heresy stirring among tertiaries and enthusiasts and put down by John was no artificial construct. The heresy of the Free Spirit, on the other hand, was. Misunderstanding, prejudice born of tensions in towns between secular and regular clergy, unpopularity of the unprotected women of the beguinages, and certain potentially perilous teaching about the mystical way stimulated authority to define a heresy and sect which, as a coherent and organized whole, never existed; the belief that it did cost innocent lives. Worse still, the bishops of France and the officers of Philip the Fair, using inquisition and torture, falsely imputed gross errors and blasphemies to the order of Templars, apparently for the sake of their money, and destroyed them. The mechanisms of repression and the fear of the enemy within put potent weapons into the hands of the ruthless.

With the partial exception of Olivi and perhaps Amaury of Bène no leading academic ever became involved in popular heresy. Accusations of heresy and

2   A principal theme of Leff, *Heresy*.

error were hazards of debate in the schools and were settled within the schools. Only John Wyclif, a first-rate intellectual, launched a popular heresy, and that in the last six years of his life. His motives, and the thinking behind his decisions may never be wholly clarified. The effects were remarkable. His followers translated the whole Bible into the vernacular, launched a rebellion designed to depose and kill the king, and contrived to put into action a movement which, despite some heavy persecutions, lasted into the Reformation epoch and played some part in bringing about religious change in England.

In the lands of the Bohemian crown his ideas fermented within an existing reform movement; suspicion of complicity with them led to the burning of Hus; that act, coupled with the passion for reform, Hus's own preaching, Czech patriotism and enthusiasm for the lay chalice sparked a rebellion against the Council of Constance, then the king, finally the pope, and a series of Rome-inspired crusades, which were all brought to nought.

For the first time the mechanisms of repression were rendered ineffective. State power and the support of a substantial body of aristocrats, moved by patriotism and indignation at Hus's fate, were mobilized. Forces were unleashed at Tabor and Horeb, where peasants and their families, climbing the hills, left behind in the plains below the divisions of society between lord and peasant, priest and layman, the world of lordship, private property and clericalism. Together, until 1434 and the decisive clash at Lipany, Tabor and nobles, in uneasy alliance, formed a shield which could not be turned aside.

In the end, the concessions wrung from authority by the success of Hussite arms proved unstable; though as late as 1485 the resilience and powers of organization of Hussites were sufficient to force from their Catholic enemies and a reluctant king an extraordinary agreement on mutual tolerance, and Utraquists even in the sixteenth century showed a dour political skill in maintaining their cause, the movement at last faded. Times changed. Ferdinand I, the Habsburg ruler of Bohemia, had dreamed that the concession of the lay chalice by the papacy would reconcile at least moderate Utraquists to his rule. It was not to be; when Pius IV made the concession in 1564, there was no major response. Other ideas occupied the central stage.

In the Reformation epoch the unity of belief of the medieval Church broke down and Europe was divided – as it has been until the present day. Research has undermined an older, simplistic interpretation that saw in the victory of the Reformers the fruit of an ever-increasing incidence of abuse and disorder in the late medieval clerical establishment. True, the papacy was unable to provide any lead, for reasons which Mandell Creighton long ago gave us;[3] yet, below that level and a 'calcified' Church leadership,[4] there was still much vitality, a profound piety, and a series of small-scale reforms and developments.

---

3 See his own summary of intentions in his classic *History of the Papacy* (above, p. 338, n. 59) in L. Creighton, *Life and Letters of Mandell Creighton D. D.* II (London, 1904), pp. 231–2.
4 F. Oakley, *The Western Church in the Later Middle Ages* (Ithaca, NY, and London, 1979), p. 315.

Luther, it has been pointed out, was himself the child of one such late medieval monastic reform.[5] What distinguished the Reformation epoch was the quality of mind of Luther himself and his successors, that fused older grievances and anticlericalisms and the regional patriotisms so vividly represented in the events of the Hussite revolution, with a doctrinal challenge more profound and far-reaching than any which emerged in the history of medieval heresy.

So old heresies were left behind. The lay chalice ceased to matter. The Waldensians, still despite heavy persecution nobly incarnating the medieval ideal of the poor wandering preacher in an age in which it was no longer greatly valued, yielded place to settled, Geneva-trained Calvinist pastors; Waldensians kept their name with its heroic associations, but in reality surrendered to Calvin. Lollards, the least organized of the movements condemned as heretical by the papacy, after playing a background part in the movement of the English towards Protestantism, lost their separate identity.

While so much else changed in the sixteenth century, the medieval concept of heresy and the overriding duty to repress it by force remained in being. Definitions of orthodoxy changed profoundly, but both Catholics and Protestants were agreed in asserting its importance and in using the power of the State to impose their versions on the recalcitrant. Friar John Forest was burnt under Henry VIII for fidelity to the medieval doctrine of the papacy; Calvin's Geneva declared itself the legitimate heir to the authority of the now discredited medieval Church by burning Servetus for his anti-Trinitarian views; in the seventeenth century Episcopalians in Scotland executed Covenanters; as late as 1697 a medical student was put to death in Edinburgh for denying the Trinity, while the reputation of the Catholic Church was long blackened by the attempts of the inquisition to repress Protestantism over centuries and by the barbaric ritual of the auto-da-fé. Perhaps this was the most baleful and lasting result of the struggles of the medieval Church with heresy.

The Christian Church in the East as well as the West was the heir to the assumptions of the pagan Roman Empire and of the whole ancient world, of the duty of the ruler to enforce right belief, and, with some hesitation, its leaders came to act on those assumptions. None the less, repression of wrongful belief in the West came during the Middle Ages to take on a dynamic quality which it did not have in the East.

Byzantine churchmen shared the horror of heresy and emperors took a direct part in the pursuit of heretics. Burning was a penalty imposed on the obdurate in the Byzantine Church as well – we have a vivid description by Anna Comnena of the burning of the Bogomil leader Basil in Constantinople – but it was less frequently used. Police action in the Byzantine world was more sporadic and less organized. The Byzantines were used to heresy. Western writers were aware of this. Guibert de Nogent attributed the higher incidence of heresy there to the fact that the air was lighter and purer, which gave the Greeks thinner bodies and more volatile minds and made them more liable to neglect the authority of their

5   Ibid., p. 318.

elders and so fall into heresies. Byzantium was the heir to the speculations of the Greeks and the proliferation of belief in the early Christian centuries. Heresy had often in the past allied with nationalist movements against the supremacy of Constantinople, and the emperor and patriarch had had to live with the consequences of past doctrinal disputes.

The West, with its experience in the Dark Ages of a comparative absence of heresy, was more crudely impatient, and, as Catharism in the late twelfth century showed its power over minds, suffered an intense feeling of fear and powerlessness. A ferocious response followed, issuing in the use of the crusade weapon against heresy, and the development of inquisitorial procedures. How those procedures, and the attitude of mind fostered by them, contributed to the witch mania and the persecution, above all, of innocent women is becoming ever more plain through modern research.[6] The persecution of the witch spanned the Reformation and afflicted both Catholics and Protestants.

Did Western churchmen of the thirteenth century and afterwards believe that if they were vigilant and energetic enough, a time would come when the Church would be entirely cleansed and there would be purity of faith? Perhaps they did. Certainly both sides in the wars of religion and in the long battle between Reformation and Counter-Reformation worked on the assumption that the use of force, deployed with adequate efficiency, could have this effect. When long before, in the 1040s, Wazo of Liège was asked for advice on the treatment of heretics, he had pleaded Scripture and argued that wheat and tares should grow together till harvest. Many lives and much suffering would have been saved had his voice been heard.

---

6   Cohn, *Inner Demons, passim*; D. Müller, 'Hexenprozess und Frauenrepression', *Heresis* XII (1989), pp. 33–51.

# Glossary of Heretics

**Adamites.**   A heretical sect imitating nakedness of Adam, described first by Epiphanius and Augustine, then by Isidore of Seville; possibly originally to be identified with licentious Gnostic sect, the Carpocratians, but as organized, persisting sect in Middle Ages, wholly imaginary. Abusive term for a Hussite group. (pp. 358–60)

**Albigenses, Albigensians.**   The term for Cathars in south of France, originally referring to adherents in the region of Albi.

**Amalriciani.**   Pantheists; followers of Amaury of Bène (condemned 1210).

**Apostolics, Apostolic Brethren.**   Exaggerated imitation of the Franciscans, with heresies on poverty and perfection, founded by Gerard Segarelli in Parma 1260; broke into rebellion under Dolcino di Novara (burnt 1307). (pp. 219–23)

**Arnoldists.**   Followers of Arnold of Brescia (executed 1155), of Donatist and anticlerical views, attempting to impose apostolic poverty on the Church as an obligation; a north Italian movement or strand of thought. (pp. 59–61)

**beghards.**   Men leading a religious life without rule or vows, similarly to the female equivalent, the beguines, but more mobile, sometimes gaining a living by begging; accused of Free Spirit heresy in early fourteenth century. See beguines, Beguins, Free Spirit. (ch. 10, s. 2)

**beguines.**   Pious women leading a religious life without rule or vows, singly or in convents, often linked to the mendicant orders; popular from the early thirteenth century, but inhibited by prejudice and accusations of Free Spirit heresy in the fourteenth century. Name originally popular and pejorative, from Albigensis. (ch. 10, s. 2) See also beghards, Beguins, Free Spirit.

**Beguins.**   A pejorative term from the same root as beguine; applied to tertiaries and others of either sex associated with Olivi and other Spiritual Franciscans, chiefly in the Franciscan province of Provence, with exaggerated views on the place of poverty; suppressed after issue of *Quorumdam exigit* by John XXII in 1318; spelling with capital and no 'e' adopted for convenience in this book to mark distinction from the beguines. (ch. 11) See also beguines, *fraticelli*, Spiritual Franciscans.

**Bogomils.** A heretical movement, so called from the name (possibly a pseudonym) of a tenth-century Bulgarian village priest, preaching opposition to the Greek Church and teaching that all matter is evil; active in Byzantium and the Balkans; spread into Western Europe to form Cathar sect. (pp. 62–4)

**Bohemian Brethren.** See *Unitas Fratrum*.

**Calixtines.** See Utraquists.

**Cathars.** Dualist heretics, teaching that all matter is evil. Derived originally from Bogomil influence and (possibly) Paulicians in Western Europe; active from twelfth to late thirteenth or early fourteenth centuries, esp. in parts of Lombardy and southern France. Term derived from kissing the cat should properly be restricted to their leading class, the *perfecti*, but is commonly applied to the whole movement. (chs 4, 6, 7)

**Flagellants.** Movements, most commonly of laymen, engaging in mass flagellation in public as a form of penance; orthodox in origin; in 1260 stimulated in Italy by diffused Joachimite expectation of the end of the world; in 1349, by Black Death (term most commonly applied to participants in this episode), esp. in the kingdom of Germany and neighbouring lands; condemned by Clement VI. (pp. 215, 218, 242–3)

**fraticelli** (also **fratricelli, fraterculi**). Spiritual Franciscans in Italy who broke away from the order to follow a literal observance; exaggerated place of poverty in religious life; condemned by John XXII in 1317; term (from the Italian *frate*) may also be used loosely for orthodox members of orders or hermits. (ch. 11)

**Free Spirit.** Adherents of supposed sect of deviant mystics, esp. among beguines and beghards, accused of libertinism and autotheism after issue of *Ad nostrum* by Clement V in 1312; no organized heretical group in fact existed, and accusations were often imaginary, particularly when levelled against beguines. (ch. 10, s. 2)

**Henricians.** Followers of Henry the Monk, preacher of penance, then heretic, influenced by Peter of Bruis, active in the first half of the twelfth century in French-speaking lands, who rejected the sacraments and the doctrine of original sin. (pp. 52–4, 56)

**Horebites.** See Orebites.

**Humiliati.** Loosely organized congregations in northern Italian towns leading a penitential life with manual labour and preaching; refusal to laymen among them by Alexander III of the right to preach led to heresy, as in the case of the Waldensians; Innocent III gave regulations to Humiliati willing to return to the Church in 1201. (pp. 74–7, 85, 100–103) See Poor Lombards.

**Hussites.** Generic term for Bohemian reform movement which challenged the papacy in the fifteenth century; originally a term of abuse; may be used in practice for the more moderate members of the movement. (chs 16–19) See also Taborites, *Unitas Fratrum*, Utraquists.

**Joachimites.** The term used in this book for writers and others, both orthodox and heretical, seriously influenced by ideas and symbols emanating ultimately (but often in false and distorted versions) from the exegetical, prophetic works of Joachim of Fiore. (chs 6, 11)

**Lollards.** (i) Imprecise popular term current in German-speaking lands, pejorative in origin and derived from *lollen, lullen* ('to sing'), applied to men leading a religious life without rule or vows; synonym of beghard.

(ii) In England relates to adherents of a popular evangelical heresy, given initial stimulus by teaching of John Wyclif, based on individual faith and supremacy of Scripture; apparently first applied in 1380 to followers of Wyclif's teaching (late in his life) in Oxford. (chs 13, 14) See beghards.

**Lyonists, Leonists.**   The moderate wing of the Waldensian movement, so called after the original centre at Lyons, that remained faithful to the tradition of Valdes and his early followers; separated from Poor Lombards from 1205; survived in France and its borderlands. (chs 5, 6, 8)

**Orebites.**   Radical Hussites from Hradec Králové (Königgrätz) in eastern Bohemia who formed a community and military force comparable to Tabor under the priest Ambrose, renaming their town after the Mount Horeb of Scripture. (pp. 353, 363, 366)

**Orphans.**   The Orebites, who gave themselves the title in token of mourning for the death of Žižka in 1424. (pp. 366, 367)

**Passagians.**   A small group, possibly only found in Lombardy, who observed to the letter OT precepts, including circumcision; condemned by Lucius III in 1184. (p. 76)

**Pataria.**   An eleventh-century reform movement in Milan, supported by the papacy. (pp. 44–6)

**Patarene.**   An Italian term for heretics, especially Cathars, current from third Lateran Council of 1179.

**Paulicians.**   A heretical sect dating back to the early centuries; dualist by the ninth century and opposed by the Byzantine Church; a possible factor in the rise of Bogomilism and Catharism.

**Petrobrusians.**   Adherents of Peter of Bruis, village priest originally from the Embrun region who preached in south-west France c.1119–c.1140, rejecting all external forms of worship. (pp. 54–6)

**Pikarts.**   A loose term of abuse for heretics, derived from beghard. (p. 359)

**Poor Lombards.**   Waldensians, based initially in northern Italy, influenced by the Lombard climate of opinion to a more radical and anti-Church attitude; formed congregations supported by manual labour under influence of Humiliati, split from the Lyonists in 1205; active missionaries, esp. in German-speaking lands. (chs 5, 6, 8)

**Runcarii.**   A synonym for Poor Lombards, derived from John de Ronco, leader in the Waldensian split of 1205; used by the Passau Anonymous about heretics prosecuted in 1266. (chs 6, 8)

**Speronists.**   A minor sect, followers of Ugo Speroni of Piacenza, who disseminated a heretical predestinarian doctrine, and rejected the sacraments and belief in original sin; condemned by Lucius III in 1184. (pp. 86–7)

**Spiritual Franciscans.**   Rigorist members of the Franciscan order who struggled for a strict observance of the rule, esp. in poverty, and appealed to Francis's Testament; extremists among them provided the starting-point for *fraticelli* and other heretics condemned by John XXII in 1317 and subsequent years. (ch. 11)

**Taborites.**   Radical Hussites who began as a religious movement with eschatological expectations, later developing into a military and political organization, whose fighting powers were vital to Hussite success; major support for drastic religious changes in lands controlled by the Hussites; name of Tabor, with scriptural echoes, given to fortress south of Prague in 1420, thereafter their base. (chs 16–18)

**Unitas Fratrum** (or **Bohemian Brethren**). A small, rigorist group within the Hussite movement influenced by pacifist ideas of Peter Chelčický, formally separated from Utraquist Church in 1467; ancestors of Moravian Brethren. (chs 18, 19)

**Utraquists**. Supporters of the lay chalice, who insisted that communion should be given to the laity in both kinds (*sub ultraque specie*), i.e. bread and wine; the usage, initiated in Prague in 1414, was condemned by the Council of Constance in 1415. The lay chalice became a symbol to the Hussite movement. (chs 17–19)

**Vaudois**. See Waldensians.

**Waldensians** (or **Waldenses**). An evangelical heresy of the late twelfth century, springing from an orthodox poverty and preaching movement launched by Valdes, a former businessman of Lyons; fell into heresy following refusal of the right to preach and subsequent condemnation by Lucius III in 1184; split into a Lyonist and Poor Lombard wing, but continued in France, Germany, parts of Eastern Europe and Italy and survived into modern times. (chs 5, 6, 8, 19)

**'Waldo, Peter'**. Form for Valdes (Lat. Valdesius) employed esp. by older historians; Peter, though used by Waldensian controversialists in the fourteenth century, was not historically Valdes's name. See Waldensians. (chs 5, 6, 8)

# Abbreviations

| | |
|---|---|
| *ABAW* | *Abhandlungen der königlichen bayerischen Akademie der Wissenschaften (Historische Klasse)* |
| *Act. Fel.* | *Les Actes du Concile Albigeoise de Saint Félix de Caraman*, ed. A. Dondaine, *Miscellanea Giovanni Mercati* v (*Studi e Testi* cxxv) (Rome, 1946), pp. 324–55 |
| *ADRSP* | *Archivio della deputazione Romana di storia patria* |
| *AFH* | *Archivum Franciscanum Historicum* |
| *AFP* | *Archivum Fratrum Praedicatorum* |
| *AHDLMA* | *Archives d'histoire doctrinale et littéraire du Moyen Age* |
| *AKG* | *Archiv für Kulturgeschichte* |
| *ALKG* | *Archiv für Literatur- und Kirchengeschichte des Mittelalters*, ed. H. Denifle and F. Ehrle |
| *AM* | *Annales du Midi* |
| *ARBB* | Académie royale de Belgique, *Bulletin de la classe des lettres et des sciences morales et politiques* |
| *ARG* | *Archiv für Reformationgeschichte* |
| *ASL* | *Archivio storico Lombardico* |
| *BC* | M. Barber, *The Cathars: Dualist Heretics in Languedoc* (Harlow, 2000) |
| *BF* | *Bullarium Franciscanum* v, ed. C. Eubel (Rome, 1898). *Epitome*, ed. C. Eubel (Ad Claras Aquas, 1908) |
| *BHL* | P. Biller and A. Hudson (ed.), *Heresy and Literacy (1000–1530)* (Cambridge, 1994; corrected, 1996) |
| *BIHR* | *Bulletin of the Institute of Historical Research* |
| *BISIAM* | *Bollettino dell'istituto storico Italiano per il Medio Evo e archivio Muratoriano* |
| *BJRL* | *Bulletin of the John Rylands Library* |
| *BK* | A. Borst, *Die Katharer* (Stuttgart, 1953) |
| Bouquet | *Recueil des historiens des Gaules et de la France*, ed. M. Bouquet |
| *BS* | *Balkan Studies* |
| *BSAHDL* | *Bulletin de la société d'art et d'histoire du diocèse de Liège* |
| *BSRS* | *Bulletin of the Society for Renaissance Studies* |
| *BSSV* | *Bollettino della società di studi Valdesi* |
| *CCM* | *Cahiers de civilisation médiévale* |
| *CDH* | *Christian Dualist Heresies in the Byzantine World c.650–c.1405*, ed. B. and J. Hamilton, with Y. Stoyanov (Manchester and New York, 1998) |

| | |
|---|---|
| *CEC* | *Cahiers des études Cathares* |
| *CF* | *Cahiers de Fanjeaux* (Toulouse): |

    I *Saint Dominique en Languedoc* (1966)

    II *Vaudois Languedociens et Pauvres Catholiques* (1967)

    III *Cathares en Languedoc* (1968)

    IV *Paix de Dieu et guerre sainte en Languedoc au XIII siècle* (1969)

    V *Les Universités du Languedoc au XIII siècle* (1970)

    VI *Le Credo, la morale et l'inquisition* (1971)

    VII *Les Evêques, les clercs et le roi (1250–1300)*

    VIII *Les Mendiants en pays d'Oc au XIIIe siècle* (1973)

    X *Franciscains d'Oc. Les Spirituels 1250–1314* (Toulouse, 1975)

    XVI *Bernard Gui et son monde* (1981)

    XX *Effacement du Catharisme? (XIIIe–XIVe s.)* (1985)

    XXIII *La Femme dans la vie religieuse du Languedoc XIIIe–XIVe siècles* (1988)

    XXVII *Fin du monde et signes des temps: Visionnaires et prophètes en France méridionale fin XIIIe–début XVe siècle* (1992)

    XXIX *L'église et le droit dans le Midi (XIIIe–XIVe s.)* (1994)

    XXXII *La Prédication en Pays d'Oc (XIIe – début XVe Siècle)* (1997)

    XXXIV *Evangile et évangélisme (XIIe–XIIIe siècle)* (1999)

| | |
|---|---|
| *CH* | *Church History* |
| *CHR* | *Catholic Historical Review* |
| *CMH* | *Cambridge Medieval History*, ed. J. R. Tanner, C. W. Previté-Orton and Z. N. Brooke (Cambridge, 1911–36), 8 vols |
| CNEC | Centre Nationale des Etudes Cathares |
| *CV* | *Communio Viatorum* |
| *DA* | *Deutsches Archiv* |
| *DHC* | *De Heresi Catharorum in Lombardia*, ed. A. Dondaine, in 'La Hiérarchie Cathare en Italie', *AFP* XIX (1949), pp. 280–312 |
| *DHGE* | *Dictionnaire d'histoire et de géographie ecclésiastiques* |
| *DLZ* | *Deutsche Literaturzeitung* |
| *DNB* | *Dictionary of National Biography* |
| *DTC* | *Dictionnaire de théologie Catholique* |
| *DZG* | *Deutsche Zeitschrift für Geschichtswissenschaft* |
| *EC* | *Etudes Carmelitaines* |
| *EcHR* | *Economic History Review* |
| *EEQ* | *Eastern European Quarterly* |
| *EETS* | *Early English Text Society* (London, 1864–). Original series (O.S.) |
| *EFV* | *Enchiridion Fontium Valdensium* I, ed. G. Gonnet (Torre Pellice, 1958) |
| *EHD* | *English Historical Documents*, ed. D. C. Douglas (London, 1953–). 13 vols |
| *EHR* | *English Historical Review* |
| *EO* | *Europe et Occitanie: les Pays Cathares; Collection Heresis* V (Arques, 1995) |
| EV | Early Version of Wyclif Bible (see pp. 262–4) |
| *FF* | *Forschungen und Fortschritte* |
| *FFor* | *Franziskanische Forschungen* |
| *FK* | H. Fichtenau, *Ketzer und Professoren* (Munich, 1992) |
| *FRB* | *Fontes Rerum Bohemicarum*, ed. J. Goll, V (Prague, 1893) |
| *FS* | *Franciscan Studies* |
| *FZ* | *Fasciculi Zizaniorum*, ed. W. W. Shirley (RS, 1858) |

| | |
|---|---|
| *GRK* | G. Rottenwöhrer, *Der Katharismus* I–IV (Bad Honnef, 1982–93) |
| | I (1) *Quellen zum Katharismus*, (2) *Anmerkungen* (Bad Honnef, 1982) |
| | II *Der Kult, die religiöse Praxis, die Kritik an Kult und Sakramenten der Katholischen Kirche*: |
| | (1) *Der Kult* (Bad Honnef, 1982); (2) *Die religiöse Praxis* (Bad Honnef, 1982) |
| | III *Die Herkunft der Katharer nach Theologie und Geschichte* (Bad Honnef, 1990) |
| | IV *Glaube und Theologie der Katharer* 1–3 (Bad Honnef, 1993) |
| *HJ* | *Hibbert Journal* |
| *HJB* | *Historisches Jahrbuch* |
| *HLB* | A. Hudson, *Lollards and Their Books* (London, 1985) |
| *HPR* | A. Hudson, *The Premature Reformation* (Oxford, 1988) |
| *HS* | *Hérésies et sociétés dans l'Europe pré-industrielle, 11e–18e siècles*, ed. J. Le Goff (Paris and The Hague, 1968) |
| *HTN* | *Heresy Trials in the Diocese of Norwich 1428–31*, ed. N. Tanner (London, 1977) |
| *HZ* | *Historische Zeitschrift* |
| *IP* | *Istoričeski Pregled* |
| *JDH* | J. Duvernoy, *Le Catharisme* II: *L'Histoire des Cathares* (Toulouse, 1979) |
| *JDR* | J. Duvernoy, *Le Catharisme* I: *La Religion des Cathares* (Toulouse, 1976) |
| *JEH* | *Journal of Ecclesiastical History* |
| *JF* | *Le Registre d'Inquisition de Jacques Fournier (1318–1325)*, ed. J. Duvernoy, I–III (Toulouse, 1965) |
| *JFD* | *Le Registre d'Inquisition de Jacques Fournier (1318–1325)*, trans. J. Duvernoy, I–III (Paris, le Haye and New York, 1978) |
| *JGMO* | *Jahrbuch für die Geschichte Mittel- und Ostdeutschlands* |
| *JMH* | *Journal of Modern History* |
| *JMRS* | *Journal of Medieval and Renaissance Studies* |
| *JRH* | *Journal of Religious History* |
| *JTS* | *Journal of Theological Studies* |
| *JWCI* | *Journal of the Warburg and Courtauld Institutes* |
| *LG* | *Lollardy and the Gentry in the Later Middle Ages*, ed. M. Aston and C. Richmond (Stroud and New York, 1997) |
| *LMA* | *Le Moyen Age* |
| *LMH* | M. D. Lambert, *Medieval Heresy* (London, 1977; Oxford and Cambridge, MA, 1992) |
| LV | Late Version of Wyclif Bible (see p. 277) |
| *MA* | *Medium Aevum* |
| Mansi | J. D. Mansi, *Sacrorum conciliorum nova et amplissima collectio* (Florence and Venice, 1759–98), 31 vols |
| *MBPH* | R. I. Moore, *The Birth of Popular Heresy* (London, 1975) |
| *ME* | G. G. Merlo, *Eretici e inquisitori* (Turin, 1977) |
| *MGH* | *Monumenta Germaniae Historica* |
| *MH* | *Medievalia et Humanistica* |
| *MLC* | M. D. Lambert, *The Cathars* (Oxford, 1998) |
| *MLK* | K. B. McFarlane, *Lancastrian Kings and Lollard Knights* (Oxford, 1972) |
| *MOPH* | *Monumenta Ordinis Praedicatorum Historica* |
| *MRS* | *Medieval and Renaissance Studies* |
| *MS* | *Mediaeval Studies* |
| *MW* | K. B. McFarlane, *John Wycliffe* (London, 1952) |
| *NMS* | *Nottingham Medieval Studies* |
| NT | New Testament |

OT          Old Testament
PBA         *Proceedings of the British Academy*
PC          *La Persécution du Catharisme XIe–XIVe siècles; Collection Heresis* VI (Arques, 1996)
PHA         *Heresy and Authority in Medieval Europe*, ed. E. Peters (London, 1980)
PL          J. P. Migne, *Patrologia Latina* (Paris, 1844–64)
PP          *Past and Present*
RB          H. Grundmann, *Religiöse Bewegungen*, 2nd edn (Hildesheim, 1961) (1st edn, 1935)
RBPH        *Revue belge de philologie et d'histoire*
Relazioni   *Relazioni del X congresso internazionale di scienze storiche* (Florence, 1955)
RES         *Revue des études slaves*
RHE         *Revue d'histoire ecclésiastique*
RHL         *Revue historique et littéraire du Languedoc*
RHPR        *Revue d'histoire et de philosophie religieuse*
RHR         *Revue de l'histoire des religions*
RMS         *Reading Medieval Studies*
RPTK        *Realencyklopädie für protestantische Theologie und Kirche*, 3rd edn (Leipzig, 1908)
RQH         *Revue des questions historiques*
RR          *Ricerche religiose*
RS          *Chronicles and Memorials of Great Britain and Ireland during the Middle Ages* (London, 1858–97) (The Rolls Series)
RSCI        *Rivista di storia della chiesa in Italia*
RSI         *Rivista storica Italiana*
RSLR        *Rivista di storia e letteratura religiosa*
RSPT        *Revue des sciences philosophiques et théologiques*
RTAM        *Recherches de théologie ancienne et médiévale*
SCH         *Studies in Church History*
            I Ed. C. W. Dugmore and C. Duggan (London, 1964)
            II Ed. G. J. Cuming (London, 1965)
            III Ed. G. J. Cuming (Leiden, 1966)
            IV *The Province of York*, ed. G. J. Cuming (Leiden, 1967)
            V Ed. G. J. Cuming (Leiden, 1969)
            VI *The Mission of the Church and the Propagation of the Faith*, ed. G. J. Cuming (Cambridge, 1970)
            VII *Councils and Assemblies*, ed. G. J. Cuming and D. Baker (Cambridge, 1971)
            VIII *Popular Belief and Practice*, ed. G. J. Cuming and D. Baker (Cambridge, 1972)
            IX *Schism, Heresy and Religious Protest*, ed. D. Baker (Cambridge, 1972)
            X *Sanctity and Secularity: The Church and the World*, ed. D. Baker (Oxford, 1973)
            XI *The Materials, Sources and Methods of Ecclesiastical History*, ed. D. Baker (Oxford, 1975)
            XII *Church, Society and Politics*, ed. D. Baker (Oxford, 1975)
            XIII *The Orthodox Churches and the West*, ed. D. Baker (Oxford, 1976)
            XIV *Renaissance and Renewal in Christian History*, ed. D. Baker (Oxford, 1977)
            XV *Religious Motivation: Biographical and Sociological Problems for the Church Historian*, ed. D. Baker (Oxford, 1978)
            XVI *The Church in Town and Countryside*, ed. D. Baker (Oxford, 1979)
            XVII *Religion and Humanism*, ed. D. Baker (Oxford, 1981)
            XVIII *Religion and National Identity*, ed. Stuart Mews (Oxford, 1982)
            XIX *The Church and Healing*, ed. W. J. Sheils (Oxford, 1982)
            XX *The Church and War*, ed. W. J. Sheils (Oxford, 1983)

XXI *Persecution and Toleration*, ed. W. J. Sheils (Oxford, 1984)

XXII *Monks, Hermits and the Ascetic Tradition*, ed. W. J. Sheils (Oxford, 1985)

XXIII *Voluntary Religion*, ed. W. J. Sheils and D. Wood (Oxford, 1986)

XXIV *The Church and Wealth*, ed. W. J. Sheils and D. Wood (Oxford, 1987)

XXV *The Churches, Ireland and the Irish*, ed. W. J. Sheils and D. Wood (Oxford, 1989)

XXVI *The Ministry, Clerical and Lay*, ed. W. J. Sheils and D. Wood (Oxford, 1989)

XXVII *Women in Church*, ed. W. J. Sheils and D. Wood (Oxford, 1990)

Subsidia I *Medieval Women*, ed. D. Baker (Oxford, 1978)

Subsidia IV *The Bible in the Medieval World*, ed. K. Walsh and D. Wood (Oxford, 1985)

Subsidia V *From Ockham to Wyclif*, ed. A. Hudson and M. Wilks (Oxford, 1987)

Subsidia IX *The Church and Sovereignty*, ed. D. Wood (Oxford, 1991)

Subsidia X *Prophecy and Eschatology*, ed. M. Wilks (Oxford, 1994)

Subsidia XI *The Medieval Church* ed. P. Biller (Woodbridge, 1999)

Subsidia XII *Life and Thought in the Northern Church*, ed D. Wood (Woodbridge, 1999)

| | |
|---|---|
| *SDAB* | *Sitzungsberichte der deutschen Akademie der Wissenschaften zu Berlin* |
| *SEER* | *Slavonic and Eastern European Review* |
| *SHF* | *Société de l'histoire de France* |
| *SHR* | *Scottish Historical Review* |
| *SM* | *Studi medievali* |
| *SSAWL* | *Sitzungsberichte der sächsischen Akademie der Wissenschaften zu Leipzig* |
| *STC* | A. W. Pollard and G. R. Redgrave, *A Short-Title Catalogue of Books Printed in England, Scotland and Ireland, 1475–1640* (London, 1926) |
| *TAPS* | *Transactions of the American Philosophical Society* |
| *TDH* | *Tractatus de hereticis*, ed. A. Dondaine, in 'La Hiérarchie Cathare en Italie', *AFP* XX (1950), pp. 234–324 |
| *TLL* | J. A. F. Thomson, *The Later Lollards 1414–1520* (Oxford, 1965) |
| *TR* | *Theologische Rundschau* |
| *TRE* | *Theologische Realenzyklopädie* (Berlin and New York, 1987– ) |
| *TRHS* | *Transactions of the Royal Historical Society* |
| *TLZ* | *Theologische Literaturzeitung* |
| *UBHJ* | *University of Birmingham Historical Journal* |
| *WEH* | W. L. Wakefield and A. P. Evans (ed.), *Heresies of the High Middle Ages* (New York and London, 1969) |
| *WHC* | W. L. Wakefield, *Heresy, Crusade and Inquisition in Southern France 1100–1250* (London, 1974) |
| WS | Wyclif Society |
| *ZFB* | *Zbornik Filozofskog fakulteta u Beogradu* |
| *ZFK* | *Zeitschrift für Kirchengeschichte* |
| *ZFZ* | *Zbornik Filozofskog fakulteta u Zagrebu* |
| *ZG* | *Zeitschrift für Geschichtswissenschaft* |
| *ZRG* | *Zeitschrift für Religions- und Geistesgeschichte* |

# Bibliographies and Translations of Texts

P. Biller, 'Les Vaudois aux xive et xve siècles: le point', *Bibliographie Sommaire*, in *Les Vaudois des origines à leur fin (xiie–xvie siècles)*, ed. G. Audisio (Turin, 1990), pp. 65–75.

T. A. Fudge, *The Magnificent Ride. The First Reformation in Hussite Bohemia* (Aldershot and Brookfield, 1998).

G. Gonnet, 'Bibliographical appendix: recent European historiography on the medieval inquisition', in *The Inquisition in Early Modern Europe*, ed. G. Henningsen and J. Tedeschi (Dekalb, IL, 1986), pp. 199–223.

H. Grundmann, *Bibliographie zur Ketzergeschichte des Mittelalters*, in *Sussidi eruditi* xx (Rome, 1967); repr. in *Hérésies et sociétés dans l'Europe pré-industrielle, 11e–18e siècles*, ed. J. Le Goff (Paris and The Hague, 1968), pp. 411–67.

H. Grundmann, *Ketzergeschichte des Mittelalters, Die Kirche in ihrer Geschichte: Ein Handbuch*, ed. K. D. Schmidt and E. Wolf, ii, G.i (Göttingen, 1963) (short analysis with extensive bibliography).

A. Hudson, *The Premature Reformation* (Oxford, 1988), pp. 520–37.

G. Leff, *Heresy in the Later Middle Ages: The Relation of Heterodoxy to Dissent c.1250–c.1450* (Manchester, 1967), ii, pp. 741–77.

B. McGinn, *Visions of the End: Apocalyptic Traditions in the Middle Ages* (New York, 1979), pp. 347–63.

G. G. Merlo, *Eretici ed Eresie Medievali nella Storiografia Contemporanea* (Torre Pellice, 1994).

J. B. Russell and C. T. Berkhout, *Medieval Heresies: A Bibliography, 1960–1979* (Toronto, 1981).

P. Segl, *Ketzer in Österreich: Untersuchungen über Häresie und Inquisition im Herzogtum Österreich im 13. und beginnenden 14. Jahrhundert* (Paderborn, 1984), pp. xvi–cxxi.

E. van der Vekené, *Bibliotheca bibliographica historiae Sanctae Inquisitionis* i–ii (Vaduz, 1982–3).

*WEH*, pp. 820–46.

J. K. Zeman, *The Hussite Movement: A Bibliographical Study Guide* (Ann Arbor, 1977).

## Texts in Translation

R. B. Brooke, *The Coming of the Friars* (London, 1975), pp. 140–59 (see also introduction, chs 3, 4, 5).

A. Hudson, *Selections from English Wycliffite Writings* (Cambridge, 1978).

B. McGinn, *Visions of the End: Apocalyptic Traditions in the Middle Ages* (New York, 1979).

R. I. Moore, *The Birth of Popular Heresy* (London, 1975).

E. Peters, *Heresy and Authority in Medieval Europe* (London, 1980).

J. B. Russell, *Religious Dissent in the Middle Ages* (New York and London, 1971). (Brief extracts.)

*WEH*. (The most extensive and varied collection in existence.)

# Select Bibliography

Abels, R. and Harrison, E., 'The participation of women in Languedocian Catharism', *MS* XLI (1979), pp. 215–51.

Albaret, L., *Recherche sur l'historiographie du Catharisme depuis 1970*, Mémoire de Maitrise (Paris-X Nanterre, 1991–2).

—— *L'Inquisition* (Paris, 1999).

d'Alverny, M. Th., 'Un fragment du procès des Amauriciens', *AHDLMA* XXVI (1951), pp. 325–36.

Amati, G., 'Processus contra Valdenses in Lombardia Superior, anno 1387', *ASI*, 3rd ser. I (1865), pp. 3–52; II (1865), pp. 3–61.

Andrews, F., *The Early Humiliati* (Cambridge, 1999).

Angold, M., *Church and Society in Byzantium under the Comneni, 1081–1261* (Cambridge, 1995).

Archer, M., 'Philip Repington, bishop of Lincoln, and his cathedral chapter', *UBHJ* IV (1954), pp. 81–97.

Arnold, J. H., 'The historian as inquisitor. The ethics of interrogatory "subaltern voices"', *Rethinking History* II: 3 (1998), pp. 379–86.

—— 'The preaching of the Cathars', in *Medieval Monastic Preaching*, ed. C. Muessig (Leiden, Boston and Cologne, 1998), pp. 183–205.

—— 'Inquisition, texts and discourse', in *Trials*, ed. P. Biller and C. Bruschi.

—— ' "A man takes an ox by the horn and a peasant by the tongue": literacy, orality and inquisition in medieval Languedoc', in *Literacy and Learning in the Middle Ages*, ed. S. Rees-Jones, F. Riddy and C. Cross (Turnhout, 2001).

Arnold, R. (ed.), *Select English Works of Wyclif* I–III (Oxford, 1869–71).

Asad, T., 'Medieval heresy: an anthropological view', *Social History* XI (1986), pp. 354–62.

Aston, M. E., 'Lollardy and sedition, 1381–1431', *PP* XVII (1960), pp. 1–44.

—— 'Wycliffe and the vernacular', *SCH* Subsidia V, pp. 281–330.

—— 'Lollardy and the Reformation: survival or revival?', *History* XLIX (1964), pp. 149–70.

—— 'John Wycliffe's Reformation reputation', *PP* XXX (1965), pp. 40–1.

—— ' "Caim's Castles": poverty, politics and disendowment', in *The Church, Politics and Patronage*, ed. R. Dobson, pp. 45–81.

—— 'Lollard women priests?', *JEH* XXXI (1980), pp. 441–61.

—— 'William White's Lollard followers', *CHR* LXVIII (1982), pp. 469–97.

—— *Lollards and Reformers: Images and Literacy in Late Medieval Religion* (London, 1984).
—— ' "Corpus Christi and Corpus Regni": heresy and the Peasants' Revolt', *PP* CXLIII (1994), pp. 3–47.
—— 'Bishops and heresy: the defence of the faith', in Id., *Faith and Fire*, pp. 73–93.
—— *Faith and Fire: Popular and Unpopular Religion* (London and Rio Grande, 1993).
—— *England's Iconoclasts* I (Oxford, 1988).
—— 'Were the Lollards a sect?', *SCH* Subsidia XI, pp. 163–91.
—— ed. with C. Richmond, *Lollardy and the Gentry in the Later Middle Ages* (Stroud and New York, 1997).
Audisio, G., *Le barbe et l'inquisiteur: Procès du barbe vaudois Pierre Griot par l'inquisiteur Jean de Roma (Apt 1532)* (Aix en Provence, 1979).
—— *Les Vaudois du Luberon: Une minorité en Provence (1460–1560)* (Gap, 1984).
—— with E. Cameron, 'Les Vaudois des Alpes: débat sur un ouvrage récent', *RHR* CCIII (1986), pp. 395–409.
—— 'Pourquoi une Bible en Français pour les Vaudois?', in *Olivétan*, ed. G. Casalis and B. Roussel, pp. 117–34.
—— *Les 'Vaudois': Naissance, vie et mort d'une dissidence* XIIe–XVIe *siècles* (Turin, 1989); trans. C. Davison, *The Waldensian Dissent: Persecution and Survival c.1170–c.1570* (Cambridge, 1999).
—— (ed.), *Les Vaudois des origines à leur fin (*XIIe–XVIe *siècles)* (Turin, 1990).
—— 'La fin des Vaudois (XVIe siècle)?', in Id., *Les Vaudois*, pp. 77–99.
—— 'Famille, religion, sexualité dans une secte: les Pauvres de Lyon (XVe–XVIe siècles)', *RHR* IV (1992), pp. 427–57.
Barber, M., 'Propaganda in the Middle Ages: the charges against the Templars', *NMS* XVII (1973), pp. 42–57.
—— 'Women and Catharism', *RMS* III (1977), pp. 45–62.
—— *Trial of the Templars* (Cambridge, 1978).
—— ' "Lepers, Jews and Moslems": the plot to overthrow Christendom in 1321', *History* LXVI (1981), pp. 1–17.
—— 'Catharism and the Occitan nobility: the lordships of Cabaret, Minerve and Termes', in *The Ideals and Practice of Medieval Knighthood* III, ed. C. Harper-Bill and R. Harvey (Woodbridge, 1990), pp. 1–19.
—— 'James of Molay, the last grand master of the order of the Temple', in Id., *Crusaders*, ch. 2.
—— *Crusaders and Heretics, 12th–14th centuries* (Aldershot, 1995).
—— 'The trial of the Templars revisited', in *The Military Orders* II, ed. H. Nicholson (Aldershot, 1998), pp. 329–42.
—— *The Cathars: Dualist Heretics in Languedoc in the High Middle Ages* (Harlow, 2000).
—— 'Moving Cathars: the Italian connection in the thirteenth century', *Library of Mediterranean History* (forthcoming).
Barone, G., 'L'oeuvre eschatologique de Pierre Jean Olieu et son influence. Un bilan historiographique', *CF* XXVII, pp. 49–61.
Bartoš, F. M., 'Apologie de M. Jean Huss contre son Apologiste', *CV* VIII (1965), pp. 65–74, 235–8; IX (1966), pp. 175–80.
—— *The Hussite Revolution 1424–37*, ed. J. M. Klassen; East European Monographs CCIII (Boulder, 1986).
Bautier, R. H., 'L'hérésie d'Orléans et le mouvement intellectuelle au début du XIe siècle', in *Actes du 95e Congrès National des Sociétés Savantes* (Rheims, 1970); *Section philologique et historique* (Paris, 1975) I, pp. 63–88.

Becamel, M., 'Le Catharisme dans le diocèse d'Albi', *CF* III, pp. 237–52.

Becquet, J., 'Erémitisme et hérésie au moyen âge', *HS*, pp. 139–45.

——'L'érémitisme clérical et laie dans l'ouest de la France', in *L'eremitismo nei secoli XI et XII* (Milan, 1965), pp. 182–211.

Benad, M., *Domus und Religion in Montaillou* (Tübingen, 1990).

Benedetti, M., 'Il Culto di Santa Guglielma e gli Inquisitori', in *Vite*, ed. Benedetti *et al.*, pp. 221–41.

Benedetti, M., Merlo, G. G. and Piazza, A. (ed.), *Vite di eretici e storie di frati* (Milan, 1998).

Benrath, G. A., *Wyclifs Bibelkommentar* (Berlin, 1966).

Betts, R. R., *Essays in Czech History* (London, 1969).

Biget, J. L., 'Un procès d'inquisition à Albi en 1300', *CF* VI, pp. 237–341.

——'L'extinction du Catharisme urbain: les points chauds de la répression', *CF* XX, pp. 305–40.

Bihel, S., 'S. Franciscus, fuitne angelus sexti sigilli (Apoc. 7.2)?', *Antonianum* II (1927), pp. 59–90.

Biller, P., 'Medieval Waldensian abhorrence of killing pre-c.1400', *SCH* XX, pp. 129–46; repr. in Id., *Waldenses*, pp. 81–95.

——'Words and the medieval notion of religion', *JEH* XXXVI (1985), pp. 351–69.

——'The oral and the written: the case of the Alpine Waldensians', *BSRS* IV (1986), pp. 19–28; *Waldenses*, pp. 159–67.

——'*Thesaurus absconditus*: the treasure of the medieval Waldensians', *BSRS* IV (1986), pp. 139–54; *Waldenses*, pp. 97–110.

——'The historiography of medieval heresy in the United States of America and Great Britain, 1945–1992', *Waldenses*, pp. 25–47.

——'*Curate Infirmos*: the medieval Waldensian practice of medicine', *SCH* XIX, pp. 55–77; *Waldenses*, pp. 49–67.

——'*Multum ieiunantes et se castigantes*: medieval Waldensian asceticism', *SCH* XXII, pp. 215–28; *Waldenses*, pp. 69–79.

——'Les Vaudois au XIVe et XVe siècles: le point', in *Les Vaudois*, ed. G. Audisio, pp. 43–59.

——'The common woman in the Western Church in the thirteenth and early fourteenth centuries', *SCH* XXVII, pp. 127–57.

——ed. with A. Hudson, *Heresy and Literacy 1000–1530. Cambridge Studies in Medieval Literature* XXIII (Cambridge, 1994).

——'Cathars and material women', in *Medieval Theology and the Natural Body*, ed. P. Biller and A. J. Minnis (York, 1997), pp. 61–107.

——'The preaching of the Waldensian Sisters', *Heresis* XXX (1999), pp. 137–68; *Waldenses*, pp. 125–58.

——'What did happen to the Waldensian sisters? The Strasbourg testimony', *Protestantesimo* LIV (1999), pp. 222–33.

——'William of Newburgh and the Cathar Mission to England', *SCH Subsidia* XII, pp. 11–30.

——'The Waldenses in the fourteenth and fifteenth centuries: the current state of knowledge', *Waldenses*, pp. 1–23.

——'The Waldenses 1300–1500', *RHR* CCXVII (2000), pp. 75–99.

——'The *Liber Electorum*', *Waldenses*, pp. 207–24.

——'Medieval Waldensians' construction of the past', *Waldenses*, pp. 191–206.

——'The *De Vita et Actibus de Lugduno*', *Waldenses*, pp. 225–31.

——'German money and medieval heresy: the wealth of the German Waldenses', *Waldenses*, pp. 111–23.

—— 'The anti-Waldensian treatise *Cum dormirent homines* of 1395 and its author', *Waldenses*, pp. 237–69.

—— 'Waldenses in German-speaking areas in the later fourteenth century: the view of an inquisitor', *Waldenses*, pp. 271–90.

—— 'The *topos* and reality of the heretic as *illiteratus*', *Waldenses*, pp. 169–90.

—— 'Northern Cathars and higher learning', *SCH* Subsidia xi, pp. 25–53.

—— 'William of Newburgh and the Cathar mission to England', *SCH* Subsidia xii, pp. 11–30.

—— *The Waldenses 1170–1530* (Ashgate and Aldershot, 2001).

—— ed. with C. Bruschi, *Trials and Treatises. Texts and the Repression of Heresy* (York, 2001).

—— 'The Waldenses in Bernard Gui's Liber Sententiarum', in *Trials*, ed. P. Biller and C. Bruschi.

—— 'The earliest heretical Englishwomen', in *Medieval Women: Texts and Contexts*, ed. J. Wogan-Browne *et al.* (Turnhout, 2000), pp. 363–76.

—— 'Cathar peacemaking', in *Christianity and Community in the West*, ed. S. Ditchfield (Aldershot, 2001).

—— 'Fat Christian and Old Peter: ideals and compromises among the medieval Waldensians', in *Pragmatic Utopias: Ideals and Communities 1200–1630. Essays Presented to Barrie Dobson*, ed. R. Horrox and S. Rees-Jones (Cambridge, 2001).

—— 'Through a glass darkly: seeing medieval heresy', in *The Medieval World*, ed. P. Linehan and J. Nelson (London, 2001).

—— with C. Bruschi (ed.), *Texts: York Studies in Medieval Theology* iv (forthcoming, Woodbridge, 2002).

Bird, J., 'Heresy, crusade and reform in the circle of Peter the Chanter, c.1187–c.1240' (DPhil, Univ. Oxford, 2001).

—— 'The construction of orthodoxy and the (de)construction of heretical attacks on the eucharist in *Pastoralia* from Peter the Chanter's circle in Paris', in *Trials*, ed. P. Biller and C. Bruschi.

Bittner, K., *Deutsche und Tschechen: Zur Geistesgeschichte des böhmischen Raumes* (Brunn, 1936).

Blaquière, H. and Dossat, Y., 'Les Cathares au jour le jour: confessions inédites de Cathares quercynois', *CF* iii, pp. 259–316.

Bloomfield, M. W., 'Recent scholarship on Joachim of Fiore and his influence', in *Prophecy*, ed. A. Williams and M. W. Bloomfield, pp. 21–52.

Bock, F., 'Studien zum politischen Inquisitionsprozess Johannes xxii', *Quellen und Forschungen aus italienischen Archiven und Bibliotheken* xxvi (1935–6), pp. 21–142; xxvii (1936–7), pp. 109–34.

—— 'Der Este-Prozess von 1321', *AFP* vii (1937), pp. 41–111.

—— 'Processi di Giovanni xxii contro i Ghibellini italiani', *ADRSP* lxiii (1940), pp. 129–43.

Böhmer, H., 'Die Waldenser', *RPTK* xx, cols 799–840.

—— *Analekten zur Geschichte des Franciscus von Assisi* (Tübingen, 1961).

Bolton, B., 'Innocent iii's treatment of the Humiliati', *SCH* viii, pp. 73–82.

—— 'Tradition and temerity: papal attitudes to deviants 1159–1216', *SCH* ix, pp. 79–91.

—— 'The poverty of the Humiliati', in *Poverty in the Middle Ages*, ed. D. Flood, *FFor* xxvii (1975), pp. 52–9.

—— 'Mulieres sanctae', *SCH* x, pp. 77–95.

—— '*Paupertas Christi*: old wealth and new poverty in the twelfth century', *SCH* xiv, pp. 95–103.

—— *The Medieval Reformation* (London, 1983).

—— ' "A show with a meaning": Innocent III's approach to the Fourth Lateran Council, 1215', *Medieval History* I (1991), pp. 53–67.

—— *Innocent III: Studies on Papal authority and pastoral care* (Aldershot, 1995).

Bonnassie, P. and Landes, R., 'Une nouvelle hérésie est née dans le monde', in *Les sociétés méridionales autour de l'an mil*, ed. M. Zimmerman (Paris, 1992), pp. 435–59.

Borst, A., *Die Katharer* (Stuttgart, 1953); trans. C. Roy, *Les Cathares* (Paris, 1974).

Bosl, K. (ed.), *Handbuch der Geschichte der böhmischen Länder* I (Stuttgart, 1967); II (Stuttgart, 1974).

Bostick, C. V., *The Antichrist and the Lollards: Apocalypticism in Late Medieval and Reformation England* (Leiden, Boston and Cologne, 1998).

Boyle, L. E., 'Innocent III and vernacular versions of Scripture', *SCH* Subsidia IV, pp. 97–107.

—— 'Montaillou revisited: *mentalité* and methodology', in *Pathways to Medieval Peasants*, ed. J. A. Raftis (Toronto, 1981), pp. 119–40.

Bozóky, E. (ed.), *Le Livre secret des Cathares. Interrogatio Johannis, Apocryphe d'origine bogomile* (Paris, 1980).

Brandmüller, W., 'Hus vor dem Konzil', in *Hus*, ed. F. Seibt, pp. 235–42.

Brenon, A., *Le vrai Visage du Catharisme* (Portet-sur-Garonne, 1988).

—— 'Les Cathares: bons Chrétiens et hérétiques', in *Christianisme médiéval, mouvements dissidents et novateurs*, ed. with N. Gouzy; *Heresis* XIII, XIV (Villegly, Aude, 1989), pp. 115–70.

—— *Les Femmes Cathares* (Paris, 1992).

—— 'La Parole Cathare', in *Actes du VIII colloque Jean Boisset* (Montpellier, 1995), pp. 99–121.

—— 'La maison cathare', *EO*, pp. 213–32.

—— *Le Dico des Cathares* (Toulouse, 2000).

—— *Les Archipels Cathares* (Cahors, 2000).

—— 'Le Catharisme dans la famille en Languedoc aux XIIIe–XIVe siècles d'après les sources inquisitoriales', in Id., *Les Archipels Cathares*, pp. 205–26.

—— 'La réponse des hérétiques: les recueils des sermons vaudois de la fin du Moyen Age', in Ibid., pp. 311–19.

—— and Gouzy, N. (ed.), *Christianisme médiéval, mouvements dissidents et novateurs*; *Heresis* XIII, XIV (Villegly, Aude, 1989).

Brigden, S., *London and the Reformation* (Oxford, 1989).

Brock, P., *The Political and Social Doctrines of the Unity of Czech Brethren in the Fifteenth and Sixteenth Centuries* (The Hague, 1957).

Brooke, C. N. L., 'Heresy and religious sentiment: 1000–1250', *BIHR* XLI (1968), pp. 115–31.

—— *Medieval Church and Society* (London, 1971).

Brooke, R. B., *Early Franciscan Government, Elias to Bonaventure* (Cambridge, 1959).

—— (ed.), *Scripta Leonis et Angeli Sociorum S. Francisci* (Oxford, 1970).

—— *The Coming of the Friars* (London, 1975).

Bruschi, C., 'Il *Liber Suprastella* (1235), fonte antieretici piacentina. L'ambiente ed il motivo di produzione', *Archivio Storico per le Province Parmensi*, 4th ser. XLIX (1997), pp. 405–27.

—— '*Liber qui Suprastella dicatur*: primi rilievi testuali sulla struttura e sulla tecnica polemica', *Storia ereticale e anticlericale del Medioevo*, *BSSV* CLXXIX, pp. 95–108.

—— '*Detur ergo Sathane*. Il tema della *Vindicta* nel *Liber Suprastella* di Salvo Burci', *Mélanges de l'École Française de Rome. Moyen Age* CXII (2000), pp. 149–82.

—— 'The critical analysis of the Inquisition hearings in the Doat MS (1238–86)', in *Trials*, ed. P. Biller and C. Bruschi

—— 'An early inquiry into an inquisition (1330)', in Ibid.

Burgess, C., ' "By Quick and by Dead": wills and pious provision in late medieval Bristol', *EHR* CII (1987), pp. 837–58.

Burr, D., 'The persecution of Peter Olivi', *TAPS*, n.s. LXVI Pt 5 (1976).

—— 'Bonaventura, Olivi and Franciscan eschatology', *Collectanea Franciscana* LIII (1983), pp. 23–40.

—— *Olivi and Franciscan Poverty: The Origins of the Usus Pauper Controversy* (Philadelphia, 1989).

—— (ed.), *P. J. Olivi, De Usu Paupere* (Perth, Australia, 1992).

—— *Olivi's Peaceable Kingdom* (Philadelphia, 1993).

Callahan, D. F., 'Ademar of Chabannes, millennial fears and the development of Western anti-Judaism', *JEH* XLVI (1995), pp. 19–35 at 27–9.

—— 'The Manichaeans and the Antichrist in the Writings of Adamar of Chabannes: the Terrors of the Year 1000', *Studies in Medieval and Renaissance History* XV (1995), pp. 163–223.

Cameron, E., *The Reformation of the Heretics: The Waldensians of the Alps 1480–1580* (Oxford, 1984).

—— *The Waldenses: Rejections of Holy Church in Medieval Europe* (Oxford and Malden, MA, 2000).

Campagnola, S. da, *L'angelo del sesto sigillo e l'alter Christus* (Rome, 1971).

Cantimori, D., 'The problem of heresy', in *The Late Italian Renaissance 1525–1630*, ed. E Cochrane (London, 1970), pp. 211–25.

Carrières, M., 'Sur la langue de la Bible de Valdo', *BSSV* LXXXV (1946), pp. 28–34.

Casalis, G. (ed. with B. Roussel), *Olivétan, traducteur de la Bible* (Paris, 1987).

Catto, J. I., 'Some English manuscripts of Wyclif's Latin works', *SCH* Subsidia V, pp. 353–9.

—— 'Wyclif and Wycliffism at Oxford 1356–1430', in *The History of the University of Oxford* II, ed. J. Catto and R. Evans (Oxford, 1992), pp. 175–261.

—— ed. with R. Evans, *The History of the University of Oxford* II (Oxford, 1992).

Cazenave, A., 'Hérésie et société', in *Christianisme*, ed. A. Brenon and N. Gouzy, pp. 7–61.

—— 'La résistance Cathare de la défaite à l'exile', in *Histoire et Clandestinité. Colloque de Paris* (Mai, 1977), *Revue du Vivarais* ed. M. Tilloy *et al.* (Albi, n.d.), p. 357.

—— 'La chasse aux Cathares', *L'Histoire* LVI (1983), pp. 22–31.

Chiffoleau, J., 'Vie et mort de l'hérésie en Provence et dans la vallé du Rhône du début du XIIIe au début du XIVe s.', *CF* XX, pp. 73–99.

Clédat, L., *Le Nouveau Testament traduit au XIIIe siècle en langue Provençale, suivi d'un rituel cathare* (Paris, 1887).

Clifton-Everest, J. M., 'The eucharist in the Czech and German prayers of Milič z Kroměřiže', *Bohemia* XXIII (1982), pp. 1–15.

Cohn, N., *The Pursuit of the Millennium* (London, 1957, 1970).

—— *Europe's Inner Demons* (London, 1975).

—— 'Medieval millenarism: its bearing on the comparative study of millenarian movements', in *Millennial Dreams in Action*, ed. S. L. Thrupp, pp. 31–43.

Colledge, E., ' "The Recluse" – a Lollard interpolated version of the "Ancren Riwle" ', *Review of English Studies* XV (1939), pp. 1–15, 129–45.

Collinson, P., 'Truth and legend: the veracity of John Foxe's Book of Martyrs', in *Clio's Mirror: Historiography in Britain and the Netherlands*, ed. A. G. Duke and C. A. Tamse (Zutphen, 1985), pp. 31–54.

Comba, E., *Histoire des Vaudois 1: De Valdo à la Réforme* (Paris, 1901).

Contini, S., 'Il matrimonio e l'eresia', in *Vite di eretici*, ed. M. Benedetti *et al.*, pp. 157–70.

Costen, M., *The Cathars and the Albigensian Crusade* (Manchester and New York, 1997).

Cowdrey, H. E. J., 'Archbishop Aribert', *History* LI (1967), pp. 1–15.

—— 'The papacy, the Patarenes and the Church of Milan', *TRHS*, 5th ser. XVIII (1968), pp. 25–48.

—— 'The Peace and the Truce of God in the eleventh century', *PP* XLVI (1970), pp. 42–67.

Cracco, G., 'Riforma ed Eresia in momenti della cultura Europa tra X e XI secolo', *RSLR* VII (1971), pp. 411–77.

—— 'Pataria: *opus* e *nomen*', *RSCI* XXVIII (1974), pp. 357–87.

—— 'Bernardo e i movimenti ereticali', in *Bernardo Cisterciense*, ed. E. Menesto (Milan, 1990), pp. 165–86.

Crompton, J., 'Fasciculi Zizaniorum', *JEH* XII (1961), pp. 35–45, 155–66.

Cronin, H. S., 'The Twelve Conclusions of the Lollards', *EHR* XXII (1907), pp. 292–304.

Cross, C., *Church and People 1450–1660: The Triumph of the Laity in the English Church* (Hassocks, 1976).

—— 'Popular piety and the records of the unestablished Churches 1460–1660', *SCH* XI, pp. 269–92.

—— 'Great reasoners in Scripture: the activities of women Lollards 1380–1530', *SCH* Subsidia I, pp. 359–80.

Cursente, B., 'La Gascogne réfractaire à l'hérésie: une société differente', *EO*, pp. 131–47.

Davies, R. G., 'Lollardy and locality', *TRHS*, 6th ser. I (1991), pp. 191–212.

Davis, G. W., *The Inquisition at Albi 1299–1300* (New York, 1948).

Davis, J. F., 'Lollards, reformers and St Thomas of Canterbury', *UBHJ* IX (1963), pp. 1–15.

—— 'Lollard survival and the textile industry in the south-east of England', *SCH* III, pp. 191–201.

—— 'The trials of Thomas Bylney and the English Reformation', *Historical Journal* XXIV (1981), pp. 775–90.

—— 'Lollardy and the Reformation in England', *ARG* LXXIII (1982), pp. 217–36.

—— *Heresy and Reformation in the South East of England, 1520–1559* (London and New Jersey, 1983).

Deanesly, M., *The Lollard Bible* (Cambridge, 1920, 1966).

Delaruelle, E., 'Les grands processions de pénitents de 1349 et 1399', in *Il Movimento dei disciplinati nel settimo centenario del suo inizio. Bollettino della R. Deputazione di storia patria per l'Umbria* (Perugia, 1962; repr. 1986), pp. 109–45.

Delmaire, B., 'Un sermon arrageois inédit sur les "Bougres" du nord de la France', *Heresis* XVII (1991), pp. 1–15.

Denis, E., *Huss et la guerre des Hussites* (Paris, 1878, 1930).

—— *Fin de l'indépendance Bohème* I: *Georges de Podiebrad. Les Jagellons*; II: *Les Premiers Habsbourgs* (Paris, 1890).

Dickens, A. G., *Lollards and Protestants in the Diocese of York* (Oxford, 1959).

—— 'Heresy and the origins of English Protestantism', in *Britain and the Netherlands*, ed. J. S. Bromley and E. H. Kossman (Groningen, 1964), pp. 47–66.

—— with D. Carr, *The Reformation in England to the Accession of Elizabeth I* (London, 1967).

—— 'The early expansion of Protestantism in England', *ARG* LXXVIII (1987), pp. 187–222.

—— *The English Reformation*, 2nd edn (London, 1989).

Dickson, G., 'The burning of the Amalricians', *JEH* XL (1989), pp. 347–69.

—— 'The flagellants of 1260 and the crusades', *JMH* XV (1989), pp. 227–67.

—— 'Encounters in medieval revivalism: monks, friars and popular enthusiasts', *CH* LXVIII (1999), pp. 268–93.

—— 'Prophecy and rationalism: Joachim of Fiore, Jewish messianism and the Children's Crusade of 1212', *Florensia* XIII–XIV (1999–2000), pp. 97–104.

—— 'Revivalism as a medieval religious genre', *JEH* LI (2000), pp. 473–96.

—— *Religious Enthusiasm in the Medieval West* (Aldershot and Burlington, VT, 2000).

—— 'Religious enthusiasm in the medieval west and the second conversion of Europe', in Id., *Religious Enthusiasm*, ch. 1.

—— 'Medieval Christian crowds and the origins of crowd psychology', *RHE* CXV (2000), pp. 45–75.

Diehl, P., 'Overcoming reluctance to persecute heresy', in *Christendom*, ed. with S. J. Waugh, pp. 47–66.

Dobson, R. B. (ed.), *The Church, Politics and Patronage in the Fifteenth Century* (Gloucester, 1984).

Döllinger, I. von, *Beiträge zur Sektengeschichte* I–II (Munich, 1890 repr. New York, 1963).

Dondaine, A., 'Nouvelles sources de l'histoire doctrinale du Néo-Manichéisme au Moyen Age', *RSPT* XXVIII (1939), pp. 465–88.

—— *Un Traité neo-manichéen du XIIIe siècle: Le Liber de duobus principiis, suivi d'un fragment de rituel cathare* (Rome, 1939).

—— 'Aux origines de Valdéisme: une profession de foi de Valdes', *AFP* XVI (1946), pp. 191–235.

—— 'Le manuel de l'inquisiteur (1230–1330)', *AFP* XVII (1947), pp. 85–194.

—— 'La hiérarchie cathare en Italie', *AFP* XIX (1949), pp. 282–312; XX (1950), pp. 234–324.

—— 'L'Origine de l'hérésie médiévale', *RSCI* VI (1952), pp. 43–78.

—— 'Durand de Huesca et la polémique anti-Cathare', *AFP* XXIX (1959), pp. 273–4.

—— 'Les hérétiques et l'inquisition XIIe–XIIIe siècles', in *Documents et Etudes*, ed. Y. Dossat (Aldershot, 1990).

Dossat, Y., 'Le clergé méridional à la veille de la croisade albigeoise', *RHL* I (1944), pp. 263–78.

—— 'La répression de l'hérésie par les évêques', *CF* VI, pp. 217–51.

—— 'L'évolution des rituels cathares', *Revue de Synthese*, n.s. XXII–XXIII (1948), pp. 27–30.

—— 'Les Cathares d'après les documents de l'inquisition', *CF* III, pp. 71–104.

—— 'Remarques sur un prétendu évêque cathare du Val d'Aran en 1167', *Bulletin Philologique et Historique du Comité des Travaux Historiques et Scientifiques, Années 1955–1956* (Paris, 1957), pp. 337–47.

—— *Les Crises de l'inquisition toulousaine au XIIIe siècle 1233–1273* (Bordeaux, 1959).

—— 'Les Vaudois méridionaux d'après les documents de l'inquisition', *CF* II, pp. 207–26.

—— 'Une figure d'inquisiteur: Bernard de Caux', *CF* VI, pp. 253–72.

—— 'De Vaudès à Saint-François à Montauban', *CF* VIII, pp. 403–13.

—— (ed.), *Documents et Etudes* (Aldershot, 1990).

Dujčev, I., 'I Bogomili nei paesi slavi e loro storia', *Medioevo Bizantino-slavo* I (Rome, 1965), pp. 251–82.

Dupré-Theseider, E., *Introduzione alle eresie medievali* (Bologna, 1953).

—— 'Le Catharisme languedocien et l'Italie', *CF* III, pp. 299–316.

—— 'L'eresia a Bologna nei tempi di Dante', *Studi storici in onore di G. Volpe* (Florence, 1958) I, pp. 363–444.

—— 'Gli eretici nel mondo comunale Italiano', *BSSV* LXXIII (1963), pp. 3–23.

Duvernoy, J., (ed.), *Le Registre d'Inquisition de Jacques Fournier (1318–1325)* I–III (Toulouse, 1965; corrections, Toulouse, 1972; trans., Toulouse, 1978).

—— *Le Catharisme* I: *La Religion des Cathares*; II: *L'Histoire des Cathares* (Toulouse, 1976, 1979).

—— 'Le Catharisme en Languedoc au début du XIVe siècle', *CF* XX, pp. 27–56.

Dykmans, M., *Les Sermons de Jean XXII sur la vision béatifique* (Rome, 1973).

Eberhard, W., *Konfessionsbildung und Stände in Böhmen, 1478–1530* (Munich and Vienna, 1981).

—— *Monarchie und Widerstand: Zur ständischen Oppositionsbildung im Herrschaftssystem Ferdinands I in Böhmen* (Munich, 1985).

—— 'Interessengegensätze und Landesgemeinde: die böhmischen Stände im nachrevolutionären Stabilisierungskonflikt', in *Europa 1500*, ed. W. Eberhard and F. Seibt (Stuttgart, 1987), pp. 330–48.

—— 'Religion and the development of estates', in *Crown, Church and Estates*, ed. R. J. W. Evans and T. V. Thomas (London, 1991), pp. 23–47.

—— 'Bohemia, Moravia and Austria', in *The Early Reformation in Europe*, ed. A. Pettegree (Cambridge, 1992), pp. 23–48.

Emery, R. W., *Heresy and Inquisition in Narbonne* (New York, 1941).

Emmerson, R. K., *Antichrist in the Middle Ages* (Manchester, 1981).

Erbstösser, M. and Werner, E., *Ideologische Probleme des mittelalterlichen Plebejertums: Die freigeistige Häresie und ihre sozialen Würzeln* (Berlin, 1960).

—— *Sozialreligiöse Strömungen im späten Mittelalter* (Berlin, 1970).

—— 'Strukturen der Waldenser in Deutschland im 14. Jahrhundert', in *Mentalität*, ed. S. Tanz, pp. 95–106.

Eršil, J., 'Les rapports administratifs et financiers de la papauté avignonaise avec les pays de la couronne de Bohème entre 1352 et 1378', *Rozpravy československá Akademie Věd* LXIX (1959), p. 130.

Esser, K., *Das Testament des heiligen Franziskus von Assisi* (Münster-i-W, 1949).

—— 'Franziskus von Assisi und die Katharer seiner Zeit', *AFH* II (1958), pp. 225–64.

Evans, N., 'The descent of dissenters in the Chiltern hundreds', in *The World of Rural Dissenters*, ed. Spufford, pp. 288–308.

Fairfield, L. P., 'John Bale and the development of Protestant hagiography in England', *JEH* XXIV (1973), pp. 146–60.

Fearns, J. V., 'Peter von Bruis und die religiöse Bewegung des 12. Jahrhunderts', *AKG* XLVIII (1966), pp. 311–35.

—— 'The *Contra Petrobrusianos* of Peter the Venerable' (PhD thesis, Univ. Liverpool, 1963).

—— edn of text, *Corpus Christianorum, Continuatio mediaevalis* X (Turnhout, 1968).

Ferreiro, A. (ed.), *The Devil, Heresy and Witchcraft in the Middle Ages: Essays in Honor of Jeffrey B. Russell* (Leiden, Boston and Cologne, 1998).

Fichtenau, H., *Ketzer und Professoren. Häresie und Vernunftglaube in Hochmittelalter* (Munich, 1992); trans. D. A. Kaiser, *Heretics and Scholars* (Philadelphia, 1998).

Fines, J., 'Heresy trials in the diocese of Coventry and Lichfield 1511–12', *JEH* XIV (1963), pp. 160–74.

—— 'The postmortem condemnation for heresy of Richard Hunne', *EHR* LXXVIII (1963), pp. 528–31.

—— 'Studies in the Lollard heresy' (PhD thesis, Univ. Sheffield, 1964).

Forde, S., 'Nicholas Hereford's Ascension Day sermons 1382', *MS* LI (1989), pp. 205–41.

Foreville, R., 'Innocent III et la Croisade des Albigeois', *CF* IV, pp. 184–217.

Fössel, A., *Die Ortlieber: eine spiritualistische Ketzergruppe im 13. Jahrhundert* (Hanover, 1993).

——with A. Hettinger, *Klosterfrauen, Beginen, Ketzerinnen. Religiöse Lebensformen von Frauen im Mittelalter* (Idstein, 2000).

Fousek, M. S., 'Spiritual direction and discipline: a key to the flowering and decay of the 16th century Unitas Fratrum', *ARG* LXII (1961), pp. 207–25.

Frassetto, M., 'Reaction and reform: reception of heresy in Arras and Aquitaine in the early eleventh century', *CHR* LXXXIII (1997), pp. 386–400.

——'Heresy, celibacy and reform in the sermons of Ademar of Chabannes', in *Medieval Purity and Piety*, ed. Frassetto (New York and London, 1998), pp. 131–48.

——'The sermons of Ademar of Chabannes and the letter of Heribert. New sources concerning the origins of medieval heresy', *Revue Bénédictine* CIX (1999), pp. 324–40.

——'The Manichaeans in the writings of Ademar of Chabannes and the origins of medieval heresy', *Revue des Études Augustiniennes* (forthcoming).

——'The writings of Ademar of Chabannes, the Peace of 994 and the "Terrors of the year 1000"', *JMH* (forthcoming).

Freed, J. B., 'Urban development and the *cura monialium* in thirteenth-century Germany', *Viator* III (1972), pp. 312–27.

Friedlander, A., 'Les agents du roi face aux crises de l'hérésie en Languedoc', *CF* XX, pp. 199–220.

——(ed.), *Processus Bernardi Delitiosi: The Trial of Fr. Bernard Délicieux*, *TAPS*, LXXXVI, pt 1 (Philadelphia, 1996).

Fristedt, S. L., *The Wycliffe Bible* I (Stockholm, 1953), II (Stockholm, 1969).

——'The dating of the earliest manuscript of the Wycliffite Bible', *Stockholm Studies in Modern Philology*, n.s. I (Stockholm, 1960).

Frugoni, A., *Arnaldo da Brescia nelle fonti del secolo XII* (Rome, 1954).

——'Filii Arnaldi', *BISIAM* LX (1958), pp. 521–4.

Fudge, T. A., 'The state of Hussite historiography', *Mediaevistik* VII (1994), pp. 93–117.

——*The Magnificent Ride. The First Reformation in Hussite Bohemia* (Aldershot and Brookfield, 1998).

Gál, G. and Flood, D. (ed.), *Nicolaus Minorita Cronica* (New York, 1996).

Garsoïan, N. G., *The Paulician Heresy* (The Hague and Paris, 1967).

Gieysztor, A., 'Mouvements para-hérétiques en Europe centrale et orientale du 9e au 11e siècle: apostasies', *HS*, pp. 159–67.

Gilmont, J. F., 'Sources et critiques des sources', in *Les Vaudois*, ed. G. Audisio, pp. 105–13.

——'Les Vaudois des Alpes: mythes et realités', *RHE* LXXXIII (1988), pp. 69–89.

——'La publication de la Bible d'Olivétan: audaces et limites d'une enterprise de précurseurs', in *Olivétan*, ed. G. Casalis and B. Roussel, pp. 31–7.

Girgensohn, D., *Peter von Pulkau und die Wiedereinführung des Laienkelches* (Göttingen, 1964).

Given, J. B., 'A medieval inquisitor at work: Bernard Gui, 3 March 1308 to 19 June 1323', in *Portraits of Medieval and Renaissance Living*, ed. S. K. Cohn Jr. and S. A. Epstein (Ann Arbor, 1990), pp. 207–32.

——*Inquisition and Medieval Society. Power, Discipline and Resistance in Languedoc* (Ithaca and London, 1997).

——'The Béguins in Bernard Gui's Liber Sententiarum', in *Trials*, ed. P. Biller and C. Bruschi.

Glaber, R., see Rodulfus.

Gonnet, G., 'La figure et l'oeuvre de Vaudès dans la tradition historique et selon les dernières recherches', *CF* II pp. 87–109.

——'Nature et limites de l'episcopat vaudois au Moyen Age', *CV* II (1959), pp. 311–21.

——'I rapporti tra i Valdesi franco-italiani e i riformatori d'oltralpe prima di Calvino', in *Ginevra et l'Italia* (Florence, 1959), pp. 1–63.

——'Casi de sincretismo ereticale in Piemonte nei secoli *xiv* e *xv*', *BSSV* cviii (1960), pp. 3–36.

——*Le Confessioni de fede valdesi prima della reforma* (Turin, 1967).

——with A. Molnár, *Les Vaudois au Moyen Age* (Turin, 1974).

——'Sur les causes de la faillite en Italie des mouvements d'opposition à l'église officielle au moyen âge et au seizième siècle', *CV* xxxvi (1983), pp. 177–93.

Gordon, J. D., 'The laity and the Catholic Church in Cathar Languedoc' (DPhil, Univ. Oxford, 1992).

Gorre, R., *Die ersten Ketzer im 11. Jahrhundert: Religiöse Eiferer – Soziale Rebellen?* Konstanzer Dissertationen 3 (Constance, 1985 edn).

Greco, A. *Mitologia Catara. Il favoloso mondo delle origini* (Spoleto, 2000).

Griffe, E., *Les Débuts de l'aventure cathare en Languedoc (1140–1190)* (Paris, 1969).

——*Le Languedoc cathare de 1190 à 1210* (Paris, 1971).

——*Les Cathares et l'Inquisition (1229–1329)* (Paris, 1980).

Grundmann, H., *Studien über Joachim von Floris* (Leipzig, 1927).

——'Der Typus des Ketzers im mittelalterlichen Anschauung', in *Kultur- und Universalgeschichte. Festschrift für Walter Goetz* (Leipzig and Berlin, 1927), pp. 91–107.

——*Neue Forschungen über Joachim von Floris* (Marburg, 1950).

——'Neue Beiträge zur Geschichte der religiösen Bewegungen im Mittelalter', *AKG* xxxvii (1955), pp. 129–68.

——*Religiöse Bewegungen im Mittelalter* (Hildesheim, 1961); trans. S. Rowan, *Religious Movements in the Middle Ages* (Notre Dame and London, 1995).

——'Oportet et haereses esse: Das Problem der Ketzerei im Spiegel der mittelalterlichen Bibelexegese', *AKG* xlv (1963), pp. 129–64.

——*Ketzergeschichte des Mittelalters. Die Kirche in ihrer Geschichte: Ein Handbuch*, ed. K. D. Schmidt and E. Wolf (Göttingen, 1963).

——'Ketzerverhöre des Spätmittelalters als quellenkritisches Problem', *DA* xxi (1965), pp. 519–75.

——*Ausgewählte Aufsätze* i: *Religiöse Bewegungen* (Stuttgart, 1976), ii: *Joachim von Fiore* (1977), iii: *Bildung und Sprache* (1978).

Guarnieri, R., 'Il movimento del Libero Spirito', *Archivio Italiano per la storia della pietà* iv (1965), pp. 351–708.

Gui, Bernard, *Practica inquisitionis heretice pravitatis*, ed. C. Douais (Paris, 1886); trans. G. Mollat, *Manuel de l'inquisition* (abridged) (Paris, 1926).

Guiraud, J., *Cartulaire de Notre Dame de Prouille, précedé d'une étude sur l'Albigéisme languedocien au xiie et xiiie siècles* i–ii (Paris, 1907).

——*Histoire de l'Inquisition* i–ii (Paris, 1935).

Gwynn, A., *The English Austin Friars in the Time of Wyclif* (Oxford, 1940).

Hagman, Y., 'Catharism, a medieval echo of Manichaeism or of primitive Christianity?' (PhD, University of Lund, 1988).

Haigh, C., 'The recent historiography of the English Reformation', in *The English Reformation Revisited*, ed. C. Haigh (Cambridge, 1987), pp. 17–33.

Haines, R. M., ' "Wild Wittes and Wilfulness": John Swetstock's attack on those "Poyswunmongerers", the Lollards', *SCH* viii, pp. 143–53.

——'Reginald Pecock: a tolerant man in an age of intolerance,' *SCH* xxi (1984), pp. 125–37.

Hamilton, B., *The Albigensian Crusade* (London, 1974).

—— 'The Cathar Council of S. Félix reconsidered', *AFP* XLVIII (1978), pp. 23–53.

—— *The Medieval Inquisition* (London, 1981).

—— 'Wisdom from the East: the reception by the Cathars of eastern dualist texts', *BHL*, pp. 38–60.

—— 'The Cathars and Christian perfection', *SCH* Subsidia XI, pp. 5–23.

—— 'The legacy of Charles Schmidt to the study of Christian dualism', *JMH* XXIV (1998), pp. 191–214.

—— 'Catholic perceptions of East European dualism in the twelfth and thirteenth centuries', in Id., *Crusades, Cathars and the Holy Places* (Aldershot, 1999), no. XIV.

Hamilton, J. and B. and Stoyanov, Y., *Christian Dualist Heresies in the Byzantine World c.650–c.1405* (Manchester and New York, 1998).

Hanssler, M., *Katharismus in Südfrankreich* (Regensburg, 1991).

Hargreaves, H., 'The marginal glosses to the Wycliffite New Testament', *Studia Neophilologica* XXIII (1961), pp. 285–300.

Harris, M. R., 'Prolégomènes à l'histoire textuelle du Rituel cathare occitan', *Heresis* VI (1986), pp. 5–14.

Haupt, H., 'Waldensertum und Inquisition im südöstlichen Deutschland bis zur Mitte des 14. Jahrhunderts', *DZG* II (1889), pp. 285–330, 337–411.

Head, T. and Landes, R. (ed.), *Essays on the Peace of God: The Church and the People in Eleventh Century France. Historical Reflections / Reflexions Historiques* XIV (3) (1987).

—— and Landes, R. (ed.), *The Peace of God: Social Violence and Religious Response in France around the Year 1000* (Ithaca and London, 1992).

Heath, P., 'Urban piety in the later middle ages: the evidence of Hull wills', in *The Church, Politics and Patronage*, ed. R. B. Dobson, pp. 209–34.

Henderson, J. M., 'Piety and heresy in medieval Orvieto: the religious life of the laity c.1150–1350' (PhD thesis, Univ. Edinburgh, 1990), pp. 70–117.

Herold, V., 'Wyklif als Reformer', in *Hus*, ed. F. Seibt, pp. 39–47.

Heymann, F. G., 'The national assembly of Čáslav', *MH* VIII (1954), pp. 32–55.

—— *John Žižka and the Hussite Revolution* (Princeton, 1955).

—— 'John Rokycana: Church reformer between Hus and Luther', *CH* XXVIII (1959), pp. 240–80.

—— 'The Hussite–Utraquist Church in the fifteenth and sixteenth centuries', *ARG* LII (1961), pp. 1–26.

—— 'The Hussite revolution and the German Peasants' War: an historical comparison', *MH*, n.s. I (1971), pp. 141–59.

Hlaváček, I., 'Zur böhmischen Inquisition und Häresiebekämpfung um das Jahr 1400', in *Häresie*, ed. F. Šmahel, pp. 109–31.

Holeček, F., 'Hussens Auffassung von der Kirche', in *Hus*, ed. F. Seibt, pp. 183–91.

Holeton, D. R., *La Communion des tout-petits enfants: Etude du mouvement eucharistique en Bohême vers la fin du Moyen-Age* (Rome, 1989).

—— ' "O felix Bohemia – O felix Constantia": the liturgical commemoration of Saint Jan Hus', in *Hus*, ed. F. Seibt, pp. 385–97.

Hope, A., 'The lady and the bailiff: Lollardy among the gentry in Yorkist and early Tudor England', *LG*, pp. 250–77.

Hrubý, K., 'Senior Communitas – eine revolutionäre Institution der prager hussitischen Bürgerschaft', *Bohemia* XIII (1972), pp. 19–43.

Hudson, A., 'A Lollard mass', *JTS* XXIII (1972), pp. 407–19.

—— 'A Lollard compilation and the dissemination of Wycliffite thought', *JTS* XXIII (1972), pp. 65–81; *HLB*, pp. 13–29.

—— 'The examination of Lollards', *BIHR* XLVI (1973), pp. 145–59.

—— *Selections from English Wycliffite Writings* (Cambridge, 1978).

—— ed. with P. Gradon, *English Wycliffite Sermons* I–V (Oxford, 1983–96).

—— *Lollards and Their Books* (London, 1985).

—— 'Wycliffism in Oxford 1381–1411', in *Wyclif in His Times*, ed. A. Kenny, pp. 67–84.

—— 'Wyclif and the English Language', in *Wyclif in His Times*, ed. A. Kenny, pp. 67–104.

—— *The Premature Reformation* (Oxford, 1988).

—— 'John Purvey: a reconsideration of the evidence', *HLB*, pp. 85–110.

—— 'A neglected Wycliffite text', *HLB*, pp. 43–65.

—— 'A Lollard compilation in England and Bohemia', *HLB*, pp. 32–42.

—— '*Poor preachers, poor men*: views of poverty in Wyclif and his followers', in *Häresie*, ed. F. Šmahel, pp. 41–53.

—— ' "No Newe Thyng": the printing of medieval texts in the early Reformation period', *BHL*, pp. 227–48.

—— (ed.), *Testimony of William Thorpe, Two Wycliffite Texts*, EETS CCCI (1993), pp. 24–93.

—— 'Lollardy and eschatology', in *Eschatologie und Hussitismus*, ed. A. Patschovsky and F. Šmahel, pp. 99–113.

—— 'Accessus ad auctorem: the case of John Wyclif', *Viator* XXX (1999), pp. 323–44.

—— 'Which Wyche? Framing of a Lollard heretic', in *Trials*, ed. P. Biller and C. Bruschi.

Hurley, M., ' "Scriptura Sola" – Wyclif and his critics', *Traditio* XVI (1960), pp. 275–352.

Ilarino da Milano, 'La "Manifestatio heresis catarorum"', *Aevum* XII (1938), pp. 281–333.

—— 'Il "Liber supra stella" del piacentino Salvo Burci contro i Catari e altre correnti ereticali', *Aevum* XVI (1942), pp. 272–319; XVII (1943), pp. 90–146; XIX (1945), pp. 218–341.

—— *L'Eresia di Ugo Speroni nella confutazione del Maestro Vacario* (Vatican, 1945).

—— 'Le Eresie popolari del secolo XI nell' Europa occidentale', in *Studi Gregoriani*, ed. G. B. Borino, II (Rome, 1947), pp. 43–89.

Iogna-Prat, D., 'L'argumentation défensive de la polémique grégorienne au *Contra Petrobrusianos* de Pierre le Vénérable', in *Inventer l'Hérésie?*, ed. M. Zerner, pp. 87–118.

Jacob, E. F., 'The Bohemians at the Council of Basel', in *Prague Essays*, ed. R. W. Seton-Watson (Oxford, 1948), pp. 81–123.

—— 'Reynold Pecock, Bishop of Chichester', *PBA* XXXVII (1951), pp. 121–53.

Jiménez-Sanchez, P., 'Relire la Charte de Niquinta, (1) Origine et problématique de la charte', *Heresis* XXII (1994), pp. 1–26, (2) 'Sens et portée de la charte', *Heresis* XXIII (1995), pp. 1–28.

—— 'Le "traité cathare anonyme": un recueil d'autorités à l'usage des prédicateurs cathares?', *Heresis* XXXI (1999), pp. 73–100.

Jurkowski, M., 'New light on John Purvey', *EHR* CX (1995), pp. 1180–90.

Kadlek, J., 'Die Bibel in mittelalterlichen Böhmen', *AHDLMA* XXXVI (1964), pp. 89–109.

Kaelber, L., *Schools of Asceticism. Ideology and Organisation in Medieval Religious Communities* (Pennsylvania, 1998).

Kaeppeli, T., 'Une somme contre les hérétiques de S. Pierre Martyr(?)', *AFP* XVII (1947), pp. 295–335.

Kalivoda, R., 'Seibts "Hussitica" und die hussitische Revolution', *Historica* XIV (1967), pp. 225–46.

—— with A. Kolesnyk (ed.), *Das hussitische Denken im Lichte seiner Quellen* (Berlin, 1969).

—— *Revolution und Ideologie: Der Hussitismus* (Cologne and Vienna, 1976).

—— 'A new approach to the post Hussite development of Hussitism', *CV* xxvii (1984), pp. 73–90.

Kaminsky, H., 'Hussite radicalism and the origins of Tabor, 1415–1418', *MH* x (1956), pp. 102–30.

—— 'Pius Aeneas among the Taborites', *CH* xxviii (1959), pp. 281–309.

—— 'The religion of Hussite Tabor', in *The Czechoslovak Contribution to World Culture*, ed. M. Reichigl (The Hague, 1964), pp. 210–23.

—— 'Peter Chelčický: treatises on Christianity and the social order', in *Studies in Medieval and Renaissance History* i, ed. W. Bowsky (Lincoln, NE, 1964), pp. 106–79.

—— 'Nicholas of Dresden and the Dresden School in Hussite Prague', in *Master Nicholas of Dresden: The Old Color and the New, TAPS*, n.s. lv, i, ed. H. Kaminsky *et al.* (Philadelphia, 1965), pp. 5–28.

—— 'The Prague insurrection of 30 July 1419', *MH* xvii (1966), pp. 106–26.

—— *A History of the Hussite Revolution* (Berkeley and Los Angeles, 1967).

Kejř, J., 'Zur Entstehungsgeschichte des Hussitentums', *Die Welt zur Zeit des Konstanzer Konzils, Vorträge und Forschungen* ix (Constance and Stuttgart, 1965).

—— *The Hussite Revolution*, trans. T. Gottheinerova (Prague, 1988).

Kenny, A. (ed.), *Wyclif in His Times* (Oxford, 1987).

—— 'Wyclif', *PBA* lxxvi (1990), pp. 91–113.

Kestenberg-Gladstein, R., 'The "Third Reich": a fifteenth-century polemic against Joachimism and its background', *JWCI* xviii (1955), pp. 242–95.

Kieckhefer, R., 'Radical tendencies in the Flagellant movement of the mid-fourteenth century', *JMRS* iv (1974), pp. 157–76.

—— *The Repression of Heresy in Medieval Germany* (Pennsylvania, 1979).

Kienzle, B. M., *Cistercians, Heresy and Crusade in Occitania, 1145–1229* (Rochester, NY, 2001).

Klassen, J. M., *The Nobility and the Making of the Hussite Revolution* (Boulder, 1978).

*Knighton's Chronicle, 1337–96*, ed. G. H. Martin (Oxford Medieval Texts) (Oxford, 1995).

Koch, G., *Frauenfrage und Ketzertum im Mittelalter* (Berlin, 1962).

Kolmer, A., *Ad Capiendas Vulpes: Die Ketzerbekämpfung im Südfrankreich in der ersten Hälfte des 13. Jahrhunderts und die Ausbildung des Inquisitionsverfahrens* (Bonn, 1982).

—— 'Christus als beleidigte Majestät: von der Lex "Quisquis" (397) bis zur Dekretale "Vergentis" (1199)', in *Papsttum, Kirche und Recht*, ed. K. Mordek (Tübingen, 1991), pp. 1–13.

Köpstein, H., 'Zu den Auswirkungen der hussitische-revolutionären Bewegung in Franken', in *Aus 500 Jahren deutsch-tschechoslowakische Geschichte*, ed. K. Obermann and J. Polisensky (Berlin, 1958).

—— 'Über den deutschen Hussiten Friedrich Reiser', *ZG* vii (1959), pp. 1068–82.

Kurze, D., 'Die festländischen Lollarden', *AKG* xlvii (1965), pp. 48–76.

—— 'Zur Ketzergeschichte der Mark Brandenburg und Pommerns vornehmlich im 14. Jahrhundert', *JGMO* xvi–xvii (1968), pp. 50–94.

—— *Quellen zur Ketzergeschichte Brandenburgs und Pommerns. Veröffentlichungen der historischen Kommission zu Berlin* xlv, *Quellenwerke* vi (Berlin and New York, 1975).

Laberge, D., 'Fr. Petri Johannis Olivi, O. F. M.: tria scripta sui ipsius apologetica annorum 1283 et 1285', *AFH* xxviii (1935), pp. 115–55, 374–407; xxix (1936), pp. 98–141, 365–95.

Lambert, M. D., *Franciscan Poverty: The Doctrine of the Absolute Poverty of Christ and the Apostles in the Franciscan Order 1210–1323* (London, 1961; S. Bonaventure, NJ, 1998).

—— 'Catharisme et bon sens populaire', in *La Persécution du Catharisme XIIe–XIVe siècles; Collection Heresis* vi (Arques, 1993), pp. 193–214.

—— 'The motives of the Cathars: some reflections', *SCH* xv, pp. 49–59.

—— *The Cathars* (Oxford and Malden, MA, 1998).

—— 'Catharism as a reform movement', in *Häresie*, ed. F. Šmahel, pp. 23–39.

Landes, R., *Relics, Apocalypse and the Deceits of History. Adémar of Chabannes, 989–1034* (Cambridge, MA and London, 1995).

—— 'The dynamics of heresy and reform in Limoges: a study of popular participation in the "Peace of God" (994–1033)', in *Essays*, ed. T. Head and R. Landes, pp. 467–511.

Lansing, C., *Power and Purity. Cathar Heresy in Medieval Italy* (New York and Oxford, 1998).

Le Roy Ladurie, E., *Montaillou: village occitan de 1294 à 1324* (Paris, 1975); trans. B. Bray, *Montaillou* (London, 1978).

Lea, H. C., *A History of the Inquisition of the Middle Ages* i–iii (New York, 1888).

Leclercq, J., 'Simoniaca haeresis', in *Studi Gregoriani*, ed. G. B. Borino, i, pp. 523–30.

Lee, H. E. *et al.* (ed.), *Western Mediterranean Prophecy: The School of Joachim of Fiore and the Fourteenth Century Breviloquium* (Toronto, 1989).

—— with M. Reeves, 'The school of Joachim of Fiore', in Ibid., pp. 3–15.

—— with M. Reeves, 'Petrus Johannis Olivi', in Ibid., pp. 17–26.

Leff, G., 'The changing pattern of thought in the earlier fourteenth century', *BJRL* xliii (1961), pp. 354–72.

—— 'The place of metaphysics in Wyclif's theology', *SCH* Subsidia v, pp. 217–32.

—— *Heresy in the Later Middle Ages: The Relation of Heterodoxy to Dissent c.1250–c.1450* i–ii (Manchester, 1967).

—— 'Wyclif and Hus: a doctrinal comparison', *BJRL* lx (1968), pp. 387–410.

Lemberg, E., *Geschichte des Nationalismus in Europa* (Stuttgart, 1950).

Lerner, R., 'The image of mixed liquids in late medieval mystical thought', *CH* xxx (1971), pp. 397–411.

—— *The Heresy of the Free Spirit in the Later Middle Ages* (Berkeley, 1972).

—— 'The Black Death and Western European eschatological mentalities', *American Historical Review* lxxxv (1981), pp. 533–52.

—— *The Powers of Prophecy* (Berkeley, Los Angeles and London, 1983).

—— Rapports, *Comité International des Sciences Historiques*, xvi *Congrès International des Sciences Historiques* (Stuttgart, 1985).

—— *The Feast of St Abraham: Medieval Millenarians and the Jews* (Philadelphia, 2000).

Leyser, H., *Hermits and the New Monasticism: A Study of Religious Communities in Western Europe 1000–1150* (London, 1984).

Limborch, P., *Historia Inquisitionis* (Amsterdam, 1692).

Lindberg, C., *MS Bodley 959* i–v (Stockholm, 1959–73).

Little, L. K., *Religious Poverty and the Profit Economy in Medieval Europe* (London, 1978).

Loades, D. (ed.), *John Foxe and the English Reformation* (Aldershot, 1997).

Lobrichon, G., 'Le clair-obscur de l'hérésie au début du xie siècle en Aquitaine: une lettre d'Auxerre', in *Essays*, ed. T. Head and R. Landes, pp. 422–44.

—— 'Arras, 1025, ou le vrai procès d'une fausse accusation', in *Inventer l'Hérésie?*, ed. M. Zerner, pp. 67–85.

Loos, M., *Dualist Heresy in the Middle Ages* (Prague, 1974).

Loserth, J., *Huss und Wiclif* (Munich and Berlin, 1884; 2nd edn 1925).

Lourdaux, W. and Verhelst, D. (ed.), *The Concept of Heresy in the Middle Ages (11th–13th C.)*; *Medievalia Lovaniensia*, Ser. i *Studia* iv (Leuven and The Hague, 1976).

Lutton, R., 'Connections between Lollards, townsfolk and gentry in Tenterden in the late fifteenth and early sixteenth centuries', *LG*, pp. 199–228.

Luxton, I., 'The Lichfield court book: a postscript', *BIHR* xliv (1971), pp. 120–5.

Maccarrone, M., 'Riforma e sviluppo della vita religiosa con Innocenzo iii', *RSCI* xvi (1962), pp. 29–72.

MacCulloch, D., *Suffolk and the Tudors* (Oxford, 1986).

—— *The Later Reformation in England, 1547–1603* (Basingstoke, 1990).

McDonnell, E. W., *The Beguines and Beghards in Medieval Culture, with Special Emphasis on the Belgian Scene* (New Brunswick, 1954).

Macek, J., 'Villes et campagnes dans le Hussitisme', *HS*, pp. 243–56.

McFarlane, K. B., *John Wycliffe and the Beginnings of English Nonconformity* (London, 1952).

—— *Lancastrian Kings and Lollard Knights* (Oxford, 1972).

McGinn, B., *The Calabrian Abbot: Joachim of Fiore in the History of Western Thought* (New York and London, 1985).

—— *Visions of the End: Apocalyptic Traditions in the Middle Ages* (New York, 1979).

—— 'Symbolism in the thought of Joachim of Fiore', in *Prophecy*, ed. A. Williams and M. W. Bloomfield, pp. 143–64.

—— *The Presence of God. A History of Western Mysticism* (New York, 1998).

McGrade, A. S., 'The medieval idea of heresy: what are we to make of it?', *SCH* Subsidia xi, pp. 111–39.

McHardy, A. K., 'The dissemination of Wyclif's ideas', *SCH* Subsidia V, pp. 361–8.

—— 'De Heretico Comburendo', *LG*, pp. 112–26.

Machilek, F., 'Deutsche Hussiten', in *Hus*, ed. F. Seibt, pp. 267–82.

McNiven, P., *Heresy and Politics in the Reign of Henry IV* (Woodbridge, 1981).

McSheffrey, S., *Gender and Heresy. Women and Men in Lollard Communities, 1420–1530* (Philadelphia, 1995).

Maisonneuve, H., *Etudes sur les origines de l'Inquisition* (Paris, 1960).

Mallard, W., 'Clarity and dilemma – the *Forty Sermons* of John Wyclif', in *Contemporary Reflections on the Medieval Christian Tradition*, ed. G. H. Shriver (Durham, NC, 1974), pp. 19–38.

—— 'Dating the *Sermones quadraginta* of John Wyclif', *MH* xvii (1966), pp. 86–105.

Manselli, R., 'Il monaco Enrico e la sua eresia', *BISIAM* lxv (1953), pp. 1–63.

—— *Studi sulle eresie del secolo XII* (Rome, 1953).

—— *La 'Lectura super Apocalipsim' di Pietro di Giovanni Olivi* (Rome, 1955).

—— 'Una designazione dell'eresia Catara "Arriana Haeresis"' , *BISIAM* lxviii (1956), pp. 233–46.

—— *Spirituali e Beghini in Provenza* (Rome, 1959).

—— 'L'Anno 1260 fu Anno Gioachimito?', in *Il Movimento dei disciplinati nel settimo centenario del suo inizio* (Perugia, 1962).

—— 'I Passagini', *BISIAM* lxxv (1963), pp. 189–210.

—— *L'Eresia del Male* (Naples, 1963).

—— 'Evangelisme et mythe dans la foi cathare', *Heresis* v (1985), pp. 9–17.

Marrou, H. I., 'L'héritage de la Chrétienté', *HS*, pp. 51–4.

—— 'Un Ange déchu, un Ange pourtant', *Satan EC* xxvii (1948), pp. 28–43.

Martin, G. H., 'Knighton's Lollards', *LG*, pp. 28–40.

Martin, J. W., *Religious Radicals in Tudor England* (London, 1989).

Matthew, F. D., 'The trial of Richard Wyche', *EHR* v (1890), pp. 530–44.

Merlo, G. G., *Eretici e inquisitori nella società piemontese del trecento* (Turin, 1977).

—— 'Pietro di Verona – San Pietro Martire', in *Culto di Santi*, ed. S. Boesch Gajone and L. Sebastiani (Aquila and Rome, 1984), pp. 471–88.

—— *Valdesi e Valdismi medievali: itinerari e proposte di ricerca* (Turin, 1984).

—— *Valdesi e Valdismi* II: *Identità valdesi nella storia e nella storiografia: studi e discussioni* (Turin, 1991).

—— 'Le mouvement vaudois des origines à la fin du XIIIe siècle', in *Les Vaudois*, ed. G. Audisio, pp. 15–35.

—— Il *Sermo Generalis* dell' inquisitore: una sacra rappresentazione anomala', in *Vite*, ed. M. Benedetti *et al.*, pp. 203–20.

—— (ed.), *Eretici ed Eresie Medievali nella Storiografia Contemporanea* (Torre Pellice, 1994).

—— '"Heresis Lumbardorum e filii Arnaldi": note su Arnaldismo e Arnaldisti', *Nuova Rivista Storica* LXXVIII (1994), pp. 87–102.

Miccoli, G., 'Per la storia della pataria milanese', *BISIAM* LXX (1958), pp. 43–123.

Mildenberger, F., 'Die böhmischen Länder im Früh- und Hochmittelalter', in *Handbuch*, ed. K. Bosl, I, pp. 165–347.

Mingroot, E. van, 'Acta Synodi Atrebatensis (1025): problèmes de critique de provenance', *Studia Gratiana* XX (1976), pp. 202–30.

Miolo, G., *Historia breve e vera de gl'affari dei Valdesi delle Valli*, ed. E. Balmas (Turin, 1971).

Mohr, W., 'Tanchelm von Antwerpen, eine nochmalige Überprüfung der Quellenlage', *Annales Universitatis Saraviensis* III (1954), pp. 234–47.

Mollat, G., *Manuel de l'inquisiteur* (Paris, 1926).

Mollat, M., 'La notion de la pauvreté au moyen âge: position de problèmes', *Revue d'histoire de l'église de France* LII (1966), pp. 6–23.

—— with P. Wolff, *The Popular Revolutions of the Late Middle Ages* (London, 1973).

Molnár, A., 'Hus et son appel à Jésus-Christ', *CV* VIII (1965), pp. 95–104.

—— with G. Gonnet, *Les Vaudois au Moyen Age* (Turin, 1974).

—— 'Die kleine und die grosse Partei der Brüderunität', *CV* XXII (1979), pp. 239–48.

—— 'Luther und die böhmischen Brüder', *CV* XXIV (1981), pp. 47–67.

—— 'La letteratura Taborita', *RSLR* XVIII (1982), pp. 3–23.

—— 'Erasmus und das Hussitentum', *CV* XXX (1987), pp. 185–97.

Montanari, P., 'Milano "Fovea haereticorum": le fonti di un' immagine', in *Vite*, ed. M. Benedetti *et al.*, pp. 203–20.

—— 'Valdesi a Milano tra XII e XIII secolo', *RHR* CCXVII (2000), pp. 59–74.

Moore, R. I., 'St Bernard's mission to the Languedoc in 1145', *BIHR* XLVII (1974), pp. 1–10.

—— 'Guibert de Nogent and his world', in *Studies in Medieval History presented to R. H. C. Davis*, ed. H. Mayr-Harting and R. I. Moore (London, 1975), pp. 107–17.

—— 'Heresy as a disease', in *Concept*, ed. W. Lourdaux and D. Verhelst, pp. 1–11.

—— *The Origins of European Dissent* (London, 1977; Oxford, 1985).

—— 'Family, community and cult on the eve of the Gregorian Reform', *TRHS*, 5th ser. XXX (1980), pp. 49–69.

—— 'Popular violence and popular heresy in Western Europe c.1000–1179', *SCH* XXI, pp. 43–50.

—— *The Formation of a Persecuting Society: Power and Deviance in Western Europe, 950–1250* (Oxford, 1987).

—— 'New sects and secret meetings', *SCH* XXIII, pp. 47–68.

—— 'Heresy, repression and social change in the age of the Gregorian reform', in *Christendom and Its Discontents*, ed. S. J. Waugh and P. Diehl, pp. 19–46.

—— 'A la naissance d'une société persécutrice: les clercs, les Cathars et la formation de l'Europe', in *La Persécution du Catharisme XIIe–XIVe siècles. Collection Heresis 6eme Session d'Histoire médiévale* (Arques, 1996), pp. 11–37.

—— *The First European Revolution, c.970–1215* (Oxford, New York, 2000).

—— 'The birth of popular heresy: a millennial phenomenon', *JRH* xxiv (2000), pp. 8–25.

—— 'Heresy and enthusiasm in "the millennial generation"', in *Imagining the End: Millennial Faith from Ancient Middle East to Contemporary America*, ed. A. Amanat and M. Bernhardsson (I. P. Tauris, 2001).

Morée, P. C. A., *Preaching in Fourteenth Century Bohemia. The Life and Ideas of Milicius de Chremsier* (Slavkov, 1999).

Morghen, R., *Medioevo Cristiano* (Bari, 1953).

Muessig, C., 'Les sermons de Jacques de Vitry sur les Cathares', *CF* xxxii, pp. 69–83.

Müller, D., 'Les beguines', in *Christianisme*, ed. A. Brenon and N. Gouzy, pp. 351–89.

—— 'Katharer', *TRE* xviii (Berlin and New York, 1988).

—— 'Hexenprozess und Frauenrepression', *Heresis* xii (1989), pp. 33–51.

—— *Frauen vor der Inquisition. Lebensformen, Glaubenszeugnis und Aburteilung der deutschen und französischen Katharismus* (Mainz, 1996).

Müller, J. T., *Geschichte der Böhmischen Brüder* i–iii (Herrnhut, 1922–31).

Mundy, J. H., *Liberty and Political Power in Toulouse, 1050–1230* (New York, 1954).

—— 'Charity and social work in Toulouse, 1110–1250', *Traditio* xxii (1966), pp. 203–87.

—— *The Repression of Catharism at Toulouse: The Royal Diploma of 1279* (Toronto, 1985).

—— 'Le mariage et les femmes à Toulouse au temps des Cathares', *Annales* (1987), pp. 136–9.

—— *Men and Women at Toulouse in the Age of the Cathars* (Toronto, 1990).

Murray, A., 'Piety and impiety in thirteenth-century Italy', *SCH* viii, pp. 83–106.

—— 'The medieval inquisition: an instrument of secular politics?', *Peritia* v (1986), pp. 161–200 (Denis Bethell Memorial Lecture).

—— 'Missionaries and magic in Dark Age Europe', *PP* cxxxvi (1992), pp. 186–205.

Nechutová, J. (ed.), *Matthiae de Janov dicti magistri Parisiensis Regularum Veteris et Novi Testamenti Liber v De Corpore Christi*, Veröffentlichung des Collegium Carolinum lxix (Munich, 1993).

Nelli, R., *La vie quotidienne des Cathares* (Paris, 1969).

Nelson, J. L., 'Society, theodicy and the origins of heresy: towards a reassessment of the medieval evidence', *SCH* ix, pp. 65–77.

Nickson, M., 'The "Pseudo-Reinerius" treatise: the final stage of a thirteenth century work on heresy from the diocese of Passau', *AHDLMA* xxxiv (1967), pp. 255–314.

Nimmo, D., *Reform and Division in the Franciscan Order 1226–1538* (Rome, 1987).

Nolcken, C. von, 'Richard Wyche, a certain knight and the beginning of the end', *LG*, pp. 127–54.

Nold, P., 'Bertrand de la Tour and Franciscan poverty' (DPhil, Univ. Oxford, 1999).

O'Day, R., *The Debate on the English Reformation* (London and New York, 1986).

Odložilík, O., 'The Reformation leaders of the Unitas Fratrum', *CH* ix (1940), pp. 253–63.

Oliger, L., *De secta spiritus libertatis in Umbria saec. xiv: disquisitio et documenta* (Rome, 1943).

—— 'Spirituels', *DTC* xiv, cols 2522–49.

Ourliac, P., 'La société languedocienne du xiiie siècle et le droit romain', *CF* vi, pp. 199–216.

Palacký, F., *Documenta J. Hus vitam illustrantia* (Prague, 1869).

Pales-Gobilliard, A., *L'Inquisiteur Geoffrey d'Ablis et les Cathares du Comté de Foix (1308–1309)* (Paris, 1984).

Pánek, J. et al. (ed.), *Husitství–Reformace–Renesance* (Prague, 1994).

Paolini, L, *L'eresia a Bologna fra xiii e xiv secolo*. i: *L'Eresia catara all fine del duecento* (Rome, 1975).

—— 'Italian Catharism and written culture', *BHL*, pp. 83–103.

Paravy, P., 'Les Vaudois du Haut-Dauphiné de la Croisade de 1488 à la Réforme', in *Christianisme*, ed. A. Brenon and N. Gouzy, pp. 255–86.

—— *De la Chrétienté romaine à la Réforme en Dauphiné: evêques, fidèles et deviants (vers 1340 vers 1530)*, Collection de l'Ecole Française de Rome, I–II, CLXXXIII (Rome, 1993).

Partner, P., *The Murdered Magicians: The Templars and Their Myth* (New York, 1982).

Pásztor, E., 'Le polemiche sulla "Lectura super Apocalipsim" di Pietro Giovanni Olivi fino all sua condanna', *BISIAM* LXX (1958), pp. 365–424.

—— 'Una raccolta di sermoni di Giovanni XXII', *Bulletino dell' Archivio Paleografico Italiano*, n.s. I–III (1956–7), pp. 265–89.

Patschovsky, A., *Der Passauer Anonymus: Ein Sammelwerk über Ketzer, Juden, Antichrist aus der Mitte des 13. Jahrhunderts* (Stuttgart, 1968).

—— with K. V. Selge, *Quellen zur Geschichte der Waldenser* (Güterloh, 1973).

—— 'Strassburger Beginenverfolgungen im 14. Jahrhundert', *DA* XXX (1974), pp. 56–198.

—— *Die Anfänge einer ständigen Inquisition in Böhmen* (New York and Berlin, 1975).

—— (ed.), *Quellen zur böhmischen Inquisition im 14. Jahrhundert. MGH; Quellen zur Geistesgeschichte des Mittelalters* XI (Weimar, 1979).

—— 'Der Ketzer als Teüfelsdiener', in *Papsttum, Kirche und Recht in Mittelalter*, ed. H. Mordek (Tübingen, 1991), pp. 317–34.

—— 'The literacy of Waldensianism from Valdes to c.1400', *BHL*, pp. 112–36.

—— with F. Šmahel (ed.), *Eschatologie und Hussitismus* (Prague, 1996).

—— 'Antichrist bei Wyclif', in *Eschatologie*, ed. A. Patschovsky and F. Šmahel, pp. 33–98.

—— 'Toleranz im Mittelalter: Idee und Wirklichkeit', in *Toleranz im Mittelalter. Vorträge und Forschungen* XLV, ed. A. Patschovsky and H. Zimmermann (Sigmaringen, 1998), pp. 391–402.

—— 'Der taboritische Chiliasmus, seine Idee, sein Bild bei den Zeitgenossen und die Interpretation der Geschichtswissenschaft', in *Häresie*, ed. F. Šmahel, pp. 169–95.

—— 'Heresy and society: on the political function of heresy in the medieval world', in *Trials*, ed. P. Biller and C. Bruschi.

Paul, J., 'Hugues de Digne', *CF* X, pp. 69–97.

—— 'La procédure inquisitionale à Carcassonne au milieu du XIIIe siècle', *CF* XXIX, pp. 361–96.

Paxton, F. S., 'The Peace of God in modern historiography: perspectives and trends', in *Essays*, ed. T. Head and R. Landes, pp. 385–404.

Peal, A., 'Olivier de Termes and the Occitanian nobility in the thirteenth century', *RMS* XII (1986), pp. 109–29.

Pegg, M. G., *The Corruption of Angels. The Great Inquisition of 1245–1246* (Princeton and Oxford, 2001).

—— 'On Cathars, Albigenses, and Good Men of Languedoc', *JMH* XXVII (2001), pp. 181–95.

Peter of les Vaux de Cernay, *The History of the Albigensian Crusade*, trans. W. A. and M. D. Sibly (Woodbridge, 1983).

Peters, E., *The Magician, the Witch and the Law* (Hassocks, 1978).

—— (ed.), *Heresy and Authority in Medieval Europe* (London, 1980).

—— *Torture* (Oxford, 1985).

—— *Inquisition* (New York and London, 1986).

—— 'Henry Charles Lea 1825–1909', in *Medieval Scholarship* I, ed. H. Damico and J. B. Zařadil (1995), pp. 89–99.

—— 'Destruction of the flesh – salvation of the spirit: the paradoxes of torture in medieval Christian society', in *The Devil*, ed. A. Ferreiro, pp. 131–48.

Pirenne, H., 'Tanchelm et le projet de démembrement du diocèse d'Utrecht vers 1100', *ARBB*, 5th ser. xiii (1927), pp. 112–19.

Piron, S., 'Petrus Johannis Olivi, epistola ad Fratrem R.', *AFH* xci (1998), pp. 33–64.

Plumb, D., 'The social and economic spread of rural Lollardy: a reappraisal', *SCH* xxiii, pp. 111–29.

—— 'The social and economic status of the later Lollards', in *The World of Rural Dissenters*, ed. Spufford, pp. 103–31.

Polivka, M., 'Nicholas of Hus', *Historica* xxviii (1988), pp. 75–121.

—— 'Popular movement as an agent of the Hussite revolution in late medieval Bohemia', in *History and Society*, ed. J. Purs and K. Herman (Prague, 1985), pp. 261–85.

Pons, T., 'Barba, barbi e barbetti nel tempo e nello spazio', *BSSV* lxxxviii (1967), pp. 47–66.

Puech, H. C., with A. Vaillant (ed.), *Le Traité contre les Bogomils de Cosmas le Prêtre* (Paris, 1945).

—— 'Catharisme médiévale et Bogomilisme', in *Oriente ed Occidente nel Medio Evo* (Rome, 1957), pp. 84–104.

Rausch, R., *Abtrünnig im Glauben. Zur Verbreitungsmöglichkeit und Kommunikationsmitteln der englischen Lollarden*, Innsbrucker Historische Studien xxii (Innsbruck, 2000).

Reeves, M. E., 'The *Liber Figurarum* of Joachim of Fiore', *MRS* ii (1950), pp. 57–81.

—— *The Influence of Prophecy in the Later Middle Ages: A Study in Joachimism* (Oxford, 1969).

—— with B. Hirsch-Reich, *The Figurae of Joachim of Fiore* (Oxford, 1972).

Reltgen, A., 'Dissidences et contradictions en Italie', in *Christianisme*, ed. A. Brenon and N. Gouzy, pp. 89–113.

Renna, J., 'Wyclif's attacks on monks', *SCH* Subsidia v, pp. 267–80.

Říčan, R., *Die Böhmischen Brüder: Ihr Ursprung und ihre Geschichte*, trans. B. Popelář (Berlin, 1961).

Richardson, H. G., 'Heresy and the lay power under Richard ii', *EHR* li (1936), pp. 1–28.

Richmond, C., 'Religion and the fifteenth century English gentleman', in *The Church, Politics and Patronage*, ed. R. Dobson, pp. 193–208.

Richter, K., 'Die böhmischen Länder von 1471–1740', in *Handbuch*, ed. K. Bosl, ii, pp. 99–143.

Roach, A., 'The Cathar economy', *RMS* xii (1986), pp. 51–71.

—— 'The relationship of the Italian and Southern French Cathars' (DPhil, Univ. Oxford, 1989).

—— *The Devil's World: Heresy and Society 1000–1320* (forthcoming, 2001).

Robson, J. A., *Wyclif and the Oxford Schools* (Cambridge, 1961).

*Rodulfus Glaber Opera*, ed. J. France et al. (Oxford, 1989).

Roquebert, M., *L'Epopée Cathare* i: *L'Invasion* (Toulouse, 1970), ii: *La Dépossession* (1977), iii: *Les Lys et la Croix* (1986), iv: *Mourir à Montségur* (1989), v: *Les Cathares de la chute de Montségur aux derniers bûchers 1244–1329* (Paris, 1998).

—— 'Le Catharisme comme tradition dans la "Familia Languedocienne"', *CF* xx, pp. 221–38.

—— 'Montségur, refuge ou quartier general?', in *La Persécution du Catharisme; Collection Heresis* vi (Arques, 1996), pp. 159–92.

—— 'Un exemple de Catharisme ordinaire: Fanjeaux', *EO*, pp. 169–211.

—— *La Religion Cathare. Le Bien, Le Mal et le Salut dans l'hérésie médiévale* (Paris, 2001).

Rottenwöhrer, G., *Der Katharismus*, i: (i) *Quellen zum Katharismus*, (ii) *Anmerkungen* (Bad Honnef, 1982), ii: *Der Kult, die religiöse Praxis, die Kritik an Kult und Sakramenten der*

*Katholischen Kirche*, (i) *Der Kult*, (ii) *Die religiöse Praxis* (1982), III: *Die Herkunft der Katharer nach Theologie und Geschichte* (1990), IV: (i–iii) *Glaube und Theologie der Katharer* (1993).

Rouse, R. H. and M. A., 'The Schools and the Waldensians: a new work of Durand of Huesca', in *Christendom*, ed. S. Waugh and P. Diehl, pp. 86–111.

Rubellin, M., 'Au temps où Valdès n'était pas hérétique: hypothèses sur le rôle de Valdès à Lyon (1170–1183)', *Inventer l'Hérésie?*, ed. Zerner, pp. 193–218.

Russell, J. B., 'Les Cathares de 1048–54 à Liège', *BSAHDL* XLII (1961), pp. 1–8.

—— 'A propos de synode d'Arras en 1025', *RHE* LVII (1962), pp. 66–87.

—— 'Interpretations of the origins of medieval heresy', *MS* XXV (1963), pp. 26–33.

—— 'St Boniface and the Eccentrics', *CH* XXXIII (1964), pp. 3–15.

—— *Dissent and Reform in the Early Middle Ages* (Berkeley and Los Angeles, 1965).

—— *Religious Dissent in the Middle Ages* (New York, 1971).

Šanjek, F., 'Le rassemblement de St Félix de Caraman et les églises Cathares au XIIe siècle', *RHE* LXVII (1972), pp. 767–99.

Scattergood, V. J., '"The two ways" – an unpublished religious treatise by Sir John Clanvowe', *English Philological Studies* X (1967), pp. 33–56.

—— (ed.), *The Works of Sir John Clanvowe* (Cambridge and Ipswich, 1975).

Schaff, D. S., *De Ecclesia. The Church, by John Hus* (Westport, CT, 1915).

Schaller, H. M., 'Endzeiterwartung und Antichrist Vorstellungen im 13. Jahrhundert', in *Festschrift für Hermann Heimpel*, II (Göttingen (Max-Planck-Institut), 1972), pp. 924–47.

—— 'Die Frömmigkeit Friedrichs II', *DA* LI (1995), pp. 493–513.

Scharff, T., 'Schrift zur Kontrolle – Kontrolle der Schrift. Italienische und französische Inquisitoren-Handbücher des 13. und frühen 14. Jahrhunderts', *DA* LIV (1998), pp. 547–84.

Schmitt, J. C., *Mort d'une hérésie, l'église et les clercs face aux beguines et beghards du Rhin supérieur du XIVe et XVe siècle* (Paris, 1978).

Schneider, M., *Europäisches Waldensertum im 13. und 14. Jahrhundert* (Berlin and New York, 1981).

Scuderi, G., 'Il problema del matrimonio nella fede, nella pietà e nella teologia del Valdismo medioevale', *BSSV* CVI (1959), pp. 31–54.

Segl, P., 'Conrad von Marburg, Inquisitor', in *Neue Deutsche Biographie* XII (Berlin, 1980), pp. 544–6.

—— *Ketzer in Österreich: Untersuchungen über Häresie und Inquisition im Herzogtum Österreich im 13. und beginnenden 14. Jahrhundert* (Paderborn and Zurich, 1984).

—— 'Die religiöse Frauenbewegung in Südfrankreich zwischen Häresie und Orthodoxie', in *Religiöse Frauenbewgung*, ed. P. Dinzelbacher and D. R. Bauer (Cologne and Vienna, 1988), pp. 91–116.

—— (ed.), *Die Anfänge der Inquisition im Mittelalter* (Cologne, Weimar and Vienna, 1993).

—— 'Ketzer im Mittelalter', in *'Ketzer' – Dissidenten – 'Volksschädlinge'*, ed. S. Krimm and U. Triller (Munich, 1999), pp. 25–50.

—— 'Gregor IX, die Regensburger Dominikaner und die Anfänge der "Inquisition" in Deutschland', in *Regensburg, Bayern und Europa*, ed. L. Kolmer *et al.*, pp. 307–19.

—— 'Berthold von Regensburg und die Ketzer seiner Zeit', in *Studien und Quellen zur Geschichte Regensburgs* IV (Regensburg, 1987), pp. 115–29.

Seibt, F., 'Johannes Hus und der Abzug der deutschen Studenten aus Prag 1409', *AKG* XXXIX (1957), pp. 63–80.

—— 'Die Hussitenzeit als Kulturepoche', *HZ* CXCVI (1962), pp. 21–62.

—— 'Communitas primogenita: zur Prager Hegemonialpolitik in der hussitischen Revolution', *HJB* LXXXI (1962), pp. 80–100.

—— *Hussitica: Zur Struktur einer Revolution* (Cologne, 1965).

—— 'Die *Revelatio* des Jacobellus von Mies über die Kelchkommunion', *DA* xxii (1967), pp. 618–24.

—— 'Die Zeit der Luxemburger und der hussitischen Revolution', in *Handbuch*, ed. K. Bosl, i, pp. 351–536.

—— 'Das Zeitalter Georgs von Podiebrady', in *Handbuch*, ed. K. Bosl, i, pp. 537–68.

—— 'Utopie im Mittelalter', *HZ*, ccviii (1969), pp. 555–94.

—— 'Bohemica, Probleme und Literatur seit 1945', *HZ*, Sonderheft iv (1970), pp. 49–99.

—— *Karl IV: Ein Kaiser in Europa 1346 bis 1378* (Munich, 1978).

—— *Hussitenstudien, Personen, Ereignisse. Ideen einer frühen Revolution* (Munich, 1987).

—— 'Peter Chelčický', in *Hussitenstudien*, pp. 209–16.

—— 'Vom Vitkov bis zum Vyšehrad', in *Hussitenstudien*, pp. 185–207.

—— 'Konrad von Vechta', in *Hussitenstudien*, pp. 241–52.

—— 'Hus in Konstanz', in *Hussitenstudien*, pp. 229–40.

—— 'Die hussitische Revolution', in *Hussitenstudien*, pp. 79–90.

—— *Kaiser Karl v und die Reformation* (Berlin, 1990).

—— 'Eine historische Anomalie?', in *Husitství*, ed. J. Pánek *et al.*, pp. 275–85.

—— (ed.), *Jan Hus. Zwischen Zeiten, Völkern, Konfessionen* (Munich, 1997).

—— 'Jan Hus – zwischen Zeiten, Völkern, Konfessionen', in *Hus*, pp. 11–26.

Selge, K. V., *Die ersten Waldenser* i: *Untersuchung und Darstellung*, ii: *Der Liber antiheresis des Durandus von Osca* (Berlin, 1967).

—— 'Caractéristiques du premier mouvement vaudois et crises au cours de son expansion', *CF* ii, pp. 110–42.

—— 'L'origine della opere di Gioacchino dà Fiore', in *L'Attesa della fine dei tempi nel medioevo*, ed. O. Capitanei and J. Miethke (Bologna, 1990), pp. 87–130.

Sheils, W. J., *The English Reformation 1530–1570* (London and New York, 1989).

Shirley, J. (trans.), *The Song of the Cathar Wars. A History of the Albigensian Crusade, William of Tudela and an Anonymous Successor* (Aldershot, 1996).

Sibly, W. A. and M. D. (ed. and trans.), *The History of the Albigensian Crusade, Peter of les Vaux-de-Cernay* (Woodbridge and New York, 1998).

Šmahel, F., 'The idea of the "nation" in Hussite Bohemia', *Historica* xvi (1969), pp. 143–347, xvii (1969), pp. 93–197.

—— *La Revolution Hussite: Une anomalie historique* (Paris, 1985).

—— 'Jan Hus – heretic or patriot', *History Today* xx (1990), pp. 27–33.

—— (ed.), *Häresie und vorzeitige Reformation im Spätmittelalter*, Schriften des Historischen Kollegs, Kolloquien xxxix (Munich, 1998).

Smalley, B., 'Wyclif's Postilla on the Old Testament and his Principium', *Oxford Historical Society*, n.s. xvi (1959–60), pp. 253–97.

—— 'The Bible and eternity: John Wyclif's dilemma', *JWCI* xxvii (1964), pp. 73–89.

Söderberg, H., *La Religion des Cathares: Etudes sur le gnosticisme de la basse antiquité et du Moyen Age* (Uppsala, 1949).

Southern, R. W., 'Aspects of the European tradition of historical writing 3: History as prophecy', *TRHS*, 5th ser. xxii (1972), pp. 159–80.

Spinka, M., *John Hus at the Council of Constance* (New York and London, 1965).

—— *John Hus' Concept of the Church* (Princeton, 1966).

—— *John Hus: A Biography* (Princeton, 1968).

—— with J. M. Pope (trans.), *The Letters of John Hus* (Manchester, 1972).

Spufford, M. (ed.), *The World of Rural Dissenters 1520–1725* (Cambridge, 1995).

Stephens, J. N., 'Heresy in medieval and Renaissance Florence', *PP* liv (1972), pp. 25–60.

Stephens, P., *The Waldensian Story. A Study in Faith, Intolerance and Survival* (Lewes, 1998).

Stock, B., *The Implications of Literacy: Written Language and Models of Interpretation in the Eleventh and Twelfth Centuries* (Princeton, 1983).

Stoodt, H. C., *Katharismus im Untergrund* (Tübingen, 1997).

Stoyanov, Y., *The Other God. Dualist Religion from Antiquity to the Cathar Heresy* (New Haven and London, 2000).

Strnad, A., 'Die Zeugen im Wiener Prozess gegen Hieronymus von Prag', in *Husitství*, ed. J. Pánek *et al.*, pp. 331–67.

Sumption, J., *The Albigensian Crusade* (London, 1978).

Svatoš, M., 'Hussens Freunde', in *Hus*, ed. F. Seibt, pp. 67–72.

Swinburne, L. M. (ed.), *The Lantern of Light*, EETS CLI (1917).

Székely, G., 'Le mouvement des Flagellants au 14e siècle, son caractère et ses causes', *HS*, pp. 229–38.

Tanner, N. (ed.), *Heresy Trials in the Diocese of Norwich 1428–31*, Camden 4th ser. XX (London, 1977).

——(ed.), *Kent Heresy Proceedings 1511–12* (Stroud, 1997)

——with S. McSheffrey (ed.), *Trials of Coventry Lollards 1486–1522* (forthcoming, 2001).

——'William White', *DNB* (forthcoming, 2004).

Tanz, S. (ed.), *Mentalität und Gesellschaft im Mittelalter* (Frankfurt-am-Main, 1993).

Taviani, H., 'Naissance d'une hérésie en Italie du nord au XIe siècle', *Annales* XXIX (1974), pp. 124–52.

Taylor, C., 'The letter of Heribert of Périgord as a source for dualist heresy in the society of early eleventh century Aquitaine', *JMH* XXVI (2000), pp. 313–49.

Thomson, J. A. F., 'Tithe disputes in later medieval London', *EHR* LXXVII (1963), pp. 1–17.

——*The Later Lollards 1414–1520* (Oxford, 1965).

——'Orthodox religion and the origins of Lollardy', *History* LXXIV (1989), pp. 39–55.

——'Knightly piety and the margins of Lollardy', *LG*, pp. 95–111.

Thomson, S. H., 'Luther and Bohemia', *ARG* XLIV (1953), pp. 160–81.

Thouzellier, C., 'La répression de l'hérésie et les débuts de l'Inquisition', in *Histoire de l'Eglise*, ed. A. Fliche and V. Martin, X (Paris, 1950), pp. 291–340.

——'Hérésie et croisade au XIIe siècle', *RHE* XLIX (1954), pp. 855–72.

——*Un Traité Cathare inédit du début du XIIIe siècle d'après le 'Liber contra Manicheos' de Durand de Huesca* (Louvain, 1961).

——*Une Somme anti-Cathare: Le 'Liber contra Manicheos' de Durand de Huesca* (Louvain, 1964).

——'Tradition et résurgence dans l'hérésie médiévale', *HS*, pp. 105–20.

——*Hérésie et hérétiques* (Rome, 1969).

——*Catharisme et Valdéisme en Languedoc*, 2nd edn (Louvain and Paris, 1969).

——*Livre des deux Principes* (Paris, 1973).

Thrupp, S. L. (ed.), *Millennial Dreams in Action* (The Hague, 1962).

Tierney, B., *Origins of Papal Infallibility, 1150–1350* (Leiden, 1972).

Tondelli, L., Reeves, M. and Hirsch-Reich, B. (ed.), *Il libro delle figure dell' Abate Gioacchino da Fiore*, 2nd edn (Turin, 1953).

Töpfer, B., *Volk und Kirche zur Zeit des beginnenden Gottesfriedensbewegung in Frankreich* (Berlin, 1957).

——'Eine Handschrift des Evangelium aeternum des Gerardino von Borgo San Donnino', *ZG* VII (1960), pp. 156–63.

——*Das kommende Reich des Friedens* (Berlin, 1964).

——'Die Anschauungen des Papstes Johannes XXII über das Dominium in der Bulle "Quia Vir Reprobus"', in *Folia Diplomatica* (Brno, 1971), pp. 295–306.

—— *Urzustand und Sündenfall in der mittelalterlichen Gesellschaft- und Staatstheorie* (Stuttgart, 1999).

—— 'Die Wertung der weltlich-staatlichen Ordnung durch John Wyclif und Jan Hus', in *Häresie*, ed. F. Šmahel, pp. 55–76.

Torrell, J-P. and Bouthillier, D., *Pierre le Vénérable et sa vision du monde* (Louvain, 1986).

Tourn, G., 'Sans nom ni lieu', in *Olivétan*, ed. G. Casalis and B. Roussel, pp. 21–9.

Trapp, D., 'Clm 27034: unchristened nominalism and Wycliffite realism at Prague in 1381', *RTAM* xxiv (1957), pp. 320–60.

Treesh, S. K., 'Europe's peasant heretics: the Waldensians 1375–1550' (PhD, Univ. Rutgers, 1988).

Tremp, K. U., 'Waldenser und Wiedergänger. Das Fegefeuer im Inquisitionsregister des Bischofs Jacques Fournier von Pamiers', in *Himmel, Hölle, Fegefeuer* (Freiburg, 1994), pp. 125–34.

—— 'Hérétiques ou usuriers? Les Fribourgeois face à Saint Vincent Ferrier', *Memoire Dominicaine* vii (1995), pp. 117–37.

—— '"Parmi les hérétiques": la Vierge Marie dans l'inquisition de l'évêque Jacques Fournier de Pamiers (1317–1326)', in *Marie. Le Cult de la Vierge*, ed. D. Iogna-Prat *et al.* (Paris, 1996), pp. 533–60.

—— 'Multum abhorrerem confiteri homini laico', in *Pfaffen und Laien – ein mittlelalterliches Antagonismus*, Freiburger Colloquium 1996, ed. E. C. Lutz and E. Tremp (Freiburg, 1999), pp. 153–89.

—— 'Les Vaudois de Fribourg (1399–1430): état de la recherche', *RHR* ccxvii (2000), pp. 121–38.

—— 'Es ist gelogen was man singet', *Freiburger Geschichtsblätter* lxxvii (2000), pp. 27–41.

—— (ed.), *Quellen zur Geschichte der Waldenser von Freiburg im Uechtland (1399–1439): MGH* (Munich, 2000).

Trusen, W., 'Von den Anfängen des Inquisitionsprozesses zum Verfahren bei der *Inquisitio haereticae pravitatis*', in *Anfänge*, ed. P. Segl, pp. 39–76.

Tugwell, S., 'Notes on the life of St Dominic', *AFP* lxvi (1996), pp. 5–200; lxviii (1998), pp. 5–116.

Turdeanu, E., 'Apocryphes bogomiles et pseudo-bogomiles', *RHR* cxxxviii (1950), pp. 22–52, 176–218.

Turley, T., 'John xxii and the Franciscans: a reappraisal', in *Popes, Teachers and Canon Law*, ed. J. R. Sweeney and S. Chodrow (Ithaca, NY, and London, 1990), pp. 74–83.

Turner, D., *The Darkness of God: Negativity in Western Mysticism* (Cambridge, 1995).

Vauchez, A., *Les Laics au moyen âge. Pratiques et experiences religieuse* (Paris, 1987); ed. D. J. Bornstein, trans. M. J. Schneider, *The Laity in the Middle Ages* (Notre Dame, 1993).

—— 'Movimenti religiosi fuori dell' ortodossia nei secoli XII e XIII', in *Storia dell' Italia religiosa* i, ed. G. de Rosa, T. Gregory and A. Vauchez (Rome and Bari, 1993), pp. 311–36.

—— 'Les Origines de l'hérésie Cathare en Languedoc d'après un sermon de l'archevêque de Pise, Frederico Visconte (1277)', in *Società, istituzioni, spiritualità: studi in onore di Cinzio Violante* ii (Spoleto, 1994), pp. 1023–30.

—— 'L'Historiographie des hérésies médiévales', in *L'Ogre historien. Autour de Jacques Le Goff*, ed. J. Revel and J. C. Schmitt (Paris, 1998), pp. 243–58.

Vekené, E. van der, *Bibliographie der Inquisition: Ein Versuch* (Hildesheim, 1963).

Venckeleer, T., 'Un recueil cathare: le manuscrit A.6.10 de la collection vaudois de Dublin, i: une glose sur le pater', *RBPH* xxxviii (1960), pp. 820–31; xxxix (1961), pp. 762–85.

Vicaire, M.-H., 'Les Cathares', *CF* III, pp. 105–28.

—— *Histoire de Saint Dominique* (Paris, 1957), trans. K. Pond as *St Dominic and His Times* (London, 1964).

—— '"L'affaire de paix et de foix" du Midi de la France', *CF* IV, pp. 102–27.

Vidal, J. M., 'Les derniers ministres de l'Albigéisme en Languedoc: leurs doctrines', *RQH* LXXIX (1906), pp. 57–107.

—— 'Doctrine et morale des derniers ministres albigeois', *RQH* LXXXV (1909), pp. 357–409; LXXXVI (1909), pp. 5–48.

Violante, C., 'Hérésies urbaines et hérésies rurales en Italie du 11e au 13e siècle', *HS*, pp. 171–98.

—— *La Pataria milanese e la riforma ecclesiastica* I: *Le Premesse 1045–57* (Rome, 1955).

Volpe, G., *Movimenti religiosi e sette ereticali nella società medievale Italiana (secoli XI–XIV)* (Florence, 1926).

De Vooght, P., *Les Sources de la doctrine chrétienne d'après les théologiens du XIVe siècle et du début du XVe* (Paris, 1954).

—— *L'Hérésie de Jean Huss* (Louvain, 1960).

—— *Hussiana* (Louvain, 1960).

—— 'Jean Huss et ses juges', in *Das Konzil von Konstanz*, ed. A. Franzen and W. Müller (Freiburg, 1964).

—— *Jacobellus de Stříbro († 1429), premier Théologien du Hussitisme* (Louvain, 1972).

Wagner, M. L., *Petr Chelčický* (Scottdale, PA, Kitchener, Ontario, 1983).

Wakefield, W. L., 'Notes on some antiheretical writings of the thirteenth century', *FS* XXVII (1967), pp. 285–321.

—— 'The family of Niort in the Albigensian Crusade and before the inquisition', *Names* XVIII (1970), pp. 97–117, 286–303.

—— 'Friar Ferrier, inquisition at Caunes and escapes from prison at Carcassonne', *CHR* LVIII (1972), pp. 220–37.

—— *Heresy, Crusade and Inquisition in Southern France 1100–1250* (London, 1974).

—— 'Heretics and inquisitors: the case of Le Mas-Saintes-Puelles', *CH* LXIX (1983), pp. 209–26.

Walsh, K., 'Preaching, pastoral care and *sola scriptura* in later medieval Ireland: Richard Fitzralph and the use of the Bible', *SCH* Subsidia IV, pp. 251–68.

—— 'Wyclif's legacy in Central Europe in the late fourteenth and early fifteenth centuries', *SCH* Subsidia V, pp. 397–417.

—— *A Fourteenth Century Scholar: Richard Fitzralph in Oxford, Avignon and Armagh* (Oxford, 1981).

—— 'Lollardisch-hussitische Reformbestrebungen im Umkreis und Gefolgschaft der Luxemburgerin Anna, Königin von England (1382–94)', in *Häresie*, ed. F. Šmahel, pp. 77–108.

Walter, J. von, *Die ersten Wanderprediger Frankreichs* I–II (Leipzig, 1903–6).

Walther, H. G., 'Ziel und Mittel päpstlicher Ketzerpolitik in der Lombardei und im Kirchenstaat', in *Anfänge*, ed. P. Segl, pp. 103–30.

Waugh, S. J. and Diehl, P. D. (ed.), *Christendom and Its Discontents* (Cambridge, 1996).

Webb, D. M., 'The Pope and the cities: anticlericalism and heresy in Innocent III's Italy', *SCH* Subsidia IX, pp. 135–52.

Welti, M., *Breve storia della riforma italiana* (Casale Monferrato, 1985).

Weltsch, R. E., *Archbishop John of Jenstein (1348–1400)* (The Hague and Paris, 1968).

Werner, E., 'Bogomil – eine literarische Fiktion?', *FF* XXXIII (1959), pp. 24–38.

—— 'Der Kirchenbegriff bei Jan Hus, Jakoubek von Mies, Jan Želivský und den linken Taboriten', *SDAB, Klasse für Philosophie* X (1967), pp. 5–73.

—— 'Häresie und Gesellschaft im 11. Jahrhundert', *SSAWL Philologischhistorische Klasse* CXVII (1975), pp. 5–83.

—— with M. Erbstösser, *Ketzer und Heilige: Das religiöse Leben im Hochmittelalter* (Berlin, 1986).

—— 'Wort und Sakrament im Identitätsbewusstsein des tschechischen Frühreformators Jan Hus (um 1370–1415)', *Sitzungsberichte der Akademie der Wissenschaften der DDR, Gesellschaftswissenschaften* XIII (1989), pp. 3–26.

—— *Jan Hus* (Weimar, 1991).

—— 'Das Altarsakrament im Religionsverständnis von Jan Hus', in *Husitství*, ed. J. Pánek *et al.*, pp. 317–28.

Wessley, S., 'The thirteenth-century Guglielmites: salvation through women', *SCH* Subsidia I, pp. 289–303.

West, D. C., 'The education of Fra Salimbene of Parma: the Joachite influence', in *Prophecy*, ed. A. Williams and M. W. Bloomfield, pp. 193–215.

Whiting, R., *The Blind Devotion of the People: Popular Religion and the English Reformation* (Cambridge, 1989).

Wilks, M. J., 'Predestination, property and power: Wyclif's theory of dominion and grace', *SCH* II, pp. 220–36.

—— 'The early Oxford Wyclif: papalist or nominalist', *SCH* V, pp. 69–98.

—— '*Reformatio regni*: Wyclif and Hus as leaders of religious protest movements', *SCH* IX, pp. 109–30.

—— 'Wyclif and the great persecution', *SCH* X, pp. 41–63.

—— 'Misleading manuscripts: Wyclif and the non-Wycliffite Bible', *SCH* XI, pp. 147–61.

—— *Wyclif: Political Ideas and Practice*, ed. A. Hudson (Oxford, 2000).

William of Tudela, *The Song of the Cathar Wars*, trans. J. Shirley (Aldershot, 1996).

Williams, A. and Bloomfield, M. W. (ed.), *Prophecy and Millenarianism* (Harlow, 1980).

Williams, G. H., *The Radical Reformation* (London, 1962).

Wilts, A., *Beginen im Bodenseeraum* (Sigmaringen, 1994).

Winn, H. E. (ed.), *Wyclif: Select English Writings* (Oxford, 1929).

Winter, E., *Frühhumanismus: Seine Entwicklung in Böhmen* (Berlin, 1964).

Wolff, P., 'Role de l'essor économique dans la ralliement social et religieux', *CF* XX, pp. 243–55.

Workman, H. B., with R. M. Pope (trans.), *Letters of John Hus* (London, 1904).

—— *John Wyclif: A Study of the English Medieval Church* I–II (Oxford, 1926).

Zambon, F., *La cena segreta. Trattati e rituali Catari* (Milan, 1997).

Zanella, G., *Itinerari ereticali: Patari e Catari tra Rimini e Verona* (Rome, 1986).

Zeman, J. K., 'The rise of religious liberty in the Czech reformation', *Central European History* VI (1973), pp. 128–47.

—— 'Anabaptism: a replay of medieval themes or a prelude to the modern age?', *Mennonite Quarterly Review* (1976), pp. 259–71.

—— *The Hussite Movement and the Reformation in Bohemia, Moravia and Slovakia (1350–1650)* (Ann Arbor, 1977).

Zerner, M. (ed.), *Inventer l'Hérésie? Discours polémiques et pouvoirs avant l'Inquisition* (Nice, 1998).

—— 'Du "Contra Hereticum" aux "Contra Hereticos"', in Ibid., pp. 119–56.

# Index